WITHDRAWN

NOV

Katie Schermerhorn

LADY MARY WORTLEY MONTAGU AND HER TIMES

BY
GEORGE PASTON

WITH TWENTY-FOUR ILLUSTRATIONS

LONDON & NEW YORK
G. P. PUTNAM'S SONS
1907

DA
501
M7
S8

PREFACE

WHEN I undertook to write a Memoir of Lady Mary Wortley Montagu, I had little hope that any considerable gleanings, in the shape of unpublished letters, would have been left by former workers in the same field. By the kindness of the Earl of Harrowby, however, I was permitted to examine the Wortley Montagu Manuscripts at Sandon Hall, and among these I found four or five hundred unpublished letters, many of great interest, relating to the first half of the eighteenth century. Lady Mary was responsible for upwards of a hundred of these, and Mr. Wortley for fifty or sixty, the remainder being written by relations, or by friends of the family. My heartiest thanks are due to Lord Harrowby for permission to copy the most interesting letters, and also to reproduce his whole-length portrait of Lady Mary by Richardson, which forms the frontispiece to this book.

I am deeply indebted to Mrs. Godfrey Clark for her kindness in allowing me to reproduce the miniature of Lady Mary in Turkish costume, the sketch of Lovere, and the crayon drawing of Lady Bute, all in her possession; and I gratefully acknowledge the valuable aid I have received from the Hon. James Home in the annotation of the unpublished letters.

PREFACE

WHEN I undertook to write a Memoir of Lady Mary Wortley Montagu, I had little hope that any considerable fragment, in the shape of unpublished letters, would have been left by former workers in the same field. By the kindness of the Earl of Harrowby, however, I was permitted to examine the Wortley Montagu Manuscripts at Sandon Hall; and among these I found four or two hundred unpublished letters, many of great interest relating to the first half of the eighteenth century. Lady Mary was responsible, for one-half of a hundred of these, and Mr. Wortley for fifty or sixty, the remainder being written by relations, or by friends of the family. My heartiest thanks are due to Lord Harrowby for permission to copy the most interesting letters, and also to reproduce his whole-length portrait of Lady Mary by Kneller, which forms the frontispiece to this book.

I am deeply indebted to Mrs. Godfrey Clark for her kindness in allowing me to reproduce the miniature of Lady Mary by Zincke, containing the sketch of Lovere, and the crayon drawing of Lady Bute, all in her possession; and I gratefully acknowledge the valuable aid I have received from the Hon. James Home in the annotation of the unpublished letters.

CONTENTS

CHAP.		PAGE
I.	FROM CHILDHOOD TO GIRLHOOD	1
II.	ENGLAND IN 1709	9
III.	ANNE WORTLEY MONTAGU	21
IV.	EARLY LOVE-LETTERS	28
V.	A DIFFICULT SUITOR	39
VI.	WEST DEAN	48
VII.	MR. WORTLEY DEPARTS	59
VIII.	A STRANGE COURTSHIP	69
IX.	LOVERS' MEETINGS	79
X.	A JEALOUS LOVER	93
XI.	QUARRELS AND FAREWELLS	104
XII.	MRS. HEWET AND MR. ADDISON	116
XIII.	A DISTASTEFUL MATCH	130
XIV.	PLANS FOR ELOPEMENT	141
XV.	A SECRET MARRIAGE	155
XVI.	"THE BRIDE IN THE COUNTRY"	163
XVII.	MOTHERHOOD	174
XVIII.	POLITICAL AMBITIONS	187
XIX.	COURT LIFE AND POEMS	200
XX.	MONTAGU BACON	214
XXI.	THE EMBASSY TO THE PORTE	227
XXII.	JOURNEY TO THE EAST	239
XXIII.	EVENTS AT HOME	252
XXIV.	LETTERS FROM TURKEY	260
XXV.	THE RECALL	270
XXVI.	RETURN TO ENGLAND	278
XXVII.	INTIMACY WITH POPE	285
XXVIII.	THE "AFFAIRE RÉMOND"	294
XXIX.	INOCULATION	302

CHAP.		PAGE
XXX.	Social Gossip	309
XXXI.	Literary Friendships	320
XXXII.	Family Troubles	329
XXXIII.	The Enmity of Pope	339
XXXIV.	Parents and Children	355
XXXV.	Journey to Venice	366
XXXVI.	Travels in Italy	377
XXXVII.	A Prodigal Son	390
XXXVIII.	Life at Avignon	400
XXXIX.	Life at Avignon (*continued*)	411
XL.	Fontenoy	418
XLI.	The Forty-Five	428
XLII.	In Italy Again	440
XLIII.	Gottolengo	453
XLIV.	Lovere	463
XLV.	Theories of Life	471
XLVI.	Novels of the Day	478
XLVII.	Critical Reflections	487
XLVIII.	Move to Venice	495
XLIX.	Letters from Venice	506
L.	Death of Mr. Wortley	514
LI.	Return to England	525
LII.	Character and Writings	539
	Titles of Published Works	547
	Index	549

LIST OF ILLUSTRATIONS

LADY MARY WORTLEY MONTAGU . . . *Frontispiece*
   From the Portrait by J. RICHARDSON
   Photo. F. C. STOATE, Stafford

                                                             PAGE

ANNE WORTLEY MONTAGU 22
   By SIR GODFREY KNELLER

SIR RICHARD STEELE 40

DR. GILBERT BURNET, BISHOP OF SALISBURY. . . 60
   By J. RILEY

LADY MARY PIERREPONT 95
   From a Miniature

JOSEPH ADDISON 119

LADY MARY WORTLEY MONTAGU 165
   By ZINCKE

SIR JOHN VANBRUGH 181
   By SIR G. KNELLER

EVELYN PIERREPONT, DUKE OF KINGSTON . . . 201
   By SIR G. KNELLER

JOHN, EARL OF MAR 219
   By SIR G. KNELLER

EDWARD WORTLEY MONTAGU 240

LADY MARY WORTLEY MONTAGU 262
   From a Miniature

LADY MARY WORTLEY MONTAGU 292
   By ZINCKE

WILLIAM CONGREVE	PAGE 310
By SIR GODFREY KNELLER	
PHILIP, DUKE OF WHARTON	318
By C. JERVAS	
FRANCES, COUNTESS OF MAR	336
By SIR GODFREY KNELLER	
ALEXANDER POPE	340
By SIR GODFREY KNELLER	
JOHN, LORD HERVEY	344
By VANLOO	
MARY, COUNTESS OF BUTE	359
From a Crayon Drawing	
HORACE WALPOLE	388
By ROSALBA	
EDWARD WORTLEY MONTAGU, JUNIOR . .	420
By GEORGE ROMNEY	
LOVERE, LAGO D'ISEO	448
From a Sketch	
MARY, COUNTESS OF BUTE	478
By SIR JOSHUA REYNOLDS	
JOHN, EARL OF BUTE	498
By ALLAN RAMSAY	

LADY MARY WORTLEY MONTAGU AND HER TIMES

CHAPTER I

FROM CHILDHOOD TO GIRLHOOD

IN the year 1789, Evelyn Pierrepont, a cadet of an ancient and distinguished family, was living with his wife Lady Mary (a daughter of William Fielding, third Earl of Denbigh) in the then fashionable district of Covent Garden. In May of this year their first child, a daughter, was born to them, and christened Mary at the parish church of St. Paul's. At this time Evelyn Pierrepont's prospects were not particularly brilliant, and he could boast of little except his lineage. His great-grandfather, the first Earl of Kingston, commonly called the "good Earl of Kingston," had been a zealous supporter of the Royalist cause, and was one of the most popular of the Cavalier commanders. In 1643 he was taken prisoner by the Parliamentarians at Gainsborough, whence he was sent by boat towards Hull. The boat was overtaken by a party of Royalists under Sir Charles Cavendish, who demanded the release of the prisoner. This being refused, they fired upon the boat, unfortunately killing both Lord Kingston and his servant.

The second Earl of Kingston remained faithful to Charles I., by whom he was created Marquis of Dorchester, but his younger brother, William, who earned the nickname of "Wise William," became the intimate friend and trusted adviser of Oliver Cromwell. He had great influence with the popular party, and is described as one of the wisest councillors and most excellent speakers in the Long Parliament. Although he had been considered by the extremists too well-disposed towards Charles I., he was not in favour of the Restoration, and retired from public life in 1661. He lived on his estate, Thoresby House, near Holm Pierrepont, Sherwood Forest, till 1678, and it does not appear that he suffered from the part he had played during the Commonwealth. Wise William's eldest son, Robert,[1] married the daughter and heiress of Sir John Evelyn of West Dean in Wiltshire, a cousin of Richard Evelyn, who has a note in his famous Diary anent "the prodigious memory of Sir John o' Wilts' daughter." The pair had one daughter (married to Lord Cheyne) and three sons, Robert, William, and the Evelyn to whom allusion has already been made. The eldest brother inherited the title of Earl of Kingston from his great-uncle, the second Earl,[2] but died young, and was succeeded by his brother William, who died without issue in 1790. Thus at thirty-five Evelyn Pierrepont became, quite unexpectedly, fifth Earl of Kingston, inheriting the paternal estate of Thoresby, and, at his mother's death, her property in Wiltshire.

If there is anything in heredity, the little Lady Mary Pierrepont ought to have succeeded to a fine mental and moral inheritance—virtue and courage from her great-great-grandfather, wisdom from her great-grandfather, and a prodigious memory from her Evelyn grandmother. Of Lady Kingston we know nothing, except that she died in 1697,[3] leaving three little girls and one boy. Lady Mary spent most of her early childhood with her grandmother at West Dean, but Mrs. Pierrepont died when the little girl was only eight years old, and she then returned to her father's house. The children were now motherless, and Lord Kingston, as a fine gentleman and man of pleasure, could bestow little time or thought upon the training of his

---

[1] William Pierrepont's second son was created Baron Pierrepont of Hanslope. His three daughters married respectively Lord Ogle, Lord Clare, and Lord Halifax. Lady Mary could therefore " call cousins " with members of these three houses.

[2] The Marquessate of Dorchester becoming extinct.

[3] According to most of Lady Mary's biographers, her mother died in 1692, but it appears from the *Dictionary of National Biography* that she was buried at Holm Pierrepont in 1697. As she left four children, the eldest of whom was born in 1689, it seems unlikely that she should have died as early as 1692.

daughters. When he remembered her existence, however, he seems to have been proud of his eldest daughter's beauty and precocious intelligence. The well-known tale of her early début as a toast of the Kit-Cat Club[1] must needs be repeated once again, and it cannot be better told than in the words of her grand-daughter, Lady Louisa Stuart.[2]

"As a leader of the fashionable world, and a strenuous Whig, Lord Kingston of course belonged to the Kit-Cat Club. One day at a meeting to choose toasts for the year, a whim seized him to nominate her [Lady Mary], then not eight years old,[3] a candidate, alleging that she was far prettier than any lady on their list. The other members demurred, because the rules of the Club forbade them to elect a beauty whom they had never seen. 'Then you shall see her,' cried he; and in the gaiety of the moment sent orders home to have her finely dressed, and brought to him at the Tavern, where she was received with acclamations, her health drunk by everyone present, and her name engraved upon a drinking-glass. The company consisting of some of the most eminent men in England, she went from the lap of one poet, patriot, or statesman to the arms of another, was feasted with sweetmeats, overwhelmed with caresses, and what perhaps pleased her better than either, heard her wit and beauty loudly extolled on every side. Pleasure, she said, was too poor a word to express her sensations; they amounted to ecstasy; never again throughout her whole life did she pass so happy a day. . . . Her father carried on the frolic by having her picture painted for the club-house that she might be enrolled as a regular toast."

---

[1] The Kit-Cat Club is supposed to have taken its name from Christopher Cat, who kept the Cat and Fiddle Tavern in Shire Lane, where the Club held its meetings. According to one account it was founded as early as 1688 by some "men of wit and pleasure," with no political object. But in 1703 it had become the rallying place of the Whig party. The Secretary at this time was Jacob Tonson, Dryden's publisher, who built a room in his house at Barn Elms (the present Ranelagh) for the summer meetings of the Club. This he desired to adorn with portraits of the members. As the walls were not high enough for whole-lengths, Kneller used a canvas 36 inches long by 28 wide, which has ever since been known as the Kit-Cat size.

[2] In her Introductory Anecdotes prefixed to Lady Mary's Correspondence.

[3] If the Club only became a Whig centre in 1703, Lady Mary was fourteen at this time.

Lady Mary has left a fragment of autobiography,[1] of which she says that although it has the air of a romance there is not a "sillable" feigned in it, except the names, which she could not bring herself to set down at length.

"I need say nothing," she writes in the style of her favourite romancers, D'Urfé and Mademoiselle Scudéry,[2] "of the Pedegree of the unfortunate Lady, whose Life I have undertaken to write. 'Tis enough to say she was daughter of the Duke of Regiavilla, to inform my reader there is no nobler descent in Portugal. Her first misfortune happened in a time of life when she could not be sensible of it, though she was sufficiently so in the course of it; I mean the death of a noble Mother, whose virtue and good sense might have supported and instructed her youth, which was left to the care of a young Father, who, tho' naturally an honest man, was abandoned to his pleasures, and (like most of those of his quality) did not think himself obliged to be very attentive to his children's education. Thus was the unfortunate left to the care of an old governess, who, though perfectly good and pious, wanted a capacity for so great a trust.

"Lætitia had naturally the strongest inclination for reading, and finding in her Father's house a well-furnished Library, instead of the usual diversions of children, made that the seat of her pleasures, and had very soon run through the English part of it. Her appetite for knowledge increasing with her years, without considering the toilsome task she undertook, she began to learn herself the Latin grammar, and with the help of an uncommon memory and indefatigable labour, made herself so far mistress of that language as to be able to understand almost any author. This extraordinary attachment to study became the theme of public discourse. Her Father, though no scholar himself, was flattered with a pleasure in the progress she made, and this reputation which she did not seek (having no end in view but her own amuse-

---

[1] Unpublished except for a few lines quoted by Mr. Moy Thomas in the Memoir prefixed to his edition of Lady Mary's Correspondence.

[2] Lady Mary possessed a whole library of these romances, which were mostly "Englished by a Person of Honour." Her chief favourite was D'Urfé's *Astrea*.

ment) gave her enviers and consequently enemies among the girls of her own age."

Leaving the autobiographical romance for the moment, we may note that the young student received guidance in her reading from no less a person than Dr. Burnet, Bishop of Salisbury,[1] who "condescended to direct the studies of a girl"; and also from her maternal uncle, William Fielding, a man of parts, with whom she was a great favourite. It was with Dr. Burnet's help and encouragement that at the age of twenty she translated the Latin version of the *Enchiridion* of Epictetus, a philosopher who had a considerable influence upon her mode of thought, though very little upon her conduct. To these early days belong also one or two fragmentary romances in the French genre, and an imitation of Ovid, said to have been written at the age of twelve, which has been printed among her poetical remains.

Lord Kingston had now a town-house in Arlington Street, but his daughters, before their début, probably spent the greater part of the year at Thoresby. Although the old house was situated in the midst of the most romantic forest scenery, where every glade holds memories of Robin Hood and his merry men, Lady Mary's early letters contain not a single word about her surroundings, save for an occasional complaint about the badness of the roads. Her days seem to have been passed in reading and writing, these occupations being only diversified by a visit to one of her few neighbours, or a jaunt to Nottingham Races. Yet in Italy, in her later years, Lady Mary displayed great taste in gardening, kept her own dairy, and taught her neighbours the English methods of making bread and butter and mince-pies. She must therefore have gained a certain amount of household knowledge in those girlish days at Thoresby, to say nothing of one all-important accomplishment—the art of carving.

"The mistress of a country-house," to quote Lady Louisa Stuart again, "had not only to invite—that is, urge and tease —her company to eat more than human throats could conven-

---

[1] Gilbert Burnet (1643-1715), the trusted counsellor of William III., was appointed Bishop of Salisbury in 1789. Lady Mary was a great admirer of the much-discussed *History of His Own Times*, which was published after his death.

iently swallow, but to carve every dish when chosen with her own hands. Each dish was carried up in turn, to be operated upon by her alone . . . since the very master of the house, posted opposite to her, might not act as croupier; his department was to push the bottle. As for the crowd of guests, the most inconsiderable among them, if suffered through her neglect to help himself to a slice of the mutton placed before him, would have chewed it in bitterness, and gone home an affronted man, half-disposed to give a wrong vote at the next election. There were then professed carving-masters, who taught young ladies the art scientifically; from one of whom Lady Mary said she took lessons three times a week, that she might be perfect on her father's public days; when, in order to perform her functions without interruptions, she was forced to eat her own dinner alone an hour or two beforehand."

Among the girlish friends of the Ladies Mary, Frances, and Evelyn Pierrepont were the pretty, flighty Dolly Walpole, sister of Sir Robert, who made amends for a stormy youth by marrying that grave and reverend statesman Lord Townshend; the unhappy Lady Anne Vaughan, daughter of Lord Carbery, who bestowed herself and her large fortune upon the Duke of Bolton, only to be neglected by him for "Polly Peacham" (Lavinia Fenton), whom he married on the death of his ill-used wife; and the Ladies Howard, daughters of Lord Carlisle. In the Forest itself there was Mrs. Hewet, née Betenson, one of Lady Mary's early correspondents, whose husband was Surveyor-General of Her Majesty's Woods and Forests; and there was Miss Banks, who lived at Scofton, and was nobody in particular, but wrote very pleasant girlish letters, and had a great admiration for the brilliant Lady Mary. But most interesting and intimate of all was the friendship with Anne and Katherine Wortley Montagu, daughters of the Hon. Sidney Montagu, who lived at Wharncliffe Lodge, about thirty miles from Thoresby. Mr. Montagu was the second son of the first Earl of Sandwich,[1] and had married

[1] Distinguished as a military commander in the Parliamentarian Army, and famous as Lord High Admiral after the Restoration. If his own deeds were forgotten, he would still be immortal as the friend and patron of Samuel Pepys.

the daughter[1] and heiress of Sir Francis Wortley. Anne Montagu, a pretty, lively girl, was the favourite sister of Mr. Edward Wortley Montagu, a gentleman of literary tastes and some political distinction, who was presently to be introduced to the Lady Mary Pierrepont. The method of the introduction is thus graphically described in the unpublished Autobiography :—

"Amongst the girls of her (Lætitia's) own age was Mlle. ——. She had a large fortune, which was enough to draw after her a crowd of those that otherwise would never have thought of her. She triumphed over Lætitia when she related to her the number of her conquests, and amongst others named to her Sebastian [Mr. Wortley Montagu] as he that was most passionately her servant, and had made most impression on her heart. Lætitia, who saw through the little vanity that agitated her, and had a very mean idea of a man that could be captivated with such charms, laughed at her panegyric, and the other, who insisted on the merit of her imagined lover, would make her a witness both of his agreeableness and passion. A party for this purpose was very easily contrived, and Lætitia invited to play where he was to tally[2] at Bassette. She was then but newly entered into her teens, but never being tall, had already attained the height she always had, and her person was in all the childish bloom of that age.

"Sebastian, who seriously designed upon the fortune of Mlle. ——, who was three years older, proposed nothing by coming there but an occasion of obliging her, and being at that time near thirty, did not expect much conversation among a set of romps. Tea came in before cards, and a new play being then acted, it was the first thing mentioned, on which Lætitia took occasion to criticise in a manner so just and so knowing, he was as much amazed as if he had heard a piece of waxwork talk on that subject. This led them into a discourse of Poetry, and he was still more astonished to find

---

[1] Anne Newcomen was the illegitimate daughter of Sir Francis, who had long been separated from his wife. She inherited her father's estates on condition that her husband assumed the name of Wortley.

[2] Literally, to mark or score. But at certain games the person who "tallied" acted as the "banker."

her not only well read in the moderns, but that there was hardly any beautiful passage in the classics she did not remember; this was striking him in the most sensible manner. He was a thorough scholar, and rather an adorer than an admirer of learning. The conversation grew so eager on both sides neither cards nor Mlle. were thought upon, and she was forced to call on him several times before she could prevail on him to go towards the table. When he did, it was only to continue his discourse with Lætitia, and she had the full pleasure of triumphing over Mlle., who was forced to be silent while they talked about what she could not understand. This day put an end to his inclination ever to see her again, and his admiration [for Lætitia] was so visible that his sisters (who are generally ready to make court to an elder brother) made all sorts of advances of friendship to Lætitia, who received them very obligingly, and the acquaintance was very soon made."

Lady Louisa Stuart gives a somewhat different version of the incident, but this may relate to one of the subsequent meetings between the pair. Mr. Wortley, she explains, chose his intimates chiefly from among the wits and politicians of the day, who formed a class distinct from that of the "white-gloved beaux." He was not at any time a "ladies' man," but meeting Lady Mary Pierrepont in his sister's room one day, he was struck by her wit and reading even more than by her beauty. "Something that passed led to the mention of Quintus Curtius, which she said she had never read. This was a fair handle for a piece of gallantry; in a few days she received a superb edition of the author, with these lines facing the title-page:—

> 'Beauty like this had vanquished Persia shown,
> The Macedon had laid his empire down,
> And polished Greece obeyed a barbarous throne.
> Had wit so bright adorned a Grecian dame,
> The am'rous youth had lost his thirst of fame,
> Nor distant Indus sought through Syria's plain;
> But to the Muses' stream with her had run,
> And thought her lover more than Ammon's son.'"

CHAPTER II

ENGLAND IN 1709

LADY MARY'S published Correspondence begins about 1709, when she had just completed her twentieth year. Before dealing with her early letters it seems desirable to take a brief survey of the society in which she found herself. Her father, a prominent member of the Whig party, had been created Lord Dorchester in 1706, and also appointed one of the Commissioners for the Union with Scotland. Born in 1665, he was still in early middle-age, and is described by a contemporary as "A very fine gentleman, of good sense, well-bred, and a lover of the ladies; is entirely in the interest of his country, makes a good figure, is of a black complexion, well-made, not forty years old."[1] Lady Mary said in after years that he might have served as a model for the lively father of Sir Charles Grandison, and that he was too complete a man of fashion to be a very tender or considerate parent. Like most fathers of that day, he seems to have regarded his children as chattels, to be kept in strict subjection to his will, and to be disposed of to the best advantage from a worldly point of view.

The mixed Government of 1706 had become a Whig Government by 1708, much against the wishes of Anne. The reign of the Whigs was short though glorious, since the year 1710 was to see the fall of Godolphin, and the return of the Tories to power, with Harley at their head. Marlborough, not yet hampered by an economical Tory Cabinet, was still astride his whirlwind, though he was unable always to "direct the storm," since his victory of Malplacquet in the autumn of this year was little less disastrous than a

[1] John Macky in his *Secret Service* (1705).

defeat. The Queen and Duchess Sarah were still "Mrs. Morley" and "Mrs. Freeman," but the relations between them were becoming strained, owing to Mrs. Freeman's habit of "speaking her mind openly on all occasions." The new favourite, Mrs. Masham, was much more soothing, and had already undermined the influence of the imperious Duchess. It was in this year that Sacheverell preached his famous sermons against the Act of Toleration, which delighted the Queen and enraged the Whigs. His trial may be described as one of the most fashionable "functions" of the period.

Lord Dorchester affected the society of wits and poets, and his daughter had the good fortune to make her début in the middle of the "Augustan age" of letters, when one magic circle included Addison, Steele, Swift, Congreve, Vanbrugh, Cibber, Maynwaring, Garth, Arbuthnot, Gay and Pope. And few of these were yet past the prime of life. Addison and Steele were still two years short of forty. The first had leapt into fame with his poem *The Campaign* just five years earlier, and had been rewarded, after the pleasant fashion of those days, with various public appointments—first a commissionership, then an Under-Secretaryship, then the Irish Secretaryship. Steele, after his taste of military life, had published his *Christian Hero*, and then counteracted its ultra-pious effect with his comedies of *The Funeral*, and *The Lying Lover*. He had been more lucky than Addison in writing for the stage (*Cato* was still in manuscript), but he had been less handsomely treated by the Government, having received nothing better than a gentleman-ushership to Prince George of Denmark and the office of Gazetteer. He had been married two years to the charming Mrs. Scurlock. Swift, at forty-two, had made his name with *The Battle of the Books* and *The Tale of a Tub*, but had yet three years to wait for his Deanery. During his visits to London in 1705 and 1707 he had been made free of the charmed circle. Pope, at twenty-one, had just come into popular notice with his Pastorals, but two or three years were to elapse before his introduction to Addison and Steele.

The chief literary event of the year 1709 was the founding of the *Tatler* by Steele, with the help of Addison. The success of the unpretending little periodical, which was brought out three times a week at one penny, probably surprised nobody more than the promoters. It found its way into the boudoirs of fine ladies and the dressing-rooms of the beaux, as well as into the clubs and coffee-houses. The gentle fun poked by "Mr. Bickerstaff" at the foibles of his countrymen had, according to Gay, an effect that was almost incredibly beneficial upon the manners and morals of the town.

The theatrical world was supposed to be in a parlous state, but then there is a "decadence of the drama" in nearly every age. In 1709 the licence of the Theatre Royal, Drury Lane, had been temporarily suspended and the house closed, owing to Rich's quarrels with his company. His best actors had seceded years before, and had been playing at the old theatre in Lincoln's Inn Fields, or at Vanbrugh's new house in the Haymarket. Now that Rich had come to the end of his tether, a new era of prosperity was to open for Drury Lane under the triple rule of Cibber, Wilks, and Doggett. Congreve, though only thirty-nine, had retired from active business as a playwright, and was living "like a gentleman" on a fat commissionership of hackney-coaches. Vanbrugh at forty-five had also finished his dramatic career, and returned to his first love—architecture. He was now employed upon the building of Blenheim Palace, and had lately been appointed Clarenceux king-at-arms. Cibber, at thirty-eight, was the most popular playwright, as well as the leading character actor of the day. Betterton was just at the end of his career, but Booth was ready to step into his shoes, while Mrs. Bracegirdle and Mrs. Barry were making way for the more youthful charms of Mrs. Oldfield and Mrs. Porter.

Italian opera was just coming into fashion, though both Addison and Steele were trying to kill it with ridicule. It was generally understood, however, that Addison was "laughing on the wrong side of his mouth," his own lyric drama, *Rosamond*, having been a dismal failure. At present opera was a hybrid form of entertainment, being performed partly in Italian and partly in English. Buononcini's *Almahide*, produced in 1710, was the first piece that was given entirely in Italian. Nicolini, the famous contralto, soon to be the idol of the public, had arrived in 1708, and negotiations were soon to be opened for the engagement of Mr. Handel, who came to England two years later. Vanbrugh's theatre in the Haymarket (finished in 1705) had been found unsuitable for the drama, and it was now to be devoted almost entirely to opera. Cibber complained that it was situated out in the country, beyond an easy walk from the City and the Inns of Court. The managers, he declared, could draw no sustenance beyond a milk diet from the pastures that surrounded it! Fortunately, the opera became a fashionable form of entertainment, patronised by the great people who had not to think of coach-hire, much less of shoe-leather.

The art of painting was almost at its lowest ebb. At sixty-three Sir Godfrey Kneller was still the leading portrait-painter, though Richardson and Jervas each had his following. There were no art schools and no exhibitions of pictures, while there was a general impression among patrons and connoisseurs that no English artist could paint a fine historical or imaginative work. This was hardly surprising, when the efforts of Highmore, Kent, and Thornhill are taken into account. Perhaps the most solid and valuable work was being done by the artist engravers, Dutchmen who had come over in the train of William III., or Frenchmen who had taken refuge in England from the troubles at home.

Women were beginning to take an active part in the game of letters, though already the curious and deep-rooted prejudice against a liberal education for "females" had begun to infect men's minds. In Elizabethan and even in Restoration days wit and knowledge were regarded as extra feathers in the feminine cap, but by the end of the seventeenth century Mrs. Astell[1] (afterwards the friend and warm admirer of Lady

---

[1] Mary Astell (1668–1731) was a remarkable woman in her way. She was the daughter of a merchant at Newcastle, but was well educated by a clerical uncle. She came to London early in life, and presently settled at Chelsea, to be near her friend and correspondent, Bishop Atterbury. It was in 1694 that she published her *Serious Proposal to the Ladies*, the proposal being for a Church of England institution which should serve at once as a place of religious retirement and an academy of learning. For this daring suggestion she suffered much abuse and insult. Later

Mary) was fulminating with a feeble violence against the male "puppies" who objected to learning in the other sex. The best of the joke was that the prejudice was purely theoretical. In actual life, on the rare occasions that men came into contact with a cultivated intelligent woman, they fell flat at her feet. Thus we have the curious anomaly that while the average man (not the big ones, such as Swift or Pope) was inveighing bitterly against "learned ladies," the girls, who instinctively knew better, were the "enviers and enemies" (to quote Lady Mary) of the few among their fellows whose superior education enabled them to hold their own in masculine society. Mrs. Astell, some two hundred years in advance of her time, urged the foundation of a college for women, an idea that was grossly ridiculed by Steele and Addison in the *Tatler*. Ten thousand pounds was promised for this object by an anonymous lady, commonly believed to be Queen Anne. Rumour says that she was dissuaded from carrying out her promise by Bishop Burnet, who thought that the public would suspect the college of being a nunnery in disguise.

Women, then as now, found their best mode of expression in fiction. Novels were still regarded rather in the light of a "foreign import," most of those published in English being translations of French or Spanish romances, which dealt in heroic fashion with the amazing adventures of princes and princesses, giants and enchanters. The pseudo-memoir, which was coming into fashion, was a change for the better, as was the *roman à clef*, even though realism might sometimes be carried too far. Mrs. Manley,[1] a too notorious lady, who

she won fame by her Platonic controversy with John Morris of Bemerton, and impressed Atterbury by the skill with which she conducted an argument with him on theological subjects. He said that if she had as much good breeding as good sense she would be perfect. It says much for her character that she was the lifelong friend of Lady Elizabeth Hastings, whom to love was "a liberal education." Among her other works were *Reflections upon Marriage* and an *Essay in Defence of the Female Sex*.

[1] Mary de la Riviere Manley (1663-1724), daughter of the Cavalier officer Sir John Manley. She made a false start in life, through being drawn into a bigamous marriage with her cousin John Manley. Besides the *New Atlantis*, she published *Memoirs of Europe*, *Court Intrigues*, and several political pamphlets. She edited the *Female Tatler*, succeeded Swift as editor of the *Examiner*, and produced several

brought out her scandalous *New Atlantis* in 1709, suffered for her boldness. Not that her scandals or her personalities would have brought her into trouble; but she chose to libel the Whigs, and the Whigs being in the ascendant the lady was arrested and brought before a magistrate, but it does not appear that she was sentenced to any punishment. Although Mrs. Manley's style is slovenly and her love-scenes " the worse for being warm," it is easy to understand that a novel about real human beings would be a refreshing change from the romances of D'Urfé or Scudéry. One other woman writer of the period deserves mention, namely Mrs. Centlivre,[1] who wrote eighteen comedies, the most successful, *The Busy-Body*, being produced in this same wonderful year—1709.

Lady Mary Pierrepont, through her father, was acquainted with the leading men of letters and artists, though it is doubtful whether she saw very much of them. They did not greatly affect feminine society, but spent their time between the tavern and the coffee-house. They wanted good wine and good talk, and they could get neither at the dreary formal assemblies which were the most fashionable form of festivity in Queen Anne's reign. Still, Lady Mary was able to affirm, from personal knowledge, that Addison was the very best of company (which proved that he was at his ease with her), that Congreve had more wit than anybody else, and that Steele was a very good-natured man. Of the last named she could hardly say less, since he acted as go-between during her secret engagement to Mr. Wortley Montagu. She sat for her portrait both to Kneller and Richardson, and she not only consulted Garth in his medical capacity, but attended dances at his house.

Mr. Wortley, who was now in his thirty-second year, enjoyed the intimate friendship of Addison, and consequently had the *entrée* into the best literary set. In early life he had spent three years on the Continent, and during a part of that period had joined forces with Addison, who had gone abroad on the travelling-pension granted him by an intelligent Gov-

---

plays, some of which met with success. She had several "protectors," Alderman Barber among others.

[1] Born about 1667, died in 1723. Her husband was cook to Queen Anne.

ernment. On his return to England Mr. Wortley entered Parliament as a member for Huntingdon, for which borough the influence of his uncle, Lord Sandwich, ensured his election. By this time he had already made a certain mark in the House, having introduced one or two useful little Bills, notably one (in 1709) for "the encouragement of learning, and the securing the property of copies of books to the rightful owners thereof." This was agitated for several years, but was lost in 1713. Mr. Wortley's friendship for Steele, to one of whose daughters he stood godfather, seems to have begun shortly after his return from the Grand Tour. He was invited to send ideas for articles to the *Tatler*, and one paper at least was written at his suggestion, his rough notes being still in existence. A yet greater honour awaited him, for the second volume of the *Tatler* was dedicated to "Mr. Edward Wortley Montagu" in the most friendly and flattering terms.[1]

Lady Mary Pierrepont's earliest published letter is written from her father's house in Arlington Street, and is addressed to Mrs. Hewet. It is undated, but probably belongs to the spring of 1709. It begins with an apology for delay in answering Mrs. Hewet's letters, and a complaint that in "this busy town" the writer has very little time at her own disposal.

[1] The dedication runs as follows :—

"SIR,—When I send you this volume I am rather to make a request than a Dedication. I must desire that if you think fit to throw away any moments on it, you would not do it after reading those excellent pieces with which you are so well conversant. The images which you will meet with here will be very faint after the perusal of the Greeks and Romans who are your ordinary companions. I must confess I am obliged to you for the taste of many of their excellences, which I had not observed until you pointed them out to me. I am very proud that there are some things in these Papers which I know you pardon; and it is no small pleasure to have one's labours suffered by the judgment of a man who so well understands the charms of eloquence and poesy. But I direct this address to you; not that I think I can entertain you with my writings; but to thank you for the new delight I have, from your conversation, in those of other men.

"May you enjoy a long continuance of the true relish of the happiness Heaven has bestowed upon you! I know not how to say a more affectionate thing to you, than to wish that you may be always what you are; and that you may ever think, as I know you now do, that you have a much larger fortune than you want.—I am, Sir, your most obedient and most humble servant, ISAAC BICKERSTAFF."

"My great pleasure is at Mrs. Selwyn's,"[1] she continues. "I came from thence just now, and I believe that I am the only young woman in town that am in my own house at ten o'clock to-night. This is the night of Count Turruca's ball, to which he has invited a few bare-faced, and the whole town *en masque*. . . . I have begun to learn Italian, and am much mortified I cannot do it of a signor of Monsieur Resingade's recommendations, but 'tis always the fate of women to obey, and my papa has promised me to a Mr. Cassotti. I am afraid I shall never understand it so well as you do—but *laissons cela*, and talk of somewhat more entertaining."

The "somewhat more entertaining" is an anecdote about the marriage of a plain, portionless old maid (also an inhabitant of Arlington Street) to a man with £7000 per annum and £40,000 in ready money. "Her equipage and liveries outshine anybody's in town. He has presented her with £3000 in jewels, and never was man more smitten with these charms that had lain invisible for these forty years. But, with all his glory, never bride had fewer enviers, the dear beast of a man is so filthy, frightful, odious, and detestable. I would turn away such a footman, for fear of spoiling my dinner, while he waited at table. . . . He professes to have married her for her devotion, patience, meekness, and other Christian virtues he observed in her: his first wife (who has left no children) being very handsome, and so good-natured as to have ventured her own salvation to secure his. He has married this lady to have a companion in that paradise where his first has given him a title."

As we have seen, Lady Mary was already, to use her own expression, a rake at reading, and Mrs. Hewet seems to have shared her taste for romances, though not for the classics. The novels the pair exchanged were more suited to the reading of a matron than a maid, but at twenty Lady Mary had left her bread-and-butter days behind her, and can certainly not

---

[1] Mrs. Hewet's sister, Albinia Betenson, was the widow of General William Selwyn of Matson. Her son, Colonel John Selwyn, aide-de-camp to the Duke of Marlborough, married his first cousin, Mary Farrington, whose mother was a Betenson. They were the parents of George Selwyn the Wit.

be regarded in the light of a "young person." In September 1709 she wrote to her friend from Thoresby—

"Ten thousand thanks to you for Madame de Noyer's Letters;[1] I wish Signor Roselli[2] may be as diverting to you as *she* has been to me. The stories are very extraordinary; but I know not whether she has not added a few *agrémens* of invention to them: however, there is some truth. . . . Don't you think that the Court of England would furnish stories as entertaining? Say nothing of my malice, but I cannot help wishing that Madame de Noyer would turn her thoughts a little that way. I fancy she would succeed better than the authoress of the *New Atlantis*. I am sure I like her method much better, which has, I think, hit that difficult path between the gay and the severe, and is neither too loose, nor affected by pride."

Mrs. Manley had brought out the first part of her *New Atlantis* in May of this year. Although it contained many scandalous anecdotes of well-known persons,[3] whose identities were but thinly veiled, it had not yet attracted the unfavourable notice of the Government.

Alluding, no doubt, to the battle of Malplacquet, which took place on 9th September, Lady Mary continues: "I take an interest in Mr. Selwyn's[4] success. In a battle like that I think it may be called so to come off alive. I should be so sensible of any affliction that could touch you or Mrs. Selwyn that I may very well rejoice when you have no occasion for any. Adieu, Madam; this post has brought me nothing but complaints without one bit of news. . . . Excuse my dulness,

---

[1] Madame Dunoyer (1663–1720) was a French Protestant who spent some time in England. She published her *Lettres Historiques et Galantes* (seven volumes) in 1704. To these were added, in an edition published after her death, her memoirs, and those of her husband, from whom she was separated. Voltaire, as a young man, was the lover of her eldest daughter, known as Pimpette, and desired to marry her, but the marriage was opposed by his godfather, the Marquis de Châteauneuf, and by the lady's mother. The affair has been described by Madame Dunoyer in one of her books.

[2] *Les Aventures de Signor Roselli, l'infortuné Néapolitain*, was published anonymously by J. Bliner. An English translation appeared in 1709.

[3] The Marlboroughs, Whartons, Shrewsburys, and Dr. Burnet were among those attacked.

[4] Mrs. Hewet's nephew, John Selwyn.

and be so good as never to read a letter of mine but in one of those minutes when you are entirely alone, weary of everything, and *inquiète* to think what you shall do next. All people who live in the country must have some of those minutes, and I know so well what they are, that I believe even my letters may be welcome when they are to take them off your hands."

On 20th October Mrs. Manley published the second part of the *New Atlantis*, which was to bring her into conflict with the authorities. But she was probably consoled by the fact that the book had a *succès de scandale*. Writing shortly after its appearance, Lady Mary says—

"You expressed a desire of seeing the second part of the *Atlantis*. I had just sent to London for it, and did not question having it last Saturday. I hoped that a book you had a mind to see might atone for the nothingness of my letter, and was resolved not to send one without the other; but, like an unfortunate projector as I am, my designs are always followed by disappointment. Saturday came, and no book. God forgive me, I had certainly wished the lady who was to send it me hanged, but for the hopes it was to come by the Nottingham carrier, and then I should have it on Monday; but after waiting Monday and Tuesday, I find it is not come at all."

To make up for the non-arrival of the book, Lady Mary concludes her letter with some morsels of gossip, true or false, which she had received by the last post. Lady Essex Saville (eldest daughter of William, second Marquis of Halifax) she hears is going to be married to Lord Lonsdale, but adds, "I won't swear to the truth of it, for people make no conscience of what they write into the country, and think anything good enough for poor us.[1] There is another story that I had from a hand I dare depend upon. The Duke of Grafton [2] and Dr. Garth [3] ran a foot-match in the Mall of 200 yards, and the latter,

[1] The report was incorrect. Lady Essex Saville died young and unmarried. Richard, the second Viscount Lonsdale, died unmarried in 1713.

[2] Charles, the second Duke, grandson of Charles II. and the Duchess of Cleveland.

[3] Dr. Samuel Garth (afterwards Sir Samuel) was in his forty-eighth year. He was a friend of all the wits, a member of the Kit-Cat Club, and best known by his poem, *The Dispensary*.

to his immortal glory, beat. I pray God you mayn't have heard this already. I am promised a cargo of lampoons from Bath, and if they come you shall share them with me."

From a letter dated 12th November we learn that Mrs. Hewet has succeeded in getting the much-coveted "second part." Her friend writes to beg for the loan of it, and in return promises to get the key to it. "But do you know," she continues, "what has happened to the unfortunate authoress? People are offended at the liberty she used in her memoirs, and she is taken into custody. Miserable is the fate of writers! If they are agreeable they are offensive, and if dull they starve. I lament the loss of the other parts which we should have had, and have five hundred arguments at my fingers' ends to prove the ridiculousness of those creatures that think it worth while to take notice of what is only designed for diversion. After this who will dare give us the history of Angela? I was in hopes her faint essay would have provoked some better pen to give us more elegant and secret memoirs. But now she will serve as a scarecrow to frighten people from attempting anything but heavy panegyric, and we shall be teased with nothing but heroic poems, with names at length, and false characters so daubed with flattery that they are the severest kind of lampoons, for they both scandalise the writer and the subject, like that vile paper the *Tatler*."

Mrs. Manley was arrested in September, but after being kept in custody for some months the charge against her was dismissed. The condemnation of the *Tatler* is curious in view of the fact that Steele and Addison were friends of Mr. Wortley's, whose literary judgment Lady Mary held in high respect. But even his own sister, as will presently be seen, spoke in contemptuous terms of the periodical. The aims of the writers, and the easy simplicity of their style, were probably misunderstood at first by many readers who were accustomed to the pedantic dulness of Grub Street.

The letter concludes: "All the news is that Mrs. Reeves is married to Colonel Herbert (if you know neither of them, I'll send you their pictures at full length), and that giddy rake Creswell, to a fortune of £2000 a year. I send you the Bath lampoons—Corinna is Lady Manchester,[1] and the other lady is Mrs. Cartwright, who, they say, has pawned her diamond necklace, to buy Valentine a snuff-box. These wars make men so violent scarce, that these good ladies take up with the shadows of them. . . . I fancy the ill-spelling of the lampoons will make you laugh more than the verses; indeed I am ashamed for her who wrote them. As soon as possible, be pleased to send me the second part of the *Atlantis*, etc."

[1] Dodington, daughter of Lord Brooke. She married Charles, the fourth Earl of Manchester, who was created Duke of Manchester in 1719.

CHAPTER III

ANNE WORTLEY MONTAGU

LADY MARY'S acquaintance with the Wortley Montagu sisters had rapidly developed into a warm friendship. Although Mr. Wortley had not yet publicly declared his passion, "Lætitia," to quote from the Autobiography, "easily saw the conquest she had made of his heart; but that merit which was so powerful with Mlle. made very small impression on her. She had a way of thinking very different from other girls, and instead of looking on a husband as the ultimate aim of her wishes, she never thought of marriage but as a bond that was to subject her to a master, and she dreaded an engagement of that sort. The little plan she had formed to herself was retirement and study,[1] and if she found any pleasure in Sebastian's company, it was only when he directed her in the choice of her books, or explained some passage to her in Virgil or Horace.

"He never spoke of his passion, perhaps thinking her too young for a declaration of that nature, and as long as he kept himself within those limits, she did not think she erred in seeing him as often as she could; it was always in his sister's company, and her youth hindered much observation being made on it.

"The whole winter passed in this manner, and when she went into the country, his sisters begged the honour of her correspondence, which she very readily granted them. She easily saw the letters were such as they could not write, though

---

[1] Lady Mary had evidently been strongly influenced in early girlhood by Mrs. Astell's *Serious Proposal to the Ladies*. In a letter written fifty years later, she says that at fifteen her favourite scheme was to found an English "monastery," and elect herself Lady Abbess.

they came in their hands. She was very regular in answering them, which was a fresh surprise to Sebastian, who had no notion that a girl of fourteen could write as good English as his friend, Mr. Addison."

Anne Wortley was the chief correspondent, and when left to her own devices, wrote careless, scrambling letters in a very bad hand. But only too soon Mr. Wortley was to be discovered at her elbow, and the correspondence was actually carried on between himself and Lady Mary with poor Anne as secretary and go-between. This is rather unfortunate for the reader, since Mr. Wortley in the early days of his courtship was anything but an easy writer. The rough drafts for his letters, some of which are still in existence, are so full of erasures and corrections as to be almost illegible. Lady Mary, on her side, was anxious to display the elegance of her style, and thus the correspondence, which must have cost both parties a great deal of time and pains, is as stiff and formal as a Court minuet.

Anne Wortley sets out gaily enough with a little note containing an anecdote about Lord Herbert,[1] who, it appears, had been anxious to obtain a token, no matter what, from his lady-love. As the article that he obtained is unmentionable to ears polite, it is certain that Mr. Wortley had no hand in this light-hearted scrawl. The next letter, dated 17th July 1709, is written in quite a different key, and we instantly detect the heavy masculine touch upon the quill.

"If transcribing were allowable,"[2] he begins, "you should have many Letters, for even the *Tatler* is better than anything I can do, but when I read yourn I am wild. But then compare your inimitable manner in everything with others. I may have hoped that that vast difference may justly make you value only the sincerity and love, without considering the style, sense, etc. Then I can be even with the author of the *Pleasure of the Imagination*.[3] Now I have raised that thought

---

[1] This may have been the second Lord Herbert of Cherbury, of the new creation (1694). His father, a nephew of the famous Edward, Lord Herbert of Cherbury, died in 1709.
[2] From the unpublished MS.
[3] Lady Mary had written a poem with this title.

Sir G. Kneller, pinxt.   *W. Greatbatch, sculp.*
ANNE WORTLEY MONTAGU

will conclude you in a labyrinth of bliss. Nothing can raise me, and I might as well endeavour to sing with the best, when mightily pleased with the song, as hope to come to any perfection in a thing so much superior to my genius. I have run into a way that you might fancy like flattery, but assure yourself that I know you to be too nice a judge to endeavour to please you that way, if my pen, or any other, could do it. Be so good as to let me hear from you, and excuse me when I only tell you that I love you dearly, and am faithfully yours,

"A. WORTLEY"

Lady Mary writes back on 21st July to assure her dear Mrs. Wortley that her letters are ever agreeable and beyond measure welcome, and to thank her for her obliging partiality, adding, "How happy must I think myself when I fancy your friendship to me even great enough to overpower your judgment! I am afraid this is one of the pleasures of the Imagination, and I cannot be so very successful in so earnest and important a wish." This letter, she truly observes, "is excessively dull," but explains that it is so "from my vast desire of pleasing you. . . . Believe me, I could scribble three sheets to —— (I must not name), but to twenty people that have not so great a share of my esteem, and whose friendship is not so absolutely necessary for my happiness, but am quite at a loss to you. . . ."

These complimentary letters soon pall on the modern reader, and therefore two or three more extracts may suffice to illustrate the relations between suitor and mistress. In August, Anne Wortley writing from the country says—

"I am now in the room with an humble servant of yours [Mr. Wortley], who is arguing so hotly about marriage that I cannot go on with my letter. I would be very glad to bring you into the argument, being sure you would soon convince us in what disturbs so many. Everybody seeks happiness; but though everybody has a different taste, yet all pursue money, which makes people choose great wigs. Because their neighbour sweats in it they dare not be easy out of the fashion. But you have dared to have wit joined with beauty, a thing so much out of fashion, that we fly after you with as much interestedness as you often see the birds do when one superior comes near them." This letter concludes with the request, "Send me word what books to read, etc."

On 8th August Lady Mary is still at Thoresby, whence she writes—

"I am now so much alone, I have leisure to pass whole days in reading, but am not at all proper for so delicate an employment as choosing you books. Your own fancy will better direct you. My study at present is nothing but dictionaries and grammars. I am trying whether it be possible to learn without a master; I am not certain (and hardly dare hope) I shall make any progress, but I find the study so diverting, I am not only easy, but pleased with the solitude that indulges it. I forget there is such a place as London, and wish for no company but yours. You see, my dear, in making my pleasures consist of these unfashionable diversions, I am not of the number who cannot be easy out of the mode. I believe more follies are committed out of complaisance to the world, than in following our own inclinations. Nature is seldom in the wrong, custom always. It is with some regret I follow it in all the impertinences of dress; but I am amazed to see it consulted even in the most important occasions of our lives, and that people of good sense in other things can make their happiness consist in the opinions of others, and sacrifice everything in the desire of appearing in the fashion."

In the next letter from Wharncliffe Lodge, the demon of jealousy rears its head. Lady Mary is gently reproached for her only fault—inconstancy. There follows an allusion to "the most happy person now in being," who, rumour said, had been favoured by a certain lady at the Nottingham Races. "You will want to know," adds the writer, "how this race comes into my head. This country, out of which many go thither, affords no other tittle-tattle at this time. Besides that, yesterday, as I was talking of it to Mrs. Sherard, she said, Lady Mary would be well diverted, for Nicolini[1] would be there. One that was by said there would be much

[1] It does not appear that Lady Mary was especially musical, but it was the fashion for fine ladies to make much of the opera-singers at this time. The fashion was to some extent justified in the case of Nicolini, who was a great artist.

better diversion there—looking upon me—as if he insinuated you would have pleasures less imaginary than those Nicolini can afford."

Lady Mary laughs off these insinuations in her reply, being guiltless of any connection with Nottingham Races or admirers thereat. "After giving me imaginary wit and beauty," she writes on 21st August, "you give me imaginary passions, and tell me I'm in love. If I am, 'tis a perfect sin of ignorance, for I don't so much as know the man's name; I have been studying these three hours, and cannot guess who you mean. I passed the days of Nottingham Races at Thoresby, without seeing or even wishing to see one of the sex. . . . Pray tell me the name of him I love, that I may (according to the laudable custom of lovers) sigh to the woods and groves hereabouts, and teach it to the echo. . . . Recommend an example to me; and above all, let me know whether 'tis most proper to walk in the woods, encreasing the winds with my sighs, or to sit by a purling stream, swelling the rivulet with my tears." The letter concludes with gentle reproof of her friend's suspicion. "Take back the beauty and wit you bestow upon me, leave me my own mediocrity of agreeableness and genius, but leave me also my sincerity, my constancy, and my plain dealing."

The friend, or rather the lover, replies in penitential style, professing to be overwhelmed by the severity of her reproofs, and wishing that those plains of Nottingham that have given him so much pain may be turned by some earthquake into mountains and rocks, and that none of its rivulets may receive the tears, nor its breezes the sighs, of a lover.[1] "But how can my dearest Lady Mary think it so wild (though an unhappy) thought in me to mention that race? You may easily recollect how either I or another rallied you upon one you met last year in that field, or —— where you dined together after the diversion was over." "But henceforward," he concludes, "I will be done with all jealous tricks. . . . I will not dare to speak, no, nor so much as think, anything of my dearest Lady Mary in a laughing way; nor will I ever presume to meddle with so high

[1] The composition of this letter must have cost the writer a great expenditure of time and trouble, for the original draft is one mass of erasures and corrections.

a subject as your pity to any of the other sex, which you outshine so far; but shall be satisfied if I am admitted into your lower entertainments, if I have the same rank among your admirers as your grammars and dictionaries among your books; if I serve only to assist you in procuring pleasures without the least hope of being ever able to give them. Let me send you what stories I collect, which you will be sure to make diverting; choose your ribbons and heads, on which you will bestow the power of enchanting. I will be contented never to soar above transmitting to you the best rules I hear for gaining languages, which, though it cannot raise a genius already so high, may yet very much enlarge your dominions by adding all that can possibly disobey you—the ignorant—who are taught to believe that learning is art."

Lady Mary justifies her resentment on the ground that the man who hears himself called a heretic without protesting, can never be esteemed a good Christian, and adds: " To be capable of preferring the despicable wretch you mention to Mr. Wortley is as ridiculous, if not criminal, as forsaking the Deity to worship a calf."

Meanwhile, her letter about the study of languages had reached Wharncliffe, and Miss Wortley explains that she could not forbear reading a few lines from it to a Cambridge Doctor (her brother, of course), who happened to be with her. " Where you talk of turning over grammars and dictionaries, he stopped me, and said, The reason why you had more wit than any man was that your mind had never been encumbered with those tedious authors; that Cowley never submitted to the rules of grammar, and therefore excelled all of his own time in learning as well as wit.[1] That without them you would read with pleasure in two or three months, but if you persisted in the use of them, you would throw away your Latin in a year or two, and the commonwealth would have reason to mourn. Whereas if I could prevail with you it would be bound to thank me for a brighter ornament than any it could boast of." There is a reproachful allusion in this

---

[1] It is said that the masters of Abraham Cowley could never force him to learn grammar, and excused him from this study on the ground that his natural quickness made it unnecessary.

letter to a remark Lady Mary had once made—that it was as easy to write kindly to a hobby-horse as to a woman, or even to a man.

"When I said it cost nothing to write tenderly," replied the lady by return of post, "I believe I spoke of another sex; I am sure not of myself. 'Tis not in my power (I would to God it was!) to hide a kindness where I have one, or dissemble it where I have none. . . . I hope my dear Mrs. Wortley's showing my letters is in the same strain as her compliments, all meant for raillery, and I am not to take it as a thing really so. But I'll give you as serious an answer as if 'twas all true——

"When Mr. Cowley and other people (for I know several have learnt after the same manner) were in places where they had opportunity of being learned by word of mouth, I don't see any violent necessity for printed rules. But being where, from the top of the house to the bottom, not a creature in it understands so much as even good English, without the help of a dictionary or inspiration, I know no way of attaining to any language. Despairing of the last, I am forced to make use of the other, though I do verily believe I shall return to London the same ignorant soul I went from it; but the study is a present amusement. I must own I have vanity enough to fancy, if I had anybody with me, without much trouble perhaps I might read."

The last letter of this series is dated 5th September 1709. Anne Wortley died shortly afterwards, and the correspondence between Thoresby and Wharncliffe Lodge temporarily ceased. However, Mr. Wortley must have made good use of his opportunities in town during the winter months, since in the spring of 1710 we find him a declared lover.

CHAPTER IV

EARLY LOVE-LETTERS

THE Autobiography may be consulted for the continuation of the love-story, though its accuracy must not be taken too much for granted. After the summer correspondence, we are told, the winter conversations were renewed. Sebastian's applications seemed more serious, but were always received by Lætitia in such a manner that he never mentioned love, for fear of losing the little complaisance she seemed to have for him. " The Duke had a seat very near the Town [at Acton], and as he never consulted the pleasures of his daughters when his own were in question, the matches at N[ewmarket] giving him an occasion of leaving the Town, he resolved to send them to his villa very early in the Spring, which was a great mortification, especially having there no Library, which would have been in lieu of everything to Lætitia.

" The night before her departure she went to the Park. Sebastian was there, and endeavoured by his looks and messages that he sent by the orangewomen to show her that this sudden remove made him very miserable. One of these Jades, who make it their business to find out people's inclinations, in order to find their account in serving them, seeing an unfeigned melancholy in his air and behaviour, told him after the farewell bow of Lætitia, that she gave him permission to write to her, and herself orders to convey the letter. Nothing could be more improbable than this message in every light, but he was so far transported with this surprising favour, he wrote a very passionate declaration of love, which he put into that woman's hand next morning, to which she brought him a very kind answer of her own invention. He was too well acquainted with the style and character of Lætitia to take it for hers, but the contents were so agreeable (however expressed) that he would believe it was wrote by her order by her chambermaid. But having very little opinion of the discretion of this messenger, he entrusted a faithful servant of his own with the answer, in which, after an acknowledgment full of transport for the happiness she gave him, he gently represented to her the danger to her reputation in employing a woman of that sort; that he was even glad she had not trusted her with a letter under her own hand, but he begged she would contrive some other method that might make their correspondence less hazardous to her.

"This letter was carried to the Duke's Villa, where the servant asked for Lætitia, and delivered it into her own hand. I cannot describe the astonishment with which she read it. She had been educated with a strictness that made her look on a love-letter as a mortal crime, and to be accused of writing one to a man she never had a tender thought for, made it doubly provoking. She looked on it as unpardonable vanity in him, and a want of esteem for her, to suppose her capable of it, and in the present hurry of her resentment wrote him a few lines, in which she expressed it in the severest manner, which she gave to his messenger.

"But this was not the whole consequence. It was a new thing in that regular Family to have an unknown person inquire for Lætitia, deliver her a letter, and receive an answer, and her governess was too attentive to let it pass without examination. She said nothing at that time, but searching her pocket at night found Sebastian's letter. The sight of a man's hand alarmed her; she sent it immediately to the Duke as an affair of the last consequence, and he made haste to his daughter, who, for the first time in his life, he severely reprimanded in so much fury that he would not hear her justification, and treated her as if she had been surprised in the most criminal correspondence.

"Poor Lætitia retired to her closet drowned in tears, and could think of no expedient to set her Innocence in a clear light but to employ Sebastian, who, she did not doubt, had too much generosity to let her suffer for his sake. She wrote to tell him her Father had surprised his letter, that he was in the utmost rage against her for receiving it, and as he had occasioned the mischief, she left it to his conduct to justify her. She got this conveyed by a maidservant, by the help of half a guinea, but it had a very different effect from what she had proposed. Sebastian had so far flattered himself with her love he did not doubt she had herself carried this letter to her Father, and it was an artifice to bring this affair to a proper conclusion. He was delighted with the wit of this contrivance, which was very far from her thoughts, and full of the most charming hopes went the next morning to her Father with a formal proposal of marriage, accompanied by the particulars of his estate, which was too considerable to be refused. The Duke gave him as favourable an answer as he could expect, and the lawyers were appointed to meet on both sides according to custom."

The autobiographical narrative breaks off here, and we have to turn to the Correspondence for a continuation of the love-story. The account contained in the last few paragraphs seems to be a mixture of romance and realism. After the exile of the Ladies Pierrepont to Acton Mr. Wortley sent Lady Mary a love-letter (with the new number of the *Tatler*), to which we have her reply. In the spring or early summer of 1710 he made proposals to Lord Dorchester for his daughter's hand. Negotiations were entered into, for the suitor was quite an eligible *parti*, but his lordship fell out with his future son-in-law about the settlements, and, in the language of the period, "the treaty was broke." Thereupon a secret correspondence was begun between the lovers, which continued down to the time of their runaway marriage in August 1712. It appears that on more than one occasion Mr. Wortley sent letters by a messenger whom Lady Mary considered untrustworthy or indiscreet, and once he received a note, written in her name, all knowledge of which she disclaimed.

Over a hundred love-letters—or "wrangle letters," as they might more accurately be termed—are preserved at Sandon. Of these only sixteen have hitherto been published. The whole correspondence is so extraordinary, and throws so strong a light upon the characters of the lovers, as well as, incidentally, upon the manners and customs of the period, that it has seemed desirable to relate the story of the next two years almost entirely through the medium of these "human documents."

Lady Mary has been described by most of her biographers and critics as a woman of cold, hard character, with an intellect that had been developed at the expense of her emotions. But her early love-letters give the impression that they were written by a warm-hearted, high-spirited girl, who was continually being chilled and wounded by the ungraciousness of the man upon whom she had bestowed her affection. Mr. Wortley, who can never have been young, was eleven years older than his lady-love. Judged by his letters, he was a well-developed specimen of the Egoist, as sketched by Mr. Meredith. To the cold and cautious nature which was held in such high esteem at that period, he added a carping, ungenerous temper, to say nothing of an uneasy vanity, which made him endeavour to draw definite avowals of love from his correspondent before he himself would "decide to engage." When Lady Mary wrote kindly, he begged her to avoid insincerity; but when she showed reserve, he declared that all he desired of woman was an open expression of tenderness and regard. If she resented his reproofs, he was convinced that she had ceased to value him, since fault-finding was always a mark of friendship; but when, goaded beyond endurance, she found fault in her turn, he professed to be delighted that she had discovered in time how entirely unsuited they were to each other. She could not even write prettily without being accused of a desire to be always witty. Eternal farewells were continually being spoken, and quite a number of the letters on both sides are stated to be "the very last."

The bosom friend of Addison and the boon companion of Swift must, however, have had some redeeming qualities, and we find that Mr. Wortley was regarded by his contemporaries as an upright, honourable man, of prudent disposition and cultivated mind. The graces of life had, to a great extent been exiled with the Stuarts, and the average Briton, more especially if he were a Whig, took William III. for his model, and was more inclined to practise Dutch boorishness than

Gallic politeness.[1] He despised women only a degree less than he despised the fops and beaux who adopted French fashions and made a regular profession of "gallantry," preferring to spend their time over a dish of Bohea in ladies' dressing-rooms rather than over a bottle of good wine in a club or tavern. Lady Mary could have had little in common with the butterflies, whose superficial attractions were quite outbalanced by her lover's sterling character and cultivated mind. In spite of the never-ending squabbles, it is impossible to doubt that there was a strong feeling on both sides, though each was chary of owning it. The words "sentiment" and "sentimental," in their modern sense, were not introduced till nearly half a century later, while "enthusiasm" was still regarded as a dangerous vice. Lovers spoke of their "friendship" for each other, and the ideal husband was one who would make a "kind and indulgent partner." Mr. Wortley was terribly afraid of the word "love." "Esteem," "preference," "respect," "value," "admire," are his warmest terms, though he occasionally alludes in pompous style to the violence of his "Passion." Lady Mary is less shy of "love," though once she crosses out the incriminating word and writes "care" above it. Perhaps there is a touch of feminine subtlety in the fact that she left "love" perfectly legible.

Nearly all the letters are written in tiny handwriting on miniature sheets of notepaper. Lady Mary writes a clear and pretty hand, while Mr. Wortley's, though more angular and crabbed, is fairly easy to read. The majority are undated, but a careful study of their contents has made it possible to arrange them, more or less, in chronological order. Mr. Wortley was obliged to send nearly all his letters by a private messenger, and they are merely addressed to

"THE LADY MARY PIERREPONT,
With Care and Speed."

---

[1] Bishop Burnet says that the English gentlemen of his time were "ill-taught, ill-bred, haughty, and insolent. . . . In their marriage they look only for fortune."

The lady was able to send her letters through the penny post, and they are addressed to

" MR. WORTLEY,
　At his Lodgings
　　Over against the Tavern
　　　In Great Queen Street
　　　　(A Looking-glass Shop)."

The spelling has been modernised in all the published letters, and to avoid confusion, the example set by former Editors in this respect will be followed here, though many words are written in a phonetic style that would delight Mr. Roosevelt. Thus " could," " would," and " should " are docked of the superfluous " l," and " been " is generally spelt " bin " by Mr. Wortley, though not by Lady Mary. On the other hand, an unnecessary " e " still lingers at the tail of most words ending in " ess "—" kindnesse," " endlesse," etc.—while " guess " retains the seventeenth-century form of " ghess."

One of the earliest love-letters that has been preserved, is from Mr. Wortley, and was received by Lady Mary when she was at Acton in the spring of 1710. It is evidently the continuation of a discussion that had taken place between the pair upon a subject which became a regular bone of contention. This was Lady Mary's supposed inability to lead a quiet, solitary existence on a small income in the country, and to regard her husband's society as recompense in full for all the joys and excitements of town life. The lady continually combated the accusation of an incurable love of gaiety and admiration which was levelled against her, but she invariably failed to convince her lover, who returned to the charge again and again. It may be noted that, with one exception, none of the letters has any formal beginning or ending.

" Did [1] I know what was likely to displease you," writes the lover, " I would obey your orders and of all things avoid to mention it. I would not say it, if I thought you could possibly dislike it, that I suppose your merits to be the very same I always did. Not that I believe your taking me would be the

[1] From the unpublished MS.

worst fortune that could happen to you. It is a great defect in me that my temper is directly contrary to what yours seems to be. You will be very unhappy if you choose one that is not pleased with a variety of friends, or that cannot bear to see others pretend to admire you. I own to you the way of living together that so many are delighted with, is what I can't think of with any patience, and if we differ we must live asunder. 'Tis my unhappiness that I avoid the company of those I see ready but to dispute with me; when I am tied to them but for a day it is a penance. And how can I think of continuing with you as long as I live when you have given me any just cause of complaint? Were you a thousand times more charming than you are, you would be in the wrong to think of living well with a reasonable man for whose sake you could not seem to forget you knew how to please others as well as him. If you consider well your own temper, you will find it can never receive so great an alteration. Would you not be the most imprudent woman on earth to leave your present condition, and lose the prospect of richer offers, and go to one with whom you have so small a chance for being easy? Now I dare own to you that I think you can never suit with one like myself. Do you imagine I cannot calmly reflect on everything I have had any time understood to be against me? And where could I live with you till you had forgot all the acquaintance I have ever wished you had not, or till your beauty was past? These are objections against your living with me that you may possibly answer, but I fear you cannot. . . ."

Lady Mary's first letter to her lover is dated 28th March, and is either an answer to the above, or to another letter in the same vein. She is not a little alarmed at her temerity in writing to a man, but the knowledge that she wrote very well probably helped to support her under this breach of etiquette.

"Perhaps you'll be surprised at this letter," she begins. "I have had many debates with myself before I could resolve upon it. I know it is not acting in form, but I do not look upon you as I do upon the rest of the world, and by what I do for you, you are not to judge my manner of acting with others. You are brother to a woman I tenderly loved; my protestations of friendship are not like other people's. I never speak but what I mean, and when I say I love, 'tis for ever. I had that real concern for Mrs. Wortley, I look with regard on everyone that is related to her. This, and my long acquaintance with you, may in some measure excuse what I am now doing. I am surprised at one of the *Tatlers* you send me. Is it possible to have any sort of esteem for a person one believes capable of having such trifling inclinations? Mr. Bickerstaff has very wrong notions of our sex.[1] I can say there are some of us that despise charms of show, and all the pageantry of greatness, perhaps with more ease than any of the philosophers. In contemning the world they seem to take pains to contemn us; we despise it without taking the pains to read lessons of morality to make us do it. At least I know I have always looked upon it with contempt, without being at the expense of one serious reflection to oblige me to it. I carry the matter yet further. Was I to choose of two thousand pounds a year or twenty thousand, the first would be my choice. There is something of an unavoidable *embarras* in making what is called a great figure in the world; [it] takes off from the happiness of life. I hate the noise and hurry inseparable from great estates and titles, and look upon both as blessings that ought only to be given to fools, for 'tis only to them that they are blessings. The pretty fellows you speak of, I own entertain me sometimes; but is it possible to be diverted with what one despises? I can laugh at a puppet-show; at the same time I know there is nothing in it worth my attention or regard.

"General notions are generally wrong. Ignorance and folly are thought the best foundations of virtue, as if not knowing

[1] The *Tatler* sent by Mr. Wortley was probably No. 143, for 7th March 1710. In this "Mr. Bickerstaff" states that he has been surprised by a visit from his sister Jenny, whose manner, he noticed, was above the simplicity and familiarity of her usual deportment. This, it appeared, was the result of her having set up her own chariot. She had received an order for £500 from her absent husband, who had bade her want for nothing that was necessary, and in her eyes an "equipage" came under the heading of necessaries of life. "I was heartily concerned," says Mr. Bickerstaff, "at her folly, whose affairs render her but just able to bear such an expense." He at once wrote to expostulate with his brother-in-law, and beg him not to indulge his wife in this foolish vanity. It is quite possible that the prudent Mr. Wortley may have contributed the suggestion for this little paper.

what a good wife is was necessary to make one so. . . . Give me leave to say it (I know it sounds vain), I know how to make a man of sense happy, but then that man must resolve to contribute something towards it himself. I have so much esteem for you, I should be sorry to hear you was unhappy, but for the world I would not be the instrument of making you so, which (of the humour you are) is hardly to be avoided if I am your wife. You distrust me—I can neither be easy, nor loved, where I am distrusted. Nor do I believe your passion for me is what you pretend it; at least I am sure was I in love I could not talk as you do. Few women would have spoke so plainly as I have done, but to dissemble is among the things I never do. . . . I wish I loved you enough to devote myself to be for ever miserable for the pleasure of a day or two's happiness. I cannot resolve upon it. You must think otherwise of me, or not at all.

"I don't enjoin you to burn this letter. I know you will. 'Tis the first I ever wrote to one of your sex, and shall be the last. You must never expect another. I resolve against all correspondence of the kind. My resolutions are seldom made, and never broken."

Mr. Wortley's answer to the above is very long, and not too definite. His ever-wakeful jealousy shows itself once again; he professes to believe that his lady has already made choice of another suitor, and seems uncertain whether to be relieved or despairing because her future may be settled before he crosses the water—he was then contemplating a journey to Spa. He is not sure that he wants her, yet he cannot bring himself to give her up altogether, and therefore he will decide nothing till he hears from her again.

"'In [1] the Humour you'—'If I am distrusted'—that is, in other words, if you love me—if you have any apprehension of losing me. My dear L[ady] M[ary], you had wronged me had you taken me to be of another Humour, had you thought otherwise of me, or believed I could think otherwise of you. Do you imagine anyone that is able to set a just value on you can under a Passion be less uneasy or insecure? I appeal even to your experience, which to my great grief is so much less than

[1] From the unpublished MS.

mine, whether anyone that loves is free from fear. Your own poet Virgil (you wonder how I should hear you was fond of him in the summer), who understood human nature so exactly, concludes it impossible to deceive a lover, because he is always alarmed, let the danger be never so remote."

After an allusion to his many rivals, and the little that each is worth in comparison with her excellence, he proceeds—

"I should not wonder to hear all is consummated before I am prepared to cross the water, which I hope I shall be in a month or six weeks. Tho' I was sure I was wholly out of the case, I should advise you rather to choose out of the diffident, if you can please yourself there. Did I not, I should be false to that engagement of friendship which we entered into when we were upon a quarrel, which was far below what I had vainly wished; but as clear as I am in preferring these [*i.e.* the diffident] I should be far from thinking it strange if you differed from me in it. It requires an uncommon greatness of mind to choose to be reduced to less than a third part of your present attendance, your apartments, your table, and to be quite stripped of all that glitters more than all the rest of those ornaments that are no part of you, the train of admirers. Did I to gain you quit the same proportion of my small trappings, I own my happiness would not arise from a self-denial, and therefore you will think me ungenerous in recommending it to you. . . .

"I ever believed the compleatest plan of felicity we are acquainted with, was to enjoy one woman friend, one man, and to think it of little moment whether those that were made use of to fill up some idle hours, were princes or peasants, wise or foolish. Had I you, I should have at one view all the charms of either sex met together. I should enjoy a perpetual succession of new pleasures, a constant variety in one. I never was fond of money, and in the humour I am I have a quarrel to it. As much as I value you, I wish there was no possibility of your having any. For then perhaps you would not say I must either not have you, or not think of you. . . . Could you really love me, we should both be happy beyond all example. Should you once seem to love me, and after cease to do it, we should, I fear, be wretched in as high a degree.

"This I write now only out of Punctilio, and not with the vanity of hoping for success. How you will rate anything of mine I dare not guess and wish I might never know. I need not tell you that you are bound to break a Resolution taken to the prejudice of one that belongs to you. You are to keep one made in his favour unless your keeping it is a wrong to another, and that I will not suppose till I hear it from yourself. So that you must write, either in justice to yourself or to me."

CHAPTER V

A DIFFICULT SUITOR

NEEDLESS to say, Lady Mary's good resolutions were made to be broken, and the secret correspondence seems to have continued briskly until the end of April, when Mr. Wortley went north, to stay with his uncle, John Montagu, Dean of Durham. In the course of the month Lady Mary fell ill with measles at Acton. There is a note purporting to be written with her knowledge by a maid or other go-between, which conveys the news of her illness to Mr. Wortley in the following terms:—

"D^R S^{IR},[1]—I ask pardon for my presumption, but the occasion that happened makes me take this liberty. My Lady Mary gave orders to let you know she received your two letters this day. The very time you went away, she went to Acton, and is very ill of the measles; and is very sorry she could not write sooner, for she had not conveniency; but as soon as she comes to London she does design to see you. Betty took a great deal of trouble, going often to Acton to see for a letter, but Lady Mary could get no conveniency to write. She gives her love and respects to you, but if it is not expressed as is proper, you will excuse it as from whence it comes, instead of my Lady. Lady Mary desires you to direct your letter for Betty Laskey at the Bunch of Grapes and Queen's Head in Knightsbridge. She had not time when Betty gave her the letters to read them. She signs her name to this, for I showed it her."

The letter is signed "M. P.," and it was apparently sent

[1] From the unpublished MS.

under cover to Steele, who, very early in the love-affair, was the confidant of Mr. Wortley. Steele, who must have delighted in the romance, sent on the missive endorsed—

"This is left here to-night with me to send to you. I send you no news, because I believe this will employ you better.—Your most obedient Servant,   RICH^D STEELE"

The above may have been the letter alluded to in the Autobiography, for it is made clear by the Correspondence that one was disowned by Lady Mary. However, Mr. Wortley accepted it as genuine, and replied at once in warmer fashion than usual—

"Tho'[1] last night I was perfectly well till I got the letter signed by you, I am this morning down-right sick. Had there been any such thing as sympathy that is occasioned by grief, I should have been sensible of it when you first fell ill. I had grieved at your illness, tho' I had been sure you hated me. An aversion may possibly be removed, but the loss of you would be irretrievable. There has not yet been, there never will be, another Lady Mary. You see how far a man's Passion carries his reflections. It makes him uneasy, because the worst may possibly happen from the least dangerous of distempers. I take yours to be so, and I think it a thousand to one I hear of your recovery when I hear of you next.

"I am not in the least concerned to fancy your colour may receive some alteration. I should be overjoyed to hear your Beauty is very much impaired, could I be pleased with anything that would give you displeasure, for it would lessen the number of Admirers. But even the loss of a feature, nay, of your Eyes themselves, would not make you less beautiful to ——.

"The sight of two such tedious long letters coming together has, I doubt, given you enough of my correspondence. If yours had not one word of your own in it, if you not only ordered in general a letter to be writ, but to be signed by another, I own it was too much while you was ill."

[1] From the unpublished MS.

SIR RICHARD STEELE

This letter is the only one signed in full, but the signature has been carefully erased. Lady Mary's next letter seems to have been one in which she reproaches him for having sent a foolish messenger, and disclaims the missive that was supposed to be signed by herself.

"Your conduct,"[1] she writes, "is more surprising every day than the other—how could you think of employing that creature? I begged you not to write again, I told you it would inevitably happen. To finish your indiscretion, you come to Acton that your name may be known. She has imposed upon you a thousand ways. I suppose she writ the letter you speak of. I know nothing of it; you have heard, I dare swear, fifty lies from her own mouth. I believe I may venture to affirm she never told you a word of truth. She has made everything public to every servant in the house. Imagine the pretty pickle I am in—I am so discomposed I don't know what I write. That I gave you no directions to anybody was because I would not, as I think I told you, keep any private correspondence.

"You accuse me in your last of a want of generosity. 'Tis a fault I never found in myself—I thought nothing so generous as telling the truth, and would not buy anything at the price of a deceit. I know not whether you can make me happy—you have convinced me you can make me miserable. Nothing is more dreadful than to live uneasy with people one must live with, and lose the good opinion of those that command one. I have said enough to you—too much. Happy only in my Innocence, and something of a temper that can bear misfortunes with patience, tho' I don't deserve 'em. Your last letter is excessively obliging, and I have a great deal of reason to be pleased with it. I find it is not enough to act generously, one should leave it to nobody's power to act otherwise.

"I read over again your last letter. I find you think very ill of me, but my Passion is abated, and upon cooler consideration I think you in the right. Yet there is something you wrong me in. Could you suppose I would willingly expose you to any inconveniences on my account? Forgive every-

[1] From the unpublished MS.

thing that is peevish in these two last letters. I writ that you received last, and great part of this, in a distraction. I knew not what I did; if my indiscretion (for I am now convinced I was indiscreet) has occasioned you any troubles, pardon it. Be so just as to believe it was not designed. I was born to be unfortunate, and shall complain of my destiny without complaining of you. Forgive and forget me, and it is all I have to require."

Mr. Wortley, who was one of those gentlemen who are always right in their own eyes, shows not the slightest regret for his indiscretion, but replies with his usual imperturbability—

"I[1] am the less troubled at your letter because I know I deserve none of the reproaches in it. Before I went out of town you know I never sent Betty but with answers to what she had brought from you—she has told me many times since I came, that you ordered her to be very frequently at Acton. The letter which you now disown orders me expressly to direct my letters to her. Had you thought her going to you improper, as I do, and assure you I always did, you would rather have told me to what friend of yours I might enclose. But you say you know nothing of this letter, and I am sorry for it, because it is more favourable than any of the rest. The first of those that are yours tells me that my Temper and yours can never agree. That I had yesterday from Durham says I can never please you. And that which came as I was going to bed by the Penny Post accuses me of very great faults and of folly.

"While I take the sense of your letters to be such, I should be altogether as indiscreet as you if I made any proposals. If I mistake the meaning of 'em, I hope you will give yourself the trouble of explaining. I can think of no bargain with another till you and I are agreed. And then I shall be more eager than you would have me in pursuing you. If you would have me go to your Father, and give him my estate as a great deal less than it is, so I may be secure of a repulse; or would have me tell all your friends I have writ to you very impertinently against your will, and you have rejected me, I will do either of 'em, as grievous as they would be to me, rather than

[1] From the unpublished MS.

that any fault should be imputed to you. But to take the best method of gaining you before I am convinced I may probably make you happy, is the only command of yours I can disobey."

This was not the kind of letter to console the lady for the "pickle" in which she found herself. She writes another reproachful letter on 5th May to the effect that—

"Your[1] indiscretion has given me so much trouble, I would willingly get rid of it at the price of my fever's returning. You employed the foolishest and most improper messenger upon earth. She has prattled all she knows and all she supposed, which goes a great deal farther. 'Tis not her custom to make secrets of names. Everything is known but my Innocence, which is never to be cleared. I could justify myself in part by showing your letters. I could not resolve to do what I thought not right, and burnt them to prevent their being seen, which was otherwise unavoidable. How unhappy am I! I think I have been scrupulously just to my Duty, I cannot as much as call to my mind an Expression I have cause to blame myself for, but I am not the less unfortunate. All commerce of this kind between men and women is like that of the Boys and Frogs in the Fables—'tis play to you but 'tis death to us—and if we had the wit of the Frogs we should always make that answer.

"I am mighty happy at Mr. St. [Steele] and his wife knowing this affair; he over a bottle and she over a tea-table has (I don't question) said many witty things upon this occasion. My answers have not (by a great good fortune) passed their hands. Upon second thoughts I half wish they had. To be sure they do you justice in supposing I would answer them, and perhaps me the injustice in supposing them other than they was. Without Authority for it, I find 'tis in your power to exclude me the Town; if I am as fond of it as you think me, I should be very angry at the cause of my going into a frightful solitude instead of repairing to London, where my Family is now persuaded I have behaved myself very ill. Were I disposed to tell the whole story, it would do me no

[1] From the unpublished MS.

good; they have reason to believe my vanity, or worse, has been more the cause of this business than any honourable design you had on me.

"Your last letter (which came safe to me by miracle) I don't understand a word of, nor what letter you speak of. I writ you one to the Deanery of Durham; it had no name to it, and was in the same hand as the first. I fear you never received it—I know of no others.

"My sickness was perhaps more dangerous than you think it. I have not lived very long in the world, but long enough to be weary of it, and in the state I am in, am very sorry I have recovered.

"By an indiscreet resentment to the foolish creature you employed do not expose me to her tongue.

"Make no attempts of writing. Either think of me no more, or think in the way you ought."

Among Lady Mary's published letters is one dated 25th April, which is evidently an answer to a criticism on her character by Mr. Wortley. Though she defends herself against some of his imputations, she clings firmly to the conventional idea of maidenly reserve and coolness of temperament, insisting the more strongly, perhaps, on her inability to be "fond," because she felt that in holding a secret correspondence with him she was sinning against the traditions of her upbringing. After alluding to the wit and beauty with which he endows her, as well as to the follies and weaknesses of which he accuses her, she continues—

"One part of my character is not so good, nor t'other so bad as you fancy it. Should we ever live together, you would be disappointed both ways. You would find an easy equality of temper you do not expect, and a thousand faults you do not imagine. You think if you married me, I should be passionately fond of you one month, and of somebody else the next. Neither would happen. I can esteem, I can be a friend, but I don't know whether I can love. Expect all that is complaisant and easy, never what is fond in me.

"If you can resolve to live with a companion that will have all the deference due to your superiority of good sense, and that your proposals can be agreeable to those on whom I depend, I have nothing to say against them. As to travelling, 'tis what I could do with great pleasure, and could easily quit London on your account. But a retirement in the country is not so disagreeable to me as I know a few months would make it tiresome to you. Where people are tied for life, 'tis their mutual interest not to grow weary of one another. If I had all the personal charms I want, a face is too slight a foundation for happiness. You would soon be tired of seeing every day the same thing."

After sagely observing that a love may be revived which absence, inconstancy, or even infidelity has extinguished, but that there is no returning from a *dégoût* given by satiety, this experienced worldling of one-and-twenty continues—

"I should not chuse to live in a crowd. I could be very well pleased to be in London without making a great figure, or seeing above eight or nine agreeable people. Apartments, table, etc., are things that never come into my head. But I will never think of anything without the consent of my family, and would advise you not to fancy a happiness in entire solitude, which you would only find fancy.

"Make no answer to this, if you can like me on my own terms; 'tis not to me you must make the proposals. If not, to what purpose is our correspondence? However, preserve me your friendship, which I think of with a great deal of pleasure and some vanity. If ever you see me married, I flatter myself you'll see a conduct you would not be sorry your wife should imitate."

This was not at all the kind of letter to appeal to the egoist in Mr. Wortley. He expected not only to have his own way about the place of living and the manner of life, should he decide to marry, but he wanted a blindly adoring wife into the bargain. Nor was he pleased with the rather broad hint about the quarter in which he should make his proposals. He replied on 5th May in that tone of unflinching candour which characterises all his so-called love-epistles. Her letter is, he observes, "in [1] every part of it a contradiction to the compliment you make me, and proves that no one is superior to you in good sense. However, I heartily thank you for it, as well

[1] From the unpublished MS.

as for your saying you could bring yourself to be easy and complaisant. I wish you had been able to stop there, and forbear telling me you could do nothing more. Had you, immediately after you said you might be easy, gone for the mention of settlements, I might only have taken you to be very prudent, and still have hoped for something above ease and complaisance. But to say there could be nothing more, and then to be so exact about the method of proposing, I refer it to yourself whether this doesn't look as if you were studying how to put yourself in the road to happiness, and not preparing to enter upon the possession of it. . . .

"I am one of those that have an idea of Felicity, and I know it can never be given by such a carriage as often proceeds from indifference. Should I, from your giving me no marks of a Preference (you have often laughed at the word, tho' now it is more than what you can come up to), conclude, as most would do, that you gave it elsewhere, can you answer for it that I or any man in such a case would not be miserable? He must be stupid that can ever have enough of your company. The satiety you speak of never happens where there is not a want of understanding on one side or the other. A very small share of reason, with a great deal of kindness, will secure a Passion longer than the perfection of it with your sort of return.

"If you say a man is not satiated when he has got rid of such an attachment, I will not say he is, nor quarrel with you about a word; but this I must beg leave to say, that I would much rather be cured, and that I should be much longer in curing by what you call satiety, than by such a coldness as yours. . . . I should be sorry to be tied to one to whom I could think myself superior, or whom I could live with as if I had any power. I would not think of it without first letting you know all I knew myself of my temper, that if it did not suit with yours, it might give you no trouble. Most others would first have secured you, and then seemed surprised you should not be satisfied in any place or company that pleased them most. That I have chose rather to love you than govern you will, I hope, give me some title to that Friendship you promised me.

"I am not sure retirement would agree with me better than with others. But a man should never run a hazard of hearing one he loves find fault with a place where she may not only have as much as she pleases of his company, but knows she has his heart wholly to herself."

CHAPTER VI

WEST DEAN

LETTERS were passing frequently at this time between Acton and Great Queen Street, though each lover seemed to write only to give pain or displeasure to the other. Thus, Mr. Wortley was so much incensed by one communication from Lady Mary that he says he was very doubtful whether he would answer it. But being ill at the time that he received it, he read it over again, and came to the conclusion that she left him at liberty to break off the affair, but did not wish herself to be responsible for the rupture.

"That you care very little,"[1] he continues, "is visible in every line you write. Could any woman write with so much wit, and be so much upon her guard, with one she was afraid of losing? I own I have endeavoured to express as little concern as I could, but you see an air of sincerity in all I tell you. Does anything of that appear in yours?" His present intention, he says, is not to take the leave she gives him of breaking off. He will wait till she sends him back a letter unopened, the most proper ceremony of parting for good and all. "I am sick," he concludes, "and write this to show I have not yet given over conversing with you. I can't answer for it that when I am well I shall think exactly as I do now."

The lady's heart was softened by the news of Mr. Wortley's indisposition, and it may be that she was a little alarmed at the temper of his letter, and his apparent inclination to take her at her word when she talked of putting an end to their secret romance. She was still ill herself, moreover, and even the proudest spirit may weaken under the influence of a bad attack of measles. Lastly, she was to be sent into the country as

[1] From the unpublished MS.

soon as she was able to travel, and it was doubtful when she would see her lover again. It is not surprising, therefore, that she writes in the following unusually sympathetic strain:—

"At[1] this minute I am so ill myself your letter has come in good time if you have a mind I should say anything soft to you. I have kept my chamber this three days, and have so much compassion for people that are ill, I am very likely to forget you are ill-natured, and only remember that you are sick, and talk with a great deal of tenderness. But I hope there is no occasion for this. You are now very well, and if I am to take your word for it, your thoughts are very much altered. I will take no notice of this, but write as if they were not, and answer your last letter, tho' perhaps by this time you have forgot you ever wrote it.

"You seem to reproach me with being upon my guard; what would I give that this reproach was just? I have been foolishly otherwise. I agree with you that you have less reason than anyone else to esteem me; no other knows so many of my weaknesses, and I cannot blame you for thinking of me as I do myself. I could wish impossibilities—that I could be what you seem to reproach me with, or you what I could wish you. This letter will be astonishingly silly, but there are several excuses for it. I am not well, there is musick in the next room that I hear whether I will or no, and—this must be my last letter. If only my own Resolution designed it so, neither you nor I have any reason to believe it. Tho' I once told you my Resolutions were never broken (and I remember I thought so at that time) yet I have broke two or three every day since, a punishment due to the vanity of that Expression.

"There is now a greater bar to our Correspondence. If I am well I leave this place the 28th of this month, and then it will be utterly impossible to send a letter to, or receive one from you. It is now a hazard, and will then be a certainty of discovery. A letter coming to my maid will be suspected, and I beg you to believe me, that I speak perfect truth, that even one Attempt of that kind would ruin me. If you wait till I send you a letter back unopened you will wait very long. I

[1] From the unpublished MS.

have not courage to do it, nor is it in my power to be rough. The softness of my temper is the most unfortunate part of my composition. No one can be thoroughly unhappy that wants it, and I think you very happy that know not what it is.

"You say you do not think to break off. If you do not, 'tis only to my Family you must speak. I can now hear no more from you, nor can I make you any other answer than what they are pleased to direct. If you do not agree with them, or if (which is most likely) you have resolved not to try, do not think of me otherwise than as of one who, wherever ill-fortune conducts her, will preserve an Esteem for you, and some unavailing good wishes, which are very sincere tho' very insignificant.

"I say nothing of my letters. I know you will burn them. Adieu; do not think of returning an answer except that you would have it fall into the hands of my Relations on purpose to make me miserable. Once more, Adieu. I would not have you persist in your causeless suspicions, but what remedy can I give to them?"

Perhaps it was this letter that induced Mr. Wortley to apply to Lord Dorchester for his daughter's hand. His offer seems to have been cordially received in the first instance, which was only natural, considering that he was a man of good family, and high character, and heir to a fine estate. But, as has been said, it was not long before father and lover, both men of obstinate will, fell out over the question of settlements. Mr. Wortley disapproved of settling property on an unborn heir, and was not too favourably disposed towards anything in the nature of jointure or pin-money, these last arrangements being of comparatively recent introduction. He desired to keep all his property in his own control, and objected to the system of "tying up" any part of it for the benefit of wife or child. Among his private papers are the headings for an article on this subject which he sent to his friend Steele, who worked them up for a paper in the *Tatler*. A character named " Honest Coupler, the conveyancer," is made to assert that the Marriage Settlements which are now used, have grown fashionable even within his memory. "Joyntures," he adds, "were never frequent till the age before his own; but the women were contented with the third part of the estate the law allotted them, and scorned to engage with men whom they thought capable of abusing their children." The practice of giving a wife pin-money was also denounced by both Steele and Addison.

Lord Dorchester, on his side, was unmoved by the suitor's arguments, and roundly declared that his grandchildren should not run the risk of being left beggars. Mr. Wortley refused to give in, and as Lady Mary was not consulted in the matter, the "treaty," as it is invariably termed, was broken off, and the lovers were supposed to acquiesce without a murmur. It was not, however, till the middle of the summer that the negotiations about a marriage to Mr. Wortley were finally dropped. It was probably to remove her from the neighbourhood of her obstinate suitor, while the wrangle about settlements was being carried on, that Lady Mary was sent down to West Dean, the Evelyn place in Wiltshire, which she had not visited since the days of her early childhood. Just before leaving town she wrote to Mrs. Hewet—

"We go next week into Wiltshire, which will be quite a new world to us. I was about eight years old when I left it, and have entirely forgot everything in it. I am sorry we shall not see you, though I am still in hopes we shall return to Nottinghamshire the latter end of the year; but all that is supposals, and I have no ground to believe it, but that I wish it very much. You can expect no news from one who has nothing at present in her head but packing up, and the ideas that naturally come upon going to a place, I may almost say I never saw, so perfectly have I forgotten it. . . . Mrs. Hewet should never talk of being rivalled; there is no such thing as not liking her, or liking anybody else better. It is a provoking thing to think so many tedious years as we have passed at Thoresby, we should always be asunder so many dirty miles, and the first summer you come nearer, I am tossed to the other side of the world, where I do not know so much as one creature, and am afraid I shall not meet with such agreeable neighbours as in Nottinghamshire. But destiny must be followed, and I own, was I to choose mine, it should never be to stay perpetually in the same place. I should even prefer little storms to an eternal calm; and tho' I am displeased not to see you, I am not sorry to see a new part of the kingdom. . . ."

West Dean, a village in a purely agricultural neighbourhood, seemed a dull little hole to a young lady who was accustomed to pass the season in the most brilliant society in town; but it is doubtful whether, in the unfortunate state of her love-affairs, she would have found any place or any neighbours wholly to her taste. Shortly after her arrival she wrote again to her Nottinghamshire friend—

"Most of the neighbours hereabouts have been to see me, but they are very few, and few of those few that are supportable—none agreeable. This part of the world is so different from Nottinghamshire, that I can hardly persuade myself it is in the same kingdom. The men here are all Sylvios, no Myrtillos. If they could express themselves, they would say, like him—

> 'Mille ninfe darei per una fera
> Che da Melampo mio cacciata fosse;
> Godasi queste gioje
> Chi n' ha di me più gusto; io non le sento.'

Though they cannot say it in Italian verse, they often speak to that purpose in English prose over a bottle, insensible of other pleasures than hunting and drinking. The consequence of which is, the poor female part of their family being seldom permitted a coach, or at best but a couple of starved jades to drag a dirty chariot, their lords and masters having no occasion for such a machine, as their mornings are spent among hounds, and the nights with as beastly companions, with what liquor they can get in this country, which is not very famous for good drink. If this management did not hinder me the company of my *she* neighbours, I should regret the absence of the Pastor Fidos, being of the opinion of Sylvio in Tasso—

> 'Altri segua i diletti dell' amore,
> Se pur v' è nell' amor alcun diletto.'

"I would fain persuade you to practise your Italian. I fear I shall forget to speak it, for want of somebody to speak it to.

Among the rest of the advantages I should have in your conversation (if I should be so happy as to be with you), I would endeavour to improve in that polite language.

"I find you are very busy about politics. We are the same here, particularly in the pulpit, where the parsons would fain become as famous as Sacheverell, and are very sorry that they cannot have the honour of being *tried* too.[1] For my part, I content myself in my humble sphere, am passive in their disputes, and endeavour to study my Italian in peace and quietness. But people mistake very much in placing peace in woods and shades, for I believe solitude puts people out of humour, and makes them disposed to quarrel, or there would not be so many disputes about religion and liberty, by creatures that never understood the first, nor have, or are likely to have, a taste of the latter—

'Crushed by the stint of thirty pounds a year.'"

Throughout this early correspondence we hear curiously little of Lady Mary's two younger sisters, Lady Evelyn and Lady Frances. The former, there is reason to believe, lived chiefly with her "Aunt Cheyne,"[2] who seems to have kept an inquisitorial eye upon the motherless family. Lady Frances was sometimes in favour with her elder sister, but more often

[1] Dr. Sacheverell (? 1674–1724) was the popular hero of the hour. On 5th November 1709 he had preached a violent sermon at St. Paul's, before the Lord Mayor and Aldermen, in which he condemned "toleration" and "occasional conformity," and attacked Bishop Burnet and Godolphin, the latter under his nick-name of Volpone. This sermon was declared by the House of Commons to be a seditious libel, and, against the advice of the more sober Whigs, he was impeached for high crimes and misdemeanours. His trial came on in March 1710. The proceedings were attended by the Queen, and the fashionable world followed her example. The mob cheered the culprit, who was regarded as an injured martyr, and were kept with difficulty from attacking the Whig leaders. Sacheverell was only suspended from preaching for three years. During the trial he was presented with a living in Shropshire, and when the three years were at an end the Queen gave him the rich living of St. Andrews, Holborn. He married a rich widow, was left a handsome estate, and died a prosperous man. No wonder that the Wiltshire parsons were sorry they could not be tried too!

[2] Lady Cheyne, *née* Evelyn, was second wife of William, the second Lord Cheyne, and Viscount Newhaven (a Scotch title), whose father had bought the manor of Chelsea from the Duke and Duchess of Hamilton. The second Lord Cheyne sold the manor to Sir Hans Sloane in 1712, but his name is still commemorated in Cheyne Walk, Cheyne Gardens, etc.

regarded as a spy on her actions, or at best as a clog upon her freedom and an undesired interloper in the family coach. For her young brother, then about eighteen, Lady Mary had more affection and sympathy. We shall see that later she made him her confidant, and that he did his best to help her to obtain her heart's desire. Lord Kingston, then at Cambridge, was a youth of promise, if we may judge from some of his letters to his father which are preserved among the family papers. A "rich match" for him was already under discussion, and so great was his dislike to the University (probably owing to the strong Tory feeling which prevailed there) that he seems to have looked upon an early marriage as a welcome means of escape, though he would have much preferred a chance of distinguishing himself with the army in Flanders. Two quaintly prim letters addressed by him to Lord Dorchester may here be quoted, as examples of his style. The first is dated 21st May 1710, and is written in an exquisite copperplate hand—

"My Lord,[1]—I believe by this time your Lordship must think I am either so entirely rapt up in my studies, and serious contemplations, or so eagerly given up to my Follies and Divertions, that I can't find one leisure hour to express my Duty and Gratitude to your Lordship. Neither of the two indeed. I have studied moderately, and have made use of those Divertions which this wretched Place affords, sparingly enough. I have not lockt myself up in my Chamber for whole days together, or excluded myself from all sort of Conversation, nor have I thrown away all my Time on the Bowling-green, or in Fruitless and Idle Discourse. The only Reason I can find for my silence hitherto, is that I have all along flattered myself with the (I'm afraid groundless) Hopes of being sent for to London, in order to go Abroad. Your Lordship may easily imagine that in a Place, where the sole Conversation is either railing at Dr. Bentley,[2] or inveighing

---

[1] From the unpublished MS.

[2] "Slashing Bentley with his desperate hook" had been elected Master of Trinity in 1700, which post he held, in spite of various efforts to eject him, till 1740. Being a Whig, he, like the ministers, was unpopular in the University, which was a stronghold of Jacobitism.

against the Ministry and Administration, there can be nothing agreeable, or indeed supportable, to one who has entertained a Friendship and Esteem for the former, and an entire settled good opinion of the Latter. I can't forbear telling your Lordship that Mr. Hervey[1] is going for Flanders in about a Month's time, and that I envy him very much in the Satisfaction he's like to take in a sight to which (without embracing this opportunity) he might very probably never see anything comparable, during his whole Life-time. I have not forgot what your Lordship told me at Newmarket concerning the Reason of my Continuance at Cambridge, which is a matter of great satisfaction to me, and I should take it as the greatest Honour Imaginable, if your Lordship would be pleased to take the Trouble to let me know in a Line or two, in what Posture the Affair stands, and whether 'tis to go forward. This would make me (if possible) more indebted to your Lordship than ever, and make me with the greatest sincerity, my Lord, your Lordship's most Dutifull and obedient Son,

"KINGSTON"

"*P.S.*—I should certainly have sent your Lordship a Theme enclosed, hadn't I been interrupted yesterday by a visit from a gentleman lately come to Town, Mr. George St. John,[2] second son to Sir Harry of that name, with whom I was formerly acquainted in London. I shall be sure to send it next post."

Early in the summer the young man made a riding tour in Norfolk with three friends, and wrote the following account to his father:—

"MY LORD,[3]—After a very pleasant Tour of ten days quite round the Coast of Norfolk, I returned hither Wednesday

---

[1] This was probably Carr, afterwards Lord Hervey, eldest son of the first Earl of Bristol. He was born in 1691, was M.A. of Cambridge in 1710, and died in 1723. He was elder brother of the more famous John, Lord Hervey, and was rumoured to be the father of Horace Walpole. One of Lady Mary's Court Eclogues is addressed to him.

[2] A son by his second wife of Sir Henry St. John, who was created Viscount St. John in 1716. The young man would be a half-brother of the famous Lord Bolingbroke.

[3] From the unpublished MS.

in the afternoon. Mr. Franke and I, with two other gentlemen of the University, sett out from hence on Monday was sennight, and passing thro' Ely, made Downham our first stage, near which Place we saw Denver sluyce, famous for the vast sums laid out upon it, and compared to those of the largest size in Holland. The Place we went to next was Lynn Regis, a Town very well worth seeing, with a fine spacious Market Place, and new-built hansom Cross, and good Trading tho' pretty much decayed. We went out at Sea three or four Leagues (for Curiosity sake) in a Yacht, prepared for us very civilly by the Custom House Officer. We fished, and went on board a Man of War that lay at Anchor in the station, tho' that was no great sight to me after having seen the *Brittannia*. From hence we went to Walsingham, much talk'd of, and mention'd in History, for its famous Abbey, nunnery and seat of the Blessed Virgin there. The Ruins are now only remaining to testifie its Ancient Grandeur. The next thing we saw worth taking notice of, was the seat of my Lord Townshend,[1] which (tho' I had heard no great Character of it) I had an earnest desire to see, as being the Patrimony of one who is like to make so great a figure both in the present and succeeding Ages. I was surprised at the first view of it. 'Tis a Noble House, standing upon an Eminence, surrounded with fine Woods and Beautifull Avenues, the agreeable Prospect was magnified by the unequal Account I had heard of it, and every Charm was enhanced by being unexpected. In short the House is magnificent and convenient. I had almost said, worthy to receive the Illustrious Owner.

"Leaving Raynam [Rainham], we went along the Coast thro' Burnham, Sherringham, Cromer, etc., till we came to N. Walsham, a Markett Town of good Accommodation where we Lodged that Night. Next Morning we sett out pretty early, and went the shortest way directly to the sea, about 5 miles from Walsham, and never left the very sands of it till we arrived at Yarmouth, after having rid 25 of the longest miles that ever were travelled. Yarmouth is a neat compact Town, with a

---

[1] This, of course, was the famous Whig statesman, Charles, second Viscount Townshend (1674–1738). At this time he was acting as plenipotentiary to the Netherlands. In 1713 he married the sister of Sir Robert Walpole.

hansom Marchee, convenient Harbour, and noble Kay. Busy and Populous, and next to Newcastle and Bristol, it has more the face of Trade in it than any I have met with in England.

"On Sunday morning we directed our course to Norwich, 20 miles from Yarmouth; however we reach'd it by ten o'clock, time enough to see the Mayor and Corporation come out of the Cathedral in all their Formalities. We saw everything in Norwich worth seeing, which indeed I can't say was very much. The Town stands upon a large Extent of Ground, but I can't say the Houses are mightily crowded. There stands in the middle of the Town (and in the lowest part of it) a Noble Shell of a House belonging to the Duke of Norfolk, and built by his Grandfather, but certainly the worst contrived Business that was ever designed. It would have stood naturally a great deal too low, yet not content with that they dugg a Hole to put it in, the Rubbidge of which cost a thousand pounds to be removed, so that now 'tis impossible it should be finished, and is entirely useless. Upon the least Flood, the water runs into the Cellars, and has weaken'd the foundation so much that (except it be pull'd down) it will fall in a year or two's time.

"On Tuesday morning we took the strait Road from Norwich to Cambridge, and lay at Thetford that night. We design'd to have seen Euston, the Dutchess of Grafton's Joynture House the next morning, but were prevented because Sir Thomas Hanmer[1] and the Dutchess were just come into the country, and strangers at such a Time must have been troublesome. . . .

"The Reason I did not send this by Sunday's Post will I hope seem sufficient, *i.e.* I was taken up the whole day in endeavouring to frustrate as much as in me lay (as being Master of Arts that is) two famous Projects. The first to send up a high-flying Address,[2] the second to expell Mr.

---

[1] Sir Thomas Hanmer (1677-1746) was the fourth baronet, and Speaker of the House of Commons in 1714-15. In 1698 he had married the widow of the first Duke of Grafton, who was Countess of Arlington in her own right. As he was a strong Tory, the young Lord Kingston—a keen party man—would be quite out of sympathy with him.

[2] The projected address had doubtless some connection with the political crisis that had been brought about by the Sacheverell case.

Ashenhurst.[1] They did not indeed propose an address in direct terms (as being conscious it wouldn't do) but design'd by voting a publick Commencement to frighten the Chancellor into it. However they lost their Aim, and 'twas carried for a private one. As for the Expulsion of Mr. Ashenhurst, there was a grace presented to the Vice-Chancellour, but rejected by Him and all the Heads, as a thing altogether unstatutable and not to be defended. I hope I shall soon hear how I am to be disposed of.—I am my Lord, your Lordship's dutifull son,

"KINGSTON"

" Nemo Repente fit Turpissimus."

A short Latin theme with the above title accompanies this letter.

In June Lord Kingston made a journey on horseback to Preston, where he stayed with his friend—possibly tutor—Mr. Francke. Manchester he describes as "a substantial trading town, which will soon pride itself upon the neatest Parochial Church this day in England, out of London." Preston is a "pretty neat town, pleasantly situate, with the convenience of a hansom large River." The young man enlarges upon the civil treatment he has received from the whole family, but concludes, " I would not have your Lordship think that, because I'm not at Cambridge, I must be idle. I have the whole morning to myself without any interruption but that of half an hour for Tea, and I have all the books I should make use of anywhere else. . . . I can't forbear saying that should I return to Cambridge it would seem as dull and disagreeable to me as Nottingham does to Monsieur Tallard, or Acton to my sisters."

[1] Ward Gray Ashenhurst, a Fellow of Trinity. He was not expelled, for he was holding College offices as late as 1714.

CHAPTER VII

MR. WORTLEY DEPARTS

DURING the early part of the summer, while the question of her marriage still hung in the balance, Lady Mary occupied herself in making the translation, already alluded to, of the *Enchiridion* of Epictetus. Perhaps she found the task peculiarly appropriate at a time when she needed all the consolations of a Stoic philosophy. To her kind adviser, Dr. Burnet, Bishop of Salisbury, she sent her translation, accompanied by the following letter, dated 20th July 1710:—

"MY LORD,—Your hours are so well employed, I hardly dare offer you this trifle to look over; but then, so well am I acquainted with that sweetness of temper which accompanies your learning, I dare even assure myself of a pardon. You have already forgiven me greater impertinences, and condescended yet further in giving me instructions, and bestowing some of your minutes in teaching me. This surprising humility has all the effect it ought to have on my heart; I am sensible of the gratitude I owe so much to your goodness, and how much I am ever bound to be your servant. Here is the work of one week of my solitude—by the many faults in it, your Lordship will easily believe I spent no more time on it. It was hardly finished when I was obliged to begin my journey, and I had not leisure to write it over again. You have it here without any corrections, with all its blots and errors. I endeavoured at no beauty of style, but to keep as literally as I could to the sense of the author. My only intention in presenting it, is to ask your Lordship whether I have understood Epictetus. The fourth chapter particularly I am afraid I have mistaken.

"Piety and greatness of soul set you above all misfortunes that can happen to yourself, and the calumnies of false tongues; but that same piety which renders what happens to yourself indifferent to you, yet softens the natural compassion in your temper to the greatest degree of tenderness for the interests of the church, and the liberty and welfare of your country. The steps that are now made towards the destruction of both,[1] the apparent danger we are in, the manifest growth of injustice, oppression, and hypocrisy, cannot do otherwise than give your Lordship those hours of sorrow, which, did not your fortitude of soul and reflections from religion and philosophy shorten, would add to the national misfortunes by injuring the health of so great a supporter of our sinking liberties.

"I ought to ask pardon for this digression. It is more proper for me in this place to say something to excuse an address that looks so very presuming. My sex is usually forbid studies of this nature, and folly reckoned so much our proper sphere, we are sooner pardoned any excesses of that, than the least pretensions to reading or good sense. We are permitted no books but such as tend to the weakening and effeminating of the mind. Our natural defects are every way indulged, and it is looked upon as in a degree criminal to improve our reason, or fancy we have any. We are taught to place all our art in adorning our outward forms, and permitted, without reproach, to carry that custom even to extravagancy, while our minds are entirely neglected, and by disuse of reflections, filled with nothing but the trifling objects our eyes are daily entertained with. This custom, so long established and industriously upheld, makes it even ridiculous to go out of the common road, and forces one to find as many excuses as if it was a thing altogether criminal not to play the fool in concert with other women of quality, whose birth and leisure only serve to render them the most useless and most worthless part of the creation. There is hardly a character in the world more despicable, or more liable to universal ridicule, than that of a learned woman: those words imply,

---

[1] Owing to the downfall of the Whigs, and the consequent triumph not only of the Tories but of the High Church party.

J. Riley, pinxt.   *J. Smith, fecit*
GILBERT, LORD BISHOP OF SARUM

according to the received sense, a tattling, impertinent, vain, and conceited creature. I believe nobody will deny that learning may have this effect, but it must be a very superficial degree of it.[1] . . ."

After quoting from Erasmus and the Abbé Bellegarde in corroboration of her theory, Lady Mary proceeds: "I am not now arguing for an equality of the two sexes. I do not doubt God and nature have thrown us into an inferior rank; we are a lower part of the creation, we owe obedience and submission to the superior sex, and any woman who suffers her vanity and folly to deny this, rebels against the law of the Creator and indisputable order of nature. But there is a worse effect than this, which follows the careless education given to women of quality—its being so easy for any man of sense, that finds it either his interest or his pleasure, to corrupt them. The common method is, to begin by attacking their religion. They bring them a thousand fallacious arguments their excessive ignorance hinders them from refuting; and I speak now from my own knowledge and conversation among them, there are more atheists among the fine ladies than the loosest sort of rakes; and the same ignorance that generally works out into excess of superstition, exposes them to the snares of any who have a fancy to carry them to the opposite extreme. . . ."

In the course of the negotiations about the marriage, and just when a dead-lock had been reached, Mr. Wortley wrote to Lady Mary—

"Had[2] I a month or two longer to consider, we should be much more at liberty to come together. Should we be of a mind now, we may both alter before I come back. I must go in the first place to the Spaw. Those waters (I know by having tried) are the quickest method of recovering an appetite. The want of one is my present indisposition, though I must pretend some greater to excuse my going away. . . . I will write at

---

[1] The same theory was held by Pope, who expressed it for all time in his lines—

"A little learning is a dangerous thing;
Drink deep, or taste not the Pierian spring."

[2] From the unpublished MS.

least once a day while I stay, and hope you will write as often, unless you can at once say that which will fix me. If I engage at all at present, it must either be upon a bargain I am to know just now, or to have you without any. But to pretend that I may comply with what your family shall demand is what I cannot come up to. I judge by your way of writing that your match is to go on, unless I break it. If I guess right I am unhappy in having so little time for so weighty an affair, but it is not my fault. I beg you will alter nothing upon what I write now, but let your treaty go on till I say more. If nothing hinders my return to England before the winter, I shall be fully disposed to close with you if the terms can be agreed between us, and I have no fresh grounds for complaint. But I don't know whether I can say anything to be depended on before I go. I will not excuse the plain-dealing of this letter. I am mistaken if you don't find a good deal of passion, tho' I avoided to mention it."

The negotiations seem to have been temporarily broken off before Mr. Wortley's departure. Another suitor had already come forward, as may be gathered from a short note written by the departing lover, in which he announces that should his lady be free on his return, "my opinion is I shall be desirous to engage, though perhaps not upon unreasonable terms. But my return is not to be depended on, and therefore I cannot agree you should dismiss the other affair on my account." From Harwich, just before the packet sailed, he wrote a long letter of explanation and apology, from which we learn how matters really stood at this time between the pair—

"Tho'[1] the treaty [his own] I fear is quite broke off, I am no longer able to forbear acquainting you that I can't lay the blame of its miscarriage on myself. The offers I made were very advantageous according to the common way of reckoning, such as I am sure any man without knowing the persons, and taking 'em to be equal, as they ought to be supposed, will not believe to have been rejected. I don't at all wonder it should be thought no rules ought to be observed in your case. I know too high a rate can't be set upon you.

[1] From the unpublished MS.

All I am worth would be as far short of your merit as what I offered. But if nothing like a proportion between the money and the land is to be observed, what would be the consequence? I must give away all I have, and be undone without the pleasure of paying you your due. And I certainly would give all were I to be insured you would be bound to live with me and yet be easy. Some are vain enough to think they are every way equal to you. With them it is that you should be treated for, and I know very well what you please will be granted you. But I that know how great the danger is of seeing all your charms lost to me by your being out of humour, cannot so readily agree to make myself incapable of any satisfaction, in case I should have none from you.

"What makes me excuse myself the more is that we differed chiefly about taking from me what was not to be given to you. Had the demand been for yourself, perhaps I could not have withstood it. It was for a larger settlement on an heir.[1] Now I don't know any man that would give £500 out of his pocket that his heir, yet unborn and that is sure to have enough, whatever he proves to be, may have £1000 a year added to his fortune after his father's death. And yet whoever settles £1000 a year of his own after his death, parts with at least £10,000. Is it not strange that a man without being in love should part with as much of his estate as is really worth £10,000 for what no one that thinks would value at £500? And for what the lady values at less? I don't know the sum we talked of in a letter, but the same way of reasoning will hold in any sum. This demand of so much from me, and so little, I think nothing for you, troubled me the more, because it might be altogether at your desire.

"You may imagine I had been desirous to know whether it was or not, and whether it will be insisted upon; but after I had so long obeyed your command of not writing, which was very severe for a time, I resolved to stay till I was got thus far on my journey, lest an answer should have in it any forbidding or favourable expressions. Such as pleased might

---

[1] Mr. Wortley seems to have had a premonition that his heir would turn out a thoroughly unsatisfactory person, only worthy of a life-annuity.

have obliged me to give myself and all I had without any further reflection; the other might have been insupportable. I shall now have your answer (if you send one) at such a distance that even your kindness could not destroy me on a sudden. And for your anger, that may be spent, or your aversion cease, before I see you again. Now that I shall reason better than I could if I were near you, it will be generous in you to tell me, not wittily as you have always done, but plainly your mind. This I make no doubt will either hasten or delay my return. For at this instant I admire you as much as ever.

"If all things besides a settlement were adjusted, I could consent to refer that to any impartial body, but I fear we differ in points of moment. Some men have parted with their fortunes to gain women, others have died with despair for the loss of 'em, but such Passions have always been raised by a strong belief of a return. The least proof of your being partial to me would, I am sure, have put me wholly in your power, for I only hope I am not. I would give a great deal to be satisfied I am not, tho' the greatest mark of distinction you have shown me is your allowing a treaty, which amounts to no more than this, that you may think my faults as supportable as those of other pretenders that have the same fortune, which cannot be very numerous. But admitting this to be a proof of esteem, or even of friendship, no man ever undid himself to gain or to continue a friendship, or died for the loss of it.

"Should you write to me it would not be a greater compliment. Every woman would write instead of dressing for any lover she had not resolved to strike out of her list, that could persuade herself she did it half so well as you. I know that when you write you shine out in all your beauty.

"It is well for you the Packet won't wait for me. Else I don't know but I should have given over. I can only add that letters are left for me at Mr. Goodwin's the Bookseller, or Mr. Steele's. My going abroad is known to few."

Lady Mary wrote a first answer to this letter directly she received it, without realising all its true inwardness, and taking its surface value for rather more than it was worth.

"I never thought to hear from you,"[1] she begins. "'Tis impossible to tell my surprise. What would you have me say? There is a great deal of generosity and good-nature in your letter, but I know not how to answer it.

"I will show you a confidence that will convince you I am at least very sincere in my Friendship. I am told my Brother is going to marry a great Fortune. Ten thousand pounds is to be settled on me, without its being possible to be recalled by anyone. A single woman may live very well on that money. The dispute I have at present with myself is whether I will, or will not marry at all. Now in my opinion you are very much obliged to me that it is a dispute. I should not hesitate upon many proposals. Were I sure you would live after a way agreeable to me, I should not be long in making my answer. But if, instead of travelling, the fancy should take you to confine me to the country, I could bear solitude, but perhaps not were it for life, and I had much rather be my own mistress as long as I live. If you really intend to travel, as it is the thing upon earth I most wish, I should prefer that manner of living to any other, and with the utmost sincerity I confess, I should choose you before any Match could be offered me. I think I have said nothing so favourable; I ought to be ashamed at it. If you expect Passion, I am utterly unacquainted with any. It may be a fault of my temper, 'tis a stupidity I could never justify; but I do not know I was in my Life ever touched with any. I have no notion of a Transport of Anger, Love, or any other. I here tell you the plain state of my heart, and more than I shall ever think it worth my while to tell another. I believe if I could dissemble I should please you better, but you must have some esteem for a woman that will not dissemble, tho' to please.

"I think I have said enough, and as much as ought to be expected. Flights of Passion I neither know how to feel or to counterfeit. I have no hand in the making of settlements; my present duty is to obey my Father. I shall so far obey blindly as not to accept where he refuses, tho' perhaps I might refuse where he would accept. If you think tolerably

[1] From the unpublished MS.

of me, you think I would not marry where I hated. For the rest, my Father may do some things disagreeable to my inclinations, but passive Obedience is a doctrine which should always be received among wives and daughters. That principle has made me cautious whom I set for my master. I ought, and I hope I should, obey a severe one, but severity is never so terrible as where it meets with a temper not made to resist. I have a softness that makes me perfectly wretched. Adieu. If you think me worth taking, it can be on no other terms than those of my Father. If not, I wish you all the happiness imaginable, and that your future wife (whoever she is to be) may not be one of those ladies so very free of their expressions of tenderness, at best withering, generally false. You would like her manner better than you do mine, till time convinced you of your mistake, but I rather choose to wish you a Happiness more lasting. . . . It is not from severity that I write no more. I should think your Correspondence a pleasure if it was among the number of the permitted. But you know it is forbidden, and I am in pain when I do anything that must be secret.

"You conclude yours with something about power. I know none that I have, nor, if that was possible, would I use it to your prejudice."

A little further study of her lover's letter brought Lady Mary to the conclusion that it was less generous and good-natured than she had at first imagined. Writing a supplementary epistle shortly after, she tells him that, having read and answered at first with "ridiculous precipitation," she had overlooked one part of his letter, and misunderstood it in others. He had said something of a packet-boat, which makes her uncertain whether he would receive it, and frets her heartily. Then, referring to his statement that her kindness would be his destruction, she remarks—

"In my opinion, this is something contradictory to some other expressions. People talk of being in love just as widows do of affliction. Mr. Steele has observed in one of his plays,[1] the most passionate among them have always calmness enough to drive a hard bargain with the upholders. I never knew a

[1] In *The Funeral; or, Grief-à-la-Mode*. The "up-holders" were the undertakers.

to know why you are at so much pains to assure me I must never expect anything of Passion from you, for you are incapable of it. I don't believe I ever said it was due to me, and I am sorry to hear from you the constant saying of a woman that would marry, or is married to one man, and has a Passion for another. A man always uses this discourse after he has married one he doesn't care for; a woman often says so beforehand that a disappointment might not make a breach. Your assurances of this calmness of temper are the more remarkable because they are not very credible. I know very well your Wit and Beauty must give you many admirers, and you will say how can you be troubled for the loss of anyone. You know it to be true that the most admired have generally had their share of concern.

"But you don't stop at these protestations you give me of your indifference; you tell me after, I must never expect to please another, and hope I shall not have one of those that are free of their kind expressions. I readily grant you I am without all those qualities that give you so much power, and yet I deny that I ought to be precluded from pretending to the favour of some. The opportunities that are gained by Money, Artifice, or Chance many times get a man above those who have the charms that nature can bestow, and this you can't but have observed. If you know me to be incapable of having success anywhere, I desire to hear no proofs, but would willingly enjoy the pleasure of thinking it is in the power of Fortune to favour me. I hope we shall meddle no more with this subject.

"Your declaiming against the country (another refuge of some women) was for aught I know meant to break off quite. You know I don't care for the town and cannot oblige myself to be there for any time. Nor is my estate sufficient for two families. It is full enough for myself, but I fear you would think it too strait if we lived together, much more if we lived asunder. It is less than you take it to be, for I resolve never to spend as much as I receive.

"You show me pretty plainly you have strong reasons against taking me, tho' you may have some reasons for it. I can assure you, it is the most rash thing you can do to meddle

CHAPTER VIII

A STRANGE COURTSHIP

MR. WORTLEY seems to have returned to England about the middle of October, for on the 19th of the month Swift records in his Journal to Stella, "Spent the evening with Wortley Montagu and Mr. Addison over a bottle of Irish wine." He found four of Lady Mary's letters awaiting him, two more, including the last piteous *cri du cœur*, having been forwarded to Spa by the kind-hearted Steele, who recognised the handwriting, and guessed that here was a soul in distress. The lovers do not appear to have met at this time (perhaps Lady Mary was still in the country), and Mr. Wortley went north to Wortley after a very brief stay in town. He waited till 24th October before he took the trouble to answer his lady's letters, and then he dealt mainly with the second, which was probably the least sympathetic of the six.

"I was no sooner got into Holland,"[1] he begins, "than I resolved to have a Truce (if it were possible) with business, politicks[2] and love, and therefore desired Mr. St[eele], who took care of all my letters to keep 'em till I sent for 'em. Four of yours I found in his hands; two that he takes to have been of the same hand (by what mistake I cannot guess) he sent beyond sea, and I must wait for 'em. It is a misfortune that I want 'em, for they might have explained or confirmed one of these; no two of 'em seem to have been writ while you was of the same mind. In some of 'em you say a great deal more, in others I think somewhat less than I deserve. I am at a loss

---

[1] From the unpublished MS.
[2] The fall of the Whig Government in the summer of this year must have temporarily destroyed Mr. Wortley's interest in politics, a subject which, curiously enough, is never mentioned in his letters to Lady Mary.

nuns that made use of that expedient to secure their own happiness; but amongst all the saints and martyrs I never read of one whose charity was sublime enough to make themselves deformed or ridiculous to restore their lovers to peace and quietness. In short, if nothing can content you but despising me heartily, I am afraid I shall be always so barbarous as to wish you may esteem me as long as you live."

Mr. Wortley, though he had promised to write every day, and had begged to hear as frequently from his lady, did not trouble himself to write again during the two months that his absence lasted, nor did he arrange to have his letters forwarded. Poor Lady Mary, her pride brought low by this neglect and unkindness, wrote no less than six letters, and was nearly distracted at receiving no answer. There is an undated note, with the superscription, "Pray send this to Mr. Edward Wortley Montagu wherever he may be," which clearly proves that Lady Mary's feeling for her lover was something warmer than the "complaisance" which alone she would admit.

"I cannot imagine,"[1] she complains, "the reason of your silence, and I am perpetually thinking of it without being able to guess whence it should probably proceed. You must think I am uneasy concerning the success of my letters, and I cannot persuade myself you are ill-natured enough to delight in it. You ordered me to direct to Mr. Godwin; he must know where to send them. Who should stop them? I use all imaginable care they should go safe from here, and I am sure they do. Am I to say you use me ill, or to be sorry for your illness? or have you forgot me so entirely you no longer remember there is such a creature in the world? I am torn with a variety of imaginations, and not one pleasing one. I conjure you to write, I beg it of you, and promise to tease you no longer upon the least intimation of being troublesome. 'Tis impossible to express the pain I write in, when I neither know whether you received my letter, or into whose hands it may fall.

"I have not heard from you since yours of the 10th of August, and have writ several times."

[1] From the unpublished MS.

lover that would not willingly secure his interest as well as his mistress; or if one must be abandoned, had not the prudence (among all his distractions) to consider a woman was but a woman, and money was a thing of more real merit than the whole sex put together. Your letter is to tell me you should think yourself undone if you married me; but if I would be so tender as to confess I should break my heart if I did not, then you'd consider whether you would or no; but yet you hoped you should not. I take this to be a right interpretation of—'even your kindness can't destroy me'—'I hope I am not in your power'—'I would give a great deal to be satisfied, etc.'"

Even Mr. Wortley's compliment to her talent for writing displeases his lady when she comes to consider it at her leisure. "As to writing," she observes, "that any woman would do so [who] thought she writ well—now I say no woman of common sense would. At best, 'tis but doing a silly thing well, and I think it is much better not to do a silly thing at all. You compare it to dressing. Suppose the comparison just: perhaps the Spanish dress would become my face very well; yet the whole town would condemn me for the highest extravagance if I went to Court in it, tho' it improved me to a miracle. There are a thousand things, not ill in themselves, which custom makes unfit to be done. This is to convince you I am so far from applauding my own conduct, my conscience flies in my face every time I think on't. The generality of the world have a great indulgence to their own follies; without being a jot wiser than my neighbours, I have the peculiar misfortune to know and condemn all the wrong things I do.

"You beg to know whether I would not be out of humour. The expression is modest enough; but that is not what you mean. In saying I could be easy, I have already said I should not be out of humour. But you would have me say I am violently in love; that is, finding you think better of me than you desire, you would have me give you a just cause to contemn me. I doubt much whether there is a creature in the world humble enough to do that. I should not think you more reasonable if you was in love with my face, and asked me to disfigure it to make you easy. I have heard of some

with me unless you are pretty secure we shall live as well together as it is possible. I am one of those that could not bear to live with you unless I were treated as well as any man was. I should choose to let our disagreeing be made publick rather than feel the burden of it at home. The difficulties that are certainly of your own raising seem great; those made (as you are pleased to say) by others, I am not yet able to get over. If I can judge right, the time for disposing of yourself is not yet come. You will have offers that you will be glad to accept of; you throw them away unless you wait till they are made.

"Your comparison of the widows making a hard bargain with the Upholders I hope I don't deserve—I am sure not of you. You are as much mistaken in saying a woman does not write on such occasions. I have heard from good hands that many have writ, and have writ to declare their Passion, which you are not the least acquainted with. I yield to you so far as to own it has not yet happened to myself. I daresay I never hinted to you I desired any such thing, but you suppose I do, only for an occasion of assuring me you don't value me over much. Your comparison of the Spanish dress is not I think well applied. I agree a woman would not go to Court in one, but would certainly find the means to be seen in it by the man she would marry if she thought that would secure him. You are out too in your Spanish story, for a young man did mangle his face that it might not charm any more.

"I think I have given full answers to all I saw in four letters. I only think I have, for I was more out of humour on reading 'em than I have been this two or three months, and don't care to open them again. Because I cannot see anything of yours with indifference, I don't oppose your proposition of corresponding no more. So that I agree with you in one thing, tho' indeed for a contrary reason.

"To say thus much by way of answer to yours I thought the respect due to 'em. I can't finish without saying one thing more that may save us both some trouble. I am very sure I can't promise to live in town, tho' I have taken no resolution against it, for I am afraid my occasions will force me to be there sometimes. I know but one that has engaged to be there every year. Such another you will easily find if you desire it. As to settlements, I thought the Propositions made were far from being equal, tho' they would be fit to be complied with by one that has a bigger estate than mine. You seem to think something new has happened in your family since, that may make an alteration. I have some reason to believe you are under a mistake.

"I have not sure done ill to argue upon everything you say, because this is the only proper time for disputes; if after all we should agree (as I am not wholly without hopes we may) you will have a proof of my being better pleased with you than with any other, and it will be my interest to do all that a reasonable man should do towards making you easy.

"I am obliged to you for some of your expressions, though they are not of a piece with the rest. You seem to think I writ my last with less humility than a man should do on such an occasion. You must distinguish; he that loves a woman whose consent is a clear demonstration of her being partial to him, will undergo a great deal to gain it, and must have violent uneasiness. A man that has not such a vanity cannot be so extravagant."

Lady Mary, her mind relieved about her lover's safety, plucks up her spirit again and answers his churlish letter with a good deal of natural resentment and some very well-deserved reproaches.

"I[1] am not surprised if you find my letters contradictory one to another, for I am not in the same mind three minutes together. You had been prodigiously ill-natured in desiring me to write and not taking some way to have the letter as soon as possible. You have caused me so much trouble, from uncertainty and difference of imagination, that I ought not to suppose you have any regards for my quiet. I despair of ever pleasing either you or myself. At this present I can't tell whether I am glad or sorry or distracted—I am now gone about half way in your letter and am answering it already—I cannot go on. I foresee I shall meet with something violently disobliging and can't answer for my calmness of temper. I see very plain what you think of me—you think me everything

[1] From the unpublished MS.

I am not—what do you not say? 'Tis impossible to speak plainer than you do—I believe I am the most unfortunate thing living. I think you so much in the right, as to think I am entirely in the wrong. I do heartily repent and am exceedingly sorry for these my misdoings. I see no way of remedying it but forgetting (as I told you before) that all these things have been. How soon I shall do it I can't tell, but I am sure as soon as I can.

"I beg you not to send me such another letter; 'tis full enough o' conscience. I understand every word of it, and am perfectly sensible that in writing this I prove myself a most extremely contemptible and ridiculous creature. But there is no necessity for your telling me so. . . . [Illegible.]

"I am certainly very humble—I have finished your letter; why did you send it? It would have been much better not to have writ, and let me remain in uncertainty of the reason of your silence. The pretty figure I make to Mr. St[eele]. I suppose this is now ended. You are mightily in the wrong if you wonder at it."

This is addressed to

"Mr. Edward Wortley Montagu
    Memb. Parliamt.
        At Wortley
            Near Sheffield
                Yorkshire. (Free)"

On the 4th of November Mr. Wortley wrote a rather more conciliatory letter, in which he defends himself against his lady's reproaches, and tries to explain his conduct. Is it possible, he asks, that she should be angry at his showing uneasiness at the sight of her hand, after being, for a long time, free from concern. He wishes that she may not be diverting herself with him, and finds his best hope in the fact that "every part of your letter contradicts all the rest, and that while you writ you was (as you say you often are) of three or four different humours in a minute." He repeats yet again that he cannot desire to be with her unless there is a prospect of their living together in perfect tranquillity.

"Should you wish for a sight of foreign countries,"[1] he continues, "I could not be against it. But to choose the ordinary place of abode surely should belong to the man, the busy part being wholly his. Most of what is spent is commonly his, and the custom does not seem unreasonable. Should we after a trial find ourselves as well-paired as many are, 'tis highly probable the places of habitation would grow indifferent. The country would be less ungrateful to you, and the town less tiresome to me than it is at present. You don't say if the treaty were to be renewed it must be on the same foot as the former. I own I heartily wish that person whom I honour very much [her father] would think I deserved what you mention. Not that I should take myself to be richer for such an addition (unless for your figure), but I should be much more encouraged to hope for your esteem. I beg you will this once try to avoid being witty, and to write in a style of business, tho' it should appear to you as flat as mine. Don't fancy it is below you to be as open and plain with me on such an occasion as you would with an intimate friend. Let me know what I might expect to hear on a second offer of myself; when such treaties end in nothing they are commonly a disadvantage to both, always to one."

In her reply Lady Mary declares that she is going to write with all the plainness of which she is capable, though she knows not what may be said upon such a proceeding. Whatever he may believe against her he is never to suspect her of being either ungenerous or ungrateful.

"I wish I could tell you what answer you will receive from some people, or upon what terms. If my opinion could sway, nothing should displease you. Nobody ever was so disinterested as I am. I would not have to reproach myself (I don't suppose you would) that I had any way made you uneasy in your circumstances. Let me beg you (which I do with the utmost sincerity) only to consider yourself in this affair; and, since I am so unfortunate to have nothing in my own disposal, do not think I have any hand in making settlements. People in my way are sold like slaves; and I cannot tell what price my master will put upon me. If you do agree,

[1] From the unpublished MS.

I shall endeavour to contribute as much as lies in my power to your happiness. I so heartily despise a great figure, I have no notion of spending money so foolishly, though one had a great deal to throw away. If this breaks off, I shall not complain of you; and, whatever happens, I shall still preserve the opinion you have behaved yourself well. Let me entreat you, if I have committed any follies, to forgive them, and be so just as to think I would not do an ill thing. . . .

"I have tried to write plainly. I know not what one can say more upon paper."

Mr. Wortley was not in the least softened by the kindness and generosity of this letter. He replies in his most surly vein that he is far from being resolved to break off, but is not yet determined to close the bargain, nor does he know what would close it.

"I was told,"[1] he proceeds, "before I went abroad, your money was to be raised by the marriage of your brother. That may for aught I know be near, but I haven't yet heard that it is over. My affairs will I believe oblige me to engage my estate for a considerable sum; it may indeed be clear again in two months, and I be the richer for doing this. But I did not know it would be so when I treated, nor did I mention it. Matters of this sort should not be long in agitation, and till there is a prospect of ending speedily, it is better to be quiet, most certainly not to engage. . . . Could I see into your heart, and find in it a partiality to me, I might break thro' all difficulties, and run the hazard of losing it soon, which you must own would be no small hazard. You can't wonder if so long an absence, variety of other acquaintance, and your unkindness, should make me less forward than I have been. But I yet think it not unlikely for us to agree and that in less than two months. If it is not before the spring, I take it for certain it will never be."

There was a sentence in the above which would touch any proud woman upon the raw, and Lady Mary replies with asperity—

" Indeed I do not at all wonder that absence and variety of new faces should make you forget me; but I am a little

[1] From the unpublished MS.

surprised at your curiosity to know what passes in my heart (a thing wholly insignificant to you) except you propose to yourself a piece of ill-natured satisfaction, in finding me very much disquieted. Pray which way would you see into my heart? You can frame no guesses about it from either my speaking or writing; and supposing I should attempt to show it you, I know no other way.

"I begin to be tired of my humility. I have carried my complaisances to you farther than I ought. You make new scruples, you have a great deal of fancy, and your distrusts being all of your own making, are more immoveable than if there was some real ground for them. Our aunts and grandmothers always tell us that men are a sort of animals that, if ever they are constant, 'tis only where they are ill-used. 'Twas a kind of paradox I could never believe; experience has taught me the truth of it. You are the first I ever had a correspondence with, and I thank God I have done with it for all my life. You needed not to have told me you are not what you have been; one must be stupid not to find a difference in your letters. You seem in one part of your last to excuse yourself from having done me any injury in point of fortune. Do I accuse you of any?

"I have not spirits to dispute any longer with you. You say you are not yet determined; let me determine for you, and save you the trouble of writing again. Adieu for ever; make no answer. I wish, among the variety of acquaintance, you may find some one to please you; and can't help the vanity of thinking, should you try them all, you won't find one that will be so sincere in their treatment, though a thousand more deserving, and everyone happier.

"'Tis a piece of vanity and injustice I never forgive in a woman, to delight to give pain. What must I think of a man that takes pleasure in making me uneasy? After the folly of letting you know it is in your power, I ought in prudence to let this go no farther, except I thought you had good-nature enough never to make use of that power. I have no reason to think so; however, I am willing, you see, to do you the highest obligation 'tis possible for me to do; that is, to give you a fair occasion of being rid of me."

It is evident that Mr. Wortley was divided between the desire to secure his mistress, and a reluctance to "engage" until he knew the amount of her fortune, and the exact terms upon which she would be disposed of. He was also anxious that she should confess her attachment to him in set terms before he actually committed himself. On 21st November he writes that were he in circumstances that would be certain to enable his lady to live suitably to her condition, he would not hesitate one minute what to say. He confesses there are some things in her letter he could never acknowledge enough if he were sure that she spoke her mind.

"But is it not wonderful,"[1] he asks, "that you are ignorant what the terms are on which you are to be disposed of? Was you ever free in any other family where discourses of that kind did not make up a great part of the conversation? Those you have to do with cannot set a low value on themselves, and must set a very high one on you. And you cannot have thought on this subject less than others. I should hope you might find out some way to know what is intended. I will, if I can, delay giving an answer till I hear from you again, and desire you will lay no stress upon anything I say at present. . . ."

Lady Mary seems to have taken the business-like part of this letter quite as a matter of course, but she was offended at the suggestion that her word was not to be relied on.

"I confess,"[1] she replies, "that women very seldom speak truth, but it is not utterly impossible, and with all sincerity I assure you I know no more of my own affairs than a perfect stranger. Nor am capable of returning you any other answer than I have already done. I do not know I ever told you a lie in my life. If you will not believe what I say, I cannot help it, nor shall not very much blame you, because I know it is improbable that a woman should be sincere; but 'tis a natural defect that even Experience can't cure me of, tho' I am convinced it is against all prudence to speak what one thinks, especially where people will not believe one. If you ask me to enquire, 'tis what I never did, nor ever will do,

[1] From the unpublished MS.

and perhaps would be unavailing if I did. I once more desire you not to act anything against the most prudent consideration, and to assure you, I am so far from the usual vanity of my sex, as not to expect any [illegible] on my account. I suppose this will pass for affectation, but I am sure there may be a woman, uninterested and artless. . . ."

CHAPTER IX

LOVERS' MEETINGS

THAT Lady Mary spent Christmas at Thoresby, is proved by a little note from one of her girl-friends, Miss Banks, written in December of this year. Mr. Banks' house at Scofton was within visiting distance of Thoresby, and here Lady Mary stayed in the early days of her marriage. Miss Banks writes in her admirable hand—

"Inclosed [1] is the verses you desired; I am ashamed of sending them so scrawled, but nothing but the commands of dear Lady Mary could have made me take the pains of transcribing them, even in the manner you see them. I must beg of you to send me the letter I left with you. And if you could spare a few moments I should be glad of the Italian you promised in answer to that of Mrs. Monk's. But if you do not write me the English of it, I shall be perfectly ignorant of all the fine things I say to her.

"My Papa commands me with his humble service to tell your Ladyship he flattered himself with the hopes of seeing you at Scofton before this; and that he has got a great parcel of choyce Pamphlets (and some books) just come out, which he fancied would have entertained you.

"In a letter he had the other day from his Grace of Canterbury,[2]

---

[1] From the unpublished MS.

[2] Archbishop Tenison (1636–1715). He had been translated from Lincoln to Canterbury in 1694. As a liberal Churchman, who advocated moderation towards dissenters, he was out of favour with Anne. He took active measures to secure the Protestant Succession, published several pamphlets, established the first public library in London, and was one of the founders of the S.P.G. He was either related to the Bankses or was a very intimate friend, and through them probably he had made the acquaintance of Lady Mary.

he tells him he does not despair (those are his words) of being with us before the end of Christmas. I must own his not despairing has given me new hopes of spending the latter end of Christmas more agreeably than I have done the beginning, for these terrible frosts and snows has made us (especially the women on this side the Forest) very unsociable, at least I find it so. . . .

"This letter I believe is of a very unusual length to be writ at so near a distance, but I beg you will pardon it from your Ladyship's most obedient humble servant,

"M. BANKS"

"I am a dutiful servant to her Majesty.—My Mamma is concerned she has not yet been able to send the penknives, but she is in hopes of doing it very soon."

By the beginning of January, 1711, our heroine is back in town, and the pseudo love-correspondence still continues, though we find that early in February she ordered Mr. Wortley to "give over" writing, as a punishment apparently for some unflattering criticism of her character and conduct. But he was not the man to allow anybody else to have the last word.

"Your resenting what I said,"[1] he points out in a letter dated 9th February, "is an argument of its being pretty near the truth. Your expressing the resentment in such a manner shows how little you value me. I need not tell you that where there is anything of friendship, no words are thought a crime which are not spoke with design to give offence. . . . But I should not wonder you say to-day you hate me—t'other night I was silly. I can't imagine you took either of these compliments to be literally true, but you thought I deserved little less or how could you have used them? . . . I own it will not grieve me much to know you have quite laid aside the thoughts of me, for indifference is to me absence. 'Tis a refusal, and everything that can relieve a passion, and this I suspected the moment you told me I must give over writing."

Mr. Wortley had desired one half hour's discourse, not apparently to plead his suit, but to convince his mistress how much greater the misfortune would be for her than himself if they should disagree when too late, and how difficult it would

[1] From the unpublished MS.

be for two with such tempers to agree. He thinks it impossible to enter into these points by letter, though he had already done so often enough. " Shall I tell you how to deceive me ? " he concludes, " if you think it worth your while. Avoid seeming witty (which all do naturally when they are serious), and say nothing that does not seem probable."

Poor Lady Mary, harassed and badgered, but still inexplicably unwilling to give up her ill-humoured lover, replied without delay—

" If[1] I reflect on what you have said, the pain you have given me, the uneasiness I have endured ever since, the disorder which you caused me, and which it was impossible wholly to suppress, so as to make it unperceived by the company I was with, ought I ever to write to you again? But I will not think it possible you could be in earnest. I freely own I cannot be angry with you without pain; the softness of my temper (which I confess to be a very great defect) makes me uncapable of Anger, and the height of my resentment falls into sorrow, and the grief from being ill-used is a more natural consequence of my being wronged, than Hatred or Revenge.

" Let me beg you never more to give me that grief. If you are weary of me, say that, but never say such a reason for it. I may want a thousand things necessary to please, but can accuse myself of no irregularities but what I have done for you, and they ought to be excusable to you.

" I should not be sorry to see you was it possible to discourse with you for half an hour. How to do that in a shop is very difficult, and I know no place where you visit. Lady Jekyll[2] has desired to be introduced to me. I think she

---

[1] From the unpublished MS.

[2] Lady Jekyll was a sister of the Whig statesman, Lord Somers. Her husband, Sir Joseph Jekyll (1663–1738) was the distinguished lawyer, who conducted the impeachment of Sacheverell, and afterwards was one of the managers of the impeachments of Lord Wintoun (1716) and Lord Oxford (1717). He was made Master of the Rolls in 1717. Pope alludes to him as

> "Jekyll, or some odd old Whig
> Who never changed his principles or wig."

There must have been something remarkable about Jekyll's wig, because Lord Mansfield said, *à propos* of his leaving £20,000 to be used as a sinking fund for the

is your Acquaintance; consider if I can see her at your house. As to my forbidding you to write, I am necessitated to do it; a letter intercepted would forfeit my eternal repose, especially with people who have entertained a suspicion that I am partial to you. I am going to speak very plain—it is very hard to alter a received opinion. I have accustomed myself to esteem you, and know not how to do otherwise. My Schemes of Happiness are pretty near what I have sometimes heard you declare yours. I am not very old, but know enough of the town to hate it, and always hate it most when I am in it. I am afraid you will think this out of the bounds of what is probable, but 'tis truth, the way I now live in is entirely disagreeable to me, from the same reasons most women would be pleased with it. I detest the crowd I am obliged to live in, and wish it in my power to be retired (you will think me too free, but I will proceed to tell you). I like your conversation; I think you have no faults but what are grounded upon mistakes that I am sure will vanish when you are better acquainted with my Inclinations. I propose to myself a Happiness in pleasing you, and do not think it impossible.

"And now—what shall I say to this declaration you would like me better if I was more reserved—but why should dissimulation be meritorious? I have told all my Heart and must leave it to you how you will like my sincerity. If you should think my behaviour too indiscreet, and that I say more than ought to be said—I can't help it. However my Actions may appear, I am conscious to myself of principles that would not suffer me to do anything, even for you, that was not in some degree justifiable.

"An Answer cannot be directed to me; two Penny Post letters would give occasion for enquiries. Direct to Lady Mary Creighton, at the Earl of Loudoun's[1] in the Pall Mall, near St. James's."

reduction of the national debt, "He might as well have attempted to stop the middle arch of Blackfriars Bridge with his full-bottomed wig."

[1] Hugh Campbell, third Earl of Loudoun (died in 1731). At this time he was Keeper of the Great Seal of Scotland. He married a daughter of Lord Stair. Crichton (sometimes spelt Creighton) was the family name of the Viscounts of Fendraught. The last Viscount was attainted in 1690, and died in 1698.

The difficulty of arranging a meeting in some place where the lovers might talk freely was really a serious one, even though Lady Mary was more her own mistress than most girls of her own age. The letters that follow illustrate, with a curious exactness, a passage in which Lord Chesterfield describes the state of society in London under Queen Anne.

"Public and crowded assemblies," he writes, "where every man was sure of meeting every woman, were not known in those days. But every woman of fashion kept what was called a Day, which was a formal circle of her acquaintances of both sexes, unbroken by any card-tables, tea-tables, or other amusements. There the fine women and fine men met perhaps for an hour; and if they had anything particular to say to one another, it would be only conveyed by the language of the eyes. One other public diversion was merely for the eyes, for it was going round and round the ring in Hyde Park, and bowing to one another slightly, respectfully, or tenderly, as occasion required. No woman of fashion could receive any man at her morning toilet without alarming the husband and his friends. If a fine man and fine woman were well enough disposed to wish for a private meeting, the execution of their good intentions was difficult and dangerous. The preliminaries could only be settled by the hazardous expedient of letters; and the only places almost for the conclusion and ratification of the definite treaty were the Indian houses in the City, where the good woman of the house, from good nature and perhaps some little motive of interest, let out her back rooms for momentary lodgings to distressed lovers."

Manlike, Mr. Wortley did not appreciate the difficulties of the situation.

"Had[1] you been so well pleased with my conversation," he writes, "you would have had it long since at forty different places. Who is there you do not visit besides Mrs. Steele and Mrs. Hampden,[2] at whose houses I am at home? Your

---

[1] From the unpublished MS.
[2] Probably the wife of John Hampden, M.P. for Wendover, the last direct descendant of the patriot. H. Walpole called him a buffoon Whig.

friend Lady Wharton[1] is continually with Mrs. Hampden; Lady Evelyn[2] must know several Buckinghamshire women that are intimate with her. She lives in Marlborough Street and visits all that neighbourhood. Mrs. Steele goes little abroad, but Mrs. Binns[3] that knows everybody is often with her. I not only visit Lady Jekyll but the Dutchesses of Grafton,[4] Northumberland,[5] Kent,[6] in all which places I have formerly met you. Besides, the Dutchess of Shrewsbury,[7] L[ady] Harvey,[8] and L[ady] Betty Germain,[9] Mrs. Chetwind,[10] and L[ady] Clarges.[11] Is there any of these you don't know? But perhaps at most of them it is not possible to whisper any

[1] Lucy, daughter of Lord Lisburne, who was the second wife of the Whig statesman, Thomas, first Marquis of Wharton. She was the mother of the notorious Duke of Wharton. From 1708 to 1710 her husband was Lord-Lieutenant of Ireland. He took Addison with him as his secretary.

[2] This seems to prove that Lady Evelyn Pierrepont lived chiefly with her aunt, Lady Cheyne. Lord Cheyne's family estate was Cogenho in Bucks.

[3] Mrs. Binns was an intimate friend and confidante of Mrs. Steele's, and often stayed with her at Hampton Court. Steele sends her polite messages, and is always "Mrs. Binns' humble servant."

[4] Henrietta, daughter of the Marquis of Worcester. She was married to Charles, second Duke of Grafton.

[5] Charles II. created his third son by the Duchess of Cleveland, George Fitzroy, Duke of Northumberland. The Duke married Katherine, daughter of Thomas Wheatley of Brecknock, and widow of Thomas Lucy of Charlcote. He died without issue in 1716.

[6] The wife of Henry, eleventh Earl of Kent (1664?-1740), who was created Duke of Kent in 1710. She was a daughter of Thomas, the second Lord Crew of Stene. She was connected with the Montagus, as her aunt Anne, a daughter of the first Lord Crew, had married Lord Sandwich, Mr. Wortley's grandfather.

[7] Adelhida, a daughter of the Marquis Paleotti. She was married to Charles, first Duke of Shrewsbury (1660-1717), who had been Secretary of State to William III. In 1710 he was Lord Chamberlain.

[8] Elizabeth, daughter of Sir Thomas Felton, Bart. of Playford. She was married in 1795 to John Hervey, created Baron Hervey of Ickworth in 1703 and Earl of Bristol in 1714. Lady Bristol figures in Lady Mary's later letters as a woman of violent temper, with an inclination to gallantry.

[9] Lady Betty Germain was a daughter of the second Earl of Berkeley. She married Sir John Germain, who was thirty years older than herself, and had been formerly married to the divorced Duchess of Norfolk. Lady Betty was a friend of Swift's and of Young's. She made her nephew, Lord George Sackville, her heir.

[10] This was probably Mary, daughter of Lord Fitzhardinge, and wife of Walter Chetwynd of Ridge, who was created Viscount Chetwynd in 1717.

[11] Lady Clarges was probably the wife of Sir Thomas Clarges, the second baronet.

longer than for making a Peace when it is broke, and renewing an old treaty, but not for finishing one that is but newly begun.

"In more than three years we have not been able to settle preliminaries. In this time what have I seen? But my eyes were of no use to me. That I should at last beg your Pardon for being abused by you! Indeed it has had this good effect. The many pretty things that it fetched from you destroyed a Resolution of never troubling you more, which I took on Saturday upon your not sending an Answer. I believed I should keep it all Sunday and yesterday till I had yours. I now own I am so far gone as to think myself obliged to you for it, tho' I know a whisper or a look may be worth a thousand such Epistles. I am thankful for it, tho' what you talk of the softness of your Temper, of your committing no irregularities, of the nicety of your principles, takes away that little air of truth which might have appeared in the rest. I am sorry to tell you I intended last night to be as long before I answered as you was, but—a money matter of moment is on my hands, and I find I cannot be at leisure to follow it without paying the duty. I have not said a word of the most material points, for I do not know when I should give over if I entered upon 'em. It is not unlikely I may write something of 'em in two or three days unless I see you, which I take to be the shortest way of ending. I saw you once (if you remember such a thing) at Colman's.[1] Why not there again? But Corticelli's [2] early after dinner might be better. Mrs. Corticelli or I might introduce you to Signora Checa [3] who lodges there, and while she sings it will be no ill compliment to talk very softly. Don't go on an Opera day, unless it be in the morning. I forgot to say the talking English is whispering before her. The Dutchess of Montagu [4]

---

[1] Probably the keeper of a toy shop.

[2] H. Walpole says that in the reign of George I. an Italian warehouse was kept in Suffolk Street by one Corticelli, much frequented by people of fashion for raffles, purchases, and gallant meetings.

[3] Signora Checa was probably a minor opera-singer. She is not mentioned by Burney.

[4] Lady Elizabeth Wriothesley, widow of the first Duke of Montagu, who died in 1709.

and Lady Bridgewater[1] visited her without any introduction. I could give her notice of your desire to see her, but it seems better to do it by Mrs. Corticelli. Lady Bridgewater is acquainted with Mrs. Hampden and can carry you to her."

Lady Mary replied a few days later—

"I[2] have no acquaintance with Mrs. Hampden, Mrs. Steele or Mrs. Binns. Lady Wharton that you call my friend, I have not seen above thrice very near this two year. The Duchesses of Grafton, Northumberland and Kent I visit seldom, and if we should meet there, it would be impossible to speak without observation. 'Tis harder for me than you imagine to meet anybody. Corticelli's I don't much care to go to. I have not been there a vast while, and if I should go, it would look odd to my sister and to Corticelli himself, who would not fail to guess the occasion of so unusual a visit.

"Lady Jekyll was presented to me last Monday. I like her very well, and hope to contrive to see you at her house, which I look upon to be the easiest and safest place. I am not acquainted with Lady Clarges, Mrs. Chetwynd, or Lady Betty Germain. I seldom see Lady Harvey and the Dutchess of Shrewsbury, and never at their Assemblies. I very well remember seeing you at Coleman's, but have not ventured again. 'Tis almost a certainty of its being discovered to be a designed thing; you do not know the ill Consequences such a matter would have. . . . 'Tis your way to blame me for everything—if you are sincere in all you say of mistrusting my nicety of principles, and doing no irregularities, I ought not to see you again, but I hope you do not, cannot speak your thoughts; that is you cannot be so entirely mistaken—at least if your Judgment is as good as I fancy it is.

"I shall go very soon to the Drawing-room. If you please it would be mighty easy to enter into discourse there with less suspicion than anywhere else. I cannot tell you what day it will be; perhaps I shan't know myself above half an hour before I go. Next Sunday I shall be at St. James' Chapel in

[1] Lady Elizabeth Churchill, daughter of the great Duke of Marlborough. She married Scrope, fourth Earl and afterwards first Duke of Bridgewater.
[2] From the unpublished MS.

the Ladies' Closet. You may lead me downstairs if you have anything to say that can be said in so short a time. It may be by then I shall be able to tell you when we will meet at Lady Jekyll's."

Mr. Wortley writes to suggest other places of meeting, and the Steeles are mentioned as friends whose good offices were at the disposal of the lovers, and whose house would be a convenient rendezvous. In those formal days there was some little difficulty about an introduction, the parties being of such different rank, though Steele was able to speak of Lord Dorchester as his good friend. Mr. Wortley's "scruples," it will be seen, were not yet removed, and he reverts yet again to the knotty points of the settlement and the manner of living after marriage.

"I[1] wish your business had not been too pressing to let you go for a minute to Lady Kent. She is my friend and I might at least have gone downstairs with you. You know before I say it I shall wait for you at the Chapel. Since you name no other place let me name one more, Mrs. Farmer's.[2] A friend of mine promised to carry me there just before I received yours forbidding me to write. But perhaps I may not suddenly find him now, and this may not suit with your affairs. I did venture to tell Mr. St[eele] I longed to say something to you and could not find the means, and therefore begged he would get his wife to visit you. You won't, I am sure, say this was a reflection upon you. He told me my Lord was his good friend, and you had talked of visiting her, and therefore she might go without being introduced. I said I thought that L. M. [Lady Mary] would suspect it was a contrivance of mine. But, sure, you that are in a higher rank may go without any ceremonies. Don't tell me again you dare not trust Sister F. [Frances]. I will for once grant it to be true, and advise you to pretend to her Mrs. St. sent you a message desiring leave to see you. She really has the nice principles you talk of, is simple enough to be in love with a husband, and thinks he is my friend. You can be

---

[1] From the unpublished MS.
[2] Probably one of the Fermors, Lord Lempster's family. The name was sometimes spelt Farmer at this period.

no where so free from observation as with her. If you must be introduced, get Lady Warwick[1] to do it. Dr. Garth, who lives near you, will tell you how you can go in an hour's time to either of 'em. He himself may introduce you, or may give Mrs. St. notice of your desire. She is visited by Mrs. Cotton; I fancy I know 'em. Before Mrs. St. we may talk for hours if you like it. Lady Jekyll has a niece, and few young women care to see others whisper, nor am I sure Lady Jekyll will not tell her brother.[2] I fear we could not talk more before her than at the Dutchess of Kent's. At Mrs. Hampden's I could call for cards and tally, or whisper with you, and it would pass for nothing. Perhaps your Aunt will not like your going thither, else you might easily get acquainted. You may write to-morrow, and by answering a few questions save some of our debates. If you don't care to send your thoughts on such high points, you may put a paper into my hands. You had better not attempt to disprove what you never can, but when a woman has been irregular as far as she could with safety, which way can she prevent ill future suspicions, or be pleased with the man who has entertained any? . . ."[3]

Lady Mary was quite willing to make the acquaintance of Mrs. Steele, though she naturally saw the obstacles in the way of an introduction more clearly than did Mr. Wortley. She was not accustomed to making the first visit, for no apparent reason, upon a woman of inferior rank, and she dreaded being examined as to why she did it. She proceeds to defend herself against the charge of irregularity which Mr. Wortley had levelled against her, and cautions him against making unreasonable demands of her father. She closes on a pathetic note, which is rarely touched throughout the correspondence.

"I[4] would have gone to Lady Kent's if I had known

[1] Charlotte, daughter of Sir Thomas Middleton, and widow of the sixth Earl of Warwick, who died in 1701. She afterwards married Addison.
[2] Lord Somers, who might pass on the gossip to Lord Dorchester.
[3] This letter concludes with a repetition of Mr. Wortley's favourite questions: Could Lady Mary submit to a narrow way of living, and why should a man be forced to settle his estate upon his heir?
[4] From the unpublished MS.

you desired it, tho' it would have given no opportunity of speaking. Mrs. Farmer's is the most inconvenient place in the world. I do not go very often; the house is always full of a mixture of giddy and malicious people. I am now here so much upon my guard, and should quite leave off them sort of Assemblies if I was so much my own mistress as not to fear disobliging a company of silly impertinent women.

"I am ready to believe the good character you give Mrs. Steele, and wish with all my Heart, you could persuade her Husband to send her to see me. I dare not make the first visit, for I should certainly be examined why I did it, and it is what I never do. I have proceeded so far as to ask a Lady, who told me she was intimate with her, to bring her to see me. Perhaps she never delivered my message, for 'twas one of those gay happy Ladies that mind nothing beside their own faces. I know no other that is acquainted with her. I would speak again to that Lady, but 'tis uncertain when I shall see her, for I don't much care to enter into an intimacy with her. She is Lady Ernley; she visited me this summer in the country.

"If you can oblige Mrs. Steele to come to see me, I shall be very glad, and after the first visit, there is no further difficulty. I can allow for her Modesty, and make the first offers of Friendship to entitle me to the freedom you speak of.

"I am now going to answer without reserve to your Questions. I beg you to put the mildest censure upon my sincerity. I am afraid you should think I say too much, but I must write, for I am sure I shall never be able to speak it.

"That irregularity you speak of, is nothing more than a native openness of temper, and something of the gaiety of youth, which is only ill-construed for want of being known, and there is nothing to be suspected where there is nothing but what is visibly undesigned. A man that had once showed a jealousy of Humour, would be only disagreeable to one that proposed all her future happiness in the Enjoyment of the foolish unsatisfactory Pleasures of the Town. A low manner of living has been my entire inclination, ever since I can remember having any inclination, and your liking that is one of the best things I like in you.

"As to the fortune, I cannot name positively what shall be given; some people love to make those things secrets. You may ask what you please, you cannot suppose I should not be glad to have your fortune increased. I should be glad if it were nothing to me; only let me give this caution, be not anything that may be thought unreasonable in your demands, for if one Person[1] is disobliged he is irreconcileable. You understand these things better than I—do what you please, but I beg you, do not disoblige one that has the disposal of me, —sure, you will not. As to Settlements, remember it is not I that has to make 'em, and my thinking you in the right, will not persuade others that you are so.

"My Love is not divided into many branches; except three or four women or relations, for the generality of my Acquaintance, 'tis equal to me whether I don't see them in 7 years or as long as I live.

"I have not answered all your Questions. 'Tis my turn to raise objections: I have but one, and that is what I think upon very often. You don't Love me. If this is really true, I shall be very unhappy; 'tis impossible to please anybody that has no inclinations to be pleased with me. To live with you, and not to please you, would be something very Miserable. I would rather stay as I am—I am not writing to dwell upon this thought—you force me upon it. Can anyone have a degree of Kindness and raise so many Objections?"

It seems that, in the end, Lady Mary made the first visit to Mrs. Steele. It took place, apparently, in the evening, and the guilty conscience of the visitor made her suffer keenly from self-consciousness and confusion. The lovers had some private conversation, in which Mr. Wortley showed himself not less cantankerous than in his letters. His jealous suspicions and reproaches must have rendered the interview anything but a pleasure to his lady-love, who wrote directly she reached home—

[1] Her father.

"*22nd February.*

"I[1] was never more out of Countenance in my Life than to-night. I certainly made a very silly figure; between Fear and Confusion it was impossible to suffer more than I did. I fancied everybody perceived the reason of my coming, and that fancy gave me a thousand disorders. I had reason for more when I came into the coach. My sister read me a long Lecture on your Account. I wish there had not been so much reason in what she said. I cannot justify my Actions on that point. Mrs. Steele and her husband certainly think me as ridiculous as she does. What recompense have I for all this? Have I the pleasure of obliging a man that I esteem? On the contrary you think me more inexcusable than they do, and that I would be the same for every man in the world. After your manner of thinking, every fresh instance of kindness is a new crime. How can you use me so? You call all things criminal, my Confusion (which I know not how to overcome when I see you) is Peevishness, and my very sincerity is designs. Am I to think you love me? I must come over to the opinion of my sister, and own that (at least) I ought not to think so.

"But to your Question. I have nothing to say, but that (which is saying all in a few words) if you have the disposal of me, and think it convenient either for your Pleasure or Affairs to pass your life in Yorkshire, I shall not be displeased with it. A Town Life in the public station I now am, is utterly disagreeable to me. I am weary of it, and should quit it with Pleasure. And now, consider with yourself the degree of inclination you have for me. Do not think of marrying me, except you think it would make you happy. I had rather never see you, than see you dislike me.

"After saying so much, permit me to say no more to you. If you are determined to think ill of me, my Arguments cannot convince you. If you think well—I need add no farther.

"I shall be very glad if Mrs. Steele would return my visit soon. I am ashamed to make many advances; she will think

[1] From the unpublished MS.

it is upon your account, and perhaps she knows you don't care for me. I wish I could be convinced one way or other; do something to show me your Partiality or Indifference. The first would give me pleasure, and the last would free me from pain."

CHAPTER X

A JEALOUS LOVER

THE fact that Mr. Wortley now felt pretty sure of his mistress made him only the more inclined to treat her ungenerously. Her avowal of the power he exercised over her, and her agitation in his presence, seem to have temporarily chilled what he was pleased to call his " Passion," and in his next letter he shows some desire to retreat from his position of serious lover.

" My conversing with you,"[1] he writes, " is no pleasure to you, and is a pain to me. My danger in doing it is great, yours is greater. Turn the love into friendship; you have prepared me for it. Own you value me very little; you will never oblige another so highly. All the services of my life would be too small a return. . . . But there is something in your composition so very ungenerous that the doing good to another is no satisfaction to you. What is yet more strange, your indiscretion is as remarkable as your wit, and you can scarce use me well, even for your own advantage." He continues by assuring her that had she allowed him to advise her, she would long since have been " fixed " (*i.e.* married) a great deal better than she is likely to be now. On the other hand, her friendship might be of great use to him. He has so high an opinion of her mind that he thinks if she were old and ugly she could forward him in any pursuit he might have, whether avarice, ambition, or love had the possession of him.

He has reached this point when her letter (already quoted) arrives, and he proceeds to discuss it in the following drastic fashion :—

" Now to your letter. Your Carriage last night was

[1] From the unpublished MS.

a fresh proof of your having no Esteem for me. When you was gone, you thought it better to consider whether you should dismiss me quite or not, and on second thoughts you writ this, which would have delighted me had I thought you sincere. Your talking in private for a whole night before a hundred people at Court, sometimes with one sometimes with another, but most of all with one who could attend you for nothing but the hopes of the continuance of an Engagement during Pleasure, gave you no Disorder or Confusion. Your sister did not chide you for it, and yet was concerned at your freedom among those you might reckon your servants, when I thought your carriage was strained into the extremes of Gravity and Reservedness. After all, be assured you do not like me. I would rather you would find proofs of it yourself; if you do not, I hope I shall convince you. The sooner I do this the better for us both.

"After all, I own every civil expression of yours is a favour. You know I am so far from being able to dislike you, that I cannot be indifferent but when you are. Mrs. Steele will visit you this afternoon; let me know when you return it."

One is glad to find that Lady Mary could still show some fight, for in answer to the above she writes one of her many letters of farewell. It is a good letter, and it must be allowed that nothing could be more just than the reproaches it contains and the indignation by which it is inspired.

[Endorsed *26th February* 1711.]

"I intended to make no answer to your letter; it was something very ungrateful, and I resolved to give over all thoughts of you. I could easily have performed that resolve some time ago, but then you took pains to please me. Now you have brought me to esteem you, you make use of that esteem to give me uneasiness, and I have the displeasure of seeing I esteem a man that dislikes me. Farewell then, since you will have it so. I renounce all the ideas I have so long flattered myself with, and will entertain my fancy no longer with the imaginary pleasure of pleasing you. How much wiser are all those women I have despised than myself! In placing their happiness in trifles, they have

LADY MARY PIERREPONT
(1710)
ENGRAVED BY CAROLINE WATSON FROM A MINIATURE

placed it in what is attainable. I fondly thought fine clothes and gilt coaches, balls, operas and public adoration rather the fatigues of life, and that true happiness was justly defined by Mr. Dryden (pardon the romantic air of repeating verses) when he says—

> 'Whom Heaven would bless it does from pomps remove,
> And makes their wealth in privacy and love.'

These notions had corrupted my judgment as much as Mrs. Biddy Tipkin's.[1] According to this scheme I proposed to pass my life with you. I yet do you the justice to believe, if any man could have been contented with this manner of living, it would have been you. Your indifference to me does not hinder me from thinking you capable of tenderness and the happiness of friendship, but I find it's not to me you'll ever have them. You think me all that is detestable; you accuse me of want of sincerity and generosity. To convince you of your mistake I'll show you the last extremes of both.

"While I foolishly fancied you loved me (which I confess I never had any great reason for, more than that I wished it), there is no condition of life I could not have been happy in with you, so very much I liked you—I may say loved, since it is the last thing I'll ever say to you. This is telling you sincerely my greatest weakness. And now I will oblige you with a new proof of generosity—I'll never see you more. I shall avoid all public places, and this is the last letter I shall send. If you write, be not displeased if I send it back unopened. I shall force my inclination to oblige yours, and remember you have told me I could not oblige you more than by refusing you. Had I intended ever to see you again, I durst not have sent this letter. Adieu."

Immense was Mr. Wortley's surprise and consternation at

---

[1] Miss Biddy Tipkin is one of the characters in Steele's comedy, *The Tender Husband; or the Accomplished Fools*, and may be regarded as the prototype of Lydia Languish. She is described as a young lady who, by being kept from the world, has made a world of her own. "She has spent her solitude in reading romances, her head is full of Shepherds, Knights, Flowery Meads, Groves and Streams, so that if you talk like a man of the world to her, you do nothing." Lady Mary would sympathise with Biddy's love for the French romances, and her admiration for *Astrea, Clelia, Cassandra,* and the rest of the high-flown heroines.

thus being taken at his word. Unfortunately, just before receiving the above letter, he had written another note, in which he had, so to speak, turned the knife in his own jealous heart by pretending to recommend a rival. For example, he says—

"I[1] am generous enough to own that the new man you have encouraged, and that attended you last night, may be very proper for any of your purposes. If his father's estate should be not less than £2000 a year (one of his countrymen told me that is the value of it; but it may be a great deal more—I shall know in a day or two) the part your lover may have of it may be very sufficient for the country, especially so far Northward—or, if you like the town, it is better living on a little there than not at all. ... You see how just I am to you, though in favour of a rival."

After writing the above he seems to have realised that he had been mistaken about the supposed rival; perhaps the gentleman was already engaged or married. At any rate, he writes again on 28th February in an unusually chastened spirit, and although he still professes to feel injured, there is actually a hint of apology in his tone—

Monday Night.

"What[1] would I not give to prove I writ the other sheet on Saturday night. I hope the colour of the ink and the folly of what I say about a Rival will convince you. How true a Prophet have I been? Had you ended with me in a better manner, I should have been extremely surprised. Since this has not fallen upon me unexpected, I am the more able to bear it After this you must never pretend to be either sincere or generous. Can it possibly be true that you are angry at a letter which showed I endeavoured to conceal a Passion but could not? Has it not appeared in almost every one of those unmannerly lines I have at any time sent you, as plainly as the want of one is seen in all your civil expressions, nay, I will add in your angry ones. How could any woman break off so suddenly with one she had lately valued? That you are not sincere is plain. Then

[1] From the unpublished MS.

for your Generosity. Could one who had any Humanity give a reason so mortifying as this must have been had I entirely believed it? But never imagine that from your former carriage I fancy you ever loved me, or that I can take this letter for anything but a proof you never did, and conclude that I shall be free from Pain sooner than you intend I should. I will, however, gratify you in this. I own I am grieved at present when I ought to be no more than angry. Since I perceive you tell me very truly, tho' you conceal the true reason, that you have laid aside the thoughts of me. All I have left to do is, as soon as I am able, to separate my Love from Esteem. I had been very long about it, could I have charged upon myself the loss of even that small appearance of your Partiality. I send you Mrs. Steele's letter to prove how diligent I have been in going and writing often about the return of your visits. I wish you could show me as clearly that my complaints, or but the last, was as groundless. And then all might be right again. I mean we might be as well together as we were before I writ the last letter. I own I could never forbear urging you to consider your danger till all was agreed. I once more beg of you what I did before, to give me for the reason of your refusal your not liking me. When you tell me this calmly, I shall be convinced I am dismissed in good earnest, and we may both bid adieu together. Your saying you resolve not to see me is too great a compliment. It is beneath you to admit I am able to raise in you so much anger. If Mrs. St.'s is not convenient, let me know at what hour you think of visiting some other. I could name a place without exception, but it is now too late for me to appoint.

"The other leaf I writ when I came home from the Opera, on Saturday. You may be sure, after sleeping (for I did sleep) I could not send it. To-day I had a different account of that man who enjoys so great and so short-lived a happiness. By that mistake about him, you see it is not fresh, and is only sent to show I do not wonder at your severity. I will leave town in a fortnight. Unless I see you first, I will never see you more till you are disposed of.

"You observe by my sending Mrs. Steele's letter, I do not

take you to be indiscreet in anybody's concerns but your own. This proves I did not mean literally all the ill I said of you."

Lady Mary's just resentment vanished before the more conciliatory tone of her lover's letter. This cold, hard woman, as she has been represented to the world, is shown in the following note as a trembling impulsive girl, conscious of her own weakness and folly, and yet unable to steel her heart against the man who had so often wounded it.

"I[1] am yet weak enough to write to you, and so ashamed of it, I know not what to say to you—this will be a very good jest between you and Mrs. Steele.

"I am sorry she did not return my visits sooner—I cannot see you without a vast Confusion, and yet I would—what shall I do? You will despise me for this; I own 'tis Impudence to think of seeing you, after so much indiscretion. I cannot blame you if you think me capable of everything.

"I will come to Mrs. Steele's early on Friday; I am afraid of finding company there. I hope it is not Mr. St.'s custom to carry his acquaintance upstairs—men are more censorious than women. I know I deserve it, but I could not bear to be showed as a sight to his friends. I hope I shall see none of them. Think as favourably of me as you can—I am very silly—what has become of my anger? Perhaps I shall be at the Play on Thursday; if I am not I shall be at Mrs. Steele's. This is nonsense—I tremble at what I am doing. I deserve your contempt, and expect to find it."

The quarrels, misunderstandings, and semi-reconciliations continued without intermission during the next few weeks, so that it becomes hard to believe that the lovers did not enjoy their own sufferings. The difficulty of meeting increased as time went on, the Steeles' house being almost the only place where the pair could meet in any security, and even there Lady Mary felt humiliated by the consciousness that her hosts knew too well the reason of her sudden friendship for them.

On 3rd March Mr. Wortley wrote—

"Every time you see me you give me fresh proof of your not caring for me; yet I beg you will meet me once more.

[1] From the unpublished MS.

How could you pay me that great compliment of your loving the country for life, when you would not stay with me a few minutes longer? Who is the happy man you went to? ... If you can't find it out that you are going to be unhappy, ask your sister, who agrees with you in everything else, and she will convince you of your rashness in this. She knows you don't care for me, and that you will like me less and less every year, perhaps every day of your life. You may, with a little care, please another as well, and make him less timorous. It is possible I too may please some of those that have but little acquaintance; and if I should be preferred by a woman for being the first among her companions, it would give me as much pleasure as if I were the first man in the world. Think again, and prevent a great misfortune from falling upon us.

"When you are at leisure, I shall be as ready to end all as I was last night, when I disobliged one that will do me hurt by crossing his desires, rather than fail of meeting you. Had I imagined you could have left me without finishing, I had not seen you. Now you have been so free before Mrs. Steele, you may call upon her, or send for her to-morrow or next day. Let her dine with you, or go to visits, shops, Hyde Park, or other diversions. You may bring her home. I can be in the house reading, as I often am, though the master is abroad. If you will have her visit you first, I will get her to go to-morrow.

"I think a man or a woman is under no engagement till the writings are sealed; but it looks like indiscretion even to begin a treaty without a probability of concluding it. When you hear of all my objections to you and to myself, you will resolve against me. . . ."

There is a good deal more in the same agreeable vein. As far as can be gathered, Lady Mary did not answer till 12th March, but meanwhile she had made an unsuccessful attempt to arrange a meeting at Mrs. Steele's.

[12*th March.*]

"I[1] have been sick ever since I was at the Opera, and

[1] From the unpublished MS.

had so great weakness in my sight, I haven't been able to read or write. It was with difficulty I read your letter which I received on Friday night. I designed to answer it by word of mouth and went Saturday in a scarf to Mrs. Steele. I found her not at home, which very much surprised me. It is not often my time is at my own disposal, and my sister is not of a Humour to suffer me to engage myself where she don't like. I am at present very much out of Humour, and doubly indisposed, from a very great Cold and some expressions in your Letter. You continue to be unjust, and to suspect my sincerity. I suffer every way; my sister reproaches me with fondness for a man that does not care for me.

"The plague of Company is added to my misfortunes. I must leave off—I will come to-morrow to Mrs. Steele's early, but cannot stay. I am engaged against my will to Lady K. Sidney."[1]

Mr. Wortley replied: "I[2] was extremely concerned to see your coach go away from Mrs. Steele's. Her husband was hindered all night from sleeping by the gout, and she could not sleep while he was in pain. She was ill and in bed when you came. This unlucky accident troubles me the more because it brings this reflection into my mind: Is there any of your acquaintance but myself whom you do not meet at more places than one? When you delayed so long, did you not expect many things might prevent our meeting? Don't imagine I am concerned for missing this conference because I hoped to be made happy by it. I am not vain enough to conclude I shall please you after you have given me so many proofs I cannot, but I am sorry your trouble about me, if you have had any, is not yet over. . . ."

In a later letter (22nd March) Mr. Wortley asks whether it is possible for Lady Mary to remove the strong suspicions he entertains of her sincerity, or to convince him that he will have no more cause for uneasiness. At the same time he

[1] Sidney (or Sydney) of Penshurst was the family name of the Earls of Leicester (James I. creation). "Lady K." may have belonged by birth or marriage to that family.
[2] From the unpublished MS.

feels bound in justice to own that it is now too late for her to say anything, and therefore she had better give him no answer. Although it might have seemed a vain task to attempt to satisfy so jealous and unreasonable a man, Lady Mary, who really played the part of a patient Griselda throughout this affair, replied no later than the 24th—

"Though your letter is far from what I expected, having once promised to answer it with the sincere account of my inmost thoughts, I am resolved you shall not find me worse than my word, which is (whatever you may think) inviolable.

"'Tis no affectation to say I despise the pleasure of pleasing people that I despise. All the fine equipages that shine in the Ring never gave me another thought than either pity or contempt for the owners, that could place happiness in attracting the eyes of strangers. Nothing touches me with satisfaction but what touches my heart; and I should feel more pleasure at a kind expression from a friend that I esteemed, than at the admiration of a whole play-house, or the envy of those of my own sex who could not attain to the same number of jewels, fine clothes, etc., supposing I was at the very top of this sort of happiness.

"You may be this friend if you please. Did you really esteem me, had you any tender regard for me, I could, I think, pass my life in any station happier with you than in all the grandeurs of the world with any other. You have some humours that would be disagreeable to a woman that married with an intention of finding her happiness abroad. That is not my resolution. If I marry, I propose to myself a retirement. There is few of my acquaintance I should ever wish to see again, and the pleasing one, and only one, is the way I design to please myself. Happiness is the natural design of all the world, and everything we see done is meant in order to attain it. My imagination places it in friendship. By friendship I mean an entire communication of thoughts, wishes, interests and pleasures, being undivided; a mutual esteem which naturally carries with it a pleasing sweetness of conversation, and terminates in the desire of making one another happy, without being forced to run into visits, noise and hurry, which serve rather to trouble than compose the thoughts of any reasonable creature. . . .

"And now let me entreat you to think (if possible) tolerably of my modesty, after so bold a declaration. I am resolved to throw off all reserve, and use me ill if you please. I am sensible, to own an inclination for a man is putting oneself wholly in his power, but sure you have generosity enough not to abuse it. After all I have said, I pretend no tie but on your heart. If you do not love me, I shall not be happy with you; if you do, I need add no farther. I am not mercenary, and would not receive an obligation that comes not from one that loves me.

"I do not desire my letter back again. You have honour, and I dare trust you.

"I am going to the same place I went last spring. I shall think of you there: it depends upon you in what manner."

Mr. Wortley replied that the secret of her esteeming him so much was safe, since were he vain enough to believe it himself, he should never hope to convince any other. After all the unkindness she has expressed, his "Passion" is still at such a height, that he would part with life itself to be convinced her "Esteem" is as she represents it. "But[1] after —— (I am still grieved at the thoughts of it, and will not say what it is) no one can be persuaded he is esteemed. I should have taken myself to have been the most fortunate man alive, whatever price I had paid for you, could I have believed you as indifferent to all others as to me. To see you too well pleased with another is the only hard condition to which I could not have submitted. . . ."

Lady Mary was moved by this letter, and though she says she thought to return no answer, she found she was not so wise as she imagined herself. "I cannot forbear," she writes, "fixing my mind a little on that expression, though perhaps the only insincere one in your whole letter—'I would die to be secure of your heart, though but for a moment.' Were this but true, what is there I would not do to secure you?

"I will state the case to you as plainly as I can, and then ask yourself if you use me well. I have shewed in every action

[1] From the unpublished MS.

of my life an esteem for you that at least challenges a grateful regard. I have trusted my reputation in your hands; I have no scruple of giving you under my own hand an assurance of my friendship. After all this, I exacted nothing from you. If you find it inconvenient for your affairs to take so small a fortune, I desire you to sacrifice nothing to me—I pretend to no tie upon your honour. But in recompense for so clear and disinterested a proceeding, must I ever receive injuries and ill usage?

"I have not the usual pride of my sex. I can bear being told I am in the wrong, but tell it me gently. Perhaps I have been indiscreet. I came young into the hurry of the world; a great innocence and undesigning gaiety may possibly have been construed coquetry, and a desire of being followed, though never meant by me. I cannot answer for the [reflexions] that may be made upon me. All who are malicious attack the careless and defenceless. I own myself to be both. I know not anything I can say more to shew my perfect desire of pleasing you, and making you easy, than to proffer to be confined with you in what manner you please. Would any woman but me renounce all the world for one? Or would any man but you be insensible of such a proof of sincerity?"

CHAPTER XI

QUARRELS AND FAREWELLS

ABOUT this time two fresh lovers appear on the scene—"Mr. K." and "Mr. D."—we learn their initials from Mr. Wortley's letters. Mr. D. gave him a good deal of uneasiness at one time, but Mr. K. was presently to be accepted by Lord Dorchester as a suitable match for his eldest daughter. Mr. Wortley's suspicions and insinuations are warmly repudiated by Lady Mary in a letter dated 2nd April, and probably written from West Dean, which she visited again this spring. The particular letter to which she refers, is only one of many, and cannot now be identified.

"To[1] receive such a Letter after all that I have said, after all I have done to find so much ill-usage, is something surprising. Had you told me sincerely you thought my fortune too little, I should have thought you like the rest of the world, and not have wondered at your proceeding. Had you told me I had behaved myself too indiscreetly in regard of you, that I have shown a fondness of you that entirely disgusted you, however hard, this would have been speaking to be believed. But this —this Dissimulation. I thank God, foolish as I am, I am not yet weak enough to fancy any man a Lover that has it in his own power to have a woman that he has reason to think does not hate him, always with him and would not. Let the pretence be what he will, want of Inclination is the true Cause. So now, since you have no thoughts of making me happy, for God's sake do not render me wretched. I know you have no Faith in what I say, but by all that is sacred, I am sincere. 'Tis with the utmost hazard I send this to you; should my

[1] From the unpublished MS.

Father find it out, he is of a humour never to forgive it. Your letter might have fallen into his Hands, and then I am ruined. And indeed, why would you write? Why will you persecute one that cannot yet persuade herself to wish you ill? Suffer me, if possible, to forget a Man that has given me all the uneasy moments of my Life. Do not fancy anything can persuade me you love me, nor is it of Importance I should believe it, except it is necessary to your repose I should be wretched. I am now of the opinion of those I once would not hear, that had you had any real Affection for me, you would have long ago applied yourself to him, from whose hand only you can receive me.

"The silly proofs of my Esteem I have given you, have been without a thought of your Estate. Could I bring myself to value a Man with no other Merit, I might be happier than I am.

"I am here alone in a place that I like, and where everything inspires peace and tranquillity. What injury have I done you to make you poison all the pleasure I should otherwise take in being alone and at quiet?

"Do not imagine I shall take it for a Compliment to say I have refused. I appeal to yourself, however partial against me, if I have ever used you like a property to my vanity. I have so little, I shall not be mortified if you tell people you have refused me. Nothing can mortify me after knowing it is so."

Mr. Wortley replies with what he is pleased to consider a letter of apology and retractation, but which is in reality a reiteration of his charges, with a few aggravating circumstances superadded. However, he begins generously enough: "At[1] last I am ready to confess my errors, to retract all I have said of you, and ask your forgiveness." But then he continues without any further expression of regret: "I own I was very uneasy at the beginning of the last winter when I saw you and Mr. K. pressing so close upon each other in the Drawing-room, and found that you could not let me speak to you without being overheard by him. What passed between you

[1] From the unpublished MS.

two at the Trial [1] confirmed my suspicions. 'Twould be useless to reckon up all the Passages that gave me pain. The second time I saw you at the Play this year, I was informed of your Passion for him by one that I knew would not conceal it from others. At the Birthnight you remember the many proofs of your affection for him, and cannot have forgot what passed in his favour at the Ball. My observing that you have since been present at the Park, Operas and Assemblies together, and absent together, and, to finish all your contriving, to have him for one of that select number that serenaded you at Acton, and afterwards danced at the Dutchess's — all this had gone a great way in settling my opinion that he and none but he possessed your heart. But I will now if you please acknowledge that all my uneasiness was owing to an excess of Passion, and that none but myself would have drawn the same consequences.

So that this dispute is now over. I confess the fault has been in my temper. But at the same time I must have some regard to what was told me by others with those three days—by two persons that neither love nor hate nor enyy you. They have met you several times in private companies with that happy gentleman, and both of 'em plainly discovered you was in love with him before they had mentioned it to each other, or heard anything of the story. They tell me it has been publick some time, and could not have escaped me had I not been taken for a Rival. They also confirmed me in an opinion I had formed from seeing Mr. D. often where you were not, that your familiarities with him were only to hide your fondness of the other. . . . The report, which they say some of your acquaintance had got about of my being in love with you, may have been of some use too in this affair, which cannot be approved by your family. . . . Whether I am likely to think of marrying you in case you would condescend to take one so contemptible as I should be, after such proofs (for you must own they are no longer suspicions), 'tis not for one in my position to guess. You can judge better than I how far my reason is able to resist my Passion. You will agree, I am sure, it is surprising the

[1] Possibly the trial of Sacheverell.

Passion, which I fairly confess, should still continue. You see it by the vexation I am in, nay by the very telling you this news.

"Your father will think I have abused him in not applying to him as I desired leave to do. Telling him the truth would reconcile him to me, but I would rather do wrong to myself than anything that may hurt or displease you. When you are married he shall know it; in the meantime tell me, shall I go to him? And what excuse shall I make? Shall I say in general I have taken exceptions to your conduct, which others might not have taken? Whatever you please I will say. I will even tell him, if you desire it, I cannot engage because I am in straits for money, tho' I would rather pay a great deal more for you than he will give with you, were it possible to hope I should be as well used as many men are. Not going near him is the most uncivil thing I can do; however, without your directions I will do nothing.

"I was to blame for saying in my last you had used me ill. You never did, for love is an excuse for breach of friendship. I am so far from being angry, tho' I am grieved, that I sincerely wish you may enjoy the present happiness of being pursued by the man you are in love with."

Lady Mary in her reply (17th April) says that she has done disputing with her lover, which would not have been surprising if it were true. But of course some last words were irresistible in her own defence, and she makes yet another attempt to justify her conduct in the eyes of a man who was determined to view it in the worst light.

"I[1] have done disputing with you. I am very sorry I attempted it; had I really the Inclination you charged me with, I should not deny it, but I cannot confess what I was never guilty of, to make your accusation appear just. I know not how to prove it to you, otherwise than by my own words, and I am now very well convinced they are of no force with you. However, I will do myself the satisfaction of solemnly protesting to you (since 'tis the last time I shall say anything to you) that Gentleman has no interest in my Heart, nor ever endeavoured

[1] From the unpublished MS.

having any. I have often seen him making Love to another, which I suppose he would not have done before my face, had he any design upon me. His coming to A⸺ was wholly without my knowledge, neither was it to wait upon me, but those that came with him. Here's enough of this Matter. I shall make none of the complaints another woman would do. I thank God I can now reflect on your proceeding without being angry at you. I have nothing further to desire but that for your own sake you would do nothing that you would one day repent of, for I am persuaded no Man of Honour (which I still believe you to be) can wrong anyone, without feeling sorry for having done it. Except in writing to you, I know nothing I have done against the knowledge of my Father. I confess I ought to be punished for that Indiscretion. I am punished, but would it be right in you to complain of a Conduct which has been only faulty upon your Account? Neither do I think he would take such an excuse for a compliment; he has now a very good opinion of you, and I wish you may always retain it. If you judge it absolutely necessary to say something, let me beg you find out some other pretence, than one that must render my Life uneasy to you. As to what you say of my Acquaintance reporting you a Lover of mine, it is a falsity I never told to anyone in the world. I have nothing more to say, but that I wish you all possible happiness, and myself the quiet of never hearing from you more.

"I am to thank you for not meeting me at Mrs. St. as I desired; it would possibly have done me some harm and could do me no good."

This letter by no means satisfied Mr. Wortley's suspicions, and he wrote from Wharncliffe on 23rd April—

"Had[1] I doubted of your Passion this letter would have convinced me. One half of it is filled with his praises, the other with your fears of losing him. To make you easy without more delay, I give you my word I will not find fault with your conduct. I told you in my last very clearly I would do nothing but by your order; as meanly as you think of me

[1] From the unpublished MS.

how could you be persuaded I was capable of changing my resolution so soon? You knew I could not disobey you. What need was there of your showing so much concern about him? You judge right that I envy him extremely, but I am not malicious enough to hurt him when it vexes you. Could I propose to succeed him I might do anything, but you have made it impossible for me to hope it. You know it is not true when you tell me your father would not be better with me did I give him the true reason of my ceasing to pursue you. You know he would esteem me for it. But I would fall out with him, and all that are as considerable as himself, rather than disobey you in the least of your commands.

"You tell me you should own an inclination for him if you had it. You are happy in having the man you think worthy of you. You say he is a lover of that Lady's; your jealousy is not quite so great—you cannot persuade yourself what no one else does or can believe. Tho' you fancy those you despise are neglected by all the world, you can never imagine those you love are welcome to every other. Could I credit what you solemnly protest of his never having aimed at you, I should be the weakest of all that know him or you. His passing most of his time among the women, his attempting to recommend himself to so many, is as well known as your desiring to be followed. We haven't a talk of him; had we been upon Mr. D. you would have denied his making love to you as solemnly, tho' by accident I have heard of the very words he has used, not to mention the whispers, looks, etc. which I have seen, and passed for strong assurances from other women. But enough of this happy man. I beg you will say no more of him. Why would you say nothing but of him?

"What you tell me of not meeting you at Mrs. St.'s was a continuation of the subject. You know you were going to dance with him when you called there, and you gave me no notice of your design to be there, tho' you spoke to me but the night before. I might have pressed you to stay too late. I beg I may hear no more of Rivals. If you have no other subject, say nothing. I cannot desire you to write at all unless to tell me by yourself or your servant you have had this. I would know I had put you out of pain. Converse with me or not according as you fancy; if you give over I know I may be more uneasy for the present but in all appearance shall be sooner free from the disease."

On 28th April Lady Mary replied, more in sorrow than in anger—

"I [1] must write if only to say I have received yours. I have always ten thousand things to say to you, and yet I solemnly and sincerely desire you to desist writing. . . . I could wish it was possible to keep a Correspondence with you without scandal or discovery, but as that cannot be, in Generosity do not make me uneasy. There is nothing I would not do to make you easy. That Gentleman has no interest in my heart, and yet I think he has as much as he deserves. I have the vanity to believe a man that could engage me must have a greater share of understanding. Had he desired it, it could never have been, but 'tis no Lie to assure you, he never attempted it. Mr. D. is one of those fine people that have the same way of talking to all the women they see, that everybody suffers and nobody esteems. I cannot deny he has often entertained me in that manner he does a thousand others, what I never took to be in earnest, because I knew he never meant it so. I believe he may have been well with some women, but I hope they have been women of a character very different to mine; all I know is, that there was never anything between us but a little raillery. I suppose it will be no hard matter for you to believe this; I wish I could as easily cure myself from the other. My word is not sufficient for that, in your opinion. Time and observation would soon do it, but then you may imagine me forsaken, or that we are broke off from some other cause, but it will be impossible to convince you of the truth.

"I have seen enough of the world, not to be very fond of it. I have seen so many Acquaintances unhappy, and heard so many secret complaints of Husbands, I have often resolved never to marry, and always not to sacrifice myself to an Estate. Having done with your Heart, I have no pretensions

[1] From the unpublished MS.

to yours. As I am, I enjoy every satisfaction but your conversation; marrying you is to part with every other for that. That I once resolved to do it, shows I set no common value on it. While I thought you loved me, I could have lived with you in any place or circumstances. I have but this satisfaction, that one time or other, I am assured you will think of me and regret you have wronged me. Adieu; I desire you not to answer.

"You have thrown away a Heart you knew not how to value. How hard it is to destroy an Idea that is once fixed! How happy had I been in any part of the world with you for my Companion."

Mr. Wortley was not softened by this touching conclusion. "To[1] tell me one of those never endeavoured to engage," he retorts, "and the other had indeed said fine things, but was never in earnest, shows how much you despise me, whether you fancy I shall believe you or not. To think I shall believe you is concluding me a fool; to write it when you fancy I shall not, proves you take me to be unworthy of the lowest degree of your friendship. When you say one of 'em has not understanding enough to charm you, besides the fondness of him you have expressed before me, you forget how you extolled his cunning to me, which I know you take to be the best sign of a great genius by the high praises I have heard you bestow on one that is thought to excel in that faculty. That the other has ever charmed the women you mean I cannot admit; I am credibly informed he has not. He may have been well with them, as you term it, but not so well as he has been with you."

After some more fault-finding, the letter concludes pleasantly—

"Adieu, dearest L[ady] M[ary], this once be assured you will not deceive me."

Among Lady Mary's papers there is nothing to show that she was engaged in a flirtation with any other admirer.[2] The

---

[1] From the unpublished MS.

[2] It must, however, be recalled that many years later she said in a letter to Lady Mar, "We wild girls make the best wives and mothers."

only note addressed to her by a man is one signed "A. Pierrepont," which was probably written by some distant cousin who had tried to claim a cousin's privileges, but had been rebuked for so doing. It has no date, but must have been written when Lady Mary was staying at Thoresby. It begins—

"DEAR CHARMER,[1]—You are very much in the right to imagine I am in perfect health, for nothing contributes so much to it as your good company and a set of fiddles, and am sorry you made so short a stay at the Ball, for I had not half the satisfaction after you was gone. I will be at Holm [2] by nine o'clock on Sunday morning to wait on you to Bellvior [Belvoir], for the Duchess will not be at home this week. . . . You see I have obeyed your commands, and have not mentioned the subject, nor dare say pray believe me to be etc. tho' without a compliment.—Yours to command,

"A. PIERREPONT"

Lady Mary's return to town was delayed by a case of smallpox in Arlington Street, opposite to her father's house. She wrote to inform her lover of the change of date, to prevent, as she says, his imagining her "lasting artifice," should he accidentally learn that she is not yet come to town. He is not to give himself the trouble of answering, for she believes it is a trouble. "Besides,"[1] she adds, "I know if you do write, 'twill be scruples, suspicions, and cross-questions. I am alone and not very well, and anything that vexes me now, vexes me too much. Then don't send me an ill-natured letter."

The answer, whatever it may have been, cannot with certainty be identified; but there is only one among Mr. Wortley's letters, which can truthfully be described as anything but ill-natured, and that belongs to the following year. In a note written about this time he remarks:[1] "You speak of gaiety and the desire to please many; don't mistake. A

---

[1] From the unpublished MS.
[2] Holm Pierrepont, the village in which Thoresby is situated.

woman is never pursued long, unless for her money, till she has given possession or very strong hopes. Why will you be thought to have gone so far with several? One with a very small share of your beauty and wit can draw as many and as deserving even as yours are after her whenever she pleases. Nay, take most of your own from you, if she will seem more fond of 'em and is a new woman."

On the road up to town Lady Mary wrote yet another letter of eternal farewell, which is an excellent example of her talent for this kind of composition.

"I[1] resolved not to answer your letter when I first read it, since I believed that the most agreeable way of answering it. After I had made this resolution it came into my Head that according to your way of interpreting things you would fancy I was so transported with going to London that I could think of nothing else. Rather than that you should have the least appearance of reason for such a thought, I write in an Inn after the most fatiguing day's journey that ever I passed in my Life. The sense of your letter I take to be this. Madam, you are the greatest Coquette I ever knew, and withal very silly; the only happiness you propose to yourself with a Husband is in jilting him most abundantly. You must stay till my Lord Hide[2] is a widower, or heaven raises up another Mr. Popham;[3] for my part, I know all your tricks. I believe you are in love with me, but don't flatter yourself— think not of me, for I shall never change my opinion of you. This is the exact miniature of your letter.

"Now to show you your mistake, tho' plain dealings have been very unfortunate to me, I will persist in it, and tell you the sort of Life I should choose to lead. The softness

---

[1] From the unpublished MS.

[2] Presumably Henry, Lord Hyde (1672–1753), second Earl of Rochester. He married a daughter of Sir William Leveson Gower. She was celebrated by the poets as one of the most beautiful women of her day, and was the mother of two beautiful daughters, Kitty of Queensberry and Lady Essex. Like all pretty women of that period, she was "talked about," and therefore Lady Mary thought Lord Hyde was an easy-going husband.

[3] Probably one of the Wiltshire Pophams, who bore a character for eccentricity. There was an Alexander Popham about that period, who was married three times.

CHAPTER XII

MRS. HEWET AND MR. ADDISON

THE miscellaneous letters for this year are few, consisting of a couple from Lady Mary to Mrs. Hewet, and a brief interchange of correspondence between Mr. Wortley and Mr. Addison. Some time in March Lady Mary wrote to Mrs. Hewet—

" 'Tis so long since I had a letter from dear Mrs. Hewet, I should think her no longer in the land of the living if Mr. Resingade did not assure me he was happier than I, and had heard of your health from your own hand; which makes me fancy that my last miscarried, and perhaps you are blaming me at the same time that you are thinking me neglectful of you. *À propos* of Mr. Resingade—we are grown such good friends, I assure you, that we write Italian letters to each other, and I have the pleasure of talking to him of Madame Hewet. He told me he would send you the two tomes of Madame de Noyer's Memoirs. I fancy you will find yourself disappointed in them, for they are horribly grave and insipid; and instead of the gallantry you might expect, they are full of dull morals.

" I was last Thursday at the New Opera, and saw Nicolini strangle a lion with great gallantry.[1] But he represented nakedness so naturally, I was surprised to see those ladies stare

[1] In the opera of *Hydaspes*. Addison makes fine fun out of the Lion in the *Spectator* for 15th March 1710-11. The first Lion, he says, was a candle-snuffer, who, being a fellow of testy choleric temper, overdid his part, and would not suffer himself to be killed so easily as he ought to have done. The second Lion was a tailor by trade, who had the character of a mild and peaceable man, and proved too sheepish for the part. Lion Number Three was a country gentleman, who performed for his diversion, and whose temper was such a happy mixture of mild and choleric that he outdid both his predecessors.

at him without any confusion, that pretend to be so violently shocked at a *double entendre* or two in a comedy, which convinced me that those prudes who would cry fie! fie! at the word *naked*, have no scruples about the thing.

"The marriage of Lord Willoughby[1] still goes on, and he swears he will bring the lady down to the Nottingham races. How far it may be true I cannot tell. By what fine gentlemen say, you know, it is not easy to guess at what they mean. The lady has made an acquaintance with me after the fashion of Pyramus and Thisbe; I mean over a wall three yards high, which separates our garden from Lady Guilford's.[2] The young ladies had found out a way to pull out two or three bricks, and so climb up and hang their chins over the wall, where we, mounted on chairs, used to have many *belles conversations à la dérobée* for fear of the old mother.[3] This trade continued several days, but fortune seldom permits long pleasures. By long standing on the wall the bricks loosened; and one fatal morning, down drops Miss Nelly;[4] and to complete this misfortune, she fell into a little sink, and bruised her poor—— self to that terrible degree, she is forced to have surgeons, plaisters, and God knows what, which discovered the whole intrigue, and their mamma forbade them ever to visit us, but by the door. Since that time, all our communications have been made in a vulgar manner, visiting in coaches etc., etc., which took away half the pleasure. You know danger gives a high *goût* to everything. This is our secret history—pray let it be so still—but I hope all the world will know that I am most entirely yours."

The only other letter to Mrs. Hewet this year seems to have been written in the autumn, as there is an allusion to the Peace of Utrecht, the negotiations for which began in September. Lady Mary was evidently at Thoresby at this time, though about to return to town.

"I have a thousand thanks to give my dear Mrs. Hewet

---

[1] Afterwards Duke of Ancaster. He married Jane, one of the four daughters and co-heiresses of Sir John Brownlow, Bart. of Belton, in May 1711.

[2] Another daughter of Sir J. Brownlow married the second Lord Guilford.

[3] "The old mother" was *née* Sherrard, and evidently tried to keep a strict hand over her daughters, even after they were married.

[4] The fourth Brownlow sister, who married her cousin, another Sir John Brownlow, who was created Viscount Tyrconnel in 1718.

for her news, and above all the letter; and I would not have delayed them, but your messenger was in haste, and I was resolved to write you a long scribble. My advices of Saturday say that a peace will positively be concluded.[1] This comes from the same hand that wrote so contrary on Thursday, and I depend very much on the intelligence. I am charmed with your *correspondante*, for I hope it is a woman; and if it is, I reckon her an honour to our sex. I am in no fear of the reflection you mention, and being perfectly innocent, God knows am far from thinking I can be suspected. Your news and no news I know not what to make of.

"At present, my domestic affairs go on so ill I want spirits to look abroad. I have got a cold that disables my eyes, and disorders me every other way. Mr. Mason has ordered me blooding, to which I have submitted after long contestation. You see how stupid I am. I entertain you with discourses of physic, but I have the oddest jumble of disagreeable things in my head that ever plagued poor mortals: a great cold, a bad peace, people I love in disgrace,[2] sore eyes, the horrid prospects of a civil war, and the thoughts of a filthy potion to take. I believe nobody ever had such a *mélange* before. Our coachman, dear man, arrived safe last night, but when we remove God only knows. If possible I will wait on you at Clipstone, but this physic may prevent all my good intentions. My companions are your servants. I had forgot the *Spectators*; one is not worth mentioning, the other is so plain and good sense, I wonder anybody of five years old does not find out that he is in the right."

The first number of the *Spectator* had appeared on the 1st of March. Presumably Mr. Wortley did not think very much of his friends' new venture, or Lady Mary would hardly have been so scornful. The relations between her lover and Mr. Addison may be illustrated by two or three letters which passed between them this summer.[3]

---

[1] It was not concluded till 1713.
[2] This may be an allusion to the Duchess of Marlborough, with whom Lady Mary was a favourite, or to some other of her Whig friends. Lord Dorchester was strongly opposed to the Peace, and signed the protest against it in the House of Lords.
[3] These letters are quoted from *Addisoniana* (1805).

On 21st July Addison wrote—

"DEAR SIR,—Being very well pleased with this day's *Spectator*,[1] I cannot forbear sending you one of them, and desiring your opinion of the story in it. When you have a son I shall be glad to be his Leontine, as my circumstances will probably be like his. I have within this twelvemonth lost a place of £2000 per annum,[2] an estate in the Indies of £14,000, and what is more than all the rest, my mistress.[3] Hear this, and wonder at my philosophy. I find they are going to take away my Irish place[4] from me too; to which I must add that I have just resigned my fellowship, and the stocks sink every day. If you have any hints or subjects, pray send me a paper full. I long to talk an evening with you. I believe I shall not go to Ireland this summer, and perhaps would take a month with you, if I knew where. Lady Bellasise[5] is very much your humble servant. Dick Steele and I often remember you.—I am, dear sir, yours eternally etc.,

"J. ADDISON"

[1] Number 123, for 21st July 1711. This consists of the story of Eudoxus and Leontine, and is designed to show the care that should be taken to educate judiciously the heir to a great estate. Eudoxus and Leontine were two intimate friends, both men of moderate fortune. The former sought places about the Court and acquired wealth; the latter improved his mind by study, conversation, and travel. When both were turned forty, they decided to retire into the country, Eudoxus on a large estate, Leontine on a small farm. The one had a son and heir, Florio; the other a daughter, Leonilla. Leontine's wife having died he felt himself incapable of properly educating a daughter, while Eudoxus reflected ruefully on the ordinary behaviour of a son who knows himself heir to a great estate. Finally, the two fathers agreed to exchange children, till the young pair arrived at years of discretion. Florio, fancying himself the son of a poor man, worked hard at school and university, and presently was called to the Bar. Leonilla did nothing in particular except fall in love with Florio, "but conducted herself with so much prudence, that she never gave him the least intimation of it. At length, when Florio had established his reputation, Eudoxus sent for him, announced to him his true parentage, and concluded by saying, 'I have no other way left of acknowledging my gratitude to Leontine than by marrying you to his daughter.' Thereupon the pair were married, and parents and children lived happily ever after."

[2] He had been Under-Secretary of State.

[3] This has been taken as an allusion to Lady Warwick, whom he afterwards married.

[4] He had been made Chief Secretary for Ireland under Lord Wharton in 1708.

[5] Presumably Anne, widow of the second Lord Belasyse. He died in 1692, when the title became extinct.

On 28th July Mr. Wortley replied, dating from his father's house at Wortley—

"Notwithstanding your disappointments, I had much rather be in your circumstances than my own. The strength of your constitution would make you happier than all who are not equal to you in that, though it contributed nothing towards those other advantages that place you in the first rank of men. Since my fortune fell to me, I had reason to fancy I should be reduced to a very small income. I immediately retrenched my expenses, and lived for six months on fifty pounds as pleasantly as ever I did in my life, and could have lived for less than half that sum, and often entertained myself with the speech of Ofellus[1] in the second satire of the second book [of Horace], and still think no man of understanding can be many days unhappy, if he does not want health. At present I take all the care I can to improve mine.

"This air is as proper for that as any I know, and we are so remote from all troublesome neighbours and great towns that a man can think of nothing long but country amusements or his books; and if you would change the course of your thoughts, you will scarce fail of effecting it here. I am in some fear I shall be forced to town for four or five days, and then we may come down together. If I stay, I shall let you know it in a week or ten days, and hope to see you very soon. You were never in possession of anything you love but your places, and those you could not call your own. After I had read what you say about them, I could not take pleasure in the *Spectator* you sent, but thought it a very good one. In two months or a little more, I think I must go the Newcastle journey. You told me you should like it; if you do not, we may contrive how you may pass your time here. I am not sure we shall easily have leave to lodge out of this house; but we may eat in the woods every day if you like it, and nobody here will expect any sort of ceremony.—Yours ever,

"EDWARD WORTLEY MONTAGU."

[1] "Even Ofellus will own there's a wide gap between
A table that's frugal and one that is mean."
Mr. Wortley was afterwards to be compared by Pope (in his imitation of the same Satire) to the miserly Avidienus.

Addison wrote on 17th August to the effect that the present posture of affairs in his office would not allow of his spending part of the summer with his friend. He was proposing to spend a month at the Bath, where he hoped to put himself into good-humour for the year, and concludes, " I hope you don't think it a compliment when I assure you that I value your conversation more than any man's living." Before this letter reached him in Yorkshire Mr. Wortley wrote again, to press for a visit from his friend, who, he hears, is at the Bath. He proposes to stay three months longer in the North, and adds that he has his choice of two or three pretty but small places, besides the house he is in (Wharncliffe). " You are almost as near to this place," he continues, " as to London. I am afraid you will not meet with an opportunity of coming in a coach. But if you have not seen Worcester, Stafford, Nottingham and Chatsworth, you may make your journey pleasant; and if you travel but eighteen or twenty miles a day, you will get here almost insensibly in five or six days, as you are taking the air. After you are a little beyond Gloucester, you will find a gravelly soil, as good in wet as in dry weather, which will not leave you till you are within fifteen miles of home. I can have one here that writes a better hand than your secretary. But if you like him better, he would be no trouble to any here. . . ."

On 13th October Addison writes his thanks for this or another letter of invitation, and adds: " You know I have put my hand to the plow, and have already been absent from my work one entire month at the Bath. I hope you will not think of staying in the country so long as you mention. Sure it will be worth your while to hear the peace treated in the House of Commons, and as you have seen *mores hominum multorum et urbes* I think you cannot have a better opportunity to shew yourself. If you will be my lodger I'll take a house in the Square at Kensington and furnish you a chamber, not forgetting a Cook and other particulars. I send you enclosed a paper of Abel Roper's,[1] which everybody looks upon as authentick. We talk of nothing but a peace. I am

[1] A Tory journalist and publisher (1665-1726). He founded the Tory newspaper known as the *Post-boy*, with which he was connected from 1695 to 1713.

heartily glad you have your health, and question not but you would find the Kensington air as good as the Wortley. . . ."

On 1st November Mr. Wortley wrote from Newcastle that it would probably be about the middle of December before he got to Kensington, " when I am very glad to hear I may be your lodger, if you will not be mine as I proposed. Should you like any other place better than Kensington, I desire you will choose it, and I shall certainly be pleased with it. The peace I should think will not be debated before Christmas. When it is, I fancy it will be accepted or refused by a very great majority, and the public would not suffer by the absence of all our friends put together. If I am mistaken in this, I desire you will let me know it. My opinion is, the nation must be ruined by such a peace as is talked of: notwithstanding I should pay for the war more than any man in the house whose fortune is not above double mine. That we may bear up the better under misfortunes, I hope you will be nice in the choice of a cook and other particulars."

The correspondence between the lovers languished, we may suppose, during the summer months, since the difficulties of communication were much greater. At any rate, no letters have been preserved between May and October of this year. The correspondence begins again on 11th October, when Lady Mary was back in town. Mr. Wortley was now contemplating a marriage with his lady on his own terms, which meant taking her without a fortune. It appears that a runaway match was in the minds of the pair for nearly a year before they took the decisive step. But first Mr. Wortley thought of renewing his negotiations for Lady Mary's hand, though there seemed little chance of changing Lord Dorchester's views about settlements. The obnoxious " Mr. K." had come forward as a serious suitor, and was prepared to agree to the terms demanded. Mr. Wortley was beginning to feel that his hand was forced, and since his doubts and scruples continued as strong as ever, he was torn between the fear of committing himself and the fear of losing the lady.

On 11th October Lady Mary had just received two letters from her lover, who was still in the country. She says that the first she opened pleased her so well that she wishes she had not opened the second, which seems to be out of humour with her.

"Perhaps[1] I am to blame," she admits, "but is there nothing to be forgiven for a woman's fears? I own I am a coward, I tremble at everything. Forgive me if I injure your fortune any way. I do not deserve you should. You speak of losing £20,000—lose nothing for me. I set you free from any engagement you may think yourself under. 'Tis too generous that you should take me with nothing; I can never deserve even that sacrifice. You shall not however have to reproach yourself or me that I have lessened your fortune. You do not know how much I think myself obliged for what you have already done: I would make you any return in my power. I beg you sincerely if you find the disobliging your F. will be of consequence to you, and that it is unavoidable if you do it, leave me. I shall blame nothing but my own fears, that the silly niceties sacrificed all my happiness. Perhaps that understanding you compliment me with, should we come to be better acquainted you will find yourself deceived in, and the silly woman appear in many instances. But I am honest, I would do right, I am naturally generous tho' I have no opportunity of showing it, and I could never forgive myself (of all mankind) an injury to you.

"I cannot answer that part of your letter with regard to Mr. ——, there is no judging what fools are capable of, or in what way he will behave himself upon any Occasion. As to my F.[ather] 'tis just the same thing how I do it. He will never see me more, and he will give me nothing, let me do it in what way I will. . . ."

Mr. Wortley did not remain in the country till near Christmas, but came back to town early in November, perhaps impelled by a desire to see his mistress again. He wrote to ask her to arrange a meeting at a friend's house, to which she replied on 13th November: "If[1] you have a mind to see me once more, I will venture it to oblige you. 'Tis better to make a ridiculous figure to a few than to the many, and having already been laughed at at Mrs. Steele's, I had rather be so there again than in new company. Give yourself no

[1] From the unpublished MS.

trouble to-day. I am not one of those foolish vain women that think nothing so important as themselves.

"Write me word what day would be most convenient, and if possible it shall be then. It cannot be Thursday; Dr. Garth's Ball is that day, I fancy, and I must feign a sickness, or I shall entirely disoblige my sister that has a mind to go, neither will it be in my power to refuse, for my Father has promised I shall be there. I don't speak this by way of excuse, for if you please I will say I am ill, and keep my chamber two or three days. Let me know what you would have me do."

"I[1] will be at Lady Jekyll's," replied Mr. Wortley, "any day you will name before the beginning of next week. If you give me leave I will tell you when we dine there, and perhaps you may get her to engage you that day at dinner or after. But how can I speak to you there without observation? Do you never walk in the Queen's Garden or Lady Ranelagh's?[2] . . . Is not Mrs. Hampden's a better place than Lady J.'s? I have seen other meetings of the same nature at Mrs. H.'s, and she is not censorious, nor in the least given to tell what she observes. She is too very much my friend."

In the same letter he expresses a hope that the marriage of a kinsman of his own has furnished an example that will put an end to the disputes about settlements. He thinks that Lady Mary's family must own themselves unreasonable if their demands are higher than those of the bride's relations, who are very prudent people, and skilful in managing their own affairs. He would be ready to close with almost any terms if he were convinced of Lady Mary's "Esteem." The expressions in her last, he admits, are extremely obliging, and adds: "I was fixed by 'em for a time, and had engaged myself could I have answered your letter the day it came. But having had time to reflect, I find there wants an air of sincerity. I think I should have some better security before I make this great change in my fortune."

[1] From the unpublished MS.
[2] Lady Ranelagh was a daughter of Lord Salisbury and wife of the first Earl of Ranelagh, who died without issue in 1712. The gardens of his estate at Chelsea were afterwards transformed into the fashionable resort, Ranelagh Gardens.

"You certainly believe me very little,"[1] returned Lady Mary. "I don't suppose my family would insist on better terms, than your kinsman. But I have already told you 'tis now to no purpose to talk of terms. I am too well convinced they will not hear of any; if you persist in disbelieving me, I know no way to be convinced but trying. I am unhappily assured of the Answer you will meet—that you speak too late. 'Tis never too late for me to save myself from Ruin, but that is not what they think of. I do not understand what you call an Air of sincerity; I speak, I am sure, with truth, I think with plainness. To what end should I deceive you? I am not persuading you to make proposals to my Family; I know (and I freely confess) it is too late for any hopes that way. I have neither folly nor vanity enough to suppose you would think of running away with me, and in my situation perhaps it would be more prudent to tell you what is doing is with my own consent, and affect to be pleased with it. I have done with my pretensions to Happiness; the Esteem I have for you makes me own it to you. As a Friend I shall ever be glad to see you, however melancholy my circumstances are. I am very sorry I don't visit Mrs. Hampden, she made some advances to me last winter, but these affairs put me so much out of humour I was not gay enough to think of making new acquaintance. I shall go to Kensington Gardens, but I cannot name exactly the day. If you have any inclination to see me you may go every evening, Saturday, Monday, or Tuesday. One of those days we may possibly meet. To a place like that I cannot go alone. You may make by your manner our meeting appear accidental to those with me. I go this evening to Lady J. [Jekyll]. I'm afraid you won't have this letter time enough to come."

In Mr. Wortley's next letter he says that it is not unlikely he may apply to Mr. White (possibly Lord Dorchester's agent or man of business) some day in the course of the week. That is, if Lady Mary will come to such terms as many other women might think unreasonable.

"You[1] must assure me you can freely comply with everything I have asked or you have promised by letter or

[1] From the unpublished MS.

word of mouth. Equipage, furniture, and all other expenses must please you in such proportion as I fancy, and that, I must acquaint you, may be very small. You should be sure you can be as well satisfied with the country as with the town, and with little company, or even without any but myself."

As for her future conduct, he is doubtful whether she can undertake to free him from jealousy. "You know," he reminds her, "I have with my own eyes seen you too familiar with some others. What is yet worse, you denied there was any harm in it; that is, you justified it, which was declaring you would always do the same thing when left to yourself. How can I hope you will confine yourself to what I think right if it is contrary to your own judgment? How can I be sure your passions will be guided by reason any more than they have been? I own, too, I am of a temper that no woman can live well with me long that does not value me much more than she does any other."

In conclusion, his heart apparently failing him, he says that he is not yet quite resolved to go to Mr. White, and that he will not take himself to be engaged till the "writings" are begun, if there are to be any. He would prefer to take her without troubling her family, since he values her fortune very little, and would rather lay an obligation on her than get a great deal more than her father is likely to give. "I would not think of you now," he adds, with amazing candour, "did I not believe I should oblige you if I agree with you. It is relieving you from distress, if there is any truth in what you say. Were you entering upon a state you had no reason to be afraid of, I should not be sorry to hear you were disposed of, and would not converse with you while you was in treaty."

Lady Mary, who does not appear to have resented this plain speaking, writes that she is going to spend the whole afternoon the following Saturday at Lady Jekyll's, where a meeting might be arranged, and continues—

"You[1] have not that confidence in me that you ought to have. I tell exactly the truth; nothing is more in my power

[1] From the unpublished MS.

than I say. Was I to choose my destiny (though I am sincere enough to acknowledge there are parts of your humour I could wish otherwise) I had rather be confined in a desert with you than enjoy the highest rank and fortune in a [? paradise] with him I am condemned to. This is trusting you with a very plain confession, but no great compliment." Lady Mary was obliged to open her letter to say that Lady Jekyll had put her off till the following week, and adds: " I begin to be persuaded there is a destiny that hinders our meeting, like every other pleasure to one so unfortunate as I."

There seems to have been at this time another of those many letters of eternal farewell, which was followed by a temporary break in the correspondence. Mr. Wortley never accepted a refusal as final; indeed, in one of his letters written about this time (3rd March) he says: "Though [1] what you write should prove your last farewell, I shall be more charmed with it than I could have been with the promises of endless love from any other. A refusal in such a manner is more than anything but your own acceptance," and so forth. He re-opens the correspondence by asking for another meeting, though he is unable to suggest a suitable place. The Steeles' fortunes were always uncertain, and their places of abode frequently changed. Mr. Wortley explains that he has not visited Mrs. Steele lately, and does not know whether the apartment she is in is proper for visitors. " I make few visits," he adds, " and can think of no other place, unless it be some China-house. The Duchess of Sh.[rewsbury's] or Lady Hervey's and the Play-house seem to be too publick, and not to allow time enough for discoursing a matter of any moment."

Lady Mary professes to have been never more surprised in her life than at seeing a letter from her quondam lover, and declares that only curiosity made her weak enough to receive it. She continues—

"In [1] the whole course of my commerce with you, I do not think you have always done right to me, but I do not think you have ever deceived me. Whatever you have to

[1] From the unpublished MS.

ask me, I shall answer you with the greatest sincerity. Nothing can be more hazardous than meeting you, but I am willing to remove some mistakes in your letter. Indian houses are too publick, nor at all proper for a long conversation. I will go Tuesday between six and seven to Sir Godfrey Kneller's. I set a real value on your friendship, and hope I shall never lose it."

The next day she writes again—

"I[1] was at Sir G. K.'s yesterday a quarter after seven. It was so long after the time I had named I went almost without expecting you, but I was unavoidably hindered coming sooner. I cannot go there again soon without giving suspicion to my Companion. If I should meet you in a private house, I must trust the mistress of it, and I know nobody I dare trust; a formal visit will not permit us to talk. I cannot speak to you, but before witnesses, and choose rather to tell you in this way, that your letter seems founded on mistake. I did not ask you to write, nor desire to see you; as circumstances are, I know no use it can be to me. I am very far from a thought of what you seem to think at the end of your Letter. My Family is resolved to dispose of me where I hate. I have made all the opposition in my power. Perhaps I have carried that opposition too far; however it is, things were carried to that height I have been assured of never having a shilling except I comply. Since the time of Mandane,[2] we have heard of no Ladies run away with without fortunes. That Threat would not have obliged me to consent, if it had not been joined with an Assurance of making my Maiden Life as miserable as lay in their power. That is so much in their power I am compelled to submit. I was born to be unhappy, and I must fulfil the course of my destiny.

"You see Sir, the Esteem I have for you; I have ventured to tell you the whole secret of my Heart. 'Tis for the last time I indulge myself in complaints, that in a little while will become indecent. By this real and sincere

---

[1] From the unpublished MS.

[2] This word is indistinctly written. But it might be read as "Mandane," a name borne by several heroines of romance, notably by the mother of Cyrus in Mlle. Scudéry's novel, *Cyrus the Great*.

Account of my Affairs, you may see I have no design of any engagement beyond friendship with you, since should we agree, 'tis now impossible, my fortune only following my obedience.

"'Tis utterly inconvenient for you to write to me—I know no safe way of conveying a letter. After this long Account, I don't suppose you have any farther enquiries to make, nor in my wretched circumstances is there room for advice. If you have anything to say (tho' I cannot imagine what it should be), I will be at Coleman's Friday between four and five. I cannot be more exact. If you have nothing to say, or that now you know the true state of my Affairs you think that advice can be of no importance, do not come. I shall ever think you my friend, and never give you occasion to be otherwise. My business is now to behave myself with my fortune in a manner to show I do not deserve it."

CHAPTER XIII

A DISTASTEFUL MATCH

ON 19th March 1712 Mr. Wortley wrote to say that he intended to take leave of the town and of all business whatever. A lawsuit that had vexed him for the last two or three years was at an end, and his health obliged him to quit London. "The man I am best pleased with,"[1] he explains, "presses me to do this [*i.e.* go abroad] for our pleasure, and unless I promise him shortly, he will seek another companion. If you and I agree, I shall not bear to have him or any other near me that I like very well. And whether I shall be so well satisfied with your carriage to me that I shall want no other, you can best tell. I must forbear going into a delightful climate for your sake if I love you. And my present circumstances are such that I cannot content myself with much less money than I have now I am single. All this would be hard upon you if I did not give you fair warnings. On my side I take the hazard to be as great."

In a long letter, which is a curious mixture of affection and practical common sense, Lady Mary answers the several objections raised by Mr. Wortley to their union from time to time, and gives her own idea of happiness in married life.

"You[1] seem not very well to know your mind," she begins. "You are unwilling to go back from your word, and yet you do the same thing in telling me you should think yourself more obliged to me for a refusal than for a consent. Another woman would complain of this unsteadiness of resolution. I think in an affair of this nature 'tis very natural to think one minute one thing and the next another, and I cannot blame you. I remember an expression in one of your letters to me

[1] From the unpublished MS.

which is certainly just. Should we not repent we should be happy beyond example; if we should [repent], we should I fear be both wretched in as high a degree. I should not hesitate one moment, was I not resolved to sacrifice everything to you. If I do it, I am determined to think as little of the rest of the world, men, women, acquaintance and relations, as if a deluge had swallowed them. I abandon all things that bear the name of pleasure, but what is to be found in your company. I give up all my Wishes to be regulated by yours, and I resolve to have no other study but that of pleasing you.

"These Resolutions are absolutely necessary if we are to meet, and you need have no doubt, but I will perform them. I know you too well to propose to myself any satisfaction in marrying you that must not be centred in yourself. A man that marries a woman without any advantages in Fortune or Alliance (as will be the case), has a very good title to her future Obedience; he has a right to be made easy every other way, and I will not impose on your Generosity, which claims the sincerest proceeding on my side. I am as sensible as you yourself can be of the generosity of your proposals. Perhaps there is no other man that would take a woman under these disadvantages, and I am grateful to you with all the warmth gratitude can inspire. On the other side, consider a little, whether there be many other women that would think as I do. The man my Family would marry me to, is resolved to live in London; 'tis my own fault if I do not (of the humour he is) make him always think whatever I please. If he dies, I shall have £1200 per ann. rent charge; if he lives, I shall enjoy every pleasure of Life, those of Love excepted. With you I quit all things but yourself, as much as if we were to be placed alone together in an inaccessible Island, and I hazard the possibility of being reduced to suffer all the evils of poverty. 'Tis true I had rather give my hand to the Flames than to him, and cannot think of suffering him with common patience; to you—I could give it without reluctance (it is to say more than I ought), but perhaps with pleasure. This last consideration determines me—I will venture all things for you—for our mutual good.

"'Tis necessary for us to consider the method the most

likely to hinder either of us from repenting. On that point our whole repose seems to depend. If we retire into the country, both your fortune and Inclination require a degree of privacy. The greatest part of my Family (as the greatest part of all families) are fools; they know no happiness but Equipage and furniture, and they judge of everybody's by the proportion they enjoy of it. They will talk of me as one who has ruined herself, and there will be perpetual enquiries made of my manner of living. I do not speak of this in regard to myself; I have always had a hearty contempt of those things, but on these and some other considerations I don't see why you should not pursue the plan, that you say you begun with your Friend; I don't mean take him with you, but why may not I supply his place? At Naples we may live after our own fashion. For my part, as I design utterly to forget there is such a place as London, I shall leave no directions with nobody to write after me. People that enter upon a solitude, are in the wrong if they don't make it as agreeable as they can. A fine country and beautiful prospects, to people who are capable of tasting them, are at least steps to promoting happiness. If I lived with you, I should be sorry not to see you perfectly happy. I foresee the Objection you will raise against this, but it is none. I have no Acquaintance, nor I will make none, and it is your own fault if I do see anyone else but yourself; your commands shall regulate that if you please. I can take with me a Lady you have heard me speak of, who, I am sure, will follow me over all the world if I please, and I don't care if I don't see anybody else but her and you. If you agree to this, there is but one point farther to be considered: whether you would make me any assurance of a provision, if I should be so unhappy as to lose you. You may think this an odd thing for me to name, when I bring you no fortune. My brother would keep me, but there is something very severe to submit to a dependence of that nature, not to mention the possibility of his Death, and then what am I to expect from the guardians of his son? I am sure I have nothing to expect from my F. ... By Assurance I only mean your word, which I dare entirely depend on.

"I know no faults that you are ignorant of; on the contrary, I believe you forgive more than you have occasion to forgive. I do not however look upon you as so far engaged that you cannot retreat. You are at Liberty to raise what objections you please. I will answer them, or freely confess any that are unanswerable. I make no reply to the accusation of having no value for you; I think it needs none when I proffer to leave the whole world for you. I say nothing of pin-money, etc., I don't understand the meaning of any divided interests from a man I willingly give myself to. You speak of my F. as if it were in my power to marry you with his consent. I know it is not; all is concluded with this other, and he will not put it off. If you are not of my Opinion, you may do what you please in it without naming me, which will only serve to expose me to a great deal of ill-usage, and force me to what he wills. . . ."

Mr. Wortley seems to have made another application to Lord Dorchester for his daughter's hand, but with no result. In a letter written about this time he begs his lady to consider whether she is likely to have a pleasant life with the husband who is designed for her, and if not, to refrain from putting herself into a situation from which there is no retreat. It is clear, he observes, that her father believes the new lover is more proper for her than the old one; otherwise he would not again have insisted on his first demands.

"He[1] knows that seldom any man can be so hard-hearted and unjust as not to make the person his heir that by the law and custom of his country has reason to expect it; and that in all appearance I shall, if I am able, leave him twice as much as what he would force me to do. He knows too there is little reason to doubt of my being able. I am so far from being a squanderer that I have, by my own management, made a large addition to my fortune. But I would have my heir thank me and not another that he is so. I am now reasoning as if I had been against complying with what is usual. So far from it, that I was willing to part with double what is customary, and he would surely accept of it if he did not prefer the other. If ever I make an offer near so advantageous in point of fortune

[1] From the unpublished MS.

to any other, condemn me for a fool that did not know your worth. . . . If your —— [Father] sets him above me for no other reason but that his proposals are better, he should have twice as much of him as he asked of me. Scarce any man would give an estate here for one twice as big there,[1] if he must change his country and often live there. The same rents will sell for near twice as much here as they will there. But I beg your pardon for entering into this, when for aught I know the bargain is quite concluded and fixed."

In March of this year Lady Evelyn Pierrepont was married to Lord Gower.[2] That Lady Evelyn had not lived at home with her sisters seems proved by the fact that there are no allusions to her in Lady Mary's letters, and also that she was not acquainted with her sister's friends in Nottinghamshire.

Miss Banks of Scofton writes on 25th March to Lady Mary in Arlington Street—

"The[3] Prints tell us Lady Evelyn Pierrepont is married to Lord Gower. Though I have not the honor to know her, I beg leave on this occasion to join my wishes with those of her acquaintance for her happiness. Our good Archbishop has, I fancy, before this in person satisfied his faithful little sister that he still remembers her, and perhaps that it would be more for his repose could he possibly forget her. But lest his unlucky stars should have deny'd the pleasure of telling it to you himself, I will give your Ladyship the answer to the last part of your letter in his own words. After naming his faithful little sister, he says, 'And I must add fair to faithful, and then hope she will never more doubt of my affection in a double capacity. As spiritual I hope I may be allowed to admire her faith, and as temporal, I think I may claim a right to adore the Fair.' I will make no excuse for this letter, since the share our good Archbishop has in it will,

---

[1] The other suitor had estates in Ireland.

[2] John, second baron. He was created Earl Gower in 1746, having been appointed Lord Privy Seal in 1742. There were ten children of this marriage, several of whom became the founders of great families, so that this Lord Gower has been described (by Mr. George Russell) as "the progenitor of all the Gowers, Cavendishes, Howards, Grosvenors, Campbells, and Russells who walk on the face of the earth."

[3] From the unpublished MS.

I believe, fully atone for any impertinence I have been guilty of.—I am, Dear Lady Mary's most devoted Humble Servant,
"M. BANKS"

About the beginning of July the plot thickened, and unless some desperate step were taken Lady Mary's fate seemed to be finally sealed. It was about this time that she made a last attempt to alter her father's decision, and begged to be allowed to live a single life rather than be forced to marry a man she hated. The result of the interview with Lord Dorchester is given in a long letter to Mr. Wortley written about 4th July 1712. The tone is at once so pathetic and resigned, that it is hard to imagine how any true and generous lover could read it unmoved.

"I am going to write you a plain long letter. What I have already told you is nothing but the truth. I have no reason to believe I am going to be otherwise confined than by my duty; but I, that know my own mind, know that it is enough to make me miserable. I see all the misfortune of marrying where it is impossible to love; I am going to confess a weakness which may perhaps add to your contempt of me. I wanted courage to resist at first the will of my relations, but as every day added to my fears, those at last grew strong enough to make me venture the disobliging of them. A harsh word damps my spirits to the degree of silencing all I have to say. I knew the folly of my own temper, and took the method of writing to the disposer of me. I said everything in this letter I thought proper to move him, and proffered, in atonement for not marrying whom he would, never to marry at all.

"He did not think fit to answer this letter, but sent for me. He told me he was very much surprised that I did not depend on his judgment for my future happiness; that he knew nothing I had to complain of, etc.; that he did not doubt I had some other fancy in my head, which encouraged me to this disobedience; but he assured me, if I refused a settlement he had provided for me, he gave me his word, whatever proposals were made him, he would never so much as enter into a treaty with any other; that if I founded any hopes upon his death, I should find myself mistaken, he never intended to leave me anything but an annuity of £400 per annum; that though another would proceed in this manner after I had given so just a pretence for it, yet he had the goodness to leave my destiny in my own choice, and at the same time commanded me to communicate my design to my relations, and ask their advice.

"As hard as this may sound, it did not shock my resolution; I was pleased to think, at any price, I had it in my power to be free from a man I hated. I told my intention to all my nearest relations. I was surprised at their blaming it to the greatest degree. I was told they were sorry I would ruin myself; but if I was so unreasonable, they could not blame my F[ather], whatever he inflicted upon me. I objected I did not love him. They made answer they found no necessity of loving; if I lived well with him, that was all was required of me; and that if I considered the town, I should find very few women in love with their husbands, and yet as many happy. It was in vain to dispute with such prudent people. They looked upon me as a little romantic, and I found it impossible to persuade them that living in London at liberty was not the height of happiness. However, they could not change my thoughts, tho' I found I was to expect no protection from them.

"When I was to give my final answer to ——, I told him that I preferred a single life to any other, and if he pleased to permit me, I would take that resolution. He replied, he could not hinder my resolutions, but I should not pretend after that to please him, since pleasing him was only to be done by obedience. That if I would disobey, I knew the consequences; he would not fail to confine me where I might repent at leisure; that he had also consulted my relations, and found them all agreeing in his sentiments. He spoke this in a manner hindering my answering. I retired to my chamber, where I writ a letter to let him know my aversion to the man proposed was too great to be overcome, that I should be miserable beyond all things could be imagined, but I was in his hands, and he might dispose of me as he thought fit. He was perfectly satisfied with this answer, and proceeded as if I had given a willing consent.

"I forgot to tell you, he named you, and said, if I thought

that way, I was very much mistaken; that if he had no other engagements, yet he would never have agreed to your proposals, having no inclination to see his grandchildren beggars. I do not speak this to endeavour to alter your opinion, but to shew the improbability of his agreeing to it. I confess I am entirely of your mind. I reckon it among the absurdities of custom that a man must be obliged to settle his whole estate on an eldest son, beyond his power to recall, whatever he proves himself to be, and make himself unable to make happy a younger child that may deserve to be so. If I had an estate myself, I should not make such ridiculous settlements, and I cannot blame you for being in the right.

"I have told you all my affairs with a plain sincerity. I have avoided to move your compassion, I have said nothing of what I suffer, and I have not persuaded you to a *treaty*, which I am sure my family will never agree to. I can have no fortune without an entire obedience.

"Whatever your business is, may it end to your satisfaction. I think of the public as you do. As little as *that* is a woman's care, it may be permitted into the number of a woman's fears. But wretched as I am, I have no more to fear for myself. I have still a concern for my friends, and I am in pain for your danger. I am far from taking ill what you say. I never valued myself as the daughter of ——; and ever despised those that esteemed me on that account. With pleasure I could barter all that, and change to be any country gentleman's daughter that would have reason enough to make happiness in privacy. My letter is too long; I beg your pardon. You may see by the situation of my affairs 'tis without design."

Mr. Wortley gives no sign of being moved by the pathos of the situation. The appeal to his feelings only influenced him to use exceptional caution in his reply.

"I have, for some time,"[1] he writes, "been grieved to hear you was to be confined to one you did not like, and in another country. But if the case is as you tell it, that you are to do as you please, I fancy the gaoler you speak of will trust you very little. I am not clear in it that you should not comply, and cannot advise you against it. But if you say this as you

[1] From the unpublished MS.

have done many other things, because it is so well said, and the real truth is that you are to be confined by such a one, follow the advice of one that knows something of mankind, and has a real concern for you, think no more of this match. There is scarce any instance of a woman so fettered that has not thought herself very miserable. Your relations, I am sure, whatever they threaten, will never treat you barbarously. They will for their own sakes, if not for yours, take as good care of you as they do now, and if they could be cruel they would however give something to dispose of you. But they cannot offer to punish you for what the world will praise you."

He points out, with perfect justice, that the worst condition of life for a woman is being tied to one she hates. "When a man is married, it may always be his own fault if he does not make himself easy, but a woman should have good reasons to be assured she can; nothing can pay her for such a venture. When a man marries for an estate, he is master of it; a woman can have no use of it if she dislikes the man, unless she can keep other company, but is in a worse state than perfect solitude can be. . . . For my part, I would not marry a queen if I did not love her as well as anyone living, were I to be debarred from choosing my company." Once more he makes a kind of semi-apology for his refusal to accept her father's terms. He concludes with the confession that he does not yet know his own mind, and begs to know as much of hers as he can, since that may govern his decision.

Letters were passing almost daily between the lovers during the next few weeks. There were so many things to be discussed before the plunge could be taken—ways and means, a place of abode, the possibilities of foreign travel, the amount of trust and "esteem" that could be expressed or demanded on either side. As a rule, the lady shows less timidity and a less calculating spirit than the man, though there is more than one letter in which she proves that she is not without thought for the morrow, and has even reflected upon the difficulties she may have to face at a period "forty years on."

"If[1] I think till to-morrow," she writes, "after the same manner I have thought ever since I saw you, the wisest thing

[1] From the unpublished MS.

I can do, is to do whatever you please. 'Tis an odd thing, but I fear nothing so much as a change in my mind when there can be none in my condition. My thoughts of you are capable of improvements both ways. I am more susceptible of gratitude than anybody living. You may manage in a manner to make me passionately fond of you; should you use me ill, can I answer that I should be able to hinder myself from reflecting back on the sacrifice I have made? An engagement for my whole life is no trifle, and should we both be so happy as to find we liked one another, yet even years of exquisite happiness when they are passed, could not pay me for a whole life of misery to come. I think perhaps farther than I have Occasion to think, but in an affair like this, all possible as well as all probable Events are to be foreseen, since a mistake is not to be retrieved. In my present opinion, I think if I was yours and you used me well, nothing could be added to my misfortune should I lose you. But when I suffer my reason to speak, it tells me, that in any circumstance of life (wretched or happy) there is a certain proportion of money, as the world is made, absolutely necessary for the living in it. I have never yet found myself in any Straits of fortune, and am hardly able to imagine the misery arising from it. Should I find myself forty years hence your widow, without a competency to maintain me in a manner suitable in some degree to my Education, I shall not then be so old I may not impossibly live twenty years longer without what is requisite to make Life easy—happiness is what I should not think of.

"After all these prudent considerations, the Bias of my heart is in your Favour. I hate the man they propose for me. If I did not hate him, my reason would tell me he is not capable of either being my Friend or my Companion. I have an Esteem for you, with a mixture of more kindness than I imagine. That kindness would persuade me to abandon all things for you—my Fame, my Family, the Settlement they have provided for me; and rather embark with you, thro' all the hazards of perhaps finding myself reduced to the last extremes of want, (which would be heavier on me than any other body), than enjoy the certainty of a plentiful Fortune with another. I can think with pleasure of giving you with my first declaration of Love the sincerest proof of it. I read over some of your first Letters, and I formed romantic scenes to myself of Love and Solitude. I did not believe I was capable of thinking this way, but I find it is in your power to make me think what you please.

"One may think this letter were determined—yet I know not what I shall do—I know if I do not venture all things to have you, I shall repent it."

CHAPTER XIV

PLANS FOR ELOPEMENT

THE difficulties of meeting had now greatly increased, and letters had to be conveyed in a still more roundabout fashion. Lady Mary says that she is very closely watched, and particularly on Mr. Wortley's account, some part of her family being persuaded that he is the cause of her resistance to their commands. Even her sister is a spy upon her, and never leaves her alone. She receives a message from her lover that he must see her, for he has something very special to say to her. She replies—

"Without[1] making a confidence of the people of the house, 'tis impossible to talk long either at Indian houses or painters. Assemblies are no more, and should I meet you at a visit, the sense of the silly figure I should make would render the very indiscretion to no purpose. . . . Direct to Mr. Cassotti[2] at Mr. Roberts, at the Queen's Head, in Lichfield Street, Soho. He is my Italian master. I have made a kind of plausible pretence to him for one letter to come that way. But I dare not trust him."

In this same month of July, the Steeles, after several ups and downs of fortune, had taken one of the large houses in the then fashionable Bloomsbury Square. The new venture, the *Spectator*, had been an even greater success than the *Tatler*, and though never actually free from duns and debts and lawsuits, the Editor was enjoying a period of comparative prosperity. Mr. Wortley, in his reply to the foregoing letter, after saying he is satisfied that what they do must be done with-

---

[1] From the unpublished MS.
[2] Already mentioned in an early letter to Mrs. Hewet.

out the sanction of Lady Mary's relations, and that he likes "that way" full as well as any other, continues: "There [1] can be no great harm in trusting some woman with seeing us both together on Tuesday and Wednesday. If you can't, get Mrs. Steele to be at home to meet you, who has now a house in Bloomsbury Square, the fifth door on the right hand as you look towards Southampton House. The Dutchess you was with is good-natured, and I fancy would never talk of such a thing."

The good-natured Duchess was probably Her Grace of Shrewsbury, to whom there are several allusions in the letters.[2] Lady Mary says in her reply: "The [3] Dutchess entertained me from the Garden to London with your praises. As nobody knows better how to make their court, I suspected she guessed she was making herself agreeable to me. However I would rather trust her than Mrs. St. for many reasons. I intend to go there to-morrow in the afternoon. If you come there, the best way of speaking to me, will be to excuse it to her with some compliment, and then ask me aloud to hear what you have to say for the last time. I will answer you, that you need not be so very solicitous about it, since with my Lady Dutchess's leave, as odd as it might look, I had something to say to you. We may go into the next room, for I believe your conversation may be very long.

"I don't believe she'll speak of it, or if she should, if we agree it signifies nothing. If we do not, I shall be so soon disposed of it can do me no harm. Going into the next room

---

[1] From the unpublished MS.

[2] The Duchess of Shrewsbury seems to have been a light-hearted, flirtatious lady. Lady Strafford, writing to her husband on 12th February 1712, says, " The town has made a story of the Duchess of Shrewsbury and Lady Oxford. The Duchess told me of it. She says they will make a story of her every year, but she likes this the best. They say she went to see Lady Oxford, and she said, 'Madam, I and my Lord are so weary of talking Politicks; what are you and your Lord?' And Lady Oxford sighed and said, 'she knew no Lord but the Lord Jehovah.' And the Duchess made answer again, 'Oh dear, Madam, who is that? I believe 'tis one of the new Titles, for I never heard of him before.'" The new titles were of course those of twelve Tory peers created in 1711 in order to overcome the opposition of the Whig majority in the House of Lords to the negotiations for a peace.

[3] From the unpublished MS.

will be more convenient for us than whispering, and I think civiller to the company."

It was probably in consequence of her father's suspicions that Lady Mary was sent to Acton at the end of July or beginning of August. Her brother had been married about the end of 1710 to Rachel, daughter and heiress of Thomas Baynton. Lady Mary considered that her father had blighted his life by marrying him to a silly, childish girl for the sake of her fortune, before he could judge for himself, or make a choice of his own. Lord Kingston seems to have lived at Acton after his marriage, and Lady Mary, who was much attached to her brother, made him the confidant of her tangled love-affairs, and desired to consult him before she took the step which would alienate her from the rest of her family, and put her completely in the power of the man whose generosity she had too little reason to trust. The day before she left town she wrote to Mr. Wortley—

"There[1] is something of ill-fortune that mixes in all my Affairs. My F. has taken a fancy to go dine with my B[rother] which will consequently prevent his coming to town. Tomorrow I go to Acton. I am willing to talk with him before I absolutely determine a thing of this consequence. If you please to permit me one day longer, since I cannot see him before, on Saturday morning I will write to you from Acton. I hope a day's delay of my answer can be no considerable injury to you any way. I tremble when I think what I am about. When I see you I am of opinion 'tis a clear case, and had there been a parson in the room with us, I had certainly married you last night, in defiance of consequences. When I come to consider, I should be glad if I could have my Brother's promise of protection in case of Accident. I know myself better since yesterday than I did before. I find my Inclinations are more your side than I imagined. But—I will write Saturday morning without fail. If I resolve to be so at all, Sunday night I believe I must be yours. Forgive the irresolution of this letter. I know not what I shall do. I know I wish you perfectly well."

[1] From the unpublished MS.

The next day she wrote again, after her arrival at Acton—

"I[1] found my B. in bed, just taken very ill of this fever. Something has been mistaken in the writings, that they must go back into Ireland, to be signed over again. This is at least a reprieve of three weeks, and if you please, allows us more time for consideration, and I hope for the establishment of your health. However, if you find it necessary you should go to the Spaw soon, I will positively determine in my next letter. I wish I could see you. Letters are an imperfect intelligence compared to conversation, and I have a great deal to say, but I know not how to contrive a meeting. I would not have you injure your health by staying in London, but you may be with your friend at Kensington,[2] and enjoy the benefit of the air and the gardens. I should be sorry (except all things were ended between us) that you was farther from me, daily unforeseen chances happening in my Affairs. I talk of three weeks; possibly these writings may be returned in the fortnight, and whenever they are, I may be pressed to marry at two days' or a day's warning.

"Sick as my Br. is, I have spoke to him concerning my Affair. He agrees with me there is nothing to be treated with my F. who is resolved upon the least suspicion, he will send me farther into the country, and put it out of our power ever to meet. Take care of your Health in the first place. Let me hear how you do, and if it is necessary for me to say what I intend to do positively in my next letter, I will do it, tho' since we have time I shall be glad to delay engaging for some little time. I own I tremble at the thought of irrevocably promising, and yet I tremble too at the thought of parting for ever. . . ."

Although Lord Kingston seems to have sympathised with his sister, he had not the courage openly to aid and abet her in her act of rebellion. Lord Dorchester had reason to think that Acton was too near London to be safe, and on the following Monday Lady Mary wrote a letter in which she consented to elope with her lover, and even suggested the practical arrangements for their flight.

[1] From the unpublished MS.   [2] Addison, no doubt.

"My F——[1] has been here to-day," she explains. "He bid me prepare to go to Dean this day sennight. I am not to come from thence but to give myself to all I hate. I shall never see you more. These considerations fright me to death. Tell me what you intend to do. If you can think of me for your companion at Naples, come next Sunday under this Garden wall, on the road some little distance from the summer-house at 10 o'clock. It will be dark, and it is necessary it should be so. I should wish you could begin our Journey immediately—I have no fancy to stay in London or near it. I will not pretend to justify my proceeding. Everybody will object to me, why I did not do this sooner, before I put a man to the charges of Equipages? I shall not care to tell them you did not ask me sooner. In short, as things have been managed, I shall never care to hear any more on't. 'Tis an odd step, but something must be ventured when the happiness of a whole Life is depending. I pretend to be happy with you, and I am sure it is impossible with him.

"If on the account of your health, or for any other reason, you had rather delay this till I return from Dean, 'tis certain I shall come hither from thence, and 'twill be then in our power to do the same thing. But as the time of my return is uncertain, you must not be far off if you intend to do it, for I own I cannot, nor dare not, resist my Father, and I know he has power over me to make me do whatever he pleases. I shall not be surprised if you have changed your mind, or even if you should change your mind after you have consented to this. I would have no tye upon you but inclination. I have nothing to do with your word or your honour, etc.

"If you come Sunday, 'tis indifferent to me, whether it is with a coach and six, or a pair. For my part I could wish to make our first stage that night—do what you please for that matter.—I say nothing of Jointure. I begin to think myself in the wrong to imagine a man so generous as to take me without a fortune, would not also be generous enough to make me easy every other way. Consult your own Heart, and let that determine you. Make no scruple about going back from your

[1] From the unpublished MS.

word, if you cannot resolve upon it. Should I go to the Garden door and not find you there, the disappointment would not be so hard as seeing you uneasy afterwards. On my side, if I find I cannot live with you at Naples without another wish, if I cannot answer for my own renouncing the pomps and vanities of this world, you shall not be troubled with me, and Saturday receive a letter that I cannot bring myself to it. In the opinion I am in this minute, I think I can abandon the whole world for you.

"Do not be apprehensive I shall take it for a mark of indifference if you delay till my return. Perhaps your health may require it, or the situation of your Affairs. I will think of it what you please, and will not reproach you if you do not do it then. Let us both be at Liberty till the Parson puts an end to it."

Mr. Wortley, who had been imploring his lady for the past two years to give him some decisive proof of her regard, shrank back in alarm when she offered to trust herself and her whole future to his care. He could not bear that any other man should marry her, but he was still undecided whether he really desired to tie himself for life. At the same time, he evidently felt that he had gone too far to retreat with honour, and his internal conflict found expression in the exceptionally surly tone of his next letter.

"If[1] you are in any doubt what to do," he writes, "I am very certain you ought to be against me. It was a great piece of folly in me to persist in leaving it for you to decide, after you had assured me you did not value me much. You know I have formerly broke with you on this point. All your letters of late have implied the contrary of what you said, or I could not have determined at last as I did. . . . However, I do not intend to go back from my word (whatever low opinion you may have of me). If I should not be so easy with you as I should have been with some other, you will be a sufferer as much as I, probably a great deal more. I repeat it, you judge very ill if you take such a one, if you like him no better, but take me if you please.

[1] From the unpublished MS.

"I have fairly told you any real or seeming infirmity of mine, which you might not have known without my making discovery. If there is any defect which can possibly give me a distaste, you ought to tell it for your own sake before we are tied. Some faults I could knowingly suffer, and yet be in the utmost concern when I am deceived or disappointed. . . . You do extremely well in asking your brother's consent. I wish too you would try with your Father to treat of this new affair. But perhaps you may think, and with some reason, that while he is treating with me you shall treat with me too, as you have done with better, whom after all I advise you to close with, and to marry this very day without giving me notice of it, unless you are entirely convinced I can have no reason to complain of your want of kindness.

"If you are sure of this, and conscious of nothing that can make me like you less, you may appoint the time and place when you please, and I will provide a coach, a license, parson, etc. A coach and six looks much better than a pair for such a service, but will it not be more likely to have company about it while it stands near your house? If we should once get into a coach, let us not say one word till we come before the parson, least we should engage in fresh disputes. But why should we meet at all if we are likely to have 'em? It is plain we should not. One word more, for your good as well as mine. You should put me out of pain one way or the other by the time I mention."

Scarcely was this letter sent than the lover's heart smote him, and he hastened to send another after it which is (for him) almost warm. "I was yesterday in a fever when I writ,"[1] he explains, "and I retract everything I said. The letter writ on Wednesday is what I stuck by. Had I been well yesterday I had told you in few words that travelling is what I love. If you cannot be easy unless at a distance from your Relations, I will, as soon as you please, go abroad, and leave you near the Spaw in case I am forced to come back for a month. When that is over I will wait on you to Italy, unless for the good of my affairs (which you shall always know as well as I)

[1] From the unpublished MS.

you should desire to return to England. This plan is more advantageous to you than I should have proposed to any other friend, for it should not have been in his power to say whether I should go forward or come back. I would rather live in any part of Italy than in England, and shall never wish to be here unless my affairs suffer too much by my absence. We can never differ, I think, upon this point. I have now complied with all your demands: have you anything more to ask?

"Too much of this short time has been spent in useless disputes. Out of tenderness to you I have forborn to state your case in the plainest light, which is thus. If you have no thoughts of [gallantry]¹ you are mad if you marry him. If you are likely to think of [gallantry] you are mad if you marry me. Surely in one minute you may tell which of us ought to be your choice. Lady H. has £400 a year pin-money, and is brought to town for some months every year, as the husband promised when he married her against her inclination, by her mother's persuasion. And yet she declares to her friends, she has done it to me among the rest, that one had better be buried alive than married to one that gives disgust. Pin-money is worse than nothing unless the husband is extravagant or you [deceive] him. My present income is better than his, and I have power to make settlements of every part of it. My reversions, I believe, are much more than his too. But perhaps the difference of our circumstances may be small; I am sure they ought not to have any weight in your decision of this great affair. If both of us are likely to be little better than gaolers in your eyes, hazard all or think of neither. And now I think I should give over arguing.

"Are you sure you will come back from Dean before you are married? You have no reason to trust to that. Some say you are to live in Ireland when you are married, but I suppose you know how that is to be. All I can say is that the two days more you are mistress of yourself and me."

Lady Mary received both the foregoing letters together. In her answer she speaks of a "kind letter" which she had

¹ Mr. Wortley uses a word of Elizabethan crudity. In her reply Lady Mary softens it down into "gallantry." Her example is here followed.

written and already despatched, or she confesses that she would never have sent it, for there were so many things in his to put her out of humour. "I would see you if I could," she continues, "(though perhaps it may be wrong), but in the way I am here 'tis impossible. I can't come to town but in company with my sister-in-law; I can carry her nowhere but where she pleases; or if I could, I would trust her with nothing. I could not walk out alone without giving suspicion to the whole family. Should I be watched, and seem to meet a man—judge of the consequence!

"You speak of treating with my father, as if you believed he would come to terms afterwards. I will not suffer you to remain in that thought, however advantageous it might be to me; I will deceive you in nothing. I am fully persuaded he will never hear of terms afterwards. You may say 'tis talking oddly of him. I can't answer to that; but 'tis my real opinion, and I think I know him. You talk to me of estates as if I was the most interested woman in the world. Whatever faults I may have shewn in my life, I know not one action of it that ever proved me mercenary. I think there cannot be a greater proof of the contrary than treating with you, where I am to depend entirely on your generosity, at the same time that I have settled on me £500 per annum pin-money, and a considerable jointure in another place; not to reckon that I may have by his temper what command of his estate I please; and with you I have nothing to pretend to. I do not, however, make a merit of all this to you. Money is very little to me, because all beyond necessaries I do not value, that is to be purchased by it. If the man proposed to me had £10,000 per annum, and I was sure to dispose of it all, I should act just as I do. I have in my life known a good deal of shew, and never found myself the happier for it.

"In proposing to you to follow the scheme begun with that friend, I think 'tis absolutely necessary for both our sakes. I would have you want no pleasure that a single life would afford you. You own that you think nothing so agreeable. A woman that adds nothing to a man's fortune ought not to take from his happiness. If possible, I would add to it; but

I will not take from you any satisfaction you could enjoy without me. . . . If we marry, our happiness must consist in loving one another; 'tis principally my concern to think of the most probable method of making that love eternal. You object against living in London; I am not fond of it myself, and readily give it up to you, tho' I am assured there needs more art to keep a fondness alive in solitude, where it generally preys upon itself. There is one article absolutely necessary—to be ever beloved, one must be ever agreeable. There is no such thing as being agreeable without a thorough good humour, a natural sweetness of temper, enlivened by cheerfulness. Whatever natural fund of gaiety one is born with, 'tis necessary to be entertained with agreeable objects. Anybody, capable of tasting pleasure, when they confine themselves to one place, should take care 'tis the place in the world the most pleasing.

"Whatever you may now think (now, perhaps, you have some fondness for me), tho' your love should continue in its full force, there are hours when the most beloved mistress would be troublesome. People are not for ever (nor is it in human nature they should be) disposed to be fond; you would be glad to find in me the friend and companion. To be agreeably this last, it is necessary to be gay and entertaining. A perpetual solitude in a place where you see nothing to raise your spirits, at length wears them out, and conversation insensibly falls into the dull and insipid. When I have no more to say to you, you will like me no longer. How dreadful is that view! You will reflect for my sake you have abandoned the conversation of a friend that you liked, and your situation in a country where all things would have contributed to make your life pass in (the true *volupté*) a smooth tranquillity. . . .

"I am not now arguing in favour of the town; you have answered me as to that point. In respect of your health, 'tis the first thing to be considered, and I shall never ask you to do anything injurious to that. But 'tis my opinion, 'tis necessary to being happy, that we neither of us think any place more agreeable than where we are. I have nothing to do in London, and 'tis indifferent to me if I never see it more. I know not how to answer your mentioning gallantry, nor in what sense to understand you. I am sure in one—whoever I marry, when I am married I renounce all things of that kind. I am willing to abandon all conversation but yours. If you please, I will never see another man. In short, I will part with everything for you, but you; I will not have you a month, to lose you for the rest of my life. If you can pursue the plan of happiness begun with your friend, and take me for that friend, I am ever yours. I have examined my own heart whether I can leave everything for you; I think I can. If I change my mind, you shall know before Sunday; after that I will not change my mind.

"If 'tis necessary for your affairs to stay in England to assist your father in his business, as I suppose the time will be short I would be as little injurious to your fortune as I can, and I will do it. But I am still of opinion nothing is so likely to make us both happy as what I propose. I foresee I may break with you on this point, and I shall certainly be displeased with myself, and wish a thousand times that I had done whatever you pleased. But, however, I hope I shall remember how much more miserable than anything else could make me, should I be to live with you and please you no longer. You can be pleased with nothing when you are not pleased with yourself. One of the *Spectators* is very just that says, A man ought always to be on his guard against spleen and too severe a philosophy; a woman against levity and coquetry. If we go to Naples, I will make no acquaintance there of any kind, and you will be in a place where a variety of agreeable objects will dispose you to be for ever pleased. If such a thing is possible, this will secure our lasting happiness; and I am ready to wait on you without leaving a thought behind me."

This effusion seems to have called forth the only love-letter, worthy of the name, that was written by Mr. Wortley during the whole period of his courtship. Even this, however, had been preceded by a note in which he thought proper still to "dissemble his love," for he begins—

"I[1] had no sooner sent away an answer to your long letter, but I accused myself of too much dissimulation in not having told you what effect it had upon me.

"I can now no longer forbear laying my heart quite open, and telling you the joy I am in for being so near the greatest happiness I am capable of enjoying. Your letter of three sheets, which would have pleased me more than the rest for being the longest, had it only been of the same kind with them, has transported me by removing the doubts which I resolve shall never rise up again. I now with the utmost pleasure own you have convinced me of an esteem. The firm resolutions you have taken of putting yourself in my power, and being pleased with any retirement in my company, I acknowledge to be such proofs of kindness as not many women of your condition would have given without some degree of Passion. These assurances which might have been acceptable from any woman of merit are given me by her I have, ever since I knew her, believed to possess more charms than any other upon earth. This very letter proves the brightness of your imagination to be far above what is to be met with in any other. That which may have ever made me give a preference to anyone before I knew you was the passion for me she either really had or counterfeited to the life. But you, I always admired for that which I took to be wonderful in you, without being prejudiced in your favour by any great shew of a partiality to me. Nay, it seemed to be so little that I confess to you during these years of my courtship, I have sometimes reflected with great satisfaction that by the strength of reason assisted with absence, I had brought myself again to be pleased with those that seemed pleased with me, and freed myself from the tyranny of those charms I had no reason to hope would ever be employed to my advantage. But now I am delighted beyond measure while I think the woman whose merit is certainly beyond that of others declares herself so much in my favour.

[On margin: " I shall wish to dye with you rather than to live without you in the highest circumstances of Fortune.]

[1] From the unpublished MS.

"You tell me of your gratitude. Be assured I will always express mine in the best manner I am able. The greatest part of my life shall be dedicated to you. From everything that can lessen my passion for you I will fly with as much speed as from the Plague. I shall sooner chuse to see my heart torn from my breast than divided from you. You have wrote as if I were about to save you from Pain; I am now to ask relief of you. Since you have given me these assurances of kindness, it is with impatience I want to know when we must begin to live together. I beg you will not recant any part of what you writ. It will now fall heavy upon me to be dismissed, and I can hope for no ease but from you.

"But I am indisposed, or I had said much more. The perplexity I was in for want of knowing what to do has made for some nights past my slumbers very short. . . . I now declare that I am already married to you, if you please, and if you will condescend to say something like it, such a declaration from both sides, is, I believe, as good a marriage as if it were done by a minister. I shall have this advantage if you make it, that you will go before one soon and with a great deal of ease, when you think you are doing but what you have already done, and is of no use but to satisfy others. I have more than once been indisposed in this manner, and therefore am in no fear of not being well in a few weeks: especially since I have your kindness, which will I believe be the best cordial. If this or any other illness carries me off, I will, if I am able, take care you shall not fancy your fortune has been diminished for my sake.

"The gaining you in such a manner seems now to be the greatest good Fortune. Each of us has now reason to believe the other is sincere in promising an inviolable friendship and lasting Affection. You will say perhaps these professions are not always made good, but when they are not it is owing to the folly of one, if not both, of the parties that engage.

"As you have more spirit I believe you are more generous than other women; otherwise I should not have trusted you with all this, for I know a warm letter is generally repaid with a cool answer. Unless you think you can oblige me more than you did in that long letter, which I could not help kissing very often, say nothing, for fear I should not think you say enough. . . ."[1]

[1] This letter must indeed have been a labour of love, for in the rough draft almost every sentence is rewritten two or three times.

CHAPTER XV

A SECRET MARRIAGE

AS the fateful day drew near, Lady Mary's courage began to fail her. Much as she loathed the idea of a loveless marriage, she shrank scarcely less from taking a step which would estrange her from her family, and draw upon her the censure of all the world.

"I tremble for what we are doing," she wrote on 15th August. "Are you sure you will love me for ever? Shall we never repent? I fear and I hope. I foresee all that will happen on this occasion. I shall incense my family in the highest degree. The generality of the world will blame my conduct, and the relations and friends of ——[1] will invent a thousand stories of me; yet 'tis possible you may compensate everything to me. In this letter, which I am fond of, you promise me all that I wish. Since I writ so far, I received your Friday letter. I will be only yours, and I will do what you please.

"You shall hear from me again to-morrow, not to contradict, but to give some directions. My resolution is taken. Love me, and use me well."

"I[2] will come to Acton on Sunday night at ten o'clock," wrote Mr. Wortley. "If you do not come yourself to take leave of me, or go with me, you may send your maid with a compliment. Till Sunday night I will leave word where I may be found every minute in the day. I have a faithful servant that is too good to wait behind me. He may meet your maid at Kensington, Acton, or where you please, if it be of any use, and letters may pass very speedily."

On the Saturday Lady Mary wrote another long letter,

---

[1] "Mr. K.," the Irish lover.
[2] From the unpublished MS.

making further arrangements for the flight, and pointing out yet again that her lover has nothing to hope from her father, and must be prepared to take her in a "nightgown and petticoat."

"I writ you a letter last night in some passion," she says. "I begin to fear again. I own myself a coward.—You made no reply to one part of my letter concerning my fortune. I am afraid you flatter yourself that my F[ather] may be at length reconciled, and brought to reasonable terms. I am convinced, by what I have often heard him say, speaking of other cases like this, he never will. The fortune he has engaged to give with me, was settled on my B[rother's] marriage on my sister and on myself; but in such a manner that it was left in his power to give it all to either of us, or divide it as he thought fit. He has given it all to me. Nothing remains for my sister, but the free bounty of my F. from what he can save; which, notwithstanding the greatness of his estate, may be very little. Possibly after I have disobliged him so much, he may be glad to have her so easily provided for with money already raised, especially if he has a design to marry himself, as I hear.

"I do not speak this that you should not endeavour to come to terms with him, if you please; but I am fully persuaded it will be to no purpose. He will have a very good answer to make:—that I suffered this match to proceed, and that I made him a very silly figure in it; that I let him spend £400 in wedding cloathes; all which I saw without saying anything. When I first pretended to oppose this match, he told me he was sure I had some other design in my head. I denied it with truth. But you see how little appearance there is of that truth. . . . He will now object against me,—why since I intended to marry in this manner, I did not persist in my first resolution; that it would have been as easy to run away from T[horesby] as from hence; and to what purpose did I put him, and the gentleman I was to marry, to expenses etc.? He will have a thousand plausible reasons for being irreconcileable, and 'tis very probable the world will be of his side.

"Reflect now for the last time in what manner you must

take me. I shall come to you with only a nightgown and petticoat, and that is all you will get with me. I told a lady of my friends what I intend to do. You will think her a very good friend when I tell you she has proffered to lend us her house if we would come there the first night. I did not accept of this till I had let you know it. If you think it more convenient to carry me to your lodgings, make no scruple of it. Let it be where you will; if I am your wife, I shall think no place unfit for me where you are. I beg we may leave London next morning, wherever you intend to go. I should wish to go out of England if it suits your affairs. You are the best judge of your father's temper. If you think it would be obliging to him, or necessary for you, I will go with you immediately to ask his pardon and his blessing. If that is not proper at first, I think the best scheme is going to the Spaw. . . .

"I again beg you to hire a coach to be at the door early Monday morning, to carry us some part of our way, wherever you resolve our journey shall be. If you determine to go to that lady's house, you had better come with a coach and six at seven o'clock to-morrow. She and I will be in the balcony that looks on the road; you have nothing to do but to stop under it, and we will come down to you. Do in this what you like best. After all, think very seriously. Your letter, which will be waited for, is to determine everything. I forgive you a coarse expression in your last, which, however, I wish had not been there. You might have said something like it without expressing it in that manner. But there was so much complaisance in the rest of it that I ought to be satisfied. . . ."

There had been some idea of consulting some other relation, probably either Mr. William Fielding or Lord Pierrepont of Hanslope, and persuading him to appeal to Lord Dorchester, but whoever he was, he seems to have proved a broken reed. Lady Mary opened her letter to slip in a note in which she explains that no help is to be looked for from that quarter, and changes the whole arrangement which she had so carefully thought out.

"Since[1] I writ the enclosed," she says, "I hear my F[ather]

[1] From the unpublished MS.

intends us a visit to-morrow. You cannot come at seven o'clock. I have had a letter from that relation I said I would speak to. He is prevented coming to me. I would if possible consult him before I do an action of this consequence. Upon second thoughts, it will not be convenient to go to the Lady I spoke of, for several reasons, both in regard to her and myself.

"I am in so much disorder, I can hardly form a letter. 'Tis very plain as you state the case, but a woman who disobliges her Family, and engages the world against her, risques a great deal. I have just received your Friday letter—a mistake may be fatal—it may indeed. How hard it is to decide a Question where my whole Happiness is depending. I must be perfectly happy, or I must be lost and ruined. I am fainting with Fear—forgive my Instability.—If I do it Love me—if I dare not, do not hate me.—You shall hear from me to-morrow morning; if I find I cannot do it, why should you come? You must not be exposed to that trouble."

The "Friday letter" from Mr. Wortley alluded to in the above, was the following brief note:—

"Before[1] you are to leave Acton, the post will go out but thrice, and I cannot omit using it every time. I have now done disputing with you. Say what you please to the contrary, I will go to Acton at the hour you name, and stand near the summer-house which looks upon the great road that goes into the town. Whatever you may tell me in the meantime, I cannot be assured how you will stand affected then. You must judge for both of us. A mistake may be fatal. I am yours till you turn me away."

Lord Dorchester had probably received some intimation of his daughter's intentions, and his surprise visit on the Sunday was not accidental. He appears to have upbraided her for carrying on a secret correspondence, and arranged that she should start for West Dean early next morning under her brother's escort. But she made yet another bid for freedom.

"I[1] cannot easily submit to my fortunes, I must have one more trial of it. I send you this letter at five o'clock, while the whole family is asleep. I am stole from my sister to tell

[1] From the unpublished MS.

you we shall not go till seven, or a little before. If you can come to the same place any time before that, I may slip out, because they have no suspicion of the morning before the Journey. 'Tis possible some of the servants will be about the house, and will see me go off, but when I am once with you, 'tis no matter.—If this is impracticable, adieu, I fear for ever."

This plan also was frustrated, and Lady Mary wrote to her lover almost in despair from the first inn on the road—

"I [1] would not give myself the pain of thinking you have suffered as much by this misfortune as I have done. The pain of my mind has very much affected my body. I have been sick ever since; yet tho' overcome by fatigue and misfortune I write to you from the first Inn.

"I blame myself for my cowardice and folly. I know not how my——[Father] received his intelligence, but out of my fright. When I reflect, I don't believe he knew of the taking out the License, since he did not name it particularly, but in general terms spoke of my keeping a correspondence, etc. I was so frighted and looked so guilty, I believe it was the worse for me. I had perhaps better have denied it, but instead of that, I foolishly made what promises he would.— I lament my folly, but would remedy it if possible, tho' I cannot blame you if, after so much trouble about it, you resolve never to think more of so unlucky a creature as I am. But if you like me, you are still determined. If possible I will write to you every post and what I can do I will.

"I suppose I shall not be removed from hence, till the night before my intended——[marriage]. If that should happen sooner than is convenient for you, perhaps sickness would serve for a pretence to delay it two or three days. I am afraid your Affairs may suffer, if you stay away from your ——[Father]; if so, do what is right for yourself in the first place. Neglect nothing upon my Account; go to him, if you can be back in ten days—to be sure I shall not be persecuted sooner. But do no harm to your health by fatigue or vexation; rather forget what becomes of me than any way injure yourself. I am distracted when I think how much trouble I have already

[1] From the unpublished MS.

given to the man on earth I have the most reason to esteem, and for whose happiness I would do everything. If on my Account your health or your fortune should ever be impaired, I should wish I had never been born.

"Write to me soon, to West Dean, near Salisbury, Wiltshire, by my own name. Did you write Sunday? I had no letter. . . ."

Addressed

"To Mr. Edward Wortley Montagu——
If not in town to be sent after him with speed."

As far as can be gathered from Lady Mary's next letter, Mr. Wortley followed his lady, and put up at one of the inns on the road, with the view of carrying her off from thence.

"We[1] have more ill-Luck than any other people. Had you writ in your first letter where you intended to be, etc., I could have ris up by myself at four o'clock and come to your chamber, perhaps undiscovered. At worst you could but have done what you resolved on at first. If it had been known, it could not have been till after it was over, all our people being in bed. After my woman was up she watched me so much it was impossible. She apprehended you was in the house, but I believe has now lost that thought. Had I not been sick, and gone to bed sooner than usual, I should have seen your Gentleman, and then he would have told me where you was. All things conspire against the unfortunate, but if you are still determined, I still hope it may be possible one way or other. Write to me always what contrivance you think on; I know best what is practicable for me. I have since asked my B. what he could have done if I had been married in that way. He made answer, he durst not have taken me with him, we must have stayed in the Inn, and how odd that would have been."

A day later she wrote again——

"If[1] there had been any Robbery lately committed, you had been taken up; they suspected you in the House for a

[1] From the unpublished MS.

Highwayman. I hope some time of our Lives we may laugh together at this Adventure, tho' at this minute 'tis vexatious enough.

"Do what is most convenient for your own Affairs, but if you intend to go to the Spaw, we are very near a seaport here, tho' if possible I would delay my flight till the night I come to Acton, or I must come quite alone. I should not much care to have that said, but if you judge it most convenient I will drop that scruple, and in everything prefer you to the world. I am sensible of what you do for me, and my thoughts of it are all you would have them.

"Pray write. If possible I would do what you desire, and say 'No,' tho' they brought a Parson, but I hope we shall not be put to that hard necessity, for I fear my own woman's weakness. Adieu; I am entirely yours if you please."

The elopement is supposed to have taken place from West Dean, but judging from the last hurried notes scribbled by Lady Mary the lovers may have fled from one of the inns on the road. Lord Kingston, sympathising as he did with his sister's troubles, probably kept but slight watch over her, or may even have secretly abetted her in her flight. Mr. Wortley, though he had screwed himself up to the adventure, did not show any very practical enterprise, and the difficulties were increased by the fact that Lady Mary had been obliged to leave her faithful maid behind at Acton. Her last three notes are almost illegible, having evidently been written with a very bad pen upon the cheapest paper, the kind of pen and paper that might be provided by a humble country inn. The scrawls are little more than a series of huge blots, in the midst of which the words are but dimly discernible. So much as can be deciphered is here given—

"Why[1] did you not bring a coach, etc., to be set up at another inn? I would fain come, but fear being stopped. If you could carry me with you, I would not care who saw me. Or if you had lodged on the same floor with me, I might have been married perhaps, and returned [illegible]."

"I[1] have no servant with me I dare trust; I was obliged

[1] From the unpublished MS.

to leave my own behind. I believe you have no conveniency for carrying me off now, nor is it very decent of me without a servant. I care not come to you, and hope not to have it known, except to meet not to part—tell me how you intended that——"

" If[1] you have provided a conveniency to carry me away decently, I will come. If not I dare not. Your way would be exposing my B[rother] to use me ill, and disoblige my Father for ever——"

[1] From the unpublished MS.

CHAPTER XVI

"THE BRIDE IN THE COUNTRY"

THE long courtship was over at last, and the couple entered upon that joint life which had been dreaded almost as much as desired. They had not married in haste; yet it is certain that they both found reason to repent at leisure. Mr. Wortley, worthy and estimable as he may have been from the point of view of the period, was not an easy man to live with. He proved, almost from the first, a cold and neglectful husband. His promises, made before marriage, were quickly forgotten. There was to be no romantic *solitude à deux* at Naples, but a great deal of prosaic loneliness in an English village. Lady Mary, with her hot temper, her warm heart, and impulsive nature, was not the person to submit meekly to unkindness and neglect. In her Account of the Court of George I. at his Accession, she writes, not without bitterness—

"I was then [1714] in Yorkshire. Mr. W. (who had at that time, that sort of passion for me, that would have made me invisible to all but himself, had it been in his power) had sent me thither. He stayed in town on the account of some business, and the Queen's death detained him there."

The young wife spent the greater part of the two years that elapsed between her marriage and her return to a Court life, in small furnished houses, either near Huntingdon, for which town her husband was member from 1707 to 1713, or near York, for which he had some thought of standing, when obliged to relinquish Huntingdon to his father. Occasionally she stayed at Wharncliffe Lodge with her husband's relations, or at Hinchinbroke, the seat of his kinsman, Lord Sandwich. Lady Louisa Stuart gives a not very alluring account of the *ménage* at Wharncliffe, founded on the recollections of her mother, Lady Bute. Mrs. Sidney Montagu, *née* Wortley, had been obliged to separate from her husband in consequence of his ill usage, but the poor lady was dead before Lady Mary became acquainted with the family. Lady Bute remembered Sidney Montagu as a "large, rough-looking man, with a huge flapped hat, seated magisterially in his elbow-chair, talking very loud and swearing boisterously at the servants. Beside him sat a venerable figure, meek and benign in aspect, with silver locks overshadowed by a black velvet cap. This was his brother, the pious Dean Montagu [of Durham],[1] who every now and then fetched a deep sigh, and cast his eyes upwards, as if silently beseeching Heaven to pardon the profane language which he condemned, but durst not reprove. Unlike as they were in their habits and their morals, the two brothers commonly lived together."[2]

The Montagu brothers had not seemingly much talent for matrimony, for John of Durham never married, while Charles (father of Edward, who became husband of the Queen of the Blue-stockings) was also separated from his wife. Among the Sandon papers is a long series of letters from Mrs. Charles to her brother-in-law Sidney, describing her husband's persecution of her, detailing her own exemplary behaviour, and imploring protection for herself and her children. From these letters, it is tolerably evident that Charles was not altogether in his right mind, and should have been placed under treatment. The poor man was, or professed to be, passionately in love with his wife, and several of his letters have been preserved, in which he implores her to return to him, and promises to reform his evil ways.

A few letters written by Lady Mary during the early years of her marriage have been published in her Correspond-

[1] John Montagu (? 1655–1728) was the fourth son of Lord Sandwich. He was elected Master of Trinity College in 1683, and appointed Dean of Durham in 1699. Trinity is said to have declined in numbers and reputation owing to the easiness of his rule.

[2] Mr. Sidney Montagu enlarged Wharncliffe Lodge, but allowed Wortley Hall to fall into decay. He built another house for a favourite mistress at St. Ellen's Well, near Carlton.

F. Zincke, pinxt.   J. Hopwood, sculp.
LADY MARY WORTLEY MONTAGU

ence, but many more remain in manuscript, and from these (as well as from the printed letters) extracts will be given. The first letter from Lady Mary to Mr. Wortley is dated from Mr. White's [1] house at Walling Wells (about eleven miles from Thoresby), 22nd October 1712. After three months of married life, her husband had left her for the first time to go to Durham on business. There is a heading to the effect that this was the earliest post by which the young wife could write, since she had been so fatigued and sick on arriving that she had gone straight to bed from the coach. The letter continues—

"I don't know very well how to begin; I am perfectly unacquainted with a proper matrimonial style. After all, I think 'tis best to write as if we were not married at all. I lament your absence as if you was still my lover, and I am impatient to hear you are got safe to Durham, and that you have fixed a time for your return.

"I have not been very long in this family, and I fancy myself in that described in the *Spectator*.[2] The good people here look upon their children with a fondness that more than recompenses for the care of them. I don't perceive much distinction in regard to their merits; and when they speak sense or nonsense, it affects the parents with almost the same pleasure. My friendship for the mother and kindness for Miss Biddy make me endure the squalling of Miss Nancy and Miss Mary with abundance of patience. I don't know whether you will presently find out that this seeming impertinent account is the tenderest expression of my love to you; but it furnishes my imagination with agreeable pictures of our future life, and I flatter myself with the hopes of one day enjoying with you the same satisfaction, and that after as many years

[1] It will be remembered that Mr. White was consulted when the question of settlements had reached an *impasse*.

[2] The number for 3rd October 1712 contains a defence of married life (No. 500). This (which was the composition of Steele) takes the form of a letter from "Philogamus," the happy father of ten children. "I cannot forbear amusing myself," he says, "with finding out a general, an admiral, or an alderman of London, a divine, a physician, or a lawyer among my little people, who are now perhaps in petticoats; and when I see the motherly airs of my little daughters when they are playing with their puppets, I cannot but flatter myself that their husbands and children will be happy in the possession of such wives and mothers."

together, I may see you retain the same fondness for me as I shall certainly mine for you, and the noise of a nursery may have more charms for us than the noise of an opera. . . .

"I check myself when I grieve for your absence, by remembering how much reason I have to rejoice in the hope of passing my whole life with you. A good fortune not to be valued! I am afraid of telling you that I return thanks for it to Heaven, because you will charge me with hypocrisy; but you are mistaken. I assist every day at public prayers in this family, and never forget in my private ejaculations how much I owe to Heaven for making me yours. 'Tis candle-light, or I should not conclude so soon."

In a fold of this pretty wifely love-letter is written, "Pray, my dear, begin at the top, and read till you come to the bottom."

Mr. Wortley seems to have delayed writing,—he was a notably bad correspondent after his marriage,—and his wife wrote again in great distress and anxiety. She imagines that he is not well, or has had a fall from his horse, or worse, that he thinks it of small importance to write. "I am peevish with you by fits," she exclaims, "and divide my time between anger and sorrow, which are equally troublesome to me. 'Tis the most cruel thing in the world to think one has reason to complain of what one loves. How can you be so careless? is it because you don't love writing? . . . Pray, my dear, write to me, or I shall be very mad."

In December Lady Mary was at Hinchinbroke, and on the 6th she writes that she had opened a closet where she expected to find a great many books, "but to my great disappointment there were only some few pieces of the law, and folios of mathematics, my Lord Hinchinbroke and Mr. Twinam having disposed of the rest. But as there is no affliction, no more than no happiness without alloy, I discovered an old trunk of papers, which, to my great diversion, I found to be the letters of the first Earl of Sandwich, and am in hopes that those from his lady[1] will tend much to my edification, being the most extraordinary lessons of economy that ever I read in my life. To the glory of your father, I find that *his*

---

[1] Jemima, daughter of Lord Crew of Stene.

looked upon him as destined to be the honour of the family.

"I walked yesterday two hours on the terrace. These are the most considerable events that have happened in your absence; excepting that a good-natured robin-redbreast kept me company almost all the afternoon, with so much good humour and humanity as gives me faith for the piece of charity ascribed to these little creatures in the Children in the Wood, which I have hitherto thought only a poetical ornament to that history. . . ."

Mr. Wortley was in London at this time, and Lady Mary's letters show her anxiety that he should try, through the good offices of her aunt, Lady Cheyne, and her uncle, Lord Pierrepont, to effect a reconciliation with her naturally infuriated father. Lord Dorchester, though he occasionally saw his daughter, never quite forgave her disobedience, and only left her £6000 for her life, with reversion to her daughter.

About the 9th of December Lady Mary wrote—

"I am not at all surprised at my Aunt Cheyne's conduct. People are seldom very much grieved (and never ought to be) at misfortunes they expect. When I gave myself to you, I gave up the very desire of pleasing the rest of the world, and am pretty indifferent about it. I think you are very much in the right in designing to visit Lord Pierrepont. . . . I continue indifferently well, and endeavour as much as I can to preserve myself from spleen or melancholy, not for my own sake—I think that of very little importance—but in the condition I am, I believe it may be of very ill consequence. Yet, passing whole days alone as I do, I do not always find it possible, and my constitution will sometimes get the better of my reason."

In a later letter Lady Mary says that the "Bishop of Salisbury writes me word that my Lord Pierrepont declares very much for us. As the Bishop is no infallible prelate, I should not depend much on that intelligence; but my sister Frances tells me the same thing. . . . If his kindness is sincere, 'tis too valuable to be neglected. If I know him, his desire of making my F. appear in the wrong will make him zealous for us. The Bishop tells me he has seen Lord

Halifax, who says, besides his great esteem for you, he has particular respects for me, and will take pains to reconcile my F[ather]. . . ."

One of the letters written by Mr. Wortley to his young wife about this time may here be quoted. It is in answer to hers describing her *tête-à-tête* with the robin, and shows him still something of the jealous lover, with a craving for news of her almost as keen as was her desire, in her solitude, for news of him.

"Tho'[1] I had no letter of yours by the last post, and tho' I have writ every day since I have been here, I cannot avoid doing it again. I cannot believe you have been too ill to write without letting me know it by another hand, and can think of no other reason for your silence but your having better company than the robin, who would not have hindered you in writing. Whoever was with you, sure your absence might have been excused for a minute to tell me of your health. Wherever I am, you see I can always be alone to write to you. But till I see you or hear from you again, I will not enter into the particulars of what concerns you, but only tell you in general what I am sure will not displease you much. Your uncle Lord P. has already said something in favour of you to your F. I am told Lord P. seems willing to mention a reconciliation as the thing proper for your father to agree to, but not as a favour he would ask. How far this is likely to weigh, you can best tell. . . ." [Addressed to Lady Mary at Hinchinbroke, near Huntingdon.]

Lady Mary was alone at Hinchinbroke at this time, without any amusements, as she says, with which to take up her thoughts, and she adds, alluding to her condition, " I am in circumstances in which melancholy is apt to prevail even over all amusements, dispirited and alone, and you write me quarrelling letters." With her usual attempt at philosophy she admits that it is no use complaining, whether of bodily or mental ills, but to those that can and will relieve them. " I know you are ready to tell me that I do not ever keep to these good maxims. I confess I often speak impertinently, but I always repent of it. My last stupid letter was not come to you, before I would

[1] From the unpublished MS.

have had it back again, had it been in my power; such as it was, I beg your pardon for it. I did not expect that my Lord P[ierrepont] would speak at all in our favour, much less show zeal upon that occasion, that never showed any in his life. I have writ every post, and you accuse me without reason. . . . Adieu! Je suis à vous de tout mon cœur."

In her solitude Lady Mary amused herself as she had done in her girlish days, with her books and her writing. The following lines are said to have been written by her on a window pane soon after her marriage:—

> "Whilst thirst of praise and vain desire of fame,
> In every age, is every woman's aim;
> With courtship pleased, of silly toasters proud,
> Fond of a train, and happy in a crowd;
> On each proud fop bestowing some kind glance,
> Each conquest owing to some loose advance;
> While vain coquets affect to be pursued,
> And think they're virtuous, if not grossly lewd:
> Let this great maxim be my virtue's guide;
> In part she is to blame that has been try'd—
> 'He comes too near, that comes to be deny'd.'"[1]

Among Lady Mary's manuscripts is a criticism of Addison's *Cato*, which is headed, "Wrote at the desire of Mr. Wortley. Suppressed at the desire of Mr. Addison." The greater part of the play had been written ten or twelve years before, and handed round among the author's friends; but owing to his fears of failure, it was not finished and produced till 1713. The criticism in question was evidently written before the play was performed, but after it was completed. It may therefore be attributed to the period we have now reached. It will be unnecessary to quote from it at any length, but one or two passages are interesting, as throwing some light on the dramatic criticism of the period.

[1] In the Conversations of Ben Jonson with William Drummond of Hawthornden, we find the following passage: "The Countess of Rutland [only child of Sir Philip Sidney and wife of Roger, fifth Earl of Rutland] was nothing inferior to her father in poesie. Sir Thomas Overbury was in love with her, and caused Ben to read his *Wyffe* to her, which he, with an excellent grace, did, and praised the author. That the morn thereafter he discorded with Overbury, who would have him to intend a suit that was unlawful. The lines my lady keeped in remembrance, 'He comes too near who comes to be denied.'"

"To[1] speak in the first place of the plot or fable; if I may believe the translations of Aristotle, or rely on the opinions of all the French critics, or Horace, in his art of Poetry, or that of Mr. Addison himself, it ought to be entire; I mean to admit of no episodes that do not naturally rise from the principal fable. This is, as I remember, the first law of dramatic poetry, which I am afraid is very much violated in this Tragedy of *Cato*. The death of Cato is certainly the principal action. As he was perhaps the greatest character amongst the Romans, a greater subject cannot be chosen for tragedy. But what relation to the carrying on of that action there is to be found in the Loves of Juba, Marcus, or Portia, I can't discover, or why indeed Marius is represented in love at all. The passion he talks with, the fine lines that are put in his mouth, and the fire of his character, prepares us for some very extraordinary event. I expected something very surprising on his discovering his beloved brother to be the lover of his mistress. I confess I was more surprised at his death in the 4th Act, which might have happened without his being in love at all. I attended a scene between the brothers to excel that of Brutus and Cassius by Shakespeare, or Troylus and Hector by Mr. Dryden, or even that of Menelaus and Agamemnon by Euripides. The passion of the gentleman puts me in mind of Mr. Bayes' petticoat and the stomach-ache,[2] who being asked what happened upon it, replied, 'Nothing at all, no earthly thing egad.'

"The love of Marcus, the rivalry of his brother, etc., had no relation to the death of Cato. He appears ignorant of it from one end to t'other, nor can I perceive one considerable event it produces. I think this hinders the play from being one action, and, in my opinion, Shakespeare's manner of progression is more pardonable. He makes his Play of *Julius*

---

[1] From the unpublished MS.

[2] In the Duke of Buckingham's farce, *The Rehearsal*. In the original version there is nothing about Mr. Bayes' petticoat or the stomach-ache, but then the actor who took the part of Bayes had always been allowed, as Cibber says, such ludicrous liberties of observation upon anything new or remarkable in the state of the stage, as he might think proper to take In other words, he might "gag" for all he was worth. One of Mr. Bayes' gags resulted in Cibber being made the hero of the *Dunciad* instead of Theobald.

Cæsar a series of actions: he begins with the death of Cæsar, and concludes with that of Brutus. He offends in point of time, but does not introduce Mark Antony making love to a Roman lady, who has nothing to do with the plot of the Play, tho' he describes him as a man addicted to his pleasures. Cæsar's death was his design, and we hear of no episode not relating to that. Marcus being son to Cato is no excuse for our hearing so much of his affairs; the loves of his sons are improperly represented in the Play, except they someway occasioned his death. I don't think Mr. Addison could have chose a greater subject. But 'tis too barren for a tragedy, which I always thought impossible to be made of it, without mixing things foreign to the principal action, and I am more than ever persuaded so since Mr. Addison could not do it. The subject of a tragedy should neither be too full of events, nor too plain; on the one 'tis impossible to avoid confusion, and crowding so many things in so short a compass must make it obscure for the audience. I hate to see a plot thicken; when too many characters appear on the stage, none can be carried on as they ought to be; anything intricate tires and grows dull. On the other hand, a barren subject will not afford five Acts without introducing persons and things foreign to it."

After these strictures comes a passage of almost undiluted praise. The young critic considers that the characters are all "well carried on," and above all she admires that of Cato. "The figure that great man makes in history is so noble, and at the same time so simple, I hardly believed it possible to show him on our stage. He appears here in all his beauty, his sentiments are great, and expressed without affectation. His language is sublime without fustian, and smooth without a misbecoming softness. I think I hear a Roman with all the plain greatness of Ancient Rome. Marcus appears impetuous, and in nothing he says deviates from himself; I am only sorry his character is formed to no purpose."

After some further commendation of the minor characters, she concludes in the best judicial style—

"I cannot omit, that I do not observe, throughout the whole tragedy, one thought improper for the person that speaks

CHAPTER XVII

MOTHERHOOD

IN May 1713 Lady Mary's first child was born, Edward Wortley Montagu junior. A new interest now came into her life, and in spite of the classical studies that were then supposed to unfit a woman for her domestic duties, she proved an anxious and devoted mother. She had probably come to London for her confinement, since in June she was writing from thence to her husband, who had just left her to go to Hinchinbrook—

"You[1] have not been gone three hours. I have called at three people's doors, and without knowing it myself, I find I have come home only to write to you. The late Rain has drawn everybody to the Park. I shall pass the whole evening in my chamber alone, without any business but thinking of you, in a Manner you would call Affectation, if I should repeat it to you. That Reflection brings me back to remember I should not write my thoughts to you. You will accuse me of deceit when I am opening my heart to you, and the Plainness of expressing it would appear Artificial. I am sorry to remember this, and cheque the Inclination that I have to give a loose to my tenderness, and tell you how melancholy all things seem to me in your Absence. How impatient I am for the end of this week, and how little possible I find it would be for me to live without you. My eyes are so weak I can go no farther.

"*Tuesday.* — My first news this morning is what I am sorry to hear. My Brother has the small-pox. I hope he will do well; I am sure we lose a Friend if he does not.

"I expect to-morrow impatiently; if you break your Word

[1] From the unpublished MS.

with me, and I have no letter, you do a very cruel thing, and will make me more unhappy than you imagine. The length of this letter will tire you. Your little Boy is very well, and would present his duty to you, if he could speak."

On 26th June she wrote again—

"My[1] B. they send me word is as well as can be expected, but Dr. Garth says 'tis the worst sort, and he fears he will be too full, which I should think very foreboding, if I did not think all Doctors (and particularly Garth) loved to have their patients thought in danger.

"Your son is at present in better health and much happier than his mother. I am very impatient of your absence. . . . My dear Life, write to me, take care of your health, and let me see you as soon as you can. Your little boy delivered me your letter. The Nurse thought it would be an acceptable present, and put it into his hands. You will laugh at this circumstance, which you will think very ridiculous, but it pleased me mightily."

Unfortunately, in this particular instance Dr. Garth proved no alarmist. Lord Kingston died on 1st July, leaving a widow and two children, though the poor boy was not yet of age. His death was a great grief to his sister, who had not yet recovered her strength after the birth of her child. Just before leaving town, she wrote to Mr. Wortley about some furnished houses, which had been recommended by her old friend Mr. Banks of Scofton. One was near Sheffield and the other at Middlethorpe, near York.

"I know not what to do," she says, "but I know I shall be unhappy till I see you again, and I would by no means stay where I am. Your absence increases my melancholy so much, I fright myself with imaginary horrors, and shall always be fancying danger for you while you are out of my sight. I am afraid of Lord H. [? Halifax], I am afraid of everything. There wants but little of my being afraid of the small-pox for you, so unreasonable are my fears, which, however, proceed from an unlimited love. If I lose you—I cannot bear that if—which I bless God is without probability; but since the loss of my poor brother I dread every evil.

[1] From the unpublished MS.

"*Saturday.*—I have been to-day at Acton to see my poor brother's family. I cannot describe how much it has sunk my spirits. . . ."

While the question of the house was being decided, Lady Mary went to stay with her husband's family at Wharncliffe Lodge. She writes thence on 12th July—

"I[1] find myself weaker than I imagine, and 'tis necessary to recover my strength. I should not be too much alone, which leads me into a melancholy I can't help, tho' I know 'tis very prejudicial to my Health. Not that I do not think myself happy in you, and, I am sure, to me you can recompense every Loss. While you are well and love me, I am insensible of every Misfortune, but 'tis impossible for me to hinder making some melancholy Reflections on the untimely death of my Brother, and the manner of it."

Towards the end of July the young wife was paying a visit to her friends, the Whites, at Walling Wells. She writes thence a short letter to her husband which, she warns him, will be all reproaches. "You know where I am," she complains, "and I have not once heard from you. I am tired of this place because I do not, and if you persist in your silence, I will return to Wharncliffe. I had rather be quite alone, and hear sometimes from you, than in any company, and not have that satisfaction. Your silence makes me more melancholy than any solitude, and I can think on nothing so dismal as that you forget me."

Lady Mary was now immersed in the troubles of house-hunting, a business which Mr. Wortley left entirely in her hands, only reserving to himself the right to grumble if the house or furniture turned out badly. In after life both husband and wife were accused by their contemporaries of extreme avarice. That Mr. Wortley was of a saving disposition is proved by the fact that he left a fortune of over a million pounds, a huge sum in those times. Even in his more youthful days, he prided himself, as we have seen, upon laying by a part of his income, and being able to live, if necessary, at the rate of a hundred a year. Again and again during his courtship he had warned his lady-love that as his

[1] From the unpublished MS.

wife, she would have to be content with a modest "equipage," and a narrow manner of living. His income was, at the time of his marriage, not quite eight hundred a year, but of course its purchasing power was double, if not treble, what it would be at the present day.

There is nothing in her girlish letters to show that Lady Mary thought or cared anything about money, except indeed her desire that some provision should be made for her widowhood. Her father's establishment had, we may suppose, been carried on in the style suitable to his rank and fortune, but as the wife of a gentleman of moderate means she desired to show that she could adapt herself to circumstances, and play the part of a notable housewife. She was nervously anxious to please the husband she both loved and feared, and she never forgot his generosity in taking her without a dowry. Thus she was led to practise a somewhat rigid economy in these early years of married life, and she may have found that the habit once gained was difficult to throw off when altered circumstances no longer required such prudent management.

On 3rd August Lady Mary had been to look at a house —a pretty house in a pretty place—but the rooms were not half-finished, and there was not a bit of furniture in them. Mr. Wortley was then at Boroughbridge,[1] a constituency for which Steele was elected in February 1715. He had probably gone there with a view to standing for the borough himself. His wife expresses her longing to see him, and begs to hear from him, "but no more ungracious letters." On 7th August she writes again about a house near York, probably the one at Middlethorpe, which the Wortleys occupied for a year or eighteen months.

"I [2] am of your opinion that the objections to Mr. Barlow's house are not very material. As to the want of Iron bars, it will give me no apprehensions in a house where I know there is nothing to be stole but chairs and stools. The small distance from York is much more convenient than was five or six miles. I have no acquaintance there, and whoever would have a mind to make me a visit would come to dinner, which we

[1] Near Malton, in Yorkshire. [2] From the unpublished MS.

would have found very troublesome. As it is, nobody will pretend farther than an Afternoon visit, which cannot be very importunate, if not repeated too often, which without an Intimacy is not probable. Especially in a place where we have no interest to manage. . . .

"I am almost ready to believe 'tis some mistake that Lord Gower is at York, but if he is, I am fully assured he will leave it as soon as possible. However I would not put meeting him to the hazard, for it would be an Adventure extremely disagreeable to me,[1] for which reason I will go to Knaresburgh, where I hope you will meet me and go with me to York, if he has gone by that time. The season for drinking the waters being over, I suppose I am in no danger of meeting company, and I imagine 'tis a place of tolerable accommodation. . . . I can delay no longer the pleasure of seeing you. If you loved me as well as I do you, it would be as uneasy to you, but I am afraid you are far from being equally dissatisfied, and perhaps have more reason to be comforted."

The next letter, which is dated York, 22nd August, throws a curious light upon the methods of housekeeping in a country village at that period.

"I[2] have once more viewed the House, but not taken it, and am determined I will not, till I hear from you, and beg you to consider in your own mind what you would have me do. There is vessels in the house, but Mr. H. tells me no vessels can be good out of constant use, and that it will be cheaper to have Beer from him than of our own brewing. And he will take care to have it to your taste, and in what quantity you please; perhaps he may speak this with an eye to his own interests. He would persuade me 'tis better to buy what is wanting in the kitchen and sell again, than hire, and I may do it with less loss. There will be very little trouble of that kind at Mr. Gill's, and it is for you to judge of other Inconveniences. . . . I have persuaded Mr. H. that the people shall remove, and we not be troubled with anybody in the house but our own servants, which I think a considerable

[1] Lady Mary's elopement had probably estranged her from her brother-in-law, Lord Gower, as well as from the rest of her family.
[2] From the unpublished MS.

point. The country round is disagreeable, and you may have sports about Rotherham you cannot have here, besides the advantage of the garden; but I fear Mr. G. will expect us to keep the gardener, and at that rate I am sure the garden will be no advantage at all. Perhaps also we shall find the price of meat much higher than here. Pray let me have your last thoughts, and don't leave it again to me. For upon farther thoughts without affectation, they are equal to me, and I have no sort of partiality to this, tho' I am grateful, as I ought to be, for your goodness in leaving me your choice, which I shall always remember with an unfeigned sense of it.

"Since I writ this, Mr. H. has come to tell me I may hire pewter plates at 2/6 a dozen for four months. I believe one or two dozen is all we shall want, and then you have plates hired for 5/— and other pewter at the rate of a penny per pound, but we are like to have a good deal of trouble to get Brazerie. . . ."

Throughout this correspondence there are many complaints of Mr. Wortley's infrequent letters, and the lack of interest that he showed in his wife and child. Thus on 30th August Lady Mary writes reproachfully—

"You[1] could send a letter to Mr. Adams, and know the same messenger would come to me, and yet neglect writing. How have I deserved this unkindness? Do what you please, I had rather you should not write, than write when you could as willingly let it alone.

"He brought hither this answer from Mr. A. I opened it, because I thought he might have changed his mind, and resolved to let or lend his house. . . . But I find that he has no such intention, tho' I believe he would willingly do it, but his Wife won't let him, who I perceive is very arbitrary in her governments. . . .

"My letter concluded in this manner, but I was angry that you had neglected me, and did not trouble you with kindness I begun to think you weary of. But a messenger has brought me two letters, and given me the pleasure of finding you think of me. Whenever you forget me, you forget one that sums up all her thoughts and wishes in you, and the desire of pleasing

[1] From the unpublished MS.

you is the real motive of all I do. I love the child, but after you, and because it is yours."

The difficulties about the "Brazerie" and the beer being overcome, the house at Middlethorpe was taken, and the following letter seems to refer to the move:—

"I [1] am equally surprised and afflicted at your long stay; for your sake I shall be sorry your absence was as uneasy to you as it was for me. I am in hopes, by your delays, that it is not. According to your orders, I have sent all our goods that are to go by water. . . . I know not what to do with the things in your closet, of which you have the key, and I dare not break it open. I hoped before this to have seen you, and have stayed at home, expecting every noise made by the wind was you coming in. At length—I am obliged to send this messenger, not knowing whether you have not changed your mind concerning your journey, which would now be inconveniently delayed because of our things being sent away. Mrs. Smith, without my desire, has officiously laid in provisions of coal and beer, I hope not in too large a quantity. If you please send back the messenger to-morrow with the key of your closet, I will faithfully put up your papers in the best manner I am able, and upon my word without looking in one of them. The carriers go out on Tuesday, and we must set out on that day, and meet you at Doncaster. If you have altered your resolution of going, pray let me know it. Whatever you please, I am too much yours not to be pleased with. Your child, I thank God, is very well, which I can't omit speaking of, tho' you never ask after him. Mrs. Smith says the Queen is ill." [2]

Presumably Mr. Wortley settled down with his wife at Middlethorpe, since there are no letters to him till the following year. Lady Mary seems to have found life in the Yorkshire village rather dull, if we may judge from a letter written by her to some woman-friend in the winter of 1713–14. This, which is couched in the vivacious style of the early letters to Mrs. Hewet, may have been addressed to her sister-in-law, Katherine Wortley.

[1] From the unpublished MS.
[2] The Queen's health was giving great anxiety about this time.

"I return you a thousand thanks, my dear, for so agreeable an entertainment as your letter.

> 'In this cold climate where the sun appears
> Unwillingly,'

wit is as wonderfully pleasing as a sunshiny day; and to speak poetically, Phœbus is very sparing of all his favours. I fancied your letter an emblem of yourself. In some parts I found there the softness of your voice, and in others the vivacity of your eyes. You are to expect no return but humble and hearty thanks, yet I can't forbear entertaining you with our York lovers. (Strange monsters you'll think, love being as much forced up here as melons.) In the first form of these creatures is even Mr. Vanbrugh.[1] Heaven, no doubt compassionating our dulness, has inspired him with a passion that makes us all ready to die with laughing. 'Tis credibly reported that he is endeavouring at the honourable state of matrimony, and vows to lead a sinful life no more. Whether pure holiness inspires his mind, or dotage turns his brain, is hard to find. 'Tis certain he keeps Monday's and Thursday's market (assembly day) constant, and for those that don't regard worldly muck, there's extraordinary good choice indeed. I believe last Monday there was two hundred pieces of women's flesh (fat and lean). But you know Van's taste was always odd; his inclination to ruins has given him a fancy for Mrs. Yarborough.[2] He sighs and ogles that it would do your heart good to see him; and she is not a little pleased, in so small a proportion of men among such a number of women, a whole man should fall to her share.

"My dear, adieu.

"My service to Mr. Congreve."

The Wortleys were in town together during the spring of 1714. Their old friend and sympathiser, Steele, was in trouble over his pamphlet *The Crisis*, for which he was expelled from

[1] Vanbrugh spent a good deal of time with Lord Carlisle at Castle Howard, of which he was the architect. On 29th October 1713 he wrote a letter to a friend from Castle Howard, in which he says that the place is so agreeable he shall have much ado to leave it.

[2] It was not until 1719, when he was fifty-five, that Vanbrugh married Miss Yarborough, a daughter of Colonel Yarborough of Haslington, Yorkshire.

the House. Mr. Wortley gave him advice and support during his trial. Lady Mary returned to Middlethorpe in July, expecting her husband to follow a little later. On her way to Yorkshire she stayed with her uncle, Lord Pierrepont, at Tong Castle, near Newport Pagnel, and she was anxious that Mr. Wortley should do the same. There was some idea of leaving Middlethorpe at this time, and she had undertaken to look out for another furnished house.

Lady Frances Pierrepont was about to be married to Lord Mar,[1] a match of "Aunt Cheyne's" making, but the wedding took place after Lady Mary's departure. In the same month Lord Dorchester was married to Lady Belle Bentinck, daughter of the Earl of Portland, and one of the most admired beauties of her day. Lady Mary's Journal, parts of which her grand-daughter, Lady Louisa Stuart, was allowed to read, gave an account of the romance in which the "fair Isabella," as she was called, played the leading rôle. "The heads of it were, a passion for a younger lover, and the combats and conflicts of love on one side, with interest and ambition on the other; until these latter, gaining a complete victory, made the offers of a man who had three married daughters older than the lady herself, appear too tempting to be refused." We must suppose that Lady Mary was not in sufficient favour with her family to be invited to the weddings of her father and sister, and this may have been the reason that she left town before either ceremony took place. There is no mention of her step-mother in the letters for this period, but there is reason to believe that she held but a poor opinion of the lady. Towards the end of July she wrote to her husband from Middlethorpe—

"I found our poor boy not so well as I expected. He is very lively, but so weak that my heart aches about him very often. . . . I suppose my sister is married by this time. I hope you intend to stay some days at Lord Pierrepont's; I'm sure he'll be very pleased with it. The house is in great

---

[1] John, eleventh Earl of Mar, the famous Jacobite leader, who earned the nickname of Bobbing John. He was thirty-seven at the time of his marriage, and had been made Secretary of State for Scotland in 1706. Allusions to the part he played in the Jacobite rising will be found in the record for 1715.

disorder, and I want maids so much that I know not what to do till I have some. I have not one bit of paper in the house but this little sheet, or you would have been troubled with a longer scribble. . . . My first inquiries shall be after a country-house, never forgetting any of my promises to you. . . . I am in abundance of pain about our dear child. Though I am convinced in my reason 'tis both silly and wicked to set one's heart too fondly on anything in this world, yet I cannot overcome myself so far as to think of parting with him with the resignation that I ought to do. I hope and I beg of God he may live to be a comfort to us both. . . ." It appears that the child, now over a year old, had not yet succeeded in cutting any teeth. His mother had been recommended to try cold bathing for him, but she adds, " I am very fearful, and unwilling to try any hazardous remedies."

Mr. Wortley was detained in town, first by an attempt to arrange a reconciliation with Lord Dorchester, but afterwards by the Queen's illness and death, which brought the Whigs into power again. Lady Mary, who was looking out for another house, found all her plans thrown into confusion by this unexpected delay. Queen Anne died on 1st August 1714, but the news had not reached Middlethorpe by 4th August, when Lady Mary wrote to express her surprise that Mr. Wortley had not yet spoken to her father, and to ask that Dr. Garth might be consulted about the use of cold baths for her child. Five days later she had learnt that the Queen was dead, and the feeling of agitation and uncertainty which was general throughout the country, was evidently shared by the inhabitants of the little village of Middlethorpe.

" I cannot forbear taking it something unkindly," she says on 9th August, " that you do not write to me, when you may be assured I am in a great fright, and know not certainly what to expect upon this sudden change. The Archbishop of York [1] has come to Bishopthorpe. I went with my cousin to-day to see the King proclaimed, which was done; the archbishop walking next the Lord Mayor, all the country

[1] Sir William Dawes, Bart. (1671–1724). He was appointed Bishop of Chester in 1708, and Archbishop of York in 1713.

gentry following, with greater crowds of people than I believed to be in York, vast acclamations, and the appearance of general satisfaction. The Pretender afterwards dragged about the streets and burned. Ringing of bells, bonfires, and illuminations, the mob crying Liberty and Property! and Long live King George!

"This morning all the principal men of any figure took post for London, and we are alarmed with the fear of attempts from Scotland, though all Protestants here seem unanimous for the Hanover succession. The poor young ladies at Castle Howard [1] are as much afraid as I am, being left all alone, without any hopes of seeing their father again (tho' things should prove well), this eight or nine months. They have sent to desire me very earnestly to come to them and bring my boy; 'tis the same thing as pensioning in a nunnery, for no mortal man ever enters the doors in the absence of their father, who is gone post. During this uncertainty, I think it will be a safe retreat, for Middlethorpe stands exposed to plunderers, if there be any at all. I dare say after the zeal the A. B. [archbishop] has shewed, they will visit his house (and consequently this) in the first place. The A. B. made me many compliments on our near neighbourhood, and said he should be overjoyed at the happiness of improving his acquaintance with you.

"I suppose you may now come in at Aldburgh,[2] and I heartily wish you was in Parliament. I saw the A. B.'s list of the Lords Regents appointed, and perceive Lord Wn. [Wharton] is not one of them; by which I guess the new scheme is not to make use of any man grossly infamous in either party; consequently, those who have been honest in regard to both, will stand fairest for preferment. You understand these things much better than me; but I hope you will be persuaded by me and your other friends (who I don't doubt will be of my opinion) that 'tis necessary for the common good for an honest man to endeavour to be powerful, when he can be the

---

[1] The daughters of Lord Carlisle. They were intimate friends of Lady Mary and her sisters. Lord Carlisle had been chosen one of the Lords Justices for the government of the kingdom till the King's arrival.

[2] Aldborough, a little Yorkshire borough.

one without losing the first more valuable title, and remember that money is the source of power. I hear that Parliament sits but six months. You know best whether 'tis worth any expense or bustle to be in for so short a time."

Mr. Wortley was too busy or too indifferent to write, and his wife felt herself extremely ill-used.

"You made me cry two hours last night," she writes a few days later. "I cannot imagine why you use me so ill, for what reason you continue silent when you know that your silence cannot fail of giving me a great deal of pain; and now to a higher degree because of the perplexity that I am in, without knowing where you are, what you are doing, or what to do with myself and my dear little boy. However (persuaded there can be no objection to it), I intend to go to-morrow to Castle Howard, and remain there with the young ladies, till I know when I shall see you, or what you would command. The archbishop and everybody else are gone to London. We are alarmed with a story of a fleet being seen from the coasts of Scotland. An express went thence through York to the Earl of Mar. I beg you would write to me. Till you do, I shall not have an easy minute. I am sure I do not deserve from you that you should make me uneasy. I find I am scolding; 'tis better for me not to trouble you with it. But I cannot help taking your silence very unkindly."

The move to Castle Howard was carried out, and there Lady Mary received the long-looked-for letter from her husband. She answered at once—

"I[1] am very glad to hear from you when I do, tho' you make me wait for that happiness. I am very much troubled (tho' not at all upon my own account) at my F.'s prodigious proceeding. I think you should let Lord Pierrepont know that he made you an offer of treating after my sister's marriage, and then flew off. I suppose it will be near three weeks before I see you, and since you say nothing against it, I am retired to Castle Howard. The ladies have no coach, and I have sent my horses to Wortley. My boy, I hope, grows better, which is a very considerable pleasure to me. Pray write often to me; I can't help flattering myself

[1] From the unpublished MS.

if you knew how uneasy your silence makes me, you would not punish me with it. I am in no pain concerning my sister M[ar] living in greater figure than myself, but I hope there is no sin in being a little pleased, if it should prove to the Town that matches of my Aunt Cheyne's making are not always extremely prudent."

CHAPTER XVIII

POLITICAL AMBITIONS

LADY MARY was quite as much interested and excited about her husband's election prospects as he could have been himself, and inclined to play an even more energetic rôle. To her quickly-working feminine mind and keenly practical temperament any delay or indecision on his own part, or on that of his powerful friends, was most unnecessary and exasperating. If only he would take *her* advice, he would put up at once for one of the seats that she considered the most hopeful, lose no time in canvassing the electors, and persuade his friends to give him their interest, even though it might already be promised elsewhere. As for his father, who was presuming to stand for Huntingdon in the place of his son, she had no patience with such unnatural conduct. This eagerness is rendered more amiable by the fact that she so firmly believed in her husband's powers, thought him so eminently fitted to help in the councils of the nation, that she longed, both on public and private grounds, to see him taking what she considered his " proper place." On 23rd August she writes again from Castle Howard—

" I [1] have at this instant so terrible a toothache, if it were not to write to you I should not be able to hold a pen, and even that consideration won't, I fear, enable me to do it long. I would not have you miss seeing the K. [King] [2] after waiting so long. Lord P. [Pierrepont], I don't doubt, is removed to Tong Castle before this time. I will go back to Middlethorpe in a few days on purpose to make what enquiries I can from the Thompsons, etc. Here we live directly as in a Convent, and

[1] From the unpublished MS.
[2] George I. came over in September.

know no more the affairs of York than those at Constantinople. If you are yet undetermined where to stand, I fancy you may meet as little opposition there as anywhere. If Lord Carlisle is unengaged, I suppose he will make no scruple of promising you his Interest, which is very great, but it would be convenient to ask for it as soon as you can. And Sr. Wm. Robinson [1] will, I daresay, be very willing to join with you. If he is in town you must speak to him about it; if at York, if you please, I may hint it to my Lady, and probably will be able to give you an Account what difficulty will arise in the undertaking. I think it prodigious your Father persists at standing at Huntingdon.

"The child is very lively, but not so strong as I could wish him. My insupportable teeth forces me to conclude."

Mr. Wortley was undecided at this time whether to stand for Newark or Aldborough, while his wife, as has been seen, thought that he had a good chance at York, if he would only act promptly. Still, she admitted that Aldburgh, with Lord Pelham's support, would be a much less expensive seat.

"I hope you are convinced," she writes, "I was not mistaken in my opinion of Lord Pelham; [2] he is very silly, but very good-natured. I don't see how it can be improper for you to get it represented to him that he is obliged in honour to get you chose at Aldburgh, and may more easily get Mr. Jessop [3] chose at another place. . . . Lord Pelham is easily persuaded to anything, and I am sure he may be told by Lord Townshend that he has used you ill, and I know he'll be desirous to do all things in his power to make it up. . . . Your father is very surprising if he persists in standing at Huntingdon; but there is nothing surprising in such a world as this."

A few days later she writes that he would certainly have been chosen for York if he had declared in time, but it is now too late, as "they are treating every night." She suggests

[1] Sir William Robinson was member for York from 1697 to 1722. He was grandfather to the Sir Thomas Robinson who became first Earl of Grantham.
[2] The second Lord Pelham, created Earl of Clare in 1714, and Duke of Newcastle in 1715. Under the latter title he became notorious as the foolish, good-natured Whig Prime Minister of George II. Horace Walpole's estimate of him agrees with Lady Mary's.
[3] Mr. Jessop was elected for Aldborough.

that it will be best to deposit a sum of money in a friend's hands, and buy some little Cornish borough, though it would undoubtedly look better to be "chose" for a considerable town. If he thinks of standing at Newark, which is a most uncertain and expensive place, he must try and get Lord Lexington's [1] interest through Lord Holdernesse,[2] who is both a Whig and an honest man. "'Tis a surprise to me," she concludes, "that you cannot make sure of some borough, when so many of your friends bring in Parliament men, without trouble or expense."

Politics do not, however, quite distract her mind from the cares of housekeeping, and the extortionate price of butcher's meat. In a note addressed to her husband at Aldborough, she remarks, after discussing the advisability of removing to another house—

"*28th August.*

"While[3] I am here, we live at great expense for no purpose. The Butchers (besides cheating in the weight) make us pay 2½d. per pound for all meat. I lost all patience with his Bill yesterday, and sent to-day to Sheffield, where in the public Market they asked but 2d. for better meat than any we have had yet. I am afraid we shall find ourselves proportionately cheated in all other things.

"I have taken care to break my little Horse of his kicking, and believe I shall like him mightily. I shall be easy in any place where your Affairs or your Pleasure makes it necessary for me to be, and upon no occasion will ever show an Inclination contrary to yours. You need be in no pain about me, farther than consulting your own mind what will please you best, and you may securely depend on its pleasing me. . . ."

Mr. Wortley's proposal to stand for Newark still exercised Lady Mary's mind, and she writes to explain that the Tory interest there is very strong.

"The[3] Duke of Newcastle[4] (who, you know, had more

---

[1] Robert Sutton, second Baron Lexington.
[2] Robert D'Arcy, third Earl of Holdernesse.
[3] From the unpublished MS.
[4] Lord Pelham's uncle (the last Duke of the Holles family), who died in 1711.

than double the power of Lord Pelham there) set up Brigadier Sutton[1] a few years ago, and he lost it after an expense of £1200, as I heard him say, but if he did not spend that, 'tis certain he spent a great deal to no purpose.

"All the interest the Duchess of Newcastle[2] now has, is thereabouts, and out of spite to Lord Pelham she will employ it all against you. My opinion is, if he doesn't appear there himself his name will signify nothing, and if he does 'tis still uncertain. It has always been famous for opposition, and I believe more Money has been spent there lately than in most of the Towns in England. . . . I should be very glad to hear you have a sure place, and in the meantime would not have you refuse Newark, tho' 'tis the very worst to be depended on. I am afraid most of the Boroughs are engaged; I am sure they are hereabouts, for I hear of treating every day.

"If Lord Pierrepont is coming to town, and it is consistent with your other Affairs, I think it is very right to stay to wait on him for fear of missing him on [illegible], and I should be glad you gave him a clear account of my F. breaking his word with you, and after that, tell him you will give him no farther trouble about it. I think it is very probable Lord Pierrepont should invite you to his House in the Country. If he does, I suppose you will take the first opportunity of going to it. Pray return him thanks for having done it, and let him know that you did not intend to go near his house without waiting on him. I am very melancholy and want to see you extremely. Everybody is at London, that keeps a Coach. I read all day."

Address.

"To Mr. Edward Wortley Montagu.
To be left at Mr. Tonson, Bookseller,
At the Shakespeare Head,
Over against Catherine St.
In the Strand,
London."

---

[1] Probably one of Lord Lexington's family.

[2] Margaret Cavendish, third daughter and co-heiress of the second Duke of Newcastle, of the older creation. Apparently she had no love for her nephew, Lord Pelham.

Mr. Wortley's letters did not always give satisfaction when, after being long waited for, they arrived at Middlethorpe. He wrote coldly and briefly, and often committed the unpardonable sin of forgetting to ask after his little son. In September Lady Mary writes with some asperity—

"I have [1] no great inclination to answer your last letter. It might have been directed to anybody else, and I had rather it had been writ to Grace or to Matthew.[2] You mention your little boy with so slight a regard, I have no mind to inform you how he does. I have had a doctor to him, and he has advised me to a cold well three mile off, whither I carried him with a beating heart t'other day. I thank God he appears to gather strength since; to-day Grace has gone with him again. He must go nine times. The Races at York have been this three days; I never went but once. Lady Betty Howard and her sisters came here to desire my company with them. There was very little company; I saw nobody I knew but Mrs. Margaret Boswell, in a mourning coach. Lady Betty told me Lord Wharton was at their house, and that he presented his service to me, and said he was obliged to go from hence to Nottingham Race, and much straitened in time, or he would have waited on me. Lord Pierrepont's house is near Newport Pagnel. I believe in the course of your journey you must come there to dinner; I believe you need not doubt being pressed to stay. Giving moderately to the servants, I daresay will please him best. . . . I hope you leave no part of your business of any kind at London unfinished, that we may have no more Expensive Journeys.

"I can't help wishing to see you, tho' you don't write as if you did."

Mr. Wortley was still without a seat, and his wife grew more and more impatient at his lack of energy and what in these days would be called "push."

"I am glad you think of serving your friends," she writes on 24th September. "I hope it will put you in mind of serving yourself. I need not enlarge upon advantages of money;

---

[1] From the unpublished MS.
[2] Matthew and Grace Northall were two of the servants. Mrs. Northall acted later as nurse to the child.

everything we see and everything we hear puts us in remembrance of it. If it was possible to restore liberty to your country, or limit the encroachments of the pre——ve [prerogative] by reducing yourself to a garret, I should be pleased to share so glorious a poverty with you; but as the world is, and will be, 'tis a sort of duty to be rich, that it may be in one's power to do good; riches being another word for power, towards the obtaining of which the first necessary qualification is impudence, and (as Demosthenes said of pronunciation in oratory) the second is impudence, and the third still, impudence. No modest man ever did, or ever will, make his fortune. Your friends Lord H[alifa]x, R. W[alpo]le, and all other remarkable instances of quick advancements have been remarkably impudent. . . .

"If this letter is impertinent, it is founded upon an opinion of your merit, which, if it is a mistake, I would not be undeceived in. It is my interest to believe (as I do) that you deserve everything, and are capable of everything. But nobody else will believe you if they see you get nothing."

The reconciliation with Lord Dorchester was not yet effected, though Lord Pierrepont was willing to act as mediator, and this failure also Lady Mary seems inclined to attribute to her husband's lack of *savoir faire*. In the following note she actually puts into his mouth the words he is to say to her uncle:—

"Undoubtedly[1] you should have told the story of my F. to Lord Pierrepont the first time you saw him, which would have looked much more natural and undesigned; but however it is necessary to tell it in these words: 'I believe I told your Lordship Lord D[orchester] bid me apply to him again, when L. F. [Lady Frances] was married. But he would not put it out of his power to dispose of her.' If he makes answer, 'No, you did not tell me so,' you may reply, 'I thought I had, but perhaps it was after you had left the town. But he did tell me so, accordingly I applied to him,' etc.

"I hope you visit Lady Dowager Denbigh.[2] She

---

[1] From the unpublished MS.

[2] Lady Mary's step-grandmother, the second wife of Lord Denbigh. She was a daughter of Henry Carey, Earl of Monmouth, and is said to have been a woman of very superior understanding.

will have reason to take it unkindly if you do not, and I promised her you should. Pray do before you leave the town."

The fact that Mr. Wortley's cousin, Lord Halifax,[1] was expected to be at the head of affairs in the new Government roused great hopes in the breasts of his numerous relations. Though Mr. Wortley thought scarcely any place short of a Secretaryship of State worthy of his notice, his ambition was somewhat checked by the fear lest his wife should think high preferment a reason for living in town at an extravagant rate. He hinted at this fear in one of his letters, to which she replied early in October—

"You do me wrong in imagining (as I perceive you do) that my reason for being solicitous for your having that place, was in view of spending more money than we do. You have no cause of fancying me capable of such a thought. I don't doubt but Lord H[alifa]x will very soon have the staff, and it is my belief you will not be at all the richer. But I think it looks well, and may facilitate your election, and that is all the advantage I hope from it. When all your intimate acquaintances are preferred, I think you would have an ill air in having nothing; upon that account only, I am sorry so many considerable places are disposed on. I suppose now you will certainly be chose somewhere or other, and I cannot see why you should not pretend to be Speaker. I believe all the Whigs would be for you, and I fancy you have a considerable interest among the Tories, and for that reason would be very likely to carry it. 'Tis impossible for me to judge of this so well as you can do; but the reputation of being thoroughly of no party is (I think) of some use in this affair, and I believe people generally esteem you impartial; and being chose by your country is more honourable than holding *any* place from *any* king."

Mr. Wortley had at last paid his respects to his wife's grandmother, Lady Denbigh, and also to her old friend, the Bishop of Salisbury. On hearing that they had asked after her boy, Lady Mary wrote—

[1] The famous Charles Montagu, first Earl of Halifax (1661–1715), the friend and patron of the "wits." He had been out of favour during Anne's reign, but became First Lord of the Treasury on the accession of George I.

"I [1] am very much obliged to my Lady Denbigh and the Bishop of Salisbury for their kind enquiries after the child, and the more because it is certainly neither of theirs. You may tell them he is very well, and has got some teeth, tho' he is not so strong as I should wish he were. He is all the comfort of my life. You say nothing of a Coachman; I hope you won't forget to bring down one with you. He that I have got, overturned me about a week ago at the side of the ditch, that 'twas the particular providence of God, or I had undoubtedly been killed. Ever since that time I have not stirred out, nor know not when I shall have courage to venture. Nobody comes hither, and 'tis not possible to live in a more melancholy solitude than I do." [2]

It will be seen that Lady Mary still expected her husband to join her in Yorkshire. But the times were far too exciting

[1] From the unpublished MS.
[2] It must have been during these solitary months of her early married life that Lady Mary wrote her poem *The Bride in the Country*, which was a parody on Rowe's ballad, *Colin's Complaint*.

A stanza or two from the parody may be quoted—

"By the side of a half-rotten wood
    Melantha sat silently down,
Convinced that her scheme was not good,
    And vexed to be absent from Town.
Whilst pitied by no living soul,
    To herself she was forced to reply,
And the sparrow, as grave as an owl,
    Sat list'ning and pecking hard by.

'Alas! silly maid that I was!'
    Thus sadly complaining, she cried;
'When first I forsook that dear place,
    'T had been better by far I had died!
How gaily I passed the long days,
    In a round of continual delights;
Park, visits, assemblies and plays,
    And a dance to enliven the nights.

'How simple was I to believe
    Delusive poetical dreams!
Or the flattering landscapes they give
    Of meadows and murmuring streams.
Bleak mountains, and cold starving rocks,
    Are the wretched result of my pains;
The swains greater brutes than their flocks,
    The nymphs as polite as the swains.'"

to allow of his leaving town, or even giving much thought to
his young wife, shut up alone with her delicate child in a
dismal country village. He may have lacked the imagination
to realise the pain that his neglect caused her, and the frequent
alarms she suffered in those unsettled times from the reports of
invasions and rebellions.

In one of her unpublished letters she writes bitterly: " I
have not heard from you this long time, but I confess from
writing such letters as you do, 'tis a very natural transition not
to write at all." In another she observes: " I wish you would
learn from Mr. Steele to write to your wife."[1] But Mr. Wortley
remained impervious to hints and veiled reproaches. By the
middle of November Lady Mary's patience gave way, and she
wrote him a formal letter of complaint, which seems to have
had some effect on his stony heart.

"I have taken up and laid down my pen several times,"
she begins, "very much unresolved in what stile I ought to
write to you; for once I suffer my inclination to get the
better of my reason. I have not oft opportunities of indulg-
ing myself, and I will do it in this one letter. I know very
well that nobody was ever teized into a liking; and 'tis
perhaps harder to revive a past one, than to overcome an
aversion; but I cannot forbear any longer telling you, I think
you use me very unkindly. I don't say so much of your
absence, as I should do if you was in the country and I in
London; because I would not have you believe that I am impatient to be in town, when I say I am impatient to be with
you; but I am very sensible I parted with you in July and 'tis
now the middle of November. As if this was not hardship
enough, you do not tell me you are sorry for it. You write
seldom and with so much indifference as shews you hardly
think of me at all. I complain of ill health, and you only
say you hope 'tis not so bad as I make it. You never enquire
after your child. I would fain flatter myself you have more
kindness for me and him than you express; but I reflect with
grief a man that is ashamed of passions that are natural and
reasonable, is generally proud of those that are shameful and

---

[1] Perhaps Mrs. Steele wished that her husband would learn prudence from Mr. Wortley.

silly. You should consider solitude, and spleen the consequence of solitude, is apt to give the most melancholy ideas. And there needs at least tender letters and kind expressions to hinder uneasiness almost inseparable from absence. I am very sensible how far I ought to be contented when your affairs oblige you to be without me. I would not have you do them any prejudice; but a little kindness will cost you nothing. I do not bid you lose anything by hasting to see me, but I would have you think it a misfortune when we are asunder. Instead of that you seem perfectly pleased with our separation and indifferent how long it continues. When I reflect on all your behaviour, I am ashamed of my own: I think I am playing the part of my Lady Winchester.[1] At least be as generous as my lord; and as he made her an early confession of his aversion, own to me your inconstancy and upon my word I will give you no more trouble about it. I have concealed as long as I can the uneasiness the nothingness of your letters has given me under an affected indifference, but dissimulation always sits awkwardly upon me; I am weary of it; and must beg of you to write to me no more if you cannot bring yourself to write otherwise. Multiplicity of business or diversions may have engaged you, but all people find time to do what they have a mind to. If your inclination is gone, I had rather never receive a letter from you than one which, in lieu of comfort for your absence, gives me a pain even beyond it. For my part as 'tis my first, this is my last complaint, and your next of the kind shall go back enclosed to you in blank paper."

It was perhaps in consequence of this trenchant letter that Mr. Wortley took a house in Duke Street, and arranged that his wife, with her child, should join him in town. Lady Mary was evidently displeased at not having been consulted in the choice of a house, for she writes on 27th November—

". . . I[2] am sorry you have taken a house in Duke Street, both from the dampness of the situation, and that I believe there is hardly one sound house that looks into the Park in that street. I know my Lord Loudoun lived in one, which he stayed in but a single week, being every moment in appre-

---

[1] Lady Mary's girlish friend, afterwards Duchess of Bolton.
[2] From the unpublished MS.

hension of having it fall upon their heads. Mr. G. Montagu left another for the same reason, which has stood empty ever since. I am very much afraid you have taken one of these houses. Pray tell me if you have, I hope not Mr. George Montagu's.

"You seem to have forgot I have no coachman. Here are none to be got, either acquainted with the roads, or that know how to drive in the streets at London. . . . I don't believe there is a pair of horses to be hired at York able to draw to London."

She writes again on 6th December—

"Pray[1] let me know what house you have taken, for I am very much afraid it should be that where Mr. George Montagu lived, and out of which Mrs. Montagu and her child both died of the smallpox, and nobody has lived in it since. I know 'tis two or three year ago, but 'tis generally said that Infection may lodge in Blankets etc. longer than that; at least I should be very much afraid of coming to a house whence anybody died of that distemper, especially if I bring up your son, which I believe I must, tho' I am in a great deal of concern about him. One saddle-horse is enough; you need not send down any more. George is very honest, I believe, and has behaved himself very well to his power. But he, and all like him, are too awkward to serve in London for visiting or anything of that nature. But I had much rather carry him up, than any other of his Countrymen, that would add to their awkwardness want of use.

"I have sent your Nightgown and the rest of your things to-day, directed to Jacob Tonson. The hire of two coach-horses and a postilion from hence to London is £6, if they bear their own charges, and £5 if you do. You can judge which is cheaper, to hire here or from London. . . ."

The question whether the child should be brought to town or left with a nurse in the country was anxiously debated by his mother at this time. She was torn between her desire to have him always with her, and the dread of the long, cold winter journey. On 12th December she writes—

"I[1] am still in great concern about the child. He has

[1] From the unpublished MS.

now a nurse about him, that I very much confide in, but she won't go to London, but would fain take him home to her house. I know no objection to it, but my own fears and the uneasiness I shall be in, for want of him, who is now company for me at all times. Mrs. Cromwell, I believe, would not care to take him again, and if she would, after so severe an illness there, I should not care to leave him. When I took him he was so extreme weak, that I durst hardly hope for his Life and he is now (as everybody thinks as well as me) as fine a child as ever was seen, and always merry, and at play from morning till night. For which reason I don't desire to change the nurse that is about him, which I must do, if I carry him from hence. I can leave him in charge with Mrs. Thompson and some other good Wives of York, that will see him every day, the same as if I left him in their houses; but I wish I could tell if you have any thoughts of coming here again, when my determination would depend a great deal on that, tho' I dread the long Winter Journey and change of air for him. I hope you will take care to have the house all over very well aired, which I am sure is particularly damp in that situation. There should be fires made in all the rooms, and if it be the house Mrs. Montagu died in (which I hope it is not), that all the bedding at least be changed. Lady Mary Montagu got the smallpox last year, by lying in blankets taken from a bed that had been laid in by one ill of that distemper some months before.

"Your sister has been here. Having occasion to say something of her, and some other *Affaire de Famille*, which I had no mind should be seen, I sent a box by the stage coach, and put a letter in the sleeve of my calico mantle."

The house was to have been ready for its new tenants by Christmas, but the former occupant, Lord Seafield,[1] was disinclined to move before the beginning of the new year. Lady Mary seems to have suspected either that her husband had not definitely taken the house, or else that he was glad to

---

[1] James Ogilvy, fourth Earl of Findlater and created first Earl of Seafield in 1701. A famous lawyer, who had held many high offices, and was now Keeper of the Great Seal in Scotland.

postpone her coming to town. In a letter endorsed 20th December she writes—

"'Tis[1] very surprising to me that you should take a house to be ready on Christmas Day, and my Lord Seafield be in it yet. I don't doubt he intends to stay till the Parliament is dissolved, and I hear that is not expected till Feb. . . . I have prepared all things for my Journey, and it will now be a considerable Expense to stay. I must lay in more coals, etc., which cannot be bought in a small Quantity. If you have really taken the house, as you told me you had, my Lord Seafield has no right to stay in it but till you please to come in it, and 'tis your business to tell the Landlady, or whoever let it, to give him warning, unless you have some particular tyes to be over and above civil to my Lord Seafield. What you are told about Linen is no sign there will be any when I come. At least I desire I may be sure of some the first night I come; sheets and table-cloths not being for show are absolutely necessary. I shan't bring the Boy, for I suppose there won't be a place to put him in, and 'tis easier for me to endure any hardship than see him do it. I can't believe but my Lord Seafield will agree to take another Lodging, or that I may not come to yours, except you want an Excuse to be without me."

The journey was only put off a few days, for on 1st January Lady Mary set out from Middlethorpe, with the prospect of arriving in town in about a week's time. "I leave,"[1] she writes on the day of her departure, "by the advice of all people my dear little one at home, who (they say) would hazard his life in travelling at this time of year. I would take the more care of him, because if you have twenty children you may never have one like him, for he is very pritty, and has more intelligence than is usual at his age."

It is fortunate, perhaps, that mothers have not the prophetic spirit. If Mr. Wortley had had twenty children it is hardly probable that the other nineteen would have brought upon him a tithe of the sorrow and disgrace caused by this one promising specimen.

[1] From the unpublished MS.

CHAPTER XIX

COURT LIFE AND POEMS

WHEN Lady Mary Wortley returned to London at the beginning of 1715, she found a very different state of affairs prevailing from that which she had left little more than two years before. Then the Tories were firmly fixed in power, with Oxford and Bolingbroke at their head, while Marlborough and his Duchess were in exile and disgrace. The Queen, it was well known, was favourably inclined towards the claims of the Pretender, and the Protestant Succession was in deadly peril. But with the death of Anne, a transformation scene was played in the political drama. The see-saw of fate had swung the Whigs into power again, and Townshend, Halifax, Marlborough, and Walpole were the men of the hour. Bolingbroke had fled to France, while the other leading Tories were waiting on events, upheld by the hope that their past backslidings would be forgiven, and that the new King would choose his advisers from moderate men of both parties.

But these hopes were soon proved vain. George I. had come over in September with his long train of German secretaries, chamberlains, intendants, cooks, and pages, to say nothing of his two plain elderly German mistresses. He was soon made aware that if he desired to keep the crown on his own head, this was not the time to dally with the disaffected, who were hindered by self-interest alone from openly declaring themselves for the Stuart cause. Risings were daily expected in the Highlands, riots had broken out in the Northern manufacturing towns, the whole West of England was a hot-bed of Jacobitism, and it was known that if the Pretender effected a landing upon our shores, thousands were ready to flock to his standard.

Even the leading Whigs were not above suspicion. Marlborough was notorious for his double dealing, and Walpole was suspected of a correspondence with the enemies of the Hanoverian dynasty. Nobody pretended to care for the new King, and he, for his part, made no pretence of affection for his new people, though he was willing to get what he could out of them. "We took him because we wanted him, because he served our turn; we laughed at his uncouth German ways, and sneered at him. He took our loyalty for what it was worth; laid hands on what money he could; and kept us assuredly from Popery and wooden shoes."[1]

The Montagus and Pierreponts shared in the general Whiggish prosperity. Lord Dorchester was created Duke of Kingston-upon-Hull in the course of this year, and later received the Garter. Lord Halifax, now at the head of the Treasury, appointed his cousin, Edward Wortley, who was returned for Westminster in January, one of the Commissioners. "It will be surprising to add," writes Lady Mary in her account of the period, "that he hesitated to accept of it, at a time when his father was alive and his present income very small; but he had that opinion of his own merit as made him think any offer below that of Secretary of State not worth his acceptance, and had certainly refused it if he had not been persuaded to the contrary by a rich old uncle of mine, Lord Pierrepont, whose fondness for me gave him expectations of a large legacy." It was supposed that Mr. Wortley would have considerable power at the King's councils, because he was the only man at the board (except perhaps Lord Halifax) who could speak French, and was thus capable of conversing with the King. But George I. left his affairs, financial and other, to be managed by his ministers, and therefore Mr. Wortley had no more personal intercourse with him than the rest.

Lady Mary Wortley now found herself in a position that the most ambitious might well have envied. The wittiest as well as one of the most beautiful women of her day, she numbered among her friends and admirers the most powerful of the statesmen and the most brilliant of the *littérateurs*; while for a time at least she was a favourite at the rival Courts of the

[1] Thackeray in *The Four Georges*.

King and the Prince of Wales. There is every reason to believe that she threw herself whole-heartedly into all the pleasures and excitements of the period. She had now tried the romantic solitude of which she had dreamed before marriage, and, unsweetened by a husband's kindness and companionship, had found it wanting. She had been prepared for retirement, but not for loneliness and neglect. Her openly expressed affection had been sneeringly rejected as "insincere" and "artificial," her craving for sympathy had been disappointed, and a domestic life, with its simple interests and pleasures, had been denied her. Now, therefore, she would take her place in the great world to which she belonged of right, would "warm both hands before the fire of life," and in social success would find her consolation for a defrauded heart.

Lady Mary and Mr. Wortley each left a fragmentary account of the state of affairs at the time of George I.'s accession, but hers deals chiefly with the Court and his with politics. The lady's work is, as might be expected, the more interesting of the two, and her opinion of the King, his son and his son's wife, are worth quoting.

"The King's character," she remarks, "may be described in very few words. In private life he would have been called an honest blockhead; and Fortune that made him a King, added nothing to his happiness, only prejudiced his honesty and shortened his days. No man was ever more free from ambition: he loved money, but loved to keep his own, without being rapacious of other men's. He would have grown rich by saving, but was incapable of laying schemes for getting; he was more properly dull than lazy, and would have been so well contented to have remained in his little town of Hanover, that if the ambitions of those about him had not been greater than his own, we should never have seen him in England; and the natural honesty of his temper, joined with the narrow notions of a low education, made him look upon his acceptance of the crown as an act of usurpation, which was always uneasy to him. But he was carried by the stream of people about him in that, as in every other action of his life. He could speak no English, and was past the age of learning it. Our customs and laws were all mysteries to him, which he neither tried to understand, nor was capable of understanding, if he had endeavoured it. He was passively good-natured, and wished all mankind enjoyed quiet, if they would let him do so."

Lady Mary gives an even less complimentary character of the Prince of Wales, though he appears at one time to have admired her. "The fire of his temper," she writes, "appeared in every look and gesture; which, being unhappily under the direction of a small understanding, was every day throwing him upon some indiscretion. He was naturally sincere, and his pride told him that he was above constraint; not reflecting that a high rank carries along with it a necessity of a more decent and regular behaviour than is expected from those who are not set in so conspicuous a light. He was so far from being of that opinion, that he looked on all the men and women he saw as creatures he might kick or kiss for his diversion." The Princess, in Lady Mary's opinion, "had that genius which qualified her for the government of a fool, and made her despicable in the eyes of all men of sense; I mean a low cunning, which gave her an inclination to cheat all the people she conversed with, and often cheated herself in the first place, by showing her the wrong side of her interest, not having understanding enough to observe that falsehood in conversation, like red on the face, should be used very seldom and very sparingly, or they destroy that interest and beauty they are intended to heighten."

In spite of the Princess's submission to her husband's will and professed devotion to his pleasures, she does not seem to have been pleased at his admiration for Lady Mary. In the famous Journal[1] she narrated how once, in a rapture, the Prince called his wife from the card-table to observe how becomingly Lady Mary was dressed. "Lady Mary always dresses well," replied the Princess dryly, and returned to her cards. Shortly after the Prince heard that Lady Mary had been at one of the King's select parties, and he not only grew cool, but taunted her with having gone over to the enemy's camp, and thenceforward she dressed becomingly in vain. An increase of graciousness on the part of the Princess made her amends.

Another anecdote is quoted by Lady Louisa from the Journal, which shows that the brilliant Lady Mary Wortley was considered an acquisition at the dull Court of George I. On a certain evening she had had a particular engagement, which made her anxious to leave the royal party early. She explained her reasons to the Duchess of Kendal, who passed them on to the King. But when she was about to take her leave, he began to battle the point, saying it was unfair to cheat him in such a manner, and many other fine things, in spite of which she contrived to escape. At the foot of the great stairs, however, she met Mr. Secretary Craggs,[1] who asked why she was leaving so early. She told him of her engagement, but dwelt with some complacency on the urgent manner in which the King had pressed her to stay. "Mr. Craggs made no remark; but when he had heard all, snatching her up in his arms as a nurse snatches a child, he ran full speed with her up-stairs, deposited her within the ante-chamber, kissed both her hands respectfully (still not saying a word) and vanished. The pages hastily threw open the inner doors, and before she had recovered her breath, she found herself again in the King's presence. 'Ah! *revoilà*,' cried he and the Duchess, and began thanking her for her obliging change of mind. The motto on all palace-gates is '*Hush*,' as Lady Mary very well knew. . . . But she was bewildered, fluttered, and entirely off her guard; so beginning giddily with, 'Oh, Lord, sir, I have been so frightened,' she told His Majesty the whole story exactly as she would have told it to anyone else. He had not done exclaiming, nor his Germans wondering, when again the doors flew open, and the attendants announced Mr. Secretary Craggs, who entered with as composed an air as if nothing had happened. '*Mais, comment donc*, Monsieur Craggs,' said the King, 'is it the custom of this country to carry fair ladies about like a sack of

---

[1] This was James Craggs the younger (1686–1721) son of the Postmaster-General. The young man was clever and good-looking, and a great favourite with George I. and Madame Platen, whose favour he had won during a visit to Hanover some time before. He was not "Mr. Secretary" at this time, but he was made Secretary at War in 1717, and Secretary of State a year later. Both he and his father were implicated in the South Sea scandals. It was said that Lady Mary and Mr. Craggs were the only English admitted to the King's evening parties, no very desirable privilege from all accounts.

wheat?' The minister, struck dumb by this unexpected attack, stood a minute or two, not knowing which way to look; then recovering his self-possession, answered with a low bow, 'There is nothing I would not do for your majesty's satisfaction.' This was coming off tolerably well; but he did not forgive the tell-tale culprit, in whose ear he muttered a bitter reproach, with a round oath to enforce it, 'which I durst not resent,' observes Lady Mary, 'for I had drawn it upon myself; and indeed, I was heartily vexed at my own imprudence.'"

It seems to have been in 1715 that Lady Mary made the acquaintance of Pope, who was winning fame and fortune with his translation of the *Iliad*, the first volume being published in that year.[1] He was introduced to her, no doubt, by one of her numerous literary friends. The earliest mention of her in the poet's correspondence occurs in a letter to Martha Blount, written in 1715. Miss Blount had asked him for news, which he professes to think unkind, since "it is not a sign two lovers are together, when they can be so impertinent as to inquire what the world does." Still, he will do his best to write her a letter of news, and after giving various items of gossip in the fashion of Dawkes and Dyer,[2] he observes: "I must stop here till further advices, which are expected from the Lady Mary Wortley this afternoon."

In a letter which probably belongs to 1715 or 1716, Jervas the painter[3] writes to Pope: "Lady Mary Wortley ordered me by express this morning, *cedente Gayo et ridente Fortescuvio*,[4] to send you a letter, or some other proper notice, to come to her on Thursday about five, which I suppose she meant in the evening."

[1] Curiously enough, the name of Wortley Montagu does not figure in the list of subscribers to the translation of the *Iliad* (perhaps it was too expensive), but that of the Duke of Kingston does.

[2] Well-known writers of public newsletters.

[3] Charles Jervas (1675?–1739), the friend of Pope, whose portrait he painted three times. He also tried to teach the poet drawing. He belonged to the literary set, and painted the portraits of Swift and Arbuthnot. Lady Mary, as appears from a later letter, was a warm admirer of his work.

[4] With the approval of Gay and the smile of Fortescue. This was William Fortescue, afterwards Master of the Rolls. He was the friend and (honorary) legal adviser of Pope, Gay, etc.

The poet was charmed and flattered by the friendship of the great lady, who was not only high-born and beautiful but witty and well-read, a most unusual combination. The feeling on his side went deeper than he at first realised, for it was not till long afterwards that he admitted, in the Epistle to Arbuthnot—

> "Once, and but once, his heedless youth was bit,
> And liked that dangerous thing, a female wit."

In those early days, however, the skies were clear, and neither the poet nor the lady had any prophetic warning of the storms that were to transform their friendship into the bitterest enmity. Stimulated by the encouragement of Pope and his brother wits, Lady Mary must have been working at this time upon her *Town Eclogues*, which somehow fell into the hands of Curll, who published them in 1716 (through his colleague Roberts) under the title of *Court Poems, by a Lady of Quality*. Only three, "The Basset-table," "The Drawing-room," and "The Toilet," were included in this volume, which was supposed to be "published faithfully as they were found in a pocket-book taken up in Westminster Hall, the last day of the Lord Winton's [1] Trial."[2]

When Curll announced his intention of printing the poems, Pope, so runs one version of the tale, sent for him to the Swan in Fleet Street, where he discussed the matter with him in the

---

[1] George, Lord Winton, who had taken part in the Jacobite rising of 1715. He was condemned to death, but contrived to escape, and spent the remainder of his days in Rome.

[2] In the Advertisement to this edition, Curll has a word or two to say concerning the author. "Upon reading them over at St. James' Coffee-house, they were attributed by the general voice to be the productions of a lady of quality. When I produced them at Button's, the poetical jury there brought in a different verdict; and the foreman strenuously insisted upon it that Mr. Gay was the man. . . . Not content with these two decisions, I was resolved to call in an umpire; and accordingly chose a gentleman of distinguished merit, who lives not far from Chelsea. [Probably Atterbury.] I sent him the papers, which he returned next day, with this answer—

'Sir,—Depend upon it, these lines could come from no other hand than the judicious translator of Homer.'

"Thus having impartially given the sentiments of the Town, I hope I may deserve thanks for the pains I have taken in endeavouring to find out the author of these valuable performances, and everybody is at liberty to bestow the laurel as they please."

presence of Lintot.[1] They drank wine together, and Curll was afterwards seized with sickness. He accused Pope of having poisoned him, and Pope admitted having given him an emetic "to save him from a beating," and afterwards published a pamphlet called *A Full and True Account of a Horrid and Barbarous Revenge by Poison on the Body of Edmund Curll*, which he thought worthy of being included among his prose works.[2]

Although the Eclogues are included in a manuscript volume of verses, which Lady Mary declared were all "wrote" by her own hand, without any assistance whatever, Pope told Spence in after years that "The Toilette" was almost wholly by Gay, only five or six lines being new set by the lady; while "The Basset-table" was published among Pope's own works in Warburton's edition. The truth seems to be that the verses were handed round in manuscript to be read and corrected by the writer's literary friends, and therefore they owe something to several different hands. Lady Mary was not unaware of the danger of this proceeding, for Richardson the painter relates that on one occasion she showed Pope a copy of her verses in which she intended to make some trifling alterations, but refused his help, saying, "No, Pope, no touching, for then whatever is good for anything will pass for yours, and the rest for mine."

It will be sufficient here to give a brief outline of the six Eclogues,[3] which are the best known of Lady Mary's poetical works. Their chief merit nowadays lies in the little intimate touches that describe the social types and manners of the period. The first, for Monday, is called "Roxana; or The Drawing-room." It takes the form of a lament by Roxana, the prudish Duchess of Roxburgh,[4] for the coldness and neglect with which she was treated by the Princess of Wales. To gain

---

[1] Pope's publisher.

[2] There are various versions of this mysterious incident, which may be altogether apocryphal.

[3] The other three were published by Horace Walpole through Dodsley in 1748.

[4] Mary, daughter of Lord Nottingham and widow of William, Marquess of Halifax. She married John, fifth Earl of Roxburgh, who was created Duke of Roxburgh in 1707. He was made Keeper of the Privy Seal of Scotland in 1714, and distinguished himself at Sheriffmuir in 1715.

the Princess's favour she had almost forgotten the duty of a prude, and had even missed her prayers to get her dressed by noon. In early youth, she explains,

> "Sermons I sought, and with a mien severe
> Censured my neighbours, and said daily prayer.
> Alas! how changed—with the same sermon-mien
> That once I prayed, the *What d'ye call't*[1] I've seen."

All this devotion proved useless, since Coquetilla's artifice prevailed. Coquetilla was the good-natured, easy-going Duchess of Shrewsbury, whose house had been made a trysting-place by Lady Mary and Mr. Wortley during their secret engagement. She had been appointed lady of the bed-chamber to the Princess in the autumn of 1714. Roxana continues—

> "That Coquetilla, whose deluding airs
> Corrupt our virgins, still our youth ensnares;
> So sunk her character, so lost her fame,
> Scarce visited before your highness came.
> Yet for the bed-chamber 'tis her you choose,
> When zeal and fame and virtue you refuse."

The lament concludes with the covert threat—

> "Despised Roxana, cease, and try to find
> Some other, since the Princess proves unkind:
> Perhaps it is not hard to find at Court
> If not a greater, a more firm support."

The Eclogue for Tuesday is called "St. James' Coffee-house," and takes the form of a dialogue between two beaux, Silliander and Patch, who like the classic shepherds rendered popular by Pope's and Phillips' Pastorals, boast of the favours that they both received from their respective mistresses. The lines are addressed to Lord Hervey—

> "Who so many favours hast received
> Wondrous to tell, and hard to be believed.
> Oh Hervey,[2] to my lays attention lend,
> Hear how two lovers boastingly contend;
> Like thee successful, such their bloomy youth,
> Renowned alike for gallantry and truth.

---

[1] Gay's successful farce, produced in 1715.
[2] Carr, eldest son of the Earl of Bristol.

> St. James' bell had tolled some wretches in
> (As tattered riding-hoods alone could sin),
> The happier sinners now their charms recruit,
> And to their manteaux their complexions suit;
> The opera queens had finished half their faces,
> And city dames already taken their places;
> Fops of all kinds to see the Lion run;[1]
> The beauties stay till the first act's begun,
> And beaux step home to put fresh linen on."

The only well-dressed youths left in the coffee-house at this hour were Patch and Silliander. Silliander boasts that he is the toast at a ladies' club, and that fair Miss Flippy, whose fan he had torn, condescended to use one that was his gift. Patch retorts—

> "Women are always ready to receive;
> 'Tis then a favour when the sex we give.
> A lady (but she is too great to name)
> Beauteous in person, spotless in her fame,
> With gentle strugglings let me force this ring;
> Another day may bring another thing."

Silliander, not to be outdone, exclaims—

> "I could say something—see this billet-doux—
> And as for presents—look upon my shoe—
> These buckles were not forced, nor half a theft,
> But a young countess fondly made the gift."

The contest continues in the same style, Patch being finally left triumphant over Silliander.

For Wednesday we have "The Tête-à-tête," in which Dancinda is wooed by the ardent Strephon. The lady, while admitting her love, remonstrates with Strephon because he had deceived her unpractised youth by swearing that no impious wishes shall offend her ear—

> "Nor ever shall my boldest hopes pretend
> Above the title of a tender friend."

But Strephon has now forgotten his platonic vows, and Dancinda complains—

> "I see too well what wishes you pursue;
> You would not only conquer but undo:

---

[1] In the opera of *Hydaspes*.

> You, cruel victor, weary of your flame,
> Would seek a cure in my eternal shame;
> And, not content my honour to subdue,
> Now strive to triumph o'er my virtue too."

The title of "The Tête-à-tête" is not altogether accurate, since when Dancinda has ceased her reproaches, Strephon took a pinch of snuff, and began—

> "'Madam, if love——' But he could say no more,
> For Mademoiselle came rapping at the door.
> The dangerous moments no adieus afford.
> 'Begone,' she cries, 'I'm sure I hear my lord.'
> The lover starts from his unfinished loves,
> To snatch his hat, and seek his scattered gloves:
> The sighing dame to meet her dear prepares,
> And Strephon, cursing, slips down the back stairs."

Thursday's Eclogue is "The Bassette-table," a dialogue between Smilinda and Cardelia, who sing, the first the misery of ill-luck in love, the second the greater wretchedness of ill-luck at cards. They lay the case before a friend, "Betty Loveit," and declare that

> "Impartial she shall say who suffers most,
> By *cards' ill-usage,* or by *lovers lost.*"

Betty adjures them to tell their griefs, and promises that attentive she will stay, though time is precious, and she wants her "tay." Cardelia stakes on her side an "equipage" or chatelaine

> "By Mathers wrought,
> With fifty guineas (a great penn'orth) bought.
> See on the tooth-pick Mars and Cupid strive,
> And both the struggling figures seem alive.
> Upon the bottom shines the queen's[1] bright face,
> A myrtle foliage round the thimble-case.
> Jove, Jove himself, does on the scissors shine,
> The metal and the workmanship divine."

---

[1] Anne is meant here, which looks as if this Eclogue had been written before the accession of George I.

Smilinda stakes a snuff-box, once the pledge of Sharper's love—

> "At Corticelli's[1] he the raffle won;
> Then first his passion was in public shown.
> Hazardia blushed, and turned her head aside,
> A rival's envy (all in vain) to hide.
> This snuff-box—on the hinge see brilliants shine—
> This snuff-box will I stake, the prize is mine."

Cardelia then describes her recent losses at bassette, which were aggravated by the fact that it was her own lord who drew the fatal card—

> "In complaisance I took the queen he gave,
> Though my own secret wish was for the knave.
> The knave won Sonica, which I had chose;
> And the next *pull*, my *septleva* I lose."

Then Smilinda relates the perfidy of Ombrelia, who stole away her lover, and adds—

> "She was my friend, I taught her first to spread
> Upon her sallow cheeks enlivening red.
> I introduced her to the park and plays,
> And by my interest Cosins[2] made her stays."

Betty Loveit very soon grows tired of this contention, and is afraid, moreover, that the tea will be too strong, so she breaks in upon the argument with a decision worthy of Solomon—

> "Attend, and yield to what I now decide;
> The equipage shall grace Smilinda's side:
> The snuff-box to Cardelia I decree.
> Now leave complaining, and begin your tea."[3]

In "The Toilette" (for Friday) the reader is introduced to a lady of forty-five named Lydia, who laments her vanished bloom and faithless lovers in the following lines:—

> "O youth! O, spring of life for ever lost!
> No more my name shall reign the fav'rite toast.
> On glass no more the diamond grave my name,
> And lines misspelt record my lover's flame.

---

[1] See the proposal for a meeting at Corticelli's in the love-letters, p. 85.

[2] Cosins, a "famous staymaker," mentioned in Pope's *Sober Advice from Horace*.

[3] Tea seems to have been indifferently pronounced "tee" and "tay," according to the exigencies of the rhyme.

> Nor shall side-boxes watch my wandering eyes,
> And, as they catch the glance, in rows arise
> With humble bows; nor white-gloved beaux encroach
> In crowds behind, to guard me to my coach."

She debates with herself what she shall do to pass the hateful day, and decides that as she is not yet old enough to appear at chapel among ancient matrons and gray religious maids—

> "Strait then I'll dress, and take my wonted range
> Through India shops to Motteux's,[1] or the Change,
> Where the tall jar erects its stately pride
> In antic shapes in China's azure dyed.
> There careless lies a rich brocade unrolled,
> Here shines a cabinet with burnished gold.
> But then, alas, I must be forced to pay,
> And bring no penn'orth, not a fan away."

In the midst of her dismal reverie, her maid appears, bandbox in hand, and flatters her mistress into good humour again—

> "'How well this ribbon's gloss becomes your face!'
> She cries in rapture; 'then so sweet a lace!
> How charmingly you look! so bright! so fair!
> 'Tis to your eyes the head-dress owes its air!'
> Straight Lydia smiled; the comb adjusts her locks;
> And at the play-house Harry keeps her box."

Saturday's Eclogue is called "The Small-pox," and describes the feelings of Flavia, an unfortunate beauty, when she looked in the glass after her recovery from the dread disease. Lady Mary was attacked by smallpox, in spite of her precautions against infection, some time in 1715, and it is supposed that she has expressed her own sensations through the mouth of her heroine. Not that her beauty was altogether destroyed, though it may have been blemished, since she was courted and admired for many years after this period, and could

[1] Peter Anthony Motteux (1660–1718), a rather remarkable Frenchman, who came to England as early as 1685. He wrote comedies and poems and edited the *Gentleman's Journal*, and (like Jervas) published a translation of *Don Quixote*. In 1712 he became an "East India merchant," but seems to have kept a retail shop in Leadenhall Street, where he sold china and tea. His poem on Tea was addressed to the *Spectator*, and a letter from him about his shop is printed in the issue for 30th January 1712. His death was mysterious, and he was commonly believed to have been murdered.

complain of no lack of lovers. But she lost her eyelashes, which made her fine eyes look too fierce and prominent. Her Flavia recalls the happier days when her beauty was undimmed, and sighs—

> "There was a time (ah! that I could forget!)
> When opera-tickets poured before my feet;
> And at the Ring where highest beauties shine,
> The earliest cherries of the spring were mine.
> Witness, O Lilly,[1] and thou, Motteux, tell
> How much japan these eyes have made ye sell."

Her only course, now that beauty is fled and lovers are no more, is to forsake mankind, and bid the world adieu—

> "Adieu, ye Parks—in some obscure recess,
> Where gentle streams will weep at my distress,
> Where no false friend will in my grief take part,
> And mourn my ruin with a joyful heart;
> There let me live in some deserted place,
> There hide in shades this lost inglorious face.
> Plays, operas, circles, I no more must view!
> My toilette, patches, all the world adieu!"

---

[1] Charles Lilly, who kept a perfumer's and fancy shop in Beaufort Buildings, Strand. He was one of the publishers of the *Tatler*.

CHAPTER XX

MONTAGU BACON

DURING the eighteen months which elapsed between the arrival of the Wortleys in town and their departure for the East, there are only two or three letters in Lady Mary's own hand, and these of no special importance. The principal topics of the day, however, are discussed in a series of interesting letters,[1] written by another member of the family, Montagu Bacon, to his cousin, James Montagu (son of the prodigal Charles), who was then M.P. for Camelford. Montagu Bacon was a first cousin of Mr. Wortley's, being the second son of Nicholas Bacon of Shrubland Hall, Coddenham, Suffolk, by Lady Catherine Montagu, youngest daughter of the first Earl of Sandwich. Montagu was born in 1688, and admitted a fellow-commoner of Trinity in 1704-5, but took no degree till 1734. When the Whigs returned to power, he was given a small sinecure, and having bad health he lived a life of leisure, frequently travelling abroad, or taking the waters at the Bath. When in London he seems to have shared chambers with one of the Onslows,[2] who was his most intimate friend. His correspondent James had been adopted by his uncle, Lord Crew, the time-serving Bishop of Durham,[3]

---

[1] Among the Sandon Papers.

[2] This may have been Arthur Onslow (1691-1768), a barrister, Whig M.P., and Speaker of the House of Commons from 1728 to 1761 ; or else Thomas, son of Sir Richard Onslow.

[3] Nathaniel Crew (1633-1722). His sister married the first Earl of Sandwich. His father was created Earl Crew of Stene in 1661 for the part he took in promoting the Restoration. Nathaniel was a favourite of the Duke of York's (James II.) because he connived at his Romish practices, and married him to Maria D'Este. He was made Bishop of Durham in 1674. When James came to the throne, he showered favours on Crew, but at the time of the Revolution the Bishop forsook his king, and tried to curry favour with the new Government. Although excepted from the general pardon of 1690, he was allowed to continue unmolested at Durham.

with whom he lived, and who left him the estate of Newbold Verdun, which afterwards came into the possession of Mr. Wortley.

Montagu Bacon was interested in politics, and also dabbled in literature, some notes by him on *Hudibras* and a *Dissertation on Burlesque Poetry* being published after his death by Zachary Grey. He prided himself on picking up news for his cousin, and his letters are written in a much more natural and spontaneous style than was common in the correspondence of the period. He possessed also the great merit (in a letter-writer) of indiscretion, and there is reason to believe that this quality got him into trouble at some period of his career.[1] The first letter of the series is dated from Paris, 27th April 1714. Montagu was then on his way to Bourbon for treatment for a distemper which his physicians agreed was "on the nerves."

"We are all in expectation,"[2] he writes, "of what your Parliament will do. They speak here very respectfully of the Queen, and laugh in their sleeves at the same time. All the English here are Tories, and most of them of the deepest dye. They use a freedom in their discourse and healths, as I am told, that seems strange to anybody that knows the Pretender is not actually on the throne. I keep company with but few of them, and those I do converse with are a little more modest. If you have occasion to mention this to anybody, don't name my name, for fear I should be looked on as a spy. Jacob Tonson[3] and I, who are the only Whigs in the town, get together to comfort one another, and bestow our best wishes upon our friends in England. My humble service to my uncles.—I am, my dear Cousin, your affec^{ate} cousin, MONTAGU BACON"

The next latter was written nearly a year later, on 14th

He succeeded to the title in 1697. Lincoln College benefited under his will, and the Creweian oration perpetuates his name.

[1] By mentioning public personages by their names in full, instead of disguising them under initials and nicknames, as was the more general habit in days when the post-office officials were spies in the service of the Government.

[2] From the unpublished MS.

[3] This was probably Jacob Tonson the younger.

February 1715. Montagu was back in London, but his cousin James had just gone to Paris.

"I[1] was very much surprised to hear from my uncle Wortley of the danger you were in at sea. No doubt it must be a little shocking to you. I can assure you it was no small uneasiness to us your friends here, tho' we heard at the same time of your escape; I hope you had better luck at your second setting out, and that this will find you safe at Paris. We have had very little news since you went. What has made most noise of late is a pamphlet published by Tom Burnet,[2] entitled *A Letter to my Lord Halifax*, showing the necessity of impeaching the last Ministry. It is a merry piece indeed, and what we are all ashamed of, especially the good Bishop, who says he would have given one thousand pounds rather than it should have come abroad.

"The parsons have grown more saucy than ever. One Dr. Bramstone, whose zeal for the cause made his name long ago be turned into brimstone by the punsters, preached a sermon at the Temple Church last Sunday, the most outrageous that ever was heard of. He described a good and a bad Prince, applied the one to the late King, and left his audience to fix the other. However, to direct them in their search, he told them they ought particularly to pray for this King, because his throne was beset with Heretics, Turks and Infidels; that one who denied the Divinity of Christ, meaning I suppose Dr. Clark,[3] was protected under the wings of the Lord's Anointed; that indeed people talk much of the King's

---

[1] From the unpublished MS.

[2] Third son of the Bishop of Salisbury. Tom Burnet, who was called to the Bar in 1715, was a wit and a profligate in his youth. Swift declared that he belonged to the Mohock gang that scared the town in 1712. He was imprisoned for one of his pamphlets by the Tories, but when the Whigs came into power he was given a consulship at Lisbon. Later he resumed his legal studies, became a Judge of the Court of Common Pleas, and was knighted. He wrote several books and pamphlets, and wrote a Memoir of his father, which was prefixed to the Bishop's *History of His Own Times*. He made fun of Pope's translation of *Homer*, and was satirised by the irritable poet.

[3] Dr. Samuel Clarke (1675–1729), the friend and disciple of Sir Isaac Newton, of whose *Optics* he published a Latin translation. He published his *Scripture Doctrine of the Trinity*, which led to his being accused of Arianism, in 1714.

wisdom and goodness, but we had seen nothing of it yet—it was all to come. And then he run out into his praises with which, after all the sedition he had vented before, he had the impudence to conclude. They say this was a concerted thing, and that there were a great many such sermons as these all over the town. Notwithstanding this the Parliament goes on as well as we could wish, and we do not doubt of a glorious majority; Spencer Compton[1] will be the man to speak. Lord Nottingham[2] has got a pension of three thousand and fifty pounds a year added to his place, which is fifteen hundred; this addition is to make up a round sum of five thousand a year. . . ."

A letter dated 17th March 1715 contains several interesting allusions to people and events of the day. James was still in Paris, but was expected back to take his seat in the new Parliament.

". . . I[3] hope we shall soon see you here now that the Parliament is so near, and the public affairs require your assistance. You will never be forgiven if you don't come and help us to hang my Lord Oxford,[4] etc. We have no news here, our eyes and thoughts are all turned towards foreign affairs, especially what is doing in your country, if you will give me leave to call it so at the present (not that we intend to part with you so easily). However as you are a Frenchman at this time, and I am an Englishman, I can't help representing to you that your lines, and camps, and fortresses give us a great deal of uneasiness. We are in hopes tho' that General Cadogan has accommodated matters at Vienna, and then we shall be the better able to deal with you. As

[1] A younger son of the third Earl of Northampton. He was Speaker of the House from 1715 to 1727, and three years later he was created Earl of Wilmington.

[2] Daniel Finch, second Earl of Nottingham (1647-1730), who succeeded his half-brother in 1729 as sixth Earl of Winchelsea. Though he had been regarded as the head of the High-Church Tories during the reign of Anne, he was named President of Council by George I. in 1714. A couple of years later he was dismissed for advocating leniency to the rebel peers.

[3] From the unpublished MS.

[4] Oxford stood his ground when Bolingbroke fled the country. It was popularly supposed that he would lose his head; but though imprisoned in the Tower till his trial (in 1717), the charges against him were dismissed. He was, however, excepted from the Act of Grace, and forbidden the Court.

to the assurances people with you seem to have of Mr. Bromley [1] being Speaker, I believe if they were to choose him he would, but I daresay he will never pass upon so honest a parliament as this is. Sir Richard Onslow [2] talked of standing, but the Court opposed it, and he was forced to give it over. Some people think it would have been as prudent in him not to have been so positive in his declarations, unless he would have been sure of carrying it through. There are two pieces of private news which I don't know whether you have heard; one that of my Lord Winchendon,[3] son to the Earl of Wharton, who has been drawn into a match with General Holme's daughter at the same time that my Lord was a'going to marry him to my Lord Godolphin's [4] daughter. As the town says, the marriage cannot be dissolved, but the General, who has played a very knavish part in this business, will feel the effect of it. The other story is of our Cousin Parkhurst, the doctor's elder brother, who has committed a most barbarous murder. The best that can be said for him is that he was certainly mad drunk with rack brandy; however, all the world can't save him from being hanged. We do what we can to comfort the poor doctor. This is all I can think of worth writing you. Marsh and Onslow both present their hearty services to you. Marsh and I join in a request to you, that you would do us the favour to buy each of us a couple of razors."

On 1st August 1715 Lady Mary's brother-in-law, Lord Mar, alias Bobbing John, had kissed hands as a loyal subject at the King's Levee, and on 2nd August had set out for the north in order to raise the Highlands for King James the

[1] William Bromley (1664–1732). He had been Speaker in 1710, and was one of the Secretaries of State 1713–14.

[2] Sir Richard Onslow (1654–1717). He had been Speaker of the House in 1708–10. He was Chancellor of the Exchequer 1714–15, and created Baron Onslow in 1716.

[3] Afterwards notorious as the wicked and witty Duke of Wharton. He was born in 1698, and therefore was only sixteen at this time. He seems to have left his wife in the country for the greater part of their married life, while he amused himself in town.

[4] The famous first Earl of Godolphin had died in 1712. The second Earl had three daughters: Henrietta, who married Thomas Pelham Holles, Duke of Newcastle; Marguerite, who died young; and Mary, who married (in 1740) the fourth Duke of Leeds.

Third. He invited the Jacobite gentlemen to a great hunting match, at which it was decided that the time was ripe for insurrection, and all present took an oath to be faithful to one another and to Lord Mar as the General of King James. The clans were called out, and it was firmly believed that if once Scotland were won, England would not long remain loyal to King George. The death of Louis XIV. on 1st September was a serious blow to the cause, but it was then too late for the Chiefs to retreat. In the West of England Lord Lansdowne and the Duke of Ormonde had been secretly fanning the flame of Jacobitism, which they hoped to kindle into open insurrection. In September Montagu Bacon was at Bath, where as a staunch Whig he found himself quite in the minority. He writes thence on the 14th—

"I[1] arrived here on Saturday night and began yesterday to take the waters. I don't know whether I shall settle into boarding or not, because there are two or three ordinaries of twelve or eighteenpence where a body may dine very well, and meet several of my acquaintance who are here at present. There is a great deal of company here, viz. Lord Plymouth,[2] Lord Windsor,[3] Lord Rochester,[4] Sir John Waters, Mr. Hampden,[5] and Ward,[6] the Lawyer. There are balls and plays and all sorts of playing. They do not forget their politics in the midst of their waters. The Tories are the majority, and have thought fit to bring up a custom of going without swords, which we Whigs, knowing ourselves to be outnumbered, can by no means submit to, so we are distinguished by that. I am lodged in the house with two or three very pretty ladies. One of them is a great acquaintance of my sisters, so you may be

---

[1] From the unpublished MS.
[2] Other, second Earl of Plymouth, of the second creation (1679–1727).
[3] Eldest son of Lord Plymouth. He was a child of eight at this time.
[4] Henry, second Earl of Rochester, and afterwards fourth Earl of Clarendon.
[5] Husband, probably, of the Mrs. Hampden whose house had been used as a meeting-place by Lady Mary and Mr. Wortley.
[6] This sounds like Sir Edward Ward, the famous Whig lawyer, who was Chief Baron of the Exchequer 1695–1714. But according to the biographical dictionaries he died in 1714, the year before the date of this letter. He left two sons, both of whom became distinguished lawyers.

sure I do not neglect the opportunity. Mr. Wycherley[1] and Mr. Pope are here too. . . ."

"To JAMES MONTAGU
Member of Parliament
At Mr. Warner's, Goldsmith
Near Temple Bar
London."

Bacon took the news of the rebellion in Scotland, as well as of the riots in the West, in the most light-hearted spirit imaginable. From his letters written at this time no one would think that Britain was suffering from invasion and civil war, or that King George's crown was tottering on his forehead. He writes again from Bath on 17th October—

"Since[2] you have stayed so long in town, I am something in hope I may meet you there when I come back, a fortnight more will make an end of my course; but hold! I had forgot there was a disturbance in Northumberland. You will be necessary to head some troops there, and I don't doubt but we shall see you return with more than one bough.[3] We were in great danger here before the soldiers came down, and really showed great magnanimity in daring to stay. I hope since the King has so many valliant friends, he will soon see his desire upon his enemies. I was very sorry to find our friend [Onslow] left out in the new Commission of the Treasury, and it is still a mystery to me. I am just going to the tavern with some honest officers, so have no time to say more."

By 27th November Bacon was back in London. The Battle of Sheriffmuir, at which Mar and his Highlanders encountered the Duke of Argyll and his English forces, took place on 13th November. Though Argyll defeated a part of the rebel army, his left wing was routed by the Highlanders.

---

[1] William Wycherley, the famous dramatist, was seventy-five at this time. His last play, *The Plain-Dealer*, had been produced as long before as 1674. He died in 1716, and was married for the second time only a few days before his death. Pope used to follow him about like a dog, and after the old man had departed, published his correspondence, which he so manipulated as to make it redound to his —the editor's—greater glory.

[2] From the unpublished MS.

[3] Alluding to the Jacobite custom of wearing green boughs on the hat.

The Duke lost touch with the main body of his army, and it was afterwards said of him that he had fulfilled the Christian precept of not letting his left hand know what his right was doing. On hearing at length of the disaster, he rallied his broken forces, but Mar gave orders for a retreat, and the Duke marched into Dunblane. The next morning the Duke appeared on the battlefield, but Mar retired to Perth with his followers. Both sides claimed a victory, and as a matter of fact each had at one time defeated the left wing of the other. Allusions to this battle and to other contemporary events will be found in the following letter, written by Montagu Bacon on 27th November :—

"We[1] have no news since my last, but what you have had by this time in the public papers, only general reflections severe enough upon the conduct of the Duke of Argyll. For a General to send a hue and cry after his left wing they say is perfectly new; indeed it seems strange to us that don't understand those matters, and we are encouraged to think so by those who do. However, perhaps it would be more discreet not to run upon him so much as they do, considering he is in a post where he may do us so much harm. They talk of sending General Cadogan into Scotland too, but how those two will set their horses together, and whether there be anything in the report, I can't tell.[2] Your friend Foster,[3] the General I mean, was found a'bed with a flagon of ale by him. 'Tis said he lays

[1] From the unpublished MS.
[2] General William Cadogan (1675–1726). He had been Quarter-Master General to Marlborough from 1701 to 1711, and had fought in all his great battles. He was sent north in 1715, and acted as second in command under Argyll. Montagu Bacon was perfectly correct in his suspicion that the two Generals would not work well together, for on 4th February 1716 Cadogan wrote to Marlborough: "The Duke of Argyll grows so intolerably uneasy that it is almost impossible to live with him; he is enraged at the success of this expedition, though he and his creatures attribute to themselves the honour of it." Cadogan was created Earl of Cadogan in 1718.
[3] An order had been issued for the arrest of six members of Parliament, among them Thomas Foster, M.P. for Northumberland, who had been the Old Pretender's General. A writ was also out against Lord Derwentwater. Rather than surrender, the "handful of North-country fox-hunters," as Scott called them, took the field with their followers, and marched to Rothbury, with Foster at their head. They were joined by Lord Kenmure, with the Earls of Nithsdale, Winton, and Carnwath. The march of the English rebels ended in the Battle of Preston, and the surrender or capture of most of their leaders.

his rebelling upon his friendship to the Duke of Ormonde. My Lord Derwentwater,[1] we fancy, had merited his pardon by something he had done before the King's troops came up. The Master of the Temple[2] preached a flaming sermon to the King and the Government last Sunday. Bentley, too, has published one against Popery, but it is so full of criticism and the usual barbarities of his style, that tho' there be good matter in it, it is very ill received. He falls upon both sides, so I suppose he does not expect he should make his court to any. It was thought before this Scotch battle that the Pretender was in Scotland, but we don't hear any more of it now. The Duke of Ormonde must be somewhere lurking about, for the news of his being castaway does not prove true. The Bishop of London[3] a little while ago received a letter telling him that he did very wrong in writing letters to his clergy, encouraging them in the interests of the king; that if he did it any more it should be the worse for him. This letter, tho' it looks like a banter, he sent gravely to the Secretary of State, and was laughed at for his pains. This is all I can pick up for you at present. Onslow has got well again; Marsh and I dine together to-day, where we shall not fail to remember you."

This letter is addressed to James Montagu at Lord Crew's house at Stene, near Brackley, Northamptonshire.

The Pretender landed at Peterhead on 22nd December. Argyll had been reinforced by Dutch and English troops, and General Cadogan had arrived with instructions to quicken the movements of the Duke, who, half-hearted in the cause, made excuses for lingering at Stirling. The march of the English army towards Perth began on 24th January, when the rebel leaders decided to retreat upon Montrose, much to the disgust

---

[1] James Radcliffe, third Earl of Derwentwater (1689–1716). He was not pardoned, but suffered death on the scaffold.

[2] Thomas Sherlock (1678–1761). He was appointed Master of the Temple in 1704. He earned a great reputation as a preacher, and was more than suspected of Jacobitism. He became successively Bishop of Bangor, Salisbury, and London.

[3] John Robinson (1650–1723). He had been chaplain to the British Embassy at the Swedish Court for twenty-five years. In 1710 he was made Bishop of Bristol, and in 1712 he was first English Plenipotentiary at the conference for the Peace of Utrecht. He was translated to the see of London in 1714.

of the Highland chieftains. Argyll and his vanguard entered Perth about twelve hours after the last of the rebels had quitted it. The Chevalier was urged by his followers to re-embark, and on 4th February it was contrived to get him on board a small French vessel, which carried him back to France in safety. His army, which had been kept in the dark about his intentions, gradually melted away, the common men returning to their homes, and the gentlemen escaping in boats to Orkney, and thence to the Continent. Ormonde had returned to France after his abortive attempt to raise an insurrection in the West of England, and Mar also escaped, though he left his wife in England.

The members of the University of Oxford had made little secret of their Jacobite sympathies. The Duke of Ormonde was their Chancellor, but on his flight and attainder, they conferred that dignity on his brother, the Earl of Arran.[1] Colonel Owen and several "broken officers" took refuge at Oxford, and were known to be busily engaged in seditious plots. But their designs were quashed by General Stanhope,[2] who sent down a company of dragoons, under General Pepper, with orders to arrest all suspected persons. The Vice-Chancellor and the heads of houses, alarmed at this proceeding, promised to give the General all the help in their power, and though Owen escaped, ten or twelve persons were taken. On 2nd December Montagu Bacon takes up the tale—

". . . I[3] will begin my letter with a piece of news which is as true as it is surprising. Mr. Lechmere[4] is turned out—

[1] Lord Charles Butler, created Earl of Arran in 1693. He married a daughter of Thomas, Lord Crew of Stene, and therefore was distantly connected with the Montagus.

[2] James Stanhope, created Earl Stanhope in 1718. This distinguished General and statesman was made Secretary of State for the southern division in 1714, and to him was entrusted the chief direction of the measures for crushing the rebellion of 1715.

[3] From the unpublished MS.

[4] Nicholas Lechmere (1675-1727). He was called to the Bar in 1798, made Solicitor-General 1714-18, Attorney-General 1718-20, and raised to the peerage as Baron Lechmere in 1721. He was commonly described by his contemporaries as an excellent lawyer, but with a temper "violent, proud, and impracticable." He was married to one of Lady Mary's friends, a daughter of Lord Carlisle. Lord Stanhope alludes to the fact that Lord Lechmere was temporarily disgraced in 1715, but says that he has been unable to discover the reason.

what may we not see! I suppose you won't be content with the bare matter of fact, but expect I should give you people's reflections upon it. All the light I can help you to in this matter is that some time ago, before the trial of the Oxford traitors, there was a squabble in Chancery between Sir J. Jekyll and him. Jekyll told him that he had an overbearing insolence; t'other answered, that Jeckyll had no merit, and was raised by accident. This passed on till the aforesaid trial, when Sir J., speaking on the evidence on the King's side, said some part of it would reflect very severely on the University of Oxford, and he was sorry to say it, but 'twas a shame that such use should be made of the influence which the care of his education gave them over the youth of the nation to pervert them from their allegiance to the King and the Government. Mr. Lechmere, when it came to his turn, said there was some part of the evidence indeed would bear hard upon some warm indiscreet people in the University of Oxford, but for reflections upon the University in general they were trifling and scandalous. The major part of that learned body were in the interest of the Government, and that these were only a few hot-headed fools. Such a ridiculous contradiction as this out of pure spite to the other, against his known opinion, has revolted everybody against him. I cannot affirm that this is the reason of his being turned out; I rather think not, for you must know there is to be a great change in the law. Lord Cowper [1] is obliged to lay down for his health, and my Lord Ch—— will certainly succeed him. The only contract the former has made for himself is that Spencer Compton shall have the certain reversion of the Master of the Rolls his place. 'Tis thought that Eyres [2] will be Chief Justice, Northey [3] is kept for the Chief Baron, when Dodd,[4] who cannot last long,

---

[1] William, first Earl Cowper. He was Lord Chancellor from 1714 to 1718, so that Bacon's information in this, as in certain other details, does not appear to have been correct.

[2] Possibly Sir Robert Eyre (1666–1735), Solicitor-General in 1708, and Lord Chief Baron in 1723.

[3] Sir Edward Northey (1652–1723). He had twice been Attorney-General—in 1701–7 and 1708–10.

[4] Sir Samuel Dodd (1652–1716). He was made Lord Chief Baron in 1714, and knighted in the same year.

dyes off. In all these changes, they say it was proposed that Lechmere should be Attorney, but it seems he thought that not sufficient, unless he could have the making of his friend Denton Solicitor, which at first sight is unreasonable, and perhaps his having flounced upon this occasion, as you know his custom is, may have brought this disgrace upon him. It is known that Walpole and he have been at variance some time, and the gentlemen that has the administration at present, resolved to show that they will not be bullied. If I should tell you that Steele is disgusted by their not making him Master of the Charterhouse, that Addison and he upon some private affairs betwixt them are fallen out, that the Duke of Argyle will shortly come up, I should tell you what is reported, but I don't know whether I should tell you truth. Indeed, as to the first, they have managed so as to let a very worthless fellow get into a very fine preferment. Steele's being married was the disqualification that was stuck at, but resolving to carry that through, they provided nobody besides who was qualified.

"We have every now and then a talk that the Pretender is in Scotland, but it vanishes again. However it is, the Tories are very uppish, and pretend they think as well of their affairs as ever. They say my Lord Mar has sent word that if they hang any of the rebels or the last Ministry, which is the same thing, he'll make reprisals out of those he has taken in Scotland, but the Government is not discouraged at this, and we believe will go briskly to work. 'Tis thought the first trial will be my Lord Lansdowne's,[1] because they are best provided for that, and the Tories will not be much concerned at it, being thoroughly nettled at him for seducing the West country gentlemen and then leaving them in the lurch at last. For he knew he was to be taken up a week before he was,

[1] George Granville (1667–1735), son of Bernard and grandson of Sir Bevil Granville. He was one of the batch of twelve peers created at once in December 1711, in order that the Government might carry through the negotiations for the Peace of Utrecht. He was committed to the Tower in 1715, because he was supposed to be concerned in a Jacobite plot for a rising in Cornwall. He was kept in the Tower till 1717, and then restored to liberty without a trial. In 1722 he went to Paris, and remained there for ten years. He was a poet in a "polite" way, and Pope professed to admire his verses.

and yet had not the courage to go down to head his friends. Those that come from Preston, say General Foster has declared that he had his Commission from the Duke of Ormonde two months after the Queen's death. I hear his brother's chambers were searched t'other day, but they found nothing of any consequence . . ."

The coolness between Addison and Steele at this time arose, it is believed, from Steele's jealousy of Addison's rapid advancement. When the Whigs came into power the author of *Cato* was made Secretary to the Regency. He married Lady Warwick the following year, and in 1717 was made Secretary of State. The author of *The Crisis*, who had suffered for his party spirit, was only made Governor of the Royal Company of Comedians at Covent Garden, and was refused the Mastership of the Charterhouse because it was against the rules to appoint a married man, whereas a grateful Government might have been expected to stretch a point in his favour.[1]

[1] Steele was knighted in this year, but he would probably have preferred some more substantial reward.

CHAPTER XXI

THE EMBASSY TO THE PORTE

EARLY in 1716 Mr. Wortley was appointed Ambassador to the Porte, with instructions to mediate, in concert with the representatives of other European powers, between the Imperialists and the Turks. Lady Mary, who, as we have seen, had long cherished a desire to travel, decided to accompany her husband, and to take her three-year-old boy with her. In April 1716 she was busy making preparations for the journey, all minor details, including the choice of a chaplain and of liveries for the servants, being left to her judgment. In the course of this month she wrote to Mr. Wortley, who was on a visit to Wharncliffe—

"By[1] your last I hope to see you in Town before this can get into Yorkshire. But, however, I will not forbear writing. The Bill was carried yesterday by more than 100.[2] Sir J. Jekyll spoke for it with great earnestness, and I hear extremely well. I have done nothing concerning Liveries, having not your particular directions about 'em. . . . I hear some people question your right of sitting in Parliament, and suspect there is somebody ready to supply your place. You know your own affairs better than I do, and I shall therefore say nothing. If you would have me bespeak Liveries, say whether you would have plain or laced. Any sort of lace will very considerably increase the Expense, but perhaps it may be necessary."

A week or two later she writes: "Dr. Clarke[3] has been spoke to, and excused himself from recommending a chaplain,

---

[1] From the unpublished MS.
[2] This may have been the Bill to strengthen the Protestant interest by enforcing the laws against Papists. This was passed on 17th April.
[3] The Dr. Samuel Clarke mentioned on p. 216.

as not being acquainted with many orthodox divines. . . . You say nothing positive about the liveries. Lord B.'s lace is silk, with very little silver in it but for twenty liveries comes to £110."

Among Lady Mary's correspondents [1] during the period of her husband's Embassy were her sister, Lady Mar, Lady Bristol, Lady Rich,[2] the Abbé Conti,[3] and Mr. Pope. Several of Pope's letters to her have also been published. These effusions are written in the artificial language of pseudo-gallantry, then commonly adopted by a man of the world when addressing a "fine woman," a fashion borrowed from France, and not improved in the transit. The poet was seeking "to naturalise a foreign style of letter-writing of which he did not understand the secret, and so fell into a manner

[1] The identity of Lady Mary's correspondents has often been a matter of guess-work with her editors. They have been guided by initials and the nature of the contents. In some cases the letters seem to have been merely exercises in com-position.

[2] Elizabeth, daughter of Colonel Griffith, Clark of the Green Board to Queen Anne. About 1710 she was married to Sir Robert Rich (1685–1768), second son of Sir Robert Rich, Bart., of Roos Hall, Suffolk. He had a distinguished military career, and also entered political life.

[3] The Abbé Conti (1677–1748) was born at Padua. He was educated for the priesthood, but though he took orders, he preferred the literary to the ecclesiastical life. He studied science and philosophy, and planned a treatise on the ancient and modern systems of philosophy, which was to include an exposition of his own theories. In order to prepare himself for this great work, he decided to travel, and visited Paris in 1713, where he established a friendship with Fontenelle and Male-branch. In 1715 the desire to see Newton took him to London, his travelling companion being a certain Monsieur Rémond, of whom more anon. Conti was well received by Newton, and also gained the favour of George 1., to whom he explained questions of mathematics and philosophy in French. In 1716 George invited Conti to accompany him to Hanover, and he remained there till 1717, when he returned with the Court to London. The following year he was back in Paris, where he remained eight years. He got into some trouble for communicating Newton's chronological system to his French friends, together with the philosopher's own explanations. In 1726, an asthma, which he had acquired in England, drove him to Italy, and he spent the last twenty-two years of his life between Venice and Padua. He wrote pamphlets on scientific subjects, tragedies (some of them imitated from Shakespeare), and a number of poems, among them translations of Pope, and *La Vita Conjugale di milady Montagu, tradotta in versi italiani*. This last was probably a translation of Lady Mary's Essay (written in French), *Sur la Maxime de M. de Rochefoucault: Qu'il y a des mariages commodes, mais point de délicieux*. Lady Mary must have made his acquaintance during her first visit to London in 1715.

which makes his correspondence with Lady Mary Wortley Montagu worthless, whether regarded as evidence of natural feeling, or as an example of literary composition. His model was Voiture, but the imitation of the *Samedis* degenerated into preciosity in France, and the case was even more hopeless in England, where the ladies had acquired little of the social influence which they afterwards exercised. No man ever excelled him in paying a compliment to a *man*; but when he seeks to make himself agreeable to a woman his style is detestable. . . . The greater portions of his letters to her [Lady Mary] are accordingly composed in the most wearisome complimentary style, with a complete absence of news, and an attempt to find a witty turn for every sentence." [1]

As has been seen by his already-quoted letter to Martha Blount, Pope considered it as little short of an insult to be asked by a woman-correspondent for "news." The secret of his style may be found in his observation that "The most politic way is to seem always better pleased than one can be —greater admirers, greater lovers, greater fools than we are. So shall we live comfortably with our families, quiet with our neighbours, favoured by our masters, happy with our mistresses."

The following letter from Pope to Lady Mary was written shortly before her departure, probably in July 1716:—

"So natural as I find it to me to neglect everybody else in your company, I am sensible I ought to do anything that might please you, and I fancied, upon recollection, our writing the letter you proposed was of that nature.[2] I therefore sat down to my part of it last night when I should have gone out of town. Whether or no, you will order me in recompense, to see you again, I leave to you; and yet if I thought I should not see you again, I would say some things here, which I could not to your person. For I would not have you die deceived in me, that is, go to Constantinople without knowing that I am,

[1] Courthope's *Life of Pope*.
[2] A joint letter, written by Pope and Lady Mary to Lady Rich and Sir Robert. Pope's share of it is printed in the unauthorised editions of his *Letters* (1735). It is headed "To a Lady, written on one column of a letter, while Lady M. writ to the lady's husband on the other." In this the poet says that their words are as a two-edged sword, "whereof Lady M. is the shining blade, and I only the handle."

to some degree of extravagance, as well as with the utmost reason, Madam, your most faithful and most obedient humble servant."

The new Ambassador, his family, and suite, set out on their long journey on the 1st of August. Lady Mary was almost always unfortunate in her experiences at sea, and the yacht in which the party sailed from Gravesend to Flushing came in for a storm. In a letter written from Rotterdam on 3rd August to her sister, Lady Mar, the new Ambassadress says that though the captain was frightened out of his wits, she suffered from neither fear nor sea-sickness. Like most novices in travelling, she was delighted with everything she saw, even at Rotterdam, and the comparisons she draws are none too favourable to her own countrymen and countrywomen. For example—

"The shops and warehouses are of a surprising neatness and magnificence, filled with an incredible quantity of fine merchandise, and so much cheaper than what we see in England, I have much ado to persuade myself that I am still so near it. Here is neither dirt nor beggary to be seen. One is not shocked with those loathsome cripples, so common in London, nor teased with the importunity of idle fellows and wenches, that choose to be nasty and idle. The common servants and little shopwomen here are more nicely clean than most of our ladies; and the great variety of neat dresses (every woman dressing her head after her own fashion) is an additional pleasure in seeing the town."

The journey through Holland and Germany to Vienna took about a month, the party arriving in the Imperial city on 3rd September. Lady Mary, who says that she fancied herself upon a party of pleasure the whole time, wrote to her friends from the principal stopping-places, Nimeguen, Cologne, Nuremberg, and Ratisbon. To Lady Bristol she sent a long letter from Nuremberg on 22nd August, in which she remarks that, after passing through a large part of Germany, "'Tis impossible not to observe the difference between the free towns and those under the government of absolute princes, as all the little sovereigns of Germany are. In the first there appears an air of commerce and plenty. The streets are well built and full of people, neatly and plainly dressed. The shops loaded with merchandise, and the commonalty clean and cheerful. In the other, a sort of shabby finery, a number of dirty people of quality tawdered out; narrow nasty streets out of repair, wretchedly thin of inhabitants, and above half of the common sort asking alms. . . . They have sumptuary laws in this town, which distinguish their rank by their dress, and prevent the excess which ruins so many other cities, and has a more agreeable effect to the eye of a stranger than our fashions. I think, after the Archbishop of Cambray [1] having declared for them, I need not be ashamed to own that I wish these laws were in force in other parts of the world."

The traveller was greatly impressed by the magnificence of the altars in the Roman Catholic churches, the rich images of the saints, and the jewelled *enchassures* of the relics, though she could not help coveting the pearls, diamonds, and rubies bestowed on the adornment of rotten teeth and dirty rags. She was somewhat consoled at Ratisbon, where she was allowed the privilege of touching the relics, by discovering that the jewels were most of them false, the original stones bestowed by kings and emperors having been converted in many instances into bits of coloured glass. It was at Ratisbon that she was shown a prodigious claw set in gold, and told that it was the claw of a griffin. " I could not forbear asking the reverend priest that showed it, whether the griffin was a saint? That question almost put him beside his gravity, but he answered, they only kept it as a curiosity."

Now began the correspondence with Pope, which he declared, on his side, should be regular and intimate, and show that honesty and sincerity of which he brags so loudly as to raise doubts of his good faith in the mind of every candid reader. In his first letter, addressed to Lady Mary at Vienna, which is dated 18th August, there is no news of the town, and no tidings of friends at home, such as a traveller might be supposed eager to hear. He tells her that his letters will be the most impartial representations of a free heart, and the truest copies of a very mean original, and she will be doing him an injustice if she looks upon anything he says as a compliment either to

[1] Fénelon.

her or himself. The freedom he will use in thus thinking aloud on paper may prove him a fool, but it will prove him one of the best sort of fools, the honest ones.

"You may easily imagine," he continues, "how desirous I must be of a correspondence with a person who had taught me long ago that it was as possible to esteem at first sight as to love; and who has since ruined for me all the conversation of one sex, and almost all the friendship of the other. I am but too sensible, through your means, that the company of men wants a certain softness to recommend it, and that of women wants everything else. . . . Books have lost their effect upon me; and I was convinced since I saw you, that there is something more powerful than philosophy, and since I heard you, that there is one alive wiser than all the sages. A plague of female wisdom! It makes a man ten times more uneasy than his own." He concludes by hoping that the person for whom she has left all the world may be so just as to prefer her to all the world; and that she may ever look upon him with the eyes of a first lover, and even with the unreasonable happy fondness of an inexperienced one."[1]

Only two days later he writes again, at almost equal length, declaring that if he were to write to his correspondent as often as he thought of her, it must be every day of his life. "I attend you in spirit through all your ways, I follow in books of travel through every stage, I wish for you and fear for you through whole folios. You make me shrink at the past dangers of dead travellers, and when I read of a delightful place or agreeable prospect, I hope it still exists to give you pleasure. . . . I communicated your letter to Mr. Congreve: he thinks of you, and talks of you as he ought; I mean as I do (for one always thinks that to be as it ought). We never meet but we lament over you; we pay a sort of weekly rite to your memory, where we strow flowers of rhetoric, and offer such libations to your name as it were a profaneness to call toasting. I must tell you too that the Duke of Buckingham[2]

---

[1] This conclusion is omitted from Pope's authorised edition of his *Correspondence*. Several of his letters to Lady Mary are slightly manipulated, so as to produce a greater effect of intimacy.

[2] John Sheffield, created Duke of Buckingham in 1703, the patron of Dryden and of

has been more than once your high priest, in performing the office of your praises; and upon the whole, I believe there are as few men who do not deplore your departure, as women that sincerely do. For you, who know how many of your sex want good sense, know also they must want generosity. . . . For my part, I hate a great many women for your sake, and undervalue all the rest. . . ."

Lady Mary replies to these extravagances in a style of good sense and good breeding, lightened by a vein of quiet humour. She was flattered by the attentions of a man whose genius she could not fail to recognise, but it is obvious that she took his compliments for what they were worth. On 14th September she replies from Vienna—

"Perhaps you'll laugh at me for thanking you gravely, for all the obliging concern you express for me. 'Tis certain that I may, if I please, take the fine things you say to me for wit and raillery, and it may be it would be taking them right. But I never in my life was half so disposed to believe you in earnest; and that distance which makes the continuation of your friendship improbable, has very much increased my faith in it, and I find that I have (as well as the rest of my sex), whatever face I set on't, a strong disposition to believe in miracles." With that the sensible woman dismisses her admirer's ardent protestations, and making none in return, proceeds to tell him of her having been on the preceding Sunday at the opera, which was given in the garden of the Favorita, the scenery and costumes costing the Emperor £30,000. No house could have held such large decorations, " but the ladies all sitting in the open air exposes them to great inconveniences, for there is but one canopy for the imperial family; and the first night it was represented, a shower of rain happening, the opera was broken off, and the company crowded away in such confusion, I was almost squeezed to death."

The lady has also been to a German comedy, based on the story of Amphitrion. She understood enough of the language to follow the greater part of the story, and declares she never

Pope. In the intervals of political affairs, he dabbled in literature, producing *An Essay on Poetry*, an adaptation of *Julius Cæsar*, and other forgotten works. He died in 1721, aged seventy-three.

laughed so much in her life, not at the wit, but at the absurdity of the treatment. The poet, however, had larded his play with such indecent expressions as would not be suffered from a mountebank by an English mob, though the Austrian nobility seemed very well pleased with their entertainment.

"I won't trouble you," she concludes, "with farewell compliments, which I think generally as impertinent as curtseys at leaving the room, when the visit has already been too long." It is a pity that Pope was incapable of taking this neatly-worded hint.

The traveller had already, on 8th September, written a long letter to Lady Mar, in which she gave her first impressions of Vienna. The town did not, she says, at all answer her ideas of it, being much smaller than she expected to find it, with narrow streets, and houses built so high that it seemed as if the builders had clapped one town on the top of another. The "flat" system, even then in vogue in Vienna, did not meet with her approval, for the apartments of the greatest ladies, and even of ministers of state, were divided only by a partition from those of a tailor or a shoemaker; while the great stone stairs were as common and dirty as the street. The furniture, however, in the abodes of the people of quality, by several of whom she had already been entertained, was surprisingly magnificent. With housewifely enthusiasm she enlarges upon the tapestry hangings, the prodigious looking-glasses in silver frames, the japan chairs and tables, the damask or velvet curtains, the vast jars of china, and the lustres of rock crystal.

More marvellous still was the lavish splendour of the dinners. "I have more than once been entertained," she writes, "with fifty dishes of meat, all served in silver, and well dressed; the dessert proportionable served in the finest china. But the variety and richness of their wines is what appears the most surprising. The constant way is, to lay a list of the names upon the plates of the guests, along with the napkins; and I have counted several times to the number of eighteen different sorts, all exquisite in their kinds. . . . I have not yet been at Court, being forced to stay for my gown, without which there is no waiting on the Empress;[1] though I am not

---

[1] Elizabeth Christina, daughter of the Duke of Brunswick.

without a great impatience to see a beauty that has been the admiration of so many different nations."

The next letter to Lady Mar, dated 14th September, gives an account of Lady Mary's first appearance at the Imperial Court, beginning with the following description, for the satisfaction of feminine curiosity, of the fashions that prevailed in Vienna at that time :—

"They build certain fabrics of gauze on their heads about a yard high, consisting of three or four stories, fortified with numberless yards of heavy ribbon. The foundation of this structure is a thing they call a *Bourle*, which is exactly of the same shape and kind, but about four times as big, as those rolls our prudent milkmaids make use of to fix their pails upon. This machine they cover with their own hair, which they mix with a great deal of false, it being a particular beauty to have their heads too large to go into a moderate tub. Their hair is prodigiously powdered to conceal the mixture, and set out with three or four rows of bodkins made of diamonds, pearls, red, green and yellow stones. . . . Their whalebone petticoats outdo ours by several yards' circumference, and cover some acres of ground."

Lady Mary thought the Austrian ladies had been too liberally endowed with natural ugliness, but she goes into raptures over the beauty and graciousness of the young Empress, her unsurpassable complexion and adorable smile, her mien of Juno, her air of Venus, and so forth. No men were admitted to the drawing-room, except the old grand-master, who came to announce the Emperor. Charles VI. spoke to Lady Mary "in a very obliging manner," but to none of the other ladies, and the whole ceremony struck her as strangely grave and formal.

The Ambassadress was also presented to the Empress mother,[1] a virtuous princess who was always performing extraordinary acts of penance, without having done anything to deserve them; and to the Empress Amelia,[2] widow of the Emperor Joseph, and her two daughters. At the palace of the Empress Amelia, outside the town, Lady Mary witnessed

[1] Widow of the Emperor Leopold I., and a princess of Palatine Newburgh.
[2] A daughter of John, Duke of Hanover.

a diversion which was quite new to her, though a common amusement at the Court. "On each side of the Empress was ranged a party of young ladies of quality, headed by the Archduchesses, all in full dress, and armed with fine light guns. At proper distances were placed three oval pictures to be shot at. . . . Near the Empress was a gilded trophy wreathed with flowers and made of little crooks, on which were hung rich Turkish handkerchiefs, tippets, ribbons, laces etc. for the small prizes. . . . All the men of quality at Vienna were spectators; but only the ladies had permission to shoot, and the Archduchess Amelia carried off the first prize. I was very well pleased with this entertainment, and I do not know but it might make as good a figure as the prize-shooting in the *Enid* [*sic*], if I could write as well as Virgil. This is the favourite pleasure of the Emperor, and there is rarely a week without some feat of this kind, which makes the young ladies skilful enough to defend a fort, and they laughed very much to see me afraid to handle a gun. . . ."

To Lady Rich, who was all agog to hear strange tales of "foreign parts," Lady Mary addressed a long letter on 20th September, in which she describes with much vivacity the social customs of the Viennese nobility. She was greatly struck by the institution of the *cicisbeo*, and even more by the vogue of the middle-aged woman.

"I can assure you," she writes, "that wrinkles, or a small stoop in the shoulders, nay, grey hair itself, is no objection to making new conquests. I know you cannot easily imagine a young fellow of five-and-twenty ogling my Lady Suff——[1] with passion, or pressing to lead the Countess of O——d [Oxford][2] from an opera. But such are the sights I see every day, and I don't perceive anybody surprised at them but myself. A woman, till five-and-thirty, is only looked upon as a raw girl, and can possibly make no noise in the world till about forty. I don't know what your ladyship may think about the matter; but 'tis a considerable comfort to me to

[1] This was probably Mary, widow of the fifth Earl of Suffolk, whom she had married as his second wife in 1791. She was a daughter of the Rev. Ambrose Upton, and had first been married to Sir John Maynard Knight.

[2] Sarah Middleton, second wife of Robert Harley, first Earl of Oxford.

know there is upon earth such a paradise for old women; and I am content to be insignificant at present, in the design of returning when I am fit to appear nowhere else."

With regard to "reputation," Lady Mary explains that the word has quite a different meaning in Vienna from that which it bears in England, while the two sects of coquettes and prudes into which London society is divided are unknown at Vienna. No woman dared appear coquette enough to encourage two lovers at a time, but none were such prudes as to pretend fidelity to their husbands, who were the best-natured set of people in the world. "In one word, 'tis the established custom for every lady to have two husbands, one that bears the name, and another that performs the duties. And these engagements are so well known, that it would be a down-right affront, and publicly resented, if you invited a woman of quality to dinner, without at the same time inviting her two attendants of lover and husband, between whom she always sits in state with great gravity. These sub-marriages generally last twenty years together, and the lady often commands the poor lover's estate even to the ruin of his family, though they are as seldom begun by passion as any other matches. . . . The first article of the treaty is establishing the pension, which remains to the lady, though the gallant should prove inconstant; and this chargeable point of honour I look upon as the real foundation of so many wonderful instances of constancy."

Lady Mary's Viennese acquaintances were much exercised because she showed no desire to follow the fashion in this respect, but they charitably excused her shortcomings on the ground that the length of her stay was so uncertain. One young Count, however, as he led her down to dinner, suggested that whether her stay were long or short, she ought to pass it agreeably, and to that end she should indulge in a little affair of the heart. She replied gravely that her heart did not engage so easily, and that she had no intention of parting with it. "'I see, madam' (said he, sighing), 'by the ill-nature of that answer, that I am not to hope for it, which is a great mortification to me that am charmed with you. But, however, I am still devoted to your service; and since I am not worthy of entertaining you myself, do me the honour of letting me know whom you like best among us, and I'll engage to manage the affair entirely to your satisfaction.' You may judge in what manner I should have received this compliment in my own country, but I was well enough acquainted with the way of this to know that he really intended me an obligation, and thanked him with a grave courtesy for his zeal to serve me, and only assured him that I had no occasion to make use of it."

CHAPTER XXII

JOURNEY TO THE EAST

INSTEAD of proceeding direct from Vienna to Constantinople, the Wortleys were obliged to retrace their steps as far as Hanover, George I. having temporarily returned to his beloved capital, much to the annoyance of his English ministers. Probably something had occurred at Vienna to make a further conference with the newly-appointed Ambassador desirable. There is an allusion to this change of plan in one of the letters, full of *fade* compliment and far-fetched wit, with which Pope continued to bombard his friend. The distance to which she is removed, he says, has so extended his notion of her value, that he begins to be impious on her account, and to wish that even slaughter, ruin, and desolation might interpose between her and a journey to Turkey.

"Is there no other expedient," he asks, "to return you and your infant in peace to the bosom of your country? I hear you are going to Hanover? Can there be no favourable planet at this juncture, or do you only come back so far to die twice? Is Eurydice once more snatched to the shades? If ever mortal had occasion to hate the king, it is I; for it is my particular misfortune to be almost the only innocent man whom he has made suffer, both by his government at home and his negotiations abroad."[1] In another letter of about the same period the poet expresses his envy of the opportunity Lady Mary enjoyed of conversing with Jean Baptiste Rousseau,[2]

[1] Pope, as a Catholic, had to pay double taxes. He implies that he suffered from the King's negotiations abroad because these involved the absence of Mr. Wortley and his wife.

[2] Jean Baptiste Rousseau (1670–1741) had been banished from France in 1712 on account of his scandalous libels against La Motte and others. In 1714 he was taken to Vienna by the Comte de Luc, and there introduced to Prince Eugene.

who, banished from France, was then living at Vienna under the protection of Prince Eugene. He alludes to the marriage of Addison to Lady Warwick, which took place on 2nd August 1716, and observes that the bridegroom has not had a single Epithalamium, and will be reduced, like a poorer and a better poet, Spenser, to make his own.

The Wortleys and their suite set out from Vienna on their long wintry journey about 14th November. Three days brought them to Prague, whence Lady Mary wrote a brief note to Lady Mar, describing the discomforts of travelling through the desert kingdom of Bohemia, where clean straw was not always to be had in the post-houses. Of Prague she formed but a poor opinion, the town being "old-built," and the picturesqueness of age and decay not being appreciated by the eighteenth century. With Dresden she was delighted, for the town was the "neatest" she had seen in Germany, and most of the houses were newly built.

"Perhaps," she remarks, "I am partial to a town where they profess the Protestant religion, but everything seemed to me with quite another air of politeness than I have found it in other places. Leipzig, where I am at present, is a town very considerable for its trade; and I take this opportunity of buying page's liveries, gold stuffs for myself, etc., all things of that kind being at least double the price at Vienna, partly because of the excessive customs, and partly the want of genius and industry in the people, who make no one sort of thing there, and the ladies are obliged to send even to Saxony for their shoes."

Arrived at Hanover, the Wortleys were allotted rooms in part of the Palace, which was a piece of good-fortune, for the town was so crowded with English that it was difficult to get a sorry room in a mean tavern. Lady Mary, in describing her impressions of the Court of Hanover, observes that she has now got into the region of beauty, since "all the women have literally rosy cheeks, snowy foreheads and bosoms, jet eye-brows and scarlet lips, to which they generally add coal-black hair. These perfections never leave them till the hour of their deaths, and have a very fine effect by candle-light; but I could wish they were handsome with a little more variety. They resemble one another as much as Mrs. Salmon's Court of Great Britain,[1] and are in as much danger of melting away by too near approaching the fire, which for that reason they carefully avoid."

The traveller in a letter to Lady Bristol (perhaps it was intended to be handed round in Court circles) assures her friend, without either flattery or partiality, that the young Prince Frederic (afterwards Prince of Wales) " has all the accomplishments that it is possible to have at his age, with an air of sprightliness and understanding, and something so very engaging and easy in his behaviour, that he needs not the advantage of his rank to appear charming. . . . I was surprised at the quickness and politeness that appeared in everything he said, joined to a person perfectly agreeable, and the fine fair hair of the Princess."

The weather remained bitterly cold, and the English visitors were astonished at the orange trees in the garden, and the ripe fruits—oranges, lemons, and ananas—that were served at the King's table, and seemed to come there by enchantment. On inquiry Lady Mary learnt that the Germans had brought their stoves to such perfection that they lengthened the summer as long as they pleased, giving to every plant the degree of heat it would receive from the sun in its native soil.

" The effect is very near the same; I am surprised we do not practise in England so useful an invention. This reflection naturally leads me to consider our obstinacy in shaking with cold six months in the year, rather than make use of stoves, which are certainly one of the greatest conveniences of life; and so far from spoiling a room, they add very much to the magnificence of it, when they are painted and gilt, as at Vienna, or at Dresden, where they are often in the shape of china jars, statues, or fine cabinets, so naturally represented they are not to be distinguished. If ever I return, in defiance of the fashion, you shall certainly see one."

The further instructions which Mr. Wortley received from the King at Hanover have been preserved among the family papers, and are as follows:—

[1] Mrs. Salmon was an eighteenth-century Madame Tussaud. Her waxwork show was long popular in London.

"ADDITIONAL [1] INSTRUCTIONS for our trusty and well-beloved EDWARD WORTLEY ESQ., whom we have appointed to be our Ambassador Extraordinary to the Grand Seigneur Given at our Court at Hanover, the   day of December 1716, in the 3rd year of our reign.

"GEORGE R.

"Whereas soon after the breaking out of the present war between the Ottoman Porte and the Venetians, it was intimated by the late Grand Vizier to Sir Robert Sutton,[2] our Ambassador Extraordinary, then residing at the Porte, that our mediation for composing the differences arisen and renewing the peace would be very acceptable to the Grand Seigneur; whereupon to show our hearty affection towards him, and to prevent the calamities of a war between Princes and States, with each of which we were in strict alliance, we immediately sent orders to our said Ambassador to offer our mediation for reconciling the differences which had happened, and to use his utmost endeavours for that purpose in the manner he should find would be most agreeable to the Porte. All which friendly offices of ours being afterwards rejected, and rendered ineffectual by the late Grand Vizier, the war was continued, and the Emperor of Germany having been engaged in it, the misfortunes which we endeavoured to prevent, have thereupon happened to the Ottoman Empire, with an immediate prospect of many more, unless both sides can at last be prevailed upon to lay aside their animosities, and hearken sincerely to the terms of a general peace.

"Notwithstanding, therefore, that our former kind offices of mediation were not regarded in the manner we had reason to expect, the event having shown the great benefits the Porte might have received from them, and that the difficulties of effecting a general peace are now rendered much greater by the advantageous situation of the Emperor's affairs, yet to manifest our sincere friendship for the Grand Seigneur, and continuing in the same disposition we formerly showed to put an end to a war among our allies, so destructive to the common good of mankind, you are hereby directed, upon any proper occasion, to represent to the Grand Seigneur and Grand

[1] From the unpublished MS.   [2] Afterwards Lord Lexington.

Vizier, that we have sent you as our Ambassador Extraordinary to reside at the Porte, with orders that whenever the Porte shall signify to you their desire of our mediation and good offices for a general peace, to use your best endeavours in our name for that purpose, with all the Princes and States engaged in the present war. That the same may be concluded in a manner the most conducing to the mutual advantage and satisfaction of all sides.

"You are from time to time to communicate what steps you shall make relating to this peace to the Ambassador of our good friends the States-General residing at the Porte, he being likewise ordered to act in concert with you upon that subject.

"(Signed) G. R."

It is unfortunate that the letters received by Lady Mary while abroad have not, with the exception of those from Pope, been preserved, and the poet, as has been seen, thought it almost an insult to send news to a lady. It is rather surprising that two such excellent letter-writers as Lady Mary and her cousin by marriage, Montagu Bacon, did not correspond, but we have it under her own hand that she had refused to keep up a correspondence with ten or twelve of her friends, who had offered to write to her regularly while she was abroad, though she believed that they would have written very entertaining letters. Bacon was still sending news from time to time to James Montagu at Durham, and from his letters some of the gossip of the day may be gleaned. On 11th October, having returned from France, he writes to his cousin—

". . . 'Tis[1] true I am come into England, and as true I have been going out of town ever since I came. I think now if I can possibly, to set out in a day or two, and how long my stay will be I can't tell. 'Tis not easy for a man so enamoured with the country as I am, to say when he shall get away. Besides I understand that you gentlemen of the House of Commons intend to cut us short in our funds, and then I don't know what charms there will be in an eleemosynary subsistence. I suppose you expect to hear something about my health. I can only say that I have brought home about as many ails as

[1] From the unpublished MS.

I carried out; I have one the less, indeed, because Onslow tells me your hearing is mended, but then the bankruptcy aforesaid of the public is a symptom that is more than fancy. Onslow has just come to town from Guildford, where they have been presenting their plum cake to the Prince. Cowper[1] is still on his honeymoon. There is no news here but of our new alliance with the French. The subjects of the Emperor begin to be very insolent, and the poor Dutch want somebody to hold their backs, for certainly never were people in this world so drained. I haven't room here to give you the political reflections I have picked up in my travels, but cannot help adding that all the Jacobites abroad cry out upon Bullingbrook [Bolingbroke] for the greatest villain that ever was born; I would have you congratulate your friends at Durham upon the sincerity of their former darling. . . ."

On 18th November he writes from Coddenham, the family home, where he is staying with his mother, who had married Mr. Gardeman, the vicar of the parish—

". . . I[2] have been here about a month, and I believe I shall stay till after Christmas at least, if not a great deal longer. In the letter that was lost by the villainy of my French servant (and I wish that had been the only penny he had robbed me of), I had acquainted you with the scheme I had proposed to myself of getting my place transferred to Dick Felton, who was to give me £70 or £75 a year, and let me have no further trouble about it; for to tell the truth, 'tis not worth confining myself for so small a matter: and I had rather live in the country for the rest of my life. . . .

"The disturbances you speak of at Newcastle, are very surprising. The Tories are as well disposed here, but I think not so insolent. They are a little arch upon me for being so small a gainer by a Government I am so zealous for; I wish my friends in the State would take this argument out of their mouths, because really it is the strongest they have against the present Administration. To be serious, I have been so plagued with disputes ever since I came down, that I, who wondered

---

[1] Lord Cowper was married, secondly, to Mary, daughter of John Clavering, Esq., of Chopwell, Durham.
[2] From the unpublished MS.

what had become of my Whiggism in London, am turned as great a party-man as ever. I knew I should have a brush with them at first, but now I see there is no good to be done, I leave them to the Civil Magistrates and retire to my studies, tho' it is as much as a Senator can do to have any patience with them. We have had pretty good weather, and that is a great happiness here, for the fresh air is all that we have to boast of. I suppose you have other diversions in so polite a place as Durham, but I believe you won't need the Sergeant-at-Arms to fetch you up. . . .

"All here give their services to you, that is to say my Mother and Mr. Gardeman. We drink our friends in the North every day after the Church and King."

To return to the Wortleys and their adventures. The visit to Hanover lasted barely a month, for we find the Ambassador and his family in Vienna again by the end of December. They were to set out on their journey to Constantinople in about three weeks' time, and meantime Lady Mary was taking part in the diversions of the Carnival, which seem to have begun early in January. Although it was then the very extremity of the winter, and the Danube was frozen over, the air was so dry and clear that colds were not half so common as in England.

"I am persuaded," writes Lady Mary to Lady Rich, "there cannot be a purer or more wholesome air than that of Vienna. The plenty and excellence of all sorts of provisions are greater here than in any place I ever was in, and it is not very expensive to keep a splendid table. It is really a pleasure to pass through the markets, and see the abundance of what we should think rarities, of fowls and venison, that are daily brought in from Hungary and Bohemia." In answer to a complaint from Lady Rich that her friend had told her no wonderful tales about her travels, an omission that she evidently attributed to laziness, Lady Mary replied that it was truth, not laziness, which prevented her from entertaining her correspondent with prodigies. "I might easily pick up wonders in every town I pass through, or tell you a long series of popish miracles; but I cannot fancy that there is anything new in letting you know that priests can lie, and mobs believe, all the world over."

The Viennese themselves are not described as particularly polite or agreeable, but as Vienna was inhabited by all nations, Lady Mary was able to form a little society of such as were completely to her own taste, and though the number was not very great, it would have been impossible, she says, to find, in any other city, so many reasonable agreeable persons. "We were almost always together," she tells her sister, "and you know I have ever been of opinion that a chosen conversation, composed of a few that one esteems, is the greatest happiness of life." Among her new friends was that dashing hero, Prince Eugene,[1] but she was as unwilling to talk of him at the Court of Vienna, as she would have been of Hercules at the Court of Omphale. Apparently he was engaged in some not too creditable intrigue, for she continues: "I don't know what comfort other people find in considering the weakness of great men (because it brings them nearer to their level), but 'tis always a mortification to me to observe that there is no perfection in humanity."

It was no doubt through Prince Eugene that Lady Mary made the acquaintance, envied by Pope, of Jean Baptiste Rousseau. "He passes here for a free-thinker," she writes, "and what is still worse in my esteem, for a man whose heart does not feel the encomiums he gives to virtue and honour in his poems. I like his odes mightily: they are much superior to the lyric productions of our English poets, few of whom have made any figure in that kind of poetry. I don't find that learned men abound here. There is indeed a prodigious number of alchymists at Vienna; the philosopher's stone is the great object of zeal and science, and those who have more reading and capacity than the vulgar, have transported their superstition (shall I call it?) or fanaticism from religion to chymistry. They believe in a new kind of transubstantiation, which is designed to make the laity as rich as the other kind has made the priesthood. . . . There is scarcely a man of opulence or fashion that has not an alchymist in his service;

---

[1] The famous General was fresh from his triumphs in the Turkish campaign. The battle of Peterwaradin, where, at the head of a small force, he had put the army of the Grand Vizier to flight, had taken place on 5th August 1716, and the capitulation of Temeswar on 13th October.

and even the Emperor is supposed to be no enemy to this folly in secret, though he has pretended to discourage it in publick."[1]

The Wortleys were repeatedly warned by their friends at Vienna of the dangers to be encountered in a mid-winter journey through Hungary, and they were urged to wait at least till the Danube was thawed, that they might travel by water. Lady Mary writes to Pope on 16th January that she is in all the hurry of preparing for her journey, and thinks she ought to bid adieu to all her friends with the same solemnity that she would use if about to mount a breach. " I am threatened at the same time," she remarks, " with being frozen to death, buried in the snow, and taken by Tartars, who ravage that part of Hungary I am to pass."

" For God's sake," exclaims the poet, " value yourself a little more; and don't give us cause to imagine that such extravagant virtue can exist anywhere else than in a romance." He implores his friend to write to him only of herself, for he cares nothing for shrines and relics, and had ten times rather go on pilgrimage to see her face than John the Baptist's head. Alluding to her journey, he continues—

" I expect to hear an exact account how, and at what places, you leave one article of faith after another, as you approach nearer to Turkey. Pray, how far are you gone already? Amidst the charms of high mass, and the ravishing trills of a Sunday opera, wha tthink you of the doctrine and discipline of the Church of England? Have you from your heart a reverence for Sternhold and Hopkins? How do your Christian virtues hold out in so long a voyage? . . . I doubt not I shall be told (when I come to follow you through those countries) in how pretty a manner you accommodated yourself to the customs of the true believers. At this town, they will say, she practised to sit on the sofa; at that village she learnt to fold the turban; here she was bathed and anointed, and there she parted with her black full-bottom.[2] At every

---

[1] Mr. Wortley's old friend, Dick Steele, had sunk a good deal of money, his own and other men's, in attempts to discover the philosopher's stone.

[2] Lady Mary had started on her journey from England in a black full-bottom wig. So at least her friends assured Pope, who was under the impression that she wore

Christian virtue you lost, and at every Christian habit you quitted, it will be decent for me to fetch a holy sigh; but still I shall follow you. . . . But if my fate be such that this body of mine (which is as ill-matched to my mind as any wife to any husband) be left behind in the journey, let the epitaph of Tibullus be set over it—

> 'Hic jacet immiti consumptus morte Tibullus,
> Messalam terra dum sequiturque mari.'
>
> (Here, stopt by hasty death, Alexis lies,
> Who crossed half Europe, led by Wortley's eyes.[1])"

The dangers of a winter journey through Hungary appear to have been much exaggerated, for on 30th January Lady Mary wrote to her sister from Peterwaradin that the whole party had suffered so little from the rigour of the weather, and had found everywhere such tolerable accommodation, that she could hardly help laughing at the recollection of all the frightful ideas given her by her Viennese friends. They had arrived at Buda-Pesth on 22nd January, having started on the 16th O.S. The whole country, once so flourishing, had been laid waste by the long wars between the Imperialists and the Turks. Buda itself was in ruins, no part of the town having been repaired since the siege, except the Castle and fortifications.

"I don't name to you," continues the writer, "the little villages, of which I can say nothing remarkable; but I'll assure you I have always found a warm stove, and great plenty, particularly of wild boar, venison and all kind of *gibier*. The few people that inhabit Hungary live easily enough. They have no money, but the woods and plains afford them provision in great abundance. They were ordered to give us all things necessary, even what horses we pleased to demand, *gratis*; but Mr. W. would not oppress the poor

a "bob." A good example of a lady's full-bottomed wig is seen in Kneller's portrait of Lady Mar, who is represented in riding costume.

[1] In this same year, in the first version of the Epistle to Jervas, Pope had written—

> "Thus Churchill's race shall other hearts surprise,
> And other Beauties envy Wortley's eyes."

After the quarrel, he changed the name to Worsley, there being a Lady Worsley who also had fine eyes.

country people by making use of this order, and always paid them the full worth of what we had from them. They were so surprised at this unexpected generosity, which they are very little used to, they always pressed upon us, at parting, a dozen fat pheasants, or something of that sort, for a present."

The Wortleys were then waiting at Peterwaradin till the negotiations were adjusted for their reception on the Turkish frontier. The next stopping place was Belgrade, which city the Ambassador and his suite entered in state, accompanied by an escort of three hundred horsemen. In a letter to Pope, dated 12th February, Lady Mary describes their journey, and how they passed over the battlefields of Carlowitz, where the scene of Prince Eugene's last great victory was still strewn with the carcases of men, horses, and camels. They had expected to proceed on their journey after only one night's delay, but were detained by the pasha till he received orders from Adrianople. The town was strongly garrisoned by turbulent janissaries, who had killed the last pasha, because he would not allow them to pillage the German frontiers. Lady Mary suffered from some uneasiness at finding herself in a town which was really under the rule of mutinous soldiery, but she consoled herself with the conversation of her host, Achmet Bey, a man of great learning, who had had the good sense to prefer an easy, secure life to all the dangerous honours of the Porte.

"He sups with us every night," she writes, "and drinks wine very freely. You cannot imagine how much he is delighted with the liberty of conversing with me. He has explained to me many pieces of Arabian poetry, which, I observed, are in numbers not unlike ours, generally alternate verse, and of a very musical sound. Their expressions of love are very passionate and lively. I am so much pleased with them, I really believe I should learn to read Arabic if I was to stay here a few months. . . . I pass for a great scholar with him, by relating to him some of the Persian tales, which I find are genuine. At first he believed I understood Persian. I have frequent disputes with him concerning the difference of our customs, particularly the confinement of women. He assures me there is nothing at all in it; only, says he, we have the advantage, that when our wives cheat us, nobody knows it."

This letter must have crossed one from Pope, dated 3rd February 1717, in which he professes to be almost distracted with anxiety about the safety of his friend. It is impossible, he declares, to write anything to divert her owing to the state in which her letter announcing her departure from Vienna has thrown him.

"Till now I had some small hopes in God and fortune; I waited for accidents, and had at least the faint comfort of a wish when I thought of you; I am now—I can't tell what—I won't tell what, for it would grieve you. This letter is a piece of madness which throws me after you in a distracted manner. I don't know which way to write, which way to send it, or if ever it will reach your hands. If it does, what can you infer from it, but what I am half afraid and half willing you should know,—how very much I was yours, how unfortunately well I knew you, and with what a miserable constancy I shall ever remember you?"

The Wortleys arrived safely at Adrianople on 13th March. The first letter extant written thence by the English Ambassadress is addressed to the Princess of Wales, and dated 1st April. This, a rather dull and stilted composition, gives some account of a seven days' journey through the forests of Servia, a naturally fertile country, the inhabitants of which had been ruined by the depredations of the janissaries. The unhappy peasants who had been hired to convey the Ambassador's baggage from Belgrade in twenty waggons, were sent back by the soldiery without any payment, though many of their horses had been killed or injured on the way. "The poor fellows came round the house weeping and tearing their hair and beards in the most pitiful manner, without getting anything but drubs from the insolent soldiery. I cannot express to your R. H. how much I was moved at this scene. I would have paid them the money out of my own pocket with all my heart; but it had been only giving so much to the aga, who would have taken it from them without any remorse."

Though the country was the finest in the world, and the

inhabitants seemed to enjoy perpetual spring, Lady Mary concludes with the reflection that "This climate, as happy as it seems, can never be preferred to England, with all its frosts and snows, while we are blessed with an easy government, under a king who makes his own happiness to consist in the liberty of his people, and chooses rather to be looked upon as their father than their master."

CHAPTER XXIII

EVENTS AT HOME

EVENTS in London, both literary and political, were still being faithfully chronicled by Montagu Bacon. On 12th February 1717 he wrote to his cousin, among other news, an interesting account of the famous quarrel between Pope and Cibber, which led twenty years later to Cibber's appearance as the hero of the new *Dunciad*, vice Theobald deposed. The mischief began with the failure of Gay's farce, *Three Hours after Marriage*, which was produced in 1717. The piece, in which both Pope and Arbuthnot [1] were supposed to have had a hand, deals with the humours of a pedantic physician, sketched from Dr. Woodward,[2] and two lovers of the Doctor's wife, who conceal themselves, the one inside a crocodile and the other inside a mummy. Cibber introduced into a revival of *The Rehearsal* a harmless "gag" to the effect that he had intended to bring on the two Kings of Brentford, one as a mummy and the other as a crocodile. This feeble joke proved too much for Pope's irritable vanity. He went behind the scenes, and abused the actor, who declared that he would repeat the gag as long as the play was acted.[3]

This is Cibber's version of the incident. Bacon's edition of the story is more explicit, and if true, shows that

---

[1] Dr. John Arbuthnot, the literary physician (1667–1735), who was intimate with all the wits, published *The History of John Bull* and contributed to the Memoirs of Martinus Scriblerus.

[2] Dr. John Woodward (1665–1728). He seems to have been a learned but eccentric man, who was as much interested in geology as in medicine. He published an *Essay towards a Natural History of the Earth*, in which he proved himself rather in advance of his times.

[3] See Cibber's published Letter to Pope.

the squabble led to actual violence between the actor and Gay.

"Nothing[1] has happened material since you went out of town. The plot[2] is where it was, horrid and bloody and barbarous, but our politicians can see no farther into it than they did some time ago. All that is known is, that the [Swedish] Envoy has bubbled the Tories of good sums of money, which he has applied to the use of his arrears, and all they can find in his letters amounts to no more than my friends have promised this, my friends have promised that, my friends have given this, my friends have given that, no persons named, so that the Ministry look like geese upon it. The Pretender is actually removed from Avignon; 'tis thought the Parliament will be still further prorogued; no news of any more Court quarrels. I heard a good thing yesterday, that Monteleoni, the Spanish Minister, said to M. Robethon[3] upon the King's first coming over. The latter went to the Prince's Levy like some others to catch a bow, and after he had almost tumbled himself over to make his reverence, the Prince passed by without taking any notice of him. Monteleoni, who saw this, came to him afterwards and told him M. Robethon, you have grown very fat. 'Fat,' says Robethon, 'I don't know that I have grown fat; the same clothes that I went out with, I have upon me still, and they are not too little.' 'Nay but,' says t'other, 'it must be so, for the Prince himself did not know you again.'

"To touch upon the polite world before I conclude, I don't know whether you heard before you went out of town, that *The Rehearsal* was revived, not having been acted before these ten years, and Cibber interlarded it with several things in ridicule of the last play, upon which Pope went up to him and told him he was a rascal, and if he were able he would cane him; that his friend Gay was a proper fellow, and that if

---

[1] From the unpublished MS.
[2] A fresh Jacobite plot.
[3] John Robethon, a Huguenot refugee. He had been employed by William III., and was now private secretary to George I. The King is said to have been considerably influenced by Robethon in his choice of ministers.

he went on in his sauciness, he might expect such a reception from him. The next night, Gay came accordingly, and treating him as Pope had done the night before, Cibber very fairly gave him a filip upon the nose, which made them both roar. The Guards came in and parted them, and carried away Gay, and so ended this poetical scuffle. . . .

"*P.S.*—All the great men of one cabal[1] and t'other met yesterday, as 'tis supposed by way of accommodation at Bothmar's[2] where they dined. Sir William Windham[3] was discharged of his bail this morning. I have heard a new edition of the story between Pope and Cibber. They say that Pope told Cibber that he was a great rascal, and that Cibber told him again that he was a little rascal, and of such a figure as not to raise the indignation of any *man*, but desired him to send Gay. *He*, he confessed, was a human creature; the rest of the story as before."

The next letters deal with the curious plot for a Swedish invasion of England, which was discovered and quashed at this time.

"*14th February* 1717

"Since[4] I writ my morning letter, great news is come to town. A ship that came in at Deal brings advice that she saw 32 sail of Swedish ships in the road near Yarmouth. This was all the buzz of the Court this morning; the Prince asked Admiral Aylmer,[5] how many men might be transported in such a fleet. He said he believed they might crowd in about 8,000. The Princess said, if 8,000 could come over in these 32 ships, what occasion was there for so many more ships at the Revolution, where there were not many more men. The

---

[1] The party that favoured the King, and the party that favoured the Prince of Wales.

[2] Baron Bothmar was one of the most influential of the Hanoverians. He had acted as agent in England for the Elector during the reign of Anne.

[3] Sir William Wyndham (1687-1740) had been Chancellor of the Exchequer 1713-14. He was a strong Jacobite, and an intimate friend of Bolingbroke's. He was arrested for complicity in the rising of 1715, but was allowed bail, and was never brought up for trial.

[4] From the unpublished MS.

[5] Matthew, Baron Aylmer (died in 1720). He was Commander-in-Chief of the fleet 1709-11 and 1714-20.

Duke of Shrewsbury[1] who stood by her, and you know was in that expedition, said they had a great many horse, ammunition and provisions, which perhaps these people had not brought over with them. This is the whole account of the matter, in which you see it is designed for our Suffolk Tories. I do not doubt the Swedes, Goths and Vandals, or any manner of barbarians will be welcome amongst them."

"14*th February* 1717

"I[2] can't help writing to you again to-day, having two or three scraps of news. They say that at the grand Assembly t'other day, as soon as they were met, Baron Bothmar began and told them very frankly, if they would not be friends, the King knew where to have another set of Ministers.[3] They all stared upon one another and promised to be very good friends for the future. When Sir William Windham was dismissed, the Attorney-General told the Court he had had orders from the King to indict that gentleman of a misprision of the same treason my Lord Lansdowne was indicted of, but a pardon being granted to the latter for the original treason, His Majesty out of the same gracious goodness was pleased to pass by the misprision. I had liked to have forgot one thing before I conclude, which is by what I understand, tho' the Court seemed to be angry at Toland's book,[4] there is good ground to apprehend that the limitations [under the Act of Settlement] will be taken off for Bothmar and Bernsdorff.[5]

"16*th February* 1717

"We[2] have heard nothing further of the ships I gave you an account of in my last. The Tories say that all their

[1] The Duke of Shrewsbury had taken a prominent part in bringing about the revolution of 1688. He had taken a considerable sum of money to Holland to aid William's enterprise, and had accompanied him to England in 1688. Therefore he would be an authority on the point in question.

[2] From the unpublished MS.

[3] The dissensions among the Whigs had already begun, which led to the removal of Townshend from the post of Secretary of State.

[4] John Toland (1670–1722), a theological and political pamphleteer. The offending pamphlet may have been one in which Toland advocates according civil and political rights to Jews in England (1714).

[5] In order that they might acquire lands, titles, etc.

terrible armament that put the Court into such a sweat, was only a fleet of colliers innocently making their way to Newcastle. However, this we may be certain of, the great people here would not have given so much credit to the testimony of a single ship, if they had not had repeated advices that such a thing is designed and ready to be put into execution. You see the Dutch have seized Baron Gortz [1] and his strong box, they are fitting out 20 men-of-war, and we as many as we can. The King of Prussia has sent the King word that he has undoubted intelligence that the King of Sweden is determined to prosecute this matter. Be it how it will, the Court is thoroughly alarmed. Embargos are laid upon all shipping whatsoever, there are to be four camps, General Cadogan with 14,000 men at Blackheath, Wills [2] at Newcastle, Carpenter [3] in Scotland, and another camp in the West, but I don't know who is to command it. Orders are sent to Chatham to make all possible expedition. . . ."

"*21st February* 1717

"I [4] am glad the little news I can pick up is acceptable to my Lord [the Bishop of Durham] and you. In such a nice juncture as this, where the news varies so much every day, I thought you would like to have frequent accounts. The papers relating to the Swedish affair were laid before the House yesterday, and though they will be printed in four or five days, perhaps it may not be unacceptable to give you some general notion of them.

"The whole was nothing but letters between Gyllenberg [5] and Gortz. Gortz, you must know, was supervisor of all the Swedish Ministers in this part of the world. It appears that the scheme was of Gyllenberg's hatching. The King of Sweden was to bring over 8,000 Foot and 4,000 Horsemen, of which 500 only were to be mounted, the remaining 3,500

---

[1] The Swedish Envoy at the Hague.
[2] Sir Charles Wills (1666–1741), a distinguished General. In concert with General Carpenter, he had defeated the rebels at Preston.
[3] General George Carpenter (1657–1732), Commander-in-Chief in Scotland. He was created Baron Carpenter in 1719.
[4] From the unpublished MS.
[5] The Swedish Minister at the Court of St. James.

to be provided with horses here. The time was to have been about the latter end of next month. Baron Gortz expresses his concern how the troops might be accommodated here, and whether there might not be some danger of their wanting provisions. To this the other answers, they would come into a plentiful country where they would find at least ten to one ready to assist them (such he imagines the affection to the present Government); that there were hopes of gaining over a very considerable man; and as a key to this, Baron Gortz asks him whether his hopes were not grounded upon the late ill-usage of that gentleman's brother-in-law. In short, it is plain they mean Mr. Walpole; to make it more plain, Gyllenberg adds there was no hopes of doing anything with Lord Sunderland[1] and Mr. Stanhope, they were so violent in their principles, and so obstinately bent to the interest of King George. In one of his letters he says, he can give him no further account of the matter at that time, because the chief manager was out of town, but would return in a week. 'Tis not expressed who the chief manager is; perhaps he may be gone to Bromley.[2]

" There is a passage in Baron Gortz' letters which will be very agreeable to every Englishman, and with which I shall conclude, that the Regent of France was inviolably attached to the present Government; no thoughts of his ever favouring the Pretender, and I think they say there is this expression, that that Prince would lay his hands at King George's feet, and you know he has just come from Paris. I have told you almost all that is material, and I hope enough to stay your stomach till the narrative comes out. It does not appear that any one potentate in Europe was privy to the expedition, or was to have aided it. The Tories say this is the fruit of the King seizing the Duchy of Bremen, but I suppose they know better what it is the fruit of. Some say the Council of Sweden disapproved of the design, but that Gortz and Gyllenberg had

[1] Charles Spencer, third Earl of Sunderland (1674–1722). He was made Lord Privy Seal in 1715, and succeeded in undermining the power of Townshend and Walpole, becoming first Lord of the Treasury in 1717. He was obliged to resign in favour of Walpole in 1721.

[2] Atterbury, Bishop of Rochester, afterwards exiled, is meant here. The Bishop's palace was at Bromley.

prevailed upon their master to undertake it. I had almost forgot to tell you that Gyllenberg in one place says, the chief business of the conspirators would be to increase the cry against the Standing Army. This is all I have heard hitherto; if I meet with anything more before night, I'll send you a postscript according to custom. . . . It is said the King of Sweden intended to conquer for himself and not for the Pretender."

"*23rd February* 1717

"The[1] same day I writ to you last, came out bad in Gyllenberg's letters. I find I was pretty right in most things, except only of the Regent of France, and I don't see anything to countenance that notion; on the contrary, I think there is one passage against it. You will wonder to see Walpole and Townshend so often in it, but I believe the mystery of that is that when Townshend was first turned out, they thought Lord Sunderland had made his interest by promising to engage the nation against Sweden in behalf of the King's hereditary territories; if so, that very thing would be a proper article to distress them upon, not knowing anything of that treasonable conspiracy. When Walpole's name was read, all the House looked upon him, and he, according to custom, laughed. There was a masquerade on Thursday last at the Haymarket Playhouse. By laying planks over the Pit, they made a continued floor as far as the Boxes, which were blocked up with pieces of fine painting, and two or three of the side Boxes left open for wine and other things. 'Twas of Heidegger's projecting, the price of tickets a guinea and a half, and not only so, but they that took them were obliged to subscribe too for the next. . . ."

This plot for a Swedish invasion had been recommended to Charles XII. by his favourite minister Baron Gortz, a Franconian by birth and an adventurer by fortune, who was at this time Swedish Envoy at the Hague. Thence he carried on a secret correspondence with the Swedish ministers in London and Paris, Count Gyllenberg and Baron Spaar. He was also in communication with the Pretender and the Duke

[1] From the unpublished MS.

of Ormonde. Money was supplied to the enterprise against England, both by Spain and by the Court of the Pretender. In October 1716 the English Government had clues to the conspiracy, but it was not till after the King's return from Hanover that decisive measures were taken. On 29th January Count Gyllenberg was arrested by General Wade, and his papers seized. These papers were published, and proved a complete justification of the high-handed action. Gortz, who was on his way to England, was arrested at Arnheim by an order of the States-General, obtained at the application of England. By way of reprisals, Charles ordered the arrest of Mr. Jackson, the British resident in Sweden. But by the mediation of the Regent, the affair was smoothed over. Gyllenborg was exchanged for Jackson, and Gortz was set at liberty in Holland.

In allusion to Bothmar and Bernsdorff,[1] the Hanoverian ministers, Lord Stanhope remarks that they " expected peerages and grants of lands, and were deeply offended at the limitations of the Act of Settlement. Robethon, the King's private secretary, whilst equally fond of money, was still more mischievous and meddling; he was of French extraction, and of broken fortunes: a prying, impertinent, venomous creature, for ever crawling in some slimy intrigue."

[1] The name is spelt in various ways—Bernsdorf, Bernstorf, etc.

CHAPTER XXIV

LETTERS FROM TURKEY

UNDER the date of Adrianople, 1st April 1717, there are no fewer than nine long letters in Lady Mary's hand. It is not likely that these were all written at one time, but they were probably compiled from the famous Diary, and sent off to various correspondents as opportunity offered for the conveyance of a package to England. They are marred to some extent by the inevitable "guide-bookishness," an excusable blemish in days when rather less was known of Turkey by the average Briton than is now known of Thibet.

The inquisitive Lady Rich was indulged with a highly-coloured account of a visit paid by Lady Mary to the famous hot baths at Sophia, one of the stopping places on the journey. The rooms were all paved with marble, and round the walls were two marble sofas, raised one above the other. On the first row, which was cushioned, sat the ladies, and on the second their slaves; but there was no distinction of rank shown by their dress, all being in a state of nature.

"There were many amongst them," she observes, "as exactly proportioned as ever any goddess was drawn by the pencil of Guido or Titian—and most of their skins shiningly white, only adorned by their beautiful hair divided into many tresses, hanging on their shoulders, braided either with pearl or ribbon, perfectly representing the figures of the Graces. I was here convinced of a reflection I had often made, that if it was the fashion to go naked, the face would be hardly observed. I perceived that the ladies with the finest skins and most delicate shapes had the greatest share of my admiration, though their faces were sometimes less beautiful than those of their companions. To tell you the truth, I had wickedness enough to wish secretly that Mr. Jervas [1] could have been there invisible." The ladies treated the traveller with the most " obliging civility," and though she wore her riding-dress, which must have appeared most peculiar to them (especially if it included her full-bottom wig) they repeated over and over again, " Uzelle, pék uzelle," which means " Charming—very charming." They were so anxious that she should undress and join them in the bath, that it was only by showing them her stays, which convinced them she was locked up in a box, that she could excuse herself from complying with their request.

In a letter to her sister, Lady Mary gives some account of the manners and customs of the Eastern ladies, and declares that the descriptions of all previous travellers must have been coloured by exemplary discretion or extreme stupidity. After describing the costume of the women, she continues : " You may guess how this disguises them, so that there is no distinguishing the great lady from her slave. 'Tis impossible for the most jealous husband to know his wife when he meets her, and no man dare follow a woman in the street. This perpetual masquerade gives them entire liberty of following their inclinations without danger of discovery. The most usual method of intrigue is, to send an appointment to the lover to meet the lady at a Jew's shop, which are as notoriously convenient as our Indian houses. . . . The great ladies seldom let their gallants know who they are, and it is so difficult to find it out, that they can very seldom guess at her name they have corresponded with above half a year together. You may easily imagine the number of faithful wives very small in a country where they have nothing to fear from a lover's indiscretion, since we see so many that have the courage to expose themselves to that in this world, and all the threatened punishment of the next, which is never preached to Turkish damsels."

With the married men the case was very different. No man of quality would use the liberty that allowed him four wives, nor would any woman of rank suffer it. If a man happened to be inconstant to his wife he kept the matter as private as he could, and it was not etiquette for a husband to

[1] The painter, who was a friend of Lady Mary's as well as of Pope's.

cast a favouring eye upon the slaves of the harem. Altogether, in spite of travellers' tales, Lady Mary considered the Turkish women the only free people in the empire.

In a letter to Pope there is a charming description of the Wortleys' new home at Adrianople and its surroundings. Lady Mary takes no notice of the poet's passionate outpourings, but writes as calmly and sensibly as if she were addressing her own sister. There is a little more polish in the composition, and to the "judicious translator of Homer" she is careful to dilate on the old Greek customs which still lingered among the country-people. The house stood on the banks of the Hebrus, in a garden full of tall cypresses, in the boughs of which the turtle-doves murmured soft nothings from morning till night. The environs of Adrianople were laid out in gardens which supplied the town with fruit and herbs. Here the people wiled away the long sunny days under the shady trees, the young shepherds weaving garlands for the lambs that lay at their feet while they sang to the music of reed instruments. It was clear that Theocritus was no writer of romances, since he had only given a plain image of everyday life among the peasants.

Lady Mary says that she has re-read Mr. Pope's *Homer* with an infinite pleasure, and found several little passages explained of which she had not before understood the full beauty. The ladies still passed their time at their looms surrounded by their maidens; the old men with their silver beards sat basking in the sun, like King Priam and his councillors, while the dances were the same that Diana danced on the banks of the Eurotas. "The great lady still leads the dance, and is followed by a group of young girls, who imitate her steps, and, if she sings, make up the chorus. The tunes are extremely gay and lively, yet with something in them wonderfully soft. The steps are varied according to the pleasure of her that leads the dance, but always in exact time, and infinitely more agreeable than any of our dances."

As seems inevitable in letters from the East, there are many descriptions in this correspondence of gorgeous processions and visits to harems, where the jewels and the dresses and furniture seem to have come out of the *Arabian Nights*. Lady Mary adopted the Turkish costume, at least for certain

LADY MARY WORTLEY MONTAGU
FROM A MINIATURE

occasions, visited the bazaars, and mixed to some degree in Turkish society. She dined with the Grand Vizier's lady, and visited the harem of his Lieutenant, but she was never admitted into the Seraglio of the Grand Seignior, though malicious rumour stated that she was once discovered therein, and that the handkerchief was thrown to her. More interesting than the highly-coloured pictures of Eastern interior, is the comparison that the traveller draws (in a letter to Lady Bristol) between the Turkish and British methods of government.

"The Government here," she writes, "is entirely in the hands of the army; and the Grand Seignior,[1] with all his absolute power, is as much a slave as any of his subjects, and trembles at a janissary's frown. Here is, indeed, a much greater appearance of subjection than among us. A minister of state is not spoken to but upon the knee; should a reflection be dropped in a coffee-house (for they have spies everywhere) the house would be razed to the ground, and the whole company put to the torture. No huzzaing mobs, senseless pamphlets, and tavern disputes about politics—

> 'A consequential ill that freedom draws;
> A bad effect—but from a noble cause.'

None of our harmless calling names! but when a minister here displeases the people, in three hours' time he is dragged even from his master's arms. They cut off his hands, head, and feet, and throw them before the palace gate, with all the respect in the world; while that Sultan (to whom they all profess an unlimited adoration) sits trembling in his apartment, and dare neither defend nor avenge his favourite. This is the blessed condition of the most absolute monarch upon earth, who owns no *law* but his *will*.

"I cannot help wishing, in the loyalty of my heart, that the Parliament would send hither a ship-load of your passive-obedient men, that they might see arbitrary government in its clearest, strongest light, where it is hard to judge whether the prince, people, or ministers are most miserable."

It is in the spring of 1717 that Lady Mary first mentions the system of ingrafting for the smallpox, which she was later

[1] Achmet III., who reigned from 1703 to 1730.

to introduce into England. In a letter addressed to " Mrs. S. C.," probably Sarah Chiswell, she writes—

"*A propos* of distempers, I am going to tell you a thing that I am sure will make you wish yourself here. The smallpox, so fatal, and so general among us, is here entirely harmless by the invention of ingrafting, which is the term they give it. There is a set of old women who make it their business to perform the operation every autumn, in the month of September, when the great heat is abated. People send to one another to know if any of their party has a mind to have the smallpox: they make parties for this purpose, and when they are met (commonly fifteen or sixteen together), the old woman comes with a nutshellful of the matter of the best sort of smallpox, and asks what veins you please to have opened. She immediately rips open that you offer her with a large needle (which gives you no more pain than a common scratch), and puts into the vein as much venom as can lie upon the head of her needle, and after binds up the little wound with a hollow bit of shell. . . . The children or young patients play together all the rest of the day, and are in perfect health till the eighth. Then the fever begins to seize them, and they keep their beds two days, very seldom three. They have rarely above twenty or thirty in their face, which never mark; and in eight days' time they are as well as before their illness. Where they are wounded there remain running sores during the distemper, which I don't doubt is a great relief to it. Every year thousands undergo this operation, and the French Ambassador says pleasantly that they take the smallpox here by way of diversion, as they take the waters in other countries. There is no example of anyone who has died in it; and you may believe that I am very well satisfied of the safety of the experiment, since I intend to try it on my dear little son.

" I am patriot enough to take pains to bring this useful invention into fashion in England; and I should not fail to write to some of our doctors very particularly about it, if I knew any one of them that I thought had virtue enough to destroy such a considerable branch of their revenue for the good of mankind. But that distemper is too beneficial to them not to expose to all their resentment the hardy wight that should undertake to put an end to it. Perhaps, if I live to return, I may, however, have courage to war with them."

In May the Wortleys removed to Constantinople, and took up their quarters in a palace at Pera. It was here that Lady Mary wrote a poem, descriptive of her surroundings, which she sent to her uncle, Mr. Fielding, who allowed copies to be taken. One of these found its way into Anthony Hammond's *Miscellany*, published in 1720. It opens with the lines—

> "Give me, great God! said I, a little farm,
> In summer shady, and in winter warm."

After a shivering allusion to the fact that

> "Our frozen isle now chilling winter binds,
> Deformed by rains, and rough with blasting winds,"

there is a glowing eulogy of the country where

> "The violet grows with odours blest,
> And blooms in more than Tyrian purple drest;
> The rich jonquils their golden beams display,
> And shine in glory's emulating day."

Then follows a long description of the view from her window, and a comparison between the past glory of Greece with the present pomp of their Eastern conquerors. But, concludes the poet, not all the temples and palaces, the woods and hanging gardens

> "So soothe my wishes or so charm my mind
> As this retreat secure from humankind.
> No knave's successful craft does spleen excite,
> No coxcomb's tawdry splendour shocks my sight,
> No mob-alarm awakes my female fear,
> No praise my mind, nor envy hurts my ear,
> Ev'n fame itself can hardly reach me here;
> Impertinence, with all her tattling train,
> Fair-sounding flattery's delicious bane;
> Censorious folly, noisy party-rage,
> The thousand tongues with which she must engage
> Who dares be virtuous in a vicious age."

But even perpetual sunshine and the *dolce far niente* of Oriental life may pall in time upon exiles from our "frozen isle," and there are unmistakable signs of home-sickness in a letter to Pope, written from Belgrade village, whither the Wortleys had gone to escape the heat of the city.

"To tell truth," writes her ladyship, "I am sometimes very weary of this singing and dancing and sunshine, and wish for the smoke and impertinences in which you toil, though I endeavour to persuade myself that I live in a more agreeable variety than you do, and that Monday setting of partridges—Tuesday, reading English—Wednesday, studying the Turkish language (in which by the way I am also very learned)—Thursday, classical authors—Friday, spent in writing—Saturday, at my needle—and Sunday, admitting of visitors and hearing music, is a better way of disposing of the week, than Monday, at the drawing-room—Tuesday, Lady Mohun's [1] —Wednesday, the opera—Thursday, the play—Friday, Mrs. Chetwynd's,[2] etc., a perpetual round of hearing the same scandal and seeing the same follies acted over and over, which here affect me no more than they do other dead people. . . ."

In the same month, June 1717, Pope sent his correspondent a long letter, accompanied by "the third volume of the *Iliad* [published 3rd June], and as many other things as fill a wooden box directed to Mr. Wortley. Among the rest you have all I am worth, that is, in my works. There are few things in them but what you have already seen, except the Epistle of Eloisa to Abelard, in which you will find one passage that I cannot tell whether to wish you should understand or not.[3]

[1] Elizabeth, daughter of Dr. Laurence, state physician to Queen Anne. She married first a Colonel Griffith, and afterwards became the second wife of the pugnacious Charles, fifth Baron Mohun, who was twice arraigned for murder. In 1712 he fought a duel with the Duke of Hamilton in Hyde Park, which proved fatal to both combatants.

[2] The Mrs. Chetwynd, already noticed, whose house was one of the suggested meeting-places for Lady Mary and her lover during their engagement.

[3] Pope alludes to the concluding lines—

"And sure if fate some future bard shall join
In sad similitude of griefs to mine,
Condemned whole years in absence to deplore,
And image charms he must behold no more;
Such if there be, who loves so long, so well,
Let him our sad, our tender story tell!
The well-sung woes will soothe my pensive ghost;
He best can paint them who can feel them most."

"For the news in London I'll sum it up short. We have masquerades at the theatre in the Haymarket of Mr. Heideker's [Heidegger's] institution; they are very frequent, yet the adventures are not so numerous but that of my Lady Mohun still makes the chief figure. Her marriage to young Mordaunt [1] and all its circumstances, I suppose you'll have from Lady Rich or Miss Griffith [Lady Mohun's daughter]. The political state is under great divisions, the parties of Walpole and Stanhope as violent as Whig and Tory.[2] The K[ing] and P[rince] continue two names; there is nothing like a coalition but at the masquerade; however, the Princess is a dissenter from it, and has a very small party in so unmodish a separation."

Travellers in out-of-the-way countries are apt to be embarrassed by commissions from friends at home who desire what they believe to be some extraordinary production of the strange country, with as much coolness as they would order a knick-knack from Paris. A lady—probably Lady Rich—sent Lady Mary a commission for a Greek slave and some balm of Mecca.

"I heartily beg your ladyship's pardon," replies the Ambassadress, "but I could not help laughing heartily at your letter, and the commissions you are pleased to favour me with. You desire me to buy you a Greek slave, who is mistress of a thousand good qualities. The Greeks are subjects, not slaves. Those who are to be bought in that manner are either such as are taken in war, or stolen by the Tartars from Russia, Circassia or Georgia, and are such miserable, awkward, poor wretches, you would not think any of them worthy to be your housemaids. . . . The fine slaves that wait upon the great ladies, or serve the pleasures of great men, are all bought at the age of eight or nine years old, and educated with great care, to accomplish them in singing, dancing, embroidery, etc. They are commonly Circassians, and their patron never sells them, except it is as a punishment for some very great fault. If ever they grow weary of them, they either present them to a friend, or give them their freedom. Those that are exposed

---

[1] Lady Mohun took for her third husband Charles Mordaunt, a nephew of the Earl of Peterborough. He was much younger than herself.
[2] Walpole resigned on 10th April 1717.

to sale at the markets are always either guilty of some crime, or so entirely worthless that they are of no use at all."

The balm of Mecca was not so easily got as was generally supposed, and Lady Mary does not advise her correspondent to make use of it, and cannot understand how it comes to have such universal applause. " I have had a present," she continues, " of a small quantity (which, I'll assure you, is very valuable) of the best sort, and with great joy applied it to my face, expecting some wonderful change to my advantage. The next morning the change indeed was wonderful; my face was swelled to a very extraordinary size, and all over as red as Lady B.'s. It remained in this lamentable condition three days, during which you may be sure I passed my time very ill. I believed it would never be otherways; and to add to my mortification, Mr. W—— [Wortley] reproached my indiscretion without ceasing. However, my face is since *in statu quo*; nay, I am told by the ladies here, that it is much mended by the operation, which I confess I cannot perceive in my looking-glass. Indeed, if one were to form an opinion of this balm from their faces, one should think very well of it. They all make use of it, and have the loveliest bloom in the world. For my part, I never intend to endure the pain of it again; let my complexion take its natural course, and decay in its own due time." [1]

Towards the end of August the Imperialist troops under Prince Eugene captured Belgrade, having completely routed the Turks. The consternation in Constantinople was indescribable, and the Sultan, fearing a revolution, took the precaution to have several persons strangled who were objects of his suspicion. He also ordered his treasurer to advance some months' pay to the janissaries, in spite of the fact that they had behaved very badly during the campaign. In September Mr. Wortley paid a visit to the Sultan's camp at Philipopoli, as recorded in the *Weekly Journal* for 21st December—

"The Lord Ambassador Wortley Montagu having received an invitation from the Porte to come to the Grand Signior's camp at Philipopoli, set out from Constantinople the 12th of

[1] If Pope and Horace Walpole may be believed, Lady Mary did not adhere to this resolution.

September, and arrived at the said camp the 21st of September, where, according to the custom of Ambassadors, he made his public entry with a great ceremony and magnificence. The next day the Grand Vizier arrived in the camp from Nizza, ordered his Excellency's tents to be pitched near his own, and a chamber of janissaries was ordered to serve and guard him." There is no mention of Lady Mary, so it must be supposed that she remained behind at Pera. This is the more likely, as she was expecting her confinement early in the new year.

CHAPTER XXV

THE RECALL

MEANWHILE, the home Government seems to have been growing dissatisfied with Mr. Wortley's conduct of affairs in the East, and while the Ambassador was enjoying his grand reception at the Sultan's camp, his recall had already been sent out. Thus, on 13th September, the following notice was issued to the Lord Onslow and the members of the Turkey Company, who were specially affected by the change, Mr. Wortley acting as Consul-General to the Levant:—

" Right [1] trusty and well-beloved Councillor, and trusty and well-beloved, we greet you well. Having taken into our Royal consideration, that the face of affairs in the Ottoman Empire is very much changed since our trusty and well-beloved Edward Wortley Montagu, Esq., was appointed Ambassador to the Porte, and thinking it requisite, that in order to facilitate a peace between the Emperor and the Turks, a person of long experience in the affairs of Turkey, in conjunction with some other person, who is well acquainted with the inclinations and disposition of the Court at Vienna should be employed in negotiating and forwarding the said peace; we do hereby think fit to acquaint you that we have accordingly made choice of our trusty and well-beloved Sir Robert Sutton, our late Ambassador in Ordinary at the Porte, together with our trusty and well-beloved Abraham Stanyan,[2] Esq., our present Envoy Extraordinary at Vienna, to act on our part at that negotiation, and likewise that we think it proper the said Abraham

---

[1] From the unpublished MS.
[2] Abraham Stanyan (? 1669–1732). He was Envoy Extraordinary to the Court of Vienna 1716–17, and Ambassador Extraordinary to the Porte 1719–20.

Stanyan should be invested with the character of our Ambassador in Ordinary at the Porte, whom we accordingly recommend to you as a person very fitly qualified for your service: We are so thoroughly satisfied with the conduct of our said Edward Wortley Montagu, as our Ambassador, that we should not have named another to succeed him so soon in that employment, had not the present conjuncture of affairs seemed to require such a disposition as is above mentioned, which we look upon as the best expedient to advance not only our own service, but likewise the benefit and advantage of the Turkey Company: wherefore we give you this notice of our Royal intention in that behalf, that you may govern yourselves accordingly: And so we bid you heartily farewell.

"Given at our Court at Hampton Court, the 13th day of October, 1717, in the fourth year of our reign.—By His Majesty's command, J. ADDISON"

Addison had this year been appointed the principal Secretary of State, in spite of his inability to speak in Parliament, and the difficulty he found in framing a despatch to suit his fastidious literary taste. When, as secretary to the Regency, he had been ordered to send to Hanover the announcement of Queen Anne's death, he found it so impossible to express himself in accordance with his own notions of the importance of the event, that the lords of the Regency were obliged to employ one of the clerks, Mr. Southwell, who boasted ever afterwards of his superiority to Addison.

The Secretary wrote on 28th September a friendly letter to his old friend to prepare him for the impending blow, and, as will be seen from the following extracts, he put as good a face on the matter as possible, and held out hopes of greater honours at home, honours which were never bestowed:—

"DEAR SIR,—Having been confined to my chamber for some time by a dangerous fit of sickness, I find, upon my coming abroad, that some things have passed which I think myself obliged to communicate to you, not as the Secretary to the Ambassador, but as an humble servant to his friend. . . . Our great men are of opinion, that upon your being possessed [of the reversion of certain places] (which they look upon as sure and sudden) it would be agreeable to your inclinations, as well as for the King's service, which you are so able to promote in Parliament, rather to return to your own country than to live at Constantinople. For this reason, they have thought of relieving you by Mr. Stanyan, who is now at the Imperial Court, and of joining Sir Robert Sutton with him in the mediation of a peace between the Emperor and the Turks. I need not suggest to you that Mr. Stanyan is in great favour at Vienna, and how necessary it is to humour that Court in the present juncture. Besides, as it would have been for your honour to have acted as sole mediator in such a negotiation, perhaps it would not have been so agreeable to you to act only in commission. This was suggested to me the other day by one of our first ministers, who told me that he believed Sir R. Sutton's being joined in a mediation, which was carried on by my Lord Paget [1] singly, would be shocking to you, but that they could be more free with a person of Mr. Stanyan's quality. I find by his Majesty's way of speaking of you, that you are much in his favour and esteem, and I fancy you would find your ease and advantage more in being nearer his person than at the distance you are from him at present. I omit no opportunity of doing you justice where I think it is for your service, and wish I could know your mind as to these several particulars by a more speedy and certain conveyance, that I might act accordingly to the utmost of my powers. Madame Kilmanseck [2] and my Lady Hervey desire me to forward the enclosed to my Lady Mary Wortley, to whom I beg you will deliver them with my most humble regards."

The news of Mr. Wortley's recall soon became public, since Pope in a letter to Lady Mary, written some time in October, says—

"I am told that fortune (more just to us than your virtue) will restore the most precious thing it ever robbed us of." Her

---

[1] William, sixth Baron Paget. He was Ambassador to the Porte 1693–1702.

[2] Or Kilmannsegg, mistress to George I. Lady Mary said she had never been a beauty, and was past forty when she came to England, but that she had an unusual vivacity in conversation for a German.

coming, he declares, will be the only equivalent the world affords for Pitt's diamond,[1] and if only they may have her from the East, the sun is at their service. He professes to think seriously of meeting her in Italy, and travelling back with her. "Allow me but to sneak after you in your train, to fill my pockets with coins, or to lug an old busto behind you, and I shall be proud beyond expression. Let people think, if they will, that I did all this for the pleasure of treading on classic ground; I would whisper other reasons in your ear."

Like Lady Rich, he desires her to bring him a fair Circassian, and she is to look in the glass to choose him one he may like. But the colours must be less vivid, the eyes less bright, for else, instead of being her master, he will be her slave. He assures her that her Eclogues are enclosed in a monument of red Turkey, written in his fairest hand, and the gilded leaves opened with no less veneration than the pages of the sibyls. Finally, she is to believe that Mr. Congreve remembers her, even in the gout. "Dr. Garth makes epigrams in prose when he speaks of you. Sir Robert Rich's lady loves you, though Sir Robert admires you. Mr. Craggs commemorates you with honour; the Duke of Buckingham with praise; I myself with something more. When people speak most highly of you, I think them sparing; when I try myself to speak of you, I think I'm cold and stupid. I think my letters have nothing in 'em, but I am sure my heart has so much, that I am vexed to find no better name for your friend and admirer than YOUR FRIEND AND ADMIRER"

In January 1718 Lady Mary was busy with preparations for the increase in her family, which, as she says in a letter to Mrs. Thistlethwaite (4th January), she is expecting daily. She is somewhat consoled for her uneasy situation by the glory that accrues to her from it, and a reflection on the contempt she would otherwise fall under. In Turkey, she explains, it is more despicable to be married, and not have children, than it is to have children before marriage in England. Most of her acquaintance who have been married ten years have twelve

[1] Bought by the Regent in June 1717 for the young King of France.

18

or thirteen children, while the old ones boast of having had twenty-five or thirty apiece. When asked how they propose to provide for such a flock, they reply that the plague will certainly kill half of them. Not to bear children was regarded as a sign of old age, while the exemption they seemed to enjoy from the curse of Eve probably encouraged the desire to prove their youth. But Lady Mary is afraid she will prove an Englishwoman in that respect, as she does in her dread of plague and fire, two evils very little feared by the natives.

On 10th March Lady Mary writes to inform Lady Mar that she is the mother of a little daughter, already five weeks old. "I don't mention this," she observes, "as one of my diverting adventures; tho' I must own it is not half so mortifying here as in England, there being as much difference as there is between a little cold in the head, which sometimes happens here, and the consumptive coughs so common in London. Nobody keeps their house a month for lying in, and I am not so fond of any of our customs as to retain them when they are not necessary."

Thereupon follows a long description of a visit that the Ambassadress had recently paid to the widow of the late Sultan Mustapha, a lady whose costume on this occasion was worth at least a hundred thousand pounds, her diamonds being as large as hazel-nuts, one of her emeralds as big as a turkey's egg (!), and her four strings of pearls enough to make four necklaces of the size of the Duchess of Marlborough's. The dinner consisted of fifty dishes of meat, each served separately, which the guest not unnaturally found rather tedious, even though the knives were of gold with hafts set with diamonds, and the cloth and napkins of the finest tiffany, embroidered with silks and gold in natural flowers. The writer is afraid that her sister will think she is copying from the *Arabian Nights*, but she explains that those tales were written by an author of that country, and (excepting the enchantments) were still realistic representations of the manners and customs.

It is pleasant to know that Lady Rich, after several vain attempts, at length sent a commission that her friend was able to carry out. This was one of the Turkish love-letters, expressed symbolically in a pearl, a clove, a straw, a hair, a grape, and other small articles, each with its own poetical meaning, so that it was possible to send letters of passion, friendship, civility, and even news without ever inking the fingers. Lady Mary gives the meaning of such a love-letter, both in Turkish and English, and imagines that her friend must be much impressed by the profundity of her learning. But, she explains, she has fallen into the misfortune common to the ambitious; while they are employed in conquests abroad, a rebellion starts up at home.

"I am in great danger," she continues, "of losing the English language. I find it is not half as easy to me to write in it as it was a twelvemonth ago. The human memory can retain but a certain number of images, and 'tis as impossible for one creature to be perfect master of ten different languages as to have in perfect subjection ten different kingdoms, or to fight against ten men at a time; so that I am afraid I shall at last know none as I should do. I live in a place that very well represents the Tower of Babel. . . . My grooms are Arabs; my footmen, French, English and Germans; my nurse an Armenian; my housemaids, Russians; half a dozen other servants, Greeks; my steward, an Italian; my janissaries, Turks; so that I live in the perpetual hearing of a medley of sounds, which produces a very extraordinary effect upon the people that are born here. They learn all these languages at once, without knowing any of them well enough to read or write in it."

Some time in March Lady Mary removed with her children to Belgrade Village, where she proposed to have them "engrafted" for the smallpox. She wrote thence to Mr. Wortley on 23rd March: "The boy was engrafted last Tuesday, and is at this time singing and playing, and very impatient for his supper. I pray God my next may give as good an account of him. . . . I cannot engraft the girl; her nurse has not had the smallpox."

She seems to have been at Adrianople on 19th April, when she wrote the following unpublished letter to her husband, which shows how much she had taken his recall to heart—

"I[1] have not mentioned to anybody whatever your design of going sooner than by the man-of-war, but it has been writ to several people at Adrianople. I was asked, and made answer (as I always do upon your affairs) that I knew nothing of it. I perceive by my F.'s letter that he is desirous to be well with us, and am very clearly of opinion (if my opinion is of any weight with you) that you should write him a civil letter. The birth of your daughter is a proper occasion, and you may date your letter as if writ during my lying-in. I know him perfectly well, and am very sure such a very trifling respect will make a great Impression on him. You need not apprehend my expressing any great joy for our return; I hope 'tis less shocking to you than to me, who have really suffered in my health by the oneasiness it has given me, tho' I take care to conceal it here as much as I can. Your son is very well; I cannot forbear telling you so, tho' you do not so much as ask after him. . . . I hear the F. A.'s [French Ambassador's] business at Adrianople is to buy the Holy Land, and there is a 1000 purses offered for it, which is to pass through his hands; I believe he neglects no opportunity. . . . Here is some table-gilt plate offered to me for the weight. It is not fine silver, but makes the same show. If you think you will want anything of that kind it may be a pennyworth."

An undated letter from Pope belongs to the spring of this year, 1718. In allusion to his former request for a fair Circassian, he says, "Don't think to put me off with a little likeness of yourself. The girl which I hear you have some way or other procured, and are bringing with you, is not fit for me; whatever you may fancy, Molyneux is married, and I am past a boy." Samuel Molyneux was the Prince of Wales' secretary, and Pope, for once condescending to gossip, relates that ' The other day, at the Prince's levee he [Molyneux] took Mr. Edgcombe[2] aside and asked, with an air of seriousness, What did the Czar of Muscovy, when he disinherited his son, do with his secretary? To which Edgcombe answered, He was sewed up in a foot-ball, and tost into the water. . . . Our

---

[1] From the unpublished MS.
[2] This was probably Richard, afterward created Baron Edgcumbe. He was one of the Lords of the Treasury at this time.

gallantry and our gaiety have been great sufferers by the rupture of the two courts here: scarce any ball, assembly, basset-table, or any place where two or three are gathered together. No lone house in Wales, with a rookery, is more contemplative than Hampton Court: I walked there the other day by the moon, and met no creature of any quality but the king, who was giving audience all alone to the birds under the garden wall." [1]

[1] A slightly different version of this anecdote occurs in a letter to Miss Blount, date of 13th September 1717.

CHAPTER XXVI

RETURN TO ENGLAND

THE Wortleys sailed from Constantinople for Tunis on 4th July 1718. On the whole, though she had sometimes suffered from home-sickness, Lady Mary returned to England with regret. So at least she assured Lady Bristol, who, she feared, would charge her with hypocrisy.

"But I am used to the air," she explains, "and have learnt the language. I am easy here; and as much as I love travelling, I tremble at the inconveniences attending so great a journey with a numerous family." In a letter to the Abbé Conti, written about the same time, after describing the exquisite interior of a royal palace, together with the enchanting beauty of its gardens, she concludes with the following reflections:—

"Thus you see, sir, these people are not so unpolished as we represent them. 'Tis true their magnificence is of a different taste from ours, and perhaps of a better. I am almost of opinion they have a right notion of life; while they consume it in music, gardens, wine and delicate eating, we are tormenting our brains with some scheme of politics, or studying some science to which we can never attain, or if we do, cannot persuade people to set that value upon it we do ourselves. . . . Considering what short-lived weak animals men are, is there any study so beneficial as the study of present pleasure? I dare not pursue this theme; perhaps I have already said too much, but I depend upon the true knowledge you have of my heart. I don't expect from you the insipid railleries I should suffer from another in answer to this letter. You know how to divide the idea of pleasure from that of vice, and they are only mingled in the heads of fools. But I allow you to laugh at me for the sensual declaration that I had rather be a rich *effendi* with all his ignorance, than Sir Isaac Newton with all his knowledge."

On 31st July Lady Mary writes from Tunis a long and rather laboured letter, designed to show her knowledge of the classical localities through which she had passed. It is evidently a compilation from her Journal, and was at first addressed to Lady Mar, but was afterwards headed " To the Abbot of ——."

She relates how on the third night of the voyage the ship anchored in the Hellespont, between Sestos and Abydos, which gave her the opportunity of meditating on

" The swimming lover and the nightly bride,
How Hero loved, and how Leander died."

After seeing the narrow straits, she found nothing improbable in the adventures of Leander, nor anything very wonderful in the bridge of boats of Xerxes. The travellers gazed on Mount Ida, saw the spot where Hecuba was buried, and wandered round the "ruins of Troy." Sailing past Mitylene and Lesbos into the Ægean Sea, her ladyship refrains, obviously with reluctance, from dwelling on the classical associations of islands, which she passes by with the reflection that " 'Tis impossible to imagine anything more agreeable than this journey would have been between two and three thousand years since, when, after drinking a dish of tea (!) with Sappho, I might have gone the same evening to visit the Temple of Homer in Chios, and have passed this voyage in taking plans of magnificent temples, delineating the miracles of statuaries, and conversing with the most polite and gay of human kind."

The journey home was by Genoa, Turin, Lyons, and Paris. At Genoa, where the party stayed a month, Lady Mary worked conscientiously at "sight-seeing," though the churches appeared so mean in her eyes after that of Sancta Sophia, she could hardly do them the honour of writing down their names. Of the old masters, Guido and Correggio were her especial favourites, and she owns that she can find no pleasure in objects of horror; in her opinion the more naturally a crucifixion is painted, the more disagreeable it becomes. But the institution of the *cicisbeo*, a form of which she had already encountered at Vienna, seems to have interested her more than all the wonders of Italian art or architecture, and she gravely states that it was a political expedient, founded by the Senate to put an end to those family hatreds which tore their state to pieces, and to find employment for those young men who had been forced to cut one another's throats *pour passer le temps*. Since the foundation of this gallant order there had been nothing but peace and good-will among these former fire-eaters.

At Lyons Lady Mary was detained by a fever, caught during a terrible journey over the Mont Cenis. The travellers were carried on men's shoulders in little seats of twisted osiers, and the long exposure to cold and mist were enough to account for an indisposition so severe as to make her believe that all her journeys were ended. It was perhaps her bad state of health that made her write to Pope on 28th September in rather a melancholy vein. Her letter, it may be premised, is in answer to one from him, filled with the most extravagant raptures at the prospect of her return.

"I received yours here, and should thank you for the pleasure you express for my return; but I can hardly forbear being angry at you for rejoicing at what displeases me so much. You will think this but an odd compliment on my side. I'll assure you 'tis not from insensibility of the joy of seeing my friends; but when I consider that I must at the same time see and hear a thousand disagreeable impertinents, that I must receive and pay visits, make courtesies, and assist at tea-tables, where I shall be half-killed with questions; on the other part, that I am a creature that cannot serve anybody but with insignificant good wishes, and that my presence is not a necessary good to any one member of my native country, I think I might much better have staid where ease and quiet made up the happiness of my indolent life."

On 29th September the Wortleys started for Paris, where Lady Mary had the pleasure of meeting Lady Mar, and the sisters spent the next two or three weeks in visiting all the most famous sights of the town and neighbourhood. Lady Mar, as the daughter of the Whig Duke of Kingston, was allowed to pass to and fro between London and Paris as often as she pleased, even though her husband was ostensibly in the service of the Pretender. But "Bobbing John" was still playing a double part, and, when it suited his own purpose, betraying his own party to the Whig Government at home.

Lady Mary's description of the Parisians and their manners in the autumn of 1718 is worthy of quotation. The French beauties she considered nauseous creatures (only she used a stronger word), "so fantastically absurd in their dress! so monstrously unnatural in their paint! their hair cut short and curled round their faces, loaded with powder that makes it look like white wool! and on their cheeks to their chins, unmercifully laid on, a shining red japan, that glistens in a most flaming manner, that they seem to have no resemblance to human faces, and I am apt to believe, took the first hint of their dress from a fair sheep newly ruddled. 'Tis with pleasure I recollect my dear pretty countrywomen."

The Abbé Conti, who acted as cicerone, informed the travellers that the women in Paris moulded the character of the men. It struck the Englishwoman forcibly that there seemed to be no intermediate state between infancy and manhood; for as soon as the boy had quit his leading-strings he was set agog in the world. "The ladies are his tutors, they make the first impressions, and they render the men ridiculous by the imitations of their humours and graces, so that dignity in manners is a rare thing here before the age of sixty." Lady Mary continues that nothing delighted her more than to see a Briton absolute at Paris. This was John Law, the financier of the Mississippi scheme, who treated the dukes and peers *de haut en bas*, and was treated by them with the utmost submission and respect.

Although she did not admire the opera or the playhouses at Paris, Lady Mary was constrained to own that the French tragedians were far better than any that London could boast. "I should hardly allow Mrs. O. [Oldfield][1] a

---

[1] Anne Oldfield (1683–1730). She made her first appearance at Drury Lane as early as 1692, but had little success till 1704, when she made a hit in the part of Lady Betty Modish. She played under Cibber's management at Drury Lane from 1711 to 1730, and was considered, *pace* Lady Mary, almost equally good in tragedy and comedy.

better place than to be confidante to La ——. I have seen the tragedy of *Bajazet* so well represented, I think our best actors can only be said to speak, but these to feel; and 'tis certainly infinitely more moving to see a man appear unhappy than to hear him say that he is so, with a jolly face, and a stupid smirk in his countenance." In general she thinks that Paris has the advantage of London, in the neat pavement of the streets, and the regular lighting of them at nights, the stone-built houses and the beautiful gardens. London might be nearly twice as big as Paris, but that, she thought, was the only way in which the English capital surpassed the French.

There is some confusion about the dates in the later letters, since two (to the Abbé Conti) appear to have been written from Dover on 31st October, whereas, according to the *Weekly Journal* of 11th October, the late Ambassador to the Porte and his lady returned to town "on Thursday sennight." But it was ostensibly from Dover on 1st November that Lady Mary wrote her answer to a letter from Pope (of 1st September), in which he relates his favourite story of the rustic lovers who were killed by lightning at Stanton Harcourt. Pope was apt to fall into sentimentality when he desired to express pathos, and the sentimentality of the eighteenth century was too artificial to be convincing. After relating his story with all due unction, he transcribes two bombastic epitaphs, which he professes to have written on the occasion. When he edited his *Correspondence*, however, he attributed the letter (or one of the many versions of it) to Gay, and he also shifted the unlucky epitaphs on to the shoulders of his brother poet.

Pope probably had no intimate personal knowledge of the manners and customs of the agricultural labourer. Like most of his literary contemporaries, he seems to have fancied that Hodge was an English counterpart of the classic shepherd who sang and piped through the Pastorals of Theocritus or of Virgil. Thus, he imagines that, before the storm broke, John had been matching several kinds of poppies and field-flowers to Sarah's complexion, with a view to making her a present of knots of ribbon for the wedding day. Charmed with his own fancy, he proceeds—

"Upon the whole, I can't think these people unhappy. The greatest happiness next to living as they would have done, was to die as they did. The greatest honour people of this low degree could have was to be remembered on a little monument; unless you will give them another—that of being honoured with a tear from the finest eyes in the world. I know you have tenderness; you must have it; it is the very emanation of good sense and virtue; the finest minds, like the finest metals, dissolve the easiest."

The poet professes to be dissatisfied with both his epitaphs, but says that the second, which here follows, is considered the most successful of the two:—

> "Think not, by rig'rous judgment seized,
>   A pair so faithful could expire;
> Victims so pure Heav'n saw well pleased,
>   And snatched them in celestial fire.
>
> Live well, and fear no sudden fate:
>   When God calls virtue to the grave,
> Alike 'tis justice, soon or late,
>   Mercy alike to kill or save.
> Virtue unmoved can hear the call,
> And face the flash that melts the ball."

Lady Mary knew a good deal more about the country and country folk than Pope, thanks to her long solitary sojourns at Thoresby, West Dean, and Middlethorpe. Being under no illusion whatever about haymakers or their mode of courtship, she ridicules the poet's pastoral dream, and with a ruthless hand tears away the web of sentiment that he had woven round the rustic tragedy.

"I must applaud your good-nature," she observes, "in supposing that your pastoral lovers (vulgarly called haymakers) would have lived in everlasting joy and harmony, if the lightning had not interrupted their scheme of happiness. I see no reason to imagine that John Hughes [actually Hewet] and Sarah Drew were either wiser or more virtuous than their neighbours . . . and I cannot help thinking that, had they married, their lives would have passed in the common track with their fellow-parishioners. His endeavour to shield her from the storm was a natural action, and what he would certainly have done for his horse, if he had been in the same situation. Neither am I of opinion that their sudden death was a reward of their mutual virtue."

Since he has desired her to try her skill in an epitaph, she sends some lines, perhaps more just, though not so poetical as his—

> "Here lie John Hughes and Sarah Drew;
> Perhaps you'll say, what's that to you?
> Believe me, friend, much may be said
> On this poor couple that are dead.
> On Sunday next they should have married,
> But see how oddly things are carried!
> On Thursday last it rained and lightened;
> These tender lovers, sadly frightened,
> Sheltered beneath the cocking hay,
> In hopes to pass the storm away;
> But the bold thunder found them out
> (Commissioned for that end, no doubt),
> And, seizing on their trembling breath,
> Consigned them to the shades of death.
> Who knows if 'twas not kindly done?
> For had they seen the next year's sun,
> A beaten wife, a cuckold swain
> Had jointly cursed the marriage chain:
> Now they are happy in their doom,
> For P. has wrote upon their tomb."

CHAPTER XXVII

INTIMACY WITH POPE

ALTHOUGH Lady Mary had left Constantinople with regret, and looked forward with no great desire to her return to a more conventional life in London society, she had no sooner arrived at home than she seems to have resolved to make the best of things, and to follow the example of the majority of her countrymen in thinking that there was no real enjoyment of life except in Old England. All that is gained by travel and study, she observes, is "a fruitless desire of mixing the different pleasures and conveniences which are given to different parts of the world, and cannot meet in any one of them. After having read all that is to be found in the languages I am mistress of, and decayed my sight by midnight studies, I envy the easy peace of mind of a ruddy milk-maid, who, undisturbed by doubt, hears the sermon with humility every Sunday.... And after having seen part of Asia and Africa, and almost made the tour of Europe, I think the honest English squire more happy, who verily believes the Greek wines less delicious than March beer; that the African fruits have not so fine a flavour as golden pippins, and the *becafiguas* of Italy are not so well tasted as a rump of beef."

The Wortleys settled down in a house in Cavendish Square, which they afterwards exchanged for one in the Piazza, Covent Garden. Mr. Wortley's recall, however it may have been glossed over by his friends, was a decided set-back to his political career, and we hear no more of any prospects of promotion. For the rest of his active life he remained, as he had begun, a steady, hard-working Member of Parliament, belonging to the party of "country Whigs." In the two years of his absence several changes had taken place in the political world, which must have been adverse to his chance of promotion. His powerful kinsman, Lord Halifax, had died the previous year, while his friend Addison resigned office in 1718, on account of declining health, and died a year later. Though the Whigs were in power, their internal dissensions greatly weakened the Government.

"The division of Whigs is so great," wrote Erasmus Lewis to Swift in January 1717, "that, morally speaking, nothing but another rebellion can ever unite them. Sunderland, Stanhope and Cadogan are of one side; Townshend, Orford, Walpole, Devonshire and the Chancellor on the other." The Sunderland faction prevailed for the time being. Townshend was dismissed from office on 10th April, and all the other Whigs mentioned by Lewis (except the Lord Chancellor Cowper) resigned office. Four years later Walpole came back to power, and entered upon a reign that was to last for twenty years. Mr. Wortley, who never admired Walpole's political methods, afterwards became his bitter adversary, and helped to bring about his downfall in 1743.

Society was suffering at this time from the breach between the King and the Prince of Wales, the great people being split up into rival camps. The Jacobite spirit, which was still keen, served to divide families and to dissolve friendships, while the constant fear and expectation of plots and risings went far to destroy all social comfort and security.

Lady Mary saw but little of her own family at this time. Her sister, Lady Gower, wasted her whole time and most of her money at the quadrille-table, her passion for cards being so strong that it is said to have shortened her life. Lady Mar settled in Paris with her worthless husband in 1721, and remained there until her mind gave way in 1728. The Duke of Kingston was never on very cordial terms with his disobedient daughter, though he did not refuse to see her. Lady Bute relates that when she was quite a little girl she was playing about the room one day where her mother was dressing, when a dignified elderly man entered, with the authoritative air of a person entitled to admittance at all times. To her great surprise, her mother started up from the dressing-table, and all dishevelled as she was, fell on her knees to ask the stranger's blessing. Afterwards the little girl (she was only eight when the Duke died) knew that she had seen her grandfather.

There is an allusion to the home-coming of Mr. Wortley in one of Montagu Bacon's letters, and some of the gossip that was floating about the town in the autumn of 1718 may be quoted from the same source. Unluckily, Montagu professes to have renounced his pleasant but dangerous habit of writing unreservedly about public affairs; possibly the custom of inspecting private letters at the post-office may have got him into trouble with the authorities. Still, he does not always keep to his resolution, and his letters generally contain some gossiping allusion to topics of the day. Thus on 20th September 1718 he writes to his cousin James at Durham—

". . . If[1] there were any news here, you know I have given over that sort of correspondence, but there is none. One piece of private news I can tell you, that Lady Musgrave is a widow; I must go and condole with her. I suppose you have seen Mr. Craggs' genuine letter, the matter of which is very good, but the style perfectly new. Anybody may perceive he does not tread servilely in the steps of the Ancients: see what work your fine speakers in the House of Commons make, what they sit down to write. . . . They say the Right Honble. author wrote it in French, and that the translator is to answer for all that is amiss in it. But anyone that understands style and translation, knows that that cannot be; there are faults which 'tis impossible a translator should fall upon unless he had found them in the original. If Addison had continued in the Secretary's office, what a fine piece we should have had. He would have have given them as thorough a defeat by land as Sir George Byng[2] did by sea. This is all we have to entertain ourselves with at present. The town is a perfect wilderness. My humble service to the Triumvirate;[3]

[1] From the unpublished MS.
[2] Admiral Sir George Byng, the famous naval officer, who was created Viscount Torrington in 1721. He held command in the Mediterranean from 1718 to 1720, and on 31st July 1718 destroyed the Spanish fleet off Cape Passaro. He was the father of the unfortunate Admiral George Byng, who was shot for neglect of duty in 1757.
[3] He means his three uncles, the Bishop of Durham, the Dean of Durham, and Mr. Sidney Wortley Montagu.

I met two or three gentlemen at Tonbridge who admired the Dean almost to a degree of idolatry. Brigadier Windsor[1] was one of them; the others, I believe, he will hardly remember, if I should name them. . . .

"As to the Fair One you mention, I must beg you to make my best compliments to her. You are acquainted with the lady, and so may easily guess how much I am her humble servant. I could give you some directions on this subject, but I trust to the fruitfulness of your invention."

"LONDON, *2nd October* 1718

"I[2] know not how to persuade you of the sincerity of my intention to have followed you to Durham, if the expectation of seeing the lady you mention in your letter, cannot convince you. I will add too, if anything can be added, the pleasure you know I take in yours and the good company you have at the Deanery, beyond that which I am now going to. If I could inform you of the melancholy afternoons and evenings I pass here in town, and how I linger still without going into Suffolk, you would think I am sufficiently punished for any remissness I may have been guilty of. I thank you heartily for the good offices you have done me with the Fair One; if the eloquence of my friend has been ineffectual to take off her suspicion, nothing I can say will do it, and to tell you the truth, there is so much kindness in it, I could half wish it may remain. But now, for the Words and the Look! How shall I express my gratitude? You cannot be so little acquainted with matters of gallantry, as not to be sensible what ecstasy such a circumstance must raise in the mind of a lover; a thousand things crowd in upon me that I could say on this chapter, a thousand things I could tell her, if I had the happiness to sit by, talk to her and look upon her; but speeches of this nature are tender in the conveyance, and fear very much the severity of a third person. Thus far you are engaged by your letter to give her my

[1] Andrews Windsor, son of the first Earl of Plymouth. He was a member of Parliament as well as a brigadier-general.
[2] From the unpublished MS.

thanks, and I beg of you to do it in the most pathetical manner.

"I hope you understood me that my objection to Mr. Craggs' letter was only with respect to the style, and I will be bold to say it is the worst-drawn piece has appeared a good while from the hands of a Minister of State. Almost all the good company, except what attends upon the two Courts, is gone to the Bath. Dr. Garth has gone down to Bristol to see how Mr. Addison does.[1] Lechmere has gone to the Bath. They talk of the King's going to Newmarket, but I fancy the alteration of the season will prevent him.... I am sorry my uncle Wortley keeps his chamber, but it is less inconvenient in so cheerful a family, and almost as good as going abroad anywhere else.... Before I conclude, I must also, very seriously and without any poetical rapture, desire you to give my hearty humble service to the lady in question. I envy you the opportunity of making so agreeable a visit."

"*21st October* 1718

"... I[2] hope that none of you think of staying much longer at Durham; 'tis a good sign that the company begins to file off. I long to hear the success of your conference; you have reason to be careful of my modesty, because even the smallest instance of the good opinion of so deserving a lady is enough to blow up a lover upon other occasions pretty well armed against self-conceit. I have not seen our Ambassador,[3] nor do I know where he lodges; they say he has come home very rich. 'Tis a long while since I left off writing news, but you are so particularly serviceable to me in the affair of my Amour, that I cannot do less than throw you in some. They talk of alterations at Court. Lord Stanhope[4] to be Master of the Horse, some say quite out, and Lord Carteret to be Secretary of State. 'Tis certain my Lord Stanhope is very

[1] Addison, whose health was already failing, had retired on a pension of £1500 a year. He had gone to Bristol to drink the waters.
[2] From the unpublished MS.
[3] Mr. Wortley.
[4] Lord Stanhope was Secretary of State in 1718. Lord Carteret afterwards Earl Granville, first held that office under Walpole, 1721-24.

uneasy. The King comes to town very soon, so then we shall see the scene opens. I know not whether Mr. Lechmere pushes at the Chancellor, but I am informed he said these words at the Bath, ' I let that fellow, meaning my Lord Parker,[1] play with the Seals for six or seven months, and then I intend to take them myself.' The expressions are so very extraordinary, I could not help transcribing them. There is likely to be a rot amongst the poets; Mr. Rowe[2] is in a dying condition at the Bath, and another that has a place under my Lord Chancellor, Mr. Hughes,[3] is not much better here in town.

"To return though from politics to matters of gallantry, Lady Kingston[4] has made a slip with Lord Lumley.[5] The same lady and her affairs are at present all the scandal of the town, but I think it is barbarous, for us, at least, to insist upon an error that proceeds only from too much kindness for our sex. This is all I can pick up. . . ."[6]

[1] Thomas Parker, afterwards first Earl ot Macclesfield (1666?–1732), was appointed Lord Chancellor in 1718. Mr. Lechmere had to content himself with the Attorney-Generalship.

[2] Nicholas Rowe (1674–1718), poet and dramatist. Among his best-known tragedies are *Tamerlane*, *The Fair Penitent*, and *Jane Shore*. He translated Lucan and edited Shakespeare. In 1715 he was appointed poet-laureate. At this time he was suffering from his last illness.

[3] John Hughes (1677–1720). He wrote *The Siege of Damascus* and other successful dramas, and contributed to the *Tatler* and the *Spectator*. He made various translations, edited Spenser, and was a good musician. He lived nearly two years after being practically "killed off" by Montagu Bacon. Swift thought him dull and mediocre, but Pope said his honesty made up for his want of genius.

[4] Widow of Lady Mary's brother. She was not a person of strong intellect. She died in 1722, her early death being supposed to be indirectly due to the heartless conduct of Lord Lumley.

[5] Richard, eldest son of the first Earl of Scarborough, whom he succeeded in 1722. He died unmarried in 1740.

[6] This is the last letter of any interest from Montagu Bacon. He took his degree at Cambridge in 1734, previously entered Holy Orders, and is supposed to have been curate at Newbold Verdun, in Leicestershire, where his favourite cousin James inherited an estate from Lord Crew. In 1743 he was presented to the Rectory of Newbold Verdun, but shortly after he became temporarily deranged, and was removed to lodgings in Chelsea. For a time he was confined in Duffield's asylum in Little Chelsea. He seems to have had lucid intervals until his death in 1749. As already stated, he amused his leisure hours with annotating *Hudibras*. A few of his letters, of no very special interest, were published in Duncombe's *Letters of Eminent Deceased Persons* (1773), and he is mentioned in Nichols' *Literary Anecdotes*.

Pope was happily exempt from the misfortunes of his brother poets. Thanks to the success of his *Homer*, he had never been in such prosperous circumstances, nor in such high esteem with the public. He moved from Chiswick to Twickenham the end of this year (1718), and eventually persuaded the Wortleys to take a house in the same village. The first letter that he wrote to Lady Mary on her arrival in England is curiously impersonal, and looks as though he wished to forget or ignore the passionate phrases that he used in the letters that he wrote to her abroad. It is true that he begins somewhat in the old style—

" 'Tis not possible to express the least part of the joy your return gives me; time only and experience will convince you how very sincere it is. I excessively long to meet you, to say so much, so very much to you—that I believe I shall say nothing. I have given orders to be sent for the first minute of your arrival (which I beg you will let them know at Mr. Jervas'). I am fourscore miles from London [at Stanton Harcourt], a short journey compared to that I so often thought at least of undertaking, rather than die without seeing you again. Though the place I am in is such as I would not quit for the town, if I did not value you more than any, nay, everybody else there; and you'll be convinced how little the town has engaged my affections in your absence from it, when you know what a place this is which I prefer to it."

Then follows a long description, partly imaginary, of the old house at Stanton Harcourt, a description which he evidently thought too valuable to be wasted on one person, for he sent another version of it to the Duke of Buckingham, in return for a word-picture of Buckingham House.

During the year or two after Lady Mary's return, she and Pope must have frequently met, and this accounts for the fact that only a few brief notes have survived of what was probably a very scanty correspondence. His attachment to Miss Blount did not hinder the expression of his "passion" for Lady Mary, and she, though without any great faith in the sincerity of his feeling, thought it incumbent on her to check his professions with an occasional word of semi-serious reproof.

So at least we may gather from two or three undated notes, written by the poet in or about 1719. Thus, in one of these he writes—

"It is not in my power to say what agitation the two or three words I wrote to you the other morning have given me. Indeed, I truly esteem you, and put my trust in you. I can say no more, and I know you would not have me."

And again: "Upon my word, I take yours, and understand you as you would be understood, with a real respect and resignation when you deny me anything, and a hearty gratitude when you grant me anything. Your will be done, but God send it may be the same with mine."

The negotiations about a house belonging to Sir Godfrey Kneller at Twickenham began as early as 1719, but the Wortleys do not seem to have decided upon taking it till a year or two later. Pope not only busied himself in house-hunting for his friends, but he also insisted that Lady Mary should sit to Sir Godfrey for her portrait, which portrait, judging from his letters, was a commission given by himself.[1]

Writing to Lady Mary about the proposed portrait (painted in 1720), Pope says: "The picture really dwells at my heart, and I have made a perfect passion of preferring your present face to your past. I know and thoroughly esteem yourself of this year; I know no more of Lady Mary Pierrepont than to admire what I have heard of her, or be pleased with some fragments of hers as I am with Sappho's. But now—I can't say what I would of you now. Only still give me cause to say you are good to me, and allow me as much of your person as Sir Godfrey can help me to. Upon conferring with him yesterday, I find he thinks it absolutely necessary to draw the face first, which, he says, can never be set right on the figure if the drapery and posture be finished before. To give you as little trouble as possible, he proposes to draw your face with crayons, and finish it up at your own house in a

---

[1] Mr. Dallaway states that this portrait was painted for Pope, but Mr. Thomas infers that it was a commission from Mr. Wortley, because it passed into the possession of his son-in-law, Lord Bute. But Lord Bute might have bought it at Pope's death.

Sir Godfrey Kneller, pinxt., 1720   *Caroline Watson, sculp*
LADY MARY WORTLEY MONTAGU

morning; from whence he will transfer it to the canvas, so that you need not go to sit at his house. This, I must observe, is a manner in which they seldom draw any but crowned heads; and I observe it with secret pride and pleasure."[1]

[1] A poor copy of verses upon a lady's portrait has been printed as a tribute from Pope to Lady Mary's picture. But as the style is quite unlike his, there is no need to quote the verses here.

air of London because "On aime tout ce qu'on aime. Je sens déjà que *I love* a un autre efficace que j'aime, et donnant une honnête liberté à mon esprit, au lieu de dire en tremblant, 'Je vous aime,' je dirai sans évaindre (*sic*), *I love you at all my heart*."

The letters continue in the same sentimental strain. "Adieu. Pensez quelquefois à moi, et sois assurée qu'aucune femme n'a jamais été aimée autant que je vous aime."

Incidentally literature and the drama come under discussion. Rémond has read the Preface to "M. Poppe's" *Homer*, and wished that an essay so useful and agreeable could be translated into French, so that it might be more generally read. It was no doubt after his visit to England that he wrote, with what seems to be ironical praise—

"Vos pièces de théâtre ont un grand mérite pour un pauvre paresseux comme moi. On y apprend, sans peine, toute la vie d'un héros, et, le conduisant d'âge en âge, il semble qu'on a passé sa vie avec lui. D'ailleurs, la scène anglaise n'est pas comme la nôtre, une personne delicate et peureuse, qui s'évanouirait si elle voyait une goutte de sang. Elle soutient avec courage les spectacles les plus terribles, et un assassinat ou un cadavre n'a rien qui l'épouvantait."[1]

During M. Rémond's stay in London Lady Mary advised him to speculate in South Sea stock, and, thinking he saw the chance of making his fortune, he left a sum of money in her hands, begging her to lay it out to the best advantage. After his departure he wrote to thank her for "cette amitié qui vous fait descendre jusqu'au détail de mes affaires domestiques, ces conseils que vous me donnez pour assurer ma petite fortune chancelante."

All was *couleur de rose* as long as the stock went up, but when it went down, and obstinately refused to rise again, M. Rémond's friendship "*chancelait*" like his fortune, and presently broke up in wrath and reproaches. But the story is best told in Lady Mary's letters to Lady Mar, who was now settled in Paris. From these we learn that her ladyship was still credulous enough to put some faith in the sincerity of her admirers, and was far from realising that their passionate

[1] The above extracts are from his unpublished letters.

protestations were merely the unmeaning coin of compliment paid by any man of the world to any woman of wit and beauty. In the first letter to her sister, undated, but probably written early in 1721, she explains that—

"A person, whose name is not necessary, because you know it, took all sorts of methods, during almost two years, to persuade me that there never was so extraordinary an attachment (or what you please to call it) as they had for me. This ended in coming over to make me a visit against my will, and, as was pretended, very much against their interest. I cannot deny I was very silly in giving the least credit to this stuff. But if people are so silly, you'll own 'tis natural for anybody that is good-natured to pity and be glad to serve a person they believe unhappy upon their account. It came into my head, out of a high point of generosity (for which I wish myself hanged), to do this creature all the good I possibly could, since 'twas impossible to make them happy in their own way. I advised him very strenuously to sell out of the subscription, and in compliance to my advice he did so; and in less than two days saw he had done very prudently. After a piece of service of this nature, I thought I could more decently press his departure, which his follies made me think necessary for me. He took leave of me with so many tears and grimaces (which I can't imagine how he could counterfeit) as really moved my compassion; and I had much ado to keep to my first resolution of exacting his absence, which he swore would be the death of him. I told him there was no other way in the world I would not be glad to serve him in, but that his extravagances made it utterly impossible for me to keep him company."

It was then that M. Rémond asked Lady Mary to take charge of the money he had made, and try to increase his little fortune. After some hesitation she accepted the trust, bought stock again after the fall had begun (on Pope's advice), and thought she had done "prodigious well" to sell out for a small profit the day after the books closed. Unfortunately, the buyers absconded before paying, leaving her with the stock on her hands.

At first M. Rémond took the news of his misfortune with

besides the cruel misfortunes it may bring upon me in my own family. If you have any compassion either for me, or my innocent children, I am sure you will try to prevent it. I think (to say nothing either of blood or affection) that humanity and Christianity are interested in my preservation."

How the matter ended can only be guessed. Each of the letters from M. Rémond to Lady Mary is endorsed by Mr. Wortley with an indication of its contents. Mr. Thomas infers that the Frenchman sent Lady Mary's letters to her husband as he had threatened, and that for her own justification she put those she had received in his hands. The last of these, written after his return to France, bears evidence to the fact that he had never been a favoured lover—

"Je ne regrette point le climat ni la société d'Angleterre," he writes, "mais bien la conversation de quelques personnes, surtout la vôtre, dont je n'ai joui que rarement. . . . Si vous venez jamais en France (en vérité c'est un beau pays) vous serez plus contente de moi. Tout cela n'est pas pour me plaindre. Je sais que les dames anglaises sont incapables d'amitié et d'amour. Je ne me soucie guère de la folie de l'un, mais je suis fort sensible à la douceur de l'autre. Je vous aimerai sans exiger de retour."

It must be supposed that Mr. Wortley took a more lenient view of his wife's folly than she expected, for the storm seems to have blown over without any open scandal. But she was not to get off without punishment. In her anguish of mind, she had doubtless appealed to her neighbour, Pope, for help and advice, and it will be seen later what cruel use he made of the knowledge thus obtained. The old scandal cropped up again years afterwards in a letter from Horace Walpole to Sir Horace Mann. Writing in August 1751, Walpole says that he has been at Woburn, where the Duchess of Devonshire borrowed for him from a niece of Lady Mary's a volume containing fifty letters from the latter to Lady Mar.

<small>night, armed with a sword and pistol, and declared his passion for her. She was obliged to summon help, and the man was tried and condemned to death, but the sentence was commuted to one of penal servitude. The incident made a great sensation at the time, and Lady Mary wrote a so-called *Epistle from Arthur Grey*, which Horace Walpole thought one of her best works.</small>

"They are charming," he declares, "have more spirit and vivacity than you can imagine, and as much of the spirit of debauchery as you will conceive in her writing. . . . Ten of the letters indeed are dismal lamentations and frights on a scene of villany of Lady Mary, who, having persuaded one Rurémond [*sic*], a Frenchman and her lover, to entrust her with a large sum of money to buy stock for him, frightened him out of England by persuading him that Mr. Wortley had discovered the intrigue and would murder him; and then would have sunk the trust. That not succeeding, and he threatening to print her letters, she endeavoured to make Lord Mar or Lord Stair cut his throat." This, as will be seen, is a most malignantly garbled account of the affair. Horace admits, however, that "in most of them the wit and style are superior to any letters I ever read but Madame Sévigné's," and adds, "It is very remarkable, how much better women write than men."

one of whom was to play a rather important part in her after life. In July 1721 she writes to Lady Mar—

"The most considerable incident that has happened a good while, was the ardent affection that Mrs. Hervey [1] and her dear spouse took to me. They visited me twice or thrice a day, and were perpetually cooing in my rooms. I was complaisant a great while; but (as you know) my talent has never lain much that way, I grew at last so weary of those birds of paradise, I fled to Twickenham, as much to avoid their persecutions as for my own health."

Even before the Rémond business had been settled, the peaceful pleasures of life at Twickenham had been broken into by the storm that arose over Lady Mary's attempt to introduce the practice of inoculation into this country. During the four or five years after her return to England, she seldom passed a day, we are told, without repenting of her patriotic undertaking; and she often declared that she would never have attempted to introduce the new treatment if she could have foreseen the vexation, the persecution, and the obloquy that it would bring upon her.

"The faculty rose in arms to a man, foretelling failure and the most disastrous consequence; the clergy descanted from their pulpits on the impiety of thus seeking to take events out of the hand of Providence; and the common people were taught to hoot at an unnatural mother, who had risked the lives of her own children." The Wortleys' son had been inoculated in Turkey, but it was not till after they returned to England that their little daughter underwent the operation. Four leading physicians were deputed by Government to watch the treatment, but they betrayed so much scepticism about its success, and such obvious unwillingness to see it succeed, that the mother never dared leave her child alone with any one of them. The Princess of Wales, who had her own children inoculated,[2] proved a powerful ally, and as the practice gradually gained

---

[1] Mrs. Hervey was the charming Maid of Honour, Molly Lepell, who married Mr., afterwards Lord, Hervey in 1720. Her friendship with Lady Mary did not last very long.

[2] The experiment was tried on six condemned criminals before the Princess submitted her own children to the operation.

in public, if not in professional esteem, Lady Mary's numerous friends and acquaintance came one after the other to beg for her advice and guidance while the operation was in progress. Thus, in a letter to Lady Mar, written in 1723, she says—

"Lady Byng[1] has inoculated both her children; the operation is not over, but I believe they will do very well. Since that experiment has not yet had any ill effect, the whole town are doing the same thing, and I am so much pulled about, and solicited to visit people, that I am forced to run into the country to hide myself." Horace Walpole, we learn from himself, was inoculated in 1724; therefore he owed something to the woman for whom he never had a good word. In another letter of the same year, Lady Mary announces the death of a little nephew (son of Lady Gower) from smallpox, and adds, "I think she has a great deal of reason to regret it, in consideration of the offer I made her two years together, of taking the child home to my house, where I would have inoculated him with the same care and safety I did my own. I know nobody that has hitherto repented the operation; though it has been very troublesome to some fools, who had rather be sick by the doctor's prescription, than in health in rebellion to the college!"

Inoculation was, of course, a much more risky operation than vaccination. The patient was given a mild attack of smallpox in the hope of saving him from a severe one in later life, and in the case of delicate children it sometimes proved fatal.[2] However, by the year 1724 the efficacy of the practice seems to have been pretty well established. In July of this year, *The Plaindealer*, a paper at one time edited by Steele, gave a most laudatory notice of the new treatment, and of the lady who had introduced it to her countrymen. The writer, who was almost certainly Mary Astell, begins by denying the commonly accepted belief that the English are fond of novelty.

"I have wondered a thousand times," she observes, "how this notion became established. For that nothing is more false in fact may be proved by our old Histories, and is every day

---

[1] Wife of Admiral Byng, already noticed.
[2] The only child of Charles, Earl of Sunderland, died from the effects of inoculation in April 1722.

remarkable in our modern and familiar practice. . . . Innovations were ever odious to us, and we chose rather to neglect advantages than to try an unbidden path for 'em. What lost England the first possession of that gold and silver world in the Spanish West Indies but her disposition to discredit *Novelty*? Our very laws depend on *Precedent*. And the defence even of rights in Parliament is supported by *What has been*, and seems unconcerned in *Why it was*. Those scandalous oppositions which are so obstinately given to the clearest Bills for publick benefit, such as *Making our rivers navigable — Putting our Lands under a Register — Promoting untried Trades* — and establishing *National Fisheries*, are all convincing instances that no nation under Heaven have so fixed an aversion to the encouragement of *Novelty*, which yet everybody is imputing to us as the Reigning Humour of our Country."

After pointing to the opposition to the process of inoculation as one more proof of our conservatism, the writer refers to a pamphlet lately published by a member of the Royal Society, who, resolving to establish or expose this practice, had informed himself of its success in all parts of the kingdom. "It is demonstrated," she continues, "in the above-mentioned Treatise, from a forty years' examination of the Bills of Mortality, that the Small-pox carries off at least one in every nine of all whom it seizes in the natural way; whereas not one in fifty (scarce one in many hundreds) of those who receive it by inoculation, have been found to die of it."

After describing the intense malignancy of the opposition, she continues (and here speaks, surely, the voice of Mary Astell): "It is the voice of some Historian — but I forget where I met with it — *That England has owed to Women the greatest blessings she has been distinguished by*. In the case we are now upon this reflection will stand justified. We are indebted to the reason and the courage of a Lady for the introduction of this art, which gains such strength in its progress that the memory of its Illustrious Foundress will be rendered sacred by it to Future Ages. This ornament of her Sex and Country, who ennobles her own Nobility by her Learning, Wit, and Vertues, accompanying her consort into Turkey, observed the Benefit of this Practice, with its frequency, even among these obstinate Predestinarians, and brought it over for the service and the safety of her native England, where she consecrated its first effects on the persons of her own fine children ! . . ."

The writer next "drops into poetry," in the shape of a description, in heroic verse, of Lady Mary being presented by the Nine Muses to Apollo, who, finding her already endowed with beauty, wit, and learning, and wishing to bestow some gift upon her, endows her with power over " Beauty's chief foe, a feared and fierce disease," and concludes—

> "Breathed in this kiss, take power to tame its Rage,
> And from its Rancour free the rescued Age.
> High o'er each Sex, in double Empire sit,
> Protecting Beauty and inspiring Wit."

Perhaps conscious of the deficiencies of her own verse, she proceeds : " It is an uncommon misfortune to her [Lady Mary's] vast genius, that the only thing in the world worth knowing, and not known to her, is her own prodigious excellence. So she is neither able nor willing to describe it herself; and no verse but her own can soar high enough for her merits. The sweetest of our English poets has endeavoured it with less success than attended any of his other compositions. . . ."

Mrs. Astell then quotes the following stanzas from Pope's poem, addressed to Lady Mary in 1720, before his friendship had begun to cool:—

> "In beauty or wit
> No mortal as yet
> To question your empire has dared :
> But men of discerning
> Have thought that in learning
> To yield to a lady was hard.
>
> Impertinent schools,
> With musty dull rules,
> Have reading to females denied ;
> So Papists refuse
> The Bible to use,
> Lest flocks should be wise as their guide." [1]

---

[1] The remainder of the poem, which was first printed in Hammond's *Miscellany* for 1720, runs as follows :—

> "'Twas a woman at first
> (Indeed she was curst)
> In knowledge that tasted delight,

>   And sages agree
>   The laws should decree
> To the first possessor the right.
>
>   Then bravely, fair dame,
>   Resume the old claim,
> Which to your whole sex does belong;
>   And let men receive
>   From a second bright Eve
> The knowledge of right and of wrong.
>
>   But if the first Eve
>   Hard doom did receive
> When only one apple had she,
>   What a punishment new
>   Shall be found out for you,
> Who, tasting, have robbed the whole tree?"

In a letter to Broome, his collaborator in the translation of the *Odyssey* (16th July 1721), Pope had said, "I showed your letter to my Lady Mary Wortley, who is not a little pleased at the zeal of Mr. Tr., and proud of the thought you seem not averse to entertain of honouring her. It would be, I think, one of the first occasions, as well as one of the justest, of writing as well as you are able; and immortality, if such a thing be in the gift of English poets, would be but a due reward for an action which all posterity may feel the advantage of. Your motto from Virgil, in relation to the world's being freed from the future terrors of the smallpox,

> 'Irrita perpetua solvent formidine terras,'

is as good an one as ever I read."

CHAPTER XXX

SOCIAL GOSSIP

DURING the next few years—1722 to 1728—Lady Mary, by her own admission, took life as it came, made the most of its pleasures, and succeeded for the most part in stifling all regrets for the more substantial happiness that she had been denied. Her health was good, she was still young enough and handsome enough to attract admiration, her high spirits and clever tongue brought her the homage of the wits and men of letters, while, her husband being out of office, she was free to choose her own society, and was neither obliged to frequent the dull Court, nor attend the assemblies of the wives of Ministers. Among her chief intimates we find the Duchess of Montagu, the witty Lady Stafford, Molly Skerret,[1] —first the mistress and later the second wife of Sir Robert Walpole,—Lord and Lady Hervey, the wicked Duke of Wharton,[2] President of the Hell-fire Club, the vivacious Lord Bathurst, Lady Rich, Sir William Yonge, and Mr. Congreve. In strange contrast to these lively ladies and rakish wits were her friends, the dull but estimable Lady Oxford, and the homely Mrs. Astell, with her strong theological interests.

The Duke of Wharton (who had been a ward of the Duke of Kingston's) was now occupied in dissipating the last remnants of his great fortune, and in coquetting with the Jacobites, though he still professed to be an ardent supporter of the House of Hanover. In his idle hours he composed society ballads and lampoons, many of which he (being an arrant coward) laid at the door of Lady Mary Wortley. Lord Hervey[3] also dealt in

---

[1] The name is also spelt Skerritt and Skirrit.
[2] The "Clodio" of Pope's satires.
[3] The "Sporus" and "Lord Fanny" of Pope.

the same kind of literary wares, and, as we may gather from his letters, exercised a pernicious influence over Lady Mary, who was afterwards to become his collaborator in an unfortunate satire. Sir William Yonge, an ardent Whig, like most of the Wortleys' friends, was otherwise a sufficiently worthless person. He was made one of the commissioners of the Treasury about this time, but was chiefly celebrated for his *vers de société*, mostly scandalous, some of which found their way into the miscellanies, while others were handed about in manuscript.[1]

Mr. Congreve, at fifty-three, was past his gay and giddy youth, and was regarded as the exclusive property of Henrietta, the young Duchess of Marlborough, who erected a monument to him at his death in 1729. A characteristic little note from the Duchess is among Lady Mary's unpublished papers. "I[2] am sure you won't dislike to have Mr. Congreve to-morrow," it runs, "if you can get him, for he is like all good things, hard to come at, and tho' I shan't add to your company, I have wit enough not to spoyle it, which you must allow as being tolerable. What hour would you have me come?"

That the Duchess's friendship for Lady Mary was only nominal, seems proved by the following allusion in a letter to Lady Mar: "The reigning Duchess of Marlborough has entertained the town with concerts of Buononcini's composition very often, but she and I are not in that degree of friendship to have *me* often invited. We continue to see each other like two people who are resolved to hate with civility."

Molly Skerret was the daughter of an Irish gentleman, an old beau of some fortune, who was a well-known figure at Tunbridge and the Bath. Lady Mary remarked years later on the curious fate that led her to make friends with a girl in a country village, who was afterwards tossed up to the top of the social wave. There is a quaint little note, unsigned, but endorsed "La Walpole," which was probably written by Miss Skerret in her maiden days. "This[2] comes to tell you, if you intended me the favour of your company to-night, 'tis impossible. Lord

---

[1] Pope, of whom we hear little at this time, is said to have been furiously jealous of these new admirers, who monopolised the society of his lady, and it is certain that he dreaded the attacks of other satirists, however inferior their literary quality.

[2] From the unpublished MS.

Sir G. Kneller, pinxt. *J. Smith, fecit*
MR. WILLIAM CONGREVE

Hunsden, Abercorn and God knows who—ten men are to be here with Papa to drink Punch, get drunk and sup. So that I am to go out at five to be out of their way. In great haste." [1]

Lady Stafford, a daughter of the Comte de Grammont and La Belle Hamilton, was much older than Lady Mary, having been married to the first Earl of Stafford as early as 1694. Lord Hervey used to say that she had " as much wit, humour and entertainment in her as any man or woman I ever knew, with a great justness in her way of thinking, and very little reserve in her manner of giving her opinion of things and people." Horace Walpole remembered seeing her when he was a child, and says, " She used to live at Twickenham when Lady Mary and the Duke of Wharton lived there, and had more wit than both of them. . . . Lady Stafford used to say to her sister : ' Well, child, I have come without my wit to-day ' ; that is, she had not taken her opium, which she was forced to do if she had any appointment to be in particular spirits."

A very different character was Lady Mary's former correspondent, Lady Rich, a foolish flighty beauty, who strove to keep up the appearance of youth by affecting a girlish simplicity, and served as a regular butt to her witty friend. On one occasion, relates Lady Louisa Stuart, the Master of the Rolls happened to be mentioned, the same old Sir Joseph Jekyll who " never changed his principles or wig," and had held the office so long that he was identified with it in everyone's mind. "' Pray who is the Master of the Rolls ? ' asked Lady Rich in an innocent tone. ' Sir Humphrey Monnoux, madam,' answered Lady Mary, naming off-hand the most unlikely person she could think of. The company laughed, and the lady looked disconcerted ; but not daring to betray her better knowledge by disputing the fact, went on in desperation to be more simple still. ' Well ! I am vastly ashamed of being so prodigiously ignorant. I dare say I ask a mighty silly question ; but pray now, what is it to be Master of the Rolls ? What does he do ? for I really don't know.' ' Why, madam, he superintends all the French rolls that are baked in

[1] The note might possibly have been written by Margaret Rolle, who (in 1724), at the age of fourteen, was married to Sir Robert Walpole's eldest son, the newly-created Baron Walpole of Wolterton.

London; and without him you would have no bread and butter for your breakfast.' There was no parrying this. Lady Rich coloured, flirted her fan, and professed herself unable to cope with Lady Mary Wortley's wit—*she* had no *wit*. 'Nay, but look you, my dear madam, I grant it a very fine thing to continue always fifteen—*that* everybody must approve of; it is quite fair; but indeed, indeed, one need not be five years old.'"[1]

With Lady Oxford, a friend of later years, the case was different. She was a dull woman, but she made no pretence to having "parts," nor did she try to make capital out of feminine silliness, like so many old-fashioned women. Nobody was ever less poetical than my Lady Oxford, yet Lady Mary seems to have clung to her friendship, and to have loved and trusted her more than any of her more brilliant companions; while Lady Oxford, who heartily detested most of the wits that surrounded her husband, cherished a warm and lasting admiration for Lady Mary. "Lady Bute confessed that she sometimes got into sad disgrace by exclaiming, 'Dear Mamma, how can you be so fond of that stupid woman?' which never failed to bring upon her a sharp reprimand, and a lecture against rash judgments, ending with, 'Lady Oxford is not shining, but she has much more in her than such giddy things as you and your companions can discern.'"[2]

To Mrs. Astell Lady Mary showed a manuscript volume compiled from the letters and journals written during her travels. This elderly friend, who had herself braved the publicity of print, was most anxious that the volume should be published, but to this the author would not consent, though she allowed one or more copies to be taken, which were probably handed round among her friends and acquaintance and brought her a certain meed of fame both as a writer

---

[1] From Lady Louisa Stuart's Introductory Anecdotes.

[2] Dr. Johnson stated, in his *Life of Pope*, that Lord Oxford's table was "infested" by Lady Mary Wortley, who contradicted him (Pope) and disputed with him, till one or the other left the house. But Lord Oxford's daughter, the Duchess of Portland, declared that no such meeting had ever taken place under her father's roof. "If *he* could have dreamed of inviting them at the same time, she said, which his good breeding made impossible, my mother, who adored Lady Mary and hated Pope, would no more have consented to it than she would have put her hand in the fire."

and a traveller. To one of these copies Mary Astell wrote a Preface (1724), in which she says—

"If these Letters appear hereafter, when I am in my grave, let this attend them, in testimony to posterity that among her contemporaries, *one* woman at least was just to her merit. . . . I confess I am malicious enough to desire that the world should see to how much better purpose the LADIES travel than their LORDS; and that, whilst it is surfeited with *male* Travels, all in the same tone, and stuffed with the same trifles, a lady has the skill to strike out a new path, and to embellish a worn-out subject with variety of fresh and elegant entertainment." Mrs. Astell, after dilating upon the delicacy of sentiment, the easy gracefulness, the lovely simplicity, and the purity of style that distinguish the letters, adjures her her own sex, at least, to do the writer justice, and to lay aside envy, malice, and all the hideous crew which are falsely said to attend the Tea-table. "Let us freely own the superiority of this sublime genius," she concludes, "as I do in the sincerity of my soul; pleased that a *woman* triumphs, and proud to follow in her train. Let us offer her the palm which is so justly her due; and if we pretend to any laurels, lay them willingly at her feet." [1]

The letters to Lady Mar, after the Rémond affair was settled, are filled chiefly with the social gossip of the day. Lady Mary was anxious to cheer and amuse her favourite sister, whose melancholy turn of mind became more pronounced as the time went on. The letters are written in the confidential style natural from one sister to another, and some of the details about contemporary scandals are told with the freedom of language affected by even the greatest ladies at that day. There is a strain of cynicism in the tone of these compositions, which suggests that the social pleasures and amusements so enthusiastically described were but an unsatisfying substitute for domestic happiness, and served rather as an opiate than a cure for a disappointed heart.

Lady Mary had already gained a not altogether enviable

---

[1] It is said that Mrs. Astell, shortly before her death, promised Lady Mary that if departed spirits were allowed to revisit those they loved on earth, she would appear to her. But the apparition never came.

reputation as a writer of satirical verses, and, as has been said, many of the anonymous skits and lampoons that dealt with the follies or misfortunes of the fashionable set were laid to her door. A certain Miss Lowther, one of Lord Lonsdale's sisters,[1] was the heroine, it appears, of an anecdote which was then fire-new, and considered "amazing droll," but which has since degenerated into the mouldiest of chestnuts. It relates to the tradesman, who called at the house of a mature spinster, and sent up word that he died for the mistress. The lady, secretly flattered, pretended to be furious at the man's impudence, but presently discovered, to her much more genuine annoyance, that the audacious lover was only a tradesman who dyed her old clothes. Some verses appeared shortly after the incident became public on "A Lady mistaking a Dying Tradesman for a Dying Lover," which were attributed to Lady Mary Wortley. In a letter to Lady Mar for 1723 she writes—

"Your old friend, Mrs. Lowther, is still fair and young, and in pale pink every night in the Parks; but after being in high favour poor I am in utter disgrace, without my being able to guess wherefore, except she fancied me the author or abettor of two vile ballads written on her dying adventures, which I am so innocent of that I never even saw them. *À propos* of ballads, a most delightful one is said or sung in most houses about our dear beloved plot,[2] which has been laid firstly to Pope, and secondly to me, when God knows we have neither of us wit enough to make it." After detailing one or two new engagements, she continues, "This is, I think, the whole state of love. As to that of wit, it splits itself into ten thousand branches; poets increase and multiply to that stupendous degree, you see them at every turn, even in embroidered coats and pink-coloured top-knots; making verses is almost as common as taking snuff, and God can tell what miserable stuff people carry about in their pockets, and offer to all their acquaintances, and you know one cannot refuse reading and taking a pinch."

[1] Presumably a sister of Henry, third Viscount Lonsdale, who succeeded in 1713, and died in 1750.
[2] The Jacobite plot in which Atterbury was concerned.

On 31st October Lady Mary comes home "piping hot from the birth-night" to write to her sister, her brain warmed, as she says, with all the agreeable ideas that fine clothes, fine gentlemen, brisk times, and lively dances can raise there. "First you must know that I led up the ball, which you'll stare at; but what is more, I believe in my conscience I made one of the best figures there. To say truth, people are grown so extravagantly ugly, that we old beauties are forced to come out on show-days, to keep the Court in countenance."

In the same letter there is a satirical sketch of the lax state of society under George I.[1]—

"The world improves in one virtue to a violent degree, I mean plain-dealing. Hypocrisy being, as the Scripture declares, a damnable sin, I hope our publicans and sinners will be saved by the open profession of the contrary virtue. I was told by a very good authority who is deep in the secret, that at this very minute there is a bill cooking up at a hunting seat in Norfolk [Houghton] to have *not* taken out of the commandments and clapped into the creed, the ensuing season of parliament. This bold attempt for the liberty of the subject is wholly projected by Mr. Walpole, who proposed it to the secret committee in his parlour. William Yonge seconded it, and answered for all his acquaintance voting right to a man. Dodington[2] very gravely objected, that the obstinacy of human nature was such that he feared when they had positive commands to do so, perhaps people would not commit adultery and bear false witness against their neighbours with the readiness and cheerfulness they do at present. This objection seemed to sink into the minds of the greatest politicians at the board; and I don't know whether the bill won't be dropped, though it is certain it might be carried with great ease, the world being entirely *revenue du* (sic) *bagatelle*, and honour, virtue, reputation, etc., which we used to hear of in our nursery, is as much

---

[1] Lord Chesterfield said that the difficulties and dangers suffered by lovers and their ladies in the prudish reign of Queen Anne, were in a great measure removed by the arrival of the Hanoverian monarch. "King George I. loved pleasures, and was not delicate in the choice of them."

[2] George Bubb Dodington (1691–1762), created Baron Melcombe in 1761. He was a Lord of the Treasury in 1724, and a favourite of Frederick, Prince of Wales. He too was a scribbler of verses, and affected the society of the wits.

laid aside and forgotten as crumpled riband. To speak plainly, I am sorry for the forlorn state of matrimony, which is as much ridiculed by our young ladies as it used to be by young fellows. In short, the appellation of rake is as genteel in a woman as in a man of quality. . . . You may imagine we married women look very silly; we have nothing to excuse ourselves, but that it was done a great while ago, and we were very young when we did it."

Society was greatly agitated at this time by the second marriage of Lady Holdernesse (a daughter of the Duke of Schomberg) to Benjamin Mildmay, afterwards Lord Fitzwalter. Lady Mary had at first disbelieved the rumour of the marriage, and had defended Lady Holdernesse from the accusation that she contemplated such a step.[1] But on 7th December 1723 she writes to her friend, Mrs. Calthorpe, a daughter of the first Lord Longueville—

"My knight-errantry is at an end, and I believe I shall henceforth think freeing of galley slaves and knocking down windmills more laudable undertakings than the defence of any woman's reputation whatever. To say truth, I have never had any great esteem for the generality of the fair sex, and my only consolation for being of that gender has been the assurance it gave me of never being married to anyone among them. But I own at present I am so much out of humour with the actions of Lady Holdernesse that I was never so heartily ashamed of my petticoats before. You know, I suppose, that by this discreet match she renounces the care of her children, and I am laughed at by all my acquaintance for my faith in her honour and understanding. My only refuge is the sincere hope that she is out of her senses, and taking herself for the Queen of Sheba, and Mr. Mildmay for King Solomon. I do not think it quite so ridiculous. But the men, you may well imagine, are not so charitable; and they agree in the kind reflection that nothing hinders women from playing the fool but not having it in their power."

Lady Mary must have written much in the same strain to

[1] The bride and bridegroom were both, it appears, in a decrepit state of health. However, the lady lived till 1751, and her lord till 1756.

the Duchess of Montagu,[1] who replies, "I[2] am very much obliged to you, dear Lady Mary, for your kind letter of the 2nd of December. I find you very sincere in saying you think I have not much curiosity, for you have writ me a letter which would have cost my Lady Chetwin (*sic*)[3] her life, considering it can't be explained in less than six weeks. Who the happy pair are, who you describe without naming to be so charming and so charmed, sounds more like heaven than hell, and yet upon the whole I am a little of your mind, that there will be nothing more than this world. Sometimes, in a fit of generosity, I think there should be something better to reward some of us, but then I don't know what to do with the rest; and I am sure if it was not for hell Mrs. C. would not know what to do with anybody.

"My Lady Holdernesse' match is the nastiest thing I ever heard in my life. There is nothing in my Lord Rotchester's verses that makes one more ashamed. I hear his daughter is at Rouen still, and keeps my Lady, being there two months in her way to England. She may be there still for anything I know. I believe she is, for I can do neither of them so much wrong as not to think they are in love. One must be very dull to be otherwise in the presence of such objects. . . ."

To her sister Lady Mary retailed the gossip about Lady Holdernesse, and a piece of scandal about Anastasia Robinson, the singer: "I find it is impossible to forbear telling the metamorphoses of some of your acquaintance, which appear to me as wondrous as any in Ovid. Could one believe that Lady Holdernesse is a beauty and in love? and that Mrs. Robinson is at the same time a prude and a kept mistress? The first of these ladies is tenderly attached to the polite Mr. Mildmay, and sunk in all the joys of happy love, notwithstanding she wants the use of her two hands by a rheumatism, and he has an arm that he cannot move. I wish I could send you the particulars of this amour, which seems to me as curious

---

[1] This was Mary, daughter of the great Duke of Marlborough. She married the second Duke of Montagu.

[2] From the unpublished MS.

[3] Mrs. Chetwynd's husband was created Viscount Chetwynd in 1717.

as that between two oysters, and as well worth the serious inquiry of the naturalists.

"The second heroine has engaged half the town in arms, from the nicety of her virtue, which was not able to bear the too near approach of Senesino in the Opera; and her condescension in accepting of Lord Peterborough for her champion, who has signalised both his love and his courage upon this occasion in as many instances as ever Don Quixote did for Dulcinea. Poor Senesino, like a vanquished giant, was forced to confess upon his knees that Anastasia was a nonpareil of virtue and beauty. Lord Stanhope, as dwarf to the said giant, joked of his side, and was challenged for his pains. Lord Delawar[1] was Lord Peterborough's second. My lady miscarried— the whole town divided into parties on this important point. Innumerable have been the disorders between the two sexes on so great an account, besides half the house of peers being put under arrest. By the providence of Heaven, and the wise cares of his Majesty, no bloodshed ensued. However, things are now tolerably accommodated; and the fair lady rides through the town in triumph in the shining berlin of her hero, not to reckon the essential advantage of £100 a month, which 'tis said he allows her."

It soon becomes apparent that Lady Mary had joined a set in which the pace was fast and furious, and in such a *milieu*, whatever her actual conduct, her indiscreet tongue and general disregard of appearances must have been a source of danger.

The first allusion to the Duke of Wharton appears in a letter written by Lady Mary to her sister early in 1724. "In general," she observes, "gallantry never was in so elevated a figure as it is at present. Twenty pretty fellows (the Duke of Wharton being president and chief director) have formed themselves into a committee of gallantry. They call themselves *Schemers*, and meet regularly three times a week to consult on gallant schemes for the advantage and advancement of that branch of happiness. . . . I consider the duty of a true Englishwoman is to do what honour she can to her native country; and that it would be a sin against the pious love I

[1] John, seventh Lord Delawarr, married a daughter of Lord Clancarty. He was afterwards created Earl Delawarr.

bear the land of my nativity, to confine the renown due to the Schemers within the small extent of this little island, which ought to be spread wherever men can sigh or women wish. 'Tis true they have the envy and curses of the old and ugly of both sexes, and a general persecution from all old women; but this is no more than all reformations must expect in their beginning."

Later we hear that "The Duke of Wharton has brought his Duchess to town, and is fond of her to distraction;[1] in order to break the hearts of all the other women that have any claim upon his. . . . He has public devotions twice a day, and assists at them in person with exemplary devotion, and there is nothing pleasanter than the remarks of some pious ladies on the conversion of so great a sinner. For my own part, I have some coteries where wit and pleasure reign, and I should not fail to amuse myself tolerably enough, but for the d——d d——d quality of growing older and older every day, and my present joys are made imperfect by fears of the future."

[1] The daughter of General Holmes, whom he had married when he was only sixteen. By 1724 he had run through his great fortune (he admitted having lost £120,000 in the South Sea Scheme), and his estates about this time were placed in the hands of trustees, who allowed him £1200 a year.

CHAPTER XXXI

LITERARY FRIENDSHIPS

LADY MARY loved to pose as a critic of letters and a patroness of authors, though, if there is any foundation for the charge of meanness so often brought against her, her patronage could not have been worth very much, even to the poorest inhabitants of Grub Street. Dr. Young, Richard Savage, and her cousin, Henry Fielding, were among her literary friends or protégés at this period. In February 1724 Dr. Young[1] wrote the following letter about his tragedy *The Brothers*, which she had read and criticised:—

" MADAM,—A great cold and a little intemperance has given me such a face as I am ashamed to show, tho' I much want to talk with your ladyship. For my theatrical measures are broken. *Marianne*[2] brought its author above £1500, *The Captives*[3] above £1000, and *Edwin*,[4] now in rehearsal, has already, before acting, brought its author above £1000. Mine, when acted, will not more than pay for the paper on which it is written; but the moment I get abroad, I will wait on your ladyship, and explain further. Only this at present, for the reason mentioned, I am determined to suppress my play for this season at least. The concern you show for its success is my apology for this account, which were otherwise very impertinent. . . ."

---

[1] Edward Young (1683-1765) was a protégé of the Duke of Wharton's, and a friend of Bubb Dodington's (which does not say much for him). He had produced his tragedy *The Revenge* with success at Drury Lane in 1721. *The Brothers* was withdrawn from rehearsal in 1728, owing to his appointment as Chaplain to George II., and not produced till 1753. It was not until 1742 that he brought out the *Night Thoughts*, by which he is now best remembered.

[2] By Elijah Fenton.   [3] By Gay.   [4] By G. Jeffreys.

In 1725 Savage[1] dedicated his Miscellanies[2] to Lady Mary, who sent him some acknowledgment in money. Dr. Young, who seems to have conducted the negotiation, wrote on 1st March: "I have seen Mr. Savage, who is extremely sensible of the honour your ladyship did him by me. You was, I find, too modest in your opinion of the present you pleased to make him, if Mr. Savage may be allowed to be a judge in the case." Later, when *The Brothers* was actually in rehearsal, we find Dr. Young admitting with humility, the force of certain criticisms on the piece made by Lady Mary. He will alter such as be alterable. "Those that are not I beg you to make a secret of," he continues, "and to make an experiment on the sagacity of the town which I think may possibly overlook what you have observed, for the players and Mr. Dodington, neither of whom were backward in finding

---

[1] Richard Savage, the poet, claimed to be the illegitimate son of Lord Rivers. He had already written a comedy and in 1723 had played the title-rôle in his tragedy *Sir Thomas Overbury* at Drury Lane. Two years after the date of this letter he killed a man in a tavern brawl, and was condemned to death, but was pardoned through the intercession, it is said, of Lady Hertford with Queen Caroline, from whom he afterwards obtained a pension. Dr. Johnson tried to help him during his last years.

[2] "*Miscellaneous Poems and Translations* by several Hands. Published by Richard Savage, son of the Earl of Rivers." The dedication is a full-blooded example of the eighteenth-century literary compliment—

"MADAM,—That I have the ambition to address my Miscellany to the loveliest Patroness in the World, is a presumption, I confess, in *me*, who have not the honour to be known to your Ladyship. But I have a motive to it still more powerful than the flattering hope of your condescending to forgive me. . . . I mean the Goodness, Tenderness and Sweetness of disposition so natural to your Ladyship. I know not how I can forbear this application; because there is scarce a possibility that I should say more than I believe when I am speaking of your excellence.

"Since our country has been honoured by the glory of your Wit, as elevated and immortal as your soul! it no longer remains a doubt whether your Sex have strength of mind in proportion to their sweetness. There is something in your *verses* as distinguished as your *Air*! They are as strong as Truth; as deep as Reason; as clear as Innocence; and as smooth as Beauty! They contain a nameless mixture of grace and force; which is at once so movingly serene, and so majestically lovely, that it is too amiable to appear anywhere but in your *eyes* and your *writings*.

"Forgive me, Madam, if (while I feel the divine influence of your Spirit, which no words but yours can display, and no form but yours could have enshrined) I presume to lay before you such unpardonable compositions as my own: Those of my Friends will, I doubt not, prove worthy of your perusal; and in some measure atone the faults of his who begs permission to subscribe himself, with the utmost Devotion, Madam, your Ladyship's most Humble and most Obedient Servant,

"RICHARD SAVAGE."

fault, or careless in attention, took no notice of the flaw in D.'s [Demetrius'] honour, or Erixene's conduct, and I would fain have their blindness continue till my business is done."

The relations that then existed between Lady Mary and her second cousin, Henry Fielding,[1] may be illustrated by a couple of letters, in which the young man consults her about the dramatic work upon which he was then engaged. The following note probably refers to his earliest comedy, *Love in several Masques*, which was produced in 1727, but not published till 1728:—

"MADAM,—I have presumed to send your ladyship a copy of the play which you did me the honour of reading three acts of last spring, and hope it may meet as light a censure from your ladyship's judgment as then; for while your goodness permits me (what I esteem the greatest, and indeed only happiness of my life) to offer my unworthy performances to your perusal, it will be entirely from your sentence that they will be regarded or disesteemed by me. I shall do myself the honour of calling at your ladyship's door to-morrow at eleven, which, if it be an improper hour, I beg to know from your servant what other time will be more convenient.—I am, with the greatest respect and gratitude, madam, your ladyship's most obedient, most humble servant."

Not less subservient is the other note, dated 4th September and attributed to the year 1731.

"I hope your ladyship will honour the scenes which I presume to lay before you, with your perusal. As they are written on a Model I never yet attempted, I am exceedingly anxious lest they should find less mercy from you than my lighter productions. It will be a slight compensation to *The Modern Husband*,[2] that your ladyship's censure will defend him from the possibility of any other reproof, since your least

---

[1] Henry Fielding was only twenty at this time, and was trying to make a career as a playwright. He got into trouble over his political skit *Pasquin* in 1736, and gave up his dramatic work to "find himself" as a novelist, his *Joseph Andrews* being published in 1742.

[2] Produced at Drury Lane in February 1732.

approbation will always give me pleasure, infinitely superior to the loudest applauses of a theatre. For whatever has past your judgment may, I think, without any imputation of immodesty, refer want of success to want of judgment in an audience. I shall do myself the honour of waiting upon your ladyship at Twickenham next Monday to receive my sentence, and am, madam, with the most devoted respect, your etc."

About this time we begin to hear more of Lady Mary's dear friends, Lady Stafford and Molly Skerret, with whom she contrived to live in intimacy without either quarrels or misunderstandings. They were, no doubt, among the select few that, as she tells her sister, she retained to supper every Sunday, after receiving the whole town in the afternoon. "If life could be always what it is now," she remarks (January 1725), "I believe I have so much humility in my temper I could be contented without anything better than this two or three hundred years. But alas,

> 'Dulness and wrinkles and disease must come,
> And age, and death's irrevocable doom.'"

Squabbles were common and public enough among the "people of quality" at that period, who were less civilised, in the sense of being less self-controlled, than their descendants of the present day.

"All our acquaintance have run mad," writes Lady Mary (February 1725). "They do such things! such monstrous and stupendous things! Lady Hervey and Lady Bristol[1] have quarrelled in such a polite manner, that they have given one another all the titles so liberally bestowed amongst the ladies at Billingsgate. Sophia and I have been quite reconciled, and are now quite broke, and I believe not likely to piece up again." Sophia was apparently her nickname for the Duke of Wharton, now a ruined man, and more than suspected of being in communication with the Jacobites abroad. Later in the year she writes—

"Sophia is going to Aix-la-Chapelle, and from thence to

[1] Lady Hervey was the daughter-in-law of Lady Bristol, who was a woman of violent temper.

Paris. I dare swear she'll endeavour to get acquainted with you. We are broke to an irremediable degree. Various are the persecutions I have endured from him this winter, in all which I remain neuter, and shall certainly go to heaven from the passive meekness of my temper."[1] With the "vivacious Lord Bathurst," too, Lady Mary says, "I have been well and ill ten times within these two months: we now hardly speak to each other."

A worse quarrel was that with Mrs. Murray, whose unfortunate adventure with the footman, Arthur Grey, had already been poetically treated by Lady Mary. An indecent ballad on the same incident, *Virtue in Danger*, had lately appeared, and it was perhaps natural that it should be attributed to the author of the *Epistle from Arthur Grey*. Mrs. Murray was much incensed at the renewed publicity given to her misfortune, and visited her wrath upon Lady Mary, who reports to her sister that—

"A very odd whim has entered the head of little Mrs. Murray; do you know she won't visit me this winter? I, according to the usual integrity of my heart and simplicity of my manners, with great *naïveté* desired to explain with her on the subject, and she answered that she was convinced that I had made the ballad upon her, and was resolved never to speak to me again. I answered (which was true) that I utterly defied her to have any one single proof of my making it, without being able to get anything from her but repetitions that she knew it. I cannot suppose that anything you have said should occasion this rupture, and the reputation of a quarrel is always so ridiculous on both sides, that you will oblige me in mentioning it to her, for 'tis now at that pretty pass, she won't curtsey to me whenever she meets me, which

---

[1] The Duke had left England for Vienna about this time, and had openly espoused the cause of the Pretender, who created him Duke of Northumberland. Later he went to Madrid on Jacobite business, and on the death of his first wife he married a Miss O'Neill, Maid of Honour to the Queen of Spain. Having served on the Spanish side at the Siege of Gibraltar, he was outlawed by the English Government, and his allowance was stopped. He wandered about Europe during the last three years of his life, subsisting on small grants from the Pretender. His health broke down in 1730, and, having become a Roman Catholic, he died in the Franciscan Monastery of Poblet in 1731, being then only thirty-three.

is superlatively silly (if she really knew it) after a suspension of resentment for two years together."

Our heroine, having now reached the mature age of thirty-six, seems to have been undecided whether to settle down into sober middle age, or to hang on to the skirts of youth and gaiety a little longer. At one moment she longs to be ten years younger, and feels with regret that she is insensibly dwindling into a spectator of life. At another she is full of youthful enthusiasm over a new horse she has acquired, which is vastly superior to any human being she knows, and she has taken ardently to stag-hunting.

"I have arrived to vast courage and skill in that way," she explains, "and am as pleased with it as with the acquisition of a new sense. His Royal Highness hunts in Richmond Park, and I make one of the *beau monde* in his train. I desire you, after this account, not to name the word of old woman to me any more. I approach to fifteen nearer than I did ten years ago, and am in hopes to improve every year in health and vivacity."

Then follows a cryptic passage, which may probably be explained by the fact that some new love-interest had come into the writer's life, which she found it difficult to conduct with prudence and discretion.

"I have such complications of things both in my head and heart that I do not very well know what I do, and if I can't settle my brains, your next news of me will be that I am locked up by my relations. In the meantime I lock myself up, and keep my distraction as private as possible. The most facetious part of the history is, that my distemper is of such a nature I know not whether to laugh or cry at it;[1] I am glad and sorry, smiling or sad;—but this is too long an account of so whimsical a being. I give myself admirable advice, but I am incapable of taking it."

The stream of lively gossip still continues. Lord Carleton[2]

---

[1] Could this have been the declaration of Pope?

[2] Henry Boyle, a younger son of the Earl of Orrery, who had been Secretary of State, 1708–10. He was created Baron Carleton in 1714. Lady Mary says that he disposed of his estate as he did his time, between Lady Clarendon and the Duchess of Queensberry, having given his affections first to the mother and then to the daughter.

has just died, holding the young Duchess of Marlborough's hand, and being fed with a fat chicken. Lady Gainsborough [1] has stolen poor Lord Shaftesbury,[2] aged fourteen, and married him to her daughter, under the pretence that he has been in love with her for years. Lady Hervey makes the top figure in town, and is so good a politician that if people were not blind to merit, she would govern the nation. Mrs. Murray has got an accomplished new lover in Bubb Dodington. My Lord Bathurst is paying assiduous court to the Prince and Princess of Wales, a fact that fills the coffee-houses with speculation.

"But I, who smell a rat at a distance," continues the chronicler, "do believe in private that Mrs. Howard [3] and his lordship have a friendship that borders on the tender." A little later, we hear that "These smothered flames, though admirably covered with whole heaps of politics laid over them, were at length seen, felt, heard and understood; and the fair lady given to understand by her commanding officer that if she showed under other colours, she must expect to have her pay retrenched. Upon which the good lord was dismissed, and has not attended in the drawing-room since. You know one cannot help laughing when one sees him next, and I own I long for that pleasurable moment."

Another piece of scandal concerned Lady Mary's old acquaintance Lady Lechmere (one of the Ladies Howard), who had "lost such furious sums at Bath that 'tis questioned whether all the sweetness that the waters can put into my Lord's blood, can make him endure it, particularly £700 at one sitting." In the next letter we hear of the melancholy catastrophe of the "discreet and sober" Lady Lechmere. "After having played away her reputation and fortune, she has poisoned herself. This is the effect of prudence!" Lady Lechmere did not succeed in her attempt, for she survived till 1739 and married again. But there is an allusion to the incident, or

---

[1] Lady Dorothy Manners, wife of Baptist Noel, third Earl of Gainsborough.
[2] Anthony Ashley, fourth Earl, who succeeded his father in 1713. Lady Susannah Noel was his cousin.
[3] The mistress of George II., and afterwards Countess of Suffolk.

so it is supposed, in the "Rosamunda's bowl" of Pope's *Epistle on the Characters of Women.* Lady Mary's comment is, "We wild girls always make your prudent wives and mothers."

Mr. Sidney Montagu being still alive, Mr. Wortley was only moderately well off, though he appears to have made money during his Turkish Embassy. Some of his capital may have been lost in the South Sea Bubble, and whatever his income, he was not inclined to give his wife a free hand in the matter of her personal expenses. She had evidently been rather extravagant in the year 1725, for anxious as she was to visit Paris during the summer in order to cheer and console her unhappy sister, she explains that she is obliged to stay in "this sinful sea-coal town" till she can dispose of some superfluous diamonds. As money is supposed to be "high" at Paris, she begs Lady Mar to inquire for what she could sell a clean thick diamond, Indian cut, and weighing thirty-nine grains.

A couple of letters from Lady Mar have been preserved, and one of them, dated 23rd November, contains the answer to the above request—

"I've[1] this moment received your letter, and to let you see how far I am from deserving your displeasure, I won't defer answering it even till next post, tho' I shall persist in thinking my reasons for silence very good, so good that I fear a time will come when I shall neither write nor see anybody. Staying at home, you say, inclines one to converse with one's friends this way. If that was so I should often have a pen in my hand; but my solitude comes from causes that you are too happy to have experienced, and gives me no other inclination but to dose upon a couch, or exclaim against my fortune, and wish, like Altamont, forgetfulness could steal upon me, to soften and assuage the pain of thinking.

"In short, I've had since my return all sorts of mortifications that you can imagine can happen to anybody, and the story of Sophia is a trifle to what I've met with. I believe most women are devils in all countries, but here they are much worse than anywhere else, having neither common honesty nor common sense. As for your project of coming, I should be

[1] From the unpublished MS.

heartily glad to see you, but before I inquire (which I won't fail to do as soon as possible) I know this is the worst time to think of getting anything here, money being so scarce that I question whether anybody could be found to buy such a diamond as you speak of. Everything is very dear, which makes people retrench their expense to what is absolutely necessary, and jewels you know cannot be comprehended under that head; but I hope that won't hinder you from making your trip. I'm at present very much out of humour with the world, but would leave my chimney corner to attend you. My house could be no entertainment to you, for I see but a few women, and no men that can divert anybody. But pray come; I'm impatient for your next letter in hopes to have a commission for taking you a lodging. Adieu."

CHAPTER XXXII

FAMILY TROUBLES

ON 7th March 1726 Lady Mary wrote to inform her sister of the "surprising death" of their father (on 5th March) and the "surprising management" of the people about him. Lady Mar, who was already in a morbid state, was much distressed at the news, but Lady Mary in a later letter remarks with philosophic calm—

"*Au bout de compte*, I don't know why filial piety should exceed fatherly fondness. So much by way of consolation. As to the management at that time, I do verily believe if my good aunt [Cheyne] and sister [Gower] had been less fools, and my dear mother-in-law less mercenary, things might have had a turn more to your advantage, and mine too. . . . I could not get my sister Gower to act with me, and mamma and I were in an actual scold when my poor father expired. She has shewn a hardness of heart upon this occasion that would appear incredible to anybody not capable of it themselves."

The Duke had expressed a good deal of kindness for his eldest daughter at the last, and even a desire of talking to her, but this "my Lady Duchess" would not permit. The said Duchess was left a rich and beautiful young widow, but she only lived to enjoy her jointure two years. Many were the family squabbles about the guardianship of the young Duke and his sister, who were now doubly orphaned, their mother having died, of a broken heart it was supposed, in 1722. The Duke was then about sixteen, and it was arranged that he should set out on his travels at once. He had been given so ill an education, in Lady Mary's opinion, that it was hard to tell what he would do. He had spirit, without his father's good sense, but as young noblemen went, it was possible he might make a good figure among them. His sister Frances, who had £400 a year for her maintenance, was finally carried off to Trentham by Lady Gower, who was always short of money, owing to her passion for crimp and quadrille.

Lady Mary only received £6000 from her father, but, for some reason or other, her affairs were in great prosperity at this season, and she herself in excellent spirits. For one thing, she had quite given up gambling on Change Alley. Wars and rumours of wars made all the conversation, and the tumbling of the stocks influenced most people's affairs, but "for my part," she writes, " I have no concern there or anywhere, but hearty prayers that what relates to myself may ever be exactly what it is now. I am in perfect health, and hear it said I look better than ever I did in my life, which is one of those lies one is always glad to hear."

Perhaps the secret of this complacency may be found in the following passage, which occurs in another letter: " We have nothing but ugly faces in this country, but more lovers than ever. There are but three pretty men in England, and they are all in love with me at this present writing. This will amaze you extremely; but if you were to see the reigning girls at present, I will assure you there is very little difference between them and old women."

A visit to Paris was again in contemplation, but was again postponed, London having grown so gay that it was impossible for a woman of fashion to exchange its delights for a sojourn in Paris which was temporarily deserted by the gay and the gallant.

"This town improves in gaiety every day; the young people are younger than they used to be, and all the old are grown young. Nothing is talked of but entertainments of gallantry by land and water, and we insensibly begin to taste all the joys of arbitrary power. Politics are no more; nobody pretends to wince or kick under their burdens; but we go on cheerfully with our bells at our ears, ornamented with ribands, and highly contented with our present condition. So much for the general state of the nation. The last pleasure that fell in my way was Madame Sévigné's Letters; very pretty they are, but I assert, without the least vanity, that mine will be full as entertaining forty years hence. I advise you, therefore, to put none of them to the use of waste paper." A letter which never came to her sister's hands she describes as a *chef d'œuvre* of a letter, crammed with news, and worth any of the Sévigné's and Grignan's.

Lady Mary's complacency was soon to receive a shock, through the misdemeanours of her son, then a boy of thirteen. He ran away from school on at least three separate occasions, the first time in 1726. "My blessed offspring," she tells her sister in June, "has already made a great noise in the world. That young rake, my son, took to his heels t'other day, and transported his person to Oxford; being in his own opinion thoroughly qualified for the University. After a good deal of search we found and reduced him, much against his will, to the humble condition of a school-boy. It happens very luckily that the sobriety and discretion are on my daughter's side. I am sorry the ugliness is so too, for my son grows extremely handsome."

In a letter written in November of this year there is the following slighting allusion to *Gulliver's Travels*, the first two volumes of which were published on 28th October: "Here is a book come out that all our people of taste run mad about. 'Tis no less than the united work of a dignified clergyman, an eminent physician, and the first poet of the age;[1] and very wonderful it is, God knows!—great eloquence have they employed to prove themselves beasts, and shew such a veneration for horses, that, since the Essex Quaker, nobody has appeared so passionately devoted to that species; and to say truth, they talk of a stable with such warmth and affection, I cannot help suspecting some very powerful motive at the bottom of it."

There is a gap of nearly six months in the correspondence with Lady Mar, and it is not till March 1727 that we have another letter from Lady Mary, who writes in low spirits because her friend Lady Stafford is going to Paris, and takes half the pleasures of life along with her.

"I am more stupid than I can describe," she writes, "and

[1] The book was thought at first to be the joint production of Swift, Pope, and Arbuthnot.

am as full of moral reflections as Cambray or Pascal. I think of nothing but the nothingness of the good things of this world, the transitoriness of its joys, the pungency of its sorrows, and many discoveries that have been made these three thousand years, and committed to print ever since the first presses."

The usual budget of gossip follows: "Our dear and amiable cousin, Lady Denbigh,[1] has blazed out on her return from Paris in cartloads of ribbons and surprising fashions, and keeps a Sunday assembly to show that she has learnt to play cards on that day." Lady Frances Fielding is the prettiest woman in town, and it makes Lady Mary's heart ache to see her surrounded by such fools as her relations. The man in England that gives the greatest pleasure and the greatest pain, is "a youth of royal blood, with all his grandmother's beauty, wit and good qualities. In short, he is Nell Gwyn in person, with the sex altered, and occasions such fracas among the ladies of gallantry that it passes description." This was Lord Sidney Beauclerk, son of the first Duke of St. Albans. Chief among his admirers was the sixty-year-old Duchess of Cleveland,[2] who had turned her daughter, Lady Grace Vane, and all her family out of doors in order to make room for him. Lady Stafford declared that there had been nothing like it since Phædra and Hippolitus, and Lady Mary concludes—

"Lord ha' mercy upon us! See what we may all come to!"

About the end of May Lady Gower gave birth to a daughter, and on 27th June she died, having never, it must be supposed, recovered from her confinement. That she had injured her constitution from her devotion to quadrille may be gathered from a letter which Lady Stafford wrote from Paris, to make her friend "a compliment" (as she oddly expresses it) on the death of her sister. "Cela est bien pitoyable," she adds, "de perdre la vie par jouer à cadrille, mais aussi, il faut considérer qu'elle ne perd que ce plaisir là, et que c'est tout ce qu'elle aurait fait dans ce monde, si elle y était restée plus longtemps."

[1] Wife of William, fifth Earl of Denbigh. She was a daughter of Peter de Jong of Utrecht.
[2] A daughter of Sir William Pulteney, and second wife of Charles, Duke of Cleveland.

Lady Mary, although she admits that the manner of Lady Gower's death had made an impression on her not easily to be shaken off, desires that Lady Mar will not give way to her grief.

"Of all sorrows," she observes, "those we pay to the dead are most vain; and as I have no good opinion of sorrow in general, I think no sort of it worth cherishing." She had other troubles, however, that touched her more nearly. "My girl gives me great prospect of satisfaction, but my young rogue of a son is the most ungovernable little rake that ever played truant." She is inclined to believe that things are more equally disposed than most people imagine, and concludes by giving her sister, whose philosophy was so lugubrious, a rule which she had found conducive to health both of body and mind. "As soon as you wake in the morning, lift up your eyes and consider seriously what will best divert you that day. Your imagination being then refreshed by sleep, will certainly put into your mind some party of pleasure, which, if you execute with prudence, will disperse those melancholy vapours which are the foundation of all distempers."

This Epicurean philosophy could not, however, be tried too far. Its consolations were of small avail to a mother who was lamenting the disappearance of an only son. In August Lady Mary wrote—

"I am vexed to the blood by my young rogue of a son, who has contrived at his age to make himself the talk of the whole nation. He is gone knight-erranting, God knows where; and hitherto 'tis impossible to find him. You may judge of my uneasiness by what your own would be if dear Lady Fanny was lost. Nothing that ever happened to me has troubled me so much; I can hardly speak or write of it with tolerable temper, and I own it has changed mine to that degree I have a mind to cross the water, to try what effect a new heaven and a new earth will have upon my spirits." An advertisement was published offering a reward of £20 for the return of the boy, who was to be identified by the inoculation marks on his arms. He was discovered a month later on board a ship about to set sail nobody knew whither.

In September Lady Mary was in a mood of gloomy resignation. She declares that it is a vile world, and that most people are made up of a mixture of fool and knave. Yet sixpenny-worth of common sense, divided among a whole nation, would, she thinks, make life roll away smoothly enough. The whole mischief arises from our making laws and following customs, since by the first we cut off our own pleasures, and by the second we are answerable for the faults and extravagances of others.

"All these things, and five hundred more, convince me (as I have the most profound veneration for the Author of Nature) that we are here in an actual state of punishment. I am satisfied I have been one of the *condemned* ever since I was born; and in submission to the divine justice, I don't at all doubt but I deserved it in some pre-existent state. I will still hope I am only in purgatory, and that after whining and grunting a certain number of years, I shall be translated to some more happy sphere, where virtue will be natural and custom reasonable; that is, in short, where common sense will reign.[1]

"I grow very devout, as you see, and place all my hopes in the next life, being totally persuaded of the nothingness of this. Don't you remember how miserable we were in the little parlour at Thoresby? We then thought being married would put us in possession of all we wanted. Then came being with child, etc., and you see what comes of being with child. Though, after all, I am still of opinion that it is extremely silly to submit to ill-fortune. One should pluck up a spirit, and live upon cordials, when one can have no other nourishment. These are my present endeavours, and I run about, tho' I have five hundred pins and needles running into my heart. I try to console myself with a small damsel who is at present everything I like—but alas! she is yet in a white frock. At fourteen she may run away with the butler. There's one of the blessed consequences of great disappointments; you are not only hurt by the thing present, but it cuts off all future hopes, and makes your very expectations melancholy. *Quelle vie ! ! !*"

Mr. Sidney Montagu died in the course of this year, and Mr. Wortley came into his inheritance. He seems to have had some idea of going to live in Yorkshire, but Wortley Hall

[1] The ideal heaven of the eighteenth century.

had been allowed to fall into decay, Wharncliffe Lodge was too small, and he naturally disliked the associations of the house at St. Ellen's Well, which Mr. Montagu had built for his mistress. So he and his wife continued to pass their time between London and Twickenham. They now enjoyed a very good income, and the economical methods that had become second nature to both of them, ensured a steady increase of fortune year by year.

George I. died in June, and on 11th October George II. was crowned. The last letter in the series to Lady Mar contains a description of the Coronation, which Lady Mary found highly diverting—

"I saw the procession much at my ease, in a house which I filled with my own company, and then got into Westminster Hall without trouble, where it was very entertaining to observe the variety of airs that all meant the same thing. . . . She that drew the greatest number of eyes was indisputably Lady Orkney.[1] She exposed behind a mixture of fat and wrinkles; and before, a very considerable protuberance which preceded her. Add to this the inimitable roll of her eyes, and her grey hairs, which by good fortune stood directly upright, and 'tis impossible to imagine a more delightful spectacle. She had embellished all this with considerable magnificence, which made her look as big again as usual; and I should have thought her one of the largest things of God's making, if my Lady St. John[2] had not displayed all her charms in honour of the day. The poor Duchess of Montrose[3] crept along, with a dozen of black snakes playing round her face, and my Lady Portland[4] (who is fallen away

[1] Lady Orkney (Elizabeth Villiers) had been one of Queen Mary's Maids of Honour, and afterwards became mistress to William III. When he dismissed her in 1694 she married Lord George Hamilton, who was created Earl of Orkney in 1696. At this time Lady Orkney was about seventy years old. She died in 1733. Swift said she was the wisest woman he ever knew.

[2] This was probably the second wife of Henry St. John, created Viscount St. John in 1716, father of the great Lord Bolingbroke. She was Angelica, daughter of George Pilesary, Treasurer-General of the Marines under Louis XVI.

[3] The wife of the first Duke of Montrose. She was Christian, daughter of the third Earl of Northesk.

[4] Jane, a daughter of Sir John Temple, Bart., of East Sheen. She married first Lord Berkeley, and afterwards became the second wife of William Bentinck,

since her dismission from Court) represented very finely an Egyptian mummy embroidered over with hieroglyphics. In general, I could not but perceive that the old were as well pleased as the young; and I, who dread growing wise more than anything in the world, was overjoyed to find that one can never outlive one's vanity."

Lady Mar's melancholy had grown upon her to such an extent that it was feared she might take her own life, and in March 1728 her lunacy was declared. The following letter, written by her to her sister in the previous November, shows the depression from which she was suffering at that time:—

"You[1] think me a strange creature, I'm sure, for being so long without writing to you. All I can say is, laziness, stupidity and ill-humour have taken such hold upon me that I write to nobody, nor have spirits to go anywhere. Perhaps a letter from you may contribute to my cure. I must tell you some part of my misfortunes, and I believe you'll own the reason I think myself born to ill-luck, and I dare say had you met with such an adventure you would complain as much as I do. You know the state of my affairs was that I owed considerably here to all sorts of people, and with much solicitation got money to pay part of my debts; but I was no sooner arrived here but an *Arrêt* came out from the Government to diminish the money a fifth part, so that I lost in one night, without dispensing a farthing, four hundred pounds. As my debts were in French livres, I must pay the same number, viz. a hundred pounds, which made three and twenty hundred Livres, and is now worth but 1800. I own no disappointment of that nature ever vexed me so much as this has done, since it might have been prevented twenty ways. Borrowing the money at London, had I had any friends to have lent it me, would have saved me, and not hurt them. Nay, could I have foreseen it, taking up the money at ten per cent. interest would have been better than staying

---

first Earl of Portland. George I. had made her governess to his grandchildren, when he removed them from the care of their parents. Consequently, George II. dismissed her as soon as he came to the throne.

[1] From the unpublished MS.

till it was sent me. This change of the money makes great confusion here, and Paris is now so dear that I don't see how 'tis possible upon our small income to stay in it, nor know I where to go out of it. But this is enough of complaints.

" Should I but mention half the things that vex me, my letter would swell to a volume. I go very seldom abroad, and have very few people that entertain me at home. My Miss Skerret, whom you've heard me talk of, is the only reasonable person in this Country, which is become very dull to me. The King has taken a fancy to pass this winter at Fontainebleau, which keeps all the Court, and Paris is dull beyond what you can imagine. I hope you pass the time better; I long to hear from you. My Lady Stafford has been in the country with my Lady Sandwich.[1] I have not inquired after her, because your commission cannot be executed at this time. The guineas you gave, which used to be five and twenty livres, go now but for eighteen. The silks and every other thing are the same price as before the fall of the money, so that I can buy nothing. I reckon you are returned by this time to London, which God knows when I shall see again, but in the meantime I beg to know what passes there, and I hope this long letter will atone for my silence. Adieu."

" (PARIS, 10th November.)—My daughter makes you her compliments. She is my constant companion, and I shall very soon have the reputation of the greatest prude and the best mother in all Paris, for I keep company with none but old women and little children. I dined with the Comte de Luc,[2] and made him your compliments, but he is grown very old and very stupid. I've often told you what you would find a truth if you were here, the young people are excessively debauched, and the old ones very censorious. . . ."

Lady Mar, who accused her husband of having driven her mad by his ill-usage, was brought to England in March. Lord Mar's brother, Lord Grange,[3] tried to obtain the

---

[1] Elizabeth, daughter of the Earl of Rochester, and wife of the third Earl of Sandwich.
[2] The Comte de Luc already mentioned as the friend and patron of Jean Baptist Rousseau.
[3] James Erskine, Lord Grange (1679–1754). He was Lord Justice-Clerk, with

custody of her, and the control of her fortune, in which aim he was strongly opposed by Lady Mary. The year before, Lord Grange had imprisoned his own wife in the island of St. Kilda, for fear, it was said, that she would disclose Jacobite secrets. Finding himself unable to get the custody of Lady Mar by legal means, he contrived to abduct the poor woman, but when upon the road to Scotland, he was stopped, and his victim arrested, to quote his own account, by a warrant procured " on the false affidavit of her sister Lady Mary, and brought back to London, declared lunatic, and by Lord Chancellor (whose crony is Mr. Wortley, Lady Mary's husband) delivered into the custody of Lady Mary." In her sister's care she remained for about ten years, when her daughter, Lady Frances Erskine, was old enough to take charge of her. Lady Frances afterwards married a son of Lord Grange's, and therefore joined the opposite camp. Lord Mar, who never obtained permission to return to England, died in France in 1732, but Lady Mar lived till 1761.

the title of Lord Grange, in 1710. Though his character was notorious, he afterwards became secretary to Frederick, Prince of Wales.

CHAPTER XXXIII

THE ENMITY OF POPE

WE have now reached the beginning of what may be called the Pope persecution period. Many and various have been the reasons assigned for the malignity with which the poet pursued his former divinity. Lady Mary told Spence[1] that she had persuaded Dr. Arbuthnot to ask Pope what she had done to offend him. He replied that Lady Mary and Lord Hervey had pressed him once to write a satire on some certain persons; that he refused it, and this had occasioned the breach between them. She, on the other hand, denied that Pope had ever been in company with herself and Lord Hervey in his life.

According to family tradition, however, the trouble arose from the poet's indiscretion in making passionate love to his lady at some ill-chosen time, when she so little expected a "declaration," that, in spite of her utmost endeavours to be angry and look grave, she burst into an immoderate fit of laughter. From that moment, there being no fury like a "poet" scorned, he became her implacable enemy.

Pope's love declaration was probably no more genuine than his love-letters, and he would have been terribly alarmed if the lady had taken him seriously and fallen into his arms. He was acting his part in a social charade, and all he asked was that his partner should "play up to him," and, by gentle reprimands and timid reproaches, appear to take him

---

[1] Joseph Spence (1699–1768). In 1728 he was appointed professor of poetry at Oxford, and in 1742 was made Regius Professor. He was acquainted with Pope and his circle, and took notes of their conversation, which were published long after his death. He was accustomed to travel with young men of rank, and in the year 1740 he met Lady Mary in Rome.

seriously, as the "most thinking rake alive." But by her ill-timed laughter Lady Mary wounded him in a cripple's tenderest point—his masculine vanity—and gave proof of the tactlessness which made her more enemies than her ruthless tongue.

The quarrel, from whatever cause it actually arose, was aggravated by Pope's jealousy of Lady Mary's friendship with the Duke of Wharton and Lord Hervey, and his belief that she and they were responsible for some of the anonymous attacks upon his poetry. In the *Epistle to Dr. Arbuthnot* the poet alludes to the broken friendship in the lines—

> "Yet soft by nature, more a dupe than wit,
> Sappho can tell you how this man was bit.[1]
> Safe as he thought, tho' all the prudent chid,
> He wrote no libels, but my Lady did."

This was a misstatement, since the first shots were undoubtedly fired by Pope.[2] As late as 1727 he was writing pleasantly in *Sandys' Ghost*—

> "Ye ladies, too, draw forth your pen,
> I pray where can the hurt lie?
> Since you have brains as well as men,
> As witness Lady Wortley."

Something must have happened about this time to rouse his resentment, for in the same year appeared the volume of Miscellanies published by Swift and Pope which contained *The Capon's Tale* addressed to a Lady who fathered her Lampoons upon her acquaintance. This tells how a Yorkshire farmer's wife had a hen—

> "With eyes so piercing yet so pleasant
> You would have sworn this hen a pheasant."

---

[1] The other version begins—

> "Once, and but once, his heedless youth was bit,
> And liked that dangerous thing, a female wit."

[2] The first published attacks were certainly by Pope, but Lady Mary may have handed round satires on her quondam friend in manuscript, or Pope may have honestly believed that some of the anonymous lampoons directed against his poetry were from her pen.

The bird having hatched more chicks than she could rear, the goodwife made a capon drunk, and clapped the brood beneath his wings. The poem concludes with the lines—

> "Such, Lady Mary, are your tricks;
> But since you hatch, pray own your chicks." [1]

But there was worse to follow the next year, in the couplet in the *Dunciad*—

> "When hapless Monsieur much complains at Paris
> Of wrongs from Duchesses and Lady Maries."

In the second edition the i's were dotted and the t's crossed by the appended note—

"This passage was thought to allude to a famous lady who cheated a French wit of £5000 in the South Sea year. But the author meant it generally of all bragging travellers, and of all whores and cheats under the name of ladies."

Lady Mary did not retaliate at once, though Pope accused her of being the author of one or two scurrilous lampoons which were directed against him—*A Pop upon Pope, The One Epistle*, etc. In a letter to Dr. Arbuthnot, written in October 1730, Lady Mary positively denies that she is the author of a skit—probably *The One Epistle*—which had been attributed to her.

"I am told," she writes, "Pope has the surprising impudence to assert he can bring the lampoon when he chooses to produce it, under my own hand; I desire he may be made to keep to this offer. If he is so skilful in counterfeiting hands, I suppose he will not confine that great talent to the gratifying of his malice, but take some occasion to increase his fortune by the same method, and I may hope (by such practises) to see him exalted according to his merit,[2] which nobody will rejoice at more than myself. I beg of you, sir, (as an act of justice) to endeavour to set the truth in an open light, and then I leave to your judgment the character of those who have attempted to hurt mine in so barbarous a

---

[1] Pope is probably alluding here to ballads published by the Duke of Wharton or Sir William Yonge, in which Lady Mary was supposed to have a finger.

[2] An allusion to the fact that, in those days, forgers were exalted on a gibbet.

fashion. I can assure you (in particular) you named a lady [1] to me (as abused in this libel) whose name I never heard before, and as I never had any acquaintance with Dr. Swift, am an utter stranger to his affairs, and even his person, which I never saw to my knowledge, and am now convinced the whole is a contrivance of Pope's to blast the reputation of one who never injured him. I am not more sensible of his injustice than I am of, sir, of [the] candour, generosity and good sense I have found in you, which has obliged me to be, with a very uncommon warmth, your real friend, and I heartily wish for an opportunity of showing I am so more effectually than by subscribing myself your very humble servant."

During the next six or eight years many and malignant were the attacks upon the Wortleys in the satires of Pope. No man could pay a more elaborate poetical compliment, and no man could pack more concentrated venom into two lines of verse. The most obscure of his enemies was not too insignificant to be immune from punishment that seemed out of all proportion to the offence. On the appearance of each successive satire some Grub Street hack or foolish lordling found himself "damned to everlasting fame." Both hacks and lordlings essayed retorts which answered their purpose at the time by infuriating the thin-skinned poet; but the retorts have long been forgotten, while the original insults are immortalised by their style.

In the later part of 1730 Lady Mary had a severe illness, brought on possibly by worry. The total rupture of Pope's friendship with her cannot have been realised by her old admirer Lord Bathurst, who wrote to the poet in September, "The newspapers say Lady Mary is very ill. Pray inquire after her in your name and mine. We have both been her humble admirers at different times. I am not so changeable as you. I think of her now as I always did."

In the *Epistle to Lord Bathurst* (published a couple of years later) Pope satirised both Lady Mary and her friend Molly Skerret, already suspected of a connection with

---

[1] "Vanessa" (Esther Vanhomrigh), whose amour with Swift is satirised in *The One Epistle*, itself a parody by Moore, Smythe, and Welsted of Dr. Young's laudatory *Two Epistles to Mr. Alexander Pope*.

Sir Robert Walpole, under the names of Sappho and Phryne—

> "Ask you why Phryne the whole auction buys?
> Phryne foresees a general excise.
> Why she and Sappho raise that monstrous sum?
> Alas! they fear a man will cost a plum."

Again, in the *Characters of Women* there is the insulting comparison between

> "Sappho at her toilet's greasy task,
> And Sappho radiant at an evening mask."

But most outrageous of all was the unquotable couplet levelled at "furious Sappho" in the *Imitation of the First Satire of the Second Book of Horace*, which appeared in February 1733. This could not be borne in silence. Lady Mary and Lord Hervey, who had also suffered under the lash of Pope (as "Lord Fanny"), determined to satirise the satirist. The intimacy between the pair had grown closer in the last few years. An extract or two from some letters written by Lord Hervey to her ladyship during a stay in Bath (October 1728) may serve to illustrate the terms upon which they then were. Lady Mary had asked for a list of the visitors at "the Bath," and Lord Hervey replied—

" The Duchess of Marlborough, Congreve and Lady Rich are the only people whose faces I know, whose names I ever heard of, or who, I believe, have any names belonging to them. The rest are a swarm of wretched beings, some with half their limbs, some with none, the ingredients of Pandora's box *personifié*, who stalk about, half-living remembrances of mortality; and by calling themselves human, ridicule the species more than Swift's Yahoos. I do not meet a creature without saying to myself, as Lady —— did of her femme de chambre, 'Regardez cet animal, considérez ce néant, voilà une belle âme pour être immortelle.' . . ."

Three weeks later he wrote again to assure his friend that her fear lest the Duchess of Marlborough should suspect their correspondence was groundless. He admitted that he had read two or three extracts from Lady Mary's last letter to the Duchess, who thought that the writer was Lord Chesterfield.

He begs that in future their correspondence may be without restraint, and concludes—

"I cannot say that my manner of passing my time here is at all disagreeable, for you must know I have an ungenteel happiness in my temper that gives me a propensity to being pleased with the people I happen to be with, and the things I happen to be doing. . . . If you do not dislike long letters, and an unstudied galimatias *tout ce qui se trouve au bout de la plume (comme dit Madame de Sévigné)*, let me know it, and if you would not have me think it flattering when you tell me you do not, encourage the trade, not only by accepting my bills, but making quick returns. . . ."

On 8th March 1733 (N.S.), an advertisement appeared in the *Daily Post* of "Verses addressed to the Imitator of Horace. By a Lady." It soon became an open secret that the joint authors of the satire were Lady Mary and Lord Hervey, though Lord Oxford declared that Mr Wyndham, who was married to Lady Deloraine [1] (the "Delia" of Pope), had a finger in the work. Professor Courthope thinks that the design and the greater part of the composition may be attributed to Lady Mary, while the versification resembles Lord Hervey's. A few lines from these Verses will be sufficient to show their aim and style. The authors begin with a sneer (which only shows that their critical judgment was blinded by their resentment) at the poet's rendering of Horace—

> "Thine is just such an image of his pen
> As thou thyself art of the sons of men,
> Where our own species in burlesque we trace,
> A sign-post likeness of the human race,
> That is at once resemblance and disgrace.
> Horace can laugh, is delicate, is clear,
> You only coarsely rail, or darkly sneer;
> His style is elegant, his diction pure,
> Whilst none thy crabbèd numbers can endure;
> Hard as thy heart, and as thy birth obscure."

After an allusion to Pope's ingratitude to the Duke of

---

[1] Mary, daughter of the Hon. Philip Howard. She was the second wife of the first Earl of Deloraine (son of the Duke of Monmouth). He died in 1730, and she married Mr. William Wyndham.

Chandos, shown by his ridicule of Canons in the *Essay on Taste*, the authors proceed—

> "If none do yet return the intended blow,
> You all your safety to your dulness owe:
> But whilst that armour thy poor corse defends,
> 'Twill make thy readers few, as are thy friends:
> Those who thy nature loathed, yet loved thy art,
> Who liked thy head, and yet abhorred thy heart;
> Chose thee to read, but never to converse,
> And scorned in prose him whom they prized in verse,
> Even they shall now their partial error see,
> Shall shun thy writings like thy company;
> And to thy books shall ope their eyes no more
> Than to thy person they would do their door.
>
> . . . .
>
> Then whilst with coward hand you stab a name,
> And try at least t'assassinate our fame,
> Like the first bold assassin's be thy lot,
> Ne'er be thy guilt forgiven or forgot;
> But as thou hat'st, be hated by mankind,
> And with the emblem of thy crooked mind
> Marked on thy back, like Cain, by God's own hand,
> Wander like him, accursed through the land."

The taste of these lines is indefensible, but then so was that displayed in Pope's attacks on Sappho. The poet had been the first to hit "below the belt," and he ought not to have complained when he received return blows of the same nature. But the satirist is always quiveringly sensitive to satire, and in spite of the literary inferiority of his opponents, Pope keenly felt their taunts, more especially the insulting allusions to his birth and figure. He appealed for sympathy and protection to Sir Robert Walpole, of all people in the world,—Sir Robert, whom he himself publicly ridiculed,—Sir Robert, who left the satirists and caricaturists of his day a free hand, treating their personal attacks in the most sensible fashion, with a shrug of the shoulders and a burst of contemptuous laughter. In a letter to Fortescue, dated 18th March 1733, Pope says—

"You may be certain I shall never reply to such a libel as Lady Mary's. It is a pleasure and comfort at once to find that with so much mind as so much malice must have to accuse or blacken my character, it can fix on no one ill or immoral thing in my life, and must content itself to say, my poetry is dull and my figure ugly. I wish you would take an opportunity to represent to the person [Sir R. Walpole] who spoke to you about that lady, that her conduct in no way deserves *encouragement* from him, or any other great persons; and that the good name of a private subject ought to be sacred, even to the highest, as his behaviour towards them is irreproachable, legal and respectful."

In an undated letter to the same, the poet adds: " I have seen Sir R. W. but once since you left. I made him then my confidant in a complaint against a lady of his, and once of my acquaintance, who is libelling me, as she certainly will one day him, if she has not already. You will easily guess I am speaking of Lady Mary. I should be sorry if she had any credit or influence with him, for she would infallibly use it to belie me; tho' my only fault towards her was, leaving off her conversation when I found it dangerous." [1]

Pope took the trouble to vindicate his birth in the *Epistle to Dr. Arbuthnot,* but the insult to his person still stuck in his throat, and in his *Letter to a Noble Lord* [2] (unpublished in his lifetime) he observes: " It is true, my Lord, I am short, not well shaped, generally ill-dressed, if not sometimes dirty. Your Lordship and Ladyship [3] are still in bloom, your figures such as rival the Apollo of Belvedere, and the Venus of Medici, and your faces so finished that neither sickness nor passion can deprive them of colour."

Mr. Wortley, as well as his wife, now became a regular object of Pope's malice, and is satirised for his miserly habits under the names of Worldly, Avidien, Gripus, and Shylock. Thus, in the *Epistle to Lord Bathurst,* after an allusion to the plenty that would ensue if ministers were paid in kind instead of in money, the poet continues—

> "Poor Avarice one torment more would find;
> Nor could Profusion squander all in kind.
> Astride his cheese Sir Morgan might we meet,
> And Worldly crying coals from street to street,

---

[1] Pope told Arbuthnot that Lady Mary and Lord Hervey had too much wit for him.
[2] Lord Hervey, who had attacked Pope in his *Letter to a Learned Divine.*
[3] He means Lady Mary, not Lady Hervey.

>Whom with a wig so wild, and mien so mazed,
>Pity mistakes for some poor tradesman crazed."

There is a note to the effect that "some misers of great wealth, proprietors of coal-mines, had entered at this time into an association to keep up coals to an extravagant price, whereby the poor were reduced almost to starve, till one of them, taking the advantage of underselling the rest, defeated the design."

Again, in the *Imitation of the Second Satire in the Second Book of Horace*, after speaking of the mean to be observed between avarice and extravagance, he points to the evil examples of Avidien and Avidien's wife, who

>"Sell their presented partridges or fruits,
>And humbly live on rabbits and on roots:
>One half-pint bottle serves them both to dine,
>And is at once their vinegar and wine.
>But on some lucky day (as when they found
>A lost bank bill, or heard their son was drowned)
>At such a feast old vinegar to spare
>Is what two souls so generous cannot bear:
>Oil, though it stink, they drop by drop impart,
>But souse the cabbage with a bounteous heart."[1]

On 3rd January 1735, Lady Mary wrote to Dr. Arbuthnot about the famous *Epistle* recently addressed to him by Pope, with its further attack upon Sappho: "I have not perused the last lampoon of your ingenious friend, and am not surprised you did not find me out under the name of Sappho, because there is nothing I ever heard in our character or circumstances to make a parallel, but as the town (except you who know better) generally suppose Pope means me, whenever he mentions that name, I cannot help taking notice of the horrible malice he bears against the lady signified by that

---

[1] In the *Essay on Man* (1733) the poet has another fling at the Wortleys in the lines—
>"Is yellow dirt the passion of thy life?
>Look but on Gripus, and on Gripus' wife."

Again, in the *Epistle to Lord Bathurst*, after asking what Riches can give, he replies that they might
>"Find some doctor that would save the life
>Of wretched Shylock, spite of Shylock's wife."

name, which appears to be irritated by supposing her writer of the verses to the Imitator of Horace. Now I can assure him they were wrote without my knowledge[1] by a gentleman of great merit, whom I very much esteem, who he will never guess, and who, if he did know, he durst not attack. But I own that design was so well meant, and so excellently executed, that I cannot be sorry they were written. I wish you would advise poor Pope to turn to some more honest livelihood than libelling. I know he will allege in his excuse that he must write to eat, and he is now grown sensible that no one will buy his verses except their curiosity is piqued to it, to see what is said of their acquaintance; but I think this method of gain so exceeding vile that it admits of no excuse at all. Can anything be more detestable than his abusing poor Moore,[2] scarce cold in his grave, when it is plain he kept back his poem while he lived for fear he should beat him for it? This is shocking to me, though of a man I never spoke to, and hardly knew by sight; but I am seriously concerned at the worse scandal heaped on Mr. Congreve,[3] who was my friend, and whom I am obliged to justify, because I can do it on my own knowledge, and which is yet farther, bring witness of it from those who were then often with me, that he was so far from loving Pope's rhyme, both that and his conversation were perpetual jokes to him, exceeding despicable in his opinion, and he has often made us laugh in talking of them, being particularly pleasant on that subject. As to Pope's being born of honest parents, I verily believe it,[4] and I will add one

[1] These lines are however contained in Lady Mary's MS. book, at the beginning of which is the plain statement: "All the verses and prose in this book were wrote by me without the assistance of one Line from any other.
"MARY WORTLEY MONTAGU."

[2] James Moore Smythe (1702–1734), a minor poet and dramatist, had incurred Pope's resentment by inserting six lines into his comedy *The Rival Modes*, which he had seen in a manuscript of Pope's. Permission to use the lines had at first been given, and then withdrawn. Pope introduces Moore into the *Dunciad*, and Moore had retorted (in conjunction with Welsted) in *The One Epistle*. It was not true, therefore, that Pope only satirised Moore after his death. Moore took the name of Smythe on inheriting his grandfather's property.

[3] In the line
"And Congreve loved, and Swift endured my lays."

[4] Alluding to the beautiful lines on his parents at the end of the *Epistle to Arbuthnot*.

praise to his Mother's character that (I only knew her very old) she always appeared to me to have much better sense than himself. I desire, sir, as a favour, that you would show this letter to Pope, and you will very much oblige, sir, Your humble servant."

With characteristic tactlessness, Lady Mary continued to fit the Sapphic cap on her own head, and went to Lord Peterborough to beg him to remonstrate with the poet. Lord Peterborough was reluctant to interfere, but, as appears from the following letter, he repeated the substance of Lady Mary's complaint to Pope, and received from him a rather lame explanation of the libel—

" I was very unwilling to have my name made use of in an affair in which I have no concern, and therefore would not engage myself to speak to Mr. Pope; but he coming to my house the moment you went away, I gave him as exact an account as I could of our conversation.

" He said to me what I had taken the liberty to say to you, that he wondered how the town would apply those lines to any but some noted common woman; that he should be yet more surprised if you should take them to yourself. He named to me four remarkable poetesses and scribblers, Mrs. Centlivre, Mrs. Haywood, Mrs. Manley, and Mrs. Ben [Behn], ladies famous indeed in their generation, and some of them esteemed to have given very unfortunate favours to their friends, assuring me that such only were the objects of his satire.

" I hope this assurance will prevent your further mistake, and any consequence upon so odd a subject. I have nothing more to add."

That Lady Mary was believed to be willing to retaliate on her persecutor, and even to join herself for that purpose with some of his Grub Street victims, seems proved by the following letter addressed to her on 11th June 1733, by Giles Jacob [1]:—

---

[1] Giles Jacob (1686–1744), minor poet and compiler. He was bred to the law, but afterwards became steward and secretary to the Hon. William Blathwaite. He published the *Poetical Register, or Lives and Characters of the English Dramatic Poets*, in 1719-20. He wrote a poem on the Court Beauties, and one or two plays, and compiled several legal reference books. Jacob had made slighting mention of

"My Lady,[1]—In my letter of thanks that I sent to your Ladyship about a week ago, for your favourable acceptance of my collection of Letters under the title of The Mirrour. I desired you would be pleased to communicate to me any Letter or other Composition as you should think fit concerning Mr. Pope, to be inserted in a second edition of the above pamphlet; but I quite forgot to mention how you might convey the same to me, which is the occasion of my giving your Ladyship this trouble, and further to send you the following rude epigram which I have lately writ on Pope, comparing him as a satirist with the famous Dryden.

> 'Dryden's just Satire rightly others blamed,
> But Pope's Scurrility himself has damned.'

"If this or my former Letter should be thought worthy of an Answer, please direct to me at my country Lodgings, at Mr. Jones's in Rufford's Buildings, beyond the Church in Islington.—I am, my Lady, your Ladyship's most obedient servant G. JACOB"

Among Lady Mary's unpublished papers is the draft of part of "A Letter to A. P. in answer to the Preface of his Letters." This seems to have been intended for publication in some such form as the pamphlet collection of Mr. Jacob, and must have been written in 1737, when Pope's authorised edition of his correspondence appeared, ostensibly called forth by Gay in his *Poetical Register*, and Pope avenged his friend in the *Dunciad* with the lines—

> "Jacob, the Scourge of Grammar, mark with Awe,
> Nor less revere him, Blunderbuss of Law."

In 1732 Jacob retorted with a Letter to John Dennis, which was reprinted in 1733 in his catchpenny publication, *The Mirrour, or Letters Satyrical, Panegyrical, Serious, etc.* In the Letter to Dennis he asks whether there is anything in Pope's Poems but senseless versification and sonorous nonsense. "I doubt not," he proceeds, "but it will be confessed that my writings in their way are more useful and beneficial to the world, and of consequence, likely to last longer than the idle nonsensical poems and maimed translations of Mr. Alexander Pope." *The Mirrour* also contains "The Legal Tryal and conviction of Mr. Pope of Dulness and Scandal before Mr. John Dennis, Mr. Lewis Theobald and Mr. Aaron Hill, Apollo's Deputy Judges of the High Court of Apollo" (!).

[1] From the unpublished MS.

Curll's editions, the publication of which the poet had so elaborately engineered. In this Preface Pope observes that "The printing private letters in such a manner [the piratical method attributed by him to Curll] is the worst sort of *betraying conversation,* as it has evidently the most extensive and the most lasting ill consequences. It is the highest offence against *Society,* as it renders the most dear and intimate intercourse of friend with friend, and the most necessary intercourse of man with man, unsafe, and so to be dreaded. To open Letters is esteemed the greatest breach of honour; even to look into them already opened and accidentally dropt, is held an ungenerous if not an immoral act. What then can be thought of the procuring them merely by Fraud, the printing them merely for Lucre."

On this passage Lady Mary comments with some force and justice in the manuscript mentioned above, and announces her suspicion, which years later was proved correct, that Pope had manipulated the correspondence of his friends to suit his own purposes.

"I agree with Mr. Pope,"[1] she observes, "in all that he says of the indecency and immorality of publishing private Letters, but what then must be said of himself, who is now become the Publisher of dead men's Letters, from whom he could have no previous leave of publication, several of which I do not doubt are wrote by himself, and falsely ascribed to them; particularly that from Dr. A[tterbury], dated 26th February, 1721–2, for I cannot believe (tho' I have no extraordinary high opinion of the Bishop's morals) that he would applaud his unjust satire on Mr. Addison, or encourage him to abuse others by telling him he had at last found out what he could write upon, and had an excellent talent at railing, etc.[2] As to his marginal note asserting his never having shewn those verses, it must make everyone laugh that has thrown away so much time as to read his Miscellanys, or his Satyr on Women [3]

---

[1] From the unpublished MS.

[2] In the letter alluded to Atterbury asks for a complete copy of the famous lines on Addison under the name of Atticus, and continues, "Now you know where your real strength lies, I hope you will not suffer that talent to lie unemployed." Pope says in a note that an imperfect copy of the lines was "got out," very much to the surprise of the author.

[3] The lines on Addison were not published in the *Characters of Women.*

published by himself. I suppose the letter said to be wrote by Mr. Wycherley, 26th May 1709, comes from the same hand,[1] and I am the more inclined to this belief, knowing so many little mean falsities published in this Monument of Friendship, as he calls it, where he has imputed a letter to poor dead Gay, which I have seen under his own hand addressed to another person,[2] and that letter which he pretends to have sent to the late Duke of Buckingham, as a jest upon his description of his house in the Park."[3]

Pope continued to stick his poisoned darts into his victim. For example, in the *Satires of Dr. Donne Versified* (first published as Pope's in 1737) there is another abominable line on Sappho, while in the Epilogue to the Satires (1738) occurs the oft-quoted couplet with its double sting—

> "And at a peer or peeress shall I fret
> Who starves a sister or denies a debt?"[4]

The bitterness of the quarrel caused Lady Mary, never an impartial critic, to under-estimate, not only the talents of Pope, but those of his friends Swift and Bolingbroke. Years afterwards, in her conversations with Spence in Rome, she declared that she admired Pope's *Essay on Man* very much when it first appeared, because she had not then read any of the ancient critics, and did not know that it was all stolen. Swift, she said, had stolen all his humour from Cervantes and Rabelais. With Lord Bolingbroke she never would become acquainted, because she looked upon him as so vile a man. "You are very wrong," she told Spence on another occasion, "in thinking that Mr. Pope could write blank verse well. He has indeed got a knack of writing the other, but was he to attempt blank verse, I dare say he would appear quite contemptible in it."

[1] In this letter Wycherley warmly praises Pope's poems in Tonson's Miscellany, and says: "The salt of your wit has been enough to give a relish to the whole insipid hotch-potch it is mingled with."

[2] The letter about the haymakers who were killed by lightning, which Pope had written to Lady Mary. Versions of the incident, the joint composition probably of himself and Gay, were sent to Fortescue and to Lord Bathurst.

[3] The description of the old house at Stanton Harcourt, which Pope sent to Lady Mary and to the Duke of Buckingham.

[4] Alluding to her alleged ill-treatment of Lady Mar, and repudiation of her debt to Rémond.

With regard to Pope's special medium, the heroic couplet, she asserted that he wrote these verses so well, that he was in danger of bringing even good verse into disrepute from his "all tune and no meaning." It need scarcely be pointed out that Lady Mary paid her enemy the sincerest flattery by imitating his style. Curiously enough, among her poetical remains is a fragment of a poem, written as early as 1713, about the Goddess of Dulness, and a visit paid by that Deity to Bolingbroke, then in power. The Goddess points out to the Minister that

> "Men must be dull who passively obey,"

and urges him to

> "Think of this maxim, and no more permit
> A dangerous writer[1] to retail his wit.
> . . . . . .
> Encourage you the poet[2] I shall bring,
> Your Granville he already tries to sing;
> Nor think, my Lord, I only recommend
> An able author, but a useful friend;
> In verse his phlegm, in puns he shows his fire,
> And skilled in pimping to your heart's desire."

Some years later Lady Mary began another poem on the Court of Dulness, in which Pope and Bolingbroke are again attacked and Addison exalted. These lines may have been handed round among her friends, and thus have come to Pope's knowledge. It will be remembered that Pope addressed his *Essay on Man* to Bolingbroke under the name of Lælius. Lady Mary has one more shot at her enemy in a poem (unpublished, so far as can be discovered, in her lifetime) called *An Epistle from Pope to Lord Bolingbroke*. The first portion consists of ironical congratulations from the poet to his Lælius on his great virtues, and the services that he has rendered to his country. Pope is then made to continue—

> "I own these glorious schemes I view with pain;
> My little mischiefs to myself seem mean,
> Such ills are humble, tho' my heart is great,
> All I can do is flatter, lie and cheat.
> . . . . . .

---

[1] Addison.   [2] Pope.

My first subscribers I have first defamed,
And when detected never was ashamed;
Raised all the storms I could in private life,
Whispered the husband to reform the wife;
Outwitted Lintot in his very trade,
And charity with obloquy repaid.
Yet while you preach in prose, I scold in rhymes,
Against th' injustice of flagitious times.
You, learned doctor of the public stage,
Give gilded poison to corrupt the age;
Your poor toad-eater I, around me scatter
My scurril jests, and gaping crowds bespatter."

CHAPTER XXXIV

PARENTS AND CHILDREN

APART from the Pope episode, we know comparatively little of Lady Mary's history between the year 1727, when her correspondence with Lady Mar was discontinued, and the year 1738, when a fairly regular correspondence was begun with Lady Pomfret. About 1730 the Wortleys' troubles with their son again became acute. As already stated, he had run away from school several times, and on one occasion he had actually worked his passage out to Oporto,[1] where he was arrested and brought home. Later, he was sent abroad with a tutor named Gibson, and visited Italy and, there is reason to believe, the West Indies. On his return he married a woman of low birth much older than himself. He was at once separated from her by his parents, and placed in Holland with Mr. Gibson, who seems to have acted as a kind of keeper. The young man, who was allowed £300 a year, occupied himself (when out of mischief) in studying Arabic and several European languages. His mother, who was never blinded by partiality, described him as an excellent linguist and a thorough liar, and so weak withal as to be capable of turning monk one day and Turk three days after. The following letter from Mr. Gibson, dated Troyes, 18th August 1732, will show the state of young Wortley at that time—

" MADAM,[2]—. . . I beg leave to tell your ladyship that your son enjoys a perfect state of health at present, but as I hinted to you some time ago, I find still in him the old intriguing

---

[1] His adventures in Spain are described in a spurious catchpenny Memoir, which appeared in 1779.
[2] From the unpublished MS.

disposition, which tho' not carried to any height, begins, however, in some measure to take him off his studies. I could therefore, with much submission, wish that Mr. Wortley and your ladyship would judge it proper to remove us to some other town. Your ladyship will take your own prudent way, without letting him know that this comes from me.

"I have here insinuated what I look upon as a very considerable failing in a young gentleman; I must, however, do your son justice, in telling your ladyship that if he is not as yet cured of the above mentioned failing, he is, I hope, entirely of one other, very near, if not fully as dangerous, I mean that of drinking, for which at present (to my great joy) he seems to have a real aversion.

"Your ladyship will easily see that I lay matters before you plainly and ingenuously without the least mask or disguise. Heaven knows all I aspire at is, the real interest of your son, and to maintain the character of an honest man. . . ."

In 1733 Lady Mary's brother-in-law, Lord Gower, married again, his second wife being the widow of Sir Henry Atkins, and daughter of Sir John Stonehouse. One of Lord Gower's daughters, Gertrude, afterwards Duchess of Bedford, writes to announce the happy event to her aunt twenty-four hours after it had happened. The Lady Fanny mentioned in her note is Lady Fanny Erskine, daughter of Lady Mar.

"I[1] give your Ladyship a great many thanks for your obliging letter. I suppose you have heard that my Papa was married yesterday morning. He orders me to tell you he was at your house the day before in order to acquaint your Ladyship with it. Lady Gower has so general a good character, and seems to be so sweet-tempered a woman, I don't in the least doubt it will be a happiness to us all that she is our mother-in-law; I hear Lady Fanny is to live with your Ladyship. I am extremely glad of it, for I have so great a value for her that everything that is for her advantage gives me pleasure. I hope she continues well, and liked walking at the wedding. I am in haste to dress for dinner, so beg you would

[1] From the unpublished MS.

forgive the faults in this, and be assured that I am, dear aunt, your most dutiful niece and obedient servant,
"G. LEVESON GOWER."

From one or two contemporary allusions it appears that Lady Mary's character had already suffered, partly from the allegations of Pope and partly from her own imprudence. Writing to her sister in March 1732, Mrs. Pendarves says: "Lady Wortley's[1] verses are pretty; how ill her actions and her words agree."[2] Again, Lady Strafford, writing to her husband from St. James' Square on 10th June 1734, says: "Lady M. Wortley came here this morning, her dress was a sack and all her jewels, and she walked here from her own house [in the Piazza, Covent Garden]; she had no news, and I was sadly tired of her before she went." In the following year appeared *Advice to Sappho*, occasioned by her *Verses on the Imitator of the First Satire of the Second Book of Horace. By a Gentlewoman*. This feminine champion of Pope's, who is inferior in literary power to his attackers, begins her exhortation with the curious rhymes—

> "When Rome was lashed by Juvenal's sharp lines,
> Each conscious breast applied them to his crimes:
> Thus Sappho, stained with faults of scarlet dye,
> Knows how each keen invective to apply,"

and concludes—

> "Cease, Sappho, cease, thy lines are not of force
> To render him or his one jot the worse.
> Whether with toil or ease you thoughts produce,
> Abortive let them die, they're of no use.
> Study yourself, search well your crooked heart,
> And banish thence each rancorous pois'nous part.

---

[1] Lady Mary is sometimes alluded to as Lady Wortley by her contemporaries, as may be seen from a line already quoted in *Sandys' Ghost*.

[2] Lady Irwin, writing to her father, Lord Carlisle, 8th April 1730, says: "The enclosed is Lady Mary Wortley's advice to me and my answer. She is here often, and contributes not a little to the enlivening conversation; her principles are as corrupt as her wit is entertaining, and I never heard a woman, let her practice be never so scandalous, maintain such arguments. She was here a night ago; the conversation turned on Constancy. Lady M. immediately attacked me for a practice so inconsistent with reason and nature; called for a pen and ink, said she found herself inspired for my service, and writ, as she pretended, the enclosed off-hand. I had the better of the argument, but not having the wit to support it, my answer fell flat."
—*Hist. MSS. Commission*, Rep. 15.

> When thus refined, court him to be your friend,
> To your repentance he an ear may lend :
> Excess of goodness with his merit joins,
> Or you'd been crushed to atoms by his lines."

In May 1734 Mr. Wortley stood for York, not, as it appears, with any hope of being elected, but with the idea of keeping out an undesirable candidate. According to the *Wentworth Papers*, he spent a good deal of money on the contest, and was "much caressed" by the neighbouring gentry for his patriotic conduct. He came out at the bottom of the poll, but, as will be seen from the following letter to Lady Mary, "moral victories" were not unknown, even in those far-off days :—

"Last [1] night the poll ended and the numbers stood thus—

Stapylton,	7884
Turner,	7880
Winn,	7714
Wortley,	5906

My number perhaps is such as no man ever had in the memory of man in any country without having asked one vote for himself. A scrutiny was demanded, and if the Sheriff could and would strike out all the votes gained by indirect practices, 'tis thought I should be the second man, not Turner.

"The endeavours used by myself and Mr. Moles hindered the appearance of any green bough or leaf during the whole elections. No party reflection was thrown out, none upon the King, Queen or any of his family, and what is yet more extraordinary no personal reflection was thrown out on any one of the four candidates. . . .

"YORK CASTLE

"I am now in the room where they are examining the books to see if they are right cast up. I have had the unanimous and hearty thanks of all our friends for the part I have acted."

In 1736 Miss Wortley was just eighteen, and though she had not as yet run away with the butler, a catastrophe her mother had jokingly prophesied, she had fallen passionately in love with the good-looking young Scotchman, Lord Bute.

[1] From the unpublished MS.

The young man, who was only five years older than his lady-love, had hitherto occupied himself in his island home with the study of botany, agriculture, and architecture. Although elected a Representative Peer in 1737, he took scarcely any part in public life till ten years later, when he was taken into favour by Frederick, Prince of Wales. It might be thought that a Scottish peer was a sufficiently good match for the daughter of Mr. Wortley Montagu, but, for some reason or other, Lady Mary set herself against the marriage. Miss Wortley had probably inherited something of her father's obstinate will and her mother's high spirit, for, young as she was, she went her own way, and married the man she loved.[1] The fact of Lady Mary's disapproval, though not the reason for it, is shown in the following note from Lord Gower, dated Trentham, 11th September 1736:—

"MADAM,[2]—Some horse-races in this country which I was obliged to attend have prevented my acknowledging sooner the honour of your Ladyship's letter. I was very much concerned to hear your daughter had given you so much uneasiness, and surprised to find she had fixt upon a husband that had not your approbation. I hope by her future conduct she will atone for her past, and that her choice will prove more happy than you and Mr. Wortley expect. I am sorry too that Lady Fanny Erskine has increased your uneasiness. I was in hopes from her letters to my daughter that everything had been settled between you in the most amicable manner. . . ."

It appears that Lady Fanny, now nearly grown up, desired the custody of her mother, Lady Mar, and as she afterwards married her cousin, a son of Lord Grange, it is probable that she sided with her father's family, and was prejudiced against her aunt. A letter from Mr. Wortley to his wife, dated 6th November, belongs to the period we have reached, 1737–38—

"I[2] do not wonder that your business with Lord G—r

---

[1] Lord Chesterfield, in his *Character of Lord Bute*, describes Lady Mary as "eminent for her parts and her vices." He adds that Lord Bute's marriage was a runaway love-match, notwithstanding which they lived very happily together: she proved a very good wife, and did in no way *matrizare.*"

[2] From the unpublished MS.

[Gower] is tiresome. I believe it will never be otherwise, and therefore you had best get out of it as fast as you can. You have done all that anyone could think reasonable in you to do for your sister, there is now no hope of her recovery; her daughter, who has a right to whatever can be saved out of her jointure, is almost a woman. She ought to choose for herself, who should preserve her mother's life, which is to be considered a part of her fortune. If she has not the prudence to take care of her mother, you cannot be blamed. I think it will be right in you and some other of her English relations to advise her whom to choose. When that is done, you are justified to the world, whatever happens to your sister and your niece.

"If you think it proper you should have some share in the care of her person, I desire to be free from the care of her estate. Perhaps my Lord Chancellor may consent to let one of the officers have the care of the estate. That I think would be best. Perhaps, Lord Chancellor will not suffer Lady Fanny to make an improper choice of trustees, but will rather choose them for her. I propose to set out for London on the 12th or 14th, and desire the beds may be aired and lain in both in London and Twickenham."

In the summer of 1738 Lady Mary began a correspondence with Lady Pomfret, one of the Ladies of the Bedchamber to the late Queen. She was a daughter of Lord Jeffreys of Wem, and had married Lord Pomfret in 1720. In 1727 he was appointed Master of the Horse to Queen Caroline, a post which he was accused of having bought of Mrs. Clayton (afterwards Lady Sundon) with a pair of diamond earrings. This transaction gave rise to a well-known *bon mot* of Lady Mary's. Hearing the old Duchess of Marlborough express surprise that Mrs. Clayton should call upon her "with her bribe in her ear," she exclaimed, "How are people to know where wine is to be sold if she does not hang out a sign?"

On the death of Queen Caroline Lady Pomfret retired from public life. In the autumn of 1738 she went abroad with her husband and daughters, and during the first year of her exile she corresponded regularly with Lady Mary, whom she frequently urged to join her on the Continent. Her ladyship, as appears from her published Correspondence with Lady

Hertford, and from the testimony of Horace Walpole, was not only a *précieuse ridicule*, but a Mrs. Malaprop into the bargain. Walpole has reported some of her solemn absurdities, such as the saying that it was as difficult to get into an Italian coach as it was for Cæsar to take Attica, by which she meant Utica; and that Swift would have written better if he had never written ludicrously.

It is difficult to believe that Lady Mary was taken in by her pretensions to learning, or that she really appreciated her dull and stilted letters. Yet we find her writing to Lady Pomfret on more than one occasion in the following flattering strain:—

"I dare not say half what I think of your delightful letter, though nobody but myself could read it, and call anything complimental that could be said of it. . . . If I had the utmost indifference for you, I should think your letters the greatest pleasure of my life; and if you deputed Lady Vane [1] to write for you, I could find a joy in reading her nonsense, if it informed me of your health."

Lady Mary professed to find it as impossible to send an equivalent out of stupid London as it would have been to return a present of the fruits of Provence out of Lapland: "We have no news, no trade, no sun, and even our fools are all gone to play at Tunbridge, and those that remain are only miserable invalids, who talk of nothing but infirmities and remedies, as ladies who are on the point of increasing the world speak only of nurses and midwives. I do not believe either Cervantes or Rabelais would be able to raise one moment's mirth from such subjects, and I acquit myself of writing stupidly, from this place, as I should do Mr. Chloë,[2] if he was condemned to furnish an entertainment out of rotten turnips and artichokes run to seed."

The Pomfrets settled at Monts, near Paris, in September, and from the letters written by Lady Mary to her friend during the following winter and spring, a few bits of contemporary gossip may be gleaned. Thus we hear of Lord

---

[1] Lady Vane was the daughter of Francis Hawes of Purley Hall, Berks. She married Lord William Hamilton in 1732. He died in 1734, and the following year she married the second Viscount Vane. Her Memoirs (written by herself) were published in *Peregrine Pickle* (1751), where she figures under the name of Lady Frail. She hated her second husband, who was devoted to her, and refused to divorce her.

[2] The Duke of Newcastle's French cook.

Townshend [1] spitting up his lungs at the Gravel Pits, while his charming spouse [2] was diverting herself with daily rambles in town, and hunted in couples with Madame Pulteney from tea-drinking till midnight. Lady Sundon dragged on a miserable life, and was said to have a cancerous humour in her throat. Lady Frances Montagu, daughter of Mr. Wortley's cousin, the first Lord Halifax, was about to renounce the pomps and vanities of the world, and confine herself to rural shades with Sir John Burgoyne,[3] whose mansion-house resembled Mr. Sullen's in *The Beaux' Stratagem*. It was also reported that a much greater lady was going to be disposed of to a much worse retreat, where she would be fifth in rank after having been the first. This was probably an allusion to the proposed alliance between Princess Mary and the Landgrave of Hesse Cassel, which took place in 1740. "Women and priests," reflects Lady Mary, "never know where they shall eat their bread."

The Duchess of Richmond [4] intended to pass the winter at Goodwood, owing, it was said, to the suspension of operas. On the other hand, fifty-three French strollers had arrived to supply their place, and M. de Cambis, the French Ambassador, was going about with great solemnity, negotiating to do them service. In October we hear that the mobs grow very horrible, there being a vast number of arms and legs that only want a head to make them a very formidable body. The public drama is carried on in the most whimsical manner, but the "northern actress [5] has very good sense; she hardly appears at all, and by that conduct almost

---

[1] The second Lord Townshend died in June 1738. If this letter is correctly attributed to September 1738, it refers to his son, who lived till 1767.

[2] Audrey, daughter of Edward Harrison of Balls, Hertford. She is frequently mentioned by Horace Walpole as a member of the "fast set," and is supposed to be the original of Lady Bellaston in *Tom Jones*.

[3] According to Burke, Lady Fanny married Sir Roger Burgoyne of Sutton Park, Bedfordshire.

[4] A daughter of the Earl of Cadogan, who married the second Duke of Richmond in 1719.

[5] Madame de Walmoden, mistress of George II., who arrived in England with her husband in June 1738. She was divorced from her husband the following year, and created Countess of Yarmouth in 1740. George II. thus early fulfilled his assurance to his dying wife : "J'aurai des maîtresses."

wears out the disapprobation of the public." As for literature, " wit and pleasure are no more, and people play the fool with great impunity; being very sure there is not spirit enough left in the nation to set their follies in a ridiculous light. Pamphlets are the sole productions of our modern authors, and those profoundly stupid."

Then follows an allusion to a *mésalliance* that had startled society, the marriage of Lady Harriet Herbert (daughter of Lord Waldegrave and widow of Lord Edward Herbert), in January 1779, to John Beard,[1] the opera-singer. Lady Mary says: " I was one of the first informed of her adventures by Lady Gage,[2] who was told that morning by a priest that she had desired him to marry her next day to Beard, who sings in the farces at Drury Lane. He refused that good office, and immediately told Lady Gage, who was frighted at this affair, and asked my advice. I told her honestly that since the lady was capable of such amours, I did not doubt, if this was broke off she would bestow her person and fortune on some hackney coachman or chair-man; and that I really saw no method of saving *her* from ruin and her *family* from dishonour, but by poisoning her; and offered to be at the expense of the arsenic, and even to administer it with my own hands, if she would write her to drink tea with her that evening." This kind offer not being accepted, Lady Harriet was taken by her relations to Twickenham, but contrived later to carry out her design, and we are told that the marriage was a happy one, Beard being a man of excellent character.

Lady Vane's vagaries, and more especially her liaison with Lord Berkeley,[3] afforded more food for gossip, while a little later, in March 1739, there is a graphic account of the invasion

[1] John Beard (1716?–1791). He had made his first appearance at Drury Lane in 1737. Afterwards he became a public favourite, more especially in the part of Captain Macheath. His second wife was a daughter of "Lun" Rich, the harlequin manager of Covent Garden. In 1761 Beard became manager of that theatre.

[2] Lady Gage was a daughter of Lord Jermyn of Edmundsbury. Her husband, Sir William, was connected with Lady Mary, since among his father's five wives were two members of the Fielding family.

[3] Augustus, fourth Earl. He was barely twenty-three at this time. Lady Vane appears to have left her husband, and lived with Lord Berkeley for some years.

of the House of Lords by a number of ladies, who resented the exclusion of their sex from the Gallery during the debate on the Conduct of the Spanish Government (1st March). Among the ladies were the Duchess of Queensberry, the Duchess of Ancaster,[1] Lady Huntingdon,[2] Lady Westmoreland,[3] and Mrs. Pendarves (afterwards Mrs. Delany). The last-named has also left us an account of the affair, which tallies very fairly with that of Lady Mary.

"They presented themselves at the door at nine o'clock in the morning," she relates, "where Sir William Saunderson respectfully informed them the Chancellor had made an order against their admittance. The Duchess of Queensberry, as head of the squadron, pished at the ill-breeding of a mere lawyer, and desired him to let them upstairs privately. After some modest refusals, he swore by G— he would not let them in. Her Grace, with a noble warmth, answered by G— they would come in, in spite of the Chancellor and the whole House. This being reported, the Peers resolved to starve them out, and an order was made that the doors should not be opened till they had raised their siege. These Amazons now showed themselves qualified for the duty of foot-soldiers. They stood there till five in the afternoon, without sustenence ... every now and then playing volleys of thumps, kicks and raps against the door, with so much violence that the speakers in the House were scarce heard. When the Lords were not to be conquered by this, the two Duchesses (very well apprised of the use of stratagem in war) commanded a dead silence of half an hour; and the Chancellor, who thought this a certain proof of their absence (the Commons also being very impatient to enter) gave order for the opening of the door; upon which they all rushed in, pushed aside their competitors, and placed themselves in the front rows of the gallery. They stayed there till after eleven, when the House rose; and

---

[1] Wife of the second Duke. She was an old friend and neighbour of Lady Mary's, being one of the four daughters of Sir John Brownlow.

[2] Selina, daughter of Lord Ferrars, and wife of Theophilus, ninth Earl of Huntingdon. In this year she became a member of the first Methodist Society in Fetter Lane. She was afterwards well known as the founder of "Lady Huntingdon's Connexion," and was the special patroness of Whitefield.

[3] Wife of the seventh Earl. She was a daughter of Lord Henry Cavendish.

during the debate gave applause, and showed marks of dislike, not only by smiles and winks (which have always been allowed in these cases) but by noisy laughs and apparent contempts, which is supposed the true reason why poor Lord Hervey spoke miserably."

Mrs. Pendarves, in her account of the affair, says that " My Lord Chesterfield spoke most exquisitely well. . . . Everything after him was dull and heavy; much circumfloribus stuff was talked of on the Court side."

In May 1739 Lady Mary was contemplating a journey to Italy, and writes to Lady Pomfret, who was then at Bologna, to thank her for an agreeable and obliging letter, adding: " I can give you no better proof of the impression it made upon me than letting you know that you have given me so great an inclination to see Italy once more, that I have serious thoughts of setting out the latter end of this summer. And what the remembrance of all the charms of music, sculpture, painting, architecture, and even the sun itself could not do, the knowledge that Lady Pomfret is there has effected; and I already figure to myself the charms of the brightest conversations in the brightest climate." After alluding to the death of Lord Halifax, Lady Mary continues: " A loss more peculiarly my own is that of poor Lady Stafford,[1] whose last remains of life I am daily watching with a fruitless sorrow. I believe a very few months, perhaps weeks, will part us for ever. You, who have a heart capable of friendship, may imagine to what a degree I am shocked at such a separation, which so much disorders my thoughts, as renders me unfit to entertain myself or any others. . . ."

[1] Lady Stafford died twelve days later at her house in Sackville Street.

CHAPTER XXXV

JOURNEY TO VENICE

IN July 1739 Lady Mary started on her lonely pilgrimage, little thinking, probably, that she would never see her husband again, and that more than twenty years would pass before she was to return to her native land. The reason for her self-imposed exile has never been ascertained, and the unpublished papers throw no fresh light upon the question. Writing to Lady Pomfret from Venice, several months after her departure from England, Lady Mary says:

I am astonished at the capriciousness of my fortune. My affairs are so uncertain, I can answer for nothing that is future. I have taken some pains to put the inclination for travelling into Mr. Wortley's head, and was so much afraid he would change his mind, that I hastened before him in order (at least) to secure my journey. He proposed following me in six weeks, his business requiring his presence at Newcastle. Since that, the change of scene that has happened in England[1] has made his friends persuade him to attend parliament this session; so that what his inclinations, which must govern mine, will be next spring, I cannot possibly foresee."

There is not a word in the letters exchanged between Lady Mary and her husband after she left England, to show that he had ever thought of joining her, or she of returning to him. The ostensible reason for her going abroad was the bad state of her health (she is said to have suffered from a disfiguring skin disease), which seems to have improved directly she found herself on the other side of the Channel. It has been suggested that the persecution of Pope, continued over the past ten years, had made her position in English society anything

[1] The declaration of war with Spain.

but pleasant, while Mr. Wortley must have bitterly resented the insulting allusions to himself, which he would naturally regard as the outcome of his wife's indiscreet dealings with the poet. There seems, however, to have been no open quarrel between the pair. They corresponded regularly until Mr. Wortley's death, and Lady Mary always spoke of her husband in terms of the highest respect. Mr. Wortley supplemented her pin-money by a small allowance, and consulted her on the subject of their son, and the arrangements that had to be made for him.

Lady Louisa Stuart, who would get her ideas on the subject from her mother, points out that if the elderly husband and wife had determined upon a separation, nothing could be more likely than that they settled it quietly and deliberately between themselves, neither proclaiming it to the world, nor consulting any third person. "It admits of little doubt," she continues, "that their dispositions were unsuitable, and Mr. Wortley had sensibly felt it even while a lover. When at length convinced that in their case the approach of age would not have the harmonising effect which it has been sometimes known to produce upon minds originally but ill-assorted, he was the very man to think within himself, 'If we cannot add to each other's happiness, why should we do the reverse? Let us be the friends at a distance which we could not hope to remain by continuing unequally yoked together.'"[1]

On 26th July Lady Mary hired a boat at Dover (for five guineas), and sailed for Calais, having her usual experience of a very rough sea. At Calais she bought a chaise for fourteen guineas, and set out upon her long journey

[1] Elizabeth Robinson, afterwards Mrs. Edward Montagu, wrote to her mother from Bulstrode in 1740 another version of the affair: "Lady Shadwell saw Lady Mary Wortley at Venice, where she now resides, and asked her what made her leave England; she told them the reason was, people were grown so stupid she could not endure their company, all England was infected with dulness; by-the-bye, what she means by insupportable dulness is her husband, for it seems she never intends to come back while he lives. A husband may be but a dull creature to one of Lady Mary's sprightly genius, but methinks even her vivacity might accommodate itself to living in the same kingdom with him; she is a woman of great family merit, she has banished her children, abandoned her husband. I suppose, as she cannot reach Constantinople, she will limit her ambition to an intrigue with the Pope or the Doge of Venice."—From *Mrs. Elizabeth Montagu, the Queen of the Blue-Stockings*, by Mrs. Climenson.

across France. Mr. Wortley, himself an old traveller, begged her for a description of her route, adding: "If you mention a few of the great towns you have passed, I shall see the whole journey. . . . I wish (if it be easy) you would be exact and clear in your facts, because I shall lay by carefully what you write of your travels." He was as good as his word, all her letters to him having been carefully preserved, and endorsed with the date of their arrival, as well as a few words summarising their contents.

The traveller made easy stages, for she did not arrive at Dijon till 13th August (N.S.). Her health was already greatly improved, and she was delighted with the improvement in the state of France under Cardinal Fleury. The roads were well mended, good care taken against robbers, and the villages filled with stout, fresh-coloured peasants in good cloth and clean linen. The only drawback to the journey was the numbers of English that she found in all the large towns, and the farther she went the more acquaintance she met, so that she might just as easily have walked incognito in Pall Mall as travelled incognito in France. In Dijon alone there were no fewer than sixteen English families of fashion. On 1st September she writes from Lyons—

"I[1] am now arrived at this place, where I find the same reasons for not staying as I did at Dijon, and am persuaded that I shall find them at every town in France, which makes me resolved for Turin, where I shall set out to-morrow morning, and hope to be unknown, and live at as little expense as I please. I have bargained to be carried there, myself and servants, for 12 Louis, which is the cheapest I could get. . . . I hastened to cross the Alps, being told that the rains very often fall in this month, which will make the passage more disagreeable. . . ."

On the road to Turin Lady Mary met Lord Carlisle, her old Yorkshire friend, who told her that, next to Rome, the best place in Italy to stay in was Venice, the impertinence of the little sovereigns in the other states being intolerable. Lady Mary determined, therefore, to try if she could stand the climate, since Rome was undesirable on an account her

[1] From the unpublished MS.

husband might guess. Lord Carlisle had told her that it was very hard to avoid meeting " a certain person " (the Pretender), and there were so many dirty little spies who wrote any lie that came into their heads, that the meeting might be dangerous.

Lady Mary arrived at Venice towards the end of September, having met nothing disagreeable in her journey but too much company. " I find," she writes to Mr. Wortley on 25th September, " (contrary to the rest of the world) I did not think myself so considerable as I am; for I verily believe, if one of the pyramids of Egypt had travelled, it could not have been more followed, and if I had received all the visits that have been intended me, I should have stopped at least a year in every town I came through. . . . I am now in a lodging on the Grand Canal. Lady Pomfret is not yet arrived, but I expect her very soon; and if the air does not disagree with me, I intend seeing the Carnival here."

The Procurator of Venice was Grimani,[1] with whom the Wortleys had made friends at Vienna. Another friend and correspondent, the Abbé Conti, was also living in Venice, and in the following letter to Mr. Wortley Lady Mary describes the renewal of old acquaintances and the making of new ones:—

(VENICE, 31st *September* 1739.)

" The [2] Procurator of St. Mark has been to see me; I found him something fatter, but in as good health and spirits as ever I saw him at Vienna. He has offered me all the services in his power, and says he will bring the most agreeable Venetian ladies to wait on me. He talked a great while of you, with large professions of regard and esteem. The Abbé Conti has been with me, in much better health than I knew him in London, and if one was to judge from the old people here, this air cannot be unwholesome. Our English Consul, who has resided, as he says, this forty years, is as cheerful an old man as ever I saw. I have had visits from the French,

---

[1] Pietro Grimani. He was Doge of Venice from 1741 to his death in 1752. He remained neutral throughout the wars that were raging in Italy during the period he was in power.

[2] From the unpublished MS.

24

Imperial, Neapolitan and Spanish Ambassador and his Lady. This last inquired first of the Consul if their visit would be agreeable for me. I believe you will think me in the right to answer, that as a stranger I desired to be thought quite neutral in all national Quarrels, and should be pleased of the honour of their company. As far as I can yet judge, this town is likely to be the most agreeable and the quietest place I can fix in. If you think so, I should be glad if you will send my things hither. Three boxes of my books, my papers and bureau No. 1, my workbox No. 2, a box of my china, and the box of my dressing-plate, which is at Mr. Child's,[1] and a small empty bookcase No. 4. In all eight boxes. I am told there is now in the River Thames the ship *Tygris*, Captain Petre master, who is a relation of Lord Petre, and a man of extraordinary good character; that his ship is an extreme good one, of 30 guns and well manned, capable of resisting a privateer, and therefore not likely to be attacked, and is bound directly for Venice. This is a happy opportunity and should not be slipped, especially since I am told that even at Leghorn I should have trouble with my books, which would be all examined by the Inquisition; and here care will be taken that I may receive them without any impediment.

"I hope you continue your good health in spite of our climate. I think my things should be sent before the French fit out privateers, which if the intelligence here is worth minding, may be very soon. I forgot to mention the box of snuff and the hair trunk of my clothes. If this ship does not put into Venice, the Consul will take care that my goods shall be put on a Dutch ship and consigned hither."

On 10th October Lady Mary wrote to Lady Pomfret a glowing description of the charm and convenience of Venice as a place of residence for foreigners. "As to cheapness," she remarks, "I think 'tis impossible to find any part of Europe where both the laws and customs are so contrived purposely to avoid expenses of all sorts; and here is a universal liberty that is certainly one of the greatest *agrémens* in life. . . . If I were writing to

[1] The banker.

Lady Sophia,[1] I would tell her of the comedies and operas which are every night at very low prices; but I believe even you will agree with me that they are ordered to be as convenient as possible, every mortal going in a mask, and consequently no trouble in dressing, or forms of any kind. I should be very glad to see Rome, which was my first intention (I mean next to seeing yourself); but am deterred from it by reasons that are put into my head by all sorts of people that speak to me of it. There are innumerable little dirty spies about, all English; and I have so often had the misfortune to have false witness borne against me, I fear my star on the occasion."

It is natural perhaps that Lady Mary, who had been somewhat under a cloud in England, should dwell with great emphasis on the honours that are done her on her travels, and the wonderful reception that she is granted by appreciative foreigners. Thus, she tells her husband that she is visited by all the most considerable people in the town, and all the foreign ministers, who had made entertainments for her as if she was an ambassadress. On the other hand, she is not expected to make any dinners in return, and thus can live very genteelly on her allowance.[2]

About the middle of October Lady Mary received a batch of letters from Mr. Wortley, and it is evident that in one of these he throws doubts upon her economical management of her journey, for she writes by the next post to clear herself, with righteous warmth, from so terrible a suspicion—

"I[3] have this day received five letters from you by Mr. Walters. I did not apprehend that you intended to direct to him, which was the reason I never wrote to him, till I received your letter directed to Dijon, which also came late to my hands. I will answer them all in order as well as I can. As for taking the pacquet boat to myself, it was done to avoid a night passage, which Mr. Hall told me I must otherwise suffer. And for the price of the chaise, tho' it appeared to me very dear, I can assure you it was the cheapest in all Calais. There was not one at the Post House, tho' I saw about forty

---

[1] Lady Pomfret's elder daughter, a great beauty, and afterwards Lady Granville.
[2] She seems to have had about £1200 a year.
[3] From the unpublished MS.

there, that they would sell under 18 guineas, and the common price asked was 25. For a fine one lined with velvet, etc. they asked me 58. I bought mine at a private house, belonging to a Mr. Francia, who pretended to sell me a pennyworth. If you make an enquiry you will find all I say to be truth. I have kept an exact Journal of my travels, and all the accidents I have met with. You guess right, that I was advised at Boulogne what road to take to Dijon by an English Gent. in the French service; his name Captain Cokely. I went from thence as I have informed you to St. Omers, then to Arras, then Laon, Rheims, Chalons-sur-Marne, and Dijon. There is no going by water from thence, the river Saone not being navigable to Chalons; I took water there to Lyons, but found it very disagreeable and not much cheaper than the post. . . . The Nuncio told me last night that his letters from England say S. R. W. [Sir R. Walpole] is dying; if that be true, I suppose he is now dead.[1] Let me know if you would have me write the news I meet with here, I hear a good many reports, this place being very *nouvellisée (sic)*.

"My chaise has lasted me to Brescia, where it broke down, and I was forced to hire another to Padua; from thence I came by water, in a Burcello, which cost me but 2 sequins. I have received to-day £100 from Mr. Walters. I have now 5 sequins left of the money I carried out, and no debt, which, I think, is not being an ill manager."

To Lady Pomfret Lady Mary continues to give the most tempting descriptions of life and society at Venice, evidently in the hope of inducing her friend to join her there. The Pomfrets were not well off, and therefore special stress is laid upon the cheapness of living, and the absence of ceremony. It is the fashion to walk everywhere, and a mask, price sixpence, with a little cloak, and the head of a domino, is a perfectly genteel dress for any occasion. The greatest equipage is a gondola, which costs as much as an English chair, and the theatre tickets are low-priced, though that is no matter, since Lady Mary has the keys of all the Ambassadors' boxes at her service for herself and her friends.

"As I am the only lady here at present," she continues,

[1] Sir Robert lived till 1745.

meaning presumably the only English one, " I can assure you I am courted as if I was the only one in the world. . . . And it is so much the established fashion for everybody to live their own way, that nothing is more ridiculous than censuring the actions of another. This would be terrible in London, where we have little other diversion; but for me, who never found any pleasure in malice, I bless my destiny that has conducted me to a part where people are better employed than in talking of the affairs of their acquaintance."

A few weeks later she informs her friend, with apparent regret, that "The Prince of Saxony[1] is expected here, and has taken a palace exactly over against my house. As I had the honour to be particularly well acquainted (if one may use that phrase) with his mother when I was at Vienna, I believe I cannot be dispensed with from appearing at the conversations which I hear he intends to hold, which is some mortification to me, who am wrapt up among my books with antiquarians and virtuosi."

When the Royalties arrived, " the Electoral Prince of Saxony, the Princess of Holstein and the Prince of Wolfenbüttel,"[2] enormous sums were spent in public and private entertainments in their honour. Lady Mary assures her husband that she takes as little share in these amusements as she can, but the Prince of Saxony's governor happened to be Count Wackerbart, with whose mother she had been intimate at Vienna, and consequently both governor and pupil showed her particular civilities. " I was last night," she writes on 25th December, " at an entertainment made for him [the Prince] by the Signora Pisani Mocenigo, which was one of the finest I ever saw, and he desired me to sit next him in a great chair. In short, I have all the reason that can be to be satisfied with my treatment in this town." This letter contains an allusion to the death of Mr. Pelham's[3] two sons in the previous

---

[1] Frederic Christian, son of August III., Elector of Saxony, who was also King of Poland.

[2] The Empress Elizabeth (wife of Charles VI.) was a daughter of the Duke of Brunswick-Wolfenbüttel, and Lady Mary seems to have corresponded with the Duchess of Wolfenbüttel while in Turkey.

[3] Henry Pelham, the great statesman, and brother to the Duke of Newcastle. He left four daughters.

November. "I am sorry," she observes, "for Mr. Pelham's misfortune, though 'tis long since that I have looked upon the hopes of continuing a family as one of the vainest of mortal prospects.

> 'Tho' Solomon with a thousand wives
> To get a wise successor strives,
> But one, and he a fool, survives.'"

It has been seen that Lady Mary chose to consider herself aggrieved by her daughter's marriage. The estrangement between herself and Lady Bute seems to have continued for a time, or it may be that fresh differences had arisen between them. This cloud, whatever its cause, passed away, and the relations between mother and daughter during the last fourteen years of Lady Mary's life were of an affectionate and confidential nature. But the following letter to Mr. Wortley, endorsed 21st January 1740 (N.S.), shows the writer to have been suffering from a sense of injury :—

"I[1] am sorry your daughter continues troubling you concerning me. She cannot believe after her behaviour to me the last time she was in town, that it is possible to persuade me of any real affection, and all beside is an affectation that is better left off, now decency no longer exacts it. I am not only conscious of having in every point performed my duty to her, but with a tenderness and friendship that is not commonly found, and I may say with truth, that as even from her infancy I have made her a companion and witness of my actions, she owes me not only the regard due to a parent, but the esteem that ought to be paid to a blameless conduct, and the gratitude that is shown by every honest mind to a valuable friend. I will say no more on this subject, which is shocking to me, and cannot be agreeable to you. If you desire it, I will write a letter to her enclosed in my next to you, not knowing how to direct to Lord B.'s agent. I had rather dropped the correspondence, being very incapable of dissembling. She need take no notice of it to the world, and I shall never be asked here whether I hear from her or no.

"The noble Venetian ladies live now very much after the

[1] From the unpublished MS.

manner of the French, and visit all strangers of quality. They come to me sometimes in the morning, and sometimes in the afternoon, as my acquaintance used to do at London. Many of them keep assemblies where they are very glad to see foreigners of distinction. I have introduced Lord Granby [1] to them as a relation of mine, at the request of his Governor, and he now visits several at their toilettes, where I believe he is very welcome, being a figure not unlike Mr. Bows, tho' but nineteen year old. They do not converse with Ambassadors out of masques, and they ask at my door if any are with me, and if they hear there are, they send me a compliment that they will defer their visits to another time. The Foreign Ministers do the same thing, and thus they avoid meeting; but at their balls, where masques are always admitted, I have seen them converse very freely with them. I have never played at any game since I came here. They have cards at their assemblies, but I do not even understand the figures and have no inclination to learn. My house is properly a meeting of Literati; the Procurator Grimani seldom fails coming when I am at home, and the Abbé Conti never. I do not go often to the Opera, tho' I have many boxes at my service, and cannot always refuse the pressing invitations of the ladies that will carry me thither. Signora Grimani, niece of the Procurator, the Isabella Pisani, niece of the Doge, the Procuratessa Pisani Mocenigo, the Cornelia 'Tepoli, the Clara Michielli, the Procuratessa Foscia, the Justiani Gradinego, and the Livia Moro are all intimate with me. I suppose you know these are the first families here."

In the next letter (endorsed 15th February) Lady Mary encloses a letter to Lady Bute, which she has written in obedience to her husband's wish, and adds—

"I [2] have kept within the bounds of truth, since it is certain that whatever reason I have to complain of my daughter's behaviour, I shall always wish her well, and if it was in my

---

[1] This was John, Marquis of Granby, afterwards distinguished as a military commander. He was barely nineteen at this time. He was the eldest son of the third Duke of Rutland, whom he did not live to succeed. His great-grandfather, the first Duke, had married (in 1658) Lady Anne Pierrepont, daughter of Henry, Marquis of Dorchester. Hence his connection with Lady Mary.

[2] From the unpublished MS.

power to give her any solid mark of it, I would do it, and shall ever be of that opinion. I wrote some time since to my son, desiring him to send his letters to Mr. Walters at Paris, who will forward them wherever I am. I think all letters are opened, and I hear other people make the same complaint. The Duke of Rutland has wrote a very handsome letter to thank me for the civilities I have shown his son [Lord Granby]. Here has been great entertainments made by all the Ambassadors for the Prince of Saxony, where I could not avoid appearing, he having been obliging to me even in a surprising manner, tho' I have been but once in his box at the Opera, after many invitations. The Senate has deputed four of their principal members to do the honours of the Republic. He has three boxes made into one in the midst of the theatre, which is finely illuminated, hung with crimson velvet, richly trimmed with gold-lace and fringe, and he has a magnificent collation there every night. He has always several noble ladies with him. Whenever he has been at any of these balls and serenatas, he is seated between me and the Spanish Ambassadress; indeed the distinctions shown me here are very far above what I could expect. The Signora Justiani Gradinego made a great supper for me this Carnival, which I am told was never done before for any stranger. She only invited five ladies of my acquaintance, and ten of the chief Senators.

"I am of opinion you would very much repent your son's removal to France. There is no part of it without English or Irish, and the first bad councillor he meets, he will return to all his former folly."[1]

[1] Mr. Wortley was inclined to grant his son's request to leave Holland, and be allowed more freedom.

CHAPTER XXXVI

TRAVELS IN ITALY

WHATEVER the charms of foreign society, Lady Mary seems to have been very much bored by the specimens of her own country people who passed through Venice on the grand tour. In a letter addressed to Lady Pomfret in February 1740, after lamenting the circumstances that kept them apart, she continues—

"I am impatient to hear good sense pronounced in my native tongue; having only heard my language out of the mouths of boys and governors for these five months. Here are inundations of them broke in upon us this carnival, and my apartment must be their refuge, the greater part of them having kept an inviolable fidelity to the language their master taught them; their whole business abroad being (as far as I can perceive) to buy new clothes, in which they shine in some obscure coffee-house, where they are sure of meeting only one another; and after the important conquest of some waiting gentlewoman of an opera queen, whom perhaps they remember as long as they live, return to England excellent judges of men and manners. I find the spirit of patriotism so strong in me every time I see them, that I look on them as the greatest blockheads in nature; and, to say truth, the compound of booby and *petit maître* makes up a very odd sort of animal."

The suicide of Lord Scarborough[1] on the eve of his marriage to the widowed Duchess of Manchester made a great sensation in English society about this time. The Duchess of Manchester was the daughter of Lady Mary's old friend, the Duchess of Montagu, while Lord Scarborough (when Lord Lumley) had been the faithless lover of her sister-

[1] Richard, second Earl of Scarborough.

in-law, the widowed Lady Kingston.[1] Lady Mary mentions the Scarborough suicide more than once in her letters of this time. Writing to Mr. Wortley on 16th March, she says, after dealing with certain business matters—

"I [2] make no expenses but what are absolutely necessary, and what I am persuaded you will approve. Lord Scarborough's terrible history is publicly known; I am of opinion his engagement with that lady was not the cause, but sign of his being mad. Count Wackerbart talked to me of it last night at the Assembly, which is three times a week for the entertainment of the Prince of Saxony, at the expense of the Senate, who gave him the most magnificent ball I ever saw, in the great Theatre on Shrove Tuesday. I could not avoid going there with a set of noble ladies. I was led in by the Procurator G. [Grimani] and placed next the Prince by his own direction. I was told since that the Princess of Holstein [3] took it ill, and as she is married into a Sovereign House, I think she had reason, but he affects giving her some mortifications in return for many that the present King and Queen [of Poland] have received from her, when she was all-powerful in the reign of the late King of Poland. I was but once at the Ridotto during the whole Carnival. A Regatta is intended after Easter for the Prince, which is said to be one of the finest shows in the world, and never given since the King of Denmark was here, which is thirty year ago. Many English and others of all nations are expected to come to see it. Lord Shrewsbury [4] is arrived in company with Prince Beauvau;[5] they came to see me as soon as they arrived, as all strangers do. I am glad if my letters can be any amusement to you, and will not fail to let you know all that passes.

[1] See Montagu Bacon's allusion to Lady Kingston's supposed liaison with Lord Lumley.
[2] From the unpublished MS.
[3] A favourite daughter (by the left hand) of Augustus the Strong married a Holstein-Beck.
[4] When the Duke of Shrewsbury died without issue, the dukedom expired, but the earldom reverted to his cousin, Gilbert Talbot, a Catholic priest, who became thirteenth Earl. He died in 1743.
[5] Charles Juste, Prince de Beauvau (1720–93). He was afterwards Governor of Languedoc and of Provence. He is frequently mentioned in the *Letters* of Horace Walpole.

"None of the canals have been froze here, tho' we have had some sharp weather; it is now so warm most people have left off fires, tho' I have not. Several ladies have invited me to their palaces for some time in the summer, but I believe I shall not accept their invitations."

To Lady Pomfret Lady Mary wrote a little later: "Have you not reasoned much on the surprising conclusion of Lord Scarborough? . . . I am almost inclined to superstition on this accident, and think it a judgment for the death of a poor silly soul, that you know he caused some years ago. . . . I could pity the Duchess of Manchester, tho' I believe 'tis a sensation she is incapable of feeling for anybody, and I do not doubt it is her pride that is chiefly shocked on this occasion; but as that is a very tender part, and she having always possessed a double portion of it, I am persuaded she is very miserable. I am surprised at the different way of acting I find in Italy, where, though the sun gives more warmth to the passions, they are all managed with a sort of discretion that there is never any *éclat*, tho' there are ten thousand public engagements."

Lady Mary explains to her friend that she had promised not to leave Venice as long as the Prince of Saxony remained, not on his account, but because there were so many entertainments made in his honour, that it would be disobliging to her friends to run away. "I can hardly believe," she continues, "that it is me dressed up at balls, and stalking about at assemblies, and should not be so much surprised at suffering any of Ovid's transformations, having more disposition, as I thought, to be hardened into stone or timber, than to be enlivened by these tumultuary entertainments, where I am amazed to find myself seated by a sovereign prince, after travelling a thousand miles to establish myself in the bosom of a republic, with a design to lose all memory of kings and courts. Won't you admire the force of destiny? I remember my contracting an intimacy with a girl in a village[1], as the most distant thing on earth from power and politics. Fortune tosses her up (in a double sense), and I am embroiled in a thousand affairs that I had resolved to avoid as long as I

[1] Molly Skerret.

lived. Say what you will, madam, we are pushed about by a superior hand, and there is some predestination, as well as a great deal of free will, in my being faithfully yours, etc."

Mr. Wortley had now decided to increase his son's allowance, and was anxious that the young man should be given a chance of showing that he was able to behave himself in a freer life than he led with his tutor-keeper in Holland. The difficulty was to find another place where he would be safe from his creditors. In the course of the spring he wrote to consult with his wife on the thorny subject. His first letter cannot be found, but we have Lady Mary's answer, dated 12th May 1740, in which she says—

". . . I[1] will obey your orders in relation to your son, tho' I shouldn't have given that advice. It is as much as Edgecombe allows his, whose behaviour (tho' very bad) has not been so despicable as ours. You will find people enough to exhort you to pay his debts. I know Gibson's way of talking, and I also know that if his wisdom had been hearkened to, your son would have run up £4,000 or £5,000, and been at this time just where he is. I have answered his letters, and will write again touching his allowance. As to his removal, it is so much against my opinion, that I shall say nothing of it till I have further orders. I can perceive by his letters he is in the same folly of thinking he can make a figure, and imagines that your immense riches will furnish him with all the fine things he has a fancy for. His offering to marry while his wife is alive, is a proof of his way of thinking.

" Lord Mansel[2] is here, and intends to stay the Ascension.

---

[1] From the unpublished MS.

[2] Thomas Mansel, grandson of the first Lord Mansel, whom he succeeded in 1723. This Lord Mansel died unmarried in 1743. There is an unpublished letter from him among Lady Mary's papers, written shortly after his return from Italy. He says (dating from Charlton), "I found Holland so very dull a place, and being impatient to see England again, I made an exceedingly small stay there. I met Sir John Shadwell and his family at Rotterdam, and had the pleasure of going in the same Packet-boat with them to England, and out of my great complaisance had the pleasure of being on the floor two nights, and I (who am never sick at sea) waited on the ladies who were naked in bed, and as sick as any poor mortals could possibly be . . . and for my pains was called the best-natured and useful young man imaginable. I waited on Mr. Wortley, but did not have the happiness of finding him at home : however, I enclosed the letter in a cover, and left it at his house. . . . We talk of nothing now

He is the most zealous patriot I ever knew, and, tho' his own master, has no vice nor extravagance. I have introduced him to the ladies of my acquaintance (who are now very numerous) in return for the civilities I received from him at Dijon. If Mrs. Blackwood falls in your way, I could wish you would tell her that I have seen no young man in my travels with so reasonable a conduct. The war seems to kindle on all sides, but if it be true that the German Councils are entirely influenced by the French, our advance is very small, and very dear bought. . . ."

On 16th May Mr. Wortley wrote the following letter, in which he goes minutely into all the details of this unfortunate affair:—

"16th May 1740.

"It[1] is with concern that I trouble you upon so melancholy a subject as our son. Gibson is convinced by his letters that he is able to live within his present allowance, and others think him not so weak as we suppose him. I therefore think it necessary he should remove, but the difficulty is how to dispose of him. He is, I fear, too weak to conceal himself anywhere, and I am assured by Lord Middleton and by Mr. Drummond, who was many years a banker at Amsterdam, that no one is protected in France or Holland against Bills of Exchange or Bonds, and I do not know in what country he can be safe out of a privileged place. Mr. Drummond thinks an Englishman may be safe in Avignon, because the Pope will take no notice of what is passed in England. It is probable that most of the Foreign Ministers and merchants at Venice can inform you how far anyone can be safe in the countries from which they come.

"He writes word he will not stir from the place he is in, but a French war. Our equipments go on with great vigour; they say Sir John Norris sails the next fair wind to attempt Ferrol—for my part I doubt it much. My reason is that yesterday the Duke of Cumberland set out from Hounslow with all his baggage for Portsmouth, and is to embark on board Sir John Norris as a volunteer. Now I fancy we should scarce venture our favourite son for an expedition so dangerous as that of attempting a fortress by sea only, and having no land forces to support their attacks. However, he certainly sails, and has twelve fireships and several bomb vessels with him. . . ."

[1] From the unpublished MS.

or go to any other without your leave or mine. And I think you are absolutely safe against his coming near you, because you could hardly keep him out of a jail if you would, and could easily get him confined anywhere but in England. You will do well to assure him his allowance will be stopped as soon as it is known he comes nearer to you than you allow him to do. He is weak enough to desire his debts may be paid, tho' no one can guess whether they are nearer to 1,000 or 10,000 pounds, and he has behaved himself so that no one ought to give the least credit to what he says or writes. You will say to him what you think proper on that head. His business is to make it appear plainly that he can act with more prudence than a downright idiot, and that is what should be replied to the greatest part of what he writes. What privileged places there are in Europe besides Avignon, and that where he is, I cannot guess, and could not learn so easily as you may do.

"He seems to me to be as void of reason as he used to be; otherwise he would have contrived how he might remove with safety. It seldom happens that any debtor cannot get license from his creditors for a certain time, and I think he may easily get it if he can but treat with them, like a rational creature. I have absolutely refused taking the least notice of him, or meddling in his affairs, and have desired he will apply to no one but you. The Germans can tell you whether a debtor may be protected at Aix-la-Chapelle or Frankfort. What he begs is to be tried where there is much company. For my part I foresee that it is likely he will again go into the hands of sharpers, or worse, if it is possible, but the place he is in is too private unless he were governed there, and I think he will go without leave if he cannot get it. As he has seemed to behave himself with more decency than he used to do, I shall be censured by many if he is not removed, and I think it right to comply with the opinion of others, unless you find it wrong by information you may receive before his removal; which perhaps cannot be settled speedily with a probability of living out of a jail. You will do well to let him know how likely it is that he will be confined for his life if once he gets into a jail, since no one will be weak enough to pay his debts. He ought not to entertain a thought of satisfying his creditors any way but out of his allowance, be it greater or less. It is his business to show it is proper to trust him with the increase I propose to make. . . ."

Mr. Wortley, who had shown so little interest in his son when a baby, seldom even inquiring after his health, was now much more inclined to be lenient towards him, and to take optimistic views about his future, than was his once devoted mother. Lady Mary thought her son a fool, and she was not one who suffered fools gladly. She put no faith in his protestations of affection or promises of reform, and she was probably less influenced than her husband by the desire for an heir in the male line to the Wortley estates. The prodigal's wife was leading an inconveniently correct life, being, as Lady Mary cynically suggests, too old to attract gallants and not rich enough to buy them. There was therefore no present hope of young Wortley's getting a divorce, and being enabled to marry more suitably. Among the family papers is a letter from Mrs. Edward Wortley, junior, to her father-in-law, in which she explains that she is in want of the bare necessaries of life, and adds—

"I[1] have with the greatest caution forbore to give any sort of uneasiness to your family, of which I have the honour to write myself a member. Neither would I at this time have given you the trouble of reading my complaints, were I not compelled to it by the strongest necessity; and give leave to a woman to say thus much in her own justification, I have not done anything as far as you are able to judge unworthy of the character I bear as the wife of Mr. Wortley Mountague. I will therefore hope that you will as soon as possible send relief to her who has the honour to subscribe herself your ever dutiful Daughter and most Obed^t humble Serv^{nt},
"S. WORTLEY MOUNTAGUE"

In hearing from his mother the news that his father intended to increase his allowance, young Wortley indited the following very plausible letter, which is dated from Ysselstein in Holland:—

[1] From the unpublished MS.

"Madam,[1]—I have been honoured with your La'ship's, and am infinitely obliged to my Father and you for your extream goodness in intending to increase my allowance. It is so much the more agreeable to me as being a certain sign [illegible] has not been distressing to you, and I assure you I shall always search all means of testifying to you my gratitude for this your great tenderness, and of rendering myself more and more worthy of your affection; and as I am persuaded nothing can acquire me that so soon as a strict course of a sober and prudent conduct, I am absolutely determined never to follow any but the strictest rules of Virtue and Honour, as I am very sensible how much my former conduct must render me suspect. My whole thoughts are continually employed in searching some efficacious way of persuading you of the sincerity of my Reformation, and have at length fallen upon one which will not leave you the least room to doubt of me, and therefore humbly beg your La'ship will be so good as to permit me to pursue it. Some days past Lord Strafford[2] passed through Utrecht, and told me your La'ship was not expected in England in less than four or five years; if so, I should be infinitely obliged to you if you would permit me to have the honour of accompanying you whilst abroad. You would then be a witness of my whole conduct, and I should have no occasion for any allowance at all, since everything would be at your La'ship's disposal. I could not express to you with how deep a sense of gratitude I should be touched if you would be pleased to grant me this favour; you would by it put it into my own power to convince you of my sincerity and my attachment to you by obeying the least of your orders, and it would be out of the power of my enemies to misrepresent my behaviour or misinterpret my actions. I should have the happiness of being continually near so tender a mother, and the satisfaction of having it in my power (by searching with the greatest zeal everything that could give your La'ship the least pleasure) to show you with how much tenderness I am, Madam, your La'ship's most dutiful Son and humble Servant,

"Ed. Wortley"

[1] From the unpublished MS.
[2] William, second Earl of Strafford, of the new creation.

The tender mother was not in the least affected by this specious letter from her "most dutiful son." On 17th June she wrote to Mr. Wortley—

"I[1] have just received yours of the 16th May. I am told that my son has several considerable debts in Italy, particularly at this place, but as he kept himself altogether in low company, he did not pass for my son. The P. G. [Procurator-General] asked me once if a young man who was here, was of your family, bearing the same name. I said slightly I knew nothing of him, and he replied he always supposed from his behaviour, that he was some sharper that had assumed that name to get credit. I was glad to have it pass over in this manner, to avoid being daily dunned by his creditors. He ran away from hence, and went to Florence, where, being received by Mr. Mann, he had more opportunity of running in debt, and exposing himself. . . . I have tried to know from the Consul whether there is any privilege place for debt, but I hear of none. If he should come where I am, I know no remedy but running away myself. To undertake to confine him would bring me into a great deal of trouble, and unavoidable scandal. I know very well how fair he can make his own story, and how difficult it would be at this distance to prove past facts.

"Mr. Mackensie,[2] younger brother to Lord Bute, is here at present. He is a very well-behaved youth; he makes great court to me, and I have shown him as many civilities as are in my power. . . ."

Lady Mary had intended joining Lady Pomfret in Florence as soon as the Prince of Saxony departed from Venice. She was detained by a domestic embarrassment. Her maid and man confessed that they had been married before they left England, and that a child would shortly be born to them. This incident postponed the journey till August, when, though suffering from a severe swelled face, Lady Mary braved "the dreadful passage of the Apennines," and arrived safely at Florence about the middle of the month. She wrote thence

[1] From the unpublished MS.
[2] James Stuart, who assumed the surname of Mackensie, on succeeding to the estates of his great-grandfather, Sir George Mackensie.

to her husband that the Pomfrets were taking great pains to make the place agreeable to her, and that she had been visited by nearly all the people of quality. Only one other letter belonging to the Florentine period has survived, and that is of doubtful authenticity, but we get glimpses of our heroine in the correspondence of Lady Pomfret and of Horace Walpole.

The former sends her friend Lady Hertford [1] an essay which Lady Mary had written in French to confute La Rochefoucauld's maxim, " Qu'il y a des mariages commodes, mais point de délicieux." On this Lady Hertford comments admiringly, " I own it gives me great pleasure to find a person with more wit than Rochefoucault himself undertaking to confute any of his maxims; for I have long entertained an aversion to them, and lamented in secret that a man of his genius should indulge so invidious an inclination as that of putting his readers out of conceit with the virtuous actions of their neighbours, and scarcely allowing them to find a happiness in their own."

Lady Hertford was less pleased with Lady Mary's pessimistic lines, beginning—

"With toilsome steps I pass thro' life's dull road," [2]

---

[1] Frances Thynne. She was born in 1699, and married Lord Hertford, afterwards seventh Duke of Somerset. Soon after her marriage she became one of the Ladies of the Bedchamber to Queen Caroline (then Princess of Wales), and continued in her office until the Queen's death in 1737. She patronised the poets, and Thomson, Shenstone, and Watts dedicated poems to her. She also tried her hand at the rhymed couplet.

[2] The poem is headed "Addressed to ——, 1736," and runs—

" With toilsome steps I pass thro' life's dull road
(No pack-horse half so tired of his load);
And when this dirty journey will conclude,
To what new realms is then my way pursued?
Say, then does the embodied spirit fly
To happier climes and to a better sky?
Or, sinking, mixes with its kindred clay,
And sleeps a whole eternity away?
Or shall this form be once again renewed,
With all its frailties, all its hopes, endued;
Acting once more on this detested stage
Passions of youth, infirmities of age?

I see in Tully what the ancient thought,
And read unprejudiced what moderns taught;

and remarks that it was a pity the writer did not look into the New Testament for the conviction that she sought in vain from Pagan authors.

"How agreeable and just are your reflections upon the verses I sent you," replies Lady Pomfret. "What pity and terror does it create to see wit, beauty, nobility and riches, after a full possession of fifty years, talk that language, and talk it so feelingly that all who read must know it comes from the heart! But indeed, dear madam, you make me smile when you propose putting the New Testament into the hands of the author. Pray how should you or I receive Hobbes' *Philosophy* if she, with all her eloquence, should recommend it for our instruction?" After remarking that she had heard a very observing person say that the first twenty years of life belong to the heart and the second twenty to the head, she continues, "According to this rule, Lady Mary Wortley has been ten years (at least) immoveably fixed. I therefore have contented myself with the amusement that arose from the genius which God Almighty has bestowed upon her, leaving to her the care and consequence of being grateful to the donor."

Horace Walpole, who was travelling in Italy with Gray this year, happened to be in Florence when Lady Mary arrived. On 31st July he wrote to Richard West: "On Wednesday we expect a third she-meteor. Those learned luminaries the Ladies Pomfret and Walpole[1] are to be joined

> But no conviction from my reading springs—
> Most dubious on the most important things.
> Yet one short moment would at once explain
> What all philosophy has sought in vain;
> Would clear all doubt, and terminate all pain.
> Why then not hasten that decisive hour,
> Still in my view, and ever in my power?
> Why should I drag along this life I hate,
> Without one thought to mitigate the weight?
> Whence this mysterious bearing to exist,
> When every joy is lost, and every hope dismissed?
> In chains and darkness wherefore should I stay,
> And mourn in prison while I keep the key?"

[1] Margaret, daughter and heiress of Samuel Rolle of Haynton, Devon. She married in 1724 (at fourteen) Robert, eldest son of Sir Robert Walpole. He had

by the Lady Mary Wortley Montague. You have not been witness to the rhapsody of mystic nonsense which these two fair ones debate incessantly, and consequently cannot figure what must be the issue of this triple alliance: we have some idea of it. Only figure the coalition of prudery, debauchery, sentiment, history, Greek, Latin, French, Italian and metaphysics; all, except the second, understood by halves, by quarters, or not at all. You shall have the journals of this notable academy."

Writing on 25th September to the Hon. Seymour Conway, Horace asks: "Did I tell you Lady Mary Wortley is here? She laughs at my Lady Walpole, scolds my Lady Pomfret, and is laughed at by the whole town. Her dress, her avarice, and her impudence must amaze anyone that never heard her name. She wears a foul mob that does not cover her greasy black locks, that hang loose, never combed or curled; an old mazarine blue wrapper, that gapes open, and discovers a canvas petticoat. Her face swelled violently on one side ... partly covered with a plaster, and partly with white paint, which, for cheapness, she has bought so coarse that you would not use it to wash a chimney."

On 2nd October Horace continues his scandalous chronicle in a letter to Richard West.

"But for the Academy," he explains, "I am not of it, but frequently in company with it; 'tis all disjointed. Madame —— [Lady Pomfret], who, though a learned lady, has not lost her modesty and character, is extremely scandalised with the two other dames, especially with Moll Worthless [Wortley], who knows no bounds. She is at rivalry with Lady W[alpole] for a certain Mr. —— [Sturges?], whom perhaps you knew at Oxford. . . . He fell into sentiments with my Lady W., and was happy to catch her at Platonic love; but as she seldom stops there, the poor man will be frightened out of his senses when she shall break the matter to him; for he never dreamt that her purposes were so naught. Lady

---

been created Baron Walpole in 1723, and on his father's death he succeeded as second Earl of Orford. Lady Walpole was a woman of notorious character, but had some intellect, and was better read than most ladies of fashion. There are numerous allusions to her in Horace Walpole's *Letters*.

Mary is so far gone, that to get him from the mouth of her antagonist, she literally took him out to dance country dances at a formal ball, where there was no measure kept in laughing at her. . . . She played at pharaoh two or three times at Princess Craon's, where she cheats horse and foot. She is really entertaining: I have been reading her works, which she lends out in manuscript, but they are too womanish: I like few of her performances."

The malicious and spiteful tone in which Horace Walpole always wrote of Lady Mary is supposed to be partly due to her friendship with Miss Skerret, the woman who had supplanted his mother; and partly to the fact that Mr. Wortley had frequently opposed Sir Robert in the House. Horace never forgot nor forgave an attack on the father who neglected him, nor a slight on the mother whose memory he adored. The scandals so wittily reported by Walpole were naturally repeated by his correspondents in England. Rumours of the undesirable notoriety acquired by his quondam enemy reached the ears of Pope, who wrote to Hugh Bethel [1]—

"You mention the fame of my old acquaintance, Lady Mary, as spread over Italy. Neither you delight in telling, nor I in hearing the particulars which acquire such a reputation; yet I wish you had just told me, if the character be more avaricious or amatory, and which passion has got the better at last."

[1] Pope addressed his *Second Satire of the Second Book of Horace* to Hugh Bethel who figures as Ofellus.

CHAPTER XXXVII

A PRODIGAL SON

THE problem of how to dispose of their son was still exercising the minds of the Wortleys; in fact, this question is continually cropping up in their correspondence, and never arrives at a satisfactory settlement. On 4th September Mr. Wortley wrote to his wife, who was still at Florence—

"In[1] mine of the 27th of May, I told you I left it to you to dispose of £25 half-yearly for our son. I meant the half year should begin from his day of payment in June, so that if he has £25 at once, he should not have it till 30th December. In a letter he writ to Mr. Gibson, he seems unwilling to leave the place where he is, says travelling will be expensive, so that he could not live on his allowance. . . . He writes his creditors want to do him mischief out of revenge; my opinion is, that some other woman or the thieves engage him to stay where he is, lest nothing should come from him when he removes. In short, whoever should think of clearing his debts would get into a labyrinth, and not find his way out. . . . Tho' he cannot tell how to manage such an affair, as most debtors can, yet any man of business can easily put him into a way. I suspect much the sense, if not the words of his letter to Mr. G. [Gibson] was given him by some of the thieves, because all it aims at is getting a sum of money for them. It seems likely he is now under the direction of Warren, who is supposed to be one of those three foot-pads that robbed Mr. Wheatley, and I am convinced he was one of them from what appeared at his friend Greenwood's trial."

[1] From the unpublished MS.

"I see plainly,"[1] replied Lady Mary, "that my son's desiring to stay where he now is is a trick, for which I suppose he is advised by some of the sharpers he corresponds with, and encouraged to it by Gibson. I don't know that Gibson has any part in it, but his silly flattery, and writing to him how fond you are of him, etc., I guess may persuade him that rather than you would suffer him to remain where he is, you will comply with all his extravagant demands. I have heard G. talk to him in my presence in that style, even when he was pursuing his ruin in the worst manner, and was very angry with me that I would not set a gloss on his actions to you, saying it was a duty as a Christian to make a father and a son well together. I made answer I thought the first duty was truth, and I would disguise nothing, and indeed I am now of opinion (as I was then) that it is to no purpose to set him free, since in a half a year's time (whatever is pretended of his reformation) he would be as deeply in debt as before. He has said nothing of his Italian debts, which are both here and at Venice. I see so little sincerity that I cannot help thinking he has again fallen into plotting against himself, either with his old acquaintance, or some new ones that are as bad. However it is, I think 'tis lucky he desires to stay where he is. I suppose you have before this received mine, in which I enclosed one from him, where he makes me a proposal of a very different nature, perhaps with a design to make me great offers in case I could prevail with you to leave him all your estates; tho' if he remembers in what manner I received his first proposal of that sort, if he had common sense he would not renew it. But he is so easily led by people that know neither you nor me, that I cannot be surprised at any of his projects."

On 22nd October Lady Mary left Florence for Rome, where she had taken lodgings for a month. She says but little of her stay here, beyond the fact that she is well diverted with viewing the buildings, but has neither made nor received a single visit. "The life I now lead," she wrote to Lady Pomfret, "is very different from what you fancy. I go to bed every night at ten, run about all the morning among the antiquities, and walk every evening in a beautiful villa; where,

[1] From the unpublished MS.

if among the fountains I could find the waters of Lethe, I should be completely happy.

> ' Like a deer that is wounded, I bleed and run on,
> And fain I my torment would hide;
> But alas! 'tis in vain, for wherever I run,
> A bloody dart sticks in my side,'

and I carry the serpent that poisons the paradise I am in."

On 23rd October Mr. Wortley had written—

"I[1] am glad you go to Rome, and think you would repent if you forbore going as far as Naples; where there is so great a crowd of people, I should think, notwithstanding what you have heard, it must be easy to find a few with whom one might pass the time as agreeably as in any other part of the world. The town which is said to have been lately found underground,[2] must be the greatest curiosity in the whole world, if it comes near to what has been printed of it. I shall be glad to hear from you how much truth you believe there is in what has been published, and how you find the place when you have seen it, or been more particularly informed at Naples by several of those who have examined this wonderful ruin.

"The only point we can hope to gain as to our son, is that he may get into a way of behaving himself as if he had a little more discretion than an idiot. This he cannot do while he cannot contrive how to appear anywhere but in a place of refuge. Almost anyone with common sense would either get his creditors to give him a license or be able to hide himself from them. . . ."

Lady Mary followed her husband's advice, and arrived in Naples on 22nd November, after a very unpleasant journey. Her chaise, for which she had given twenty-five good English pounds, broke all to pieces, and it was only by great good

---

[1] From the unpublished MS.

[2] In 1706, the first fragments of mosaic from Herculaneum were brought up on the occasion of deepening a well, but little seems to have been done in the way of excavation till 1738, when regular explorations were begun. Even then the work had to be carried on with great caution, owing to the fear of undermining the houses on the surface. The theatre was cleared, two temples, and a villa from which pictures and statues were recovered. It was left for the more scientific excavators of the nineteenth century to bring the city to light.

luck that she escaped with whole bones. She remained at Naples for about six weeks, and was so charmed with the climate and the people that she had some thoughts of settling down there. But the expense of living deterred her; two coaches, two running footmen, four other footmen, a gentleman usher and two pages, being as necessary at Naples as a single servant in London. Again, the affairs of Europe were, owing to the death of Charles VI. and the struggle over the Austrian Succession, in such an uncertain state that the traveller thought it prudent to wait a little before fixing on a place of residence, or otherwise she might find herself settled in the theatre of war.

In compliance with her husband's wishes, Lady Mary made great efforts to gain information about the " new ruin," as she calls Herculaneum. "Since the first discovery," she writes, " no care has been taken, and the ground fallen in, so that the present passage to it is, as I am told by everybody, extreme dangerous." Some English gentlemen had, however, been let down the year before, and declared that the whole account, as given in the newspapers, was literally true. She tried in vain to gain permission to see the pictures and other rarities taken from " Hercolana," which were preserved in the King's palace at Portici, but he kept the key in his own cabinet, and would not part with it to anyone. "The Court in general," she concludes, " is more barbarous than any of the ancient Goths. One proof of it, among many others, was melting down a beautiful copper statue of a vestal found in the new ruin, to make medallions for the late solemn christening."

By the middle of January the traveller was back in Rome, where she stayed for another month, and only quitted it, according to her own account, from being " too much courted." On 4th February 1741 she wrote thence to Mr. Wortley—

" I[1] received this post yours of 23rd December, and at the same time one from your son, which is very absurd. He still professes obedience, but seems to think it reasonable you should get him chose in the next Parliament. I have wrote to him, representing to him in mild, but very plain terms, his true condition, and telling him how creditable it would be to

[1] From the unpublished MS.

him to set apart some of his allowance towards making his creditors easy. The rest of my letter was as near as I could what I thought you would have me say. . . . I am not surprised at Lady F. Erskine's marriage;[1] she had always a false cunning which generally ends in the ruin of those that have it, but I am amazed at Mr. Erskine's impudence at pretending to be ignorant of it. I have received a letter from my poor sister, in which she calls it a match of her making, which would be a very plain proof of her lunacy, if there were no other."

The dreaded meeting with the Pretender did not take place, though Lady Mary saw his two sons at a public ball. "The eldest," she says, "seems thoughtless enough, and is really not unlike Mr. Lyttelton[2] in his shape and air. The youngest is very well made, dances finely, and has an ingenuous countenance; he is but fourteen years of age. The family live very splendidly, yet pay everybody, and (wherever they get it) are certainly in no want of money. . . .

"The English travellers in Rome behave in general very discreetly. I have reason to speak well of them, since they were all exceeding obliging to me. It may sound a little vain to say it, but they really paid a regular court to me, as if I had been their queen, and their governors told me that the desire of my approbation had a very great influence on their conduct. While I stayed, there was neither gaming nor any sort of extravagance. I used to preach to them very freely, and they all thanked me for it."

After her return to Rome Lady Mary wrote to inform Lady Pomfret that she had found Mr. Sturges[3] with the face of a lover who has been kicked out of doors, and declares that she pities his good heart, though she despises his want of spirit. Lady Pomfret had evidently accused her of a *tendresse* for Lady Walpole's cast-off admirer, for she proceeds: "I confess I am amazed (with your uncommon understanding) that you are capable of drawing such false consequences.

---

[1] To the son of Lady Mary's old enemy, Lord Grange.

[2] Thomas, son of the first Lord Lyttelton, whom he succeeded in 1747. He was known as the "wicked" Lord Lyttelton.

[3] Lady Walpole's admirer.

Because I tell you another woman has a very agreeable lover, you conclude I am in love with him myself; when God knows I have not seen one man since I left you, that has affected me otherwise than if he had been carved in marble. Some figures have been good, others have been ill-made, and all equally indifferent to me."

The whole disclaimer, with its qualification " since I left you," comes curiously enough from a woman of fifty-two, who, if we may believe contemporary records, neglected to make the best of such charms as remained to her.

In February Lady Mary left Rome and travelled to Turin *via* Leghorn. A good many letters written during this period were lost, owing to the confusion that reigned in the country. As the post-office officials were notoriously inquisitive, it is not surprising that but little public news was retailed by foreigners travelling in Italy. On 17th March Lady Mary wrote to her husband from Turin—

"I[1] arrived here last night, after very bad roads. I hope you have received my letters relating to the town of Hercolana, which perhaps, tho' not very satisfactory, are all truth. Sir John Shadwell[2] can know nothing concerning it; the discovery of it happened six months after he had left Naples. You know he is famous for romancing. I left Rome really from being too much courted there, since I found that (in spite of all my caution) if I had stayed, it had been impossible for me to escape suspicions I no way deserved, and the spies are so numerous, and such foolish rogues, a small matter would have served for accusation. I will be more particular on this subject the first opportunity I find of sending a letter by a safe hand."

In an unpublished letter for 19th March Mr. Wortley informs his wife that he intends in future to make up her "interest money," which might be regarded as pin-money, to

[1] From the unpublished MS.
[2] Sir John Shadwell (1671–1747) had been physician in ordinary to Queen Anne, and held the same post under George I. and George II. He was in Italy at the same time as Horace Walpole, and had a pretty daughter whom the Italians called " Mademoiselle Mees Molli." Lady Shadwell's report of Lady Mary at Venice has already been quoted, as well as Lord Mansel's allusion to the Shadwell family, as his travelling companions.

three hundred a year. As she had been travelling about so much he thought that the addition was not unreasonable. He was not in the habit of sending news, but he concludes with the information that "Lady Townshend and my Lord agreed to live separately about a fortnight ago.[1] The Duchess of Bedford[2] and the Duke parted last summer. She lives in the little house next to mine that has always stood empty, tho' the Duke gives her the income of her estates."

On 11th April Lady Mary was able to send a more confidential letter by the hand of Mr. Mackensie. "The English politics," she observes, "are the general jest of all the nations I have passed through, and even those who profit by our follies cannot help laughing at our notorious blunders, though they are all persuaded that the minister[3] does not act from weakness but from corruption, and that the Spanish gold influences his measures. I had a long discourse with Count Mahony on this subject, who said very freely, that half the ships sent to the coast of Naples that have lain idle in our ports last summer would have frightened the Queen of Spain into a submission to whatever terms we thought proper to impose."[4] Lady Mary formed a very low opinion of the British ambassadors and consuls, who, she said, were "entirely wanting in common sense, and knew no more of the country they inhabited than that they ate and slept in it."

In June or July the traveller moved to Genoa, where she proposed to settle for a time on account of the cheapness of house-rents. A palace fit for a prince could be hired for fifty pounds a year. Though the republic was poor, many of the private families were rich, and lived at great expense. All the people of the first quality kept coaches "as fine as the Speaker's," though the streets were so narrow that they could

---

[1] The separation was probably due to the indiscreet conduct of Lady Townshend. Her intrigues were a matter of common knowledge.

[2] John, fourth Duke of Bedford, had married in 1737 (as his second wife) Lady Mary's niece, Gertrude, daughter of Lord Gower. The story of the separation was not true, for in 1750 H. Walpole says that the Duchess governs the "little Duke" entirely.

[3] She means Sir Robert Walpole.

[4] Elizabeth Farnese, wife of Philip v., was a lady of far-reaching ambitions, who had placed her eldest son on the throne of Naples, and was about to attempt to seize Milan for her second son, Don Philip.

only use them outside the town. Lady Mary says that she has been visited by all the first people in the town, and invited to several fine dinners, but the expense of chair-hire, eighteen francs a week, seems to have marred her pleasure. On 8th September she wrote to Mr. Wortley a long and "sensible" letter, with the object of dissuading him from a contemplated reconciliation with their son.

"I[1] should not be surprised," she observes, "if our son was sincerely an Enthusiast. Mr. Anderson told me that at Troyes he had a fit of praying for four or five hours together, and that he was with difficulty hindered from going into a Convent. Tho' I think his last letter to me, of which I have given you an account, does not look like it, since he desires to marry, tho' his wife is alive. 'Tis true no inconsistency is to be wondered at in such a head as his. I expect nothing from him but going from one species of folly to another. Folly (as Mons. Rochefoucault remarks) is the only incorrigible fault. This is a very nice subject for me to write on, but I think it my duty to put you in mind, that in so near a relation as that of father and son, there is no medium between a thorough displeasure and a thorough reconciliation. If you take the latter part, I am persuaded there is nothing you can do for him, and that he will find people to be of his mind. I very well know him; he is capable of making up a fine story to move pity, and can behave himself so, to the eye of a stranger, as to make a tolerable figure even to a man of sense, that does not give himself the trouble of a nice observation, which very few people do in a matter that does not personally concern them. I have no regard for what Murray[2] says: he is a professed patron of Pope's, very likely to be prejudiced by his lies, and not a sincere man, of which I know a very strong instance, which perhaps I never told you, it being related to me in confidence very little before I left England. In general, most people are readily disposed to be (what they call) good-natured and

[1] From the unpublished MS.
[2] This was probably William Murray, afterwards the great Lord Mansfield (1772–93). He was Solicitor-General in 1742, Attorney-General in 1754, and Lord Chief-Justice in 1756.

generous at the expense of another. Add to this, the lavish promises of eternal service and friendship which your son is ready to make to everybody he sees.

"I am clearly of opinion, that whoever you send over to him, you will have no just information. I speak on this subject without any prejudice whatever. I hope and believe I shall never know who is your heir; consequently in regard to myself, it is a thing quite indifferent. But I should think I was guilty of breach of trust to you if I concealed my real thoughts on this occasion. Anger and compassion are equal weaknesses, and a wise man never suffers himself to be influenced by either in an action of consequence. I think your only error has been too much lenity to him. If he had been forced again to sea when he first deserted it, after making it his request to be placed there, it had hindered a long train of succeeding mischief. Mr. Edgecombe takes the most prudent method with his son in keeping him at a distance, tho' he has not committed half the notorious follies of ours, and is a youth of bright parts. His allowance is no more than £300 per annum. If you are reconciled to him, you must resolve to pay his debts. If you are determined otherwise, I would hear nobody speak on that subject.

"I desire you to forgive the liberty I have taken, in explaining myself so fully. My intention is good, and if I mistake, it is a fault of judgment."

Genoa proved no abiding-place, on account of the rumoured approach of the Spanish troops. Lady Mary decided to cross the Alps once more, and take refuge in Geneva, where, she had been assured, it was possible to live very cheaply. On 18th September she wrote to her husband: "I[1] am frightened out of Italy, by the increasing of the report of the coming of the Spaniards, who are now expected here daily. I am not apt to credit public report, but I perceive it is more generally believed than ever. The Imperial Minister retired from this place yesterday, so that I think it would be imprudence to stay. I go to Geneva; if the circumstances alter I may return. William and Mary both declare that they will not pass the Alps, which puts me to a great deal of trouble, they not

[1] From the unpublished MS.

making this declaration till half my things were packed up. The truth is, they have both behaved very ill for above a twelvemonth, in hopes to provoke me to turn them away, that I might be at the expense of their journey to England, but I have suffered all their sauciness with the temper of Socrates, knowing that a great many faults are to be overlooked for the sake of having people about me that at least would not rob or murder me. But there being a Dutch ship arrived in port, who has offered them a cheap passage, they have made the bargain without giving me any warning. As to William, I can easily enough find another in his place, but I should be sorry to be without an English maid, that I could in some measure depend on in the case of sickness or other accidents. I therefore wish that Mary, the housemaid, who lived with me when I left London, might be sent to Geneva. There are great conveniences of travelling cheap through France; I desire you would take the charges of her journey out of the next quarter's allowance. This vexation hindered my sleeping last night, and has discomposed me so much, that I am afraid I have wrote a very sad letter, but I hope it is intelligible.

"If Mary will not come, I do not desire any other to be sent in her room. I think of her because I know her to be sensible and handy."

The services of Mary the housemaid were not required. The day after the foregoing letter was written, William and Mary repented them of their faithlessness with tears. Their mistress was only too glad to accept their promises of amendment, and they remained with her several years longer.

CHAPTER XXXVIII

LIFE AT AVIGNON

LADY MARY arrived at Geneva on 11th October, but here again she found no rest for her perturbed spirit. Everything, she complained, was quite different from what she had been led to expect. The way of living was exactly the reverse of that which obtained in Italy. " Here," she remarks, " there is no show, but a great deal of eating; there [in Italy] is all the magnificence imaginable, and no dinners but on particular occasions; yet the difference of the prices renders the total expense very nearly equal." The unexpected dearness of provisions and the sharpness of the air made her decide against spending the winter at Geneva, as she had originally intended. On 22nd October she wrote to Mr. Wortley—

" I[1] have this minute received yours of the 17th September. I am not at all surprised my son should say that it is my fault you are not reconciled to him. He told his sister so, and I perceived he had said the same thing to G. tho' he did not tell it to me in so plain terms as the others. He had before said it to myself, when he was hot-headed at the periwig-makers in St. Alban's Street, adding that everybody was of that opinion. I thought then that this was put into his head by Forester from Pope. I am very sorry you should have had any uneasiness on the account of my not writing often to him. I wrote from Turin; since that I have wrote twice from Genoa. During the whole time I was at Genoa, there was not one English merchant ship put into that port. I have now left a box for the Duchess of Portland in the hands of the Consul, who does not expect any opportunity of sending it, till it is determined whether or no the Spaniards

[1] From the unpublished MS.

intend for Italy, which I hear differently spoke of here. This place is exactly like an English country-town, the prospects very pretty to any eye that had not seen Naples or Genoa. I should prefer the first to any other place of residence, in consideration of the beauty and climate, if the customs were more agreeable, or our nations on better terms. But in all arbitrary Courts the subjects dare not have a long or familiar acquaintance with any stranger that is not well with the Government. I believe the Councils all over Europe change very often; a short time however must determine them. In general it is a melancholy reflection to see how far our national esteem is sunk, in all foreign Courts in particular. I have found everywhere more regard than I had occasion to expect. Your busy time is now approaching; I hope no engagement whatever will occasion you to hazard your health."

In November Lady Mary moved to Chambéry, where she proposed to spend the remainder of the winter. "Here is the most profound peace and unbounded plenty," she assures Lady Pomfret, "that is to be found in any corner of the universe, but not one rag of money. For my part, I think it amounts to the same thing, whether one is obliged to give several pence for bread, or can have a great deal of bread for a penny, since the Savoyard nobility keep as good tables without money as those in London, who spend in a week what would be here a considerable yearly revenue. Wine, which is equal to the best Burgundy, is sold for a penny a quart, and I have a cook for very small wages, that is capable of rivalling Chloë.[1] Here are no equipages but chairs, the hire of which is about a crown a week, and all other matters proportionable. I can assure you I make the figure of the Duchess of Marlborough, by carrying gold in my purse; there being no visible coin but copper. Yet we are all people that can produce pedigrees to serve for the order of Malta. Many of us have travelled, and 'tis the fashion to love reading. We eat together perpetually, and have assemblies every night for conversation."

There are very few letters relating to this period, the

[1] The Duke of Newcastle's French cook, who seems to have made a strong impression on Lady Mary's mind.

majority of those which were written failing to reach their destination, in consequence of the disturbed state of Europe. There are a few unpublished notes of no particular interest or importance, since to send "news," or discuss the position of affairs, ensured the non-delivery of a letter. Lady Mary spent the winter at Chambéry in health and tranquillity, but in April she was driven away by a report that the French troops were coming. Moving to Lyons, she was there faced by the prospect of being blocked up in a besieged town, and, not knowing how else to avoid the terrors of war, she took refuge in Avignon, where she could live "under the protection of the Holy See."

Meanwhile, young Wortley had been allowed to return to England, where he had spent three months, and from all accounts, was improved in his manners if not in his morals. He was anxious to join the army in Flanders, and had hopes of getting a commission through one of his influential relations. Mr. Wortley, who had refused to see his son, wished to have an impartial account of him, and evolved the plan of sending him to meet his mother at some place within easy reach of her present abode. He was to go under a feigned name, and with only just enough money to pay his travelling expenses. Lady Mary was requested to talk to him in a calm and gentle way, so as to win his confidence. According to Mr. Gibson the tutor, the young man's behaviour and conversation had entirely changed in the past four years, and though he might always be a weak man, there seemed reason to hope that he would avoid bad company in future, and be no ill manager of his money.

Such was the gist of a long letter addressed by Mr. Wortley to his wife on 22nd March 1742. Lady Mary was by no means enamoured of the suggestion that she should arrange an interview with her son, and she had little faith in the reality of his reformation. However, in accordance with her husband's express desire, she reluctantly consented to meet the repentant prodigal at Orange, which was within easy reach of Avignon.

"Both nature and interest," she assures her husband in a letter on the same subject, "were I inclined to follow blindly the dictates of either, would determine me to wish him your heir rather than a stranger; but I think myself obliged both by honour, conscience, and my regard for you, no way to deceive you; and I confess hitherto I see nothing but falsehood and weakness through his whole conduct. It is possible his person may be altered since I last saw him, but his figure then was very agreeable and his manner insinuating. I very well remember the professions he made to me, and do not doubt he is as lavish of them to other people. Perhaps Lord C[arteret][1] may think him no ill match for an ugly girl that sticks on his hands. The project of breaking his marriage shows at least his devotion counterfeit, since I am sensible it cannot be done but by false witnesses."

Early in May Lady Mary arrived at Avignon, where, as she tells Lady Pomfret, she hopes she may while away an idle life in great tranquillity, the only ambition that is left to her. Her interview with her son took place at Orange at the beginning of June, and on 10th June she writes the following account, the "most exact" of which she is capable, to Mr. Wortley:—

"He is so much altered in his person I should scarcely have known him. He has entirely lost his beauty, and looks at least seven years older than he is; and the wildness that he always had in his eyes is so much encreased it is downright shocking, and I am afraid will end fatally. He is grown fat, but is still genteel, and has an air of politeness that is agreeable. He speaks French like a Frenchman, and has got all the fashionable expression of that language, and a volubility of words which he always had, and which I do not wonder should pass for wit with inconsiderate people. His behaviour is perfectly civil, and I found him perfectly submissive, but in the main no way really improved in his understanding, which is exceedingly weak, and I am convinced he will always be led by the person he converses with either right or wrong, not being capable of forming any fixed judgment of his own. As to his enthusiasm, if he had it, I suppose he has already lost it; since I could perceive no turn of it all in his conversa-

[1] Lord Carteret (afterwards Lord Granville), the new Secretary of State, showed a disposition to patronise the young man. He had four daughters by his first wife, who all married well.

tion. But with his head I believe it is possible to make him a monk one day, and a Turk three days after. . . . He began to talk to me in the usual silly cant I have so often heard from him, which I shortened by telling him I desired not to be troubled with it, that professions were of no use where actions were expected, and that the only thing could give me hopes of a good conduct was regularity and truth. He very readily agreed to all I said (as indeed he has always done when he has not been hot-headed)."

Lady Mary was careful to point out to the ne'er-do-weel how very liberally he had been treated. The Prince of Hesse had lived at Geneva for some years on an allowance of £300, and Lord Hervey had given his son a travelling pension of but £200. If her son had chosen, he might, while living at Ysselstein, have saved £100 a year, which would have gone near to paying his debts in four or five years. He excused himself by replying that Mr. Gibson had told him it became Mr. Wortley's son to live handsomely, to which his mother replied that the only becoming part he could now act would be owning the ill use he had made of his father's indulgence, and endeavouring to be no further expense to him, instead of making scandalous complaints, and being always at his last shirt and his last guinea. The young man responded with promises of good behaviour and economy, and showed great delight at the prospect of going into the army, Lord Carteret having promised him a commission. He was anxious to know if Mr. Wortley had already settled his estates, and insinuated that his mother might expect great things from his gratitude if she would persuade his father to settle everything on him. She replied that nothing should ever make her act against her honour or her conscience, and that she would never persuade his father to do anything for him till she thought he deserved it. "The rest of his conversation," she concludes, "was extremely gay. The various things he has seen has given him a superficial universal knowledge. He really knows most of the modern languages, and, if I could believe him, can read Arabic, and has read the Bible in Hebrew."

Lord Hervey still kept up an intermittent correspondence

with his old friend and poetical collaborator. In Croker's biographical notice, prefaced to the *Memoirs of the Reign of George II.*,[1] two or three of the letters to Lady Mary are quoted. In 1737 Lord Hervey had replied to the lady's complaint that she was too old at forty-seven to inspire a passion, " I should think anybody a great fool that said he liked spring better than summer merely because it is further from autumn, or that they loved green fruit better than ripe only because it was further from being rotten. I ever did, and believe I ever shall like woman best

> 'Just in the noon of life—those golden days
> When the mind ripens ere the form decays.'"

On 20th May 1742 he wrote from Kensington Gravel Pits—

" I must now (since you take so friendly a part in what concerns me) give you a short account of my natural and political health; and when I say I am still alive, and still Privy Seal, it is all I can say for the pleasure of one or the honour of the other;[2] for since Lord Orford's retiring, as I am too proud to offer my service and friendship where I am not sure they will be accepted of, and too inconsiderable to have these advances made to me (though I never forgot or failed to return any obligations I ever received), so I remain as illustrious a nothing in this office as ever filled it since it was erected. There is one benefit, however, I enjoy from this loss of my Court interest, which is, that all those flies which were buzzing about me in the summer sunshine and full ripeness of that interest, have all deserted its autumnal decay, and, from thinking my natural death not far off and my political demise already over, have all forgot the death-bed of the one and the coffin of the other. I must let you know, too, that since the death of my mother[3] and my mother-in-law, my circumstances are so easy, or rather affluent, that

---

[1] Written by Lord Hervey, and edited by Croker.
[2] Lord Hervey was Lord Privy Seal 1740-42. On Walpole's fall in February 1742, he clung to his office while professing to despise it, but was dismissed in July, when he joined the Opposition.
[3] Lady Bristol died in May 1741. His father outlived him.

with regard to my pecuniary interest in being in or out, I am as indifferent as I can be whether my hat is laced or plain; and with regard to any ambitious view almost as indifferent from age and infirmity about the honour of one or the look of the other."

For 15th August there is a letter from Lady Mary to her husband, in answer apparently to one of his which contained a criticism or appreciation of Lord Bute. She seems completely to have forgotten the fact that she was violently opposed to her daughter's marriage.

"You[1] give Lord Bute the character I always believed belonged to him from the first of our acquaintance, and the opinion I had of his honesty (which is the most essential quality) made me so easily consent to the match. The faults I observed in his temper I told my daughter at that time. She made answer (as most people do while they are blinded with a passion) that she did not dislike them. I have nothing to desire of her. I never wished anything but her affection, and if I were to owe the appearances of it to the solicitations of another, it would give me no pleasure. I am very glad she continues her intimacy with the Duchess of Portland,[2] whose company will never injure her, either by advice or example. I have always answered her letters very regularly, and if she shows them to you, you will see in them nothing but kindness.

"I do not doubt that in case of a war with France, the notice you mention would be given to all the English, but I know enough of the nation to be persuaded it would be very disagreeable living amongst them in such a circumstance."

Lady Bute was staying with her father during part of this year, and Lady Mary hopes that her obedience and affection will make Mr. Wortley's life agreeable to him. "She cannot have more than I have had," concludes the exile, with an unwonted touch of pathos. "I wish the success may be greater." This confession of failure gives some colour

---

[1] From the unpublished MS.

[2] Daughter of Lady Mary's old friend, Lady Oxford. She was the "amiable Duchess" who figures so largely in Mrs. Delany's Correspondence.

to the idea that the separation had been brought about of set purpose, and was not merely an accidental arrangement.

The shortcomings of the post-offices are a frequent subject of comment in the letters of this period. Writing to Lady Pomfret in November 1742, Lady Mary explains that a certain letter has gone astray, and continues—

" I am not surprised at it, since I have lost several others, and all for the same reason ; I mean mentioning political transactions. 'Tis the best proof of wisdom that I know of our reigning ministers, that they will not suffer their fame to travel into foreign lands; neither have I any curiosity for their proceedings, being long ago persuaded of the truth of that histori-prophetical verse, which says—

> 'The world will still be ruled by knaves
> And fools, contending to be slaves.'

I desire no other intelligence from my friends but tea-table chat, which has been allowed to our sex by so long a prescription."

The traveller had now settled down at Avignon, where at last she had found peace and quiet, though the place was not without its disadvantages. Writing to Mr. Wortley on 8th January 1743, she says—

" I[1] am sorry to hear you complain of your health, particularly at the beginning of the Sessions. I hope you are by this time convinced that the attendance in Parliament is not worth hazarding a fever or even a cold. December has been sharp cold, but always clear till this last fortnight, when we have had a great fall of snow, which lay some days on the ground. The oldest people say they never remember the like, but now we enjoy the usual sunshine, tho' the air is cold and piercing, which I am told will continue till February, which is commonly spring. If the soil here was as good as the climate, we should have all the advantages of Italy, but the barren sands afford little herbage, and often a scarcity of wheat, which makes bread dear, but excellent in its kind. Mutton very good, beef rare and bad, wine good of various sorts. In general it is what the French call *Un pays de bonne*

[1] From the unpublished MS.

but it is not placed, and perhaps never shall be."[1] The inscription is an adaptation of Cowley's *Epitaphium vivi auctoris*. It must be presumed that one of the workmen employed in the building was the lucky man who met his end suddenly, probably by some accident.

From one or two unpublished notes we learn that young Wortley had joined the army in Flanders this summer, and that his mother hoped the rashness which had ruined him in other affairs might be lucky to him in his new profession. In November she has received a letter from him, which she sends on to Mr. Wortley with the comment—

"I[2] think the style is rather better than ordinary, and probably he was helped in it; but the sense is as usual, mistaking civility for approbation in the behaviour of his commanders, and saying nothing is done without him, when I know nothing is done with him. I am very sorry for the death of the Duke of Argyll,[3] on the account of my daughter, her Lord losing a great support. He dies a young man in the account of this country, where nobody is old till four-score years and ten."

[1] The inscription was not used, as Mr. Wortley objected to it.
[2] From the unpublished MS.
[3] The Duke of Argyll was Lord Bute's uncle. He was born in 1678, and was therefore sixty-five at the date of his death.

CHAPTER XXXIX

LIFE AT AVIGNON (*continued*)

LADY Mary's accounts of Avignon and the mode of life there are interesting, but her theories about the history and antiquity of the town can hardly be accepted as correct by the light of modern knowledge. For example, she was of opinion that " Avignon was certainly no town in the time of the Romans; nor is there the smallest remains of any antiquity but what is entirely Gothic.[1] The town is large, but thinly peopled. Here are fourteen large convents, besides others. It is so well situated for trade, and the silk so fine and plentiful, that if they were not curbed by the French not permitting them to trade, they would certainly ruin Lyons; but as they can sell none of their manufactures out of the walls of the town, and the ladies here, as everywhere else, preferring foreign stuffs to their own, the tradespeople are poor, and the shops ill furnished."

That the climate was healthy, in spite of the sharp north winds, seemed to be proved by the great numbers of old people, who appeared at the assemblies, ate great suppers, and kept late hours, without showing any visible infirmity. The price of provisions was high for strangers, but the gentry, who kept all their land in their own hands, and had wine, oil, and corn for the cost of production, were able to keep splendid tables at very small expense.

In the spring of 1744 the servant difficulty came to a crisis once more; William and Mary, now the parents of two children, having decided to spend the remainder of their days in their native land. In a letter to Mr. Wortley, endorsed

[1] Avignon was the capital of the ancient Cavares, and has, of course, many Roman remains.

Lady Mary describes the discomfort of her situation at Avignon, then a hotbed of Jacobitism, in consequence of the suspicion with which she was regarded by the authorities. "It is natural," she observes, "and (I think) just to wish well to one's religion and country, yet as I can serve neither by disputes, I am content to pray for both in my closet, and avoid all subjects of controversy as much as I can. However, I am watched here as a dangerous person, which I attribute chiefly to Mrs. Hay,[1] who, having changed her own religion, has a secret hatred against every one that does not do the same."

Lady Mary had been afraid to remain in Rome, lest unavoidable meetings with the Pretender and his family should rouse suspicions of her loyalty in the minds of her own party. At Avignon she was feared and disliked in consequence of her well-known Whig proclivities. There is an allusion to this unfortunate state of affairs in a letter to Mr. Wortley, dated 15th May—

". . . I[2] am particularly acquainted with the young Lady Carteret. She is beautiful and engaging, and has reason to think herself much obliged to me, but I have so often seen prosperity cause an entire oblivion, that I do not expect she should either remember or acknowlege it.[3]

"I am sorry but not surprised at the conduct of my son, being fully persuaded he is incapable of acting right on any

[1] Mrs. Hay was a daughter of Lord Stormont, and married Colonel Hay, brother of the seventh Earl of Kinnoull, and brother-in-law of Lord Mar. He took part in the Jacobite rising of 1715, and afterwards joined the Pretender's Court at St. Germains. He is said to have betrayed Mar's double-dealing, and succeeded him as secretary to the Chevalier in 1724. He was created (by the Pretender) Earl of Inverness in 1725. Mrs. Hay, a handsome, ambitious woman, was believed to be the mistress of James Edward.

[2] From the unpublished MS.

[3] Lady Sophia Fermor, daughter of Lady Pomfret. She married Lord Carteret in 1744, when he was fifty-four and afflicted by gout. Although she was young and one of the chief beauties of her day, it was considered an excellent match, he being then at the head of affairs. It was supposed that she had been jilted by Lord Lincoln. The following epigram on the match is quoted by Horace Walpole:—

> "Her beauty, like the Scripture feast,
> To which the invited never came,
> Deprived of its intended guest,
> Was given to the old and lame."

She died after only eighteen months of marriage, leaving a daughter.

occasion. The weather here has had some similitude with that in England, being more rainy than has been known for several years, drought being the usual complaint of this climate. We find the benefit of this uncommon weather, in the goodness of the garden stuff, which is very delicious, but of a very short duration, the heat of the sun soon burning it. Fruit, excepting olives, grapes, and figs, is always very scarce, the spring winds generally destroying the blossoms. Upon the whole, this town has been very agreeable to me till of late, that I am very coldly looked upon, on the account of the late disturbances, Mrs. Hay (who is here called Lady Inverness) whispering that I am a spy, which I see makes some afraid to converse with me, and others drop speeches on purpose to hear my reply, in which they are always disappointed by my being invincibly silent. However, it makes my residence so uneasy, that if I knew where to go, I believe I should quit the town. But France is now forbidden, and a journey to Italy impracticable while the Spaniards are everywhere on the frontier."

Lady Mary's old enemy, Pope, died on 30th May 1744. As late as 10th August she has heard no more than a rumour of the event, for she says in a letter to Lady Oxford of that date: "I hear that Pope is dead, but suppose it is a mistake, since your ladyship has never mentioned it. If it is so, I have some small curiosity for the disposition of his affairs, and to whom he has left the enjoyment of his pretty house at Twickenham, which was in his power to dispose for only one year after his decease."[1]

Lady Mary was not given to wearing her heart upon her sleeve, but her dependence upon Lady Oxford's friendship is expressed in her anxiety about her friend's failing health. "If I am so unhappy as to lose you," she writes about this time, "I shall look upon myself as a widow and an orphan, having no friend in the world but yourself. If you saw the tears with which these lines are accompanied, you would be convinced of the sincerity of them; let me beg you on my knees to take care of your life, and let no other regard whatever occasion the neglect of it."

[1] Pope's villa was bought after his death by Sir William Stanhope.

From the letters of this year we learn that young Wortley, after the interview with his mother at Orange, which he had solemnly vowed to keep secret, had visited a chance acquaintance at Montelimart, and, throwing off his incognito, had babbled of himself, his family, and his private affairs. On 24th December Lady Mary wrote to her husband, who was gratified by his son's behaviour in Flanders—

"I[1] am very glad if my son can act reasonably, tho' I own I very much doubt it, after his behaviour at Montelimart against his word solemnly given, and without any reason to induce him to such a conduct but downright levity and folly. I have lately seen Madame St. Auban, who informed me of all the circumstances of his nonsense. He told her his whole history (mixing however some notorious lies in it), and showed her my letters to convince her he was the person he pretended to be, which she very much doubted by his extravagant discourse. If you think the enclosed proper to be sent to him, I leave it to your discretion."

The enclosed letter runs as follows:—

"You[1] mention in your letter of 7th August many that you have wrote to me; I have never received any other. I shall be very glad to hear of your good behaviour, and that you know how to value your character. I cannot help distrusting it, when I reflect on the many solemn promises you made me at Orange of taking care to keep yourself concealed. You saw how much precaution I used to that purpose, and pretended to be very well satisfied with the reasons I gave you (though I think my commands ought to have been sufficient) why I thought it would be disadvantageous to me you should be known in this country. Yet after all this, on your leaving me, at only half a day's journey distant, you showed my likeness to Madame St. Auban, and told her a long story of yourself and family, with several falsehoods mixed in it. It will be very fruitless to deny this; I had it from her own mouth with so many circumstances I can make no doubt of it. I wish you would consider there is nothing meaner or more unworthy a gentleman than breach

[1] From the unpublished MS.

of promise, and that tattling and lying are qualities not to be forgiven even in a chambermaid. I speak to you plainly as one more interested in your welfare than any of your companions can be, and it is the best proof I can give you that I am your affec^ate Mother, M. WORTLEY"

By the beginning of the eventful year, 1745, Lady Mary was heartily tired of her residence at Avignon, but as long as the war lasted it seemed rash to quit a place of security. On 27th January she writes to Mr. Wortley—

". . . In[1] these changing times every day presents something of new difficulty. It is reported here that the taking of Maréschal Bellisle[2] will make the residence of France very unsafe to all the English. I am very secure here, which is all the recommendation of this place. I should have changed it long since if I had known where to remove, but I know of no part of Europe, except this little spot, and the Isle of Malta, which is not likely to be disturbed by the ravage of troops. The Pope's state in Italy has suffered so much, that I am informed it is almost ruined. We feel some part of the inconvenience by the dearness of provision. . . ."

[1] From the unpublished MS.
[2] In 1744 the Maréchal de Belle-Isle and his brother were captured while passing through Hanover on their way to Berlin. They were taken to England and kept in captivity for a year.

CHAPTER XL

FONTENOY

YOUNG WORTLEY, who was now on General Sinclair's[1] staff, recommended by the Duke of Cumberland, took part in the Battle of Fontenoy, besides seeing other active service. He was not allowed to communicate directly with his father, but his letters are addressed to Mr. Gibson, who acted as intermediary. On 12th May (O.S.) the young man wrote the following account of the Battle of Fontenoy, which was fought on 30th April (N.S.):—

"Since[2] His Royal Highness has thought proper to appoint me to assist General Sinclair in doing his duty as Quarter-Master General, this is the first moment I have had to myself; and I can't let it slip, for we may perhaps march in an hour or two, and God knows when I shall have another opportunity. We always go to reconnoitre before the army, and then regulate the march rout, and afterwards march again before the army to mark out the camp, by which means we are almost continually on horseback. Yesterday, as soon as we came to this ground, before we marked out our camp we were alarmed by a few shot, upon which General Sinclair sent me to reconnoitre, so I went to the place where the firing came from, and found some of our Houssards exchanging shot at about 16 yards distance with the French Pandoures.[3] I only stayed, as I had no other business there, long enough to know as well as I could, their number. However, I saw some

---

[1] James Sinclair (who died in 1762) was the Lieutenant-General commanding the forces in Flanders in 1745. Later in life he was our Ambassador at Vienna and Turin.
[2] From the unpublished MS.
[3] A Hungarian word for a cavalry soldier resembling our Huzzar.

execution done; they were not at one post above 300. We continued firing at one another the whole day; we lost three Houssards, the enemy a Captain and more than 20 dead, and five prisoners. We see very plainly the French camp, that is the advanced camp, which is not above a mile and a half from ours, but as there is a wood between us, it will render the attack difficult. However we expect an action hourly. In the meantime we have continual skirmishes; our Houssards have taken 20 prisoners.

"Monday morning. His Royal Highness[1] thought proper to go himself to reconnoitre, and the whole day passed in skirmishes between our Houssards and their Pandoures. That night we made proper passages through the wood, and on Tuesday at 2 in the morning, the whole army marched off by the right, and about 5 was drawn out in two lines on the plain which lies between Vesin and Antoing, having Vesin on our right and Fontenoy on our left. Before we were well drawn up, the enemy played very briskly upon us from a battery they had on an eminence on their left, which did us very considerable damage, and shot Sir James Campbell's[2] leg off. I was very near him. When we were drawn up, they played upon us from several batteries they had in the centre, but we soon silenced them, and advanced upon them. We then attempted taking the village of Fontenoy, the churchyard of which is extremely well fortified, and where there was also a redoubt, but notwithstanding our greatest efforts, we were forced off by dint of cannon, with a very considerable loss. The Foot then came to Platoon firing, and behaved with the greatest bravery, but after having twice obliged the enemy to retire, the heat of the fire from them on our right and left as well as centre, obliged us to retreat in good order, and the same night we marched here without being pursued in the least.

'His Royal Highness was everywhere in the heat of the action with all the coolness of an old General. I was the whole

---

[1] The Duke of Cumberland.

[2] Sir James Campbell of Lawers (1667-1745). He had served at Malplacquet thirty-six years before, as Lieutenant-Colonel of the Scots Greys. He was knighted at Dettingen in 1742. His injury at Fontenoy cost him his life.

acted up to the character which was so well established in Queen Anne's war. And whoever were only to hear the great and heroic behaviour of the Duke mentioned by all men with admiration, would be apt to imagine that all divisions were ended among us here, as I am persuaded they are by His Royal Highness's prudence in the army. . . ."

In the pride and gratification of his heart, Mr. Wortley sent an account of his son's adventures to his wife, who received it in rather sceptical fashion.

"I[1] am much obliged to you," she replied, "for the account you have given me of my son. If I could depend on his relation, I should hope that his behaviour in the profession he has chose, would in some measure re-establish his character, but as I have a too long experience of his idle vain way of talking of himself, I do not much regard what he says on any subject. I have heard the wind of a cannon will dismount a man, and that may be his meaning, tho' it is possible it may be entirely invented. However it is something that he has not behaved himself as ill as several of the French. Here are now two men of quality in this neighbourhood who ran away while their companies fought."

Prompted, no doubt, by Mr. Wortley, Mr. Gibson had written to the young officer, now promoted to be "captain lieutenant," affecting to cast doubts upon some parts of his account of the battle, and asking for more exact details. This brought a long explanatory letter, dated Liège, 17th July, which gives a description of the writer's later adventures with his regiment.

"If[1] my letters appear equivocal and obscure, I assure you it is not what I intend; I hope you have a better opinion of me than to think me capable of the first, and if I do not explain myself clearly, 'tis not my fault, for I really attempt it, but I am often obliged to write in a hurry, for otherwise, from our different employments, I should scarce ever write at all.

"When the shots clattered on my furniture behind me, and against my pistols before me, some were, I suppose, partly spent, and some might come in such a line of direction, that as the furniture is always in motion, they might only glance

[1] From the unpublished MS.

off it. That they did no harm is most certain, to my great satisfaction.

"When I mention having attempted to rally some battalions, they had had some officers killed, and many more carried off wounded, and those employed in rallying them were but few whom I assisted. As to my being thrown by a cannon-ball, when I heard a shot clatter in my furniture, my horse reared, and I thought him wounded, so lest he should fall upon me, I got my feet as soon as I could out of the stirrups, so that I was not fast on horseback; yet I believe I should not have fallen if a- cannon-ball had not come so near me. However, as my horse was on his mettle, 'tis very possible I might have been dismounted without it; however, I cannot affirm either. When I got up I was a good deal stunned, either from my fall, or the wind of the ball, or both; the ball was so near me that everybody was surprised to see me alive.

"I have writ to the Duke of Montagu and Lord Granville, but have not expatiated on my own behaviour. And with regard to my promotion, I know 'tis to General Sinclair's testimony of me alone I owe it, since neither his Royal Highness or Sir E. Fawkener [1] has received any letter with regard to me. Now I am on the subject, I cannot help telling a mistake that happened at the beginning of the campaign. The late Colonel D—— [illegible] told me Marshal Wade had writ to his Royal Highness about me, but he mistook, for it was a letter which I had writ to the Marshal, which he had sent to the Duke. His Royal Highness often honours me with his commands, and sometime since was pleased to say my behaviour was worthy commendation.

"I am extremely glad to hear my mother is anxious about me, not only as it is a mark of her affection, than which nothing can be more dear to me, but as it also assures me that she herself is well, for, as I told you in my last, I was

---

[1] Sir Everard Fawkener (1684-1758). He began life as a London merchant, but in 1735 he was knighted and sent as Ambassador to Vienna. He was afterwards Secretary to the Duke of Cumberland, and for his services in Flanders was made joint Postmaster-General. He was a friend of Voltaire's, who stayed with him in 1726-29.

think as to my own person, I have been pretty lucky, for had I been with the regiment, I must have been taken.

"There is a report that Traun [1] is got into Alsatia, and that the French have detached from their army here 2500 under the command of Lowendal; [2] if so, I hope we shall give a good account of those that remain here, but I cannot say that I believe this news; I wish it were more probable than it is. I shall be a very considerable loser by this affair, for everything I have is at Ghent, but my regimentals and ten shirts I have with me, for everybody left their baggage at Ghent when we took the field, so it is a terrible stroke for the officers. But what cannot be helped must be borne with; I am not alone in this misfortune, tho' you know the clothes you have seen, all my linen of which I had a great stock, gold watch, diamond ring, and many other things, are what I shall not in years be able to buy again; in short I am now quite stripped. . . ."

Some passages from her son's letters which were forwarded to Lady Mary inclined her to take a more favourable view of his conduct. She seemed to think that because he wrote better there was more chance that he might behave better.

"I [3] was very agreeably surprised," she tells Mr. Wortley, "by the extracts you were so good to send me of my son's letters. His style is very much mended; I hope his conduct may be so too. As you seem to wish I should write to him, I have done it in a manner according to your intention. This is the copy—

"'I am very well pleased with the accounts I have had of your behaviour this campaign. I wish nothing more than that your future conduct may redeem your past. You are

---

[1] The celebrated Austrian general (1677-1748). In 1745 he was serving in Germany under Prince Charles of Lorraine. Frederic the Great regarded him as his own instructor in the art of war.

[2] Count Ulric de Lowendal (1700-55). One of the most distinguished and successful military commanders of the period. He had fought against the Turks under Prince Eugène, and had afterwards entered the Russian service. Later he joined his old comrade Marshal Saxe, and the campaign in the Netherlands was a series of brilliant successes for him, beginning with Fontenoy, where it was he who charged the English column that penetrated to the centre of the French army, and ending with the capture of Berg op Zoom.

[3] From the unpublished MS.

now in a station where you will be observed, and may have opportunity of acquiring a character that may cause your indiscretions to be forgotten or forgiven. I have always heard that the best and worst company in the world are to be found in the army; I hope you will take care to choose the first. Your Colonel Sir John Cope [1] is a man of sense and honour; I shall be glad to hear that you had obtained his approbation and confidence. I hope experience will correct that idle way of talking that has done you so much injury. I have not heard from you since your arrival in Flanders, tho' I have wrote more than once. Your welfare is always wished by your affect^{ate}, etc.'

"I have directed this to Rotterdam, to the banker, who I do not doubt will take care of it, if he receives it, but my letters are all opened here, and many stopped. 'Tis one of the reasons makes this place disagreeable, but I know not where or how to remove. They are all here enthusiastically devoted to the interests you may guess, and notwithstanding my real indifference, and perfect silence on all political accounts, I am looked upon as a very deep politician that has very great designs, and am watched on all occasions."

[1] Sir John Cope was Commander-in-Chief in Scotland later in the year. He marched against the rebels in August, and was defeated by them at Prestonpans on 21st September.

CHAPTER XLI

THE FORTY-FIVE

ON 22nd July Mr. Wortley went abroad, and remained on the Continent for more than two months, but he did not think it necessary to inform his wife that he had left England, nor did he make any attempt to join her. He seems to have spent the greater part of the time at Pyrmont, where he drank the waters. Meanwhile, on 25th July, Prince Charles had landed in Scotland, and the Highlanders had flocked to his standard. By the middle of September, thanks to the blunders of our generals, the rebels had defeated Sir John Cope at Prestonpans, had seized Edinburgh and proclaimed the Pretender. On 26th September Mr. Gibson wrote Mr. Wortley a long account of the progress of the insurrection, which is prefaced by the latest news from Flanders—

"If[1] anything relating to your son had occurred since you left this place, worth communicating to you, I would have given you the trouble of a letter before now. I have frequently heard from him, and find he keeps up his spirits very well, and by the manner he is treated, it appears that they have confidence in him, for he has had for some time a very honourable command, tho' not a very great one. It seems that most of the officers of that battalion of General Sinclair's regiment, which was in Flanders, were made prisoners of war at Ghent, and the men so dispersed, that what remains could not appear again in their place in the army, being without tents, etc. Therefore they were sent to guard some post in or about Brussels, and your son ordered to command them, which it seems he has hitherto done with reputation.

"I doubt not that before this comes to hand, you will

[1] From the unpublished MS.

be surprised to hear what state things are in at home. A very small spark at the beginning, either not credited, or neglected, or not prudently guarded against, is now unhappily become a very great flame, which tho' at present it seems to increase, yet I hope by God's providence and the prudent measures taken to extinguish it, will soon turn to the confusion of them who kindled it. It would be too troublesome to you to tell you the rise and progress of this unhappy affair, and probably you have it from better hands. I shall only take the liberty to tell you briefly what you may depend upon in case other intelligence does not come to hand before this. The Pretender's son having landed with a very few persons in the Highlands towards Lochaber, had the address to persuade a great many people to join him, who daily increasing, Sir John Cope, Commander-in-Chief, had orders to go and suppress them. He marched with 2000 men to Stirling, and perhaps for want of due intelligence, or some other reasons, too much time was lost. From thence he marched into the Highlands, and unhappily so entangled himself, that he neither could engage the rebels, nor safely return to Stirling, for the rebels, knowing the country better, gave him the slip, and got between him and Stirling, so that he was obliged to march to Inverness, and from thence to Aberdeen, where there were ships waiting for him to bring him southwards.

"In the meantime, the rebels still increasing, came down to the Lowlands, made themselves masters of Perth, proclaimed the Pretender, sent detachments to Dundee and other places, advanced to Stirling, and crossed the Forth some miles higher, made a motion as if they intended to march to Glasgow, but turned to the left, marched straight to Edinburgh, and on the 17th entered the city by a sort of capitulation. It seems that two regiments of Dragoons, which Sir John Cope had left, being all the troops then in the neighbourhood, thought fit to decline coming into the city, and assist on foot to defend it, but thought it better to march eastward. This, and some other incidents, which are too tedious to relate, broke the whole disposition made for defending the town, and indeed, it being in a manner open without provisions for three or four days, and defended only by an undisciplined multitude, might be either forced, burnt, or starved by three or four thousand men in a very short time. The rebels took possession of the gates, proclaimed their Pretender, and for the most part encamped without observing exact discipline. Sir John Cope debarqued at Dunbar, the wind not permitting him to come to Leith. The two regiments of Dragoons joined him, and as soon as he could, he marched towards the rebels. They marched also to meet him, and at Preston Pans, about seven miles east of Edinburgh, they met, and on the 14th instant fought what I think ought not to be called a *Battle*, for the Dragoons mostly ran away after the first fire, and tho' some of the Foot behaved exceeding well, yet they were totally routed by the rebels. What numbers are killed or taken prisoners, I know not. All I hear for certain is, that Sir John Cope was not killed; some say he is wounded. There were 400 Dragoons ran away in a body, and are at Lauder with some of the Foot and Volunteers. I don't hear that Sir John's troops were above 3000. This is a very unlucky affair, and the unhappy consequence of marching into the Highlands, till a sufficient force was got together to oppose the march of the rebels towards the South.

"Now I shall tell you what appears to be doing towards quelling this insurrection, or at least checking its progress. The Government has very wisely brought over ten battalions of our own troops, which all landed last Monday, having set sail from Holland the Saturday before. The greatest part of the Dutch auxiliaries are also arrived, and they are mostly marching northward. General Wade sets out this day, and as the weather is extremely good, 'tis hoped they will make great haste. I hope the Dutch troops which sail for Scotland will not go there but stop at Newcastle; 'tis said that some of them stopped in Burlington Bay. This city is putting all things into a good disposition. The Militia and other troops will be raised in a great many places, and they say there is a very great assembly of gentlemen to meet very soon at York, and will no doubt take care of the peace and safety of that country. And it is hoped that more troops from abroad will soon arrive if there be occasion.

"Although at this present time this is a very unlucky affair, yet I see no reason why so powerful a nation should be much alarmed at the defeat of 3000 troops, all of which are not lost. And tho' the success of the rebels is rapid, yet if our counsels are not infatuated, and the nation given up to destruction for their sins, I cannot think that, morally speaking, this evil can be of long duration, for 'tis quite certain even where the rebels are masters, ten to one are against the Pretender. I am sorry that by this time you are gone from home, both for the sake of the public, and your own private affairs; for as upon other occasions of this nature, you and your ancestors have done great services to your country, so now your presence would be of very great use. The Parliament meets the 17th October. . . ."

Mr. Wortley's cousin, Edward Montagu (husband of the Queen of the Blue-Stockings), was one of the gentlemen who went north to take part in a great meeting of Yorkshire landowners, convened for the purpose of making preparations for the defence of the town. On 24th September he wrote from his house at Allerthorpe to his brother James at Newbold Verdun—

". . . The[1] affair of the Pretender has now grown more serious than I ever expected, and takes up the thoughts and time of all in these parts. The Duke of Atholl[2] passed through Allerthorpe last Thursday, and brought the melancholy news that the rebels had actually entered the town of Edinburgh last Tuesday. He said he was pursued by the rebels, and was forced to ride for his life, and was posting to London to give an account of it. It is thought this could not have happened but by the treachery of the magistrates, and our own General is reflected on, but with what justice I do not pretend to know. I hear the magistrates of Newcastle have not imitated those of Edinburgh, but have taken all proper

[1] From the unpublished MS.
[2] James, second Duke of Atholl. He succeeded his father (though second surviving son) owing to the attainder of his elder brother William, who took part in the rebellion of 1715 and of 1745. His younger brother George was Lieutenant-General of Prince Charles Edward's forces in 1745, and marched into England with the rebels. He too was attainted, but escaped to the Continent.

precautions, and have ordered a Roll wherein every person that was willing might enter their names, together with the number of men they would send for the defence of the town upon any emergency. They are shutting up some entrances into the town, and the only ones will be the bridge, Newgate, and Sandgate, and Barracks are making there for the Militia.

"On Tuesday next there is to be a great meeting of the gentlemen and clergy at York to take measures to extinguish this rebellion. The Militia, to be sure, will be raised, which is the Constitutional force of this Kingdom, but which has for this last fifty years been neglected, and laughed out of countenance, with what views I will not say, but wish now that we may not want them. The taking of Edinburgh, I hear, is gaining arms for 2000 men, besides several pieces of cannon, which must be a great advantage to the enemy. I hear, however, that with what forces we have at Newcastle and Berwick, we have about 3000 men, which together with Cope's 3000 (if any are come from Holland, as is imagined there are) will make no contemptible army. I pray Heaven they may meet with success. . . ."

On 10th January 1746 Lady Mary writes to thank her husband for sending her Sarah Fielding's novels, and observes with some acerbity that she has only learnt two days before of his trip to Pyrmont. She concludes that his absence, of which he had given her no notice, had occasioned the loss of many of her letters.

"I am very impatient to leave this town," she continues, "which has been highly disagreeable to me ever since the beginning of this war, but the impossibility of returning into Italy, and the law in France, which gives to the king all the effects any person deceased dies possessed of, and I own that I am very desirous my jewels and some little necessary plate that I have bought, should be safely delivered into your hands, hoping you will be so good as to dispose of them to my daughter.[1] The Duke of Richelieu flattered me for some time that he would obtain for me a permission to dispose of my

[1] The writer has lost her way in the middle of this sentence, but her meaning is clear.

goods, but he has not yet done it, and you know the uncertainty of Court promises."

Without deigning to give any explanation of his conduct, Mr. Wortley replied on 4th March—

"Since[1] my arrival at London from abroad, I have received yours of the 10th January and 11th February. From the time of my going, which was on the 22nd July, till my return I had only one of the 19th July and another of the 25th August. The reason of your letters not coming was not my being out of Cavendish Square, for letters that came thither were always brought to me. I have taken a small house there for a year, and shall keep it longer, if I find it convenient.

"Lord and Lady Bute came out of Scotland after she had asked my opinion, which I gave against their coming. They chose to be at Twickenham without asking my opinion, and have for the next year taken the house which was Mr. Stones' for £45 a year, which you will think extremely cheap. She tells me they design to lay down their coach, and that Scotch Estates bring little to London.

"The Pyrmont waters and travelling agreed with me very much. In coming from Warwick I sprained my shoulder by the over-turning of a post-chaise, which I think occasioned my being out of order for above two months. I have since been much better, but my shoulder is not yet quite well, but I have been able to be on horseback for about 3 weeks. . . ."

The chief political event of the new year was Lord Granville's failure to form a ministry, owing to his refusal to call Pitt to his assistance. The situation is sketched at first hand by Edward Montagu in a letter dated 10th February 1746—

"The[1] resignation of a whole Ministry at once, and at such a critical time as this, is something so extraordinary and uncommon, that I should hold myself inexcusable, if I did not send you the earliest account of it, together with such causes for it, and such reflections upon it, as I have been able to collect.[2]

---

[1] From the unpublished MS.

[2] Lord Granville, who had lost the confidence of the nation, owing to his Hanoverian sympathies, had resigned in 1744, but had remained in high favour with George II. He had been succeeded by Mr. Pelham, whose timid and vacillating

28

"When I went yesterday to the House of Commons, to my great surprise, I heard that the Duke of Newcastle and Lord Harrington[1] had resigned, and this day at the same place, that the Lords of Treasury, Admiralty and Trade either had or would do the like. Lord Chancellor, it is said, will resign on Thursday, when the term will be over, and his example will be followed by the Dukes of Richmond, Grafton, Dorset, Montagu, Lord Pembroke, and I know not how many others; in a word, by everybody that is of any rank and holds any place of consequence under His Majesty.

"Lord Granville is to be at the head of those that come in, and is to be either at the head of the Treasury or Secretary of State, tho' I believe the latter. It is thought that Lord Winchelsea will be the other Secretary, or if not Lord Cholmondeley. Lord Carlisle, First Lord of the Admiralty; there was also some talk of the Marquis of Tweeddale and Lord Bath coming in amongst them, but in what posts I know not. I hear the latter of these Lords and the Duke of Bolton spent a great deal of time last Sunday at my Lord Granville's.

"You will easily guess, without my mentioning his name, that this is owing to that person[2] whom the King so unwillingly parted with, and who has been his chief favourite ever since. He, they say, has by his intrigues undone at night what they had been doing in the Council Chamber by day, and has involved them in such difficulties by forcing them into Hanover's measures that they could go on no longer. Some have been for imputing the resignation to another cause, viz. His Majesty's refusing Mr. Pitt to be Secretary at War, but this, I cannot think to be the true cause, for it is most probable if there had been no other reason but this, they

policy was obnoxious to the King, who disliked the other chief members of the party, Newcastle, Chesterfield, and Pitt. Early in 1746 he communicated privately with Granville and Bath. The Ministry, learning the fact, resigned at once, and Bath and Granville were entrusted with the task of forming a new Government. This they failed to do, and the Pelhams returned to power, at the end of forty-eight hours, with their position greatly strengthened.

[1] The Duke of Newcastle and William Stanhope, first Lord Harrington, were the two Secretaries of State.

[2] Presumably Lord Granville, though the writer has already mentioned his name.

might have prevailed upon him to withdraw his pretensions, and make him easy some other way.¹ However all this be, the reign of these new people it is thought will be of short duration, as they will have no interest in the House of Commons, nor be able to raise those vast sums they will want. I hear the merchants waited upon Mr. Pelham to-day, and will not now lend two millions and a half, as they promised. A new Parliament is talked of, but that, I think, cannot supply their present wants, nor perhaps be more favourable to them than the present; so that I see nothing but confusion, but if it be such a one as shall produce order, and such as may benefit our country, I shall not be sorry. . . ."

A few days later Mr. Montagu was able to write again, and state that the attempt to form a Granville administration was a failure, that the Pelham ministry was re-instated, and everything was to go on as before. Horace Walpole is very amusing on the subject of this little interlude, and says that the Granville faction goes by the name of the Grandvillains. The following is Mr. Montagu's account of the matter:—

"DEAR BROTHER,² — . . . When I writ last I little thought I should so soon have it in my power to let you know that Lord Granville's reign was at an end, and that the Ministry, and all those that had resigned their places were restored to them again, and that everything is to go on in the old channel. This news we heard yesterday about 3 o'clock, after the House of Commons rose, who expected to be adjourned this day, but now will not, as there is no occasion for it, but go on, as I suppose, raising the supplies as fast as possible. This surprising turn of affairs has set the minds of a great many people at ease, who dreaded Lord Granville's schemes; and I hope will be attended with good. I am sure, after what has happened, the Ministry cannot plead want of power to promote the happiness of the nation, and if they do not do it, they will be the most inexcusable of all men upon earth.

¹ The King persisted in his refusal to make Pitt Secretary at War, even after the return of the Pelhams, but he suffered him to hold other important posts.
² From the unpublished MS.

"I am told that Lord Granville had formed the following scheme, which was to let the Ministry continue and go on raising the supplies; which after they had done, and got the King all the money they wanted, then they were to be turned out, and he was to go abroad with His Majesty. But the Ministry smelling out his design, they from time to time delayed the supply, and formed their project of a general resignation, which has, I believe, entirely ruined Lord Granville as a Statesman, and perhaps may keep him out of power as long as he lives.

"I cannot forbear making some reflections upon this Lord, whom all men own to have great parts and abilities, and who has still been twice overcome by his antagonists. It is surprising that such a one should twice split upon the same rock, and think if he had the King's favour, without any Parliamentary interest or support from any considerable body of men, that he could govern this country. In a Government perfectly arbitrary, such a scheme might succeed, but where there are any remains of liberty, as I hope there will always be some in this country, it is impossible for it not to miscarry. My Lord is, I think, a strong instance that there is no such thing as perfection in mortals, and that strong passions often get the better of the best understandings, and that bright parts and judgments do not always go together. . . ."

Lady Mary had begun at this time to keep up a regular correspondence with her daughter. The first letter to Lady Bute is dated Avignon, 3rd March, and may be attributed to this year. The Butes were apparently in some financial embarrassment, owing to the falling of stocks, and the general scarcity consequent on the war[1]—

"I[2] will not trouble you with repetitions of my concern for your uneasy situation," writes Lady Mary, "which does not touch me the less for having foreseen it many years ago; you may remember my thoughts on that subject before your marriage. God's will be done. You have the blessing o

---

[1] There was also a terrible murrain among the cattle at this time.
[2] From the unpublished MS.

happiness in your own family, and I hope time will put your affairs in a better condition. The mortality of cattle was in this country the last year, but as to milk and butter, I have long learned to live without them, the cows in this part of the world being too ill fed to afford either. I am flattered here with the hopes of Peace. I pray heartily for it, as what can only put an end to your troubles, which are felt in the tenderest manner by your most affec^{ate} mother,

"M. Wortley"

To Mr. Wortley his wife wrote on 20th March—

"I[1] have not heard from you for so long that I should be in great pain for your health, if I had not this post a letter from my daughter, who informs me that you are well. . . . I had a letter from my son the last post, very much to his own advantage (if he tells truth). I have sent him a very kind letter, believing it proper to give him some encouragement if his behaviour deserves it.

"The King of France has employed a great number of workmen to remove the earth round the ancient Temple of Diana, that is near Nismes. They have made great discoveries, particularly the foundation of a very large palace, which is supposed that of Agrippa, when he was Governor of Gaul. They have found many medals and other pieces of antiquity; the greatest part were carried to the king, and some privately sold in this country. A peasant brought me a very curious piece of a mixed metal, on which are the figures of Justice, a Roman officer, and several other groups. I have shown it to several persons, who cannot guess for what use it was designed. I will send it to you by the first opportunity. I will not pretend to decide the value, but I think I can be sure it was really found very deep amongst the ruins of the palace I have mentioned. . . ."

Since the insurrection of the previous year, increased numbers of Scotch and Irish Jacobites had found their way to Avignon, where they were protected by the vice-legate. The fear and suspicion with which they regarded Lady Mary, rendered her situation so intolerable, that in August 1746 she seized the

[1] From the unpublished MS.

opportunity which was suddenly held out to her of returning to Italy. A young Count of Palazzo, who had been recommended by her old friend, Count Wackerbart, heard her lamenting the impossibility of attempting a journey to Italy, and at once offered his services. He suggested that if she would permit him to accompany her to his native town of Brescia, whither he was returning, she might pass on the journey as a Venetian lady. The plan was agreed upon, and the pair went by sea to Genoa, whence they took post-chaises for Brescia.

"We were very much surprised," relates Lady Mary in a letter to Mr. Wortley dated Brescia, 23rd August, "to meet on the Briletta or Pochetta,[1] the baggage of the Spanish army, with a prodigious number of sick or wounded officers and soldiers, who marched in a great hurry. The Count of Palazzo ordered his servants to say we were in haste for the service of Don Philip, and without further examination they gave us place everywhere; notwithstanding which, the multitude of carriages and loaded mules which we met in these narrow roads, made it impossible for us to reach Scravalli[2] till it was near night. Our surprise was great to find, coming out of that town, a large body of troops surrounding a body of guards, in the midst of which was Don Philip in person, going a very round trot, looking down, and pale as ashes. The army was in too much confusion to take notice of us, and the night favouring us, we got into the town; but when we came there, it was impossible to find any lodging, all the inns being filled with wounded Spaniards. The Count went to the Governor, and asked a chamber for a Venetian lady, which he granted very readily; but there was nothing in it but the bare walls, and in less than a quarter of an hour after, the whole house was empty, both of furniture and people, the Governor flying into the citadel, and carrying with him all his goods and family. We were forced to pass the night without beds or supper.

"About day-break the victorious Germans entered the

[1] The Bochetta, a pass leading through the mountains to Genoa. The French and Spaniards, after their defeat at Piacenza in June 1746, had been gradually forced from their positions in Italy. The Spaniards were being driven through Genoa, while the French retreated over the Alps.
[2] Serravalle.

town. The Count went to wait on the generals, to whom, I believe, he had a commission. He told them my name, and there was no sort of honour or civility they did not pay me. They immediately ordered me a guard of huzzars (which was very necessary in the present disorder) and sent me refreshments of all kinds. Next day I was visited by the Prince of Badin Dourlach,[1] the Prince Loüestein,[2] and all the principal officers, with whom I passed for a heroine, showing no uneasiness, though the cannon of the citadel (where was a Spanish garrison) played very briskly. I was forced to stay there two days for want of post-horses. . . . At length I set out from thence the 19th instant, with a strong escort of huzzars, meeting with no further incident on the road, except at the little town of Vogherra, where they refused post-horses, till the huzzars drew their sabres. The 20th I arrived safe here. It is a very pretty place, where I intend to repose myself at least during the remainder of the summer. . . . I am now in a neutral country, under the protection of Venice. The Doge is our old friend Grimani, and I do not doubt meeting with all sort of civility."

[1] Baden Durlach. [2] Löwestein.

over my head. I should not complain of the preferment of people who had served longer, were they of the lowest rank, so that if I cannot have as much favour shown me as other people, I beg to retire. When you go to the Secretary, I suppose the Company in the Guards will be what you mention, for as one seldom gets what one asks for, I might by that means get a troop of Horse or Dragoons, and if only a troop were asked for, it would probably degenerate into a Company; which is not worth stirring about.

"I am very sensible how detrimental my not being able to be in England is to me, and consequently very sorry my creditors will do nothing; but alas! what can I do? I must wait with patience till my father pleases to set me at liberty. I imagine my father could easily get me into next Parliament without laying out much money, and then my creditors could not hinder me from appearing in England."

Mr. Gibson, acting for Mr. Wortley, saw the Secretary for War, and presumably steps were taken to obtain the young man's release. In October the intermediary wrote to Mr. Wortley that he would ask the Secretary for War to represent the contents of the above letter to the Duke of Cumberland, and continues—

"As[1] he knows your son, and expressed himself so favourably towards him, when the Secretary mentioned him, I doubt not upon proper application His R.H. will promote him. You will see by both letters that he desires some assistance extraordinary because of the charges he will be at for clothes, if he stays at Breda till His Majesty's birthday; and in his last letter he says, that he thinks of withdrawing, if he has no extraordinary supply. I have told him in my letter that I would represent it to you, and that I doubted not that you would take it into consideration, and give orders as you think proper. As my Lord Sandwich has received him so kindly, it would be a real loss to him to withdraw so soon from so good company, and if he stays at Breda, he cannot avoid being at extraordinary expenses for several reasons. . . . We had a mail last night from Holland, but it brought very little more than

[1] From the unpublished MS.

what was contained in the *Gazette*. The news from Admiral Lestock[1] and General Sinclair comes from Paris to Holland, and I do not hear that there is any account directly from themselves; so that we know almost nothing of particulars, tho' the thing in general may be depended upon, but they will scarcely give us any true account of particulars from Paris. There is a report to-day that they had not succeeded at Fort Louis, and that General Sinclair's being wounded, they were obliged to retire, but I hope this is but a story."

Some months elapsed before the Parliamentary scheme could be carried out, and meanwhile we must return to Brescia and Lady Mary. In the letter to her husband written only three days after her arrival, she had remarked that in spite of the hardships of the journey, her health was better than it had been for some time. In the next letter, written three months later (24th November), she says that she had bragged too soon, since only two days after the date of her last, she was seized with so violent a fever that she was surprised any woman of her age could be capable of it. She had been obliged to keep her bed for two months, and was then only allowed to get up for a few hours during the day. It appears that the Countess Palazzo, mother of Lady Mary's travelling companion, had met her on arrival, and taken her into her house, till a lodging could be hired. Just as the lodging was found, the illness began, which made it impossible for the invalid to think of moving.

" The Countess Palazzo," continues Lady Mary, " has taken as much care of me as if I had been her sister, and omitted no expense or trouble to serve me. I am still with her, and indeed in no condition of moving at present. I am now in a sort of milk diet, which is prescribed to me to restore my strength. From being as fat as Lady Bristol, I am grown leaner than anybody I can name. For my own part I think myself in a natural decay. However, I do what I am ordered. I know not how to acknowledge enough my obligations to the

---

[1] Richard Lestock, a veteran sailor. He had been court-martialled after the breaking of the blockade at Toulon, when he was charged with refusing to obey Admiral Matthew's orders, but was acquitted. He died this year.

Countess ; and I reckon it a great one from her who is a *dévote*, that she never brought any priest to me."

This incident probably gave rise to an " obscure history " of Lady Mary's being detained in a Brescian palace, which reached Horace Walpole as late as 1751. " A young fellow," to quote the Horatian version of the rumour, " whom she set out with keeping, has taken it into his head to keep her close prisoner, not permitting her to write or receive any letters but what he sees: he seems determined, if her husband should die, not to lose her, as the Count [Richecourt][1] lost my Lady Orford." Lord Wharncliffe, in his edition of the *Correspondence*, gives the following explanation of the scandal :—

" Among Lady Mary's papers there is a long document written in Italian, not by herself, giving an account of her having been detained for some time against her will in a country-house belonging to an Italian count, and inhabited by him and his mother. This paper seems to be drawn up, either as a case to be submitted to a lawyer for his opinion, or to be produced in a court of law. There is nothing else to be found in Lady Mary's papers referring in the least degree to this circumstance. It would appear, however, that some such forcible detention as is alluded to did take place, probably for some pecuniary or interested object ; but like many of Horace Walpole's stories, he took care not to let this lose anything that might give it zest, and he therefore makes the person by whom Lady Mary was detained, ' a young fellow whom she set out with keeping.' Now, at the time of this transaction taking place, Lady Mary was sixty-one years old." [2]

It was not until 1st March 1747 that Lady Mary was

---

[1] Count Richecourt was a Lorrainer and chief minister of Florence. He was supposed to be governed by Lady Orford.

[2] From Lord Stanhope's *Miscellanies* (2nd series) we learn that this paper was a Memoir, extending over ten years of Lady Mary's life, 1746–56. It gave details of her unfortunate acquaintance with Count Palazzo and his family, by whom she was duped, cheated, and intimidated, but not forcibly confined. Her letters were intercepted by them, and her jewels purloined, but she refused to make any official complaint, even when convinced of the Count's perfidy. This document appears to have been lost or mislaid.

able to write to Lady Oxford that she was quite recovered, which was really almost a miracle at her age. On 17th March she informs Mr. Wortley that ". . . My [1] health is much mended; I ride out every morning, which has very much contributed to my recovery. I am at present in a little house I have taken some miles from Brescia, for the sake of the air. [2]

" I wish good company may reform my son, as bad debauched him. Here is a great penn'orth to be had, if the Duchess of Marlbro' were living to take advantage of it. The purchase being 100 thousand guineas, for which, I am told, the investiture of Guastalla is to be bought."

The project for getting young Wortley into Parliament was actually carried out at the general election of July 1747, through the interest of Lord Sandwich. The question of borough reform had not yet become prominent, or it would be difficult to imagine a stronger argument in its favour. The candidate's own mother was the last person to be deceived by his alleged reformation.

" I wish nothing more than the reformation of my son," she assured Mr. Wortley on 18th May, " but I own I cannot yet believe it from any of the appearances I know. His leaving Lord S[andwich] is a plain proof to me that he is not much in his favour, or has lost that part of it he has had. I know my son, he is a showy companion and may easily impose on anyone for a short time. I am persuaded if Lord S. had a good opinion of his character, he would have wrote to you in his favour. As to the civilities of the great I look upon them as mere Court nothings."

However, Mr. Wortley was not alone in his belief in his son's altered character, for on 9th July Mr. Edward Montagu wrote to his brother—

" . . . The [3] sudden dissolution of the Parliament, the hurry occasioned thereby, and my journey to Huntingdon, were the

[1] From the unpublished MS.
[2] At Gottolengo, a village about eighteen miles from Brescia.
[3] From the unpublished MS.

principal reasons of my not acknowledging the favour of yours. Our election for the town came on Wednesday was Sennight, when Mr. Courtenay, brother-in-law to Lord Sandwich, along with me, was without opposition chosen for the Borough. That for the County will come on the 18th, and will, it is not doubted, be carried with the same ease for young Wortley and Mr. Fellowes.

"It may perhaps somewhat surprise you that Lord Sandwich should lay aside his brother, Capt. William Montagu, but I believe his Lordship had very good reasons for so doing, and his generosity to his cousin Wortley I am sure cannot be sufficiently commended, and will, I hope, be attended with the happiest consequences, for the young man behaves with great prudence and discretion, and gives great satisfaction to the County. Before my Lord proposed him, he had the consent of his father, who has furnished him with money, tho' as yet there has been no interview between father and son, but I hope that will be brought about afterwards.

"By the elections that are already over, as well as those that are yet to come on, it is thought the Court party will be stronger than ever. Many of the Prince's people have lost their elections, amongst whom I am sorry our cousin Charles Montagu is one. He was to have come in for Ockington, but was opposed by Mr. George Lyttleton [1] of the Treasury, and lost it. Some accuse Mr. L. of unfair play in this matter, but as I have not yet seen the other gentleman, I know not the truth. In things of this nature, most people, particularly Ministers, think everything lawful, and therefore, as Mr. M. is a Prince's man, and the dissolution of the Parliament was, I believe, principally levelled at and designed to demolish such as he, I am nothing surprised at what has happened. . . ."

On 25th July Mr. Wortley was able to announce to his wife the return, unopposed, of their son for the County of Huntingdon. Something of his paternal gratification may be discerned beneath his cold and laconic style—

"I [2] mentioned to you in my last that Lord Sandwich

---

[1] Created Baron Lyttelton in 1756. He was a Lord of the Treasury at this time. Known as the good Lord Lyttelton in contradistinction to his son.

[2] From the unpublished MS.

proposed to bring our son into Parliament. He then seemed not determined whether to bring him for the town or county. My Lord's brother served before for the county. As he thought it not proper his brother should be chosen again, our son was named as the next of the family to his brother, except myself, who would not have quitted Peterborough. He was chosen without opposition for the County on the 18th. As my Lord's brother is Captain of a Man-of-war, and has been lucky in prizes, perhaps my Lord may think it more for his interest that he should not be in Parliament, because he will be in less danger of being unemployed. Some think, but I do not know, that he has someway disobliged my Lord. When he mentioned to me his intention to bring in our son, he seemed to think he might depend on his discretion, and should not repent of his having done him that favour."

It is not probable that this letter can have reached Brescia by 18th August, when Lady Mary wrote to her husband, without making any mention of the new member—

". . . The [1] apprehension that what I write may never reach you is so discouraging, it takes off all satisfaction I should otherwise find in writing. I gave you thanks for the poetry you sent me in a long letter, and I have sent my daughter such particular accounts of my country amusements and way of life, she could not know more of it if she was in the neighbourhood. I am very glad she passes her time so agreeably, and in a manner that may be advantageous to her family. We are both properly situated, according to our different kinds of life, she in the gaieties of the Court, I in the retirement, where my garden and dairy are my chief diversions.

"Here has been the finest auction, fifteen miles from hence, that has been known of for a long time, being the whole furniture of the Palace of Guastalla.[2] I could not forbear going

---

[1] From the unpublished MS.

[2] The Duchy of Guastalla was given to Don Philip, together with Parma and Piacenza, at the Peace of Utrecht. The Duke was dead, but the Duchess, a princess of Hesse - Darmstadt, seems to have been a lively lady, who once paid Lady Mary a most unwelcome informal visit.

to see it; there were several pictures of the first masters that went off for a song, and a crucifix of silver, said to be the work of Michael Angelo, sold for little more than the weight. The greatest part fall into the hands of the Jews.

"I am very much obliged to you for the offer of the London Pamphlets. I should be glad to see the *Apology for the late Resignation*.[1] Now the sea is open, I may easily have things by way of Venice. If you would order me six dozen of Nottingham ale, it would be very acceptable amongst my neighbours. Be pleased to take the money due for it out of my allowance."

In July Lady Mary had been ordered by her doctor to drink the waters at Lovere, a little town on Lago D'Iseo about forty miles from Brescia. Writing to her daughter on 24th July, she says that she has found here a good lodging, good company, and a village resembling Tunbridge Wells, not only in the quality of the water, but also in the manner of the building, most of the houses being built on the sides of hills, though these hills were six times as high as those at Tunbridge.

"We have an opera here," continues Lady Mary, "which is performed three times in the week. I was at it last night, and should have been surprised at the neatness of the scenes, goodness of the voices, and justness of the actors, if I had not remembered I was in Italy. Several gentlemen jumped into the orchestra, and joined in the concert, which is, I suppose, one of the freedoms of the place, for I never saw it in any great town. I was yet more amazed (while the actors were dressing for the farce which concluded the entertainment) to see one of the principal among them, and as arrant a *petit-maître* as if he had passed all his life at Paris, mount the stage, and present us with a cantata of his own performing. He had the pleasure of being almost deafened with applause."

After explaining that she never stayed for the ball which finished the entertainment, though the opera did not begin till ten o'clock, she concludes: "I am much better pleased with

[1] Believed to be by Lord Chesterfield.

LOVERE, LAGO D'ISEO
FROM A SKETCH

the diversions on the water, where all the town assembles every night, and never without music; but we have none so rough as trumpets, kettle-drums and French horns; they are all violins, lutes, mandolins and flutes *doux*. Here is hardly a man that does not excel in some of these instruments, which he privately addresses to the lady of his affections, and the public has the advantage of it by his adding to the number of the musicians."

By September Lady Mary was back again in the house that she had taken at Gottolengo, a few miles from Brescia. Writing to Lady Oxford on 1st September, she says: " I have lived this eight months in the country, after the same manner (in little) that I fancy you do at Welbeck, and find so much advantage from the air and quiet of this retreat, that I do not think of leaving it. I walk and read much, but have very little company except that of a neighbouring convent. I do what good I am able in the village round me, which is a very large one; and have had so much success that I am thought a great physician, and should be esteemed a saint if I went to mass."

In the autumn of this year Horace Walpole arranged to have Lady Mary's *Town Eclogues* published by Dodsley, though it does not appear that he had any authority for so doing. On 24th November he writes to inform Mann of his complicity in the publication of the *Eclogues*, and adds, " They don't please, though so excessively good. I say so confidently, for Mr. Chute agrees with me: he says, for the Epistle to [from] Arthur Grey, scarce any woman could have written it, and no man; for a man who had had experience enough to paint such sentiments so well, would not have had warmth enough left. Do you know anything of Lady Mary? her adventurous son is come into Parliament, but has not opened."[1]

Lady Hertford, herself a poetaster, was one of the warmest admirers of the *Eclogues*. " There is more fire and wit in

---

[1] Horace explains in a footnote that "Some of these Eclogues had been printed long before: they were now published with other of her poems by Dodsley in quarto, and soon after with others reprinted in his *Miscellany*."

all the writings of that author [Lady Mary Wortley]," she declares in a letter to Lady Pomfret, "than one meets with in almost any other; and whether she is in the humour of an infidel or a devotee, she expresses herself with so much strength that one can hardly persuade oneself she is not in earnest on either side of the question. Nothing can be more natural than her complaint of the loss of her beauty [*vide* the "Saturday" in her *Town Eclogues*]; but as that was only one of her various powers to charm, I should have imagined she would only have felt a very small part of the regret that many other people have suffered on a like misfortune, who have nothing but the loveliness of their persons to claim admiration; and consequently, by the loss of that, have found all their hopes of distinction vanish much earlier in life than Lady Mary's :—for, if I do not mistake, she was near thirty before she had to deplore the loss of beauty greater than I ever saw in any face beside her own."

In November the new Parliament met, and young Wortley came over to take his seat. There is an account of the state of affairs at the opening of the session, and also of the relations between the Wortley father and son, in one of Mr. Edward Montagu's letters, written about this time—

". . . The[1] first day that Parliament met, there was a very numerous appearance of Members, many new faces and young gentlemen of fortune. The Court have a vast majority, and will carry everything they please. In such a time as this, it is surprising that so large a sum of money should be subscribed as was at Sir J. Barnard's.[2] Already great sums are granted towards the deficiencies of last year's supplies. The number of seamen granted for the year 1748 are 40,000, and a million given towards the discharge of the Navy debt, which amounts to 4 millions, 500 or 600 pounds. The land men are to be within a trifle of 50,000, about 190 more than last year, upon account of the East India Expedition. Mr.

---

[1] From the unpublished MS.

[2] A leading merchant, a financial expert, and M.P. for the City of London, 1722-61. The previous year a statue of him had been erected on the Royal Exchange.

Pelham, upon some of these occasions, said he wished he could say the money wanted for the current service of the year would be less than 11 millions: how the interest upon so large a sum is to be raised, is not yet made public. There is a talk of a new duty of 2s. additional upon every quarter of malt, also of a tax upon sugars and tobacco, and a Stamp Duty upon Bills of Exchange, Receipts, etc., but which or how many of these are to take place, I cannot learn. There has been a great deficiency on the window lights; it is said upwards of £100,000. That affair will again come before the House, and will be collected after a new and more equal manner.

"The melancholy situation of affairs on the Continent alarms everybody, and is owned by the Ministry in their speeches, as well as insisted on by those in the Opposition. Mr. Pelham said it had been happy if it had been well considered before it was gone into, proper alliances formed, and the quotas agreed on, but now nothing was to be done but to look forward, and put ourselves in the best condition we can to obtain a peace the best that could be got. Lord Granville is the person here reflected on. But whoever has been the author of these mischiefs, the consequences are likely to be very fatal. Many are afraid the French will overrun and conquer the seven provinces, and are already under apprehensions of what may happen if hard weather comes. It is said the Duke is in a few days to sail for Holland to be in readiness to oppose them, if the French should make any attempts.

"Young Wortley came over from Lord Sandwich and was present at the opening of the Parliament. He was to have spoke on the subject of the address, but others having said a good deal upon it he let it alone. There has been an article in the papers about a person of distinction, who was very unequally married when young, being about getting a divorce, which made a good many think it was him, but I asked him, and he is about no such matter. He is trying to get out of the army, and is then to return to Lord Sandwich at Aix, to whom I believe he has been very useful. His father has a little augmented his allowance, but has not made it sufficient for a Knight of the Shire. He has not yet admitted him into his company, and he has orders to sit on a different side of the House from him, but these things I desire you not to mention. . . ."

CHAPTER XLIII

GOTTOLENGO

AS Mr. Wortley's letters grew fewer and curter, and his interest in his wife's proceedings palpably diminished, Lady Mary's correspondence with Lady Bute became year by year fuller and more intimate. These letters are by far the best that she wrote during the period of exile. They are easy and natural (unlike those to Lady Pomfret and Lady Oxford), and are full of interesting details about her mode of life and the customs of the country. The writer's knowledge of the world, her reminiscences of bygone days, her social philosophy, and her criticisms on contemporary books and authors, all contribute towards the fascination and value of this remarkable correspondence, carried on during the uneventful years that were passed in an Italian village. Some of the most interesting and striking passages may be quoted in illustration of Lady Mary's personal history at this period. On 17th December she wrote to congratulate Lady Bute on the birth of a second son, James Archibald Stuart, who, she hopes, may grow up to be a blessing to his mother.[1]

"I amuse myself here," she continues, "in the same manner as if at London, according to your account of it; that is, I play at whist every night with some old priests that I have taught it to, and are my only companions. To say truth, the decay of my sight will no longer suffer me to read by candlelight, and the evenings are now so long and dark that I am forced to stay at home. I believe you'll be persuaded my gaming makes nobody uneasy, when I tell you that we play only a penny a corner. 'Tis

[1] He inherited the Wortley estates from his mother, and assumed the surname of Wortley. His son was the first Lord Wharncliffe.

now a year that I have lived wholly in the country, and have no design of quitting it. I am entirely given up to rural amusements, and have forgot there are any such things as wits or fine ladies in the world. However, I am pleased to hear what happens to my acquaintance. I wish you would inform me what is become of the Pomfret family, and who Sir Francis Dashwood[1] has married. I knew him at Florence: he seemed so nice in the choice of a wife, I have some curiosity to know who it is that has had charms enough to make him enter into an engagement he used to speak of with fear and trembling."

Lady Bute, who had reached the advanced age of twenty-nine, was already beginning to moralise on the great changes that she had observed in the world about her since the days of her youth. Her mother replies that this is merely owing to her being better acquainted with the world, and proceeds—

"I have never in all my various travels seen but two sorts of people, and those very like one another; I mean men and women, who always have been, and ever will be, the same. The same vices and the same follies have been the fruit of all ages, though sometimes under different names. I remember when I returned from Turkey, meeting with the same affectation of youth amongst my acquaintance that you now mention amongst yours, and I do not doubt but your daughter will find the same twenty years hence among hers. . . ."

Although she was then (5th January 1748) as far removed from the world as it was possible to be on this side the grave, Lady Mary explains that this isolation is one of choice, not of necessity, the way of living in the Italian province resembling that of England a hundred years before, and of Scotland as it still remained.

"I had a visit," she relates, "in the beginning of these holidays, of thirty horse of ladies and gentlemen, with their servants (by the way, the ladies all ride like the

---

[1] Sir Francis Dashwood, ex-president of the Hell-fire Club (afterwards Lord Le Despenser), married the widow of Sir George Ellis, and the daughter of George Gould. H. Walpole calls her a "poor forlorn Presbyterian prude."

Duchess of Cleveland).[1] They came with the kind intent of staying with me at least a fortnight, though I had never seen any of them before; but they were all neighbours within ten miles round. I could not avoid entertaining them at supper, and by good luck had a large quantity of game in the house, which, with the help of my poultry, furnished out a plentiful table. I sent for the fiddles, and they were so obliging as to dance all night, and even dine with me next day, though none of them had been in bed; and were much disappointed I did not press them to stay, it being the fashion to go in troops to one another's houses, hunting and dancing together, a month in each castle. I have not returned any of their visits, nor do not intend it for some time, to avoid this expensive hospitality. The trouble of it is not very great, they not expecting any ceremony."

These free-and-easy customs, idyllic as they sound, could hardly have appealed to a lady who had become notorious for her parsimony; indeed, the most liberal-minded might have found it difficult to rejoice at the opportunity of entertaining thirty self-invited guests, with their retinue and horses, for a fortnight at a time.

The exile still took a keen interest in the social history of her native land. She was greatly exercised about the marriage of her old acquaintance, the Duchess of Manchester,[2] to a young Irishman, Mr. Hussey. The *mésalliance* (for so it was regarded) afforded material to all the wits of the period, the more so because the Duchess had always prided herself on being the most fastidious and exclusive of fine ladies. That brilliant satirist, Sir Charles Hanbury Williams,[3] wrote a ballad on the Duchess, which brought him a challenge

---

[1] Presumably with the cross-seat. The Duchess of Cleveland of that day was Lady Henrietta Finch, daughter of Lord Winchelsea, but Lady Mary may refer to the Dowager Duchess, who was a Pulteney.

[2] Daughter of the Duchess of Montagu.

[3] *The Conquered Duchess* was the title of Sir Charles' ballad, and he seems to have written an answer to it, vindicating the match, which is published with his other works. He was in the diplomatic service, and was Envoy to the Court of Dresden about this time. His satirical and topical verses are worth studying by anyone interested in his period. Sir Charles committed suicide in 1759.

from the fiery Irish bridegroom, but Sir Charles was too prudent to fight. Lady Mary begged her husband to send her Sir Charles' latest effusions, though, at the same time, she denies that there is anything in his writings to distinguish him from the tribe of common versifiers. She admits, however, that she has been much entertained by his ballad on Tar-water, the new remedy made popular by Bishop Berkeley's [1] *Siris*.

"I find," she writes to Mr. Wortley on 24th April, "tar-water succeeded to Ward's drop.[2] 'Tis possible by this time that some other quackery has taken the place of that; the English are, easier than any other nation, infatuated by the prospect of universal medicines, nor is there any country in the world where the doctors raise such immense fortunes. I attribute it to the fund of credulity which is in all mankind. We have no longer faith in miracles and relics, and therefore with the same fury run after recipes and physicians. The same money which, three hundred years ago, was given for the health of the soul, is now given for the health of the body, and by the same sort of people—women and half-witted men."

Mr. Wortley seems to have mentioned in the letter to which the above was in answer, that Lord Sandwich had again taken up their son, and also that the Butes were emerging from the retirement in which they had hitherto lived, and beginning to play a more prominent part in the great world. This new departure was, of course, owing to the fact that Lord Bute was in high favour with the Prince and Princess of Wales. In the course of her comments on these matters Lady Mary observes—

"I should be extremely pleased if I could entirely depend on Lord Sandwich's account of our son. As I am wholly unacquainted with him, I cannot judge how far he may be either deceived or interested. I know my son (if not much altered) is capable of giving bonds for more than he will ever be worth in the view of any present advantage. Lord Bute and my daughter's conduct may be owing to the advice of the

---

[1] The famous Bishop of Cloyne, who strongly advocated the use of Tar-water.

[2] Joshua Ward, a quack doctor, who made his fortune out of a "drop and pill" chiefly composed of antimony.

Duke of Argyll. It was a maxim of Sir R. Walpole's that whoever expected advancement should appear much in public. He used to say, whoever neglected the world, would be neglected by it, though I believe more families have been ruined than raised by that method."

Horace Walpole remarks in his *Memoirs of the Reign of George II.*, that Lord Bute, "having no estates of his own, had passed his youth in studying mathematics and medicines in his own little island, then simples in the hedges about Twickenham, and at five and thirty had fallen in love with his own figure, which he produced at masquerades in becoming dresses, and in plays which he acted in private with a set of his own relations." In the early part of the spring of 1748 the Butes and their friends gave a performance of Young's play, *The Revenge*. Lady Bute sent an account of the affair to her mother, who, replying on 10th May, says that she remembers the play well, and supposes that Lord Bute must have acted Alonzo by the magnificence of his dress.

"I have had here," she continues, "(in low life) some amusements of the same sort. . . . The people of this village (which is the largest I know: the curate tells me he has two thousand communicants) presented me a petition to erect a theatre in my saloon. This house had stood empty many years before I took it, and they were accustomed to turn the stables into a playhouse every carnival; it is now occupied by horses, and they had no other place proper for a stage. I easily complied with their request, and was surprised at the beauty of their scenes, which, though painted by a country painter, are better coloured, and the perspective better managed, than in any of the second-rate theatres in London. I liked it so well, it is not yet pulled down. The performance was yet more surprising, the actors being all peasants; but the Italians have so natural a genius for comedy, they acted as well as if they had been brought up to nothing else, particularly the Arlequin, who far surpassed any of our English, though only the tailor of the village, and I am assured never saw a play in any other place. It is a pity they have not better poets, the pieces being not at all superior to our drolls. The music, habits and illumination were at the expense of the parish, and the whole entertainment, which lasted the three last days of the Carnival, cost me only a barrel of wine, which I gave the actors, and is not so dear as small beer in London."

It seems to have been in this year that Lady Mary bought the house in which she lived at Gottolengo. This was the shell of a palace which had been begun about fifty years before. Although the walls were sound, and the rooms conveniently arranged, the place had been neglected, and the owners were glad to part with it for a nominal sum. In fact, in the language of that day, it was a good " penn'orth." As there was not much ground about it, Lady Mary hired a garden about a mile away, where she fitted up a farm-building as a dairy-house, and here she spent most of her time in the summer months. The garden was situated on a high bank above the river Oglio (which was as broad as the Thames at Richmond), and its owner declared that she was as proud of it as a young author of his first play, when it has been well received by the town. It was but a plain vineyard when it first came into her hands, and though the whole measured no more than three hundred and seventeen feet by two hundred, neither my Lord Bathurst at Cirencester nor Mr. Pope at Twickenham could have dwelt more complacently on their horticultural triumphs.

The walks between the festooned vines had been converted into covered galleries of shade, and a "dining-room of verdure" had been constructed to hold a table of twenty covers. The garden abounded in all sorts of fruit and produced a variety of wines! Then there were parterres, terraces, a great walk, and espaliers crammed with roses and jessamine, to say nothing of a kitchen garden, where tea was grown with great success, though not so strong as the Indian leaf. In a surrounding wood fifteen "bowers" had been constructed with seats of turf commanding different views; while on the river bank there was a camp kitchen, where her ladyship might dress and eat her fish as soon as she had caught it, and watch the ships that passed daily from Mantua, Guastalla, or Pont de Vie.

Lady Mary's account of her idyllic method of spending a summer's day is worth giving in her own words—

"I generally rise at six, and as soon as I have breakfasted, put myself at the head of my weeder women, and work with them till nine. I then inspect my dairy, and take a turn among my poultry, which is a very large inquiry. I have at present two hundred chickens, besides turkeys, geese, ducks and peacocks. All things have hitherto prospered under my care; my bees and silkworms are doubled, and I am told that, without accidents, my capital will be so in two years' time. At eleven o'clock I retire to my books: I dare not indulge myself in that pleasure above an hour. At twelve I constantly dine, and sleep after dinner till three. I then send for some of my old priests, and either play at piquet or whist till 'tis cool enough to go out. One evening I walk in my wood, where I often sup, take the air on horseback the next, and go on the water the third. The fishery of this part of the river belongs to me; and my fisherman's little boat (where I have a green lutestring awning) serves me for a barge. He and his son are my rowers without any expense, he being very well paid by the profit of the fish, which I give him on condition of having every day one dish for my table. . . . We are both placed properly in regard to our different times of life: you amidst the fair, the gallant, and the gay; I in a retreat, where I enjoy every amusement that solitude can afford. I confess I sometimes wish for a little conversation; but I reflect that the commerce of the world gives more uneasiness than pleasure, and quiet is all the hopes that can reasonably be indulged in at my age."

The prudence and tact shown by Lady Bute in her now conspicuous position as wife of the Prince's favourite, was the subject of a letter from Mr. Wortley in July of this year, to which his wife replied—

"I am glad my daughter's conduct justifies the opinion I always had of her understanding. I do not wonder at her being well received in sets of company different from one another, having myself preserved a long intimacy with the Duchesses of Marlborough and Montagu, though they were at open war, and perpetually talking of their complaints. I believe they were both sensible I never betrayed either. . . . What I think extraordinary is my daughter's continuing so many years agreeable to Lord Bute; Mr. Mackensie telling me, the last time I saw him, that his brother frequently said among his companions, that he was as much in love with his wife as before he married her."

To her daughter, in a letter written about the same time, Lady Mary says: "I am very glad you are admitted into the conversation of the P[rince] and Ps [Princess]: it is a favour that you ought to cultivate for the good of the family, which is now numerous, and it may one day be of great advantage. I think Lord Bute much in the right to endeavour the continuance of it; and it would be imprudent in you to neglect what may be of great use to your children."

The following letter to Lady Bute, written on 6th May 1748, may be quoted in full:—

"I[1] am very much obliged to you (dear child) for yours of February the 20th, which came to my hands but yesterday May 5th. I am glad to hear that you are so well diverted and that Lady Jane[2] has got so well over the Smallpox. I think Lady L. Wentworth[3] is better married than I expected. She is of an age to be weaned from the vain part of life and with a prudent conduct, may be very happy in a moderate fortune. I have seen Gen. Howard's name very often in the newspaper, and supposed him to be Brother to Lord Carlisle, but he was not married (at least did not declare himself so), when I left England. The death of the D. of Bridgewater will make Lord Trentham's[4] marriage yet more advantageous; I heard at Avignon that the young Duke had marry'd himself very unluckily, as also the D. of Chandos,[5] Lord Salisbury,[6] and

---

[1] From the unpublished MS.

[2] Lady Jane Stuart, second daughter of Lady Bute.

[3] Lady Lucy Wentworth was a daughter of Thomas, Earl of Strafford. She married in 1747 Sir George Howard, a distinguished soldier, who fought at Fontenoy and Culloden, and commanded a brigade in Germany during the Seven Years' War.

[4] Lord Trentham, eldest son of Lord Gower, married in 1748 (as his second wife) Lady Louisa Egerton, daughter of Scrope, first Duke of Bridgewater, who died in 1745. Her brother, the second Duke, died unmarried in 1748. His brother, the next Duke, was never married.

[5] This was the second Duke, son of the "princely Chandos." He married Anne Jeffreys in 1744. She was the second of his three wives.

[6] James, sixth Earl of Salisbury, married in 1743 a sister of the Rev. John Keet, Rector of Hatfield. This *mésalliance*, as Lady Mary would probably consider it, was thus five years old.

Lord Bristol,[1] but have had no confirmation of it. I am surprised you mention Lady Townshend's[2] giving a ball; I thought she was parted from her Lord and not in circumstances of giving public entertainments. I pray for a peace which may make our correspondence more regular, and give me more frequent opportunities of telling you that I am ever (dear child) your most affec^{ate} mother,

"M. WORTLEY"

The preliminaries of peace were signed this year at Aix-la-Chapelle, and young Wortley was appointed one of the Commissioners and secretary to our Ambassador, Lord Sandwich. On 10th September his mother wrote to Mr. Wortley—

"I[3] saw in the newspaper last week that our son is one of the Secretaries to the Embassy of Lord S. I hope he may succeed in that business better than he has yet done in the professions he has undertaken. I know not whether he has had the answer I made to the last letter I received from him. I sent it to you with a copy of my return to it, which I fear never reached you; I will therefore repeat it as near as I can remember it.

"'I am very glad to hear of your health, but sorry to find you still continue in the vain way of thinking that has been your ruin. I will not ask your father to increase your allowance; it is amply sufficient for all the show you ought to make. Your past extravagances are known to all that know your name; a modest behaviour and a frugal expense are necessary to persuade the world you are convinced of the folly of your former conduct. The very reasons you give for desiring a larger income prove you do not want it, since Lord Sandwich's presenting you as his relation entitles you to more respect than an embroidered coat or a rich livery, which gain no

---

[1] The old Lord Bristol, father of Lord Hervey, did not die till 1751. His grandson, who succeeded him, died unmarried. The next brother, Augustus Hervey, did not succeed till 1775, but Lady Mary may have had him in her mind, as he was married privately to the much too celebrated Miss Chudleigh in 1744, the same lady who married bigamously Lady Mary's nephew, the last Duke of Kingston, in 1769.

[2] Lady Townshend was quite capable of giving a ball without the support of her husband, though the company may not have been very select.

[3] From the unpublished MS.

esteem but amongst the weakest of both sexes, and only serves to draw the eyes of the mob, and even by them is oftener ridiculed than admired. The true figure a man makes is in proportion to the opinion people have of his honesty and understanding. Your father's example ought to have the greatest weight with you; his real generosity and perfect disinterestedness have gained him the applause of all those whose applause is worth having. Public tables and great equipages are only becoming in those who bear public characters. Prudence and decency will recommend you to the thinking part of mankind, and make you a blessing as you have hitherto been a misfortune to your affect^{ate}, etc.' "

The record for this year may be concluded with another letter to Lady Bute, written on 25th December—

"DEAR CHILD,[1]—I find all my long letters to you have miscarried, neither have I heard from you for many months. I know not where the fault lies, but have resolved to change the method of our correspondence, to try at least if it be possible to fix it in a more regular manner.[2] I wish you would let me know the chief heads of those you have last received, being unwilling to trouble you with repetitions. Since the Peace is concluded, I suppose you may safely send me the first book of Campbell's *Vitruvius Britannicus*.[3] I desire Lord Bute would be so good to choose for me the best book of practical gardening, and at the same time a little Windsor chair no larger than a plaything. You may imagine I design it as a model, having a mind to place some in my garden, and not knowing how to explain to the workmen here what I mean. . . . I am ashamed to have promised Lady Mary[4] a token so long without performance. The first safe hand shall bring it to her."

[1] From the unpublished MS.

[2] It afterwards appeared that letters were intercepted by the Count Palazzo and his mother.

[3] By Colin Campbell, the architect (d. 1729). He published his *Vitruvius Britannicus* between 1717 and 1725.

[4] Lady Mary Stuart, eldest daughter of Lady Bute.

CHAPTER XLIV

LOVERE

LADY BUTE'S elder children were now of a schoolroom age, and it is significant, considering the popular views of Lady Mary's character, that she turns to her mother for advice about the training of young people, and more especially of girls.

"Almost all girls of quality," says Lady Mary, in one of several letters on this subject, "are educated as if they were to be great ladies, which is often as little to be expected as an immoderate heat of the sun in the north of Scotland. You should teach yours to confine their desires to probabilities, to be as useful as is possible to themselves, and to think privacy (as it is) the happiest state of life. I do not doubt your giving them all the instructions necessary to form them to a virtuous life; but 'tis a fatal mistake to do this without proper restrictions. Vices are often hid under the name of virtues, and the practice of them followed by the worst of consequences. Sincerity, friendship, piety, disinterestedness and generosity are all great virtues; but pursued without discretion become criminal. I have seen ladies indulge their own ill-humour by being very rude and impertinent, and think they deserved approbation by saying, 'I love to speak the truth.' One of your acquaintance made a ball the next day after her mother died, to show she was sincere."

Lady Mary proceeds to beg her daughter to moderate the fondness she has for her children, or at any rate to prepare herself for disappointments in connection with them. She confesses, speaking out of bitter experience, that there are few misfortunes more difficult to support than such disappointments, but adds that imagination has a great share in the suffering, and concludes that, "strictly speaking, there is but one real evil—I mean acute pain; all other complaints are so considerably diminished by time, that it is plain the grief is owing to our passion, since the sensation of it vanishes when that is over."

Another mistake, common to mothers, she is careful to point out. "If any of their daughters are beauties, they take great pains to persuade them they are ugly, or at least that they think so, which the young woman never fails to believe springs from envy, and is perhaps not much in the wrong. I would, if possible, give them a just notion of their figure, and show them how far it is valuable. It is the common doctrine of (what are called) good books to inspire a contempt of beauty, riches, greatness, etc., which has done as much mischief among the young of our sex as an over-eager desire of them. They should look on these things as blessings where they are bestowed, though not necessaries that it is impossible to be happy without." Lady Mary points her moral with the case of her own niece, Lady Fanny Pierrepont, who had eloped with Mr. Medows (third son of Sir Philip Medows) in April 1734.[1] Her "ruin," as her aunt terms the marriage, is attributed to "the notions given her by the silly good people that had the care of her."

There is a long letter to Lady Bute, dated 6th March 1749, containing congratulations on the birth of a fourth daughter, Lady Augusta Stuart.

"You[2] are in a place," continues the exile, "that every day may furnish you with a new subject to write. I have little to say from hence (having already sent you the description of my garden). My time passes as regularly as that of a clock, the returning seasons bringing with them their country business, which is all the variety of my life. I am now employed with the care of my silk-worms' eggs; the silk is generally spun the latter end of May. I wish you would tell me the price it bears at London." After asking

---

[1] Lady Fanny's son succeeded to the estates of his uncle, Evelyn, last Duke of Kingston, in 1773. He was raised to the peerage as Baron Pierrepont, Viscount Newark, and Earl Manners.

[2] From the unpublished MS.

yet again for the books on architecture and gardening, she proceeds—

"If there is anything come out that you think would amuse me, you may put it in the same pacquet, taking the price of Mr. Child, which I insist on your doing. I saw in the newspaper the death of Lord Monson.[1] I should be glad to know if my sister continues in his family, and what other changes happen among my acquaintance. I suppose Miss Rich is now a great fortune, and probably married to somebody or other. The ladies of my neighbourhood are most of them preparing clothes and equipage to assist at the Entry of Don Philip into Parma,[2] which is forty miles from hence. However I do not intend to give myself the trouble and expence of the journey to see a ceremony which I guess will not differ much from the many I have seen; my curiosity is not only lessened but almost abolish'd, and peasants as agreeable to me as Princes. This sounds very oddly to you, but my age will give you the same sentiments. We that stand on the Threshold of Life (as Mr. Waller calls it) see everything in a very different light from what they appear in youth and vigour."

On 1st May Lady Mary wrote to her husband about his recent acquisition of Newbold Verdun, left to him by his cousin, James Montagu.

"I[3] wish you joy of your new seat. I have been told that the gardens and plantations are in the best taste of any in that country; long may you enjoy it in health and happiness! I give you many thanks for the ale, which is in great esteem here by reputation, for it is otherwise unknown. I would send you some wine of my own making in return, if I thought it would arrive good, and be worth paying the Customs.

"I cannot readily answer your question concerning the passage of letters, being eighteen miles from Brescia, and there is nobody in this neighbourhood that has any foreign

---

[1] John, first Baron Monson, died in 1748. Presumably Lady Mar, after her daughter's marriage, had been placed in the charge of some member of his family.
[2] Don Philip made his formal entry into Parma in March 1749.
[3] From the unpublished MS.

correspondence. I have always dated my letters from Brescia, being the nearest post-town. But I have been there but twice, and that only for a few days, since my recovery from that terrible fit of sickness at my arrival. I find this air agrees very well with me, and amuse myself with my little country business.

"I am very glad my daughter's conduct answers the opinion I ever had of her understanding. I do not say it to lessen the praise she deserves, but I really think there is some due to Lord Bute. It is seldom that the affections of a man of his age continue so many years; may she always possess them and every other blessing. I think her much in the right to cultivate the princess's favour, but in general have no great faith in Court friendships, and remember Lord Bathurst's epigram that Princes are the sons of Kings."

Although Lady Mary had little or no belief in the miraculous cures effected by her friends' favourite quacks or nostrums, her scepticism was easily vanquished by a medical wonder of her own discovery, as may be seen by the following letter to Lady Bute (11th August):—

". . . The [1] very next day after I wrote my last, my fever seized me again, which has now tormented me four months off and on. My woman's returned also the same day, who has it eight months. I was recommended to the physician of this place [2] with much said in his praise as master of several secrets, of which I did not believe one word; however, I was prevailed on to take his advice. He gave both her and me a small dose of powder, which is a preparation of the bark of his invention, how composed I cannot tell, but so it is that after once taking, neither of us had any return of the ague; on the contrary, are restored to health and strength as if by miracle. 'Tis true we continued to take one dose per day twelve days altogether, but without any confinement, having always been about partaking of all the diversions. I cannot help giving you this information, tho' I am afraid you will think it like Ward's drops or Tar Water, but 'tis certainly true,

---

[1] From the unpublished MS.
[2] This letter was written from Lovere, on Lago D'Iseo, which Lady Mary frequently visited as a health resort.

that since I have been here, I have seen such miraculous success of his medicines in various cases, that I think I ought to let you know it, particularly of a mouth-water for the scurvy in the teeth, which I have seen experienced by an Abbé past fifty, who came from Ferrara on purpose to be under his care, and who had not one tooth that did not shake, and his gums seemed perish'd. They are come again, and all his teeth firm. The Doctor says this water will keep its virtue two or three years, and bear transportation, which if true might be of great use in England, where that distemper is almost epidemical. The tryal can hurt nobody, since the water is not to be swallowed. I believe you will think I have been very long on this subject. I intend staying here the remainder of this month; 'tis impossible to be in a more agreable place, in regard of the situation, goodness of provisions and abundance of the most excellent fruits of all kinds. 'Tis true I could wish there was less company, being heartily tired of the eternal hurry of operas, puppet-shows, etc. Here is a gaming room, but I have never been at it, nor do I know any ladies that go there, being a rendezvous of mixed company."

In the course of the summer Mr. Wortley went to France, and on 8th September his wife wrote to him at Paris—

". . . It[1] was Miss Carter (daughter of Mr. Carter who I have heard you speak as a relation of Lady Bellasis) that gave me the description of Newbold Hall. I know not what is become of her since her foolish marriage that I sent you a long account of. I seldom saw Mr. Hewet[2] at Venice; I fancy he was displeased with me for not introducing him to the noble ladies, which was out of my power. They look upon all Governors as servants, and will not receive their visits.

"If it were possible to transport houses, I could send you very fine palaces which you might purchase at 10 per. cent. I was offered the other day one of the most agreeable houses I ever saw in a delightful situation for nothing, if I would buy the land about it, valued at 20,000 crowns, and I believe they would have thrown me in the furniture into the bargain, tho'

[1] From the unpublished MS.
[2] Probably a son of the Mrs. Hewet to whom several of Lady Mary's early letters were written.

it is almost new, with some good pictures. I am still at Lovere, tho' the high season for drinking the waters is over, but my health is so much mended by them, that I intend to stay some time longer. There is a constant courier goes between this place and Brescia, which is more secure for letters than when I am at Gottolengo, where they must always come by a private messenger."

It says much for the air and waters of Lovere that Lady Mary, now in her sixty-first year, was still able to lead an active outdoor life. She rode on horseback every day, and declares that she is a better horsewoman than she had ever been in her life, having complied with the fashion of the country, which was much better than the English. "I cannot help being amazed," she exclaims, "at the obstinate folly by which the English ladies venture every day their lives and limbs." In a letter to Lady Bute, dated 5th September, she gives a brief account of the manner in which she passes her time at Lovere—

"I[1] rise early, take the air on the water every evening, and generally land at some parts of its banks, and always find some new walk amongst the Mountains, which are covered with vines and fruit trees, mixed with several natural Cascades and embellished with variety of beautiful prospects. I think I have already described this place to you; it really answers all the delightful ideas of romance. I could not be persuaded to leave it for the Fair of Bergamo, tho' half engaged to do so. I play at whisk an hour or two every afternoon; the fashion here is to play for the collation, the losers having at least the consolation of eating part of their money. I am extremely pleased with your Father's kindness to you, I do not doubt of your gratitude and affection. He speaks to me much of the beauty of your sons; I cannot help wishing it had fallen to the share of your daughters, but I believe it is the destiny of Lord Bute's family. I never heard his Mother's[2] much celebrated, tho' both her brothers have been remarkable for their figure. . . ."

Now that the war was over, boxes of new books could be

---

[1] From the unpublished MS.
[2] Lord Bute's mother was Anne, daughter of Archibald, first Duke of Argyll.

sent out from England to the exile at Gottolengo, who never lost her taste for fiction, even of the flimsiest kind. On 1st October she writes to thank Lady Bute for a batch of new novels which had amused her very much.

"I gave a ridiculous proof of it," she writes, "fitter indeed for my grand-daughter than for myself. I returned from a party on horse-back; and after having rode twenty miles, part of it by moonshine, it was ten at night when I found the box arrived. I could not deny myself the pleasure of opening it; and falling upon Fielding's works, was fool enough to sit up all night reading. I think *Joseph Andrews*[1] better than his *Foundling*." Lady Mary adds that she was the more struck by the book for having a "Fanny" in her own service, a girl of extraordinary beauty, joined to a yet more extraordinary understanding. But though the young woman never stirred from her mistress's chamber, and was always at her needle, there had been no peace in the house, or even the parish, since her arrival, all the women having declared open war with her, and all the men endeavouring at treaties of a different sort.

It must be owned that as the years went on Lady Mary became more, rather than less, censorious, especially where the conduct of her relations and friends was concerned, while the sharpness of her tongue, or rather of her pen, lost nothing of its point. In one unpublished letter she expresses her amazement at her half-sister Carolina's[2] marriage to Mr. Brand,[3] and declares that, considering her great fortune, this absurd match shows that she has "a great deal of Dutch in her composition."[4] Again, in a letter to Lady Bute (22nd June 1750) there is an amusing passage on the subject of Sir John Rawdon,[5] who had lately been created Lord Rawdon of

---

[1] *Joseph Andrews* had appeared in 1742, but apparently Lady Mary had not been able to secure it before. *The Foundling*, otherwise *Tom Jones*, was published in 1749.

[2] Daughter of the Duke of Kingston by his second wife, Lady Belle Bentinck.

[3] Thomas Brand, Esq., of the Hoo, Hertfordshire. He seems to have been a worthy man, and the marriage was a happy one.

[4] Her grandfather, the first Earl of Portland, had been William Bentinck, a Dutchman, who came over with William III., to whom he was confidential adviser.

[5] Sir John Rawdon was created Earl of Moira in 1761.

Moira. She refuses to believe that Sir John's promotion was owing to his own merit, but observes—

"Ever since I knew the world, Irish patents have been hung out to sale, like the laced and embroidered coats in Monmouth Street, and bought up by the same sort of people; I mean those who had rather wear shabby finery than no finery at all, though I do not suppose this was Sir John's case. That good creature (as the country saying is) has not a bit of pride in him. I dare swear he purchased his title for the same reason he used to purchase pictures in Italy; not because he wanted to buy, but because somebody or other wanted to sell. He hardly ever opened his mouth but to say, 'What you please, sir';—'At your service';—'Your humble servant,' or some gentle expression to the same effect." There is another anecdote to the effect that, Sir John having received a blow from one of his countrymen, his friend Lord Mansel tried to spirit him up to make some show of resentment, and represented to him very warmly that no gentleman could take a box on the ear. Sir John replied with great calmness, "I know that, but this was not a box on the ear, it was only a slap of the face."

CHAPTER XLV

THEORIES OF LIFE

IN the autumn of 1750 Lady Mary was persuaded to forsake Lovere, and pay a visit to Salo on the Lake of Guardia, where she was able to hire a magnificent palace at a nominal rent. She describes it as the finest place she ever saw, much larger than the royal palace of Naples, or any of those in Germany or England. It had been built by Cosmo de Medici, and was surrounded by gardens, diversified with fountains and statues, covered walks, and orange trees as large as lime trees in England. The present owner, to whose ancestor the Grand Duke had presented it, had lost a noble estate by gaming, and was glad to let it for a trifle. There were other palaces, also to be had at a bargain, within a radius of ten miles, and Lady Mary, who had begun to think the air of Gottolengo unsuited to her health, found the choice quite embarrassing, which is perhaps the reason why she did not buy a house and settle down at Salo.

Lord Bute had just been appointed Lord of the Bedchamber to the Prince of Wales, and his mother-in-law sends warm congratulations on his good fortune. His appointment only lasted a few months, however, since the Prince died on 20th March. Lord Bute had been seriously ill himself just before, and on 2nd April Lady Mary wrote to her daughter—

"I[1] am sorry for the uneasiness you are under on the account of Lord Bute's health, though I hope it was over long before I received the news of it. I wish you many years' continuance of the happiness you possess in one another. It is what sweetens all the accidents of life, and can be made up by no other advantage where it is wanted. I dare swear you

[1] From the unpublished MS.

have examples enough amongst your acquaintance to convince you that the greatest affluence of fortune is but a splendid wretchedness where there is no satisfaction at home. I bought not long since the pictures of the Prince and Princess, which now adorn my Gallery. Hers does not do her justice, but his represents him as naturally as a looking-glass. They belong'd to a gentleman lately dead, who had been a sort of Favourite to the Duke of Saxe Gotha, who made a present of them to him, being copies of those sent from England to that Court. I have lately lost a Friend;[1] I may say the only one I had in this country, to whom I had uncommon obligations, having been sick two months in her house, in all which time she serv'd me with so much care, as if I had been her Sister.[1] This accident has touched me very sensibly. She was carry'd off in three days' illness; tho' I think it much happier than a lingering sickness, yet there is something shocking in observing the short interval between life and death."

The news of the Prince's death seems to have taken several weeks to reach Gottolengo, for it is not till 8th May that Lady Mary writes to Mr. Wortley—

"I[2] am very much concerned at the death of the Prince, which I fear will have an ill effect on my daughter's affairs. Many people will be sufferers on this occasion, perhaps a great number of creditors. If Mr. Littleton remembers his dispute with me on the first separation of the Royal Family, he will now think my opinion not so absurd, that all debt should be avoided, it being possible for a young man to die before his father. I suppose Prince George will have a household fixed, and methinks his father's servants should have preference. However that is, the disappointment must still be very great to Lord Bute. I do not doubt his hopes were very high. *Nescia mens hominum sati, sortisque futura.* As I have a good opinion of his honesty, I think it a national misfortune that he has lost the prospect of having a share in the confidence of a king. My daughter will probably regret the pleasures of a Court, and yet more the advantages she might expect for her children. . . ."

[1] This seems to be an allusion to the Countess Palazzo.
[2] From the unpublished MS.

During this year young Wortley was disporting himself in London, and, free from fear of arrest, was astonishing the town by his extravagance. In February Horace Walpole wrote to Mann: " Our greatest miracle is Lady Mary Wortley's son, whose adventures have made so much noise; his parts are not proportionate, but his expense is incredible. His father scarce allows him anything: yet he plays, dresses, diamonds himself, even to distinct shoe-buckles for a frock, and has more snuff-boxes than would suffice a Chinese idol with an hundred noses. But the most curious part of his dress, which he has brought from Paris, is an iron wig; you literally would not know it from hair—I believe it is on this account that the Royal Society have just chosen him of their body." For once Horace's account does not seem to have been exaggerated. Young Wortley was said to have " walked," what with his buttons and buckles, worth £2500. In the course of the year he went through a form of marriage with a Miss Ashe, who figures in Walpole's letters under the nickname of the Pollard Ashe, and later went with her and some of his boon companions to Paris, where he had further adventures hereafter to be recorded.

His extravagance seems to have been concealed from his mother, who wrote to her husband on 24th May: " I can no longer resist the desire I have to know what is become of my son. I have long suppressed it from a belief that if there was anything of good to be told, you would not fail to give me the pleasure of hearing it. I find it now grows so much upon me, that whatever I am to know, I think it would be easier for me to support, than the anxiety I suffer from my doubts. I beg to be informed, and prepare myself for the worst with all the philosophy I have."

While in chronic expectation of hearing ill news, the mother consoled herself with her taste for " baubles," which she says she cultivated with all the art she was mistress of. " I should have despised them," she observes, " at twenty, for the same reason that I would not eat tarts or cheesecakes at twelve years old, as being too childish for one capable of more solid pleasures. I now know (and alas! have long known) all things in this world are almost equally trifling, and our most secret [? serious] projects have scarce more foundation than

the hero of a gambling scandal. It appears that he went to Paris in the autumn with Miss Ashe,[1] Lord Southwell[2] and Theobald Taaffe, M.P. for Arundel. According to Horace Walpole, Wortley and Taaffe had frequently acted as pharaoh-bankers to Madame de Mirepoix, the French Ambassadress, and having presumably made London too hot to hold them, they migrated to France in the hope of finding fresh victims. Shortly after their arrival, the two members of Parliament, together with Lord Southwell, were accused of making a Jew drunk, and then cheating him of 870 louis d'or. The victim, Abraham Paybas, alias James Roberts, declared that they had forced him by menaces to give drafts for the money, and that after he had left Paris they broke into his lodgings and carried off gold and jewels.

Both Wortley and Taaffe were locked up in prison, pending the trial, but the Jew's action against them failed, and they afterwards sued him for false imprisonment. He was condemned to pay each of the injured parties 100,000 livres, and also to make "reparation of honour" before twelve witnesses. It is stated that the judgment was reversed later, but no further proceedings were taken against the Englishmen. Young Wortley wrote an account of the matter, in which he complains bitterly of the treatment he has undergone, and asks whether it is probable that "after having lived hitherto without stain or reproach upon my character, I should start all at once into such a pitch of wickedness as to fuddle a man with a premeditated design to rob him of his money?"

Horace Walpole gives a lively account of the affair, and declares that the two accused would be reduced to keep the best company on their return to England, because nobody else would converse with them. "Their separate anecdotes are curious," he continues. "Wortley, you know, has been a perfect Gil Blas, and, for one of his last adventures, is thought to have added the famous Miss Ashe to the number

---

[1] Miss Ashe was supposed to be the daughter of a "high personage." After all her adventures she ended by marrying a Captain Falconer.

[2] Thomas, second Baron Southwell.

of his wives. Taaffe is an Irishman, who changed his religion to fight a duel; as you know in Ireland a Catholic may not wear a sword. . . . He is a gamester, usurer, adventurer, and of late has divided his attentions between the Duke of Newcastle and Madame Pompadour; travelling with turtles and pine-apples in post-chaises to the latter—flying back to the former for the Lewes races—and smuggling Burgundy at the same time. I shall finish their history with a *bon mot*. The Speaker was railing at gambling and White's *à propos* to these two prisoners. Lord Coke,[1] to whom the conversation was addressed, replied, 'Sir, all I can say is, that they are both members of the House of Commons, and neither of them of White's.'"

[1] The ne'er-do-weel son of Lord Leicester. His treatment of his wife, Lady Mary Campbell, had made a public scandal.

imposed on foreign ministers by telling them the naked truth." To the confounding of sense with cunning was due, she believed, the unjust custom of debarring women from the advantages of learning, the men fancying that the improvement of the feminine understanding would only furnish their wives with more art to deceive them, whereas fools are always enterprising, through not seeing the difficulties of deceit or the consequence of detection. " The same characters are formed by the same lessons, which inclines me to think (if I dare say it) that nature has not placed us in an inferior rank to men, no more than the females of other animals, where we see no distinction of capacity; though I am persuaded if there was a commonwealth of rational horses (as Dr. Swift has supposed), it would be an established maxim among them that a mare could not be taught to pace."

Lady Bute, it appears, disagreed with her mother's view on the education of girls, and there is something rather pathetic in the fact that her youngest daughter, Lady Louisa Stuart, who inherited her grandmother's passion for reading, her genius for letter-writing, and something of her talent for versifying, was harshly discouraged by her elders for trying to indulge her taste for intellectual pursuits. Lady Louisa says that she was constantly accused (by her brothers and sisters) of showing self-conceit and affectation of wisdom by reading books with which she had no sort of business. " I know you have got it into your head that you are to be like your grandmother," was their cry; whereas it was this reproach that first informed her that she ever had a grandmother, and the poor girl not unnaturally hated her very name.

The arrival of a box of new novels from England was something of a festival in the monotonous existence at Gottolengo. Lady Mary described herself once as " a rake at reading," and she seems to have been guilty of a literary " orgy " as often as opportunity occurred. Instead of making her books last for months or weeks, she fell upon them with the ferocity of the long-famished, and devoured nearly all at once, sometimes sitting up half the night to finish a particularly fascinating story. It was a fortunate period for the impassioned novel-reader, Fielding, Richardson, and Smollett being all at work, besides a host of minor lights, who gave good measure (five volumes at least), though their quality left something to be desired.

In February of this year (1752) a particularly appetising box arrived, containing *Peregrine Pickle, Roderick Random, Clarissa Harlowe, Pompey the Little,* and other less-known works. Next to reading novels, Lady Mary enjoyed giving her opinion on them, and as contemporary criticism is always interesting, even when its conclusions have not been ratified by posterity, some of her remarks may be quoted here.

The Memoirs of Lady Vane (under the name of Lady Frail), which were inserted in *Peregrine Pickle*, contained, in our critic's opinion, more truth and less malice than anything she had ever read. " Her history rightly considered," she continues, " would be more instructive to young women than any sermon I know. They may see there what mortification and variety of misery are the unavoidable consequences of gallantry. I think there is no rational creature that would not prefer the life of the strictest Carmelite to the round of hurry and misfortune she has gone through." Lady Mary imagines that the book was written by some subaltern admirer of Lady Vane's, with whom she says she had no acquaintance, though the adventurous lady had been married to two of her (Lady Mary's) relations. Mr. Shirley, Lady Orford's second husband, had been one of Lady Vane's many admirers, and Lady Mary comments on his uncommon fortune in making conquests of two such extraordinary ladies, equal in their heroic contempt for shame, and eminent above their sex, the one for beauty and the other for wealth.

Having rushed through another novel, *The Fortunate Parish Girl*, the critic, her eyes now weary, took up *Pompey the Little* (by Coventry), which, she fancied from its title, would not engage her long; but it diverted her so much more than any of the others, that she could not go to bed till she had finished it. In this once popular story, which professes to recount the adventures of a Lap-dog, Lady Mary found " a real and exact representation of life, as it is now acted in London, as it was in my time, and as it will be (I do not doubt) a hundred years hence, with some little variation of dress, and perhaps government. I found there many of my acquaintance. Lady T[ownshend] and Lady O[rford] are so well painted I fancied I heard them talk, and have heard them say the very things there repeated."[1]

In one of the characters in *Pompey the Little*, Mrs. Qualmsick,[2] Lady Mary says that she saw herself as she then was, though hitherto she had never suffered from vapours or weak nerves. But the physician of the parish, "a grave, sober, thinking, great fool," had persuaded her that she ate so little, that it was a miracle she was still alive. The "stuffing system" seems to have been known at Gottolengo in the eighteenth century, judging from the following dietary—which Lady Mary actually followed till Pompey convinced her that she was in no danger of starvation :—

"I wake generally about seven, and drink half a pint of warm asses' milk, after which I sleep two hours; as soon as I am risen, I constantly take three large cups of milk coffee, and two hours after that a large cup of milk chocolate. Two hours more brings my dinner, where I never fail swallowing a good dish (I don't mean plate) of gravy soup, with all the bread, roots, etc. belonging to it. I then eat the wing and the whole body of a large fat capon, and a veal sweetbread, concluding with a competent quantity of custard, and some roasted chestnuts. At five in the afternoon I take another dose of asses' milk, and for supper twelve chestnuts (which would weigh twenty-four of those in London), one new-laid egg, and a handsome porringer of white bread and milk. With this diet, notwithstanding the menaces of my wise doctor, I am now convinced I am in no danger

[1] *Pompey the Little* was published in 1751. The dog is made to relate his own history. He was brought over from Italy by a young Englishman of fashion (perhaps meant for Mr. Shirley), and passed into the possession of Lady Tempest (Lady Townshend), a sprightly lady who had married a young lord of great estate but inferior understanding. She soon got tired of her husband, and amused herself with other lovers. Among her friends was Lady Sophister (Lady Orford), who had read Locke and Hobbes, and asked everybody she met whether he believed in the immortality of the soul.

[2] Mrs. Qualmsick had "neither stomach, strength, appetite nor anything in the world." She tells her doctor, "I drank a little chocolate yesterday morning, and got down a little bason of broth at noon, and eat a pigeon for my dinner and made a shift to get down another little bason of broth at night—but I can't eat at all."

of starving, and am obliged to Little Pompey for the discovery."

For the works of her cousin Fielding Lady Mary had a strong admiration, and a proportionate contempt for Richardson, though she could not resist the latter's pathos. "I was such an old fool," she writes a few weeks later, "as to weep over *Clarissa Harlowe* like any milk-maid of sixteen over the *Lady's Fall*. To say truth, the first volume softened me by a near resemblance of my maiden days; but on the whole, 'tis miserable stuff. Miss Howe, who is called a young lady of sense and honour, is not only extreme silly, but a more vicious character than Sally Martin, whose crimes are owing at first to seduction, and afterwards to necessity; while this virtuous damsel, without any reason, insults her mother at home, and ridicules her abroad; abuses the man she marries, and is impertinent and impudent with great applause. Even that model of affection, Clarissa, is so faulty in her behaviour as to deserve little compassion. Any girl that runs away with a young fellow without intending to marry him, should be carried to Bridewell or to Bedlam the next day. Yet the circumstances are so laid as to inspire tenderness, notwithstanding the low style and absurd incidents; and I look upon this and *Pamela* to be two books that will do more general mischief than the works of Lord Rochester." About *Pamela* she had written the previous year, remarking that it had met with "a very extraordinary (and I think undeserved) success. It has been translated into French and into Italian; it was all the fashion at Paris and Versailles, and is still the joy of the chambermaids of all nations."

On 22nd July 1753 Lady Mary wrote to her husband—

"I[1] received yours of 28th May, which gave me great pleasure on many accounts. I could send you in return stories of the Courts round me, that would perhaps amuse you, but I dare not venture on anything of that kind, for reasons I need not mention; and have no other subject to write on, but my insignificant self, my frequent indispositions confining me almost wholly to this village. Indeed, everybody has been confined this summer, the great snows that fell in the winter being melted by excessive rains in the spring, have occasioned

[1] From the unpublished MS.

such general inundations as have not been known of many years. The bridges have been broken down in most places, a great number of cattle and many houses with their inhabitants destroyed, the roads are yet scarce practicable, and several rivers not yet retired. This misfortune has been in some measure repaired for the country people by an extraordinary fertility. Their harvest has been so abundant, the rich farmers complain of it; and the appearance of the vintage is so great, excellent wine is now to be sold for half a crown (English) a barrel, and finds no buyers. I am assured a great deal will be literally thrown away to empty the vessels. The silkworms have succeeded so well they have enriched all those that have bred them. If I could establish a correspondence with some English merchant that would take the silk at a fixed price at Venice, it would be very advantageous to me. But I know not to whom to address myself about it. I believe I could buy a hundredweight of silk in this town for 15s. per pound (their pound is only 12 ounces), but the hazard of the sea is what I am not willing to venture on. . . ."

In June of this year Lady Caroline Brand died of rheumatic fever, after a brief but very happy married life. Commenting upon the event in a letter to Lady Bute, Lady Mary says that she cannot feel much touched by it, and adds—

"It is true she was my sister, as it were in some sense; but her behaviour towards me never gave me any love, nor her general conduct any esteem. The confounding of all ranks and the making a jest of order, has long been growing in England; and I perceive by the books you send me, has made a very considerable progress. The heroes and heroines of the age are cobblers and kitchen wenches. Perhaps you will say I should not take my ideas of the manners of the times from such trifling authors; but it is more truly to be found among them, than from any historian: as they write merely to get money, they always fall into the notions that are most acceptable to the present taste. It has long been the endeavour of our English writers to represent people of quality as the vilest and silliest part of the nation, being (generally) very low-born themselves. I am not surprised at their propagating this doctrine; but I am much mistaken if this levelling principle does not, one day or other, break out in fatal consequences to the public, as it has already done in many private families. You will think I am influenced by living under an aristocratic government whose distinction of rank is carried to a very great height; but I can assure you my opinion is founded on reflection and experience, and I wish to God I had always thought in the same manner. Though I had ever the utmost contempt for *mésalliances*, yet the silly prejudices of my education had taught me to believe I was to treat nobody as an inferior, and that poverty was a degree of merit. This imaginary humility has made me admit many familiar acquaintances, of which I have heartily repented every one, and the greatest examples I have known of integrity and honour have been among those of the highest birth and fortune."

The most influential person in the neighbourhood of Brescia was the learned and benevolent Cardinal Querini.[1] He had long been an intimate friend of Lady Mary's, but in October she writes to her daughter that she is much out of humour because she is on the edge of a quarrel with the Cardinal. One of his chaplains had lately come to her with a request that she would send his master copies of her works, which were to occupy a conspicuous place in a bookcase devoted to English authors. Lady Mary made answer that she was sensible of the honour designed her, but had never

---

[1] Girolamo Querini (1680–1759). He was born at Venice, where both his father and grandfather were Procurators. Against the wishes of his parents he became a Benedictine monk, but he did not allow his ecclesiastical vocation to interfere with his literary vocation. He associated on intimate terms with the savants of Florence of his day, and in 1710 he set out on a journey through Europe, the learned men and the libraries of the various countries that he visited being the chief objects of his pilgrimage. In England he was cordially received by Newton, Bentley, and Burnet. On his return to Italy he was requested by the chapter of his Order to write the history of the Benedictines in Italy. He spent much time in collecting materials for his great work, which was never finished, the Pope, Clement XI., having forbidden its publication. In 1727 he was made Bishop of Brescia and Cardinal, and later he was appointed librarian to the Vatican. He distinguished himself as a generous and enlightened patron of letters, he repaired the Church of St. Mark at Rome, and, thanks to his efforts, the Cathedral of Brescia became one of the most beautiful in Italy. He continued his theological and historical studies, and published several learned works in Latin. In his leisure hours he wrote a number of fugitive pieces, and translated part of *La Henriade* into Italian. Voltaire, in acknowledgment, dedicated his tragedy *Semiramis* to the Cardinal.

printed a line in her life. This was perhaps literally true, but the chaplain, who probably knew that there were poems published under her name, the authorship of which was not denied, replied coldly that his Eminence could of course send to England for her works, but he had flattered himself she would not refuse him the favour he had asked. It was useless to attempt to convince him that she had spoken the truth, and Lady Mary was ready to cry with vexation when she realised that the Cardinal would regard her as a monster of ingratitude. No one, she declares, ever had such provocations to print as herself, for she had seen her literary offspring so mangled and falsified that she had scarcely known them, while poems that she had never even read had been published with her name at length.

While in Italy she had often been complimented, she explains, on the books she had published, and at first had denied the imputation with warmth, but latterly had contented herself with laughing, "knowing that the character of a learned woman is far from being ridiculous in this country, the greatest families being proud of having produced female writers; and a Milanese lady being now professor of Mathematics in the university of Bologna. . . . To say truth, there is no part of the world where our sex is treated with so much contempt as in England. I do not complain of men for having engrossed the government. In excluding us from all degrees of power, they preserve us from fatigues, many dangers, perhaps many crimes . . . but I think it the highest injustice to be debarred the entertainment of my closet, and that the same studies which raised the character of a man should [be supposed to] hurt that of a woman. We are educated in the grossest ignorance, and no art omitted to stifle our natural reason; if some few get above their nurses' instructions, our knowledge must rest concealed, and be as useless to the world as gold in the mine. I am now speaking according to our English notions, which may wear out some ages hence, along with others equally absurd."

CHAPTER XLVII

CRITICAL REFLECTIONS

EARLY in the spring of 1754 Lady Mary had another dangerous illness, and her life being despaired of by the physician at Gottolengo, some of her neighbours sent for the wonder-working doctor of Lovere, whose first prescription was that she should be removed to that village, though his colleague swore that she would die on the road. By litter and by boat she was conveyed the forty miles, and three days after her arrival found herself restored to health. The Lovere doctor declared that her illness was due to the fact that she had omitted to drink the waters for the past two years, and ordered her to make a long stay on the lake.

The little town had originally been founded by those who sought a refuge during the wars between the Guelphs and the Ghibellines. It had prospered till the year 1626, when the inhabitants had been decimated by the plague, and since that time it had only been frequented in the bathing season, its marble palaces either standing empty or being converted into lodging-houses. In a letter to Lady Bute, dated 23rd June 1754, Lady Mary confesses with some trepidation that she has bought one of these half-ruined abodes. The noise of a lodging-house, she explains, was disagreeable to her in her present infirm state of health, and the total cost of her purchase was only a hundred pounds, there being no rent, rates, or taxes to pay. It was true that the apartments were in a most "tattered condition," without doors or windows, that the great staircase was too dangerous to climb and the state bedroom given over to spiders. But the walls and ceilings were good, and it was possible to fit up six rooms with lodgings for five servants. The great saloon was forty-two feet by twenty-five, opening on to a balcony of the same length, and there was a pretty garden in terraces down to the water. The inhabitants of Lovere were delighted to welcome the English lady as a citizen, hoping that she would attract other travelling foreigners, though, as she has no correspondents outside her own family, she "might be buried here fifty years, and nobody know anything of the matter."

Another box of books had been received, containing Lord Orrery's *Remarks on the Life and Writings of Swift*, among other new works. Lady Mary was always strongly prejudiced against Swift on account of his friendship with Pope, but her remarks on his character are interesting as coming from one who was intimately acquainted with the set of Queen Anne wits in which Swift associated during his visits to London. Lord Orrery she had also known as one of those "danglers after wit" who are laughed at, though encouraged, by those who aim at being publicly distinguished for talent or genius.

"D[ean] S[wift]," writes Lady Mary, "by his lordship's own account, was so intoxicated with the love of flattery, he sought it amongst the lowest of the people and the silliest of women, and was never so well pleased with any companions as those that worshipped him while he insulted them. . . . There can be no worse picture made of the Doctor's morals than he has given us himself in the letters printed by Pope. We see him vain, trifling, ungrateful to the memory of his patron, the E[arl] of Oxford, making a servile court where he had any interested views, and meanly abusive when they were disappointed, and, as he says (in his own phrase), flying in the face of mankind, in company with his adorer, Pope. It is pleasant to consider that if it had not been for the good nature of these very mortals they contemn, these two superior beings were entitled, by their birth and hereditary fortune, to be only a couple of link-boys. I am of opinion their friendship would have continued, though they had remained in the same kingdom; it had a very strong foundation—the love of flattery on the one side, and the love of money on the other. Pope courted with the utmost assiduity all the old men from whom he could hope for a legacy, the Duke of Buckingham, Lord Peterborough, Sir G. Kneller, Lord Bolingbroke, Mr. Wycherley,

Mr. Congreve, Lord Harcourt, etc., and I do not doubt projected to sweep the Dean's whole inheritance, if he could have persuaded him to come to die in his house; and his general preaching against money was meant to induce people to throw it away that he might pick it up. There cannot be a stronger proof of his being capable of any action for the sake of gain, than publishing his literary correspondence, which lays open such a mixture of dulness and iniquity, that one would imagine it visible even to his most passionate admirers."

In her next letter Lady Mary deals in not less drastic fashion with the character and genius of Bolingbroke, whose *Essays* she has just been reading. She owns that she has small regard for him as an author, and the highest contempt for him as a man. Lord Orrery had spoken in praise of his literary style, but Lady Mary observes: "Well turned periods or smooth lines are not the perfection either of prose or verse; they may serve to adorn, but can never stand in the place of good sense. Copiousness of words, however ranged, is always false eloquence, though it will ever impose on some sorts of understandings. How many readers and admirers has Madame de Sévigné, who only gives us in a lively manner and fashionable phrases, mean sentiments, vulgar prejudices, and endless repetitions?[1] Sometimes the tittle-tattle of a fine lady, sometimes that of an old nurse, always tittle-tattle; yet so well gilt over by airy expressions and a flowing style, she will always please the same people to whom Lord Bolingbroke will shine as a first-rate author. . . . His confederacy with Swift and Pope puts me in mind of that of Bessus and his swordmen in the *King or no King?*[2] who endeavour to support themselves by giving certificates of each other's merit. Pope has triumphantly declared that they may do and say whatever silly things they please, they will still be the greatest geniuses nature ever exhibited."

It is difficult to repress a smile when we read Lady Mary's

---

[1] Lady Mary seems to have felt a kind of professional jealousy of Madame de Sévigné.

[2] Bessus, a cowardly, bragging soldier, is one of the characters in Beaumont and Fletcher's play of *King or no King?*

boast that she must really be considered an uncommon kind of creature, being an old woman without peevishness, censoriousness, or superstition. From superstition she was undoubtedly free, but there were few of her contemporaries who did not come under the ban of her censure. To do her justice, she always alludes to Mr. Wortley in terms of the highest respect and consideration. Thus, on 15th April 1755, she assures her daughter that no news can be so agreeable to her as the continuation of Mr. Wortley's health, and adds, "You see in him the good effect of a strict abstinence and regular exercise. I am much pleased (but not at all surprised) at his kindness to you: I know him to be more capable of a generous action than any man I ever knew."

A very different idea is given of Mr. Wortley a little later by Horace Walpole, who, while staying at Wentworth Castle in August 1756, wrote to Richard Bentley an account of the " seats " he had visited. After describing Wentworth, he says:

"Well! you have had enough of magnificence; you shall repose in a desert. Old Wortley Montagu lives on the very spot where the dragon of Wantley did, only I believe the latter was much better lodged: you never saw such a wretched hovel; lean, unpainted, and half its nakedness barely shaded with harateen stretched till it cracks. Here the miser hoards health and money, his only two objects: he has chronicles in behalf of the air, and battens on tokay, his single indulgence, as he has heard it is particularly salutary. But the savageness of the scene would charm your Alpine taste: it is tumbled with fragments of mountains, that look ready laid for building the world. One scrambles over a huge terrace, on which mountain-ashes and various trees spring out of the very rocks; and at the brow is the den, but not spacious enough for such an inmate. However, I am persuaded it furnished Pope with this line, so exactly it answers to the picture—

"'On rifted rocks, the dragon's late abodes.'

"I wanted to ask if Pope had not visited Lady Mary Wortley here during their intimacy, but could one put that question to *Avidien* himself?"

Walpole's statement about Mr. Wortley's excessive preoccupation with his health, is borne out by some letters to and from his friend Samuel Bracebridge, which deal chiefly with diet and the merits of cocoa, then comparatively a novelty, and how it should be prepared. In a letter dated from Bath, 10th January 1759, to Mr. Bracebridge, Mr. Wortley says—

"To[1] convince you I approve of your brevity, I will try to be as short. The laconic style, if it be not obscure, is the best, as it saves trouble both to the writer and the reader. I applaud your diet, your drinking steel water, and river bathing. A friend of mine here, who was intimate with Dr. Cheney,[2] assures me that the doctor preached to him constantly that as his case was the scurvy, his surest refuge was in a diet chiefly of milk-meat and vegetables. He now eats very little meat, and drinks no wine; he is a strong man at 66, but is still scorbutic to a certain degree. I incline to think your travelling 30 miles a day must make you easy under almost any regimen.

"Tho' I am not at all scorbutic, I frequently travel 20 miles a day and think it makes me easier than I could be with any diet if I had not the exercise. I commonly at dinner begin with fish to lessen my appetite, then take a little quantity of meat, and end with something of the farinaceous kind. After dinner I take half a pint of Hungarian wine. I breakfast at 8, dine at 1, and drink sage or balm tea in the evening, and go to bed soon after 9. My chocolate is plain, drunk without milk or cinnamon or any other drug.

"Whenever you come into England, you should not be long without visiting Bath; it is entirely altered, and I believe within these ten years, as many new houses have been built, as might be thought sufficient to make another city. The number of visitors increases every year, the subscribers to the *News* at the Coffee House were in 1758 above 1000. There are Plays, Concerts and Assemblies, just as in London, and some call it a second London. Many invalids come to pass

---

[1] From the unpublished MS.
[2] Dr. George Cheyne (1671-1743). He advocated a spare diet, and was in favour of vegetarianism.

the whole winter here, and I believe an infirm man has a better chance to be easy here than on any other spot in England. . . ."

In September 1755, Lady Mary heard of the death of her cousin and favourite author, Henry Fielding.[1] " I am sorry for H. Fielding's death," she writes to her daughter, " not only because I shall read no more of his writings, but I believe he lost more than others, as no man enjoyed life more than he did, tho' few had less reason to do so, the highest of his preferment being raking in the lowest sinks of vice and misery.[2] I should think it a nobler and less nauseous employment to be one of the staff officers that conduct the nocturnal weddings. His happy constitution (even when he had, with great pains, half demolished it) made him forget everything when he was before a venison pasty, or over a flask of champagne; and I am persuaded he has known more happy moments than any prince upon earth. . . . There was a great similitude between his character and that of Sir Richard Steele. He had the advantage, both in learning and, in my opinion, genius; they both agreed in wanting money, in spite of all their friends, and would have wanted it, if their hereditary lands had been as extensive as their imagination; yet each of them was so formed for happiness it is pity he was not immortal."[3] In another letter she remarks that since she was born no original had appeared except Congreve and Fielding, but the latter was forced by necessity to publish without correction.

Dr. Johnson's *Rambler*, which made its first appearance in 1750, does not seem to have reached Lovere till five years later. There is truth and justice in Lady Mary's criticism that " *The Rambler* is certainly a strong misnomer; he always plods in the beaten road of his predecessors, following the *Spectator* (with the same pace a pack-horse would a hunter) in the style that is proper to lengthen a paper. These writers may, perhaps, be of service to the public, which is saying a great deal in their favour. There

---

[1] Fielding died the previous year.   [2] As a police-magistrate.
[3] The admiration was mutual, for Fielding said of Lady Mary, " She is the glory of her own sex and the marvel of ours."

are numbers of both sexes who never read anything but such productions, and cannot spare time, from doing nothing, to go through a sixpenny pamphlet. Such gentle readers may be improved by a moral hint, which, though repeated over and over from generation to generation, they never heard in their lives. I should be glad to know the name of this laborious author."

Sir Charles Grandison was among the books sent out in the autumn of 1755.[1] "This Richardson is a strange fellow," says our critic. "I heartily despise him, and eagerly read him, nay, sob over him in a most scandalous fashion. The two first tomes of *Clarissa* touched me, as being very resembling to my maiden days; and I find in the pictures of Sir Thomas Grandison and his lady what I have heard of my mother and seen of my father." Her strictures, however, are much more severe than her praise is liberal. Richardson shows his ignorance of Italy by making Sir Charles' amour with Clementina begin in her father's house, which is as repugnant to custom as it would be in London for a young lady of quality to dance on the ropes at Bartholomew Fair. She strongly disapproves of Sir Charles' offered compromise about the education of the children of a mixed marriage—the girls to be brought up as Catholics, the boys as Protestants. "He seems to think," she observes, "that women have no souls by agreeing so easily that his daughters should be educated in bigotry and idolatry."

Richardson, it appears, had repeated in one of his books a saying of Lady Mary's, and given a description of her person which resembled her as much as one of the giants at Vauxhall. She is not aware how she can have incurred his indignation, but it is certain that he, perhaps by the above description, had incurred hers. She is convinced that he has only been used to the lowest company, "and should confine his pen to the amours of housemaids and the conversation at the steward's table, where I imagine he has sometimes intruded, though oftener in the servants' hall. Yet if the title be not a puff, this work has passed three editions. I do not forgive him his disrespect for old

[1] It was first published in 1753.

china, which is below nobody's taste, since it has been the D[uke] of Argyll's, whose understanding has never been doubted either by his friends or enemies. Richardson never had probably money enough to purchase any, or even a ticket for a masquerade, which gives him such an aversion to them. . . . He has no ideas of the manners of high life: his old Lord M. talks in the style of a country justice, and his virtuous young ladies romp like the wenches round a maypole. Such liberties as pass between Mr. Lovelace and his cousins are not to be excused by the relation. I should have been much astonished if Lord Denbigh should have offered to kiss me;[1] and I dare swear Lord Trentham never attempted such an impertinence to you."

In December 1755 Lady Oxford died. Lady Mary, who had received a small legacy, wrote to her daughter *à propos* of the loss of her best friend: " I have passed a long life, and may say with truth have endeavoured to purchase friends; accident has put it in my power to confer great benefits, yet I never met with any return, nor indeed any true affection but from dear Lady Oxford, who owed me nothing. . . . The little good I now do is scattered with a sparing hand against my inclination; but I now know the necessity of managing hopes, as the only links that bind attachment, or even secure us from injury."

[1] Lord Denbigh was Lady Mary's first cousin, and Lord Trentham (son of Lord Gower) her daughter's.

CHAPTER XLVIII

MOVE TO VENICE

IN the summer of 1756 Lady Mary travelled to Venice on some business errand, the nature of which is not disclosed. So far as can be ascertained, she never returned to Lovere or Gottolengo, and what became of her old palaces does not appear. On 22nd August she writes to Lady Bute from Mantua, where she had stopped a night on the road to Venice—

"I[1] received with great pleasure yours of 29th June yesterday, 21st August. You are too grateful for trifles, but you are no woman of business. When you send me a box you should at the same time send me a bill of lading, and take care it is noted in the Captain's book. I had some difficulty in obtaining the last, and am afraid I shall never get this at all, at least as I collect from your letter that you have sent it to Mr. Prescot without having any receipt from him. It is impossible to be too cautious in dealings with mankind, especially with merchants, who are often supposed rich and break the next day. I know nothing of him; his correspondent here I met accidentally at the Waters of Lovere. As I then complained to everybody I saw of the interruption of our correspondence, he heard of my distress, and assured me that he knew how to remedy it, and that he would take care any letter, or whatever else I was pleased to send, should be safely delivered to your own hand. I snatched at this opportunity, and sent that bauble of a ring to Lady Jane, as an essay to venture something of higher value to your self. About the time that I received

[1] From the unpublished MS.

your notice of its arrival I heard from the D[uke] of Portland the death of my dear friend Lady Oxford, and the kind remembrance she had bequeathed me. I wrote immediately a letter to him and another to the Duchess, in which I told them I intended to employ it in the purchase of a ring inscribed with both our names, and after I had worn it my short remainder of life, I desired her Grace would accept it in memory of us both. To neither of these letters have I had any answer. Soon after Signor Pitrovani wrote to me to say he heard I had a legacy to receive in England, and as he was obliged to pay a sum of money and should lose by the exchange, he hoped in consideration of his care and faithful delivery of the ring, I would favour him with a bill on the person who was to pay it. I made answer I would not draw a negociable note on the D[uke] of Portland as on a common Banker, but on his pressing me, I wrote a respectful demand payable to the bearer. Since that time I have no notice of its being paid, as I do not doubt but it was. I hope the Duke has had the precaution of taking the receipt, and will let me know the name of the merchant to whom he paid it.[1] I have already told you, I asked your Father's permission to dispose of the money in the manner I have mentioned; I did not doubt readily obtaining it, but have never heard either from him or you on this subject. I am determined to go to Venice myself to try to settle our commerce in a better manner. I am actually on the road, and this is wrote from an Inn in Mantua, the 22nd of August by (dear child) your most affec^{ate} Mother,

"M. WORTLEY

"My compliments to Lord Bute; both his and your conduct is so obliging to me, whatever I can do shall be wholly for you and yours. I have a necklace for you which you need not be ashamed to wear."

In October 1756 Lord Bute was appointed Groom of the

---

[1] In the Italian memoir already mentioned Lady Mary stated that the Count Palazzo concealed from her the name of the merchant whom he had empowered to receive for her Lady Oxford's legacy, with the intention, she supposed, of keeping the money for his own use.

Stole to the young Prince of Wales, an office which he held till the year 1761, when he was made Secretary of State. On 23rd November Lady Mary writes to wish her daughter joy of her new situation, and observes—

"Lord Bute has attained it by a very uncommon road; I mean an acknowledged honour and probity. I have but one short instruction (pardon the word) to give on his account; that he will never forget the real interest of prince and people cannot be divided, and are almost as closely united as that of soul and body. . . . [28th December.] The present ministry promises better counsels than have been followed in my time. I am extremely glad to hear the continuation of your father's health, and that you follow his advice. I am really persuaded (without any dash of partiality) no man understands the interest of England better, or has it more at heart. . . . I shall only repeat the Turkish maxim, which I think includes all that is necessary in a *court*-life: 'Caress the favourites, avoid the unfortunate, and trust nobody.' You may think the second rule ill-natured: melancholy experience has convinced me of the ill-consequence of mistaking distress for merit; there is no mistake more productive of evil."

During her short visit to Venice Lady Mary stayed at the house of an old friend, General Graham. She very soon moved to Padua, where, as she tells Mr. Wortley in an unpublished letter dated 8th December, she took a pretty convenient house at a very reasonable rent.

"Venice is too expensive," she continues, "and this air is deemed the best in Italy. I have reason to think well of it, having my health better than it has been for a long time." She explains in another letter (to Lady Bute) that she left her hermitage in order that what effects she had might not be dissipated by her servants, as they would probably be if she died there. She has no one to confide in, the British Minister at Venice[1] being such a scandalous fellow that he is not to be

[1] His name was John Murray. He and Lady Mary were at daggers drawn during the remainder of her stay. Among the State Papers Lord Stanhope found the following passage in a despatch from Murray to the Secretary of State: "Lady Mary Wortley Montagu arrived here two days ago. She has been for some years past, and still continues, in the hands of a Brescian Count, who, it is said, plunders her of all her riches."—Venice, 10th September 1756.

trusted to change a sequin. "I wish," she continues, "the maxims of Queen Elizabeth were revived, who always chose for her foreign ministers men whose birth and behaviour would make the nation respected, people being apt to look upon them as a sample of their countrymen. If those now employed are so, Lord have mercy upon us."

Mr. Wortley seems to have written very rarely to his wife during the last few years of his life. His eyesight was rapidly failing, and he naturally shrank from sending any confidential communication through a secretary. But in January 1757 he was inspired by his gratification at Lord Bute's promotion to write a brief note. He begins by explaining that the last letter he had received from his wife was dated December 1754, and that any others she had written must have miscarried in the post.

"I have now," he continues, "something to mention that I believe will be agreeable to you. I mean some particulars relating to my Lord Bute, which you have not learned from the prints, or from our minister at Venice. He stood higher in the late P[rince] of Wales' favour than any man. His attendance at Leicester House, where this young prince has resided ever since his father's death, continued without intermission till new officers were to be placed about him. It is said that another person was designed to be groom of the stole, but that the prince's earnest request was complied with in my lord's favour. It is supposed that the governors, preceptors, etc., that were before about him are now laid aside, and that my lord is his principal adviser.

"It is not easy to express how well-bred and reasonable the young prince always appears at his public levee every Thursday, and on all other occasions. The King of France and Empress of Germany always show themselves to great advantage, and this young prince's behaviour is equal to that of either of them. He is supposed to know the true state of this country, and to have the best inclinations to do all in his power to make it flourish."

Owing possibly to Mr. Wortley's custom of sending two servants with his letters to the post, this epistle arrived safely only nineteen days after it was written. On 24th January 1757 Lady Mary writes to her husband from Padua—

"Yours[1] of the 4th instant came to me this morning, which is quicker than I have ever received any from England. It brought me the most sensible pleasure, both as a proof of your health, and the account of Lord Bute's prosperity. God continue those blessings to me. But you know Court favour is no more to be depended on than fair weather at sea. I intend to send my daughter my jewels, as I see occasion offers. You were so good as to promise me at Avignon that she should have them after my death; I hope you will permit me to give them to her now; they may be in some degree necessary in her Court attendance. . . . I write this post to my daughter. I cannot help telling her the advantage I know it will be to her Lord to consult you in his conduct; it is possible there is no occasion for my advising what his own good sense already dictates, but I think they cannot take amiss the zeal I have to serve them."

In April Lady Mary was again in Venice, where she had been persuaded to take a little house, though she still retained her *pied-à-terre* at Padua, and intended to reside there the greater part of the year.[2] In the meantime she was amusing herself with buying and placing furniture, and sometimes indulged her taste for baubles, which she thought as excusable in a second childhood as in a first. She sends her daughter a long list of new novels, which she desired to have sent out to her — *The Fortunate Mistress*, *The Accomplished Rake*, *The History of a Lady Platonist*, *Memoirs of David Ranger*, and other forgotten works of contemporary fiction. Lady Bute seems to have criticised her mother's taste in literature, for in a later letter Lady Mary exclaims: "Daughter! daughter! don't call names; you are always abusing my pleasures, which is what no mortal will bear. Trash, lumber, sad stuff, are the titles you give to my favourite amusement. If I called a white staff a stick of wood, a gold key gilded brass, and the ensigns of illustrious orders coloured strings, this may be philosophically

[1] From the unpublished MS.
[2] It appears that Lady Mary had permitted the Count Palazzo to accompany her to Mantua and Padua, though she had discovered his real character. On returning from Venice to the house she had taken at Padua, she heard that the Count was living there. She sent him word that she did not keep an inn, whereupon he went back to Gottolengo.

true, but would be very ill received. We have all our playthings; happy are they that can be contented with those they obtain."

The exile often complained that she had lost all her correspondents, owing to the uncertainty of the post, and indeed for all this period her only letters seem to be those from her husband and daughter, with the exception of one long epistle from a Miss Wilhelmina Tichborne, dated 25th July 1757, which may be quoted in full—

"MADAM,[1]—I should appear to myself as well as to your Ladyship still more unworthy of the honor you have done me, if I could neglect even for a day, to return my thanks for it, and yet 'tis certain that I should never dare to do so otherwise than by Mr. B——, but from the persuasion that the great superiority your Ladyship has over every other correspondant must have taught you long ago, to read their letters with indulgence. Severity more commonly belongs to superficial judgement than to the perfection of it; and I am too much flattered by your permission to address you to let even my fears prevent my doing so. Your Ladyship is at too great a distance to have known (except by letters which tell them imperfectly) the numerous changes that have happened in our ministerial affairs;[2] Three or four different parties with each their separate views, have long been trying to prevail against each other, and fit themselves in the great employment. The world was prepared for seeing victory declared on the side of any one of them; but nothing could be more astonishing than their all coming in together, which is now the case, and though their professions have been exactly opposite while they were out, they now undertake to agree in everything. It put me in mind of a friend of mine who had a large family of favorite animals; and not knowing how to convey them to his country house in separate equipages, he ordered a Dutch mastiff, a cat and her kittens, a monkey and parrot to be packed together in one large hamper, and sent by a waggon. One may easily

---

[1] From the unpublished MS.
[2] The formation of a coalition ministry, which included such opposing elements as Newcastle, Pitt, Fox, and Temple.

guess how this set of company made their journey;[1] and I have never been able to think of the present compound Ministry without the idea of barking, scratching and screaming. 'Tis too ridiculous a one (I own) for the gravity of their characters, and still more for the situation this Kingdom is in; for as much as one may encourage the tone of laughter, 'tis impossible to be indifferent to the interests of the Country one lives in. Never could this or any other have given a more ample field for wit than we have lately; never were more attempts, nor never with so little success. Drawing pictures on cards in caricature has been the fashionable humour for which (if one could be obliged at all) it would be to the hand rather than the head of the author; for nothing surely can be lower than to ridicule the nose of a man because his heart is corrupt, or his genius insufficient for the place he fills. At this time of year everybody is dispersed, and very little private news is talked of; the quarrels of the young married couples have supplied all the conversation. The Duke and Duchess of Richmond[2] have had several in publick, though they have been married but a few months; their tempers do not suit, and time is not the remedy for that, though for everything else; so 'tis probable they will not continue long together. Lord and Lady Coventry[3] have used themselves and the town to their disputes; they can never live long without them, but are likely always to make them up; for though her indiscretion gives sufficient cause for resentment, her great good humour hinders it from lasting. Lady Harrington[4] would indeed have some merit if even her grief for her father was affected, but I give her the credit of being sincere in this, as she has never taken the trouble to impose on the world in anything. He was a very indulgent parent, but showed his fondness with so little judgment, that he ruined all his children except Lady

---

[1] Lady Mary quotes this anecdote in one of her own letters.

[2] Charles, third Duke of Richmond, married Mary, daughter of Lord Ailesbury, in April 1757.

[3] George, sixth Earl of Coventry, married Maria, the eldest of the two Miss Gunnings, in 1752. She died in 1760.

[4] The second Earl of Harrington married (in 1746) Caroline, eldest daughter of Charles, second Duke of Grafton. She was a very rapid lady, whose name frequently appears in the scandalous chronicles of Horace Walpole.

Hertford,[1] whose natural reserve and humility were not to be got the better of. He was certainly the proper ornament for a Court, and the more so for having only an outside. There was one line in your Ladyship's letter that mortified me, which was an excuse for its length; how then can I be forgiven for presuming to take up so much of your time, which could be employed in giving pleasure to others? Yet I should have been tempted to transgress still further if my little retirement would have furnished anything entertaining; for I am far from thinking that trifles may not be so, particularly to those at a distance. Lord and Lady Cardigan[2] pass a good deal of time here in the house that belonged to the late Duke of Montagu, and seem to be fond of it. I much regret that those days which your Ladyship calls the happiest of your life are over; for if they were still to be passed here, I might have some chance for the honour of knowing a person, to whom I can only now at a distance profess that I am, Madam, your Ladyship's most obliged and obedient Servant,

"WILHELMINA TICHBORNE

"We live in daily expectation of the news of battles. May I hope for the continuance of the happiness your Ladyship has given me.

"Black Heath, 25th July 1757."

Lady Mary continued to take a keen interest in the character and prospects of her grand-daughter. In the autumn of 1757 her namesake, Lady Mary Stuart, was presented, and there seems to have been a rumour that she was going to marry Lord Elgin. On 12th April 1758 Lady Mary writes to Lady Bute—

"The last newspapers informed me Lord Elgin[3] is likely to be one of your family, which I am very glad to

---

[1] Isabella, second daughter of Charles, Duke of Grafton, married Francis Seymour Conway, first Marquess of Hertford.

[2] George, first Earl of Cardigan, married Lady Mary's kinswoman, the third daughter and co-heir of John, Duke of Montagu. Lord Cardigan, who assumed the surname of Montagu on the death of his father-in-law, was created Duke of Montagu in 1776.

[3] Charles, fourth Earl of Elgin and third Earl of Ailesbury. He was married three times, but Lady Mary Stuart became the wife of the first Earl of Lonsdale.

hear. I have seen no young man more proper to adorn a Court, having an agreeable figure, with a large proportion of good humour and good breeding. I do not doubt you have had good success in presenting *our* daughter to the Princess. I can judge of your anxiety by what I felt on the same occasion. I had the pleasure to hear you universally commended, and believe to this day you deserv'd it. I flatter myself I shall find an opportunity this Ascension to send you a pacquet; hitherto I have had none since Mr. Anderson left. I wish you could find some way of serving that honest man, but I suppose I need not commend it to you whenever it is in your power. . . ."

Though she was aware that nothing could be more imprudent than undertaking the management of another woman's child, Lady Mary often wished that her daughter would spare her one of her many girls. She was convinced that if she had carried six daughters abroad with her she could have disposed of them all advantageously.

"The winter I passed at Rome," she continues, "there was an unusual concourse of English, many of them with great estates, and their own masters. As they had no admittance to the Roman ladies, nor understood the language, they had no way of passing their evenings but in my apartment, where I had always a full drawing-room. Their governors encouraged their assiduities as much as they could, finding I gave them lessons of economy and good conduct; and my authority was so great, it was a common threat amongst them, 'I'll tell Lady Mary what you say.' I was judge of all their disputes, and my decisions always submitted to. While I stayed, there was neither gaming, drinking, quarrelling, nor keeping. The Abbé Grant[1] (a very honest, good-natured North Briton, who has resided several years at Rome) was so much amazed at this uncommon regularity, he would have made me believe I was bound in conscience to pass my life there for the good of my countrymen."

[1] Peter Grant (d. 1784), a Scotch Roman Catholic, educated at the Scotch College at Rome. In 1737, after the murder of the Roman agent, Stuart, Grant was appointed to fill that post. He became very popular with British travellers, and was a great favourite of Clement XI.

The letters from Venice during this period are full of complaints of persecutions suffered from the British Resident, John Murray, and it is evident that the writer thinks Lord Bute, or one of his political friends, might have given Mr. Murray a hint to mend his manners. In May 1758 Sir James Stuart of Coltness and his wife Lady Frances (*née* Wemyss) arrived in Venice. Sir James, who had assumed the name of Denham in 1733, had taken a prominent part in the rising of 1745, and was excepted by name from the Act of Oblivion in 1747. He had spent nearly twenty years on the Continent, his chief study being Political Economy. He was permitted to return to his native country in 1763, partly, it would appear, through Lady Mary's influence with Lord Bute, and in 1767 he published his most considerable work, *Inquiry into the Principles of Political Economy.*

Sir James' name and literary reputation attracted Lady Mary's attention, tired as she was of "boys and governors," and she hastened to wait upon the new arrivals. "I was charmed to find," she tells Lady Bute (13th May), "a man of uncommon sense and learning, and a lady that without beauty is more amiable than the fairest of her sex. I offered them all the little good offices in my power, and invited them to supper; upon which our wise minister has discovered that I am in the interests of Popery and slavery. As he has often said the same thing of Mr. Pitt, it would give me no mortification, if I did not apprehend that his fertile imagination may support this wise idea by such circumstances as may influence those who do not know me."

The annoyance from Murray, and the stories that he was alleged to circulate against her, induced Lady Mary to retire to Padua for the summer. She tells her daughter that he has propagated the scandal that "your nurse left her estate, husband and family to go with me to England, and then I turned her out to starve after defrauding her of God knows what. I thank God witches are out of fashion, or I should expect to have it deposed, by several credible witnesses, that I had been seen flying through the air on a broomstick."

Though willing that her wrongs should come to the ears of Mr. Pitt, she urges Lady Bute not to tell Mr. Wortley these foolish squabbles, adding: "It is the only thing I would keep from his knowledge. I am apprehensive he should imagine some misplaced raillery or vivacity of mine has drawn on me these ridiculous persecutions. 'Tis really incredible they should be carried to such a height without the least provocation." She begins to be of opinion that the surest way of preserving reputation and having powerful protectors is by being openly profligate and scandalous. "I will not be so censorious as to take examples from my own sex," she writes. "But you see Doctor Swift, who set at defiance all decency, truth or reason, had a crowd of admirers, and at their head the virtuous and ingenious Earl of Orrery, the polite and learned Mr. Greville, with a number of ladies of fine taste and unblemished character; while the Bishop of Salisbury (Burnet I mean), the most indulgent parent, the most generous churchman, and the most zealous assertor of the rights and liberties of his country, was all his life defamed and vilified, and after his death barbarously calumniated, for having had the courage to write a history without flattery. I knew him in my very early youth, and his condescension in directing a girl in her studies is an obligation I can never forget."

CHAPTER XLIX

LETTERS FROM VENICE

DURING her retirement at Padua Lady Mary amused herself with reading, riding, walking, and writing the history of her own time.

"It has been my fortune," she observes, "to have more exact knowledge both of the persons and facts that have made the greatest figure in England in this age, than is common; and I take pleasure in putting together what I know, with an impartiality that is altogether unusual. Distance of time and place has totally blotted from my mind all traces either of resentment or prejudice; and I speak with the same indifference of the court of G. B. [Great Britain] as I should do of that of Augustus Cæsar. I hope you have not so ill an opinion of me as to think I am turning author in my old age. I can assure you I regularly burn every quire as soon as it is finished, and mean nothing more than to divert my solitary hours."[1]

About this time Lady Mary began a correspondence with Sir James Steuart, which continued until her death, but these letters, with which she evidently took great pains, are for the most part dull and laboured. Here and there, however, her sarcastic humour flashes out, as in her remarks on the conduct of the "heroic countess," Lady Orford, whose amusements were worthy of the generosity of a great soul.

"If I really was so skilled in magic as I am generally

[1] The autobiographical fragment printed in the early part of this work may have been written at this time. It is unfortunate that so few sheets escaped the fire. Lady Mary's history of her own time would have been neither accurate nor impartial (in spite of her boast), but it would certainly have been amusing.

supposed," she observes, "I would immediately follow her footsteps in the figure of fair fifteen, acknowledge the errors of my past life, and beg her instructions how to behave to that tyrannical sex, who with absurd cruelty first put the invaluable deposit of their precious honour in our hands, and then oblige us to prove a negative for the preservation of it. I hate mankind with all the fury of an old maid (indeed, most women of my age do), and have no real esteem but for those heroines who give them as good as they bring."

The end of 1758 was marked by a humiliating and annoying incident, which our heroine was persuaded could never have happened to anybody but herself.

"Some few months before Lord William Hamilton married," so runs her tale, "there appeared a foolish song, said to be wrote by a poetical great lady,[1] who I really think was the character of Lady Arabella in the *Female Quixote*[2] (without the beauty): you may imagine such a conduct at Court made her superlatively ridiculous. Lady Delawarr,[3] a woman of great merit, with whom I lived in much intimacy, showed this fine performance to me: we were very merry in supposing what answer Lord William would make to these passionate addresses; she begged me to say something for a poor man who had nothing to say for himself. I wrote *extempore* on the back of the song, some stanzas that went perfectly well to the time. She promised they should never appear as mine, and faithfully kept her word. By what accident they have fallen into the hands of that thing Dodsley, I know not, but he has printed them as addressed by me to a very contemptible puppy,[4] and my own words as his answer. I do not believe either Job or Socrates ever had such a provocation."

In the sixth volume of Dodsley's *Collection of Poems*, published in 1756, the two sets of verses are published with the headings respectively of "Lady Mary W*** to Sir W*** Y***, and Sir W*** Y***'s Answer." The first set, written

---

[1] Lady Hertford, afterwards Duchess of Somerset.
[2] Mrs. Lennox' novel.
[3] Charlotte, first wife of the seventh Lord Delawarr. She was a daughter of Lord Clancarty.
[4] Sir William Yonge.

by Lady Hertford, contains an avowal of love to Lord William, beginning—

"Dear Colin, prevent my warm blushes,
　Since how can I speak without pain?
My eyes oft have told you my wishes,
　Why don't you their meaning explain?"

There are five verses in the same strain. The answer, written for Lord William by Lady Mary, runs as follows—

"Good Madam, when ladies are willing,
　A man must needs look like a fool;
For me I would not give a shilling
　For one who would love out of rule.

You should leave us to guess by your blushing,
　And not speak the matter so plain:
'Tis ours to write and be pushing,
　'Tis yours to affect a disdain.

That you're in a terrible taking,
　By all these sweet oglings I see;
But the fruit that can fall without shaking
　Indeed is too mellow for me."

For 7th March 1759 there is a letter to Lady Bute, which was hastily written in order that it might be entrusted to the care of an English gentleman, Mr. Gregory, who was just leaving for England.

"I [1] believe you will think it very odd," remarks the writer, "that he has been here this fortnight without my hearing of it, but our politick Resident is so very ministerial that he makes it a point to hinder all commerce (as far as he can) amongst the English, excepting in his own house. I could tell you several very pleasant stories if the subject was not too low for entertainment.

"Your description of London gives me no envy of the young and gay, who seem undistinguished from old women. Cards was formerly the refuge of age and wrinkles, and it was the mark of a prude when a young lady passed her time at Quadrille. I am very happy in Mrs. Wright's conversation, who (notwithstanding her youth) seems pleased with mine. I have some Venetian acquaintance very agreeable, and in

[1] From the unpublished MS.

general make a shift to slide along the day without the necessity of paying for a seat in Assemblies. This Carnival has been particularly brilliant from the promotion of Procurators and Cardinals which are always accompanyed with much pageantry and very fine Balls. You will wonder to hear I have had my share of them, but I could not well avoid the invitations of my friends, and the privilege of masking made it not disagreeable to me. The magnificence has been beyond anything you ever saw; I know no people exceed the Venetians with splendour. The entry of the new Patriarch made me wish extremely that my grand-daughters had been amongst the spectators. . . ."

Among the books that were sent out to Venice in this year was Swift's *History of the last four years of the Reign of Queen Anne*, which was published in 1758, just thirteen years after the author's death. Lady Mary wrote to her husband to ask his opinion of the book, since some of the facts were evidently false, and others partially represented. He replied on 29th December 1759—

". . . The [1] weakness of my eyes, which grows worse and worse, puts me in mind of Lady Ferrers,[2] who has been quite blind for some years, and my aunt, Lady Catherine,[3] who was blind several years before her death. She had read a good deal before her blindness came on.

" Besides the saving my eyes, I have another reason which makes me much less willing to send a letter abroad. It is first opened in England, then by post-offices abroad, both by friends and enemies, who all want to get intelligence. And by the skill of their decipherers, they can put almost any construction upon the most insignificant words.

" I don't remember particularly at present what Swift, whom you mention, has written about the four last years of Queen Anne, but I know that I thought it not worth remembering, and filled with false facts as well as my Lord Bolingbroke's works. Probably Swift was not thought of consequence enough

---

[1] From the unpublished MS.
[2] The Montagus were connected, apparently, with the Shirleys of Tamworth. Sir Robert Shirley was created Earl Ferrers in 1711.
[3] Lady Catherine Bacon (*née* Montagu), mother of Montagu Bacon.

to be let into the true account of things, but only such as my Lord Oxford desired to have published. . . ."

Lady Mary, like all people who find their chief solace in reading and writing, had an intense dread of blindness. " That evil," she says in one of her letters to Sir James Steuart, " is of so horrid a nature, I own I feel no philosophy that could support me under it, and no mountain girl ever trembled more at one of Whitfield's pathetic lectures than I do at the word blindness, though I know all the fine things that may be said for consolation in such a case: but I know also that they would not operate on my constitution."

Early in 1760 she replied to her husband's letter about his decayed sight in more than usually sympathetic terms: " Having [1] had no opportunity of writing by a private hand till now, I have delayed some time answering your last letter, which touched me more than I am either able or willing to express. I hope your apprehensions of blindness are not confirmed by any fresh symptoms of that terrible misfortune. If I could be of any service to you on that, or any other occasion, I shall think my last remains of life well employed.

" I am sorry to mention a person that we can neither of us remember with pleasure.[2] He sent me lately a very sorry book, printed in his name, but no letter or direction to write to him, which I am very glad excuses me from that trouble."

The above note was enclosed in a letter to Lady Bute, in which Lady Mary says—

" I [1] believe I shall not write you many more letters. The vexations I have here will hasten the end of all vexations, and I shall have no regret in leaving a world I have long been weary of, but the apprehension that it will be a real misfortune to you. I received a letter from your Father last post that cuts my heart. He says he has great reason to fear blindness. A few days before, I received from an unknown hand, without any letter of advice, a very nonsensical book, printed with your brother's name to it, which only serves to prove to me that he has private correspondencies here and that he is still a Knavish Fool. This is no news to me; I have

[1] From the unpublished MS.   [2] Their son.

long wept the misfortune of being mother to such an animal. This is a nice subject to speak of to you, and what I never touched before, but I think I ought now to explain all my thoughts to you. You are now of an age more able to give me advice, than I am to direct, being in that time of life when the mind is in the greatest vigour. If your Father should fall into the hands of servants (as all blind people must necessarily do), how far he may be imposed on I tremble to think. I know by experience how magnificent your Brother can be in his promises, and tho' I was never moved by them, you may see daily examples of mercenary tempers in those of much higher rank than domestics. I dare not say more; I hope I say enough to be understood. I have the most perfect confidence in Mr. W.'s probity and the highest opinion of his understanding—yet—'tis possible—— I have no view of my own in what I am saying; my life is so near a conclusion, that where or how I pass it (if innocently) is almost indifferent to me. I have outlived the greatest part of my acquaintance, and to say truth, a return to crowd and bustle after my long retirement would be disagreeable to me; yet if I could be of use either to your Father or your Family, I would venture shortening the insignificant days of your most affec^{te} Mother,

"M. WORTLEY"

"12*th February*.—I have wrote the enclosed to your Father. You are more able to judge than myself, if it is proper to be given him. I only mean what appears to me right; if he should misunderstand it, it would be the highest affliction to me and a real injury to yourself."

The "nonsensical book" alluded to above was *Reflections on the Rise and Fall of the Ancient Republicks*, published in 1759, ostensibly by Edward Wortley Montagu jun. It was supposed to have been written, either wholly or in part, by a former tutor (probably Anderson), but the fictitious interest given by so notorious a name brought it some temporary success, four editions being called for. The young man had been little heard of since his Paris adventure. There are several unpublished letters from him to Mr. Gibson, asking for money to enable him to leave Paris, where he was detained after his release by the fact that he owed a considerable sum to a banker who had stood surety for him. From 1754 till 1762 he sat in Parliament for Bossiney, a Cornish borough. Lady Mary says she received no letter of advice with the book, but among her papers is the following epistle, written apparently in answer to her acknowledgment of his work :—

"MADAM,[1]—The deep Sense I have of my past ill conduct, for which I have long felt and ever shall feel the most painful self-abhorrence, deters me from sending a letter with my book to your Ladyship. So bold a step I fear would tend to increase that just displeasure which I have so repeatedly incurred, and might have prevented you from looking into the book, which I most ardently wished you would condescend to peruse. Not that I presumed to offer it as worthy of your Ladyship's attention in any other light, than as a proof of my turn of mind and application to study; and as I judged a proof of that nature would carry a more convincing evidence of a thorough change of my way of thinking, as well as way of life, than all the assurances I could make by letter. I thank God it has in some measure had the wished for effect, as it has procured me the honour of a letter from your Ladyship; a blessing which I had the less reason to expect, as I was truly conscious how little I deserved it. I had long reflected with anguish of soul that I was in a manner cut off as an alien and an outcast from my parents; and what grieved me still more deeply was the consciousness that the blame lay wholly upon myself, and that I had nothing to plead in mitigation of what I had been guilty of. Judge then, Madam, of the joy I must feel on the receipt of your letter. It was a joy too big for utterance, and was I to inform your Ladyship of the effects it produced they would appear extravagant. I shall only assure you that no one thing ever affected me so much. Your Ladyship will see by my preface and introduction the true reason of my choice of that subject; which seemed to me the best adapted to the state of our affairs at the time both at home and abroad. How I have acquitted myself in the

[1] From the unpublished MS.

execution of my plan, I beg leave to submit to your Ladyship's greatly superior judgment. I have some years since bid a final adieu to the hurry and dissipation of a town life. My thoughts have been entirely turned upon the past, and I now labour to make all the atonement in my power for my former follies, and to form such a character as I should wish to die with. Reflections of this nature must unavoidably lead me to weigh seriously the duty I owe to God, to my country, to my parents, and to myself, and I make it my daily study to know the extent of those duties and to discharge them as far as I am able. Your Ladyship's kind wishes that my amusements may be innocent, if not useful, seem to imply a hint that I might have been happier in the choice of my subject. Would your Ladyship but honour me so far as to point out one which you judge proper, I shall gladly exert the utmost of my poor abilities on so pleasing an occasion. Accept, Madam, the sincerest wishes and prayers for your Ladyship's health which the warmest duty and gratitude can inspire; for I had so often abused your goodness, that till now I despaired of regaining that maternal affection which will be the chief happiness of my life. Encouraged, therefore, by this fresh instance of your goodness, I take the liberty to send the second edition of my book (which I have corrected) as some proof of the indulgence with which it was received by the publick. I cannot leave off without informing your Ladyship of the deep sense I have of my Father's goodness, who has been pleased to place me in the present, and assure me of a seat in the next Parliament; in which, as well as in every other station of life, it is the highest object of my ambition to appear in a character worthy of your son, and to support which shall be the constant study of, Madam, your Ladyship's for evermore most dutiful son and faithful servant,

"ED. WORTLEY MONTAGU"

CHAPTER L

DEATH OF MR. WORTLEY

ON 25th October 1760 George II. died, and on 18th November Lady Mary wrote to thank her daughter for sending her early information of the event. "I do not doubt," she says, "you are sufficiently tormented by pretensions and petitions. I hope you will not forget poor Mr. Anderson, and I desire Lord Bute to take care that Sir James Steuart's name is not excluded in the Act of Indemnity. This is a very small favour, yet it will make the happiness of a man of great merit. . . . I bless God I have lived to see you so well established, and am ready to sing my *Nunc Dimittis* with pleasure."

On 1st January 1761 Mr. Wortley died, and was buried in the chapel at Wortley. A memorial tablet was put up to his memory some years later by Lady Bute, which contains the following inscription—.

"In a vault near this place lie the remains of Edward Wortley, Esq., born 8th February 1678; he departed this life 1st January 1761. He was the son of Sidney Montagu, the son of Edward, the first Earl of Sandwich, by Anne, daughter and heir of Sir Francis Wortley, Bart. He married the Lady Mary Pierrepont, eldest daughter of Evelyn, Duke of Kingston. In his earlier years he held considerable public employments, and through his life preserved the strictest regard to honour and integrity. This inscription is placed here by his grateful daughter and sole heir, Mary Wortley, Countess of Bute and Baroness Mountstuart of Wortley."

Mr. Wortley, unlike his wife and son, has not been honoured with a niche in the Biographical Dictionaries. His abilities, of which his contemporaries spoke highly, can only now be judged by his letters and speeches. One curious literary attempt is preserved among his papers, namely, a number of "Maxims after the manner of Mons. de la Rochefoucauld," which were written at Tonbridge, 7th July 1729. It cannot be said that these are very brilliant specimens. For example—

"(1) Wit[1] is an entertaining sentiment well expressed.

"(2) We are all as witty as we are judicious; but we show our wit only in proportion to our knowledge and vivacity.

"(12) As hard as it may be to cure a strong passion without success, it is far more difficult to preserve one long for a person to whom there is a constant and easy access.

"(14) Our constant and steady pursuit should be our ease. Pleasure flies from us when much pursued. But an easy mind is never long without pleasure.

"(23) Frugality is the daughter of prudence and the mother of generosity.

"(25) In a proposal of marriage, a man's prudence should be inserted in the particulars of his estate."[2]

Writing to Sir Horace Mann on 27th January 1761, Horace Walpole says that he is sending out two sets of the *Royal and Noble Authors*, one for Mann and the other for Lady Mary.[3] "The set for Lady Mary," he continues, "will probably arrive too late, as her husband is dead, and she will now probably return to England. I pity Lady Bute: her mother will sell to whoever does not know her, all kinds of promises and reversions, bestow lies gratis and wholesale, and make so

---

[1] From the unpublished MS.

[2] Lord Stanhope says that Mr. Wortley appears to have combined very moderate talents with most overweening vanity, and adds: "It is asserted that there still exists in MS. a speech of his which he intended to read from his hat. It has certain notable hints for the delivery carefully arranged along the margin, such as, 'Here pause a minute,' 'look round,' 'low,' 'loud,' 'cough.'"

[3] Lady Mary had more than once asked her daughter to send her a copy of this book, and mentions that Mr. Walpole had been very civil to her at Florence.

much mischief that they will be forced to discard her in three months, and that will go to my Lady Bute's heart, who is one of the best and most sensible women in the world; and who, educated by such a mother, or rather with no education, has never made a false step. Old Avidien, the father, is dead, worth half a million. To his son, on whom six hundred a year was settled, the reversion of which he has sold, he gives £1000 a year for life, but not to descend to any children he may have by any of his many wives. To Lady Mary, in lieu of dower, but which to be sure she will not accept, instead of the thirds of such a fortune, £1200 a year; and after her to their son for life; and then the £1200 and the £1000 to Lady Bute and her second son; with £2000 to each of the younger children; all the rest, in present, to Lady Bute, then to her second son, taking the name of Wortley, and in succession to all the rest of her children, which are numerous; and after them to Lord Sandwich, to whom, in present, he leaves about £4000.[1] . . . Admiral Forbes told me yesterday, that in one of Lady Mary's jaunts to or from Genoa, she begged a passage of Commodore Barnard. A storm threatening, he prepared her for it, but assured her there was no danger. She said she was not afraid, and going into a part of the gallery not much adapted to heroism, she wrote these lines on the side—

> 'Mistaken seaman, mark my dauntless mind,
> Who, wrecked on shore, am fearless of the wind.'

On landing, this magnanimous dame desired the commander to accept a ring: he wore it as a fine emerald, but being overpersuaded to have it unset before his face, it proved a bit of glass."

On 2nd February Horace asks George Montagu, "Have you heard what immense riches old Wortley has left? One million three hundred and fifty thousand pounds. It is all to centre in Lady Bute; her husband is one of fortune's prodigies." And again, on 17th August, he informs Mann

---

[1] These details must be taken as only approximately correct. Lord Wharncliffe says that if Edward Wortley Montagu, junior, had had a legitimate son, the child would have inherited the Wortley estates.

that "The great prince of the coal-pits, Sir James Lowther,[1] marries the eldest infanta of the adjoining coal-pits, Lord Bute's daughter. You will allow this Earl is a fortunate man; the late King, old Wortley, and the Duke of Argyle, all dying in a year, and his daughter married to such an immense fortune! He certainly behaves with great moderation, and nobody has had reason to complain of him."

The following extracts are from letters written by Lady Mary to her daughter between the dates of her husband's death and her departure from Venice in September 1761:—

"You[2] will be surprised to hear I have only finished the reading of the will this morning, the 5th of March 1761. I think your brother has far more than he deserves. I wish I had been left mourning, being out of cash at present, which, if I had not been, I had begun my journey, thinking it my duty to risk my life, if I can contribute to the due execution of your honoured Father's will and testament. You must not offer to compound with your brother, if you take my advice. His grandfather Sidney had only an annuity for life of £500 from his family. He had an eldest son, Francis Wortley, Esq., on whom I believe the Wortley estate (I mean only the Manor of Wortley and woods) was entailed. He died unmarried, and the estate came by law to your late respected Father. All the rest are acquired by him, by true and lawful purchase. My head is too bad to be prolix. . . ."

"11th March 1761.

"MY DEAR CHILD,[3]—My health is a little mended, very little God knows. I have in a great degree lost my sleep and appetite. What I most dreaded (the greatest part of my life) has now happened. I never thought to survive your (ever honored) Father, and was perfectly persuaded, I should see my Family torn to pieces and myself involved in difficulties very hard to struggle with at my time of life. I desire nothing but peace and retirement. I have catalogues of the books, household stuff and plate given me by your Father

---

[1] Afterwards Earl of Lonsdale.   [2] From the unpublished MS.

when I left England. I believe you would not counsel me to authenticate the Will in such a manner as to deprive me of the benefit, tho' perhaps they are of little use, the witnesses being (it may be) all dead. Adieu, my dear Child. I conclude with Mr. Earle's[1] toast, God bless you whatever becomes of me. . . ."

"*3rd April* 1761.

"I[2] made my Will last Wednesday, which is witnessed by Lord Torrington, Mr. Horten James, Mr. Wytton and Mr. Jennings, all the English gentlemen who are now at Venice. I have had no lawyer to assist me, yet as it is wrote by my own hand, I think it is so worded as to admit of no dispute. You will laugh (perhaps) at so much caution about a trifle, yet I confess I am weak enough to be solicitous about it. I think Lord Bute behaves very generously to your Brother; I fear there is little gratitude to be expected. If I live to September, I intend to set out for England. You need not apprehend my being troublesome by solicitations; I have only two engagements, something for poor Mr. Anderson, who I think has suffered by his attachment to an unworthy pupil, and your indemnity of S^{ir} J. Stewart, who I think a very deserving man. I can say on my deathbed I have had clean hands, never having taken (in any shape) either premium or gratification for any service that I have rendered to any of my acquaintance or supposed friends.

"I congratulate you on the return of Lord Marischal,[3] who is (in my opinion) a truly worthy and agreeable companion. Mr. Mackensie[4] has sent me the pacquet to which I imagine you have already an answer. I received in it a letter from

---

[1] Giles Earle (? 1678–1758). He was a great friend of Sir Robert Walpole's, and was considered a wit. He was a Lord of the Treasury from 1737 to 1742, and held other places. Lady Mary quotes his toast more than once.

[2] From the unpublished MS.

[3] George Keith, tenth Earl Marischal (1693?–1778). He had been attainted for taking part in the Jacobite Rebellion in 1715. He retired to the Continent, and became a favourite of the King of Prussia, who sent him as Ambassador to the Court of France, and later to that of Spain. He was pardoned by George II. in 1759, and permitted to hold property in England. He returned to Berlin in 1764, at the request of Frederick, and died at Potsdam at the age of eighty-six.

[4] Brother of Lord Bute.

will. There are many other things in his epistle that I do not understand, and consequently have made no return to it. I have wrote to Mr. Anderson to desire him to advise his pupil to give you no trouble, and to rest contented with the ample provision bequeathed him. I hope you have no other impediment to writing, but the flurry which is natural to your situation. I beg you would suspend your pleasures or business one quarter of an hour, to give satisfaction to an affectionate Mother. I delay the preparations for my journey, till I hear from you. I would willingly put all my little affairs into your management, having the most entire dependance on your discretion and good will towards me, tho' I own I am sometimes weak enough to be moved at the reports set about amongst the English here by M. and Comp. The truth is, I can expect neither advice nor assistance from any one; I seldom see the young travellers, and if I did, there are few of them that I would consult on any subject whatever. I ought to distinguish Mr. Pitt,[1] who appears to me a youth of uncommon understanding, and such as I wish my Lord Mount Stewart. He set out for Rome last week. I am too low spirited to write a long letter; I will only once more repeat that I expect no comfort but from you. You have at least three daughters that may write in your name, if your affairs allow you not time to do it with your own hand. May you ever be happy whatever becomes of your unfortunate mother. . . ."

" MY DEAREST CHILD,[2]—I do not love to break the most trifling promise, and would willingly write every post, but my eyes are now so bad, I can hardly see to read. The fine gentleman may defame and even break an indulgent mother's heart, but shall never make her guilty of hurting an innocent daughter and a worthy son-in-law. You would not wonder at my writing mysteriously if you knew all, but I (for your sake) don't tell you all that passes here. When I can get a safe conveyance, you shall know my heart as clear to

---

[1] Probably the son of George Pitt, afterwards Lord Rivers, whom Lady Mary had admired (according to H. Walpole) twenty years before.
[2] From the unpublished MS.

you as it has ever been. God send us a happy meeting. I wish you joy of a L. H. C.,[1] who I believe as strictly just as any ever graced the Bench, not excepting Sir T. M.,[2] who died a martyr. I would write to W. if my head permitted; perhaps it is better let alone in the present circumstances. I know all will be told you of my great avarice, etc. You ought to know me better."

[1] Lord High Chancellor. He was Lord Henley.
[2] Sir Thomas More.

CHAPTER LI

RETURN TO ENGLAND

AS soon as she received the news of her husband's death, Lady Mary seems to have made up her mind to return to England, and her prompt decision gives some colour to the theory that it was her relations with Mr. Wortley that had kept her in exile. Be that as it may, it was natural that she should desire to see her daughter and her grandchildren before she died, and she may already have been aware that her health was failing. On 1st September 1761 she began her homeward journey, taking the route through Germany and Holland, instead of the easier one through France, with which country we were again at war. On October the 1st she had only reached Augsburg, whence she wrote to Sir James and Lady Francis Steuart that she hoped to meet them in Holland. The journey was both dangerous and exhausting owing to the disturbed state of the country, and Lady Mary was detained at Rotterdam by the severe illness of her maid, who had been broken down by the perils and fatigues that she had endured on the way. Her mistress was made of sterner stuff.

"I am dragging my ragged remnant of life to England," she wrote to Sir James on 20th November. "The wind and the tide are against me; how far I have strength to struggle against both, I know not; that I am arrived here is as much a miracle as any in the golden legend, and if I had foreseen half the difficulties I have met with, I should not certainly have had courage to undertake it."

On the next day she wrote to Lady Bute—

"I[1] received your welcome letter of the 13th instant last

[1] From the unpublished MS.

night. You need not doubt I shall make all the haste I can to embrace you, which has been long the desire of my life, as you very well know. I have so far forgot Great George Street, I do not remember I ever saw it. I hope you have taken the house only for one year certain, or that it is such I may easily let, if the air should not agree with me. I heartily wish you may close my eyes, but to say truth, I would not have it happen immediately, and should be glad to see my other grand-daughters as happily married as Lady Mary. I hope you have my letter in which I wished her and you joy of so advantageous a match. I am told here that Lady Jane is also disposed of; I may perhaps not be at her wedding, but I flatter myself with the view of seeing Lady Anne's. Forgive this old woman's tattle, as one of the many weaknesses you will see in your most affec[t] mother, M. WORTLEY "

" I do not wonder you know nothing of the insolence of Custom House Officers. I have been so frighted with them, that I dread their name, tho' I once more solemnly assure you neither I nor my servants have any contreband. I have not learnt the art of smuggling from our worthy Minister at Venice, nor ever try'd to attempt it: yet the D[uke] of Devonshire can tell you from what distress he rescued me at the gates of Turin, where I verily believe I had died if Mr. Villette had been as little instructed in his duty as I have since found M[urray]. I design to come up the river if I can find a vessel that takes that route. I repeat once more, God send us a happy meeting, notwithstanding the lies that have been told (I believe) to us both with the impious design of setting us at variance. They have had no effect on me otherwise than making me more impatient to see you. I think I know your heart. I shall without reserve tell you what is in mine."

Lady Mary was detained at Rotterdam for nearly two months. During this period she made the acquaintance of the English chaplain, Mr. Sowden, to whom she gave one of the manuscript copies of her Letters from Constantinople. By 12th December her maid was well enough to travel, but then a hard, impenetrable frost hindered the voyage. Towards the end of

December she actually sailed for England, but as usual played the part of a Jonah on board. The captain was forced to return to harbour, owing to the mountainous sea that obstructed the passage. A second attempt was made a few days later, and early in January the traveller arrived in London, where Lady Bute had hired a small furnished "harpsichord" house for her in Great George Street.[1] After her spacious Italian palaces these new quarters must have seemed cramped indeed, but Lady Mary accommodated herself to circumstances, and jokingly declared that she was very comfortably lodged, with two closets and a cupboard on each floor.

Horace Walpole was one of the earliest callers at the little house in Great George Street, and on 29th January he wrote the following account of his visit to Sir Horace Mann:—

"I went last night to visit her [Lady Mary]; I give you my honour, and you who know her would credit me without it, the following is a faithful description. I found her in a little miserable bed-chamber of a ready-furnished house, with two tallow candles, and a bureau covered with pots and pans. On her head, in full of all accounts, she had an old black-laced hood, wrapped entirely round, so as to conceal all hair or want of hair. No handkerchief, but up to her chin a kind of horseman's riding-coat, calling itself a *pet en l'air*, made of a dark-green (green I think it had been) brocade, with coloured and silver flowers, and lined with furs; boddice laced, a foul dimity petticoat sprig'd, velvet muffeteens on her arms, grey stockings and slippers. Her face less changed in twenty years than I could have imagined; I told her so, and she was not so tolerable twenty years ago that she need have taken it for flattery, but she did, and literally gave me a box on the ear. She is very lively, all her senses perfect, her languages as imperfect as ever, her avarice greater. She entertained me at first with nothing but the dearness of provisions at Helvoet. With nothing but an Italian, a French, and a Prussian, all men servants, and something she calls an *old* secretary, but whose age, till he appears, will be doubtful, she receives all the world, who go to homage her as Queen Mother, and crams them into this kennel. The Duchess of Hamilton, who came

---

[1] Lord Bute then had a house in South Audley Street.

in just after me, was so astonished and diverted, that she could not speak to her for laughing. She says that she has left all her clothes at Venice. I really pity Lady Bute; what will the progress be of such a commencement!"

This compassion was wasted, as Horace himself admits in a letter written a couple of months later. He has just been meeting Lady Mary at a party at Bedford House. She was then dressed in yellow velvet and sables, with a decent laced head and a black hood, almost like a veil over her face. "She is much more discreet than I expected," says the gossip, "and meddles with nothing — but she is wofully tedious in her narrations."

Another early visitor was Mrs. Edward Montagu, the Blue-Stocking, who has also recorded her impression of her kinswoman by marriage. Writing to her sister-in-law at Naples on 16th February, she says—

"You have lately returned to us from Italy a very extraordinary personage, Lady Mary Wortley. When Nature is at the trouble of making a very singular person, Time does right in respecting it. Medals are preserved when common coin is worn out; and as great geniuses are rather matters of curiosity than of art, this lady seems reserved to be a wonder for more than one generation. She does not look older than when she went abroad, has more than the vivacity of fifteen, and a memory which perhaps is unique. Several people visited her out of curiosity, which she did not like. I visited her because her cousin and mine were cousins german. Tho' she had not any foolish partiality for her husband or his relations, I was very graciously received, and you may imagine entertained by one who neither thinks, speaks, acts nor dresses like anybody else. Her *domestick* is made up of all nations, and when you get into her drawing-room you imagine you are in the first storey of the Tower of Babel. An Hungarian servant takes your name at the door: he gives it to an Italian, who delivers it to a Frenchman, the Frenchman to a Swiss, and the Swiss to a Polander; so that by the time you get to your ladyship's presence you have changed your name five times without an Act of Parliament."

Lady Mary's last months were embittered by the behaviour of her son. Besides entering a false caveat to his father's will, he seems to have issued forgeries in his mother's name, and calumniated her in various ways. On 16th March 1762 she writes to him in the following uncompromising terms:—

"SON,[1]—I know not how to write to you, and scarcely what to say. Your present conduct is far more infamous than the past: it is a small sign of reformation of manners when you durst attempt to disturb an indulgent (too indulgent) Father's dying pangs on mercenary considerations; and are now defaming a too fond mother by the most impudent forgery. I think no single man deserves bread that cannot live decently and honourably on £1600 per annum rent-charge: I lived on less than half that sum with your worthy Father when you was born, and some time after, without ever borrowing or raising money on contingencies, or even on certainties, which was in some measure our case. I can add no more; you have shortened your Father's days, and will perhaps have the glory to break your Mother's heart. I will not curse you—God give you a real, not an affected repentance.   M. W. MONTAGU

"You say you know Venice; I am sorry to say Venice knows you, and I know all your criminal extravagances."

The following tragic little note in Lady Mary's handwriting is undated, and has neither beginning nor ending, but is obviously addressed to Lord Bute, and contains a further allusion to the persecutions she suffered from her son:—

"MY LORD,—I beg your pardon for this liberty I take. I really feel my head light. I swear to you (so may my soul find peace with God) I know nothing of these infamous libels

[1] An extract from this letter is published in Mr. Thomas' prefatory Memoir to Lady Mary's *Correspondence*. The remainder is from the unpublished MS.

my son has produced in my name. I dare be poor, I dare not be dishonest. I own I am weary of fighting with one hand ty'd behind. Do what you think fitting with the plate and jewels, etc. . . .

> 'To dare in fields is valour, but how few
> Dare have the real courage to be true?'"

Of Lady Mary's correspondence at this time only one other letter has been preserved. This is from a person named J. Lane, who seems to have been a humble admirer, not to say sycophant, with literary enthusiasms and aspirations. The effusion is quaint enough to be quoted in full—

"HON^D MADAM,[1]—I no sooner left your Ladyship's door than I stole a peep at your lines even in the street, as I confess desire got the better of delicacy. I trust your Ladyship's love of sincerity will pardon this offence. That transient glimpse fascinated me, and nothing but an attempt to answer would, I found, lay the *Cacoethes* which had seized me. Nothing is more true than that Poets must be born so; 'tis equally true that one real Poet, such is the Muse's enchantments, produces a thousand pretenders. Be pleased to rank me, as I truly am, in that group; that done, I am sure compassion will follow, as 'tis to your Ladyship I owe my seduction. Thus much truly prepared, I have only left to apologise for presuming to offer my poor incense at so exalted a shrine in the Republic of Belles Lettres, but the honours your Ladyship has laid upon me emboldens me to expose my weakness, and tho' the infant I present is ill favoured and scarce half made up of its due proportions, yet if it produces one smile of approbation, I shall esteem myself amply rewarded, and as all allow your Ladyship the virtues of humanity, I flatter myself your Ladyship will be so kind after a cursory review (for the enclosed is worth no more) to commit it to the flames, and forget that I ever sent that to you which the remembrance of must lessen me in your Ladyship's estimation. I cannot with truth say that it was wrote extempore, tho' nothing less can apologise for its

[1] From the unpublished MS.

imperfections. At the same time I can truly say that it was wrote before I sat down to supper. The subject ought to have been carried further, but I found myself unequal to the task. Your Ladyship's living to see your deserved darling Daughter bless'd with a numerous and hopefull progeny of nobility from a father, who is not only the most amiable of men in domesticated life, but who is now giving shining proofs of his being truly the most patriotick Minister this country was ever blessed with, are unanswerable reasons for preferring existence to annihilation—and this thought would have made a fine finish to my *petit* performances had the poesie deserved and I been equal to it. As I have put my reputation in your Ladyship's power, I trust your Ladyship will treat me with your wonted generosity, and conceal the weakness of, Madam, your all-admiring and most devoted faithful humble servant, J. LANE
" 1st *June* 1762 "

About this time it became known that Lady Mary was suffering from cancer, though she concealed her trouble as long as possible. In June she grew rapidly weaker, and on 2nd July wrote her last letter to Lady Frances Steuart. In this she says that she has been ill for a long time, and is little capable of writing, but would not pass for stupid or ungrateful in her friend's opinion. She died on 21st August at her house in Great George Street, being then in her seventy-fourth year, and was buried in Grosvenor Chapel.[1]

On 29th August Horace Walpole wrote to Mann—

"Lady Mary Wortley is dead, as I prepared you to expect. Except some trifling legacies she has given everything to Lady Bute, so we shall never know the sum—perhaps that was intended. It is given out for inconsiderable, besides some rich baubles. . . .

"[26th September.] I told you of Lady Mary's death and will, but I did not then know that, with her usual

[1] Grosvenor Chapel had a cemetery and vaults. In 1789 a cenotaph was erected to Lady Mary's memory by Mrs. Henrietta Inge in the Cathedral at Lichfield. The inscription commemorates her introduction of inoculation.

maternal tenderness, and usual generosity, she has left her son one guinea."[1]

On 3rd October he reports again: "Lady Mary Wortley has left twenty-one large volumes in prose and verse, in manuscript; nineteen are fallen to Lady Bute, and will not see the light in haste. The other two Lady Mary in her passage gave to somebody in Holland, and at her death expressed great anxiety to have them published. Her family are in terror lest they should be, and have tried to get them: hitherto the man is inflexible. Though I do not doubt but they are an olio of lies and scandal, I should like to see them. She had parts, and had seen much. Truth is often at the bottom of such compositions, and places itself here and there without the intention of the mother [? author]. I dare say, in general, these works are like Madame del Pozzo's[2] *Mémoires*. Lady Mary had more wit, and something more delicacy; their manners and morals were a good deal more alike."

In the course of the same month Mrs. Montagu wrote to her sister-in-law: "Lady Mary Wortley Montagu returned to England, as it were, to finish where she began. I wish she had given us an account of the events that filled in the space between. She had a terrible distemper; the most virulent cancer I ever heard of, which carried her off very soon. I met her at Lady Bute's in June, and she then looked well. In three weeks, at my return to London, I heard she was given over. The hemlock kept her drowsy and free from pain; and the physicians thought if it had been given early, might possibly have saved her. She left her son one guinea. He is too much of a sage to be concerned about money, I presume. When I first knew him, a rake and a beau, I did not imagine he would addict himself at one time to Rabbinical learning, and then travel all over the East, the great Itinerant Savant of the World. One has read that the believers in the trans-

[1] A proof of Lady Mary's talent for doing the wrong thing may be seen in this legacy. It would have been so much simpler and more dignified to have left her son nothing at all.

[2] Madame del Pozzo had been mistress of the Regent of France, and was celebrated for her wit, and notorious for the coarseness of her language. She wrote the Memoirs of her life, which, according to Horace Walpole, were seized by Elizabeth Farnese, Queen Dowager of Spain, of whom Madame del Pozzo had related scandals.

migration of souls suppose a man who has been rapacious and cunning does penance in the shape of a fox. . . . I believe my poor cousin, in his pre-existent state, having broken all moral laws, has been sentenced to suffer in all the various characters of human life. He has run through them all unsuccessfully enough. . . . He has certainly very uncommon parts, but too much of the rapidity of his mother's genius."

In 1763 three volumes of Lady Mary's letters, written during her husband's Embassy to Constantinople, were published under the editorship, it is supposed, of John Cleland. The manuscript copy given to Mr. Sowden at Rotterdam had been bought by Lord Bute, but there were other copies in circulation, one of which had been given to Mr. Molesworth, an old friend of the Wortleys, at Venice. Four years later another volume appeared, which was supposed to be a fabrication by Cleland, though Lady Bute believed that the contents were genuine. On 10th May 1763 Horace Walpole writes—

"We have just got three volumes of Lady Mary Wortley's *Letters*; of which she had given copies at Venice. They are entertaining, though perhaps the least of all her works, for these were written during her first travels, and have no personal history. All relating to that is in the hands of Lady Bute, and I suppose will never see the light. These letters, though pretty well guarded, have certain marks of originality—not bating freedoms both of opinion and with regard to truth, for which you know she had little partiality."

Lady Craven, afterwards Margravine of Anspach, who also wrote verses, travelled in the East, and kept up a voluminous correspondence, seems to have felt some jealousy of Lady Mary Wortley's posthumous fame, and even refused to believe that her rival had written any of the published letters that were attributed to her. "Lady Mary," she observes, "was sensible and accomplished, and had a style of her own that would have been easily distinguishable from that of another woman who wrote well. Judge, then, if I can consent to acknowledge that I take the soft, graceful hand of a lady when I feel the scratches of the cloven claw of a male scholar in every line.

Lady Bute told me that Horace Walpole and two other wits joined to divert themselves at the expense of the credulity of the public by composing these letters." [1]

Among the manuscript volumes that passed into Lady Bute's hands was the famous Diary, of whose existence the daughter had no knowledge till a few days before her mother's death. This had been kept since the time of Lady Mary's marriage, and was naturally voluminous. Lady Bute " kept it always under lock and key, and though she often looked over it herself, and read passages aloud to her daughters and friends, yet she never trusted any part of it out of her own hands, excepting the first five or six copy-books, which, at a late period, she permitted Lady Louisa Stuart to peruse alone, upon condition that nothing should be transcribed." Lady Bute burned the Diary in 1794, when she felt the close of her life drawing near, having always expressed her resolution to destroy it as a sacred duty to her mother's memory. She had often been entreated to forego her design; but, though she always spoke of Lady Mary with great respect, yet she was aware that it had been too much her mother's custom to note down and enlarge upon all the scandalous rumours of the day, without weighing their truth or even their probability. Lady Louisa acknowledges that, even in the earlier volumes, there appeared traits of satire which showed what might ensue when the vexations of advancing life should have soured the mind, and made further demands upon a Christian charity not at all likely to have increased in the meantime.[2]

It was hardly to be expected that the immediate descendants of such an exceptional couple as Lady Mary and Mr. Wortley should be ordinary, everyday people.

---

[1] This, of course, was pure imagination.

[2] Fortunately, Lady Bute did not burn her mother's miscellaneous correspondence. A portion of this, together with the letters from abroad, was published by Mr. Dallaway (with the permission of the Marquis of Bute) in 1803, with an inaccurate Memoir, and very scanty notes. In 1837 a new edition, with additional letters, corrections of Mr. Dallaway's Memoir, and the very valuable and interesting Introductory Anecdotes by Lady Louisa Stuart, was published by Lord Wharncliffe. In 1861 Mr. Moy Thomas brought out a revised edition of Lord Wharncliffe's book, in which he substituted an accurate Memoir for Mr. Dallaway's attempt, and contributed a large number of corrections and new notes. Each edition was accompanied with a selection from Lady Mary's poems.

Of the subsequent career of Edward Wortley Montagu much might be said, but a brief summary will suffice. In 1762 he started for the East, where he conformed to Turkish food, religion, and costume. He went through a form of marriage with various women, a Nubian among others, and became the father of several children. In 1775 he came to Italy, where he made friends with Romney, who painted him in Eastern costume. Hearing of the death of his wife (in 1776) he started for England, intending to marry again at once, in the hope of having a legitimate son to inherit the Wortley estates. But he had got no farther than Padua when he died suddenly, choked, it was said, by the bone of a small bird.[1]

It is pleasant to turn from the consideration of this unhappy man, who was probably the victim of some mental warp, to his sister, one of the few great ladies of her period against whom none of her contemporaries (not even the scandal-mongering Horace) had a word to say. She must have had a difficult part to play, as the wife of the most unpopular man of his day, but we are told that she never made a false step. Lord Bute was hated as a Scotchman and as a favourite of the Princess of Wales. The mob called him her lover, and the pair were unmercifully caricatured under the symbols of The Boot and The Petticoat. He was supposed to exercise far too strong an influence over the young King, whom he imbued with the belief that monarchs should govern as well as reign. His measures were all unpopular, from the peace with France down to the cider tax, and when he resigned in 1763, after only two years of power, he declared that he would rather live on bread and water than suffer the miseries of office a day longer. For a time he remained at Court, the King's trusted friend and adviser, but his influence was thought to weaken the position of ministers, and Grenville insisted that he should be driven from Court, and that the King should cease to consult him on any public matters. Henceforth, he occupied himself with his building at Luton Hoo and his gardens at Highcliffe, but it is evident that he was a disappointed, embittered man,

---

[1] Two or three spurious memoirs of him were published after his death.

and that to some extent his wife and children suffered with him.

In the delightful book, *Gleanings from an Old Portfolio*,[1] which contains letters exchanged between the various members of the family, we are enabled to follow the fortunes of the Stuarts, and realise how dull it was at Luton Hoo, the neighbours not being considered worth cultivating, and how the father's habitual gloom hung like a cloud over the whole household. Yet, though they grumbled at the dulness, they were in reality a high-spirited and original set of young people, gifted with a keen sense of humour, and an hereditary talent for writing amusing letters about the most trifling incidents of everyday life.

Eleven of the Stuart children lived to grow up, and as nearly all were married and several had families, the number of Lady Mary's great-grandchildren would have done credit to a patriarch of old.[2] Her godchild, Lady Louisa Stuart (youngest daughter of Lord Bute), who died in 1851 at the age of ninety-four, inherited her grandmother's taste for literary pursuits. That this taste was discouraged by her family is a real calamity, as all will agree who are familiar

---

[1] Edited by Mrs. Godfrey Clark, and privately printed 1895-1898.

[2] Of the five sons and six daughters, the eldest, John, was created Marquess of Bute in 1796. By his first wife, a daughter of the last Lord Windsor, he had seven children. In 1800 he married a daughter of Thomas Coutts, Esq., and had another son, Lord Dudley Stuart, and a daughter, who married the second Earl of Harrowby.

The second son, James Archibald, succeeded to the Wortley estates, and was the father of five children, his second son becoming the first Lord Wharncliffe.

The third son, Frederick, died unmarried in 1802.

The fourth son, Sir Charles Stuart, C.B., a distinguished soldier, married a daughter of Lord Vere Bertie, and had two sons, the eldest, who was created Baron Stuart de Rothesay, being the father of the two beautiful sisters, Lady Waterford and Lady Canning.

The fifth son was William, who became Archbishop of Armagh. He married a daughter of Thomas Penn of Stoke Poges, and left four children. Lady Louisa relates that during the period that William Stuart was Rector of Luton, a terrible epidemic of smallpox broke out in the neighbourhood. The mortality increased so fast that the Rector offered at length to have every person who was still uninfected inoculated at his own expense, and although many people had religious scruples on the subject, above two thousand came to the Rectory to undergo the operation. With but one country doctor and a few country nurses to depend on, it was impossible that all the patients could be properly prepared or attended to. Yet

with the *Selections from her Manuscripts* (*Essays and Verses*), and the *Letters to Miss Clinton*.[1] Her sketch of the family of John, Duke of Argyll, is a biographical gem, and her youthful letters read as if they had been written by one of Jane Austen's most charming heroines. Her satire so sweet-tempered that it is evident she likes her victims none the less for her laughter; while her common-sense philosophy, with its sub-acid flavour of gentle cynicism, may be studied with advantage even in these enlightened days.

A glimpse of Lady Mary's daughter and grand-daughter may be obtained from the Diary of Miss Burney, who met the two ladies at Mrs. Delany's in 1787. "Lady Bute," she records, "with an exterior the most forbidding to strangers, has powers of conversation the most entertaining and lively where she is intimate. She is full of anecdote, delights in strokes of general satire, yet with mere love of comic, not insidious ridicule. She spares not for giving her opinions, and laughs at fools as well as follies, with the shrewdest derision. Lady Louisa Stuart, her youngest daughter, has parts equal to those of her mother, with a deportment and appearance infinitely more pleasing; yet she is far from handsome, but proves how well beauty may be occasionally missed, when understanding and vivacity unite to fill up her place. . . . They seem both to inherit an ample

---

out of all the multitude only three died—a man of eighty, an infirm, unhealthy woman, and an infant who had already caught the disease.

Of Lord Bute's daughters, Mary, the eldest, was married to Sir James Lowther, afterwards first Earl of Lonsdale. He does not appear to have been a desirable husband, and there were no children of the marriage.

Jane, the second daughter, married Sir George Macartney, the distinguished diplomatist, who was created Earl Macartney in 1792.

Anne, the third daughter, married Lord Percy, afterwards second Duke of Northumberland, but there were no children of this marriage, and Lord Percy divorced his wife in 1779.

Augusta, the fourth daughter, married a Captain Corbet, and died as early as 1778, leaving one son.

Caroline, the fifth daughter, who was a clever artist, married Lord Carlow, afterwards created Earl of Portarlington, and had nine children.

Lady Louisa, the youngest daughter, died unmarried in 1851. As a girl, she was attached to her cousin, Colonel (afterwards General Sir William) Medows, but her parents refused to allow the marriage.

[1] Edited by the Hon. James Home.

portion of the wit of their mother and grandmother, Lady Mary Wortley Montagu, though I believe them both to have escaped all inheritance of her faults." On the occasion of another and a later meeting, Miss Burney writes: " Lady Bute and Lady Louisa were both in such high spirits themselves, that they kept up all the conversation between them with such a vivacity, an acuteness, and an observation on men and manners so clear and so sagacious, that it would be difficult to pass an evening of greater entertainment."

CHAPTER LII

CHARACTER AND WRITINGS

ALTHOUGH the *dossier* of Lady Mary Wortley is voluminous enough in all conscience, the problem of her complex "personality" still remains unsolved. Her character has stood its trial now for a century and a half, but when the evidence for the prosecution and the defence is impartially examined, an open verdict must be pronounced. Was she a woman of gallantry, heartless and shameless, as described by Pope and Horace Walpole, or was she a brilliant specimen of the eighteenth-century great lady, witty, charming, and beautiful, as she appeared to her numerous admirers? Or yet again, was she the intelligent, thoughtful woman, of exceptional culture and blameless conduct, who won the friendship of such irreproachable dames as Mary Astell, Lady Oxford, and the Duchess of Portland? Contemporary witnesses contradict each other so flatly that the answer to each of these questions must be "not proven."

Lady Mary's personal correspondence only confuses the points at issue, for she was mistress of a bewildering variety of styles. As one of her critics has pointed out, when writing to her sister and her early friend, Mrs. Hewet, she is giddy, sarcastic, and sometimes coarse; to Lady Oxford she talks the language of a grave and formal friendship; to Lady Pomfret she intersperses her chit-chat with scraps of learning; to her late and transient acquaintances, the Steuarts, her letters are verbose and empty; towards her husband she employs a sober, business-like style; to her daughter she mingles maternal tenderness with a decent complacency and much good sense; and, finally, in the Letters during the Embassy, which she intended for the world at large, there is a combination of the easy grace, the polished wit, the light humour, the worldly shrewdness of the clever and not over-scrupulous woman of fashion.[1]

Considering how powerfully she was influenced by her surroundings, it is not surprising that Lady Mary's character underwent a marked change after her marriage. The discipline of life with the worthy and estimable Mr. Wortley taught her to stifle her natural feelings, to check her more generous impulses, and to realise, temporarily at least, that the practice of petty economies was the chief aim and object of a woman's existence.

It was just when she became finally convinced that the quiet domestic happiness to which she had looked forward during the years of courtship were not for her, that she was tossed back again into the social whirlpool, where she snatched for consolation at sticks and straws, as represented by the pleasures and amusements of the Town. As a young married woman, handsome, witty, and neglected by her husband, she was naturally surrounded by admirers, who required but the slightest encouragement to become lovers in form. It was no easy task for such a woman to steer a safe course through the rocks and breakers that threatened her. The tone of society was laxer than in the preceding reign, but the whispering tongues were none the less merciless. Lady Mary, in the arrogance of her youth and beauty, was imprudent, tactless, and wholly wanting in finesse. Sometimes she was too kind to her admirers, and sometimes she ruthlessly laughed at them. She heartily despised the generality of her own sex, and she took no pains to hide her opinion of them.

As we have seen, the jokes, satirical ballads, and other lampoons, which passed from mouth to mouth or hand to hand in fashionable society, were none too decorous, and although Lady Mary was not responsible for all the skits that were placed to her account, several of her acknowledged productions are characterised by warmth of colouring and freedom of expression. There was something masculine in her breadth of view, her cynical humour, and her indifference

[1] *The Quarterly Review*, February 1737.

to the finer points of social diplomacy. Her follies and indiscretions, one feels convinced, were magnified and multiplied by her enemies—the many enemies that she had made by her bitter tongue, her dangerous pen, and her difficult temper.

It is difficult, however, to believe, after a careful examination of the Wortley Montagu correspondence, published and unpublished, that there was any ground for the worst accusations that Pope brought against Lady Mary.[1] For example, the following sentence in the letter to Mr. Wortley about Lady Bute (24th January 1740) could hardly have been addressed by a woman of open immorality to the husband she had wronged: "I may say with truth, that as even from her infancy I have made her [Lady Bute] a companion and witness of my actions, she owes me not only the regard due to a parent, but the esteem that ought to be paid to a blameless conduct, and the gratitude that is shown by every honest mind to a valuable friend." Again, it will be remembered that Lady Mary's letters to her daughter on the subject of Lady Vane, Lady Orford, and other women of profligate character, are warm with virtuous indignation, and stiffened by the most uncompromising condemnation of vice. She dwells with especial emphasis on the mortifications that are the unavoidable consequences of such a mode of life, mortifications far more humiliating than anything that the most austere order of nun is ever called upon to bear.

Whatever her moral conduct may have been, Lady Mary seems to have held the same religious views as the "sensible men" of her period, which is not crediting her with any exceptional piety. She thought that "religion" was a useful instrument for keeping the "mob" in order, and in consequence she considered it incumbent upon the upper classes to patronise the established church, and to refrain, at any rate in public, from expressing doubts on the subject of divine revelation. Enthusiasm, in her eyes, was an absurdity that might easily degenerate into a vice, and she would have been in hearty agreement with the Bishop of London,[2] who preached on "The great Folly and Danger of being Righteous overmuch." At

---

[1] That is, if he really intended her every time he mentions "Sappho."
[2] Dr. Trapp.

the same time, she strongly condemned Lady Orford for her open professions of atheism, which she considered a danger to the community. A long residence in Italy rendered Lady Mary more orthodox in her later days. She was very angry indeed with Richardson for making Sir Charles Grandison consent that his daughters should be brought up as Catholics (in the event of his marriage with Clementina). In the letter containing her criticism on the book, there is a long digression concerning her frequent theological controversies with the Italian priests, in which, by her own account, she invariably got the best of it. "When they thunder with the names of Fathers and Councils," she remarks, "they are surprised to find me as well (often better) acquainted with them than themselves."

It will hardly be contended nowadays, even by her most ardent admirers, that Lady Mary was a "poet," for her mind was the reverse of poetical. Her verses are always fluent, often lively, and sometimes forcible. She is at her best when she paints the manners of her times, as in the *Town Eclogues*, for her serious satires, even at their highest level, are but a far-away imitation of Pope. The prose Essays that are published with her other Remains, are trite enough, and show that her talent did not work easily in that form. It is to the Letters, and the Letters alone, that she owes her little niche in the Temple of Fame. And yet Lady Mary was lacking in many of the qualities that are generally found in famous letter-writers. She had little sympathy or imagination, and no sentiment. She was not even strikingly witty in the modern sense of the word, for her writings contain no fireworks, and few bons-mots or set epigrams. But then the "wit" of the eighteenth century was nothing so trivial as the cracking of jokes; it might better be defined as the felicitous expression of a glorified common sense. Lady Mary, in her youth, wrote in a dashing, high-spirited, vigorous style; she was not always accurate, consistent, or impartial, but she dealt freely and fearlessly with the people she knew, and with the social topics of the day. It was, of course, her good fortune to live in exciting times and among famous people, but it is her own keen interest in the life about her that compels the interest of her readers. In her later letters, when her high spirits had sobered down, and the philosophy that she fondly believed to be founded on the purest Stoicism, was tinctured by the natural bitterness of the disappointed elderly woman, she makes less effort to entertain. She gives out the fruits of her long experience of the narrow clique that to her represented "the world," and of her eager though not impartial study of the fashionable folk that to her represented "human nature." She does not attempt to shine, but there is something curiously impressive in her downright, matter-of-fact, forcible style, as she records her opinions and recollections, or chronicles some dramatic incident from the life in her Italian village.

Lady Bute used to say that her mother was not a great talker, rather silent, in fact, in mixed society, unless the conversation took an interesting turn. "If it did, she spoke with force and gaiety, as the subject prompted, and though not ill-natured would make cutting repartees, for she had very little patience with folly, and less with any kind of affectation." Certainly, in her younger days Lady Mary's associates were not of the type that suffers bores gladly, and in her old age we find that distinguished men were glad to be numbered among her intimates. Even Horace Walpole admits that her conversation was most entertaining, and considering his hatred of her, this tribute can hardly be overestimated. But few of her "good things" have come down to us. There was the joke about Lady Sundon's ear-rings, already chronicled, and her oft-quoted division of mankind into "men, women and Herveys," and her remark, à propos the suggestion that men and women should take each other in marriage for a term of years,—that it should be "a repairing lease." Her spécialité seems to have been the purveying of "news," which may or may not have meant scandal. Thus we have seen that Pope, in answer to Patty Blount's letter asking for news, says, "I must stop here till further advices, which are expected from the Lady Mary Wortley this afternoon"; and that Lady Strafford records a visit from Lady Mary Wortley, who for once had no news, and, as a natural consequence of this misfortune, thoroughly bored her hostess.

As a literary critic Lady Mary was quite untrustworthy, since she allowed her opinion of contemporary works to be biassed by her opinion of their authors. This failing, however, she shared with the great majority of professional critics of her period. "Most people will admit," writes Lady Louisa Stuart, "that Pope betrayed unmanly and mean malevolence in his attacks upon her [Lady Mary]; yet when she pronounced his verses to be 'all sound and no sense,' she was aiming a pointless arrow at a poet who, whenever he judged it expedient, could compress more meaning into fewer words than almost any other in our language. Not Pope alone, however, but the larger half of that noble band of authors that rendered the literary age of Anne illustrious, lay for her as under an interdict, a species of taboo, obnoxious both as Tories and as his confederates. She forbade herself to relish the wit and humour of Swift and Arbuthnot; and could not, or would not, be sensible that the former, Bolingbroke and Atterbury, ranked with her own Addison as the standard writers of English prose."

This "rake at reading," self-confessed, left only a scanty library. There were her early favourites, the French romances, a well-worn copy of Theobald's *Shakespeare*, and Dryden's works in folio, as they were first published. She had quite a modern admiration for the old English drama, and possessed several volumes of ill-printed plays, for which in after years the "collector" Duke of Roxburgh would have given their weight in gold. But Lillo's domestic tragedies were her chief favourites, and she was accustomed to say that whoever did not cry at *George Barnewell* deserved to be hanged. Among her books at Sandon are a number of the mid-eighteenth-century novels that were sent out to her during her later years of exile, including the works of Fielding and Richardson. On the title-pages of most of these she has written a brief word of comment, such as, "Sad Trash," "Charmingly Written," or "Wretched Stuff." In her copy of *Tom Jones* she wrote "Ne plus ultra," but *Clarissa Harlowe*, over which she admitted that she had sobbed in a most scandalous manner, is contemptuously dismissed as "Miserable Ideas meanly expressed."

CHARACTER AND WRITINGS

Something of Lady Mary's philosophy of life and love may be gleaned from her poem *The Lover*, one of her most sprightly effusions. In the published version this is addressed to Congreve, but in her manuscript book the invocation is to "Molly," possibly Molly Skerret. This poem, perhaps the most personal of all Lady Mary's writings, may bring her life-story to a characteristic conclusion—

"At length, by so much importunity pressed,
Take, Molly, at once the inside of my breast.
This stupid indiff'rence so often you blame,
Is not owing to nature, to fear, or to shame:
I am not as cold as a virgin in lead,
Nor are Sunday's sermons so strong in my head:
I know but too well how time flies along,
That we live but few years, and yet fewer are young.

But I hate to be cheated, and never will buy
Long years of repentance for moments of joy.
Oh! was there a man (but where shall I find
Good sense and good nature so equally joined?)
Would value his pleasure, contribute to mine;
Not meanly would boast, nor loudly design;
Not over severe, yet not stupidly vain,
For I would have the power, yet not give the pain.

No pedant, yet learned; no rake-helly gay,
Or laughing because he has nothing to say;
To all my whole sex obliging and free,
But never be fond of any but me;
In public preserve the decorum that's just,
And show in his eyes he is true to his trust!
Then rarely approach, and respectfully bow,
But not fulsomely pert, nor yet foppishly low.

But when the long hours of public are past,
And we meet with champagne and a chicken at last,
May every fond pleasure that moment endear;
Be banished afar both discretion and fear!
Forgetting or scorning the airs of the crowd,
He may cease to be formal, and I to be proud,
Till lost in the joy, we confess that we live,
And he may be rude, and yet I may forgive.

And that my delight may be solidly fixed,
Let the friend and the lover be handsomely mixed;
In whose tender bosom my soul may confide,
Whose kindness can soothe me, whose counsel can guide.

From such a dear lover as here I describe,
No danger should fright me, no millions should bribe;
But till this astonishing treatment I know,
As I long have lived chaste, I will keep myself so.

I never will share with the wanton coquette,
Or be caught by a vain affectation of wit.
The toasters and songsters may try all their art,
But never shall enter the pass of my heart.
I loathe the lewd rake, the dressed fopling despise:
Before such pursuers the nice virgin flies;
And as Ovid has sweetly in parable told,
We harden like trees, and like rivers grow cold."

TITLES OF LADY MARY WORTLEY MONTAGU'S PUBLISHED WORKS

PROSE.

Translation of the *Enchiridion* of Epictetus.
Account of the Court of England at the Accession of George I.
A Letter from the other World, to a Lady, from her former Husband.
Essay in a Paper called *The Nonsense of Common Sense*. Published 24th January 1738.
Carabosse. A L'Abbé Conti. (Fragment.)
Sur la Maxime de M. de Rochefoucault, Qu'il y a des Mariages Commodes, mais point de Délicieux.

POEMS.

Julia to Ovid. Written at twelve years of age, in imitation of Ovid's *Epistles*.
Irregular Verses to Truth. Written at fourteen years of age.
Song, "How happy is the harden'd heart."
The Lady's Resolve. Written on a window, soon after her marriage.
Town Eclogues. Written about the year 1715.
Verses. Written in the chiosk of the British Palace at Pera, overlooking the city of Constantinople, 26th December 1717.
Epilogue to Mary Queen of Scots. Designed to be spoken by Mrs. Oldfield.
Epilogue to the Tragedy of *Cato*.
To a Friend on his Travels.
To the Same.
Fragment to ———.
To Mr. ———.
John, Duke of Marlborough.
A Character.
An Answer to a Love-letter, in Verse.
Lord Hervey to Mr. Fox. Written at Florence, 1729, in imitation of the Sixth Ode of the Second Book of Horace.
Continuation. By Lady M. W. Montagu.
An Epistle to the Earl of Burlington.
Verses. Addressed to the Imitator of the First Satire of the Second Book of Horace.
Unfinished Sketches of a larger Poem.
The Court of Dulness. (A Fragment.)

An Epistle from Pope to Lord Bolingbroke.
Lady Hertford, to Lord William Hamilton.
Answered, for Lord William Hamilton, by Lady M. W. Montagu.
Epistle from Arthur Grey, the Footman, to Mrs. Murray.
Imitation of the Fourth Ode of the First Book of Horace.
Imitation of the Fifth Ode of the First Book of Horace.
The Lover: A Ballad. To Mr. Congreve.
On seeing a Portrait of Sir Robert Walpole.
An Elegy on Mrs. Thompson.
On the Death of Mrs. Bowes.
A Man in Love.
A Ballad. To the tune of "The Irish Howl."
A Hymn to the Moon. Written in July, in an arbour.
The Same. Translated into Italian by herself.
The Bride in the Country. A Parody on Rowe's Ballad, "Colin's Complaint."
Melinda's Complaint. (Another Version of the above.)
Song, "Why should you think I live unpleas'd?"
Song—Rondeau, "Finish these languors!"
Epithalamium.
Imitation of the Ninth Ode of the Third Book of Horace. 1736.
A Summary of Lord Lyttelton's Advice to a Lady.
Song, "Why will Delia thus retire?" (Addressed to Lady Irwin.)
The Same. Translated into Italian by herself.
The Politicians.
Ballad on a Late Occurrence. (Among Lady Mary's papers, but of doubtful authorship.)
Verses written in a Garden.
Song, "Fond wishes you pursue in vain."
Impromptu, to a Young Lady Singng.
Advice.
Answer.
Lady M. M***'s Farewell to Bath. (From the *Gentleman's Magazine*, July 1731.)
Epistle to Lord Hervey on the King's Birthday.
Epigram. 1734.
An Answer to a Lady who advised Lady M. W. Montagu to retire.
Lines written at Lovere.
Conclusion of a Letter to a Friend, sent from Italy, 1741.
To the Same.
Lines written at Lovere, 1755.
Lines written in a blank page of Milton's *Paradise Lost*.
Addressed to ———, 1736.
To Clio. Occasioned by her Verses on Friendship.

INDEX

Abercrombie, Colonel, 425.
Act of Toleration, The, 10.
Addison, Joseph—
  Contributions to *Tatler*, 11.
  Lady Mary's opinion of, 14.
  Travels with Mr. Wortley, 15.
  His English, 22.
  Dinner with Swift and Mr. Wortley, 69.
  Correspondence with Mr. Wortley, 119–22.
  Criticism of his *Cato* suppressed, 169.
  Quarrel with Steele, 225–26.
  Letters to Mr. Wortley, 270–73.
  Resignation, 286.
  Visit to Bristol, 289.
Advice to Sappho, 357.
Almahide, 12.
Amelia, Empress-Dowager of Germany, 235, 236.
Ancaster, Jane, Duchess of, 364.
Anderson, Mr., 397, 503, 514, 518.
Apology for the Late Resignation, 448.
Arbuthnot, Dr. John, 10, 252, 339, 544.
Argyll, John, Duke of, 220–22, 225, 457, 478, 493, 517, 537.
Ashe, Miss, 473, 476.
Ashenhurst, Mr., 57, 58.
Astell, Mary, 12, 13, 21 (*note*), 305, 307, 309, 312–13.
Atholl, James, Duke of, 431.
Atkins, Sir Henry, 356.
Atterbury, Dr. Francis, Bishop of Rochester, 13 (*note*), 257, 544.
"Avidien," 346, 347.
Aylmer, Admiral, 254.

Bacon, Lady Catherine, 509.
Bacon, Montagu, 214–25, 243, 252–58, 287–90.
Bacon, Nicholas, 214.
Baden Durlach, Prince of, 439.
Balm of Mecca, 268.
Banks, Miss, 6, 79, 80, 134.
Banks, Mr., 79.
Barnard, Commodore, 516.
Barnard, Sir John, 450.
Bath, William, Earl of, 434.

Baths of Sophia, 260.
Bathurst, Allen, Lord, 309, 321, 326, 342.
Battle of the Books, The, 10.
Baynton, Rachel (*see* Kingston, Lady), 143.
Beard, John, 363.
Beauclerk, Lord Sidney, 332.
Beauvau, Charles, Prince de, 378.
Bedford, Gertrude, Duchess of, 396.
Bedford, John, Duke of, 394.
Belasyse, Lady, 119, 467.
Belle-Isle, Marechal de, 417.
Bentinck, Lady Isabella, 182.
Bentley, Dr. Richard, 54, 222.
Bentley, Richard, 490.
Berkeley, Augustus, Earl of, 363.
Bernsdorff, Baron, 255, 259.
Betenson, Albinia, 16 (*note*).
Bethel, Hugh, 389.
Betterton, Thomas, 11.
"Bickerstaff, Mr.," 11.
"Biddy Tipkin," 95.
Binns, Mrs., 84, 86.
Blackwood, Mrs., 381.
Bligh, General, 425.
Blount, Martha, 205, 229, 291.
Bolingbroke, Henry, Viscount (*see* St. John), 200, 353, 544.
Bolton, Charles, Duke of, 6, 434.
Booth, Barton, 11.
Boswell, Mrs. Margaret, 191.
Bothmar, Baron, 254, 255, 259.
Bracebridge, Mr., 491.
Bracegirdle, Mrs., 11.
Bramstone, Dr., 216.
Brand, Lady Caroline, 484.
Brand, Thomas, 469.
Bride in the Country, The, 194 (*note*).
Bridgewater, Elizabeth, Countess of, 86.
Bridgewater, Scrope, Duke of, 460.
Bristol, John, Earl of, 461.
Bristol, Elizabeth, Countess of, 228, 229, 241, 278.
Bromley, William, 218.
Brothers, The, 320, 321.
Buckingham, Catherine, Duchess of, 408.
Buckingham, George, Duke of, 170 (*note*).

Buckinghamshire, John, Duke of, 170 (*note*), 273.
Buononcini, Giovanni, 12, 303, 310.
Burgoyne, Sir Roger, 362.
Burnet, Dr. Gilbert, Bishop of Salisbury, 5, 13, 31 (*note*), 59, 167, 193, 194, 505.
Burnet, Sir Thomas, 216.
Burney, Fanny, 537-38.
Busybody, The, 14.
Bute, John, Earl of, 358, 385, 406, 433, 456, 457, 459, 460, 466, 471, 478, 496-98, 518, 529, 535.
Bute, Mary, Countess of (*see* Wortley Montagu, Mary)—
　Recollections, 164, 286, 312.
　Marriage, 358-59.
　Estrangement of her mother, 374-76.
　Stays with her father, 406.
　Uneasy situation, 436.
　Moralising, 454.
　Amateur theatricals, 457.
　Tact and prudence, 459.
　Praise of her conduct, 466.
　Father's kindness, 468.
　Ideas on education, 480.
　Court life, 497.
　Presentation of daughter, 503.
　Description of London, 508.
　Erects tablet to her father, 514.
　Inherits Wortley estates, 516.
　Burns her mother's diary, 534.
　Conversational talent, 537-38.
Byng, Sir George, 287.
Byng, Lady, 305.

Cadogan, General, 217, 221, 222, 256, 286.
Calthorpe, Miss, 316.
Cambis, M. de, 362.
Campaign, The, 10.
Campbell, Sir James, 419.
Capon's Tale, The, 340.
Carbery, John, Earl of, 6.
Cardigan, George, Earl of, 502.
Cardigan, Countess of, 502.
Carleton, Henry, Lord, 325.
Carlisle, Charles, Earl of, 6.
Carlisle, Henry, Earl of, 368.
Caroline, Princess of Wales (afterwards Queen), 203, 208, 250, 254, 304, 326.
Carpenter, General, 256.
Carter, Miss, 467.
Carteret, John, Lord (*see* Granville, Earl), 289.
Carteret, Sophia, Lady (*see* Fermor, Lady Sophia), 414.
Cartwright, Mrs., 20.
Carving, The art of, 5.

Caryll, John, 173.
Cassotti, Mr., 16, 141.
Cato, 10, 169-73.
Cavendish, Sir Charles, 1.
Cenotaph to Lady Mary, 531 (*note*).
Centlivre, Mrs., 14.
Chandos, James, Duke of, 345, 460.
Characters of Women, 343.
Charles VI., Emperor of Germany, 235.
Charles XII., King of Sweden, 257, 258.
Charles Edward, the Young Pretender, 428-29.
Checa, Signora, 85.
Chesterfield, Philip, Earl of, 83, 343.
Chetwynd, Mrs., 84, 266.
Cheyne, Gertrude, Lady, 53, 167, 182, 186, 329.
Cheyne, William, Lord, 2.
Cheyne, Dr., 491.
Child, Mr., 370.
Chiswell, Sarah, 264.
Chloë, Mr., 401.
Cholmondeley, George, Earl of, 434.
Christian Hero, The, 10.
Chute, Mr., 449.
Cibber, Colley, 10, 11, 12, 253, 255.
Cicisbei, The, 280.
Circassian slaves, 267.
Clare, Charles, Viscount, 2 (*note*).
Clarges, Lady, 84, 86.
Clarissa Harlowe, 481-82, 493.
Clarke, Dr. Samuel, 216, 227.
Clayton, Mrs. (*see* Sundon, Lady), 360.
Cleland, John, 533.
Cleveland, Anne, Duchess of, 332, 465.
Coke, Edward, Lord, 477.
Compton, Hon. Spencer, 217, 224.
Congreve, William, 10, 11, 14, 181, 232, 273, 302, 309-10, 343, 545.
Conti, The Abbé, 228, 278, 281-82, 291, 369, 375.
Conversations of Ben Jonson, 169 (*note*).
Conway, Hon. Seymour, 388.
Cope, Sir John, 417, 429, 430.
Corticelli, Signor, 85, 86, 211.
Corticelli, Signora, 86.
Cotton, Mrs., 88.
Court Poems, 206.
Coventry, George, Earl of, 501.
Coventry, Maria, Countess of, 501.
Cowley, Abraham, 26, 27, 410.
Cowper, William, Earl, 224.
Craggs, James, the younger, 204, 205, 273, 287, 289.
Craon, Princess, 389.
Craven, Elizabeth, Lady, 533.
Crew, Nathaniel, Lord, Bishop of Durham, 214.
Crichton, Lady Mary, 82.

INDEX

Crisis, The, 181.
Croker, John Wilson, 405.
Curll, Edmund, 206, 207.

Dashwood, Sir Francis, 454.
Dawes, Sir William, Archbishop of York, 183-84.
Delany, Mrs. (see Pendarves), 408 (note), 537.
Delawarr, Charlotte, Lady, 507.
Delawarr, John, Lord, 318.
Deloraine, Mary, Countess of, 344.
Denbigh, Isabella, Countess of, 192-94.
Denbigh, Mary, Countess of, 332.
Denbigh, William, Earl of, 1.
De Noyer (Dunoyer), Mme., 17.
Derwentwater, James, Earl of, 222.
Devonshire, William, Duke of, 526.
Dodd, Sir Samuel, 224.
Dodington, George Bubb, 315, 321, 326.
Doggett, Thomas, 11.
Dorchester, Evelyn, Marquis of. See Pierrepont, Evelyn.
Dorset, Lionel, Duke of, 434.
Drew, Sarah, 283-84.
Drummond, Mr., 381.
Dulness, Goddess of, 353.
Dunciad, The, 341.

Earle, Giles, 518.
Edgecombe, Mr., 398.
Edgecumbe, Richard, Lord, 276.
Education, Ideas on, 463, 478-80.
Elgin, Charles, Earl of, 502.
Elizabeth Christina, Empress of Charles VI., 234, 235.
Embassy to the Porte, The, 227.
Epistle from Pope to Lord Bolingbroke, 353.
Epistle to Dr. Arbuthnot, 340.
Epistle to Arthur Grey, 324, 449.
Epistle to Lord Bathurst, 342.
Ernley, Lady, 89.
Erskine, Mr., 395.
Erskine, Lady Fanny, 333, 356, 359, 395.
Essay in Defence of the Female Sex, 13 (note).
Essay on Man, 353.
Essay on Maxim of La Rochefoucauld, 386.
Eugene, Prince, 240, 246, 268.
Evelyn, Sir John, 2.
Evelyn, Richard, 2.
Eyre, Sir Robert, 224 (note).

Farmer, Mrs., 87, 88.
Fawkener, Sir Everard, 423.
Female Quixote, The, 502.

Fenton, Elijah, 320 (note).
Fenton, Lavinia, 6.
Fermor, Lady Sophia (see Lady Carteret), 371.
Ferrers, Countess of, 509.
Fielding, Lady Frances, 332.
Fielding, Henry, 320, 469, 492, 544.
Fielding, Lady Mary, 1.
Fielding, Sarah, 432.
Fielding, Hon. William, 5, 157, 265.
Fleury, Cardinal, 368.
Fontenoy, Battle of, 418-20.
Forbes, Admiral, 516.
Fortescue, William, 345.
Fortunate Parish Girl, The, 481.
Foscia, Signora, 375.
Foster, General Thomas, 221, 225.
Franke, Mr., 56, 58.
Frederick, Prince of Wales, 359, 471-72.
Frederick Christian, Prince of Saxony, 373, 376, 378-79, 385.
Funeral, The; or, Grief à la Mode, 10.

Gage, Lady, 363.
Gainsborough, Dorothy, Countess of, 326.
Garth, Dr. Samuel, 10, 14, 19, 175, 182, 273, 289.
Gay, John, 10, 11, 252-54, 282, 302-3.
George I., 242, 277, 286, 335.
George II., 335.
George, Prince of Wales (afterwards George II.), 203, 253-54, 286, 326.
George, Prince of Wales (afterwards George III.), 472, 497-98.
George, Prince of Denmark, 10.
George Barnwell, 544.
Germain, Lady Elizabeth, 84, 86.
Gibson, Mr., 355, 381, 390, 391, 402, 418, 422, 428, 442, 511.
Gleanings from an Old Portfolio, 536.
Godolphin, Francis, Earl of, 218.
Godwin, Mr., 64.
Gordon, Lord Adam, 441.
Gortz, Baron, 256-59.
Gottolengo, Life at, 458-59.
Gower Evelyn, Lady (see Pierrepont, Lady Evelyn), 286, 305, 329, 330, 332.
Gower, John, Earl, 134, 178, 356.
Gradinego, Signora, 375, 376.
Grafton, Charles, Duke of, 18.
Grafton, Henrietta, Duchess of, 57, 84, 86.
Graham, General, 497, 520.
Grammont, Comte de, 299.
Granby, John, Marquis of, 375.
Grandison, Sir Charles, 9.
Grange, James, Lord, 337, 338, 359.
Grant, Abbé, 503.

Granville, John, Earl (see Carteret, Lord), 423, 433-36, 451.
Gray, Thomas, 387.
Gregory, Mr., 508.
Greville, Mr., 505.
Grey, Arthur, 324.
Grey, Zachary, 215.
Griffith, Miss, 267.
Grimani, Pietro, 369, 375, 378, 439.
Guilford, Alice, Countess of, 117.
Gulliver's Travels, 331.
Gwyn, Nell, 332.
Gyllenberg, Count, 256-59.

Halifax, Charles, Earl of, 168, 192-93, 200-1, 286.
Halifax, George, Earl of, 365.
Halifax, William, Marquis of, 18.
Hamilton, Lord Archibald, 521.
Hamilton, Elizabeth, Duchess of, 527.
Hamilton, Lord William, 507, 508.
Hammond, Anthony, 265.
Hampden, John, 83, 219.
Hampden, Mrs., 83, 86, 88, 124, 125.
Handel, George, 12.
Hanmer, Sir Thomas, 57.
Harcourt, Simon, Viscount, 489.
Harley, Robert (see Oxford, Earl of), 9.
Harrington, Caroline, Countess of, 501.
Harrington, William, Lord (see Stanhope), 434.
Hastings, Lady Elizabeth, 13 (note).
Hay, Mrs., 414-15.
Heidegger, John James, 258, 267.
Henley, Robert, Lord, 524 (note).
Herbert, Colonel, 20.
Herbert, Lord Edward, 363.
Herbert, Lord, 22.
Herbert, Lady Harriet, 363.
Herculaneum, 392, 395.
Hertford, Frances, Countess of, 386, 449, 502, 507 (note), 508.
Hervey, Carr, Lord, 55, 208.
Hervey, Elizabeth, Lady (see Bristol, Countess of), 84, 127.
Hervey, John, Lord, 309, 311, 339, 340, 343-44, 365, 404-5, 408-9.
Hervey, Mary, Lady, 304, 309, 326.
Hesse Cassel, Landgrave of, 362.
Hewet, John, 283-84.
Hewet, Mr., 467.
Hewet, Mrs., 6, 15, 16, 17, 18, 51, 116, 117.
Highmore, Joseph, 12.
Hinchinbroke, John, Lord, 166.
Holdernesse, Frederica, Countess of, 316-17.
Holdernesse, Robert, Earl of, 189.
Holmes, General, 218.
Holstein, Princess of, 373, 378.

House of Lords, Scene at, 363-64.
Howard, Lady Elizabeth, 191.
Howard, General Sir George, 460.
Howard, Mrs., 326.
Hughes, John, 290.
Huguenots of Nismes, The, 413.
Huntingdon, Selina, Countess of, 364.
Hussey, Mr., 455.
Hyde, Henry, Lord (afterwards Earl of Rochester), 113.

Imitation of the First Satire of the Second Book of Horace, 343, 357.
Inoculation, 264, 304-7.
Introductory Anecdotes, 3, 5, 312 (note).
Irwin, Anne, Lady, 357 (note).
Italian Opera, 12.

James, Edward, the Old Pretender, 357-58, 394, 413-14, 428, 431.
Jeffreys, G., 320 (note).
Jeffreys, George, Lord, of Wem, 360.
Jekyll, Sir Joseph, 81 (note), 224, 227, 311.
Jekyll, Lady, 81, 84, 86, 87, 88, 124, 125, 126-27.
Jervas, Charles, 12, 205, 261.
Jessop, Mr., 188.
Johnson, Dr. Samuel, 492.
Joseph Andrews, 469.
Journey to England (1761), 524-27.
Journey to Italy (1739), 366.

Kendal, Melusina, Duchess of, 204.
Kent, Jemima, Duchess of, 84, 86, 88.
Kent, William, 12.
Kilmannsegg, Madame, 272.
Kingston, Evelyn, first Duke of. See Pierrepont, Evelyn.
Kingston, Evelyn, second Duke of, 329.
Kingston, William, Lord, 54, 55, 58, 143-44, 161, 175.
Kingston, Isabella, Duchess of, 329.
Kingston, Mary, Countess of, 2.
Kingston, Rachel, Lady (see Baynton), 290, 378.
Kingston, Robert, Earl of, 1, 478.
Kit-Cat Club, The, 3.
Kneller, Sir Godfrey, 12, 14, 128, 292.

"Lætitia," 4, 7, 8, 21, 28, 29.
Lane, J., 530-31.
Lansdowne, George, Lord, 219, 225, 255, 299.
Lansdowne, Mary, Lady, 299.
Law, John, 281.
Lechmere, Elizabeth, Lady, 326.
Lechmere, Nicholas, Lord, 223-25, 289, 290.
Lestock, Admiral, 443.

INDEX

Letters to Miss Clinton, 537.
Lewis, Erasmus, 286.
Lexington, Robert, Lord, 189.
Ligonier, Sir John, 441.
Lillo, George, 544.
Lilly, Charles, 213.
Lonsdale, Henry, Viscount, 314.
Lonsdale, Richard, Viscount, 18.
Loudoun, Hugh, Earl of, 82, 196.
Lover, The, 545.
Lovere, Account of, 448.
Lowendal, Count Ulric von, 426.
Löwestein, Prince, 439.
Lowther, Sir James (afterwards Earl of Lonsdale), 517.
Lowther, Miss, 314.
Luc, Comte de, 337.
Lumley, Richard, Lord (*see* Scarborough, Earl of), 290.
Lying Lover, The, 10.
Lyttelton, George, Lord, 446.
Lyttelton, Thomas, Lord, 394.

Mackenzie, Lady Betty, 521.
Mackenzie, Hon. James Stuart, 385, 396, 459, 519, 520, 526.
Macky, John, 9 (*note*).
Mahony, Count, 396.
Malplacquet, Battle of, 17.
Manchester, Dodington, Countess of, 20.
Manchester, Isabella, Duchess of, 377, 379, 455.
Manley, Mrs., 13, 14, 17, 18, 19.
Mann, Sir Horace, 301, 385, 515, 522, 527.
Mansel, Thomas, Lord, 380, 470.
Mar, Frances, Countess of (*see* Pierrepont, Lady Frances)—
  Marriage, 182.
  Lady Mary's correspondence with, during the Embassy, 228, 229, 234, 248, 261, 274.
  Meets Lady Mary in Paris, 280.
  Letters from Lady Mary to, 297-336.
  Melancholy, 313.
  Letters from, to Lady Mary, 327-28, 337.
  Lunacy declared, 337-38.
  Death of, 519.
Marischal, George, Earl, 518.
Marlborough, John, Duke of, 9, 200-1.
Marlborough, Henrietta, Duchess of, 310, 326, 343, 459.
Marlborough, Sarah, Duchess of, 10, 274, 360, 445.
Mary, Princess, 362.
Masham, Mrs., 10.
Mason, Mr., 118.
Matthews, Admiral, 413.
Maynwaring, Arthur, 10.

Medows, Mr., 464.
Medows, Sir Philip, 464.
Memoirs of the Reign of George I., 405.
Memoirs of the Reign of George II., 457.
Memoirs of Lady Frail, 481.
Michielli, Signora Clara, 375.
Middleton, Francis, Lord, 381.
Mildmay, Benjamin, 316, 317.
Mocenigo, Signora, 373, 375.
Mohun, Elizabeth, Lady, 266, 267.
Molesworth, Mr., 533.
Molyneux, Samuel, 276.
Monk, Mrs., 79.
Monnoux, Sir Humphrey, 311.
Monson, John, Lord, 465.
Montagu, Lady Catherine, 214.
Montagu, Hon. Charles, 164.
Montagu, Mrs. Charles, 164.
Montagu, Edward, 164, 431, 433-34, 436, 445-46, 450-52.
Montagu, Elizabeth, Duchess of, 85.
Montagu, Mrs. Elizabeth, 367 (*note*), 528.
Montagu, Lady Frances, 362.
Montagu, George, 197.
Montagu, Mrs. George, 197-98.
Montagu, James, 214, 216-17, 222, 243, 287, 431, 465.
Montagu, John, Duke of, 423, 434, 502.
Montagu, Hon. John, Dean of Durham, 39, 164.
Montagu, Mary, Duchess of, 309, 316, 377, 459.
Montagu, William, Captain, 446.
Monteleoni, Senor, 253.
Montrose, Christian, Duchess of, 335.
Mordaunt, Charles, 267.
Moro, Signora Livia, 375.
Morris, John, 13 (*note*).
Motteux, Peter, 212, 213.
Mount Stuart of Wortley, John, Lord, 519.
Murray, Mrs. Griselda, 298-99, 325.
Murray, John, 497 (*note*), 504, 521, 526.
Murray, William (afterwards Lord Mansfield), 397.
Musgrave, Lady, 287.

New Atlantis, The, 14, 17-20.
Newcastle, Margaret, Duchess of, 190.
Newcastle, Thomas, Duke of, 424, 434, 440.
Newcomen, Anne, 7 (*note*).
Nicolini, 12, 24, 25, 116.
Norris, Sir John, 381 (*note*).
Northey, Sir Edward, 224.
Northumberland, Katherine, Duchess of, 84, 86.
Nottingham, Daniel, Earl of, 217.
Novels, Criticisms on, 481-83.

Ogle, Henry, Lord (afterwards Duke of Newcastle), 2 (*note*).
Oldfield, Mrs., 11, 281.
One Epistle, The, 341.
Onslow, Richard, Lord, 270.
Onslow, Sir Richard, 218.
Orford, Margaret, Countess of (*see* Walpole), 474, 481-82, 523.
Orford, Edward, Lord, 286.
Orkney, Elizabeth, Countess of, 335.
Ormonde, James, Duke of, 219, 222, 223, 226.
Orrery, John, Earl of, 488-89, 509.
Overbury, Sir Thomas, 169 (*note*).
Owen, Colonel, 223.
Oxford, Robert, Earl of (*see* Harley), 200, 217, 488, 510.
Oxford, Henrietta, Countess of, 309, 312, 413, 415, 445, 449, 494, 496.

Palazzo, Count, 438, 444, 496 (*note*), 499 (*note*).
Palazzo, Countess, 443, 472 (*note*).
Pamela, 483.
Parker, Thomas (afterwards Earl of Macclesfield), 290.
Paybas, Abraham, 476.
Peace of Aix-la-Chapelle, The, 461.
Peace of Utrecht, The, 117, 118.
Pelham, Henry, 373-74, 435, 451.
Pelham, Thomas, Lord (*see* Newcastle, Duke of), 188.
Pembroke, Herbert, Earl of, 434.
Pendarves, Mrs. (*see* Delany), 357, 364-65.
Pepper, General, 223.
Peregrine Pickle, 481.
Peterborough, Charles, Earl of, 318.
Petre, Captain, 370.
Petre, Robert, Lord, 370.
Philip, Don, 413, 438, 465.
Phipps, Constantine (afterwards Lord Mulgrave), 408 (*note*).
Pierrepont, A., 112.
Pierrepont, Evelyn (successively Earl of Kingston, Marquis of Dorchester, and first Duke of Kingston)—
Family, 1.
Becomes Earl of Kingston, 2.
Toasts Lady Mary at Kit-Cat Club, 3.
Appearance, 9.
Created Marquis of Dorchester, 9.
Friendship with Wits, 10.
Quarrels with Mr. Wortley over settlements, 50-51.
Letters to, from son, 54-58.
Renewed application from Mr. Wortley to, 133.
Lady Mary's interview with, 135-37.
Comes to Acton, 145.

Pierrepont, Evelyn—*continued*.
Discovers plan for elopement, 158-59.
Attempted reconciliation with, by runaway couple, 167-68.
Second marriage, 182.
Created Duke of Kingston, 201.
Prospect of reconciliation, 276.
Visit from, 286.
Death of, 329.
Small legacy to Lady Mary, 310.
Pierrepont, Lady Carolina, 469.
Pierrepont, Lady Evelyn (*see* Gower, Lady), 6, 53, 84, 134.
Pierrepont, Lady Fanny, 464.
Pierrepont, Lady Frances (*see* Mar, Countess of), 6, 53, 87, 182, 192, 330.
Pierrepont, Gervase, Lord, of Hanslope, 157, 167, 182, 187, 190, 191, 192, 201.
Pierrepont, Lady Mary. *See* Wortley Montagu.
Pierrepont, Robert, 2.
Pierrepont, Mrs. Robert, 2.
Pierrepont, William, 1, 78.
Pisani, Signora Isabella, 375.
Pitrovani, Signor, 496.
Pitt, William (afterwards first Earl of Chatham), 434, 504.
Plaindealer, The, 305.
Pleasure of the Imagination, The, 22.
Plymouth, Other, Earl of, 219.
Pomfret, Henrietta Louisa, Countess of, 355, 360-61, 365-66, 369, 370-72, 377, 379, 385-88, 391, 402, 406, 450.
Pomfret, Thomas, Earl of, 360.
Pompey the Little, 481-82.
Pop upon Pope, A, 341.
Pope, Alexander—
Pastorals, 10.
Introduction to Lady Mary, 205.
Treatment of Curll, 207.
Epistolary style, 228-29.
First note to Lady Mary, 229-30.
Extravagant letters, 231-32.
Fears for Lady Mary's safety, 247, 250.
Quarrel with Cibber, 252-54.
Epistle of Eloisa to Abelard, 266.
Desire for Lady Mary's return, 272.
Epitaph on rustic lovers, 282-83.
Description of Stanton Harcourt, 291.
Professions to Lady Mary, 292-93.
Speculates in Bubble, 294.
Lines on Lady Mary, 302.
Verses addressed to Lady Mary, 307-8.
Supposed declaration, 339-40.
Quarrel with Lady Mary, 340-52.
Poetical persecution, 339-52.
Championed by Lady, 357.

INDEX

Pope, Alexander—*continued*.
  Curiosity about Lady Mary, 389.
  Death, 415.
  Alleged avarice, 488–89.
Popham, Mr., 113.
Portland, Margaret, Duchess of, 400, 406.
Portland, Henry, Duke of, 496–97.
Portland, Jane, Countess of, 335.
Pozzo, Madame del, 532.
Pulteney, Mrs., 362.

"Qualmsick, Mrs.," 482.
Queensbury, Katherine, Duchess of, 364.
Querini, Cardinal, 485.

Rambler, The, 492.
Ranelagh, Countess of, 124.
Rawdon, Sir John, 469, 470.
Rebellion of 1715, 218–23.
Rebellion of 1745, 428–32.
Reeves, Mrs., 20.
Reflections upon Marriage, 13 (*note*).
Reflections on the Rise and Fall of the Ancient Republicks, 511.
Rehearsal, The, 252.
Remarks on the Life and Writings of Swift, 488.
Rémond, Mons., 295–301, 303.
Resingade, Mr., 16, 116.
Rich, Christopher, 11.
Rich, Elizabeth, Lady, 228, 229 (*note*), 237, 261, 267, 273, 275, 309, 311–12, 343.
Rich, Miss, 465.
Rich, Sir Robert, 273.
Richardson, Jonathan, 12, 14, 207.
Richardson, Samuel, 483, 493–94.
Richelieu, Duc de, 412–13, 433.
Richmond, Charles, Duke of, 434, 501.
Richmond, Mary, Duchess of, 362, 501.
Robethon, Mons., 253, 259.
Robinson, Anastasia, 303, 317–18.
Robinson, Dr. James, Bishop of London, 222 (*note*).
Robinson, Sir William, 188.
Rochester, Henry, Earl of, 219.
Roderick Random, 481.
Romney, George, 535.
Roper, Abel, 121.
Rosamond, 12.
Roselli, Signor, 17.
Rousseau, Jean Baptiste, 239, 246.
Rowe, Nicholas, 194 (*note*), 290.
Roxburgh, Mary, Duchess of, 207.
Royal and Noble Authors, 515.
Rutland, Elizabeth, Countess of, 169 (*note*).
Rutland, John, Duke of, 375 (*note*), 376.

Sacheverell, Dr. Henry, 10, 53.
St. Auban, Madame, 416.
St. John, Angelica, Lady, 335.
St. John, George, 55.
St. John, Henry (*see* Bolingbroke, Viscount), 9.
Salisbury, James, Earl of, 460.
Salo, Visit to, 471.
Sandwich, Edward, Earl of, 6, 166, 478.
Sandwich, Elizabeth, Countess of, 337.
Sandwich, John, Earl of, 442, 445, 446, 451, 456, 461, 516.
Sandys' Ghost, 340.
"Sappho," 340, 343, 347, 352, 357.
Saunderson, Sir William, 364.
Savage, Richard, 320–21.
Saville, Lady Essex, 18.
Saxe, Marshal, 441.
Scarborough, Richard, Earl of (*see* Lumley), 377–79.
"Schemers, The," 318.
Scudéry, Mlle., 4, 14.
Scurlock, Mary, 10.
Seafield, James, Earl of, 198–99.
"Sebastian," 7, 21, 22, 28, 29, 30.
Seignor, The Grand (Achmet III.), 242, 263, 268.
Selections from the MSS. of Lady Louisa Stuart, 537.
Selwyn, George, 16 (*note*), 17 (*note*).
Selwyn, Mrs., 16, 17.
Selwyn, Colonel John, 16 (*note*).
Selwyn, General William, 16 (*note*).
Senesino, Francesco, 303, 317–18.
Serious Proposal to the Ladies, A, 13 (*note*).
Shadwell, Sir John, 395.
Sherard, Mrs., 24.
Sherlock, Thomas, 222 (*note*).
Shirley, Hon. Sewallis, 474, 481.
Shrewsbury, Adelhida, Duchess of, 84, 86, 127, 142, 208.
Shrewsbury, Charles, Duke, 255.
Shrewsbury, Gilbert, Earl of, 378.
Sidney, Lady K., 100.
Sinclair, General, 418, 421, 423, 424, 440, 443.
Sir Charles Grandison, 493.
Skerret, Molly, 309, 310, 342, 389.
Smallpox, 212.
Somers, John, Lord, 81 (*note*).
South Sea Bubble, 294.
Southwell, Thomas, Lord, 476.
Sowden, Rev. B., 526, 533.
Spaar, Baron, 258.
Spectator, The, 118, 120, 141, 151, 165.
Spence, Joseph, 339.
Stafford, Claude-Charlotte, Lady, 299, 309, 311, 331–32, 337, 365.

Stair, John, Earl of, 299, 301.
Stanhope, James, Earl of, 223, 257, 267, 286, 289, 479.
Stanyan, Abraham, 270, 271.
Steele, Sir Richard—
  Founds the *Tatler*, 11.
  His good-nature, 13.
  Mr. Wortley godfather to his daughter, 15.
  Endorses Lady Mary's letter, 40.
  Lady Mary objects to his connivance, 43.
  Mr. Wortley sends him an article, 50.
  Forwards Mr. Wortley's letters, 64.
  His play, *The Funeral*, 66.
  His house as a trysting-place, 87.
  Lady Mary's first visit to, 90–91.
  Elected for Boroughbridge, 177.
  His pamphlet, *The Crisis*, 181.
  His habit of writing to his wife, 195.
  Disappointment about Charterhouse, 225–26.
  Attempts to discover philosopher's stone, 247 (*note*).
  Compared with Henry Fielding, 492.
Steele, Mrs. (afterwards Lady)—
  Goes little abroad, 84.
  Her nice principles, 87.
  Proposed introduction to Lady Mary, 88–89.
  Lady Mary's first visit to, 90.
  Lady Mary's desire of a visit from, 91.
  Her house as a meeting-place, 98–99.
  Indisposed, 100.
  Lady Mary's dread of her ridicule, 123.
  Change of abode, 127.
  House in Bloomsbury Square, 142.
Steuart, Lady Frances, 504, 520, 525, 531.
Steuart, Sir James, 504, 506, 510, 514, 518, 520, 525.
Stonehouse, Sir John, 356.
Strafford, Anne, Countess of, 357 (*note*), 543.
Strafford, William, Earl of, 384.
Stuart, Lady Augusta, 464.
Stuart, Hon. James Archibald, 453.
Stuart, Lady Jane, 460, 526.
Stuart, Lady Louisa, 3, 5, 8, 163, 182, 204, 367, 480, 534, 536–38, 544.
Stuart, Lady Mary, 462, 526.
Sturges, Mr., 394.
Suffolk, Mary, Countess of, 236.
Sunderland, Charles, Earl of, 257, 286.
Sundon, Charlotte, Lady (*see* Clayton, Mrs.), 362–63.
Sutton, Sir Robert, 242, 270, 271.
Swift, Jonathan, 10, 30, 69, 340, 480, 488–89, 505, 509.

Taaffe, Theobald, 476–77.
Tale of a Tub, The, 10.
Tatler, The, 11, 13, 15, 19, 22, 30, 35, 50.
Temple of Diana, 437.
Tender Husband, The, 95 (*note*).
Tenison, Thomas, Dr., Archbishop of Canterbury, 79.
Tepoli, Signora Cornelia, 375.
Thistlethwaite, Mrs., 273.
Thornhill, Sir James, 12.
Three Hours after Marriage, 252.
Tichborne, Wilhelmina, 500–2.
Toland, John, 255.
Tonson, Jacob, 3 (*note*), 197.
Tonson, Jacob, the younger, 215.
Town Eclogues, 206–7, 449, 542.
Townshend, Audrey, Lady, 362 (*note*), 396, 461, 482.
Townshend, Charles, Viscount, 56, 183, 200, 286.
Traun, Count Otho von, 426.
Trentham, Lord (afterwards Marquis of Stafford), 460, 494.
Turruca, Count, 16.
Tweeddale, John, Marquis of, 434.

Vanbrugh, Sir John, 10, 11, 12, 181.
Vane, Frances, Lady, 363.
Vaughan, Lady Anne, 6.
Verses addressed to the Imitator of Horace, 344.
Villette, Mr., 522, 526.
Vizier, The Grand, 242, 263, 269.

Wackerbart, Count, 373, 378, 438.
Wade, General, 257, 430.
Waldegrave, James, Earl of, 363.
Walmoden, Madame de, 362 (*note*).
Walpole, Dorothy, 6.
Walpole, Horace (fourth Earl of Orford)—
  Account of Lady Mary's letters to Lady Mar, 301.
  Inoculation, 305.
  Description of Lady Pomfret, 360.
  Account of Lady Mary at Florence, 387–89.
  Scandal about Count Palazzo, 444.
  Publishes *Town Eclogues*, 449.
  Allusion to Lord Bute, 457.
  Gossip about E. W. Montagu, junior, 473.
  Account of gambling scandal, 476.
  Description of Wharncliffe, 490.
  Account of Mr. Wortley's will, 515–16.
  Visit to Lady Mary, 527–28.
  Remarks on death of Lady Mary, 531–32.
  Reads her letters, 533.

INDEX

Walpole, Margaret, Lady (*see* Orford), 387–88, 394.
Walpole, Sir Robert, 6, 192, 200–1, 225, 257–58, 267, 280, 310, 315, 343, 345–46, 372, 389, 405.
Walters, Mr., 371, 372.
Ward, Joshua, 456.
Warwick, Charlotte, Countess of, 88, 226.
Waters, Sir John, 219.
Wentworth, Lady Lucy, 460.
Wentworth Papers, The, 358.
West, Richard, 387–88.
Westmoreland, Mary, Countess of, 364.
Wharton, Lucy, Countess of, 84, 86.
Wharton, Philip, Duke of, 309, 311, 318–19, 340.
Wharton, Thomas, Earl of, 184, 191, 218.
What d'ye call 't, The, 208.
White, Mr., 125, 126, 164, 176.
Wilks, Robert, 11.
William Augustus, Duke of Cumberland, 419–20, 423.
William, Sir C. Hanbury, 455–56.
Willoughby, De Eresby, Peregrine, Lord, 117.
Wills, Sir Charles, 256.
Winchelsea, Daniel, Earl of, 434.
Winchendon, Philip, Lord (*see* Wharton, Duke of), 218.
Winchester, Anne, Lady, 196.
Windsor, Brigadier, 288.
Windsor, Other, Lord, 219.
Winton, George, Lord, 206.
Wolfenbüttel, Duke of, 373.
Woodward, Dr. John, 252.
Wortley, Sir Francis, 7.
Wortley, Francis, 517.
Wortley Montagu, Anne, 6, 22, 23, 26, 27.
Wortley Montagu, Mrs. Edward, 383.
Wortley Montagu, Edward—
First meeting with Lady Mary, 7–8.
Friendship with Addison and Steele, 15.
Writes to Lady Mary in his sister's name, 21–27.
Difficult temper, 31.
Early love-letters, 33, 36–38.
Employs indiscreet messenger, 41.
A candid letter, 45–47.
Indisposition, 48.
Disagreements about settlements, 50–51.
Goes to Spa, 61.
Letter about settlements, 62–64.
Return to England, 69.
Argument by correspondence, 69–78.
Fault-finding, 80.
Suggestions for meeting-places, 83–88.

Wortley Montagu, Edward—*continued.*
Jealousy, 93.
Apology, 96.
Suspicions and reproaches, 104–12.
Correspondence with Addison, 119–22.
Renewed proposals, 122.
Doubts and hesitations, 130.
Elopement discussed, 138.
Plans for the future, 147–48.
A genuine love-letter, 152–54.
The flight, 161.
Attempts reconciliation with Lord Dorchester, 167–68.
Economical tastes, 176.
A neglectful husband, 179–85.
As parliamentary candidate, 185–95.
Appointed Ambassador to the Porte, 227.
Additional instructions, 242–43.
State entry into Belgrade, 249.
Visit to Grand Vizier's camp, 268–69.
Recall, 270–72.
A working M.P., 285.
Satirised by Pope, 346–47.
Stands for York, 358.
Letter about Lady Mar, 360.
Supposed reasons for separation from wife, 366–67.
Correspondence with his wife, 368.
Desires to reconcile wife and daughter, 374–75.
Anxiety about son, 380–83, 390.
Addition to wife's allowance, 395–96.
Suggests meeting between wife and son, 402.
Letter to General Sinclair, 421–22.
Goes to Pyrmont, 428.
Takes house in Cavendish Square, 433.
Relations with son, 452.
Inherits Newbold Verdun, 465.
Goes to France, 467.
Journey to Vienna, 475.
Visited by H. Walpole at Wharncliffe, 490.
Letter on health, 491.
Letter in praise of Lord Bute, 498.
Weakness of sight, 509.
Death, 514.
Maxims, 515.
Items from will, 516.
Wortley Montagu, junior, Edward—
Birth, 174.
Delicacy, 183, 191.
Intelligence, 199.
Inoculation, 275–76.
Plays truant, 331.
Runs away, 333.

Wortley Montagu, junior, Edward—*contd.*
  Sent abroad, 355–56.
  Difficulties with creditors, 381–83.
  Letter to mother, 384.
  Plans for his future, 390–91.
  Mother's opinion of him, 397–98.
  Interview with mother, 402–4.
  Joins army in Flanders, 410.
  Letter from Lady Mary, 416–17.
  His account of Fontenoy, 418–27.
  Prisoner, 440–41.
  Seat in Parliament, 450–52.
  Secretary to Lord Sandwich, 461–62.
  His extravagance, 473.
  Hero of gambling scandal, 476–77.
  Publishes a book, 511.
  Letter to mother, 512–13.
  Enters false caveat, 523.
  Forgeries, 529.
  Last years and death, 537.
Wortley Montagu, Katherine, 6, 180.
Wortley Montagu, Lady Mary—
  Birth, 1.
  Kit-Cat Club, Election to, 3.
  Education, 4.
  Meeting with Mr. Wortley, 7.
  Letters to Mrs. Hewet, 15–20.
  Friendship with the Wortley Montagus, 21.
  Correspondence with Miss Wortley, 22–27.
  Autobiography, 28–30.
  Early love-letters, 31–38.
  Ideas of happiness, 35.
  Illness, 39.
  Indiscreet messenger, 41–43.
  Reproaches, 49.
  Settlements, 50–51.
  Visit to West Dean, 51.
  Letters to Mrs. Hewet, 51–53.
  Translation of Epictetus, 59.
  Letter to Dr. Burnet, 59–61.
  Correspondence with Mr. Wortley, 65–78.
  Difficulties of meeting, 81–90.
  Visit to Mrs. Steele, 90–92.
  Mr. Wortley's jealousy, 93.
  Farewell letter, 95.
  Reconciliation, 98.
  Ideas of friendship, 101.
  Quarrels, 104–11.
  Another farewell, 113.
  Letters to Mrs. Hewet, 116–18.
  Hopes of a settlement, 122.
  A distasteful match, 128–38.
  Plans for elopement, 141–60.
  A runaway marriage, 161.
  Loneliness, 163–69.
  Criticism of *Cato*, 169–73.
  Birth of son, 174.

Wortley Montagu, Lady Mary—*contd.*
  Death of brother, 175.
  House-hunting, 176–80.
  Mr. Wortley's neglect, 180–86.
  Political ambitions, 187–93.
  Reproaches, 195–96.
  Return to London, 199.
  Court life, 200–5.
  Introduction to Pope, 205.
  Town Eclogues, 206–13.
  Journey to Vienna, 230–33.
  Correspondence with Pope, 231.
  Impressions of Vienna, 234–38.
  Journey to Hanover, 240.
  Departure for the East, 248.
  Arrival at Adrianople, 250.
  Life in Turkey, 260.
  Birth of daughter, 274.
  Journey home, 278–82.
  Intimacy with Pope, 291–93.
  Portrait by Kneller, 292.
  Persecution by Rémond, 296–300.
  Inoculation, 264, 304–8.
  Circle at Twickenham, 309–12.
  Letters to Lady Mar, 297–336.
  Social gossip, 314–19.
  Literary friendships, 320–23.
  Quarrel with Mrs. Murray, 324.
  Troubles with her son, 331–35.
  Account of coronation of George II., 335.
  Persecution by Pope, 354.
  Marriage of daughter, 359.
  Letters to Lady Pomfret, 361–65.
  Journey to Venice, 366–69.
  Society at Venice, 369–79.
  Consultation about son, 380–83.
  Move to Florence, 386.
  Meeting with H. Walpole, 388.
  At Rome and Naples, 392–94.
  At Genoa and Geneva, 396–401.
  Winter at Chambéry, 401–2.
  Move to Avignon, 402.
  Meeting with son, 403–4.
  Life at Avignon, 407–11.
  Discomfort of situation, 432.
  Journey to Brescia, 438.
  Illness, 443.
  Relations with the Palazzos, 444.
  At Lovere, 448.
  Begins correspondence with Lady Bute, 453.
  Life at Gottolengo, 458–59.
  Ideas on education, 463–64, 478–80.
  Proposed statue of, 474.
  Criticism of novels, 481–83.
  Diet, 482.
  Treatment of women, 486.
  Literary opinions, 488–89, 492–93.
  Move to Venice, 495.

INDEX

Wortley Montagu, Lady Mary—*contd*.
  Friendship with the Steuarts, 504.
  Quarrels with Murray, 504.
  Anxiety about Mr. Wortley, 510–11.
  Letter from son, 512–13.
  Death of Mr. Wortley, 514.
  Proposed return to England, 517.
  Last letters to Lady Bute, 517–24.
  Journey home, 525–27.
  Description of, by H. Walpole, 527.
  Interview with Mrs. Elizabeth Montagu, 528.
  Misconduct of son, 529.
  Illness and death, 531.
  Publication of letters, 533.
  Burning of diary, 534.
  Character, 539–41.
  Religion, 541–42.

Wortley Montagu, Lady Mary—*contd*.
  Literary talent, 542–43.
  Conversation, 543.
  Favourite books, 544.
  Poem, *The Lover*, 545.
  Published Works, 447–48.
Wortley Montagu, Mary (*see* Bute, Countess of), 358–59.
Wortley Montagu, Hon. Sidney, 6, 164, 289, 334–35.
Wright, Mrs., 508.
Wyndham, Sir William, 254, 255.
Wyndham, William, 344.

Yarborough, Mrs., 181.
Yonge, Sir William, 309, 310, 315, 507 (*note*).
York Election, The, 358.
Young, Dr. Edward, 320, 321.

Printed by
MORRISON & GIBB LIMITED
Edinburgh